T0361045

Routledge Library Editions

POLITICAL ARITHMETIC

ECONOMICS

Routledge Library Editions – Economics

WELFARE ECONOMICS AND ECONOMIC POLICY
In 8 Volumes

POLITICAL ARITHMETIC

A Symposium of
Population Studies

EDITED BY LANCELOT HOGBEN

Routledge
Taylor & Francis Group

LONDON AND NEW YORK

First published in 1938

Reprinted in 2003 by
Routledge
2 Park Square, Milton Park, Abingdon, Oxon, OX14 4RN

Transferred to Digital Printing 2007

Routledge is an imprint of the Taylor & Francis Group

The publishers have made every effort to contact authors/copyright holders
of the works reprinted in *Routledge Library Editions – Economics*. This has
not been possible in every case, however, and we would welcome
correspondence from those individuals/companies we have been unable to
trace.

These reprints are taken from original copies of each book. In many cases
the condition of these originals is not perfect. The publisher has gone to
great lengths to ensure the quality of these reprints, but wishes to point
out that certain characteristics of the original copies will, of necessity, be
apparent in reprints thereof.

British Library Cataloguing in Publication Data
A CIP catalogue record for this book
is available from the British Library

Political Arithmetic
ISBN 0-415-31407-0
ISBN 0-415-31402-X

Miniset: Welfare Economics and Economic Policy

Series: Routledge Library Editions – Economics

Printed and bound by CPI Antony Rowe, Eastbourne

POLITICAL ARITHMETIC

A SYMPOSIUM OF POPULATION STUDIES

EDITED BY

LANCELOT HOGBEN, F.R.S.

Routledge
Taylor & Francis Group

LONDON AND NEW YORK

FIRST PUBLISHED IN 1938

"It was by him stiled Political Arithmetick in as much as things of Government . . . and the happiness and greatness of the People are by the Ordinary Rules of Arithmetick brought into a sort of Demonstration. He was allowed by all to be the Inventor of this method of instruction, where the perplexed and intricate ways of the World are explaned by a very mean science; and had not the Doctrines of this Essay offended France, they had . . . found followers as well as improvements before this time to the advantage perhaps of mankind . . ."—Shelborne's Preface to Petty's *Politicall Arithmitick*, 1691.

"I profess to learn and to teach anatomy, not from books but from dissections, not from the positions of philosophers but from the fabric of nature."—WILLIAM HARVEY.

"I profess to learn and to teach economics, politics, sociology, not from books but from observations, not from the positions of philosophers but from the conduct of mankind."—SIR WILLIAM BEVERIDGE.

PUBLISHERS' NOTE

THE present volume sets forth some of the inquiries undertaken by the Department of Social Biology during the Editor's tenure of office therein. Accounts of some of the work carried out have already been published in journals which are only accessible to a small circle of specialists. About half of the material is presented for the first time. Any profits arising from the sales will be devoted to publication of other *factual* social studies.

CONTENTS

PART I

THE SURVIVAL MINIMUM

PART II

THE RECRUITMENT OF SOCIAL PERSONNEL

A*

PART I

THE SURVIVAL MINIMUM

INTRODUCTION TO PART I
PROLEGOMENA TO POLITICAL ARITHMETIC
by
LANCELOT HOGBEN

THE study of population is the only branch of social research with its own logical technique for the detection and co-ordination of *factual* data. This is not surprising when we recall the circumstances of its origin. The men who brought it into being were actively associated with the group which laid the foundations of the British empirical tradition of naturalistic inquiry. Some little-known information about the three founders of British demography—Graunt, Petty, and Halley—is given in a later chapter by Dr. Kuczynski. The social context which brought them together is a theme worthy of more comment. A brief account of their relations to the intellectual life of their time suggests a fitting introduction to the investigations which follow.

The names of all three are found in the original list of Fellows of the Royal Society when it received its charter in 1662. The "ingenious author of the *Bills of Mortality*" referred to in Sprat's History was of course John Graunt, the first writer on vital statistics. The first life table—that of Halley—was published in the *Philosophical Transactions* of 1693. Halley's position in the world of natural science is made memorable by the comet which bears his name. The presence of Graunt and of Petty, author of the *Politicall Arithmitick*, demand an explanation. Especially is this true of Petty. Petty is sometimes claimed as an economist. The association of economics with science jars harshly on the modern ear.

The issue of the Lansdowne Collection of unpublished fragments (1927) has thrown new light on the intellectual outlook of Petty. "By turns cabin boy, hawker of sham jewellery, seaman, inventor, physician, Fellow and Vice-Principal of Brasenose, Professor of Anatomy at Oxford, and of Music at Gresham College, Surveyor, Member of Parliament, landed proprietor, philosopher, statistician and political economist," the author of the *Politicall Arithmitick* was in short *a man of affairs*. What is less known about him is that some of the earliest meetings, perhaps the first, of the "Invisible Colledge" met in Petty's rooms at Oxford.[1] The group so called included besides Boyle and Petty, Christopher Wren, Bishop Wilkins, Seth Ward the astronomer, and later Hooke. It was the parent body of the Royal Society, and Petty may justly rank with "the father of chemistry and the uncle of the Earl of Cork" as one of its co-founders. Two circumstances conspired to encourage fruitful collaboration between men who, like Graunt and Petty, were pioneers of realistic social inquiry with men who, like Hooke and Newton, made Britain supreme in the domain of natural science. In the *Century of Inventions*[2] leaders of theoretical science were in close touch with inventors, sea captains, surveyors, and architects. They were acutely interested in the material forces propitious to the advancement of scientific knowledge or otherwise. They were equally alive to the ideological obstacles which hindered the progress of discovery. In active revolt against the scholastic tradition of the universities the Invisible College had begun its informal sessions within a decade of the death of Galileo. Less than half a century had elapsed since the Parliament of Paris—so Voltaire tells us—enacted a law by which the chemists of the Sorbonne must conform to the teachings of Aristotle on pain of death and confiscation of goods. Shortly after Newton's death Voltaire wrote that Descartes "quitta la France parce qu'il cherchait la verité qu'était persecutée alors par *la misérable philosophie de l'école.*" Newton "a vécu honoré de ses compatriotes et a été enterré comme un roi qui aurait fait du bien a ses sujets . . . heureux et honoré dans sa patrie. Son grand bonheur a été non seulement d'être né dans un pays libre mais dans un temps où *les impertinences scolastiques* étant bannies la raison seule était cultivée."

Close association of scientific theory and social practice is a feature of the "adventurous hopefulness" of early English capitalism, sufficiently documented by Hessen in his essay on the *Economic Roots of Newton's Principia*, in Professor G. N. Clark's recent lectures, and

[1] It would appear that the earliest meetings were in Petty's rather than in Boyle's rooms. In the introduction to their new edition of the Hooke Diaries, Robinson and Adams state: "They held a weekly meeting 'first at Dr. Petty's (in an apothecaries house) because of the convenience of inspecting drugs, and the like, as there was occasion; and after his removal to Ireland (though not so constantly), at the lodgings of Dr. Wilkins . . . and after his removal to Trinity College, Cambridge, at the lodgings of the Honourable Mr. Robert Boyle.'"

[2] Deliberate metalepsis. The Marquis of Worcester's title refers to the actual number listed.

in the Preface of the new volume of Hooke's Diaries edited by Robinson and Adam. The founders of the Invisible College were among the earliest apostles of the social creed of nineteenth-century capitalism. In his own words, Boyle's gospel was that "the goods of mankind may be much increased by the naturalist's insight into the trades." In a letter to a friend named Marcombes he says:

The other humane studies I apply myself to are natural philosophy, the mechanics and husbandry, according to the principles of our new philosophical colledge that values no knowledge but *as it hath a tendency to use*. And therefore I shall make it one of our suits to you that you should take the pains to enquire a little more thoroughly into the ways of husbandry . . . which will make you extremely welcome to our invisible colledge.

In tracing the origins of the Invisible College during the years which immediately preceded the first revolution of Stuart times, Sprat remarks:

I shall only mention one great man who had the true imagination of the whole Extent of this Enterprise as it is now set on foot, and that is the Lord Bacon in whose books there are everywhere scattered the best arguments that can be produced for the Defence of experimental philosophy, and the best Directions that are needful to promote it.

Bacon's defence of experimental philosophy is now a well-thumbed brief. One of his directions to promote it is forgotten, though "adorned with so much art" as Sprat appraised. It would be hard to find a better statement of what Hessen calls the unity of theory and practice than the passage which opens with the following words in the *Novum Organum*:

The roads to human power and to human knowledge lie close together, and are nearly the same; nevertheless, on account of the pernicious and inveterate habit of dwelling on abstractions, it is safer to begin and raise the sciences from those foundations which have relation to practice and let the active part be as the seal which prints and determines the contemplative counterpart.

In this spirit the Royal Society began its labours.

They design [Sprat tells us] the multiplying and beautifying of the mechanick arts. . . . They intend the perfection of graving, statuary, limning, coining and all the works of smiths in iron or steel or silver.

. . . They purpose the trial of all manner of operations by Fire. . . .
They resolve to restore, to enlarge, to examine Physick. . . . They have
bestowed much consideration on the propagation of Fruits and trees.
. . . They have principally consulted the Advancement of Navigation.
. . . They have employed much Time in examining the Fabrick of
Ships, the forms of their sails, the shapes of their keels, the sorts of Timber,
the planting of Fir, the bettering of pitch and Tar and Tackling.

The design included a conspectus of all the principal technological
problems which affected British mercantile supremacy and the
theoretical issue relevant to their solution. Of all these "histories"
the most illuminating compilation is the *Heads of Enquiries* into the
state of British Agriculture. Twenty-six major questionnaires were
printed that they might be "the more universally known" and that
persons skilful in husbandry might be "publickly invited to impart
their knowledge herein for the common benefit of the country."
The topics included "the several kinds of the soyls of England"
(sandy, gravelly, stony, clayie, chalky, light mould, heathy, marish,
boggy, fenny or cold weeping ground), when each was "employed
for arable"; "what peculiar preparations are made use of to these
soyls for each kind of grain, with what kind of manure they are
prepared; when, how and in what quantity the manure is laid on";
"what kinds of ploughs are used"; "the kinds of grain or seed usual
in England"; "how each of these is prepared for sowing," "there
being many sorts of wheat . . . and so of oats . . . which of these
grow in your county and in what soyl, and which of them thrive
best there . . ."; "how they differ in goodness"; "what kinds of
grain are most proper to succeed there"; "some of the common
accidents and diseases befalling corn in the growth of it, being
blasting, mildew, smut, what are conceived to be the causes thereof
and what the remedies"; "annoyances the growing corn is subjected
to, as weeds, worms, flies, birds, mice, moles, etc., how they are
remedied"; "waies of preserving the several sorts of grain"; "how
the above-mentioned sorts of soyl are prepared when they are used
for Pasture or Meadow"; "the common annoyances of these pasture
and meadow grounds."

Such are samples of the questions. The replies to them were
placed after discussion in the archives from which they have been
lately rescued by Lennard, who analyses them in an article in the
Economic History Review (iv, 1932). Here deliberately and systematic-
ally organized science takes stock of the common experience of

mankind to formulate problems for which precise solutions are now available. Truly "a brave attempt to link up book learning and scientific research with the experience of practical farmers" as Lennard says. We may go further and say that it is the first comprehensive vision of a rationally planned ecology of mankind.

The direct affiliations of the Invisible College with sociological inquiries are less well known. Sprat gives an eloquent list of the "qualities which they have principally required in those whom they admitted." First he insists on freedom for different schools of religion or philosophical persuasion. "This they were obliged to do or else they would come far short of the largeness of their own declarations. For they openly profess not to lay the Foundation of an English, Scotch, Irish, Popish or Protestant philosophy, but a philosophy of mankind." Nationality was to be no barrier. "By this means they will be able to settle a constant intelligence throughout all civil nations and make the Royal Society the general bank and free port of the world." The third and most significant for our present theme was "the equal balance of all professions." Seeing that "so much is to be found in men of all conditions of that which is called pedantry in scholars," they were to take care lest "Mechanicks alone were to make a philosophy . . . and force it wholly to consist of springs and wheels and weights."

To be sure there were "some Arts on which they have no mind to intrench as the Politicks, Morality and Oratory . . . because the reason, the Understanding, the tempers, the Will, the Passions of Men are so hard to be reduced to any certain observations of the senses and afford so much room to the observers to falsify or counterfeit." This omission was to be transitional. "Man's soul and body . . . are one natural engine of whose motions of all sorts there may be as certain an account given as those of a watch and a clock." Later on "when they shall have made more progress in material things they will be in a condition of pronouncing more boldly on them too." Where the facts were accessible to the senses there was to be no barrier to common intercourse between the natural and social sciences. "That they are likely to continue this comprehensive Temper hereafter, I will shew by one instance, and it is the Recommendation which the King himself was pleased to make of the judicious author of the *Observations on the Bills of Mortality*, in whose election it was far from being a prejudice that he was a shopkeeper of London. . . . His Majesty gave his particular charge to his Society, that if they find any more such Tradesmen they should be sure to admit them all without any more ado."

Of the ideological milieu in which men like Graunt or Petty rubbed shoulders with Newton and Boyle, Flamsteed and Hooke, Sprat has much to say. There was then what there is not to-day, and perhaps has never since been in the history of English social culture. Copernicus had made a common platform for students of nature and society by showing that you cannot build a science on the shifting sands of self-evident principles. Sprat spoke for Graunt when he contrasted the Baconian method with that of their predecessors who

began with some general definition of the things themselves according to their universal natures. . . . But though this notional war had been carried on with far more care and calmness amongst them than it was: yet it was never able to do any great good towards the enlargement of knowledge, because it relied on general terms which had not much foundation in knowledge. That this insisting altogether on established axioms is not the most useful way is not only clear in such any conceptions which they managed but also in those things which lie before every man's observation. . . . To make a prudent man in the affairs of state there must be a sagacity of judgment in particular things, a dexterity in discerning the advantages of occasion, a study of the humour and interests of the people. . . . The very way of disputing itself and inferring one thing from another alone is not at all proper for the spreading of knowledge. . . . For if but one link in the whole chain be loose, they wander far away and seldom or never recover their first ground again. It may easily be proved that those very themes on which they built their most subtile webs were not all collected by a sufficient information from the things themselves, which if it can be made out, I hope it will be granted that the Force and Vigour of their wit did more hurt than good.

In England the scholastic tradition of the universities was sufficiently strong to frustrate the rapprochement which Petty favoured. How strong it still is may be judged by contrasting Sprat's remarks with the following citation from a recent book ostensibly composed to divulge *The Nature and Significance of Economic Science*. In it Professor Robbins writes:

It will be convenient, therefore, at the outset of our investigations if, instead of attempting to derive the nature of economic generalizations from the pure categories of our subject-matter, we commence by examining a typical specimen. It is a well-known generalization of elementary Price Theory that, in a free market, intervention by some outside body to fix a price below the market price will lead to an excess of demand over supply. . . . Upon what foundations does it rest? . . . It should not be necessary to spend much time showing that it cannot rest on any appeal to History. . . . It is equally clear that our belief does not rest upon the results of controlled experiment. . . . In the last analysis, therefore, our proposition rests upon deductions which are implicit in our initial definition of the subject-matter of Economic Science (p. 72).

Lest it might be thought that this is an isolated passage wrested from its context, a further quotation states that "the truth of a particular theory is a matter of logical derivation from the general assumptions of the subject" (p. 106).

The author of the *Politicall Arithmitick* had anticipated a proper remedy for this notional warfare and *"les impertinences scolastiques"* by prescribing the education for a man prudent in the affairs of state.

Hindrance [he says] of the advancement of learning hath beene because thought, theory, and practice, hath beene always divided in severall persons; because the ways of learning are too tedious for them to be joyned. And whereas all writings ought to be descriptions of things, they are now onely of words, books know little of things, and the practicall men have not language nor method enough to describe [them] by words.

To remedy this he proposes "a supellex Philosophica worth 500£. Let the Students of the Schoole," he says,

have Languages, exercises and Draught, with a competency of Arithmetic, Algebra, Geometry, Geography and Chronology. Of motions and Mechanics. Of sounds, echoes, and Musick. Of Opticks, visions, and scenes. Of Magneticks. Of ships and sailing. Of Howsing. Of Land carriages. Of Pumps. Of Mills. Of Clocks and Clepsydras. Of Guns, Powder, and fireworks. Hydrostatics. Colorations. Figurations. Cloath, Leather, Hats, paper. Spining, Kniting, weaving. Meteors and Tides. Astronomy and Dialls. Ayre, fier, water. Ballisticks. Analysis of the People. Principall salts. Chymicall operations. Metalls, Quick silver. Glass and Gems. Fabrick of Animalls. Synopsis of Diseases. Botanicks. Georgicks. Insects. Bees, spiders, and silkworms. To expound the Museum of Gresham Colledge. To be performed in an yeare of 40 weekes. Each week to consist of 5 dayes, and each day of 3 howers. In all 600 howers. Let the Collegium consist of 20, under 3 masters, at 20£ per head. The Council of the Royall Society to bee Sponsores.

He suggests separate curricula for the education suitable to a man of affairs, a fop, and a courtier. For the first he recommends thirteen disciplines:

Latine, French, etc. To write any hand. Printing and designing. Fencing and gymnastics. Singing at sight. Geometry, Arithmetic and Algebra. Anatomy and Chirugery. History of Trades. Cookery and Pharmacy. [Ars Veneris] Jugling and Legerdemain. Physicall secrets, receipts and experiments. Optics, Magnetics, Jewelling.

For the fop he recommends only:

Dancing and Vaulting. To understand a horse and riding. To Play at severall games. The Art of Treating and dressing. The small moralls. Histrionic. Hunting and Hawking.

The reader will recognize which of these alternatives corresponds most closely to the intellectual preparation esteemed proper for a twentieth-century economist.

Petty's educational interests ranged over a wide field. He believed in teaching algebra as a branch of grammar. A delightful letter in which he discusses what algebra is might well be reproduced in every elementary text-book without excluding the quaint conclusion:

Archimedes had Algebra 1,900 yeares ago but concealed it. Diophantus had it in great perfection 1,400 yeares since. Vieta, DesCartes, Roberval, Harriot, Pell, Outread, van Schoten and Dr. Wallis, have done much in this last age. It came out of Arabia by the Moores into Spaine and from thence hither, and W[illiam] P[etty] hath applyed it to other than purely mathematicall matters, viz. to policy by the name of *Politicall Arithmitick*, by reducing many termes of matter to termes of number, weight, and measure, in order to be handled Mathematically.

Part of his programme for educational reform anticipated Bentham and C. K. Ogden. There is a project (No. 46, op. cit.) for "The Dictionary of Sensible Words" setting forth "what words have the same meaning, what words have many meanings . . ." and "words which by having too many meanings have none." Whereto he appends *inter alia* God, gentleman, beauty, courage, martyr, and duty. We can well imagine the following excerpt from a modernized edition: ECONOMIST (a) American *see* AFFAIRS (man of), (b) English *see* METAPHYSICIAN (British).

The Lansdowne Collection contains several fragments of a prolegomena to social biology. Petty proposes a *scala naturae* and discusses wherein man differs from and resembles other brutes from a strictly behaviourist standpoint:

Man being the first or Topp of this Scale, the question is what Animall shall bee next. . . . In the Opinion of most men, the Ape or rather the Drill (which is the largest and most manlike species of Apes) should claim the 2d. place unto which we have preferred the Elephant, 1st because his shape is far neerer to that of Man than any other Animall's is, and for that his Actions as they have been reported by those who pretend to know them do in many points resemble those of a Man. Nevertheless [since] it be true that an Elephant can understand the language better then a Drill, and that the *Mens* of an Elephant doth come neerer the *Mens* of a man, although the shape of a Drill comes neerer the shape of a man, I shall choose (as I have done) to give preference unto the Elephant. Speech is more peculiar unto, and copious in a Man than in any other Animall, and consequently wee might in that respect give the 2d. place to Parrots, or that species of them in which the formation of Articular sounds and the imitation of Man's Speech is most conspicuous. Nor is an Ape so considerable to mee for imitating the externall and visible motions of the parts and Organs of a Man, as speaking Birds are for imitating, by a sort of reason and internall sence, the motion of the hidden and unseen instruments of speech, which are the Muscelle of the Lungs and Larynx. But it is plain that although Parrotts do pronounce words, that they do it but as sounds, and not like men, as the signs of things, Actions and Notions; and consequently this faculty of speaking birds extending onely to sounds and not to the Conceptions of the Mind. . . . Haveing admitted the Parrott to a right or Competition, I will not exclude the Bee, referring you to what Virgil and many observant Men have seriously and experimentally, not vainly or fabulously, spoaken of them; and among all the admirable operations of the Bee, I preferr his pollicy, assigning that faculty for the thing wherein hee comes neerest to Man. And pollicy or the Art of Government seems to bee the most considerable faculty of a Man.

Having reflected on the differentiae of the human species, he forestalls the exploits of Malthus in the significant assertion:

A man doth differ from all other animals in use of the female, and generation. By using the same without designe or desire of generation, and when generation is needless or impossible. In making such rules and lawes concerning the same, as no other animall doth; and all this while making all the acts and instruments thereof ridiculous, shamefulle and filthy, so as not to bee seen or spoken of in the company and presence of [others without?] laughter.

Most remarkable of all the fragments are proposals for sex reform in Nos. 91 to 94 in the Lansdowne Collection. These include polygamy and family allowances. An elaborate exercise in *Politicall Arithmitick* is appended to the proposal that

> 50s. per annum bee allowd for keeping a child till full 7 yeares old, and 20s. for a woman lying in, to the publicq places or to each woman herselfe in particular. That at 7 yeares old the children bee disposed for 14 yeares after, and bee then free, having been taught some Trade. That every man and woman have a livelyhood *ut alibi*. That a woman is not bound to declare the father, but to the officer who was privy to the contract and *habet sub sigillo*. That this liberty for short marriages do not take away the present way, nor other covenants of cohabitation, estate, rewards, etc. That both parties shall sweare they [are] free from any fowle disease.

In a different context he applies the *Politicall Arithmitick* to the simple machines: "By a common Pump a man can raise 32 gallons 30 (feet) high in a minute, or 8 tons in an hour." In short, Petty was a pioneer of Social Technology. He anticipated the only rational basis for costing the resources of human welfare in his papers on Taxation:

> Our Silver and Gold we call by several names, as in England by pounds, shillings, and pence, all which may be called and understood by either of the three. But that which I would say upon this matter is, that all things ought to be valued by two natural Denominations, which is Land and Labour; that is, we ought to say, a Ship or garment is worth such a measure of Land, with such another measure of Labour; forasmuch as both Ships and Garments were the creatures of Lands and mens Labours thereupon.

Needless to say, Petty had his comic side. You cannot make spiritual omelettes without breaking metaphysical eggs. Like Hooke and Boyle he had the knack of proffering his most radical proposals within the framework of the prevailing ideology. He was scarcely in advance of his time in advocating "simple death" as a penalty for bankrupts and bedlam for "scepticall hereticks." In fairness, it may be added that a mark of interrogation was placed against the last. His views on religious and sexual freedom display the same devotion to business principles. Polyandry was permissible provided that "none copulate without a covenant." Polyandry without covenant was to be punished with death. For polygamy without covenant he proposed death expedited by gonadectomy without anaesthesia.[1] Heresy was permissible provided that a business contract preceded it and due notice of fresh deviations from theological rectitude was given:

> That the Persons desiring liberty must put themselves into tribes or Classes, by exact declaration, wherein they respectively differ in doctrine or worship from the State Religion; with a protestation that they beleive the said doctrine and worship necessary to the quiet of their Conscience here, and their Eternall Welfare after Death. . . . Upon all which there must bee a mutuall assurance, that such Liberty and Indulgence shall bee perpetuall, or not alterable but upon cleere conditions and long warning.

Before the publication of the Lansdowne Collection we had known of Petty as a pioneer and as a man of affairs. We now see him in a new light. The tireless versatility and consuming curiosity of men like William Petty and Robert Hooke can only prosper when social circumstances sustain high hopes in those whose brains have not been addled by a cloistered sophistication. If Petty is justly claimed as the father of Political Economy, the character and interests of no man could differ more conspicuously from those of a university professor of economics. He had the first desideratum of a genuine man of science—the itch to discover things for himself. He could hunt for them in unexpected places. Valuing above all knowledge "as it hath a tendency to use" he made no bones about admitting when he wanted to get something done. An impartial contemporary comparing the *Politicall Arithmitick* with the *Sceptical Chymist* might have been at pains to forecast whether the progress of chemistry would justify the comparison which Jeremy Bentham made a century later. Referring to Lavoisier's discoveries and the state of social inquiries Bentham exclaims, "Think of what chemistry was before that time—think of what it has since become!"

The training of an English economist makes no provision for studying the "history of trades, receipts and experiments, pharmacy and jewelling." So it will not be profitless to pursue Bentham's counsel. Between the work of Boyle and that of Lavoisier the course of chemistry did not run smooth. The reason why the *Sceptical Chymist* signalizes the dichotomy between modern chemistry and alchemy is that the air pump of "the immortal Mr. Boyle" had proved beyond dispute the existence of the third state of matter. Aristotle's self-evident doctrine that air is weightless had been conclusively disproved. The spirits of the retort were for the first time recognized as matter in an attenuated form, compressible—as Boyle had shown—according to ascertainable laws. The new laws of gas mechanics were established by the ungentlemanly process of manual experimentation without assistance from the original definitions of the subject. After nineteen centuries of Aristotelian futilities the common pump had come into its own. The doctrines which Aristotle had exercised the full powers of his ingenuity to discredit had been spread abroad by Gassendi's commentaries on Epicurus. Hooke's experiments on gunpowder and Mayow's work on breathing had set the stage for a correct understanding of combustion and oxidation. It seemed as if the world of science was ready for the recognition that matter, contrary to self-evident principles, is not continuous.

Seemingly every obstacle to useful knowledge about the most ancient of chemical industries had been removed. It was now known that metals gain weight when heated in air to form a calx (metallic oxide). A straightforward explanation of this fact is that they combine like charcoal or sulphur with Hooke's nitro-aerial particles of the air itself. "The atoms of Democritus and Newton's particles of light" as Blake sung of them later were destined for tardy recognition. While the English empirical school were making the discoveries indispensable to fruitful definitions and salutary principles, Teutonic sophistication had anticipated Professor Hayek's belief that principles must be settled before realistic inquiry can be undertaken with impunity.[1] A school of Continental chemists staked the claim for preserving the purity of their subject from contamination with the new theoretical principles derived from the study of heat in the first phase of steam technology by fabricating a doctrine of elegant ingenuity. This last attempt to sustain the elemental nature of fire in Aristotle's system provides an instructive model. The argument runs as follows. It is self-evident that if things burn, they must contain the fire principle. A combustible substance is therefore a compound of a calx or non-combustible material with the fire principle *phlogiston*. Since the escape of phlogiston, when a combustible substance burns or a metal is oxidized, is accompanied by production of non-combustible material which actually weighs

[1] *Economica*, 1937.

more than its predecessor, it is equally self-evident that phlogiston is endowed with the opposite of weight, i.e. *levity* or the power to make a body weigh less. The social circumstances of the time provided matters too weighty to sustain the "levity" of Becher and Stahl. From the middle of the eighteenth to the first decades of the nineteenth century a succession of chemical industries was founded to meet the exhaustion of fuel supplies. Commercial production of sulphuric acid (1740) followed by Keir's alkali factory (1780), hydrogen balloons in the same decade, Murdoch's coal gas, bleaching powder, beet sugar, and phosphorus matches—all these preceded the revival of a robust materialism in England. The new theoretical leadership demanded by the circumstances of the time was supplied by such as Dalton, Davy, Faraday, who were largely recruited from a new fund of social personnel while the echoes of the phlogiston doctrine still reverberated in the established universities. It now provides the comic relief of an early stage in the teaching of chemistry. When political arithmetic is as firmly rooted as chemistry in the social needs of mankind, marginal utility will have joined the same limbo with *entelechy* and the *caloric*.

If we compare the progress of chemistry with that of political arithmetic during the two centuries which separate us from Boyle and Petty, can we regard the record of social studies with more complacency than Bentham? No Minister of Defence could now hold office if he rejected the advice of expert chemists. No well-educated people need disagree about who the good chemists are, and what is good chemistry is not, as in Priestley's day, a party issue. By that token chemistry is recognized as an authentic science. Can we say that no Chancellor of the Exchequer can afford to reject the advice of an expert economist? If so, who are the experts? Are well-educated people of all political persuasions able to agree about who they are? To ask the question is to answer it, and to anticipate the customary defence. We shall be told that human society, and more especially the operation of the banking system, is a more complex universe of discourse than the processes with which chemistry deals. We shall be satisfied that the truth of this statement is commensurate with its relevance when we have pursued Bentham's counsel more fully.

In a printed lecture which will not have come before the notice of most who read this book I have suggested that we might explore other differences between chemistry and social inquiries before we advance an answer to these questions. In it I have enumerated three characteristics which cannot fail to impress a student of natural science when he is brought into professional contact with the conduct of social studies in English universities. Following the *Novum Organum*, I have called two of them the Idol of Logic and the Idol of Purity.

The story of phlogiston reminds us that chemistry occupies its present position of prestige and power because it has learned the hard lesson that logic which may be a good servant is always a bad master. In their turn each of the natural sciences has had to learn the same lesson which Bacon stated in immortal phraseology: "It cannot be that axioms established by argumentation can suffice for the discovery of new works, since the subtlety of nature is greater many times over than the subtlety of argument." Bacon was referring to external nature. His words are still more true of human nature and the institutions which arise from its peculiarities. Citations already given from the works of a contemporary economist sufficiently show how little the new humanistic studies have renounced the idolatry of logic. The theologians of the Sorbonne confined their speculation within the legal conventions of Aristotle's logic. Economic theory with more specious pretensions reverts to the Number Magic of the Pythagorean brotherhoods. The following is a representative specimen from a book by Dr. Hicks:[1]

> If now the employer's concession curve cuts the resistance curve on the horizontal part, the union will generally succeed in maintaining its claim; but if it cuts it at a lower point, compromise will be necessary and it is over such compromises that misunderstanding and strikes easily arise.

Readers who lack intellectual self-confidence may be trapped into believing that such exercises in draughtsmanship displayed in books on economics record the results of real measurements, as do curves in books on physics or biology. In contradistinction to realistic inquiries on how trade unions actually behave, economics is therefore inferred to be an "exact" science. The epithet is not a happy one. All genuine science is as exact as needs be for the tasks it undertakes and as exact as it can be with the instruments at its disposal. It is equally concerned with the qualitative and quantitative character-

---

[1] *Theory of Wages.*

istics of behaviour, and all new sciences must traverse a wide territory of natural history before useful measurements can be made or fruitful hypotheses based on them can be tested. The relevant issue is whether the curves of the economists correspond to any measurements which have been made by them. An employer's concession "curve" is not a graph in which a set of co-ordinates lay off the measured concessions which employers can or do make. A "curve" of trade union resistance is not a graph in which a set of co-ordinates correspond to observations of the behaviour of trade unionists or their executives.

To see what relation this has to the methods of scientific inquiry it is only necessary to recall a "concession" curve or the resistance curve for a piece of wire. A curve which tells us how much a wire spring concedes to the load applied exhibits a series of points each based on the mean of careful measurements of the observed length of a particular spring when an observed load of guaranteed weight is suspended from it. A curve which tells us the relation of resistance to heat exhibits a series of points each based on a Wheatstone bridge observation of the conductivity of a real piece of metal and a reading obtained from a reliable and tangible thermometer. The corresponding measurements of the employers' concession and the trade union resistance curves exist in the brain of Dr. Hicks. Since he does not suggest any substitute for the thermometer, balance, Wheatstone bridge, or micrometer scale, his ingenious artistry lacks the merit of a speculative hypothesis for more enterprising investigators to test. True science is *par excellence* such knowledge *as hath a tendency to use*. A scientific law embodies a recipe for doing something, and its final validification rests in the domain of action.

The immense confidence which certain scientific generalizations rightly command depends on large-scale opportunities for testing their capacity to bear fruit in the commonplace activities of everyday life. Speculative extrapolations concerning the age of the universe change from day to day as astronomical knowledge advances, and we should be justified in treating astronomers with the same suspicion as politicians if the credentials of astronomy had no firmer basis. Our reliance on astronomy is justified by the fact that it provides the farmer with a calendar of the seasons, the fisherman with a table of tides, the statesman with a map, the Union Castle Line with the means of navigating a ship into port, and the Minister of Transport with fines from motorists who fail to light up after civil twilight ends. The only valid distinction between pure and applied research in natural science lies between inquiries concerned with issues which *may eventually* and issues which *already do* arise in the social practice of mankind. Consequently the pure scientist knows that he has everything to gain from encouragement of applied research, and if the last survivors of Darwin's generation still murmur doubts about Mendelism, the experimental geneticist goes on his way serenely confident that the *Feathered World* will continue to advertise day-old sex-linked chicks, or that rabbit furriers now know how to make pure lilac from blue beveren-chocolate havana crosses, and how to fix "Rex" on any colour pattern in two generations.

In science the final arbiter of truth is not the self-evidence of the initial statement nor the façade of flawless logic which conceals it. A subject which admits to the dignity of law statements based on logical manipulations of verbal assertions is not a science. What then is it? The newest apology of the Viennese school is that economics, as Professor Robbins conceives it, does not claim to be a science. It is a logical technique which stands in much the same relation to realistic social studies as does Newtonian mechanics to experimental physics. It may be hoped that those who advance the analogy have examined how the principles of dynamics emerged from problems suggested by the introduction of artillery warfare and the technology of clock-making in an age when the determination of longitude at sea was a pivotal issue in maritime undertakings. Science does not settle its technique of discourse in isolation from the process of discovery. Men did not invent the calculus and then proceed to investigate the laws of motion. They discovered the need for a new logical technique in the process of discovering the laws of motion, and declared that the pre-existing logic was faulty in the teeth of derision from the official logicians like Berkeley. Need we say more if we but recall the historic reflection of Newton, prince of scientific logicians. His first correct calculations of the earth's gravitational pull on the moon remained buried for a decade or more, because of what seemed to be a 10 per cent error due to a faulty figure for the moon's earth distance as then recorded. *Hypothesis non fingo* was the epitaph with which they were laid aside.

Whether the suggested similarity between mechanics and economics is pertinent is a matter susceptible to historical examination. This is somewhat unfortunate, because one of the axioms of the London and Vienna school is that history cannot teach them. Since history does not repeat itself, history (they say) cannot become a science. Accordingly (we presume) palaeontology is not a science, nor is petrology. Need we even stop with physics, in which, as Professor Levy reminds us, no experiment is ever repeated in *exactly* the same way?

We might have hoped that the substantial scholarship and English empirical common sense of the Webbs would have produced a more healthy attitude to social research. If the Webbs ever flattered themselves that they would find a following in the universities, they failed to reckon with the Idol of Purity. The special province of the Idol of Purity is to protect its worshippers against dangerous thoughts. Chemists want to make new compounds and to discover new elements. If those who pursue the social sciences really wanted to make new institutions and discover new modes of social living, the social sciences might advance with equal rapidity. The plain truth is that the academic value of social research in our universities is largely rated on a futility scale. A social inquiry which leads to the conclusion that something has to be done or might be done is said to be "tendencious." In daily hymns to the Idol of Purity this refrain recurs with soporific solemnity like *selah* in the Psalms of David. If natural scientists prohibited all investigations when the research worker was suspected of wanting to find how to do something, science would come to a standstill.

Besides ensuring innocuous aimlessness when social inquiries make contact with the real world, the Idol of Purity prescribes a gentlemanly understanding that every discipline in the university curriculum is sufficient in its own right. Political science, economics, and sociology are entitled to arrive at incompatible conclusions so long as each refrains from examining the credentials of the others. During the evolutionary controversy biologists did not take this view of professional ethics. There were giants in those days. In natural science the greatest advances often occur in the region where two traditional disciplines overlap. No chemist is now anxious to tell you that what he is doing is too pure to have any connection with physics. The crippling effect of the Continental phlogiston doctrine, at a time when English physicists had set the stage for great theoretical developments, has taught the student of natural science that he cannot afford to circumscribe the boundaries of his inquiries in advance.

It is therefore difficult for a naturalist to understand why

Professor Robbins is so anxious to convince us that Austrian economics, which, if a science, is presumably concerned with aspects of human behaviour, has nothing to do with psychology, which, if a science, is also concerned with characteristics of human behaviour. The urgency with which he defends the purity of his subject from contamination with empirical studies is perhaps explained by his pre-Baconian conviction (p. 132) that "the relation of pork to human impulses . . . is verifiable by introspection." Genuine scientific knowledge of the biological basis of human nature, and the search for the laws which condition social habits and social preferences, are perforce dismissed with the assertion that in choosing between alternative systems of society "only a complete awareness of the implications of modern economic analysis can confer the capacity to judge rationally" (p. 139). If economists displayed a more becoming modesty towards their own intellectual limitations, it would be harsh to add that a rational judgment on the choice of social organization would demand considerably more knowledge of electricity, biochemistry, and genetics than writers on economics usually possess.

The fruitful association of social and naturalistic inquiries in the programme of the Invisible College was possible because Petty and others like him realized that what is a "weighty matter" is also a social question. Speaking of the origins of its successor, Sprat says "and from this Institution and Assembly it had been enough if no other advantage had come but this, that by this means there was a race of young men provided against the next age." If the present teaching of the new humanistic studies in our universities falls short of this, we need not seek the remedy afar. The exaltation of "pure" thought which bears no fruit in action exacts its own penalty in the growing disposition to regard reason and progress as exploded liberal superstitions. The younger generation have found out their teachers. A pitiable predilection for action without thought is the legitimate offspring of thought divorced from action.

There are two ways in which scientific principles can be applied to social practice. One, the condition of expanding knowledge is to discover the ways and means of getting something done. This was Boyle's way, when he declared that the "goods of mankind may be much increased by the naturalist's insight into the trades." The other, the signal of decadence, is to devise ingenious arguments for not doing something. This was the way of Malthus, whose essay was written to discredit Condorcet's belief that war, poverty, and disease are eradicable nuisances. Biology furnishes us with examples of both ways of using scientific theories. The *Heads and Enquiries* of the Royal Society in its early days, the present *Medical Research Council*, and Sir John Orr's studies on mulnutrition illustrate the first. The *Rassen hygiene* of Dr. Frick and his professional hirelings in Hitler Germany illustrate the second. *Rassenhygiene* is the offspring of the crude selectionism whose first parent was Malthus.

It is symptomatic of the temper of social studies that the phlogistonist of demography is far better known than Petty or Graunt, both of whom made enduring contributions to the science of human welfare. The Essay on Population is a fitting footnote on the Baconian theme that "radical errors in the first concoction of the mind are not to be cured by the excellence of functions and remedies subsequent." The Malthusian argument, as we all know, was based on a self-evident principle inherent in the original definitions of human ingenuity and parenthood. For these he went back to the Rhind papyrus in which the scribe Ahmes—seemingly prompted by the reflection that slaves fill a granary slowly and mice multiply rapidly—gives one of the earliest recorded examples of arithmetical and geometrical progressions. Intervening advances in technology and biology did not suggest to Malthus the need for clarifying either the limits of human ingenuity (a matter of thermodynamics) or the limits of human reproductive capacity (a matter of social physiology).

His views about the former were based on implicit assumptions which still obtrude themselves in the teaching of economics. Lacking the imaginative insight of the men who drew up the *Heads and Enquiries*, he was unable to foresee the possibility that biotechnology could make land a secondary asset of food production. His estimates of potential reproductive capacity were based on an adventitious remark of Benjamin Franklin. This we now know was certainly wrong. From the first to last page of his apology of misery there is no single constructive suggestion for research nor hint of the scientific curiosity which we find in the pages of Graunt and Petty. Further attention to the substance of the Malthusian apology is unprofitable. In the second edition Malthus introduced a host of qualifications and negations to meet the criticisms which greeted the first. So most of his statements can be offset with others in the contrary sense, and when his disciples fall back from this line of defence they can reinforce their faith by the assurance that Malthus was less concerned to demonstrate fact than to disclose a "tendency." If the word *tendency* has any use in genuine science, it is to describe something that can be made to happen by isolating the appropriate situation. Apparently the disciples of Malthus think that what Malthus described would happen if they did not practise what Malthus presumably scheduled as "vice."[1] The evidence marshalled by Carr Saunders leads one to doubt whether a situation described by the arithmetical jingle of the gloomy parson has any basis in recorded experience of human societies.

As phlogistonism failed to meet the social needs dictated by expanding chemical industry, current events are now compelling us to take up the problems of political arithmetic, where Petty left them. Contrary to everything Malthus taught, productivity has increased beyond the most optimistic forecast of Robert Owen, while the rate of reproduction in all highly industrialized countries of the West has steadily declined. Since the rate of reproduction has sunk below the limit compatible with continued survival in many countries, the problem of how to arrest further decline has become, as Shelborne would say, "a matter of government and the greatness of the people."

Unless otherwise specified the word fertility is used in this book in a purely descriptive sense without reference to influences variously classified as genetic, psychological, mechanical, or social. For the benefit of readers who are not familiar with certain elementary considerations relevant to the study of fertility, it is necessary to emphasize the fallacy of drawing conclusions about changing fertility from a rising or falling birth-rate. The birth-rate gives the number of children born per annum per 1,000 members of the population. By itself a fall or rise in this tells us nothing about the reproductive capacity of a population. This is easily seen if you consider two populations both composed exclusively of parthenogenetic females who have had or will have the same number of children in the course of their lives. If in the same year one community is exclusively composed of women of child-bearing age and the other is half made up of individuals younger than fifteen years or older than fifty years of age, the number of births in the second will be roughly half as great as the number of births in the other. Consequently the birth-

[1] The only category which the celibate author left free for contraceptive practice.

rate of the first (i.e. number of births per 1,000 population) for that year will be twice as great as that of the second.

Even if the birth-rate were a reliable index of fertility it would not be an explicit one. By itself it could not tell us whether a community is replacing its numbers. The right way to decide whether a community is capable of replacing itself is to measure fertility by the number of girl children born on the average to one woman in the course of her reproductive life. This can be done when public statistics record the age of the mother at the birth of each child. In England and Wales at the present level of fertility one hundred women on the average have eighty-five daughters in the course of the entire child-bearing period. There would thus be a 15 per cent deficit of replacement in each generation even if every daughter herself survived to become a mother. In other words, no further fall in mortality can arrest a continuous decline, and nothing short of immortality can safeguard us against extinction unless fertility is raised by considerably more than 15 per cent. This would not be achieved even if all women married unless the average married woman had more children.

You may ask: Why, then, do the Registrar-General's returns still show a slight annual increase in the population of Britain? Leaving migration out of account, the reason for this is that there is a necessary time-lag before a fall in fertility exerts its full effect if mortality is falling at the same time. That such a time-lag may occur is easy t' see with the help of a fictitious illustration. Imagine a community in which every woman died at the age of sixty and produced one female offspring in the course of her life. The female section of this community would be numerically stable so long as this fictitious state of affairs lasted. If a certain proportion of women became sterile while mortality remained the same, the annual births in the succeeding year would be less than the number of deaths. It might happen that mortality would not remain the same. For instance, we can imagine that all women of nearly sixty might live to be nearly sixty-one. The number of annual deaths would suddenly drop in the ensuing year. So there might be an excess of births over deaths in spite of the contemporary drop of fertility. If mortality persisted at the new level, the proportion of older people in the population would increase to a certain limit and the population would continue to grow for some years; but if the average number of girls reared by the women remained less than one apiece, the

B

population would eventually begin to decline and continue to do so. The character of population growth in modern industrial communities resembles this fictitious situation in so far as it depends on a simultaneous fall of fertility and mortality. The fall in the latter can only check the effect of the former temporarily. An extension of the average duration of life beyond the child-bearing period has no effect on the *capacity* for replacement.

A simple and direct method of measuring fertility with due regard to the fact that the proportion of women of child-bearing age in the population is not fixed, and that the number of children borne by women varies at different ages during the period of reproductive life, was devised first by Boekh, and thereafter neglected for many years. It has been developed by R. R. Kuczynski and applied by him to an analysis of recent changes of fertility in all countries for which reliable statistics are available. The technical issues which arise in connection with the calculations involved have been set forth in his three volumes on *The Balance of Births and Deaths* and in his more recent *Measurement of Population Growth*.[1] A more compact and elementary account is given in Dr. Enid Charles's *Twilight of Parenthood*.[2] In the first chapter of the present volume Dr. Kuczynski reviews the situation from an international standpoint. In the second Dr. Charles examines the effect of changing fertility on the age composition of Britain and the prospects of an early decline of its population.

These excursions into political arithmetic show that continued survival can only be accomplished by raising the level of fertility. Dr. Kuczynski finds that fertility cannot be raised to the survival minimum by an increase of nuptiality alone. Hence "it becomes a matter of government and of the greatness of the people" to discover how to devise incentives. As a first step to this it is necessary to discover what social agencies are at present operating to accentuate the decline. A method which approximates to the conditions of a controlled experiment was suggested in a pioneer publication of Sir William Beveridge published in 1925. In his study on *Declining Fertility of European Races* Beveridge drew attention to some consistent differences which emerge on comparing rural and urban communities, or communities with a high and low proportion of Roman Catholics. To devise the perfectly controlled experiment in dealing

---

[1] Sidgwick & Jackson.
[2] Recently reissued under the title *The Menace of Underpopulation* (Watts).

with human communities is a task which calls for caution and patience, and the difficulties of studying differential fertility are increased by the defective character of official statistics. Consequently a vast field of research must be covered before far-reaching conclusions can be drawn. To this pool of information two chapters in this book (Chapters III and IV) have contributed the most extensive materials as yet placed on record. One by Dr. Charles and Miss Moshinsky deals with recent changes in differential fertility. An investigation subsequently undertaken by Mr. David Glass deals with conditions at the time when net fertility began to fall in Britain.

Though more information about the social agencies which are responsible for reducing fertility may help to suggest measures which would arrest a further decline, it is by no means certain that such information will be sufficient to show us what incentives would reverse the present drift and re-establish fertility at the survival minimum. Experiment alone will decide the issue, and the real choice lies between experiments intelligently undertaken to test likely hypotheses and policies of despair undertaken at random. To get a clearer perspective of the issues involved it is necessary to look at the purely quantitative aspect of population from another angle. A low general fertility might result from a large fall of the mean size of the family in some sections of the population without a corresponding fall in others. It is therefore important to know the relative changes in families of different sizes. This cannot be done for Britain because of the inefficiency of public records. It can be done for Australia; and in Chapter V we have a picture of the changing size of the Australian family during a period of declining fertility.

The materials set forth in the first ten chapters do not exhaust the ways in which the problem of re-establishing a survival minimum can be made the subject of political arithmetic. A preliminary statistical survey of social policies which have been implemented in the hope of encouraging fertility has been published by Mr. David Glass. Further work of this type should be prosecuted. A more experimental approach might be made by selecting random groups of parents with large and small families in the same occupational groups and applying an arbitrary method of scoring to the social circumstances of their lives.

One of the features of declining fertility associated with fixed or falling mortality is a shift in the relative age composition of the population, more particularly an increase in the proportion of older and decrease in the proportion of younger people. Changes of demand, of social mores, and of political outlook arising therefrom are not easy to treat with exactitude. What is clear is that a rapid change in age composition must appreciably affect the recruitment of social personnel for different occupations. This raises other issues, such as how far differential fertility with respect to occupation impedes social mobility, and how far social mobility accentuates differential fertility. Before we can answer such questions and before we can make much headway in further studies concerning the characteristics of differential fertility, it will be necessary to bring the treatment of social structure and the machinery of social selection within the scope of political arithmetic. The chapters contained in Part II are a step towards this. Here again let me insist how much remains to be done. We need only reflect on the warmth with which the numerical strength of the wage-earning classes or the growth of salaried occupations is debated by partisans of different persuasions to realize how little real light is available about a question which can only be answered in numerical terms.

As soon as you ask yourself *what would have to be done* to increase, diminish, or maintain at some fixed level the population of a community you discover that you need to know a host of different things which would not occur to you if you set yourself the more general question, "How do populations grow?" The objection commonly raised to this reorientation of social studies is that men are not agreed about what they want. This objection is part of our theological heritage. It rests on the belief that man is naturally sinful and can be morally reclaimed by an act of faith or a course of ethics. The fact that there are some hypochondriacs who prefer to be ill does not prevent biologists from studying what you have to do to keep people healthy. Likewise the fact that some people still believe, like St. Francis, that poverty is a good thing need not prevent sociologists from studying how to get rid of it. We may expect social studies to enjoy the same prestige as the natural sciences when they are as firmly rooted in an accepted and acceptable social objective as the researches financed by the Medical Research Council. Medical science accepts the task of keeping individuals alive and treats arguments about whether it is worth while doing so as frivolous. Social science must undertake the responsibility for keeping the body politic alive or confine its claim for endowment to misanthropic millionaires.

About a year ago I prepared a draft of *Heads of Enquiries* into the growth of population. Its aim was to set down the main topics on which we need information before it is possible to devise any social policy which would re-establish fertility at the survival minimum. Subsequently modified by suggestions from a small group[1] who met to discuss the financial needs of realistic social research in the universities, it was as follows:

HEADS OF ENQUIRIES INTO THE POPULATION OF GREAT BRITAIN

I. AGENCIES INFLUENCING THE GROWTH AND DISTRIBUTION OF NUMBERS IN A COMMUNITY

1. Biological and social agencies related to
   (a) Fertility differentials.
   (b) Changes in character of marriage and in structure of the family group.
   (c) Differential mortality.
2. Resources available for maintaining population of a given size.
   (a) Basic material resources (biotechnical and metallurgical).
   (b) Unused physical productive capacity.
   (c) Unemployed human resources: their transferability and adaptability.
3. Regional distribution of population with respect to
   (a) Location and localization of industry.
   (b) Agencies determining present distribution of population, intra- and international movements of population growth of large towns.
   (c) Social consequences of increasing density of population and of occupational specialization.
4. Aggregate consumption of the community and demand for various types of labour as affected by regional and occupational distribution of population.

II. HOW RESOURCES OF GIFTED SOCIAL PERSONNEL ARE BIOLOGICALLY CONSERVED AND SOCIALLY UTILIZED

1. The educational recruitment of social classes.
2. Relation of maximal to initial earnings in the wage-earning and salaried classes.

[1] The group included Professor Carr Saunders, Professor Sargant Florence, G. D. H. Cole, and Colin Clark.

3. Changes of occupation at various ages of life.
4. Vertical, horizontal, and regional mobility within industrial and social
   units (including the recruitment of administrative and political
   personnel).

III. INTER-RELATIONSHIP OF QUANTITATIVE AND QUALITATIVE ASPECTS OF THE POPULATION PROBLEM

1. Growth and delimitation of social classes.
2. Relation between total and employable population.
3. Effect of urban concentration (housing policy to be taken into account)
   and of occupation upon fertility and public hygiene.
4. Relation of population density to administrative and industrial
   efficiency.
5. Change in general standards of health, education, and social efficiency.

The Heads of Enquiries set down here include many issues not
touched on in this volume. We had hoped to include another
chapter on a topic directly connected with the growth of population.
Unfortunately an enquiry into differential mortality of mothers and
infants was prevented by the refusal of the Ministry of Health to
extend to us the same courtesy which we received from the
Registrar-General. Although Lord Eustace Percy offered to use his
good offices on our behalf, we were met with a blank refusal to our
request for access to printed reports in the library of the Ministry.
Their refusal is the more remarkable because the material could
have been easily obtained if we had had sufficient time and funds
at our disposal. Since Sir John Orr's researches reflect little credit
on the efforts of the Ministry, we do not find it difficult to understand the official attitude. It calls for comment only as a warning
against confusing the aims of a scientific investigation with the
considerations which dictate what the higher officials of the Ministry
are allowed (or see fit) to include in their reports.

Some of the themes mentioned in the first part of our Heads of
Enquiries are included there because circumstances already known
justify a suspicion which may or may not be confirmed by subsequent enquiry. The phenomena of differential fertility dispose of
the illusion that mere spending capacity favours a high reproductive
capacity. Hence it is not likely that any changes in the distribution
of spending power by such means as family allowances will suffice
to re-establish the survival minimum. Other social circumstances of
parenthood must be taken into account. In particular the urban

rural differential prompts enquiry into the spacing of population. Urban congestion commends itself to enquiry for other sufficient reasons. The distribution of population in Britain has taken place during the past century with no prevision of aerial and chemical warfare. So the vast hypertrophy of London in recent years now constitutes one of the pivotal problems of national defence and the international repercussions of rearmament are commensurate with its urgency.

The distributive aspect of population best described as *metropolitanization* illustrates a difference between political arithmetic as Petty conceived it and the trivial issues which sometimes prompt laborious collections of economic statistics. The scholastic aims of the London and Vienna School justify us in restating Bacon's plea for searching out new facts. It is equally necessary to insist that science is not an indiscriminate collection of unrecorded facts. In science hypothesis is suggested by facts, tested by the arbitrament of other facts, refined in the process of testing facts hitherto unknown, and so instrumental in exposing new ones to view. Without judgment in the choice of a problem worthy of our efforts and experience to guide profitable enquiry the fact-loving temperament is as useless as it is indispensable. Thus the study of how population is distributed especially demands the outlook of what Petty would call a man of affairs.

Two (of many) considerations which might throw light on the urban proliferation of the London area suggest hypotheses which might be tested. One is the relative strength of trade union organizations in emigrant and immigrant districts, the provision of amenities which compete with the attractions offered by employees' organizations, and other circumstances which influence the policy of firms towards those they employ. The other is the extent to which the localization of industry is influenced by a large local demand which reduces transport costs. This raises a wider issue involved in more general aspects of the distribution of population, and one which would naturally escape the attention of those who take a teleological view of the monetary system. In the last resort the rational basis for costing the social efficiency of a transport system is a balance sheet of human effort expended and material resources made available by it. Since thermodynamics is not at present an educational prerequisite for social studies, it is not likely that enquiries of this kind will be undertaken in our universities for many years to come. In the meantime a realistic study of interlocking directorates might throw more light on what determines the concession of transport amenities than considerations relevant to price economics are likely to do.

Petty's plea for a balance sheet based on energetics also claims our attention when we consider the technical amenities available for planning a redistribution of population for the maintenance of the survival minimum. In our provisional Heads of Enquiries this class of problems is referred to as *resources available for maintaining population*. Naturally we cannot rely on much enlightenment from those who advertise their limitations by recording "a sense almost of shame . . . at tedious discussions of technical education" and recoil with debutante sensibility from "spineless platitudes about manures."[1] Enquiries of this kind demand knowledge of "the history of trades" supplemented by "magnetics, optics, recipes, and jewelling."

We blundered into the age of coal and steel with no prevision. We are now blundering on the threshold of an era of technical changes which may have far more drastic consequences. Here are a few already in being: the production of mobile power from unlimited supplies of natural energy; electrical communications; the replacement of the heavy metal economy by the light metal alloys from universally distributed sources which can be made available for use without the necessity of high-temperature processes; the replacement of crude traditional building and clothing materials by synthetic plastics and cellulose derivatives; a vast increase in the realizable productivity of field and pasture, crop and stock through synthetic fertilizers, control of soil bacteria, genetic selection for fertility and disease resistance, elimination of parasites and the application of Gericke's water culture or tank-gardening.

In these circumstances men of affairs like Sir Josiah Stamp have the wit to realize that the impact of science on society is a cardinal issue for a science of wealth. Alas, few professors are men of affairs in Petty's sense. Unpleasantly aware that the infusion of a little genuine scientific knowledge would compel them to undertake researches for which they lack both requisite training and social inclination, orthodox economists have adroitly entrenched themselves behind a barricade of paradox which, stripped of rhetoric, reads like this:

[1] *Nature and Significance of Economics*, p. 65.

(i) Wealth is what you have and the man next door has not;
(ii) If he had it, what you have would not be wealth;
(iii) Hence there can be no wealth without scarcity;
(iv) Since there cannot be scarcity if there is plenty, there cannot be plenty if there is wealth;
(v) If there were no wealth, there would be no economics;
(vi) Since we have economics, we cannot have plenty.

I offer no apology for using a plain English word in the plain sense in which Englishmen have always used, and will probably continue to use, it. If the word wealth is to be given a more precise meaning for scientific discussion, the necessary desideratum is to define human needs consistently with the Darwinian doctrine. The biologist is at one with the wholesome wisdom of Professor Tawney when he says that clever men emphasize the differences which separate them from their fellows and wise men emphasize what they have in common. Man is an animal. He has certain needs which he shares with all other animals, e.g. the need to reproduce if he is to survive as a species. He has needs which he shares with particular groups of animals, e.g. his common mammalian needs. He has species needs, which any individual shares with all other members of *Homo sapiens*—diet, shelter, and protection from disease. Finally, he has idiosyncratic requirements, which result partly from the fact that individual members of the species do not have the same hereditary make-up, and probably in greater part because they do not share the same uterine, post-natal, and social environment. Whether you call these requirements "wants" or "needs," it is obvious that in plain English a plain Englishman who has the power to collect Persian carpets is not what is ordinarily called a wealthy man unless he also has the power to order a square meal.

Unless we have been permanently incapacitated for lucid discourse by prolonged preoccupation with the gold standard, the first questions which arise in seeking a basis of public enquiry are whether the common needs of men as members of the same species, phylum, and type of matter are at present satisfied, what resources for satisfying them exist, and how far these resources are used. Thermodynamics supplies the only kind of answer which a scientist can recognize as appropriate. A human being of a given size and age living at a given temperature requires among other things so many calories of organic materials of particular constitution and a certain

B*

amount of material of specified heat conductivity to compensate surface loss by convection and radiation. Whether a community has actual or potential plenty is therefore a calculus for which the materials exist in a world of discourse which Sir Josiah Stamp's recent lecture[1] nowhere penetrates.

Man can secure the requisite minimum of free energy by his own activities with or without the assistance of other species like the horse. He can secure it by liberating the potential energy stored in the earth's surface by the heat engine, in which case there is a permanent calorie debt of human effort entailed in overcoming gravitation. He can also secure it by harnessing natural forces to the production of mobile power. Taking these three major categories, the energy debt in human calories is greatest in the first and least in the last. The word plenty defined with reference to man's species needs has therefore a perfectly clear social meaning which remains in spite of the continued existence of Austrian economists. *Plenty is the excess of free energy over the collective calorie debt of human effort applied to securing the needs which all human beings share.* In this sense the statement that we are living in an age of vast potential plenty as compared with our grandfathers is a truism. It is convenient to conceal it beneath an avalanche of Austrian sophistication, because a very large number of Englishmen and their families are not receiving the bare minimum of daily calories which the British Medical Council prescribes. If they were equipped with the education which Petty prescribed, it would therefore be the business of those who profess a "science of wealth" to undertake enquiries like those of Sir John Orr.

It need hardly be said that exploration of the nature of universal human needs and the means of satisfying them includes many issues which lie outside the scope of Sir John Orr's investigations. This truism does not imply that they cease to be topics for realistic research or that they therefore become the proper perquisites of a scarcity dialectic. When the existence of a universal need is recognized the problem of satisfying it is a joint matter for public accountants and technicians. Health is a universal need. Radium is a necessary reagent of the modern health laboratory. If there is not enough available radium to supply the need, or if the balance sheet of human effort expended in securing supplies shows an inordinate item on the debtor side, nothing is gained by diverting funds from

[1] *The Calculus of Plenty.*

research into the bombardment of sodium atoms by helium nuclei to endow chairs in tautology. That the issue is not essentially different when we have to deal with universal needs which lie outside the scope of biological enquiry is easily seen with the aid of a plausible illustration.

From the late palaeolithic onwards men collected glittering objects such as meteorites and gold nuggets. Women painted their eyelids with malachite in predynastic Egypt, and the practice is believed to have led to the discovery of copper metallurgy. To-day Bantu tribes use clay as a cosmetic, and in recent history native chiefs have bartered away a mining concession for brass bangles. Hence a case might be made for regarding adornment of the person as a species need of *Homo sapiens*. We may assume that this is true for argumentative usage. To clarify the illustration, let us also make the unlikely assumption that mankind has a universal craving for pearls as a means of satisfying it. It is quite clear that the demand for pearls has two components. One is the intrinsic appeal they exert as objects pleasing to the eye. The other depends on knowing that they have monetary value. Its existence is clearly shown by the fact that culture pearls can only be distinguished from "real" ones by the use of laboratory tests. Since at most a few dozen scientists in England can carry out such tests, the price difference has nothing to do with intrinsic appeal of the objects. The existence of culture pearls shows that the supply side of the intrinsic preference does not lie beyond the capacity of technical skill. The preference for real ones calls for the services of the psychologist. His problem is how to educate people to enjoy available sources of satisfaction undistracted by an itch for extraneous ostentation. At present education encourages girls to regard it as "vulgar" to wear "imitations" and ladylike to wear the real article. So the problem of pearl scarcity is essentially one of educational technique. It calls for what Petty called "a dictionary of sensible words." It would present no insuperable difficulties if children were brought up to know that the correct meaning of the adjective vulgar is "of or pertaining to monetary values."

One objection which will at once be raised is that social psychology is not yet sufficiently advanced to give us much information about species needs which lie outside the field of biology, or to show us how to educate tastes. This is self-evident, and what needs to be done is equally obvious. The correct course is to call a moratorium on mere talk and see that more psychological research is prosecuted energetically. It may also be urged that some human needs are not universal, and that they cannot be neglected from a public symposium, because their satisfaction may involve the efficiency of individuals whose special gifts are essential to social welfare. About this two things may be said. First, there can be no acceptable basis for a science of preventive social medicine unless the satisfaction of known universal needs is its first concern. Second, psychologists should have every encouragement to explore the distribution of human capabilities in their relation to the idiosyncratic requirements of individual human beings.

The belief that scarcity is an inescapable condition of settled social existence rests on one of two implicit assumptions. One is that the attempt to educate the human race so that ostentation is not a significant feature of man's social behaviour is an infringement against personal *freedom*. Psychological anti-vaccinationists who use the word freedom to signify the natural right of men and women to be unhappy and unhealthy through scientific ignorance instead of being healthy and happy through the knowledge which science confers need not detain us. The professional economist who is too sophisticated to retreat into the obscurities of libertarian mysticism will prefer the alternative assumption that the need for ostentation is a universal species characteristic. All attempts to eradicate the unconscionable nuisance and discord which arise from hypertrophied craving for personal distinction artificially fostered by advertisement propaganda and good breeding are therefore destined to failure. It may be earnestly hoped that those who entertain this view have sought divine guidance. No rational basis for it will be found in text-books of economics. Whatever can be said about human preferences with any plausibility rests on the laboratory materials supplied by anthropology and social history.

Graduates in the art of normative social surgery are invariably ready with a reason for the hope that is within them when anyone proposes radical operations on the body politic. The hope, needless to say, is that nothing will be done, and the reason, which is always the same, is that, if anything were done, it would not "pay." The crushing cogency of the rebuke depends on the time-honoured recipe of metalypsis inherent in all purely dialectical disputation. Instead of inventing a scientific nomenclature free from extraneous associations, economics, like theology, borrows its terms from common speech, defines them in a sense different from and often opposite to their accepted meaning, erects a stone wall of verbal logic on craftily concealed foundations, and defies the plain man to scale it. According to Professor Robbins, the part of the real world with which economics is concerned is bounded above and below by the two covers of a dictionary. So when the engineer says that a social amenity is technically realizable, and the economist replies that it would not pay, the issue involved is merely one which concerns the "original definitions of the subject-matter."

When there is a science of *social technology* it will give us a balance sheet of human effort, materials, and natural resources expressed in the established equivalence between the various physical units of heat, kinetic energy, and potential energy. If it is complete, the balance sheet will include the necessary minimum of calorie debt involved in the human activity of administration. It need not include the large wastage of calories involved in maintaining the body heat, sudorific and motor activity of speculators, a surfeit of solicitors, and a multiplicity of middlemen. As the word is used in its anti-social sense by the academic apologists of salesmanship, the armament industry "pays" better than a system of scientific food production socially planned to meet the known dietetic minimum needs of a population. When the thermodynamic balance sheet shows that the result of adopting a new process is to increase the free energy of the social system, and the social system operates to pile up a calorie debt of human effort in the manufacture of poison gas, thermite bombs, gas masks, and subterranean concrete shelters the professional employees of the banker exempt neither themselves nor us from the universal conservation of energy by asserting that the new process will not pay. All they contribute to the discussion is the information that they agree among themselves to use the verb to pay in an anti-social sense. In effect they tell us that the system of costing adopted by the Bank of England does not exhibit the social adjustment of human effort to available sources of free energy. That is another way of saying that the existing credit system is not based on the laws of nature like the accountancy of the engineer and biologist.

These pages were written after my resignation from a chair which was founded because Sir William Beveridge subscribes to Petty's plea for the association of naturalistic research with social enquiries. The optimism with which I have outlined the need for enquiries foreshadowed in Petty's writings might therefore seem inconsistent with my conduct. Although six years of an unsuccessful attempt to convince my professorial colleagues that some knowledge of natural science should be part of the training of those who specialize in social studies cured my belief that a new orientation can begin in our universities, they have not destroyed the hope that a science of society will develop. A university is a good house for an accredited science. It is not a lying-in hospital. Fundamental changes in our social culture must have the support of a social movement outside their walls. So was it when men like Priestley, Davy, Faraday, Dalton, and Joule provided the new theoretical leadership of natural science in the latter half of the eighteenth and the first half of the nineteenth century. I believe it will be so when social circumstances once more compel men of scientific training to examine social impediments to scientific discovery. Such were the circumstances of the time when Petty wrote the Political Arithmetic. Sir Gowland Hopkins's retiring address from the presidential chair of the Royal Society may be the portent of a return to the same temper.

CHAPTER I

THE INTERNATIONAL DECLINE OF FERTILITY

by

R. R. KUCZYNSKI

I. NUMBER OF BIRTHS

THE decline of fertility started in France apparently in the second
half of the eighteenth century. But the decrease was so slow that
for a long time it was more than offset by the decrease of mortality,
and, owing to the increase of the population, the actual number of
births did not begin to decline until about 1885. The decline of
fertility started in England in the 1880's. The decrease was here
much more rapid than in France, and the births began to decline
around 1909. In other countries, such as Bulgaria, where a decisive
decline in fertility started only twelve years ago, the decline was
precipitated so much that births began to decrease almost at once.
In the Union of South Africa, on the other hand, where fertility
among the whites has been declining for three or four decades, the
number of births was higher in 1936 than in any preceding year
because population growth, due in part to immigration, offset the
effects of the decrease in fertility. In Ireland, finally, births probably
began to decline before fertility declined because the population
decreased owing to an enormous emigration. Table I shows for a
number of countries the average number of births in 1871–75, the
maximum number of births ever attained (excluding 1920–21), the
minimum number of births since 1850 (excluding 1915–19), and
the number of births in 1936. Table II shows the trend of the number
of births in Western and Northern Europe, in Central and Southern
Europe, and in the whole of Europe, excluding Soviet Russia.

It appears that the number of births in Western and Northern
Europe increased from 3,422,000 in 1841–50 to 4,648,000 in 1901
and decreased thereafter to 4,181,000 in 1914. It dropped to
2,978,000 in 1915–19, rose to 4,335,000 in 1920, and decreased to
2,973,000 in 1933. It thus was slightly lower in 1933 than in the
war period 1915–19. Since 1933 it increased again and numbered
in 1936 3,255,000, that is about as much as in 1930–31. But this
increase was due exclusively to recent developments in Germany,

POLITICAL ARITHMETIC

TABLE I

BIRTHS IN VARIOUS COUNTRIES

Country (Present Territory)	1871–75 Number	Maximum		Minimum since 1850		1936 Number
		Year	Number	Year	Number	
WESTERN AND NORTHERN EUROPE						
Belgium	171,000	1901	202,000	1936	125,511	125,511
Denmark	60,000	1909	81,000	1851	46,000	66,418
England and Wales	831,735	1903	948,271	1933	580,413	605,292
Scotland	120,376	1903	133,525	1933	86,546	88,928
Ireland	144,924	1845	250,000[1]	1932	81,347	83,929
France	981,118	1859	1,041,000	1936	630,059	630,059
Germany	1,420,000	1901	1,810,000	1933	971,174	1,277,052
Holland	133,661	1923	187,512	1855	102,815	171,166
Norway	53,724	1901	67,303	1935	41,321	42,842
Sweden	131,033	1887	140,169	1933	85,020	88,672
Switzerland	81,833	1901	97,028	1855	60,000	64,966
Total[2]	4,141,533	1901	4,648,000	1933	2,973,496	3,254,835

CENTRAL AND SOUTHERN EUROPE

Austria	160,447	1902	191,926	1936	88,264	88,264
Bulgaria[3]	116,000[4]	1924	207,117	1890	113,000	158,800
Czechoslovakia[5]	453,887[6]	1902	472,618	1936	264,647	264,647
Finland	68,319	1909	95,005	1868	43,757	68,895
Italy[8]	1,040,000[9]	1887	1,200,000	1936	962,676	962,676
Poland[15]	1,092,000[16]	1902	1,158,800	1933	868,675	892,320
Spain[10]	600,228[11]	1903	685,265	1880	598,152	631,561[17]

OCEANIA

Australia[12]	65,586	1914	137,983	1860	47,726[13]	116,073
New Zealand[12]	11,978	1922	29,006	1855	1,460[14]	24,837

[1] Rough estimate.
[2] Including Faroe Islands, Iceland, Islands in the British Seas, and Luxemburg.
[3] No data available prior to 1888.
[4] 1888–90.
[5] No data available prior to 1901.
[6] 1901–05.
[7] 1935.
[8] No data available prior to 1872.
[9] 1872–75.
[10] No data available prior to 1878.
[11] 1878–80.
[12] Excluding Aborigines.
[13] Minimum since 1859.
[14] Minimum since 1854.
[15] No data available prior to 1895.
[16] 1895–1900.

TABLE II
MEAN POPULATION, BIRTHS, AND BIRTH-RATES IN EUROPE, EXCLUDING SOVIET RUSSIA

Years	Mean Population	Yearly Births	Birth-rate	Years	Mean Population	Yearly Births	Birth-rate
WESTERN AND NORTHERN EUROPE*				CENTRAL AND SOUTHERN EUROPE†			
1841–45	107,674,000	3,427,455	31·8	1922	170,000,000	5,445,000	32·0
1846–50	110,874,000	3,416,551	30·8	1923	172,250,000	5,444,000	31·6
1851–55	112,783,000	3,463,061	30·7	1924	174,025,000	5,388,000	31·0
1856–60	115,471,000	3,653,409	31·6	1925	176,018,000	5,366,000	30·5
1861–65	119,825,000	3,832,920	32·0	1926	178,104,000	5,339,000	30·0
1866–70	123,688,000	3,959,796	32·0	1927	179,961,000	5,199,000	28·9
1871–75	126,857,000	4,141,533	32·6	1928	181,785,000	5,274,692	29·0
1876–80	132,648,000	4,342,776	32·7	1929	183,550,000	5,159,481	28·1
1881–85	137,628,000	4,309,691	31·3	1930	185,350,000	5,352,442	28·9
1886–90	142,405,000	4,292,983	30·1	1931	187,594,000	5,131,666	27·4
1891–95	147,600,000	4,382,912	29·7	1932	189,912,000	5,128,913	27·0
1896–00	154,518,000	4,530,761	29·3	1933	192,066,000	4,924,562	25·6
1901–05	162,194,000	4,598,673	28·4	1934	193,893,000	4,952,033	25·5
1906–10	169,720,000	4,497,965	26·5	1935	195,622,000	(4,855,223)	24·8
1911–14	176,329,000	4,247,157	24·1	1936	197,260,000	(4,847,346)	24·6
1915–19	176,741,000	2,978,293	16·9				
1920	176,909,000	4,335,031	24·5		TOTAL		
1921	178,400,000	4,137,491	23·2				
1922	179,653,000	3,847,759	21·4	1922	349,653,000	9,292,759	26·6
1923	181,002,000	3,722,754	20·6	1923	353,252,000	9,166,754	25·9
1924	182,398,000	3,635,423	19·9	1924	356,423,000	9,023,423	25·3
1925	183,558,000	3,634,654	19·8	1925	359,576,000	9,000,654	25·0
1926	184,696,000	3,537,112	19·2	1926	362,800,000	8,876,112	24·5
1927	185,606,000	3,377,795	18·2	1927	365,567,000	8,576,795	23·5
1928	186,520,000	3,415,033	18·3	1928	368,305,000	8,689,725	23·6
1929	187,403,000	3,324,954	17·7	1929	370,953,000	8,484,435	22·9
1930	188,573,000	3,345,725	17·7	1930	373,923,000	8,698,167	23·3
1931	189,666,000	3,195,908	16·9	1931	377,260,000	8,327,574	22·1
1932	190,492,000	3,104,314	16·3	1932	380,404,000	8,233,227	21·6
1933	191,254,000	2,973,496	15·5	1933	383,320,000	7,898,058	20·6
1934	192,095,000	3,220,231	16·8	1934	385,988,000	8,172,264	21·2
1935	192,944,000	3,240,878	16·8	1935	388,566,000	8,096,101	20·8
1936	193,774,000	3,254,835	16·8	1936	391,034,000	8,102,181	20·7

* Present territory of Belgium, Denmark (including Faroe Islands and Iceland), United Kingdom (including islands in the British Seas), Irish Free State, France, Germany, Holland, Luxemburg, Norway, Sweden, Switzerland.

† Present territory of Austria, Bulgaria, Czechoslovakia, Danzig, Estonia, Finland, Gibraltar, Greece, Hungary, Italy, Latvia, Lithuania, Maltese Islands, Poland, Portugal, Rumania, Spain, Yugoslavia. Not included are Albania (population about 1,100,000), European Turkey (about 1,300,000), and also Andorra, Liechtenstein, Monaco, San Marino, Vatican, (total population about 55,000), for which areas no birth data are available. The 1922–27 birth figures for Greece have been estimated. We have further assumed that the 1935–36 birth figures of Yugoslavia were the same as for 1934 and that the 1936 birth figures of Spain were the same as for 1935.

where the number of births, after a decline from 1,810,000 in 1901 to 971,000 in 1933, rose to 1,277,000 in 1936 (1925–26: 1,278,000). In Western and Northern Europe, excluding Germany, the births in 1936 numbered only 1,978,000 as against 2,002,000 in 1933. In some Central European areas, such as Austria, Czechoslovakia, and Finland, the decline in the number of births began likewise before the World War, but the total number of births in Central and Southern Europe probably was never higher than in 1922–23, when it amounted to about 5,445,000. It declined to about 4,850,000

TABLE III

MEAN POPULATION, BIRTHS, AND BIRTH-RATES IN GERMANY AND IN THE REST OF WESTERN AND NORTHERN EUROPE, 1933–36

Years	Germany			Rest of Western and Northern Europe		
	Mean Population	Births	Birth-rate	Mean Population	Births	Birth-rate
1933	66,027,000	971,174	14·7	125,257,000	2,002,322	16·0
1934	66,409,000	1,198,350	18·0	125,686,000	2,021,881	16·1
1935	66,871,000	1,263,976	18·9	126,073,000	1,976,902	15·7
1936	67,346,000	1,277,052	19·0	126,428,000	1,977,783	15·6

in 1935–36. The decline in Central and Southern Europe from 1922–23 to 1935–36 was 11 per cent, or slightly larger than the decline in Northern and Western Europe from 1901 to 1914.

II. BIRTH-RATES

It is generally believed that the birth-rate, i.e. the yearly number of births per 1,000 inhabitants, was fairly constant for Western and Northern Europe as a whole until about 1876, and then began to decline. I do not quite share this view. The birth-rate prior to 1815 showed frequent ups and downs; it apparently decreased in the twenty-five years following the Napoleonic wars; and after that it was fairly constant up to about 1886. From 1841 to 1880 the average quinquennial birth-rate oscillated between 30·7 and 32·7; it amounted to 31·3 in 1881–85. There was, to be sure, a decrease in

TABLE IV

BIRTH-RATES, 1881–85, 1930–32, AND 1933–36

Country (Present Territory)	1881–85	1930–32	1933–36
Austria	32·9[1]	15·9	13·5
Belgium	30·9	18·3	15·8
Bulgaria	39·4[2]	30·7	27·7
Czechoslovakia	35·1[3]	21·7	18·3
Danzig	—	20·9	21·5
Denmark	32·4	18·2	17·6
England and Wales	33·5	15·8	14·7
Scotland	33·3	19·1	17·8
Northern Ireland	24·7[5]	20·4	19·6
Irish Free State	22·9[5]	19·5	19·5
Estonia	—	17·5	15·9
Finland	35·5	19·6	18·0
France	25·0[6]	17·6	15·7
Germany	36·8[7]	16·2	17·7
Greece	—	30·3	29·1
Holland	34·8	22·4	20·4
Hungary	44·4[8]	24·2	21·3
Italy	38·0	25·1	23·3
Latvia	—	19·5	17·7
Lithuania	—	27·0	24·4
Norway	31·0	16·5	14·6
Poland	41·9[9]	30·5	26·3
Portugal	—	30·5	28·9
Rumania	42·2[8]	34·7	31·6
Spain	36·4	28·3	26·4[4]
Sweden	29·4	14·9	13·8
Switzerland	28·7	16·9	16·0
Yugoslavia	46·8[10]	34·0	31·4[11]
Canada	—	23·1	20·3
United States	—	18·1	16·8
Australia	35·2	18·3	16·7
New Zealand	36·4	18·1	16·5
Union of South Africa	—	25·3	23·8
Japan	—	32·5	31·0[4]

[1] Pre-war territory, 38·3.
[2] Pre-war territory, 1888–90 (corrected figure).
[3] 1901–05.
[4] 1933–35.
[5] 1881–90.
[6] Pre-war territory, 24·7.
[7] Pre-war territory, 37·0.
[8] Pre-war territory.
[9] 1881–82.
[10] Serbia.
[11] 1933–34.

the late 'seventies and early 'eighties, but this decrease was not greater than had occurred on numerous previous occasions. The decisive factor was that the decrease of the birth-rate did not stop in the 'eighties, but proved to be continuous. The average birth-rate in 1911–14 amounted only to 24.

The World War did not essentially change the trend of the birth-rate. During the war the birth-rate was very low, being only 17 in 1915–19. Immediately after the war the occurrence of many marriages which had been postponed caused the birth-rate to rise temporarily. But even in 1920–21 it was not quite 24, and by 1932–33 it had fallen to 16. Owing to the recent increase in the number of births in Germany it rose to 17 in 1934–36.

But the drop of the birth-rate was by no means confined to Western and Northern Europe. It occurred in North America, in Oceania, and finally also in Southern and Eastern Europe. With the exception of Russia, where natality, while being lower than before the World War, probably is still higher than it was in Western and Northern Europe fifty years ago, practically all countries inhabited by whites have by now passed the stage through which Western and Northern Europe went in the 1880's and 1890's. It is, moreover, noteworthy that in countries where the decrease of the birth-rate started particularly late the decrease was particularly rapid. While it took France over seventy years to experience a drop in her birth-rate from 30 to 20, while this process lasted about forty years in Sweden and Switzerland and about thirty years in England and Denmark, in the last twelve years (from 1924 to 1936) the birth-rate has fallen in Bulgaria from 40 to 26, in Poland from 35 to 26, in Czechoslovakia from 26 to 17. While in 1922 and 1923 the birth-rate of Central and Southern Europe was still at least as high as in Western and Northern Europe in 1881–85, it had dropped by 1935–36 to the level held by Western and Northern Europe in 1911.

III. GROSS REPRODUCTION RATES

Fertility, however, has decreased even more than the fall of the birth-rate indicates, since the proportion of women at child-bearing age has increased with the decrease in the number of children. In order to measure fertility it is necessary indeed to take account of the sex and age composition of the population, and the best method of doing so is to compute the gross reproduction rate by adding

TABLE V

Country	1871–75	1876–80	1881–85	1886–88	1889–90
Austria	—	—	—	—	—
Denmark	—	2·220[1]		—	—
England and Wales	2·344[3]	—	2·278[4]	—	—
Finland	2·388	2·420	2·363	2·400	
France	—	—	—	—	—
Germany..	—	—		2·459	
Norway	2·221[29]	—	2·202	—	—
Russia, European	—	—	—	—	—
Baltic Provinces	—	—	—	—	—
Ukraine	—	—	—	—	—
Sweden	2·147	2·163	2·081	2·049	

Country	1901	1902–03	1904–05	1906–07	1908–09
Austria		2·393		·	2·266
Bulgaria		3·242			3·155
Czechoslovakia	—	—	—	—	—
Western Provinces	—	—	—	—	—
Eastern Provinces	—	—	—	—	—
Denmark..		1·954			1·851
England and Wales	1·725[6]		—	—	—
Scotland	—	—	—	—	—
Estonia	—	—	—	—	—
Finland			2·140		
France	1·393[7]		1·310		
Germany..			2·126		
Saxony	—	—	—	—	—
Hungary	2·605[14]		2·477		
Croatia-Slavonia	2·683[14]		2·668		
Italy	—	—	—	—	—
Norway		2·064[8]		—	—

GROSS REPRODUCTION RATES, 1870–1936*

1891	1892	1893–94	1895	1896–97	1898	1899	1900
—	—	—			2·485		
2·140[2]					2·042		
2·043[5]		—	—	—	—	—	1·725[6]
			2·278				
—		1·447				1·393[7]	
			2·366				
2·142		—	—	—	—	2·064[8]	
—	—	—	—	3·44	—	—	—
—	—	—	—	1·85	—	—	—
—	—	—	—	3·65	—	—	—
	1·968					1·944	

1910	1911–12	1913	1914–15	1916–19	1920	1921	1922
	—	1·999	—	—	—	—	—
	—	—	—	—	—	2·731	
—	—	—	—	—	1·664		—
—	—	—	—	—	1·463		—
—	—	—	—	—	2·273		—
		1·671		1·523		1·384[9]	
1·469	—	—	—	—		1·326	1·213
—	—	—	—	—		1·545	—
—	—	—	—	—	—		1·204[10]
			1·716			1·569	
1·232				0·766		1·233[11]	
—	1·472[12]		0·772[13]			1·141[11]	
2·396			—	—		1·829	—
2·518		—		—	—		—
—	—	—	—	—	—	—	2·0
1·853[16]	—		—	1·661	1·632		—

TABLE V—*continued*

Country	1901	1902-03	1904-05	1906-07	1908-09
Poland[16]	—	—	—	—	—
Russia, European	—	—	—	—	—
Serbia	2·750[14]	—	—	—	—
Sweden		1·881		1·799	
Canada, excluding Quebec ..	—	—	—	—	—
United States[17]	—	—	—	—	—
Australia	—	—	—	—	—
New Zealand	—	—	—	—	—

Country	1923	1924	1925	1926	1927
Austria	—	—	—	—	—
Bulgaria		2·502[19]		2·217	
Czechoslovakia		1·579[9]			1·307
Denmark..		1·384[9]			
England and Wales	1·176	1·120	1·086	1·062	0·992
Scotland	—	—	—	—	—
Estonia			1·133[20]		
Finland				1·402[22]	
France	—	—		1·146	
Germany..	—	—	1·116		—
Prussia	—	—	—	—	—
Saxony	—		0·891		—
Greece	—	—	—	—	—
Holland	—	—	—	—	—
Hungary..	—	—	—	—	—
Italy	—	—	—	—	—
Latvia	—	—	—	—	—
Lithuania	—	—	—	—	—
Luxemburg	—	—	—	—	—
Norway	—	—	—	1·33	1·27
Poland[16]	2·121	1·959	1·983	1·853	1·95

GROSS REPRODUCTION RATES, 1870–1936*

1910	1911–12	1913	1914–15	1916–19	1920	1921	1922
—	—	—	—	—	—	2·241	2·206
—	3·0		—	—	—	—	
		1·594		1·414		1·413	1·280
						1·698	
—	—	—	—	—	1·411	1·36[33]	
1·677						1·517	
—		1·541		1·445		1·442	

1928	1929	1930	1931	1932	1933	1934	1935
0·969	—	—	0·865		0·804		0·77[18]
—	—	1·86		—	—	—	
		1·215		1·116		—	—
1·166			1·069	1·070	1·013	1·039	1·029[30]
0·994	0·961	0·963	0·930	0·899	0·845	0·869	0·866[31]
—	—	—	1·18	—	—	1·098	—
1·018			1·00[21]		0·901		
			1·207[21]	1·1	—	—	
	1·096[23]		1·103[21]	1·03	1·05	1·00	
—	0·971	—	0·862	—	0·82	0·982	1·06[18]
—	—	0·873		—	—	—	
0·796			0·654		0·57	—	—
—	—	1·87		—	—	—	
—	—	1·429	—	—	—	1·262[34]	
—	—	1·356	—	1·238	1·200		
—	—	1·570	1·477[32]				
—	1·093		1·005[24]				
1·850	—	—	—	1·65	—	—	
—	—	1·156	—	—	—		
—	1·041	0·938	0·882				
1·87	1·87	1·72	1·62	1·48[24]			

TABLE V—continued

Country	1923	1924	1925	1926	1927
Portugal	—	—	—	—	—
European R.S.S.R.	—	—	—	2·72	
Ukraine	—	—	2·61	2·485	
Spain	—	—	—	—	—
Sweden	1·221	1·169	1·121	1·069	1·013
Switzerland	—	—	—	—	—
Canada	—	—	—	1·649	
Canada, excluding Quebec		1·596[9]		1·455	
Quebec	—	—	—	2·25	
United States,[27] Whites		1·36[33]	1·292	1·243	1·237
United States,[27] Coloured	—	—	—	—	—
Chile	—	—	—	—	—
Australia	—	1·459	1·437	1·383	1·358
New Zealand				1·301	
Union of South Africa, Whites	—	—	—	1·717	1·692
Japan	—	—	2·506	—	—

FOOTNOTES TO TABLE V

* Italics indicate that the distribution of births by age of mothers has been estimated.

Sources, in so far as rates are not computed by the author:

Statistical Year-Book of the League of Nations, 1936–37, pp. 50–51: Austria, 1933–34; Bulgaria, 1921–22; Czechoslovakia, 1921–33; Estonia, 1922–30; Finland, 1921–22, 1930–32; France, 1930–32; Germany, 1934; Holland, 1930–31; Hungary, 1930–35; Luxemburg, 1930–32; Norway, 1921, 1930–35; Portugal, 1931–32; Switzerland, 1932–36; Canada, 1921–22, 1930–32; United States, 1929–31; Chile, 1930–32; Japan, 1925, 1930.

Danmarks Statistik, *Statistisk Aarbog,* 1937, p. 27: Denmark, 1931–36.

Statistique générale de la France, *Statistique du mouvement de la population, Année 1933,* Première partie, p. 68: Bulgaria, 1930–32; Estonia, 1930–32; Greece, 1931–32; Spain 1928–30; *1935,* I, p. xlvii: France, 1933–35.

Maandschrift van het Centraal Bureau voor de Statistiek, 1937, p. 154: Holland, 1935. *Bevolkingsstatistiek, Mededeeling,* No. 5: Holland, 1936.

Metropolitan Life Insurance Company, *Statistical Bulletin,* December 1937, p. 5: United States, 1920–24, 1930–34.

New Zealand, *Monthly Abstract of Statistics,* September 1937, p. xx: New Zealand, 1936.

Dr. Enid Charles, this volume, Ch. II: Scotland, 1921–34.

L. I. Dublin and A. J. Lotka, "The True Rate of Natural Increase of the Population of the United States," *Metron,* vol. viii (1930), pp. 110–13: United States, 1925–28.

GROSS REPRODUCTION RATES, 1870–1936*

1928	1929	1930	1931	1932	1933	1934	1935
—	—	1·868		1·894[25]	—	—	—
—	2·4	—	—	—	—	—	—
2·24	1·98	—	—	—	—	—	—
	1·75	—	—	—	—	—	—
1·001	0·936	0·945	0·900	0·880	0·821	0·815	—
—	—	—	—	0·964	—	0·898[26]	—
—	—	1·554	—	—	—	—	—
—	—	—	—	—	—	—	—
2·21							—
1·188		1·106			1·04[35]		—
—		1·101	—	—	—	—	—
—	—		2·261	—	—	—	—
1·338	1·274	1·255	1·145	1·062	1·053	1·029	1·030
			1·179	1·077	1·053	1·030	1·013[28]
1·623	1·644	1·647	1·576	1·485	1·427	—	—
—	—	2·324	—	—	—	—	—

David Glass, this volume, p. 168: England and Wales, 1870–1912.

Hansi P. Pollak, "European Population Growth since Union," *The South African Journal of Economics*, vol. 4, p. 21: Union of South Africa, 1926–33.

S. H. Wolstenholme, "The Future of the Australian Population," *The Economic Record*, December 1936, p. 197: Australia, 1924–35.

[1] 1878–84.
[2] 1885–94.
[3] 1870–72.
[4] 1880–82.
[5] 1890–92.
[6] 1900–02.
[7] 1898–1903.
[8] 1899–1905.
[9] 1921–25.
[10] 1922–23.
[11] 1920–23.
[12] 1911–14.
[13] 1915–19.
[14] 1900–01.

[15] 1910–11.
[16] 1921–26, Provinces of Poznań and Pomorze only.
[17] Whites in 23 Registration States only.
[18] 1935–36.
[19] 1921–26.
[20] 1922–26.
[21] 1930–32.
[22] 1921–30.
[23] 1928–31.
[24] 1933–36.
[25] 1931–32.

[26] 1934–36.
[27] 1925–28, in 22 Registration States only; 1929–32, excluding South Dakota and Texas.
[28] 1936: 1·044.
[29] 1871–76.
[30] 1936: 1·042.
[31] 1936: 0·874.
[32] 1936: 1·40.
[33] 1920–24.
[34] 1936: 1·256.
[35] 1930–34.

TABLE VI

TREND OF GROSS REPRODUCTION RATES, 1880–1935

	About 1880	About 1895	About 1910	About 1925	About 1935
Over 3·2	Russia	Russia			
2·8–3·2		Poland	Bulgaria Russia		
2·4–2·8	Austria Germany	Austria	Croatia	Russia Japan	
2·2–2·4	Denmark England Finland Norway	Finland Germany	Hungary	Bulgaria	Japan
2·0–2·2	Sweden	Denmark Norway	Austria	Poland	
1·8–2·0		Baltic Prov. England Sweden	Finland Germany Norway		
1·6–1·8	France		Denmark Sweden Australia	Canada Union S. Africa	Bulgaria Greece Portugal
1·4–1·6		France	England New Zealand	Czechoslovakia Finland Australia	Italy Lithuania Poland Canada Union S. Africa
1·2–1·4			France	Denmark Norway United States New Zealand	Holland
1·1–1·2				France Germany Sweden	Finland Hungary
1·0–1·1				England Estonia	Czechoslovakia Denmark Germany Latvia Scotland United States Australia New Zealand
0·9–1·0					Estonia France
0·8–0·9					England Norway Sweden Switzerland
0·7–0·8					Austria

the specific fertility rates (ratio of female births to female population) of the individual years of age. The sum thus obtained shows the average number of girls born to a woman who lives through child-bearing age.

Until fifty years ago the gross reproduction rate exceeded 2 in every European country except France and Ireland. By 1895 it had dropped below 2, for example, in England and Sweden. By 1910 it was below 2 in every country of Western and Northern Europe, and also in Australia and New Zealand. By 1925 it still exceeded 2 in Russia, in the Balkan States, in Poland, and it exceeded 1 in every country of Europe as well as in every overseas area predominantly inhabited by whites. By 1935 Russia, apparently, was the only European country in which it exceeded 2, and it was below 1 in England, Norway, Sweden, Belgium, France, Switzerland, Austria, and Estonia.

In Western and Northern Europe as a whole the gross reproduction rate exceeded 2 until about 1890. By 1914 it had declined to about 1·5. It dropped below unity in 1931 and has been below unity ever since. In Central and Southern Europe it still exceeded 2 in 1922–23. By 1935 it had declined to about 1·5.

IV. NET REPRODUCTION RATES

Wherever the gross reproduction rate is constantly below 1 the population must die out even if every newly born girl reaches the age of fifty. Wherever the gross reproduction rate is constantly above 1 the population will reproduce itself if a sufficient number of newly born girls passes through child-bearing age. The best method of ascertaining the net reproduction consists in multiplying the specific fertility rates (ratio of female births to female population) of the individual years of age by the numbers of females living at those ages according to the life table. The sum of these products is the net reproduction rate. It shows (on the basis of present fertility and mortality) the average number of girls born to a newly born girl, or, what amounts to the same, the average number of future mothers born to a mother of to-day.

The net reproduction rate, of course, must always be smaller than the gross reproduction rate. Both rates could only be equal if all newly born girls reached child-bearing age and passed through child-bearing age. The proportion of such girls has increased

TABLE VII

Country	1871–80	1881–84	1885–90	1891–1894	1895
Austria	—	—	—	—	
Bulgaria	—	—	—	—	—
Denmark	—	—	1·463		
England and Wales	1·519[2]	1·572[3]	—	1·419[4]	—
Finland	—	1·485		—	--
France	—	—	—	—	—
Germany	—	1·448			
Hungary	—	—	—	—	—
Croatia-Slavonia	—	—	—	—	—
Norway	1·571	1·513	—	—	
Russia, European	—	—	—	—	—
Baltic Provinces	—	—	—	—	—
Ukraine	—	—	—	—	—
Serbia	—	—	—	—	—
Sweden	1·454	1·455			
United States[10]	—	—	—	—	—
Australia	—	—	—	—	—
New Zealand	—	—	—	—	—

FOOTNOTES TO TABLE VII

* Italics indicate that the distribution of births by age of mothers has been estimated.

Sources, in so far as rates are not computed by the author:

Statistical Year-Book of the League of Nations, 1936–37, p. 50: Japan, 1930.

Statistique du mouvement de la population, 1933, I, p. 83: Bulgaria, 1930–32; Czechoslovakia, 1929–30; Denmark, 1930–32; Estonia 1930–32; Finland, 1930–32; France, 1930–32; Greece, 1931–32; Luxemburg, 1930–32; Spain, 1928–30; Switzerland, 1932; New Zealand, 1930–32; Chile, 1930–32; *1935*, I, p. xiv: France, 1933–35.

Statistisches Jahrbuch für das Deutsche Reich, 1937, p. 93; *Wirtschaft und Statistik*, 1937, pp. 246, 279: Germany, 1932–36.

Bevolkingsstatistiek, Mededeeling, No. 5: Holland, 1930–36.

Norges Offisielle Statistikk, Folkemengdens Bevegelse, 1921–1932, p. 114; *1935*, p. 41: Norway, 1899–1900, 1920–31, 1935.

Sveriges Officiella Statistik, Befolkningsrörelsen, 1933, p. 38*; 1934, p. 39*: Sweden, 1931–34.

Population Index, 1937, p. 214: United States, 1935.

New Zealand, *Monthly Abstract of Statistics*, September 1937, p. xx: New Zealand, 1936.

NET REPRODUCTION RATES, 1870–1936*

1896–97	1898–99	1900	1901	1902–05	1906–10	1911–15	1916–20
1·411			1·428		1·410	1·305[1]	—
—	—	—	1·878		1·760	—	—
1·509			1·524		1·486	1·372	1·228
—	—	1·295[5]				1·132[6]	—
—	—		1·433			1·161	
—		0·979[7]			0·930[8]		
1·512			1·480		—	—	
—	—	1·445		—	—	—	—
—	—	1·416		—	—	—	—
—	1·570[8]		1·556			1·365	
1·65	—	—	—	—	—	—	—
1·15	—	—	—	—	—	—	—
1·96	—	—	—	—	—	—	—
		1·613		—	—	—	—
1·435			1·429		1·288	1·111	
—	—	—	—	—	—	1·159[11]	
—	—	—	—	—	1·396[12]	—	
—	—	—	—	—	1·357	—	

Dr. Enid Charles, this volume, Ch. II: Scotland, 1934.
David Glass, this volume, p. 168: England and Wales, 1870–1932.
Ryoichi Ishii, *Population Pressure and Economic Life in Japan*, p. 112: Japan, 1925.
Alfred J. Lotka "Modern Trends in the Birth-Rate," *The Annals* (Philadelphia), November 1936, p. 7: United States, 1925–34.
E. P. Neale, *The Commerce Journal*, September 25, 1937, p. 1: New Zealand, 1935.
Pollak, p. 35: Union of South Africa, 1926.
Stefan Scule, "Le mouvement naturel de la population en Pologne depuis 1895 jusqu'à 1935," *Statistique de la Pologne*, Série C, Fascicule 41, p. 124: Poland, 1927–34.
S. H. Wolstenholme, p. 198: Australia, 1911, 1932–34.

[1] 1913.	[13] 1926–27.	Poznań and Po-
[2] 1870–72.	[14] 1926–30.	morze only.
[3] 1880–82.	[15] 1920–22.	[25] 1934: 0·703.
[4] 1890–92.	[16] 1934–36: *0·76*.	[26] Prior to 1933 not all
[5] 1900–02.	[17] 1934.	States included.
[6] 1910–12.	[18] 1933–35.	[27] 1934: 0·980; 1935:
[7] 1898–1903.	[19] 1921–30.	0·961.
[8] 1908–13.	[20] 1920–23.	[28] 1932–34.
[9] 1899–1900.	[21] 1934: 0·82; 1935:	[29] 1932–34: 1935: 0·780
[10] Whites in 23 Registra-	0·88; 1936: 0·89.	[30] 1935: 0·94; 1936:
tion States only.	[22] 1935; 1936: 1·097.	0·967.
[11] 1920.	[23] 1920–21.	[31] 1934: 0·90; 1935:
[12] 1911.	[24] 1921–26: Provinces of	0·87.

TABLE VII—*continued*

	1921	1922	1923	1924	1925
Austria	—	——	—	—	—
Bulgaria			1·534		
Czechoslovakia	—	—	—	—	—
Denmark..			1·186		
England and Wales	1·113[15]		—	—	—
Scotland	—	—	—	—	—
Estonia	—	0·877		—	—
Finland					1·074[19]
France		0·977[20]	—	—	
Germany..	—	—	—		0·924
Prussia	—	—	—	—	
Saxony	—	—	—		0·757
Greece	—	—	—	—	—
Holland	—	—	—	—	—
Hungary	1·127[23]	—	—	—	—
Italy	—	—	—	—	—
Latvia	—	—	—	-	—.
Luxemburg	—	—	..	—	—.
Norway	1·337[23]	—	. —	—	—
Poland[24]	1·506	1·559	1·523	1·434	1·467
Portugal	—	—	—	—	—
European R.S.F.S.R.	—	—	—	—	—
Ukraine	—	—	—	—	—
Spain	—	—	—	-	—
Sweden			1·058		
Switzerland	—	—	—	—	—
Canada	—	—	—	—	—
United States,[26] Whites.. ..	—	—	—	—	1·128
Chile	—	—	—	—	—
Australia	1·319[15]		—	—	—
New Zealand	1·291	—	—	—	—
Union of South Africa	—	—	—	—	—
Japan	—	—	—	—	1·495

NET REPRODUCTION RATES, 1870–1936*

1926	1927	1928	1929	1930	1931	1932	1933
—	—	0·782	—	—	0·714		0·67
—	1·446[13]	—	—		1·27		—
—	—	—	0·96				—
1·012[14]					0·96		0·91
—	—	—	—		0·807		0·73 4[16]
—	—	—	—	—			0·912[17]
—	—	—	—		0·79		0·728[18]
					0·97		0·9
0·929		—	—		0·93		0·88[31]
—	—	0·818		—	0·748	0·71	0·70[21]
—	—	—	—		0·755		—
—	—	—	—	—		1·25	0·5
—	—	—	—	1·25			1·102[22]
—	—	—	—	1·011		—	—
—	—	—	—	—	1·209	—	1·18
—	—	—	—	0·890			—
—	—	—	—	0·97			
—	—	—	—	0·890		0·82[29]	
1·323	1·303	—	—	—		1·186	1·114
—	—	—	—	1·33 ι		—	1·29
	1·7		—	—	—	—	—
	1·676	1·63	1·39	—	—	—	—
—	—	1·24		—	—	—	—
	0·857				0·777	0·758	0·706[25]
—	—	—	—	—		0·85	
—	—	—	—	1·319	—	—	
1·084	1·096	1·049	—	1·079	—	0·997	0·940[27]
—	—	—	—	1·30			—
—	—	—	—	—		0·956[28]	
—	—	—	—	1·06			0·978[30]
1·449	—	—	—				—
—	—	—	—	1·571	—	—	—

TABLE VIII

TREND OF NET REPRODUCTION RATES, 1895–1935

	About 1895	About 1910	About 1925	About 1935
Over 1·8	Ukraine			
1·6–1·8	Poland Russia Serbia	Bulgaria	Russia Ukraine	
1·4–1·6	Austria Denmark Finland Germany Hungary Norway Sweden	Denmark Germany Norway	Bulgaria Poland Union S. Africa Japan	Russia (?) Japan
1·2–1·4	England	Austria Finland Sweden Australia New Zealand		Bulgaria Portugal Ukraine Canada Chile Union S. Africa
1·0–1·2	Baltic Prov.	England	Denmark Finland Hungary United States	Holland Iceland Irish Free State Italy Lithuania Poland Spain
0·8–1·0	France	France	Austria England Estonia France Germany Sweden	Czechoslovakia Denmark Finland France Germany Hungary Latvia Luxemburg Northern Ireland Scotland United States Australia
Under 0·8				New Zealand Austria Belgium England Estonia Norway Sweden Switzerland

considerably in the course of the last hundred years. In England, for instance, according to the mortality of 1838–54, 697 out of 1,000 newly born girls reached the age of 15, and 473 the age of 50, while for 1933–35 the corresponding figures are 910 and 799.

Fifty years ago the net reproduction rate in England, Germany, and the Scandinavian countries was 1·4 or 1·5. This means an increase of 40 or 50 per cent within a generation. Conditions were more or less the same in the other countries of Western and Northern Europe with the exception of France and Ireland, where the net reproduction rate was about 1; the population there merely held its own. In some Eastern countries, such as Bulgaria and the Ukraine, it was nearly 2, which means almost a doubling of the population within a generation. At present the rate is below 1 in all countries of Western and Northern Europe, with the exception of Holland and the Irish Free State; it is likewise below 1 in Austria, Czechoslovakia, Hungary, Finland, Estonia, Latvia, the United States, Australia, and New Zealand. It is below 0·8 in England, Norway, Sweden, Belgium, Switzerland, Austria, and Estonia. The only European countries in which it is above 1·2 are Portugal, the Balkan States, and Soviet Russia.

In Western and Northern Europe as a whole the net reproduction rate has dropped from 1·3 in the 1880's to 0·8 in 1933–36. In Central and Southern Europe as a whole it still is about 1·15. For the whites as a whole it may also be around 1·15; but excluding Soviet Russia it probably has not been above unity since 1932.

V. EFFECTS OF CHANGING MORTALITY

Owing to the reduction of mortality the difference between the gross and the net reproduction rate has decreased very much in the course of time. If no newly born girl died before 50 years of age they would all live 35 years in child-bearing age (15 to 50 years). In Western and Northern Europe, a hundred years ago, the average number of years lived in child-bearing age was about 20. It now is about 30. The ratio of the net to the gross reproduction rate has therefore increased from about 20 : 35 to about 30 : 35 or from about $\frac{4}{7}$ to $\frac{6}{7}$. In New Zealand, according to mortality of 1933, the average number of years lived in child-bearing age was as high as 32 years and 2 months. The net reproduction rate is here only about 7 per cent lower than the gross reproduction rate. The effects

TABLE IX

FEMALE SURVIVORS AND YEARS LIVED IN
CHILD-BEARING AGE

| Country | Period | Females Surviving out of 1,000 Live-born | | Years lived between 15 and 50 Years |
		15 Years	50 Years	
Austria	1931–32	867	738	28·41
Bulgaria	1926–27	728	549	22·38
Czechoslovakia	1929–32	823	689	26·76
Denmark	1931–35	915	805	30·53
England and Wales	1933–35	910	799	30·25
Scotland	1930–32	875	744	28·76
Northern Ireland	1925–27	867	683	27·52
Irish Free State	1925–27	880	703	28·11
Estonia	1932–34	861	728	27·93
Finland	1921–30	846	665	26·57
France	1928–33	884	727	28·47
Germany	1932–34	903	796	30·11
Holland	1921–30	913	797	30·31
Hungary	1930–31	790	635	25·06
Italy	1930–32	822	693	26·80
Latvia	1929–32	866	733	28·20
Norway	1921–30	924	771	29·80
Portugal	1930–31	773	629	24·71
Sweden	1926–30	916	779	29·89
Switzerland	1929–32	926	800	30·54
European R.S.F.S.R.	1926–27	696	558	22·17
Ukraine	1926–27	734	583	23·22
Canada	1931	890	767	29·31
United States (Whites)	1929–31	921	788	30·38
Australia	1932–34	940	837	31·51
New Zealand	1933	956	863	32·17
Union S. Africa (Whites)	1925–27	890	763	29·36

which a further reduction of mortality may have here upon net reproduction are negligible. In some countries of Central and Southern Europe, on the other hand, it is conceivable that the net reproduction rate might rise substantially through a reduction of mortality if fertility were not to decline any further. But for the future net reproduction in the total territory comprised by Western civilization changes in mortality will no longer play a very important part. The decisive factor will be the trend of fertility.

VI. EFFECTS OF CHANGING NUPTIALITY

Many people believe that an increase of nuptiality would have a considerable effect on fertility, and the recent experience of Germany may at first sight seem to confirm this opinion. Owing mainly to the grant of marriage loans the number of marriages rose from 516,793 in 1932 to 638,573 in 1933 and to 740,165 in 1934. At the same time the number of births rose from 971,174 in 1933 to 1,198,350 in 1934, to 1,263,976 in 1935, and to 1,277,052 in 1936.[1] The net reproduction rate thus increased from 0·7 in 1933 to nearly 0·9 in 1935 and 1936. But this increase, which was relatively large although not sufficient to ensure a replacement of the population, was due only in part to the increase of nuptiality, and as early as March 1935 the vital statistician of the German Statistical Office, Friedrich Burgdörfer, called attention to the fact that the high level of marriages could not possibly be maintained:

The large increase of marriages can last, of course, only as long as, so to say, "the stock lasts." This stock of marriageable young people is, it is true, still extraordinarily large, firstly, because in the time of the preceding economic depression more than 300,000 marriages which normally were due before 1933 had been postponed and are only now being contracted, and secondly, because the marriageable age-groups at present are still recruited from the large generations born before the war. But the stock of marriageable young people will shrink very considerably in the years following 1936, because at present the small generations born during the war are entering the marriageable age. The generations which now will become marriageable reach only 50 or 60 per cent of the numerical strength of the young generations which now furnish the bulk of those who get married. Since also after the World War the number of births has decreased extraordinarily (to less than one million as against two million before the war), *the subsequent marriageable generations will not for a long time again reach the present strength*.[2]

The number of marriages decreased actually from 740,165 in 1934 to 651,435 in 1935, and although 171,460 marriage loans were

---

[1] All these figures include the Saar Territory.

[2] Friedrich Burgdörfer, "Zur Kritik der neuesten deutschen Bevölkerungsentwicklung," *Deutsche Allgemeine Zeitung*, March 3, 1935.

TABLE X

MARRIAGES AND BIRTHS IN GERMANY, 1933–37*

Year	First Quarter	Second Quarter	Third Quarter	Fourth Quarter	Total
		UNASSISTED MARRIAGES			
1932†	99,935	135,545	119,804	154,313	509,597
1933†	94,878	158,453	133,032	103,230	489,593
1934†	86,543	113,088	135,093	172,088	506,812
1935†	92,260	150,496	111,487	134,110	488,797
1935‡	93,884	152,437	112,718	135,023	494,613
1936‡	79,337	128,154	103,677	128,555	438,171
1937‡	81,922	120,815	107,140		
		ASSISTED MARRIAGES			
1933†	—	—	24,849	116,710	141,559
1934†	51,895	83,044	43,545	46,135	224,619
1935†	34,559	39,237	37,541	42,800	154,277
1935‡	34,560	39,662	38,364	44,202	156,822
1936‡	35,739	43,450	43,378	48,824	171,460
1937‡	35,153	47,097	45,699		
		TOTAL MARRIAGES			
1932†	99,935	135,545	119,804	154,313	509,597
1933†	94,878	158,453	157,881	219,940	631,152
1934†	138,438	196,132	178,638	218,223	731,431
1935†	126,819	189,733	149,028	176,910	643,074
1935‡	128,444	192,099	151,082	179,225	651,435
1936‡	115,076	171,604	147,055	177,379	609,631
1937‡	117,075	167,912	152,839		
		BIRTHS EXCLUDING THOSE TO ASSISTED MARRIAGES			
1932†	262,868	250,135	237,370	227,837	978,210
1933†	246,915	243,425	237,184	215,781	943,305
1934†	251,526	264,638	265,061	269,993	1,051,218
1935†	289,923	287,088	263,828	248,640	1,092,140
1935‡	294,290	291,369	268,051	252,435	1,108,907
1936‡	283,774	283,188	265,148	260,261	1,090,358
1937‡	276,402	272,409	251,131		
		BIRTHS TO ASSISTED MARRIAGES			
1933†	—	—	536	13,074	13,610
1934†	29,498	31,181	34,606	34,676	129,961
1935†	38,904	38,343	39,415	37,800	154,625
1935‡	38,904	38,356	39,535	38,265	155,069
1936‡	44,724	47,086	47,014	47,830	186,694
1937‡	52,791	57,242	55,119		
		TOTAL BIRTHS			
1932 †	262,868	250,135	237,370	227,837	978,210
1933†	246,915	243,425	237,720	228,855	956,915
1934†	281,024	295,819	299,667	304,669	1,181,179
1935†	328,827	325,431	303,243	286,440	1,246,765
1935‡	333,194	329,725	307,586	290,700	1,263,976
1936‡	328,498	330,274	312,162	308,091	1,277,052
1937‡	329,193	329,651	306,250		

* The quarterly figures are in part provisional and therefore are not in agreement with the totals for the year.

† Excluding the Saar Territory.   ‡ Including the Saar Territory.

granted in 1936 as against 156,822 in 1935, the total number of marriages dropped further to 609,631.

One must distinguish indeed between the temporary and the permanent increase of births obtainable through an increase of marriages. The temporary increase may be enormous, but the permanent increase is limited not only by the number of females at marriageable age, but also by the proportion of girls who with present nuptiality never marry. The best method of ascertaining this proportion consists in computing a nuptiality table which is calcu-

TABLE XI

FEMALE NUPTIALITY TABLE OF ENGLAND, 1930-32

Years of Age	Remaining Unmarried	Years of Age	Remaining Unmarried	Years of Age	Remaining Unmarried	Years of Age	Remaining Unmarried
16	1,000·0	25	532·3	34	233·6	43	186·9
17	997·9	26	464·8	35	224·5	44	184·6
18	988·5	27	408·2	36	216·8	45	182·5
19	962·5	28	362·1	37	210·6	46	180·5
20	919·0	29	325·7	38	205·2	47	178·8
21	859·9	30	297·0	39	200·0	48	177·1
22	776·2	31	275·0	40	196·3	49	175·6
23	693·1	32	·258·3	41	192·8	50	174·2
24	610·4	33	244·4	42	189·7		

lated in the same manner as a life table of the female population, the only difference being that the number of single females is substituted for the number of all females, and the number of first marriages for the number of deaths. Such a nuptiality table for England, 1930-32, shows that out of 1,000 girls reaching marriageable age, 826 got married before having passed through child-bearing age, while 174 remained unmarried.

The gross reproduction rate of England, 1933, was about 0·845. Of the 845 girls borne by 1,000 females passing through child-bearing age about 40 were illegitimate children. Since, according to the nuptiality table, 826 out of 1,000 females reaching the age of 50 years had married, the gross reproduction rate of women who married (once or more), if measured by legitimate births only, was $\dfrac{0·805}{0·826} = 0·97$.

If, however, we assume that about one-half of the illegitimate girls were borne (either before, or during, or after marriage) by women who had married, the gross reproduction rate of married women would reach unity. If we further assume that the 174 girls who remained single had married at the same ages as those who did marry and had displayed the same fertility, the gross reproduction rate for all females would have been 1. But the last assumption evidently leads to an overestimate of the effect of universal marriage upon the reproduction rate, since the proportion of sterile women is probably larger among those who remain single than among those who do marry.

An approach to universal marriage might have a stronger effect upon reproduction, for instance, in the Free State of Ireland and in Northern Ireland, where the proportion of girls who do not marry is much larger than in England. The effect probably would be less marked in Sweden, where nuptiality, it is true, is low but where the proportion of illegitimate children is very high. It would be negligible in countries like France and Germany, where nuptiality is high and the proportion of illegitimate children also is rather high. In such countries the number of births may increase temporarily if marriages are promoted, but marriages could not be kept permanently on a much higher level than heretofore, since anyway only a very small proportion of girls remained unmarried.

We thus reach the conclusion: No conceivable decrease of mortality or increase of nuptiality will have a decisive effect upon the future net reproduction in the total territory comprised by Western civilization. The decisive factor will be the trend of matrimonial fertility.

CHAPTER II

THE EFFECT OF PRESENT TRENDS IN FERTILITY AND MORTALITY UPON THE FUTURE POPULATION OF GREAT BRITAIN AND UPON ITS AGE COMPOSITION

by

ENID CHARLES[1]

I. INTRODUCTION

FROM the beginning of the nineteenth century until the outbreak of the World War the population of England and Wales increased by 1·25 per cent per annum. The rate of growth during this period was larger than for any other country in Europe. From mid-year 1914 until mid-year 1924 the average yearly increase was 0·47 per cent, and from mid-year 1924 to mid-year 1934 only 0·44 per cent.

The enormous population growth prior to the World War occurred in spite of considerable emigration. The slowing down of the population increase in 1914–24 was due to the high war mortality and the decrease of fertility. The smallness of the population increase in 1924–34 was due to a further decrease of the latter. In recent years immigration has exceeded emigration. The *gross reproduction rate* of England and Wales is now less than unity. This fertility index is the total of the specific fertility rates for each year of age multiplied by the proportion of female births to total births. It indicates the number of girls that would be born on the average to a woman passing through the child-bearing period, provided fertility remained constant. The estimated figure for 1933 was 0·845. This means that whatever changes in mortality ensue, *nothing can arrest a continuous decline of the total population, unless something happens to increase fertility above its present level*

Although the gross reproduction rate of Scotland in recent years has been higher than that of England and Wales, there has been a large outward balance of migration, resulting in a decrease of about 40,000 in the census population of 1931 as compared with that at the census of 1921. More recently the balance of migration has been inwards, resulting in an increasing population. In 1933 fertility

---

[1] Leverhulme Research Fellow.

in Scotland was sufficiently high to maintain an almost stationary population, but previously the rate of decline had been as rapid as in England and Wales.

Although a gross reproduction rate below unity would eventually lead to extinction, there may be a considerable time-lag before a population which has attained such a level of fertility begins to decline in numbers. The present situation thus raises three issues of considerable social significance. The first is how soon a decline of population will set in if fertility does not rise above the level of the last five years. The second is how rapid such a decline will be if nothing occurs to restore the gross reproduction rate to unity or to increase it above unity. The third is what immediate effect upon the age composition of the population will result from the conditions of fertility and mortality prevailing now. Since a considerable change in age composition must intervene during the time-lag before an actual decline sets in, the last is very relevant to any projected social legislation affecting housing, educational policy, and pensions. In addition, it suggests the further question: Will the shift in the proportion of the wage-earning population be so great as to evoke serious economic consequences?

Among the secondary effects of a considerable shift in age composition the future of the crude mortality rate raises interesting problems. For many years improved sanitation and the progress of medical science have borne fruit in a sustained drop in the annual proportion of deaths. With an increasing proportion of old people in the population no conceivable advance in biological knowledge can suffice to maintain this decline of the crude mortality rate, which until now has been a rough index of social well-being. The average yearly excess of births over deaths in England and Wales amounted in 1838–1913 to 300,000, in 1914–23 to 220,000, in 1924–33 to 176,000. In 1933 it numbered only 84,000. The decrease in 1933 was due to the fact that the number of births (580,850) was lower than in any year since 1849, and that the number of deaths (496,550) was higher than in any year since 1919 with the exception of 1929. The death-rate in 1933 was 12·3, or practically the same as in 1920–22. But it would be a mistake to conclude that mortality was practically as high in 1933 as in 1920–22. The mean expectation of life at birth had in the meantime increased from 57·55 to 60·8 years, and the death-rate derived from the life table had decreased from 17·4 to 16·5. The ageing of the population had reduced the gap between the death-rate derived from the life table and the crude death-rate computed by relating the number of deaths to the total population. If fertility and mortality remain what they are, the crude death-rate will approach more and more to the death-rate derived from the life table and will ultimately exceed it. Or, to put it otherwise: if the rate of mortality for each year of age remains what it is, the number of deaths will show a large increase. The ageing of the population will at the same time reduce the number of births, which is bound to decrease considerably if fertility remains at its present level.

Clearly it is beyond the province of social science to predict what the total population of a community will be at some future date. On the other hand, it is a legitimate and profitable task to examine what consequences must ensue if no unforeseen social agencies intervene to raise fertility. We can at least state:

(i) What results would occur if the future growth of population is determined by present fertility and mortality rates, or what results would occur if fertility and mortality continue to fall in the manner suggested by the experience of recent years.

(ii) What effect the falling fertility of the past few years will have upon those age-groups whose size cannot be affected by current or future births. Since there is no likelihood that there will be a spectacular change in mortality figures, such an estimate in the absence of war is capable of providing a substantial basis for legislative policies. A further necessary limitation to any estimate of population is our ignorance of the extent of future migration. However, this only affects the issue in one way. Unless there is a very decisive change with regard to immigration policy, the effect of migration will not greatly magnify the figures computed, though it might conceivably diminish them. While estimates based on such assumptions do not entitle us to predict what the size of the population or its age composition will be after the lapse of a given number of years, we can:

(a) assign certain limits within which the population must lie unless unforeseen social agencies are brought to bear upon its maintenance or unless active steps are taken to avoid the consequences of present conditions;

(b) make a reasonable forecast of how the changing age composition will affect the numbers of children, persons over the age of retirement, etc., during the next ten or twenty years.

The scope of this investigation is to make such computations on different assumptions which may reasonably be taken to circumscribe the likely course of events. Two estimates in the sense defined above have been computed separately, first for England and Wales and also for Scotland. In making the first estimate, (a), it is assumed that fertility and mortality rates from 1935 onwards will be the same as they were in 1933, this being the most recent year for which the necessary data are available. In estimate (b) account is taken of the fact that fertility and mortality rates have been falling continuously over a number of years, and it is therefore assumed that they continue to fall in a manner suggested by recent experience and which will be described in detail in the next section. These two estimates may therefore be regarded as giving upper and lower limits for the future population on the basis of present experience. Finally, it must be remembered that no account is taken of emigration or immigration after January 1, 1935. Details of the assumptions made will be set forth in the next section.

2. METHOD

(i) In both estimates the estimated male and female population at each year of age on January 1, 1935, was taken as the starting-point. The data available for making this estimate were for England and Wales.

(a) The population by years of age according to the census of April 27, 1931.[1]

(b) The population by years of age up to five, and by quinquennial age-groups from five onwards, for mid-year 1931, 1932, and 1933.[2]

(c) The total births from July 1933 to the end of the third quarter of 1934.[3]

The population by years of age at mid-year 1931 was estimated by assuming that the proportion of persons 5, 6, 7, 8, and 9 years old in the group 5–9 was the same as at the census in April 1931, the total number in the group 5–9 being given by the Registrar-General's estimate. The same assumption was made for each year of age.

The population at mid-year 1932 was obtained by assuming that

[1] By courtesy of the Registrar-General's Office.

[2] Vide *The Registrar-General's Statistical Review of England and Wales for the Year 1931*. Text, p. 108. Idem 1932 and 1933, Tables, Part I, Medical.

[3] *Quarterly Returns of the Registrar-General*, 1934.

the proportion of persons 5, 6, 7, 8, and 9 years old in the 5–9 group in 1932 was the same as the proportion of persons 4, 5, 6, 7, 8 in the 4–8 group in 1931. The numbers at each year from 0 to 5 are given by the Registrar-General.

The population at mid-year 1933 was arrived at in the same way as that for 1932.

In estimating the population at mid-year 1934 it was assumed that the number of children under one year of age at that date was equal to the number of births from July 1, 1933, to June 30, 1934, multiplied by the stationary population under one according to the life table for 1933 (vide infra). It was assumed that the difference between the number of children aged 1–2 on July 1, 1934, and the number aged 0–1 on July 1, 1933, was the same as the difference between these two age-groups in 1933 and in 1932. A similar assumption was made for the other years of age.

The population on January 1, 1935, was estimated by the same method as that used to calculate the population of 1934. The births for the last quarter of 1934 not having been published at the time the calculations were made, they were estimated on the basis of the first three quarters of 1934. It has since been seen that this figure was somewhat too low. The assumption underlying the estimates for 1934 and 1935 was that mortality and migration were the same between July 1933 and January 1935 as they were between July 1932 and July 1933.

(ii) First estimate.

(a) The assumptions on which the first estimate is based are that fertility and mortality rates continue to be the same as in 1933. No specific fertility rates for England and Wales are available, only the total number of births being known. It was therefore assumed that the total births in 1933 were distributed among the women of different ages (obtained as above) in the same proportion as they were distributed in Sweden, 1931.[1] The gross reproduction rate (vide p. 73) thus obtained for England and Wales, 1933, was 0·845. The gross reproduction rate for Sweden, 1931, was 0·895.

The specific death-rates for each year of age in 1933 were available.[2] From these, in conjunction with the computed population at each year of age, abridged life tables for each sex were prepared

---

[1] Vide *Sveriges Officiella Statistik, Befolkningsrörelsen, Ar 1930, 1931.*

[2] *The Registrar-General's Statistical Review of England and Wales for the Year 1933,* Part I, p. 124.

according to the method described by Kuczynski.[1] The mean expectation of life at birth derived from these tables was 58·9 years for males and 62·8 years for females. The net reproduction rate for 1933 was found to be 0·734. The net reproduction rate is obtained by multiplying the specific fertility rates for each year of age by the number of females living at each year of age in the stationary population and multiplying the total by the proportion of female births to all births. It indicates the number of girls who will eventually be born to each newly born girl, according to the fertility and mortality rates prevailing at the time the net reproduction rate is calculated.

(b) Computation of deaths in 1935.

Since the population at age 0–1 in January will be at age $\frac{1}{2}$–$1\frac{1}{2}$ in mid-year, it was necessary to calculate mortality rates at ages $\frac{1}{2}$–$1\frac{1}{2}$, etc. The mortality rate at age $\frac{1}{2}$–$1\frac{1}{2}$ was assumed to be the average of the mortality rates at ages $\frac{1}{2}$–1 and 1–2. The mortality rate at age $1\frac{1}{2}$–$2\frac{1}{2}$ was assumed to be the average of the mortality rates at ages 1–2 and 2–3 and so on. The number of deaths during 1935 was computed as follows:

Let a = number of females at age 5–6 on January 1, 1935
 m = death-rate of females at age $5\frac{1}{2}$–$6\frac{1}{2}$
 D = deaths during 1935 of females at age 5–6 at beginning of year

$$\text{then } D = a \times \frac{2m}{(2+m)}$$

Finally, the population at each year of age, except 0–1 on January 1, 1936, is obtained by subtracting from the number at the previous year of age in 1935 the deaths during 1935, and similarly for subsequent years.

(c) Computation of births in 1935.

The procedure is similar.

Let a = number of females at age 15–16 on January 1, 1935
 D = deaths during 1935
 f = fertility rate of females at age $15\frac{1}{2}$–$16\frac{1}{2}$
 B = births during 1935 to females at age 15–16 on January 1, 1935

$$\text{then } B = \left(a - \frac{D}{2}\right) \times f$$

[1] Kuczynski, *Fertility and Reproduction*, p. 17.

The sex ratio between male and female births was assumed to be the same as in 1933.

(*d*) Computation of population between 0 and 1 on January 1, 1936.

The female population was obtained by multiplying the number of female births for 1935 by the female stationary population under one year of age according to the life table. The male population was calculated in the same way.

(*e*) Abridged method.

The population up to 1965 was computed in the manner described above. For the period 1965 to 2035 an abridged method was used which takes very much less time to compute. The population was calculated by quinquennial age-groups. The numbers at age 5–9 in 1970 were assumed to be in the same ratio to the numbers at age 0–4 in 1965 as these age-groups are to each other in the stationary population according to the 1933 life table. The births between January 1, 1965, and January 1, 1970, were obtained by applying quinquennial fertility rates to the average female population in each quinquennial age-group during these years. The population at age 0–4 in 1970 was obtained by multiplying the births during the previous five years by the stationary population under 5. The abridged method is a cruder method than that which proceeds by single years, since the age distribution within a quinquennial group is assumed to be that of the stationary population. In order to test the correspondence of the two methods, both were used on the population from 1935 to 1965 according to estimate (*a*). The results are shown in Table I.

It will be seen that in estimating the total population the abridged method is sufficiently accurate. For the quinquennial age-groups the difference was in no case more than 1 per cent.

The details of computation were the same for all the estimates, so that it only remains to describe the assumptions on which estimate (*b*) was based.

(iii) Second estimate.

In estimate (*b*) an attempt was made to project into the future the fall in fertility and mortality rates that has occurred during past years. As no accurate specific fertility rates were available, the quite arbitrary assumption was made that fertility rates for females under 20 would remain constant, that the fertility rates for females at age 20–24 would be decreased by 5 per cent every five years, for females 25–39 by 15 per cent every five years, and for females 40–49 by 25 per cent every five years, the fall continuing until 1985 and rates thereafter remaining constant. The distribution of the fall between the different age-groups was suggested by a consideration of the way in which Swedish specific fertility rates changed between

TABLE I

Year	Yearly Method	Quinquennial Method	Difference	
			Amount	Percentage
		MALES		
1940	19,621,829	19,620,006	− 1,823	−0·009
1945	19,673,805	19,666,821	− 6,984	−0·035
1950	19,609,784	19,598,777	−11,007	−0·056
1955	19,420,527	19,407,176	−13,351	−0·069
1960	19,109,261	19,096,487	−12,774	−0·067
1965	18,693,693	18,680,706	−12,987	−0·069
		FEMALES		
1940	21,205,862	21,208,513	+ 2,651	+0·013
1945	21,202,561	21,201,264	− 1,297	−0·006
1950	21,068,281	21,064,053	− 4,228	−0·020
1955	20,786,688	20,781,715	− 4,973	−0·024
1960	20,358,359	20,357,392	− 967	−0·005
1965	19,810,242	19,812,378	+ 2,136	+0·011
		TOTAL		
1940	40,827,691	40,828,519	+ 828	+0·002
1945	40,876,366	40,868,085	− 8,281	−0·020
1950	40,678,065	40,662,830	−15,235	−0·037
1955	40,207,215	40,188,891	−18,324	−0·046
1960	39,467,620	39,453,879	−13,741	−0·035
1965	38,503,935	38,493,084	−10,851	−0·028

1921 and 1931. In England and Wales the estimated gross reproduction rate fell between 1923 and 1933 from 1·176 to 0·845, a drop of about 28 per cent.

According to estimate (b) the gross reproduction rate would fall from 0·737 in the period 1935–40 to 0·566 in the period 1945–50, a drop of 23 per cent, so that it will be seen that the error in extrapolating thus from the present trend is on the conservative side. The final gross reproduction rate reached in estimate (b) for the period 1980-85 was 0·259. A curve of the type $y = Ae^{-Kx} + C$ fitted to the gross reproduction rates for 1921-33 would give a considerably steeper fall.

It was further assumed that mortality rates for persons under 1 year would fall by 20 per cent every five years, for those between 1 and 70 by 10 per cent every five years, the fall ceasing in 1965. Mortality rates for 70 and over were assumed to remain unchanged. The final mortality reached in 1965 resulted in a mean expectation of life at birth of 68·3 for males and 71·1 for females. The computations for estimate (b) were made by single years up to 1965, and thereafter by the abridged method.

The population figures upon which the Scottish estimates were based were those for mid-year 1934, obtained from the Registrar-General for Scotland, to whom acknowledgments are due. They were adjusted to January 1935 by the method already described, and from that date onwards the estimates take no account of emigration or immigration. The specific death-rates used were those for 1933. Life tables constructed by the abridged method on the basis of these rates resulted in an expectation of life for males of 56·66 years and for females of 60·32. These may be compared with the Registrar-General's life tables, 1934, based on the census of 1931 and on mortality for 1930, 1931, and 1932, which give the expectation of life for males and females as 56·0 and 59·5 respectively.

The specific fertility rates used were those for 1934. They were obtained by adjusting the births according to the age distribution of fertility in Sweden in 1926. The gross reproduction rate thus obtained was 1·098 and the corresponding net reproduction rate 0·912. Estimate (a) is thus based on the fertility of 1934 and the mortality of 1933, and these rates are assumed to remain constant thereafter. In 1921 the gross reproduction rate of Scotland was 1·545, and in 1931 it was 1·18. This is a drop of 23·6 per cent. The drop since 1931 has been rather steeper. A consideration of the rates of change of the gross reproduction rates in England and Wales and in Scotland made it appear that the change was sufficiently similar in both countries to justify the application to Scotland of the same assumptions as to future rate of fall as those used for England and Wales. In estimate (b), therefore, the same assumptions are made about the future fall in fertility and mortality rates as were made for estimate (b) for England and Wales. The populations in future years are calculated by the quinquennial method.

3. RESULTS

The total population of England and Wales at 5-yearly intervals from 1935 to 2035 according to estimates (*a*) and (*b*) is shown in Tables II and III. Figures for the separate age-groups for England and Wales have been published elsewhere.[1]

TABLE II

TOTAL POPULATION (IN THOUSANDS) OF ENGLAND AND WALES, JANUARY 1935–2035. FIRST ESTIMATE

1935	40,563	1970	37,343	2005	27,090
1940	40,828	1975	36,038	2010	25,736
1945	40,876	1980	34,614	2015	24,467
1950	40,678	1985	33,106	2020	23,268
1955	40,207	1990	31,559	2025	22,121
1960	39,468	1995	30,019	2030	21,019
1965	38,504	2000	28,522	2035	19,969

TABLE III

TOTAL POPULATION (IN THOUSANDS) OF ENGLAND AND WALES, JANUARY 1935–2035. SECOND ESTIMATE

1935	40,563	1970	33,787	2005	15,058
1940	40,655	1975	31,452	2010	12,628
1945	40,392	1980	28,857	2015	10,456
1950	39,766	1985	26,087	2020	8,563
1955	38,777	1990	23,258	2025	6,940
1960	37,441	1995	20,440	2030	5,567
1965	35,799	2000	17,685	2035	4,426

The total populations according to both estimates are shown in Fig. 1 in the form of a graph. Fig. 1 shows that, however steep the future fall in fertility may be, there will, owing to our present abnormal age composition, be a considerable period before there is any marked decrease in the total size of the population, but that thereafter the decrease is rapid. This point will be referred to again in a later section.

The corresponding figures for Scotland are given in Tables IV and V. The figures for separate age-groups are deposited in the Archives of the Royal Society of Edinburgh. The totals are shown

[1] Special Memorandum No. 40. London and Cambridge Economic Service.

graphically in Fig. 2. The present rate of reproduction in Scotland is sufficiently high to maintain the population at a practically

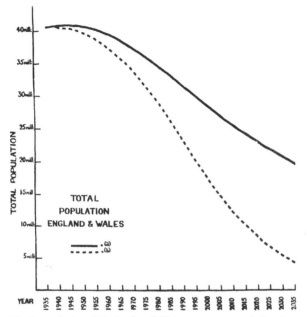

FIG. 1.—Total population of England and Wales, 1935–2035, calculated according to two different assumptions.

stationary level for a very long time. On the other hand, if the rate of fall seen in past years were to continue, it would eventually result in a steeply declining population.

TABLE IV

TOTAL POPULATION (IN THOUSANDS) OF SCOTLAND, JANUARY 1935–2035. FIRST ESTIMATE

1935	4,945	1970	5,361	2005	5,014
1940	5,053	1975	5,345	2010	4,950
1945	5,151	1980	5,314	2015	4,890
1950	5,235	1985	5,270	2020	4,831
1955	5,299	1990	5,213	2025	4,770
1960	5,341	1995	5,149	2030	4,709
1965	5,360	2000	5,081	2035	4,647

TABLE V

TOTAL POPULATION (IN THOUSANDS) OF SCOTLAND,
JANUARY 1935–2035. SECOND ESTIMATE

1935	4,945	1970	4,772	2005	2,600
1940	5,050	1975	4,558	2010	2,258
1945	5,114	1980	4,295	2015	1,935
1950	5,133	1985	3,989	2020	1,638
1955	5,110	1990	3,657	2025	1,369
1960	5,044	1995	3,309	2030	1,131
1965	4,935	2000	2,953	2935	925

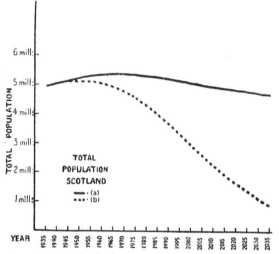

FIG. 2.—Total population of Scotland, 1935–2035, calculated according to two different assumptions.

4. AGE COMPOSITION

It has been seen that any effect of declining fertility on the total size of the population will not be very considerable for some years. On the other hand, decided changes in age composition are now taking place as a result of the declining fertility of previous years and are of some immediate social interest. The percentage age composition of the total population of England and Wales from 1935 to 2035 according to estimates (*a*) and (*b*) is given in Tables VI and VII.

TABLE VI—PERCENTAGE AGE COMPOSITION.
TOTAL POPULATION, ENGLAND AND WALES. FIRST ESTIMATE

Year	0–4	5–14	0–14	15–19	20–59	15–59	60 +
1935	7·05	16·27	23·32	7·39	56·84	64·23	12·45
1940	6·58	14·22	20·80	8·63	56·85	65·48	13·72
1945	6·45	13·18	19·63	7·30	58·23	65·53	14·84
1950	6·30	12·71	19·01	6·74	58·44	65·18	15·81
1955	6·07	12·57	18·64	6·40	58·36	64·76	16·60
1960	5·83	12·32	18·15	6·40	57·86	64·26	17·59
1965	5·62	11·96	17·58	6·38	56·95	63·33	19·10
1970	5·47	11·60	17·07	6·26	56·01	62·27	20·66
1975	5·39	11·33	16·72	6·11	55·28	61·39	21·89
1980	5·38	11·19	16·57	5·98	55·27	61·25	22·18
1985	5·37	11·17	16·54	5·91	54·06	59·97	23·50
1990	5·35	11·20	16·55	5·90	53·80	59·70	23·74
1995	5·32	11·22	16·54	5·94	53·92	59·86	23·60
2000	5·31	11·20	16·51	5·97	54·21	60·18	23·32
2005	5·31	11·16	16·47	5·97	54·32	60·29	23·23
2010	5·32	11·15	16·47	5·95	54·27	60·22	23·31
2015	5·33	11·15	16·48	5·93	54·13	60·06	23·46
2020	5·33	11·17	16·50	5·92	54·03	59·95	23·55
2025	5·32	11·18	16·50	5·93	54·02	59·95	23·55
2030	5·32	11·18	16·50	5·94	54·08	60·02	23·48
2035	5·32	11·17	16·49	5·95	54·16	60·11	23·40

TABLE VII—PERCENTAGE AGE COMPOSITION.
TOTAL POPULATION, ENGLAND AND WALES. SECOND ESTIMATE

Year	0–4	5–14	0–14	15–19	20–59	15–59	60 +
1935	7·05	16·27	23·32	7·39	56·84	64·23	12·45
1940	5·84	14·33	20·17	8·68	57·25	65·94	13·90
1945	5·11	12·67	17·78	7·42	59·38	66·80	15·42
1950	4·46	10·94	15·40	6·96	60·62	67·58	17·01
1955	3·83	9·73	13·56	5·94	61·87	67·81	18·63
1960	3·23	8·57	11·80	5·37	62·13	67·50	20·69
1965	2·68	7·43	10·11	4·84	61·40	66·24	23·64
1970	2·20	6·33	8·53	4·30	60·19	64·49	26·97
1975	1·81	5·34	7·15	3·77	58·84	62·61	30·24
1980	1·56	4·49	6·05	3·25	58·07	61·32	32·63
1985	1·36	3·85	5·21	2·79	55·11	57·90	36·88
1990	1·24	3·41	4·65	2·40	52·66	55·06	40·29
1995	1·12	3·10	4·22	2·15	49·81	51·96	43·83
2000	1·01	2·87	3·88	1·97	47·66	49·63	46·49
2005	0·93	2·59	3·59	1·87	45·61	47·48	48·93
2010	0·88	2·49	3·37	1·77	43·64	45·41	51·22
2015	0·84	2·36	3·20	1·67	41·75	43·42	53·37
2020	0·81	2·28	3·09	1·60	40·03	41·63	55·28
2025	0·79	2·23	3·02	1·56	38·69	40·25	56·74
2030	0·78	2·20	2·98	1·54	37·90	39·44	57·58
2035	0·77	2·19	2·96	1·53	37·75	39·28	57·75

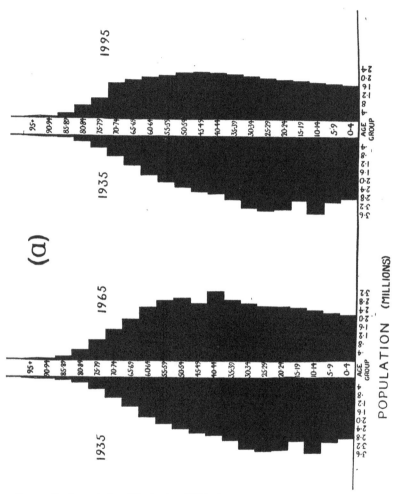

FIG. 3.—Total population of England and Wales by 5-year age-groups, 1935, 1965, 1995.
Estimate (a).

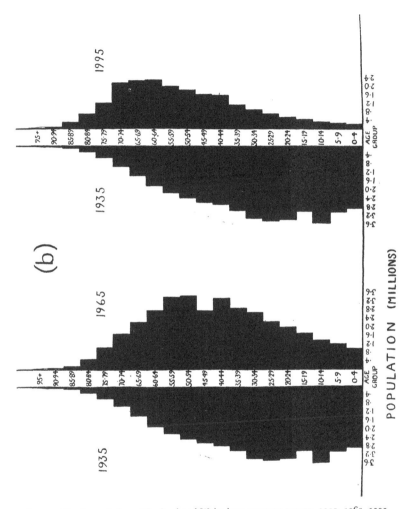

FIG. 4.—Total population of England and Wales by 5-year age-groups, 1935, 1965, 1995.
Estimate (*b*).

(a)

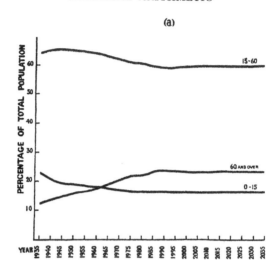

FIG. 5.—Percentage of the total population of England and Wales in the age-groups 0–15, 15–60, 60 and over, 1935–2035. Estimate (a).

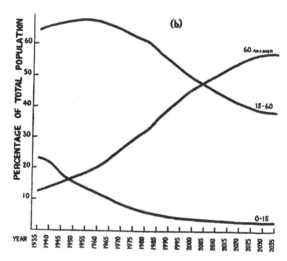

FIG. 6.—Percentage of the total population of England and Wales in the age-groups 0–15, 15–60, 60 and over, 1935–2035. Estimate (b).

The total numbers of both sexes by 5-year age-groups are shown diagrammatically in Figs. 3 and 4 for the years 1935, 1965, and 1995. Graphs of the three large age-groups, 0–15 years, 15–60 years, and 60 and over are shown in Figs. 5 and 6. It will be seen from Fig. 5 that, if present fertility and mortality remain constant, the proportion of persons aged 15–60 years will not be materially affected. The relative proportions of children and old people in the community will be reversed. With continually declining fertility, on the other hand, the preponderance of old people increases enormously. According to estimate (b) persons aged 60 years and over would eventually constitute more than half the total population. Figs. 3 and 4 would appear to indicate that the changing age composition of a declining population may be of greater social consequence than the change in the total number of people.

As in the case of England and Wales, the changes in the age composition of the Scottish population, which are taking place as a result of the falling fertility of past years or which might take place as a result of a future fall, are of more immediate interest than changes in the size of the total population. The age composition of the population in 1935, 1965, and 1995 is shown diagrammatically in Figs. 7 and 8. Graphs of the percentages in three large age-groups are shown in Fig. 9.

With fertility and mortality constant at their present level there is practically no change in the proportion of people aged 15–60. The percentages of children and old people approach more nearly to each other, but do not change places as they do in England and Wales in the same circumstances. The graph of age composition in conditions of declining fertility and mortality is very similar to that for England and Wales, and shows the same steeply rising percentage of old people.

5. THE EDUCATIONAL AGE-GROUPS

On account of the importance of estimating the numbers of children at different levels of the educational ladder, the age-groups 4–14, 11–18, and 18–22 have been treated separately for England and Wales. The totals for these age-groups for 1935 to 1965 are shown graphically in Fig. 10, while the percentages of the total population are given in Table VIII.

The most significant facts which emerge from a consideration of the foregoing figures are (a) that, unless fertility increases, the

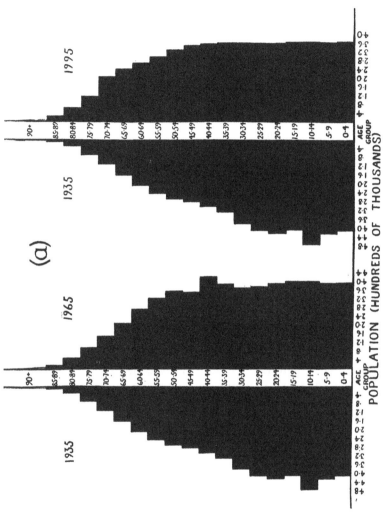

FIG. 7.—Total population of Scotland by 5-year age-groups, 1935, 1965, 1995.
Estimate (a).

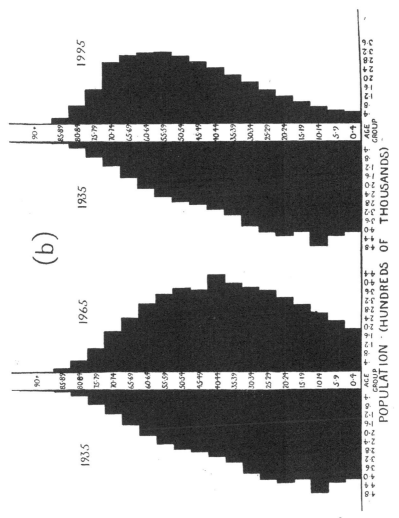

FIG. 8.—Total population of Scotland by 5-year age-groups, 1935, 1965, 1995. Estimate (b).

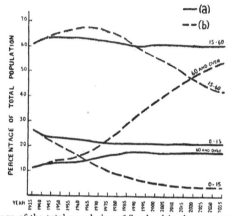

FIG. 9.—Percentage of the total population of Scotland in the age-groups 0–15, 15–60, 60 and over according to estimates (a) and (b), 1935–2035.

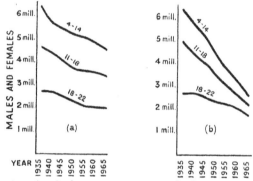

FIG. 10.—Total numbers in the age-groups 4–14, 11–18, 18–22, 1935–1965. Estimates (a) and (b). England and Wales.

TABLE VIII

PERCENTAGE AGE COMPOSITION OF TOTAL POPULATION, ENGLAND AND WALES. EDUCATIONAL GROUPS

Age-group		1935	1940	1945	1950	1955	1960	1965
4–14	(a)	15·68	14·02	13·06	12·72	12·55	12·24	11·82
	(b)	—	13·95	12·24	10·67	9·47	8·23	6·84
11–18	(a)	11·40	10·78	9·96	9·07	8·95	8·91	8·76
	(b)	—	10·85	9·96	8·72	7·73	6·91	5·90
18–22	(a)	—	6·60	6·12	5·66	5·16	5·15	5·18
	(b)	6·54	6·63	6·21	5·83	5·10	4·55	4·01

number of children in the elementary and secondary school population is going to decrease steadily *from now* onwards; and (*b*) that
the proportion of persons belonging to the age-groups of wage-
earners will not change greatly in the near future, because the
inflation of the later age-groups is largely compensated by the
diminution of the juvenile population.

As the population of Scotland was not calculated by single years,
no details of educational groups can be given, but as the numbers
of children aged 5–15 correspond fairly nearly to the elementary
school population, the totals at these ages are shown graphically in
Fig. 11. The effect of the declining fertility of past years is shown

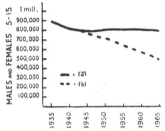

FIG. 11.—Total numbers in the age-group 5–15, 1935–1965. Estimates (*a*) and (*b*).
Scotland.

in a rapid decline in the school population during the next ten
years. On the assumption that fertility continues to fall, this decline
would also continue. In estimate (*a*) the effect of constant fertility
is to produce a practically stationary school population between
1945 and 1965, after which it would begin to decline slowly.

6. CRUDE BIRTH- AND DEATH-RATES

The crude annual birth- and death-rates for England and Wales
resulting from the two alternative assumptions adopted are shown
in Table IX. The crude death-rate is affected by changes in the
age composition of the population. In the light of the previous
section it will be obvious that the increasing preponderance of older
people tends to offset the decreasing risk of death. The crude death-
rates for both sexes are shown in graphical form in Fig. 12. In
estimate (*a*) no further fall in specific death-rates was assumed. It
will be seen that in this event the crude death-rate would rise

TABLE IX

ANNUAL BIRTH- AND DEATH-RATES (CRUDE) PER THOUSAND, ENGLAND AND WALES, 1935–2035

Years.	Birth-rate.									Death-rate.								
	Male.			Female.			Total.			Male.			Female.			Total.		
	(a).	(b).	(c).	(a).	(b).	(c).	(a).	(b).	(c).	(a).	(b).	(c).	(a).	(b).	(c).	(a).	(b).	(c).
1935–1939	15·10	13·21	16·49	13·33	11·67	14·58	14·18	12·41	15·50	13·50	12·46	11·68	12·31	11·51	10·73	12·88	12·07	11·19
1940–1944	14·74	11·39	15·86	13·06	10·09	14·10	13·87	10·72	14·95	14·27	12·39	10·93	13·12	11·42	10·49	13·67	11·88	10·70
1945–1949	14·34	9·79	15·14	12·74	8·67	13·55	13·51	9·21	14·32	15·03	12·63	10·57	14·03	12·05	10·35	14·52	12·33	10·46
1950–1954	13·76	8·30	14·30	12·26	7·39	12·88	12·98	7·83	13·57	15·72	12·99	11·36	14·96	12·76	11·29	15·32	12·87	11·32
1955–1959	13·12	6·91	13·59	11·74	6·18	12·33	12·40	6·53	12·95	16·34	13·48	12·08	15·86	13·61	12·27	16·10	13·55	12·17
1960–1964	12·58	5·66	13·19	11·31	5·09	12·05	11·92	5·37	12·61	16·98	14·06	12·72	16·73	14·59	13·17	16·85	14·33	12·95
1965–1969	12·18	4·60	12·96	11·01	4·15	11·94	11·58	4·37	12·44	17·71	15·58	13·37	17·58	16·27	13·99	17·64	15·94	13·69
1970–1974	11·95	3·75	12·84	10·85	3·41	11·93	11·39	3·57	12·38	18·58	17·57	14·17	18·42	18·20	14·77	18·50	17·89	14·47
1975–1979	11·86	3·18	12·76	10·81	2·90	11·89	11·32	3·04	12·34	19·53	20·18	15·07	19·25	20·42	15·69	19·39	20·25	15·38
1980–1984	11·80	2·77	12·64	10·79	2·53	11·83	11·28	2·64	12·27	20·41	22·78	15·84	19·99	22·85	16·12	20·19	22·82	15·98
1985–1989	11·72	2·49	12·52	10·82	2·28	11·79	11·26	2·38	12·17	21·06	25·39	16·25	20·66	25·25	16·43	20·86	25·31	16·34
1990–1994	11·64	2·23	12·44	10·70	2·04	11·82	11·12	2·13	12·12	21·46	28·13	16·48	20·88	27·74	16·53	21·16	27·93	16·50
1995–1999	11·59	2·01	12·45	10·67	1·83	11·86	11·12	1·92	12·12	21·71	31·20	16·61	21·00	30·46	16·50	21·35	30·83	16·55
2000–2004	11·58	1·84	12·45	10·67	1·67	11·89	11·14	1·75	12·15	21·83	34·33	16·53	21·03	33·38	16·30	21·42	33·84	16·42
2005–2009	11·60	1·71	12·46	10·70	1·55	11·90	11·14	1·63	12·17	21·80	37·22	16·45	21·00	36·28	16·13	21·39	36·74	16·28
2010–2014	11·63	1·63	12·44	10·72	1·47	11·90	11·17	1·55	12·17	21·71	39·53	16·45	20·86	38·80	16·05	21·28	39·15	16·25
2015–2019	11·63	1·57	12·41	10·73	1·41	11·87	11·17	1·49	12·14	21·68	41·69	16·61	20·76	40·93	16·10	21·21	41·30	16·35
2020–2024	11·61	1·53	12·39	10·71	1·37	11·85	11·15	1·45	12·12	21·75	43·74	16·78	20·76	42·95	16·24	21·27	43·34	16·51
2025–2029	11·60	1·50	12·39	10·70	1·34	11·85	11·14	1·42	12·12	21·83	45·73	16·84	20·80	44·93	16·31	21·35	45·32	16·57
2030–2034	11·60	1·48	12·40	10·69	1·32	11·87	11·14	1·40	12·13	21·85	47·43	16·79	20·89	46·75	16·28	21·39	47·08	16·53

steadily until a stable age composition was reached. In estimate (b) a very marked fall in specific death-rates was assumed. In spite of this the fall in the crude death-rate is insignificant. Thus the effect of the present age composition of the population on the crude death-rate is such that further decreases in the risk of death are not

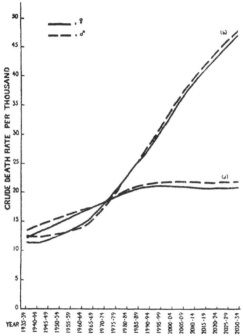

FIG. 12.—Crude annual death-rates per thousand of males and females, England and Wales, 1935–2035. Estimates (a) and (b).

likely to do more than maintain it at a more or less stationary level, while any slackening of progress in this direction would be followed by a rapidly rising death-rate.

The effect of age composition is also seen on the crude birth-rate. In estimates (a) and (b) fertility is assumed to be constant, but the crude birth-rate falls until an approximately stable age composition is reached.

The crude birth- and death-rates are shown together in graphical form in Fig. 13. This figure gives an alternative representation of

the population changes resulting from the different assumptions.
The point at which the birth- and death-rate curves cross indicates

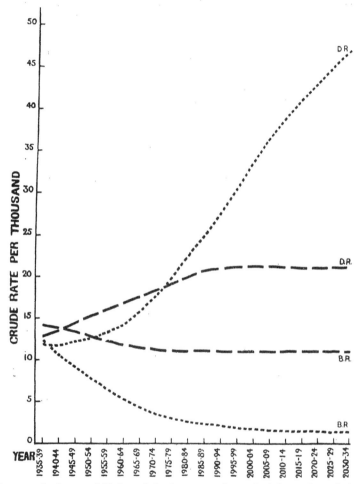

FIG. 13.—Crude annual birth- and death-rates per thousand of the total population,
England and Wales, 1935–2035. Estimates (*a*) and (*b*)

the point at which the population begins to decrease. The vertical
distance between the two curves indicates the relative rates of

decrease of the total population and the way in which these rates of decrease change.

The estimated crude birth- and death-rates for the total population of Scotland from 1935 to 2035 are shown graphically in Fig. 14. The main changes are similar to those in England and Wales.

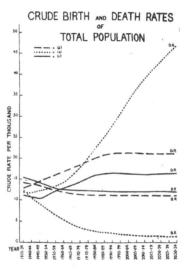

FIG. 14.—Crude annual birth- and death-rates per thousand of the total population Scotland, 1935–2035. Estimates (a) and (b).

7. THE SEX RATIO

The number of males born is greater than the number of females, but from birth onwards the death-rate at each year of age is higher for males than for females, the gap between the two rates being greatest at the older ages. It follows that the preponderance of males over females at birth is eventually replaced by a preponderance of females over males. The sex ratio in the total population is determined by the specific death-rates together with the age composition of the population. The sex ratios for certain age-groups according to estimates (a) and (b) and for the total population according to (a) and (b) are given in Table X for England and Wales. They are shown graphically for (a) and (b) in Figs. 15 and 16. It will be seen that the sex ratio for persons between 20 and 50 was abnormally

D

disturbed by the World War. During these years, at which the sex ratio is perhaps of most significance, all three alternatives lead quite rapidly to a very slight excess of males over females.

The ratio of females to males in different age-groups and in the

TABLE X

THE SEX RATIO (FEMALES TO MALES) IN SPECIFIC AGE-GROUPS
AND THE TOTAL POPULATION, ENGLAND AND WALES

Year	(a)			(b)			(a)	(b)
	0–20	20–50	50 +	0–20	20–50	50 +	Total	Total
1935	0·980	1·099	1·204	0·980	1·099	1·204	1·084	1·084
1940	0·978	1·073	1·232	0·977	1·073	1·228	1·081	1·081
1945	0·976	1·044	1·262	0·974	1·043	1·253	1·078	1·078
1950	0·975	1·019	1·284	0·970	1·017	1·268	1·075	1·075
1955	0·976	1·011	1·262	0·968	1·009	1·240	1·071	1·071
1960	0·976	1·000	1·246	0·966	0·996	1·217	1·066	1·067
1965	0·976	0·899	1·229	0·964	0·984	1·194	1·061	1·061
1970	0·976	0·988	1·205	0·963	0·981	1·165	1·055	1·055
1975	0·976	0·987	1·179	0·962	0·978	1·135	1·050	1·050
1980	0·976	0·986	1·164	0·962	0·975	1·118	1·046	1·046
1985	0·976	0·986	1·154	0·962	0·973	1·105	1·043	1·045
1990	0·976	0·986	1·147	0·962	0·971	1·098	1·041	1·044
1995	0·976	0·986	1·142	0·962	0·970	1·094	1·039	1·045
2000	0·976	0·986	1·138	0·962	0·969	1·094	1·038	1·048
2005	0·976	0·986	1·136	0·962	0·969	1·095	1·037	1·053
2010	0·976	0·986	1·134	0·962	0·968	1·098	1·037	1·058
2015	0·976	0·986	1·133	0·962	0·968	1·100	1·036	1·060
2020	0·976	0·986	1·134	0·962	0·968	1·102	1·037	1·063
2025	0·976	0·986	1·135	0·962	0·968	1·106	1·037	1·067
2030	0·976	0·986	1·135	0·962	0·968	1·110	1·037	1·070
2035	0·976	0·986	1·135	0·962	0·968	1·114	1·037	1·073

total population of Scotland according to both estimates is shown in Figs. 17 and 18. The curves closely resemble those given for England and Wales. The principal difference seen is that, owing to higher mortality in Scotland, there are relatively fewer females in the older age-groups, and hence the numbers of males and females in the total population tend to become more nearly equal.

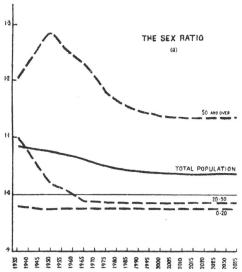

FIG. 15.—The sex ratio (females to males) in the age-groups 0–20, 20–50, 50 and over and in the total population, England and Wales, 1935–2035. Estimate (a).

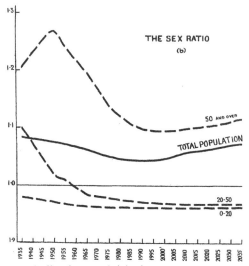

FIG. 16.—The sex ratio (females to males) in the age-groups 0–20, 20–50, 50 and over and in the total population, England and Wales, 1935–2035. Estimate (b).

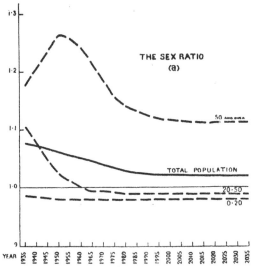

Fɪɢ. 17.—The sex ratio (females to males) in the age-groups 0–20, 20–50, 50 and over
and in the total population, Scotland, 1935–2035. Estimate (a).

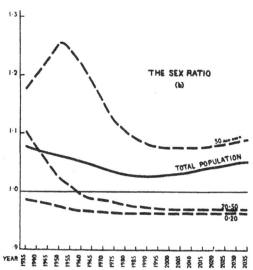

Fɪɢ. 18.—The sex ratio (females to males) in the age-groups 0–20, 20–50, 50 and over
and in the total population, Scotland, 1935–2035. Estimate (b).

8. THE STABLE POPULATION

The population figures calculated according to estimate (a) are of some statistical interest in that they illustrate the approach to a stable population. Lotka, among other workers,[1] has endeavoured to show that a population with constant fertility and mortality rates

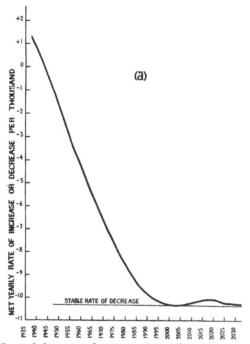

FIG. 19.—Net yearly increase or decrease per thousand, 1935–2035. Estimate (a). England and Wales.

must eventually reach a stable age composition and a constant rate of increase or decrease, and has given methods based on the calculus for determining this age composition and rate of increase. Kuczynski[2] has worked out a numerical example in which he shows that under somewhat similar conditions to estimate (a) a period of steady decrease is followed by an oscillatory period during which the oscillations become smaller and smaller, though they are still apparent after two centuries. Fig. 19 shows the yearly rate of increase

[1] *Journ. Am. Stat. Ass.*, 1925, vol. xx. [2] Kuczynski, *Fertility and Reproduction*.

or decrease of the population of England and Wales calculated according to estimate (a). It will be seen that a condition of comparative stability is reached in about sixty years after fertility and mortality rates become constant. The mean rate of decrease for the years 1995–2035 is 10·19 per thousand, and the maximum deviation from the mean is under 1 per cent. Dr. Kuczynski has calculated the ultimate stable rate of decrease of the population according to the formulae of Lotka and has found it to be 10·29 per thousand per annum. Fig. 19 may be compared with Fig. 20,

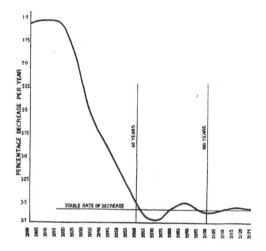

FIG. 20.—Change in annual rate of decrease of hypothetical population. (Drawn from table in Kuczynski's *Fertility and Reproduction*.)

which is drawn from Kuczynski's hypothetical numerical example. It will be seen that, in this example, after sixty years the rate of decrease oscillates about the stable level and that after a hundred years the magnitude of the oscillations is negligible. The stability of the age composition was also indicated in Fig. 5, in which it will be seen that there is very little change after 1995.

9. SUMMARY

1. Estimates of the population of England and Wales and of Scotland covering the next hundred years have been made on the following assumptions:

(a) that fertility and mortality for each year of age remain
    constant at the 1933 level;
(b) that fertility and mortality continue to fall in the manner
    suggested by the figures available for the last decade.

2. It is pointed out that (a) is a conservative estimate of the
immediate prospect of a declining population, and that (b) represents
a more reasonable forecast of the trend of population, if no new
social agencies intervene to check declining fertility.

3. An actual decline in numbers of the population of England
and Wales will ensue in 1943 according to estimate (a), and in 1939
according to (b). Even a rapid fall of fertility below the present
level will produce no spectacular changes in the size of the net
population before twenty years have elapsed. The population of
Scotland will begin to decline in numbers about 1970 according to
estimate (a), and about 1950 according to estimate (b). According
to (a) it will not fall below its present level until the period 2010–2015.

4. In England and Wales the future fall will be rapid on any
assumption which would seem plausible in the light of present
experience. According to estimate (a) the population will be halved
a century from now. According to (b) it will be reduced to one-tenth
of its present size. At the end of half a century (by 1985) it will be
reduced to 82 per cent of its present size according to (a) and to
64 per cent according to (b).

In Scotland according to (a) a long period during which the
population would be practically stationary would be followed by a
slow decline. At the end of a hundred years the population would be
94 per cent of its present size. According to (b) a period of rapid
decline would set in after about thirty years. In this estimate the
population would be 81 per cent of its present size in fifty years from
now and 19 per cent of its present size a hundred years from now.

5. Although no considerable decline in total numbers is imminent
in the next two decades, a marked fall in the total numbers of the
school age population and a marked rise in the total numbers of
persons of 60 years and over will occur in the same period.

6. In England and Wales, according to estimate (a), the age-group
4–14 (i.e. the age-group to which elementary school children belong)
will decrease to 79 per cent of the present figure twenty years from
now. According to (b) it will decrease to 57 per cent. The age-group
of 60 years and over (pensioners) will increase to 132 per cent of

the present figure twenty years from now according to estimate (a). According to estimate (b) it will increase to 143 per cent. In Scotland, according to estimate (a), the age-group 5–15 will decrease to 90 per cent of the present total twenty years from now. According to estimate (b) it will decrease to 72 per cent. The age-group of 60 and over will increase to 123 per cent of the present figure twenty years from now according to estimate (a). According to estimate (b) it will increase to 133 per cent.

7. In England and Wales twenty years from now, according to estimate (a), the age-group 4–14 will constitute 12·6 per cent of the total population. According to estimate (b) it will constitute 9·5 per cent. The age-group of 60 years and over will constitute 16·6 per cent of the total population according to (a) and 18·6 per cent according to (b).

In Scotland twenty years from now the age-group 5–15 will constitute 15·3 per cent of the total population according to estimate (a) and 12·7 per cent according to estimate (b). The age-group of 60 years and over will constitute 13·5 per cent of the population according to estimate (a) and 15·2 per cent according to estimate (b).

8. In England and Wales in 1935 the percentage of all persons under 15 and over 60 years of age was 36. According to estimate (a) it will be 35 per cent in 1955 and 40 per cent in 1985. According to estimate (b) it will be 32 per cent in 1955 and 42 per cent in 1985.

In Scotland in 1935 the percentage of persons between 15 and 60 years of age in the population was 61·8 per cent. According to estimate (a) it will be 63·3 per cent in 1955 and 60·7 in 1985. According to estimate (b) it will be 66·7 in 1955 and 62·7 in 1985.

9. Independently of any improvement in public hygiene, the changing age composition of a declining population will produce a considerable rise in the crude death-rate, which will become increasingly more misleading as an index of social well-being. The crude death-rate is unlikely to fall much below its present level on any plausible estimate, and will probably begin to rise continuously in the near future.

10. On estimates (a) and (b) for England and Wales the crude birth-rates per thousand, twenty-five years from now, will be approximately 12 and 6 respectively. The crude death-rates will be 16·5 and 14 respectively. Fifty years hence, according to (a), the

crude birth-rate will be 11 and the crude death-rate 20·5. According to estimate (*b*) the corresponding figures are 2·5 and 24.

On estimates (*a*) and (*b*) for Scotland the crude birth-rates per thousand fifty years from now will be 15·7 and 3·35 respectively, and the death-rates 17·87 and 20·73 respectively.

11. The effect of declining fertility is to raise the sex ratio of the total population owing to the preponderance of females in the older age-groups. Between the ages of 20 and 50, which cover the greater part of the period of active sex life, the present ratio of females to males is 1·099. This appears to be abnormally disturbed on account of the loss of male lives in the World War, since according to all three alternatives there are fewer females than males in this age-group in 1965 and thereafter.

12. According to the first alternative, which assumes constant fertility and mortality rates from now onwards, the percentage age composition of the population begins to oscillate about a stable level after about 60 years. The annual rate of decrease also becomes nearly stable in this time and appears to be slightly over 1 per cent per annum in England and Wales. According to the second alternative the annual rate of decrease would be nearly 3 per cent per annum in sixty years and about 4·6 per cent per annum in a hundred years.

In Scotland, according to estimate (*a*), the annual rate of decrease at the end of a hundred years would be 0·26 per cent per annum. According to the second alternative the annual rate of decrease at the end of a hundred years would be 4 per cent per annum.

CHAPTER III

DIFFERENTIAL FERTILITY IN ENGLAND AND WALES DURING THE PAST TWO DECADES[1]

by
ENID CHARLES
and
PEARL MOSHINSKY

I. INTRODUCTION

CONSIDERABLE attention has recently been paid to the rapid decline in fertility of England and Wales. Since its continuance must eventually lead to a rapidly dwindling population, it is becoming imperative to ascertain what social agencies are associated with diminishing reproductive capacity. Foremost among social phenomena which may throw light on them are differences of fertility related to regions, occupations, and racial stocks. Unfortunately, information of this kind is somewhat difficult to obtain in this country because of the paucity of details recorded at the registration of births.

Studies of differential fertility, both regional and occupational, have already been undertaken by using the materials supplied by the census.[2] Since they have been mainly concerned with families as they existed at the time of the census, the conclusions drawn from them are open to the objection that the record of surviving families is not necessarily representative of fertility prevailing when the parents were first married. In this communication the technique of measuring fertility by *gross reproduction rates* will be used to estimate regional changes in England and Wales between 1911 and 1931. Current differences between rural districts, urban districts, large towns and London can then be compared without incurring the criticisms which have been raised against the use of census data. Indirectly, as will appear, some light will be thrown on the extent and persistence of occupational differences, concerning which annual registration provides no explicit information.

---

[1] Reprinted from *Ann. Eugen.*
[2] Newsholme, *Elements of Vital Statistics; Annual Report of the Registrar-General*, 1912. Stevenson.

II. METHOD AND DATA

In a previous chapter the significance of the *gross reproduction rate* was outlined together with a method adopted for obtaining an approximation to it for England and Wales by applying the appropriate Swedish specific fertility rates. This procedure is necessary because the age of mother at birth has not been recorded at the registration of births. For the gross reproduction rates given in this paper the populations were obtained from the census returns and the births from the Registrar-General's annual returns. The Swedish specific fertility rates used were in the first instance those most appropriate for England and Wales as a whole for the given year. These were for 1911, Sweden 1916–20; for 1921, Sweden 1922; and for 1931, Sweden 1931. The Swedish fertility rates used are given by Kuczynski.[1] Kuczynski[2] has shown that the maximum error likely to arise in using inappropriate fertility rates is about 6 per cent, but an error as big as this will only occur in quite exceptional circumstances. In order to minimize any such error some gross reproduction rates were recalculated from more appropriate fertility rates as a check on noteworthy differences between actual births and those given by the Swedish fertility rates. The maximum differences found in the gross reproduction rates thus calculated in two different ways was under 2 per cent.

The years 1911, 1921, 1931 have been selected for comparison because they were census years, for which accurate information concerning the age composition, regional and occupational distribution of the population is therefore known. Nineteen-twenty-one, however, was a year of abnormally high fertility following on the postponement of births during and immediately after the World War. The figures recorded for this year are therefore of no value in connection with the general trend of fertility during the period. The figures obtained are presented as they might be of use in a study of post-war fluctuations in fertility.

For the convenience of readers unfamiliar with the topographical subdivision of this country a brief account of the regions studied follows. The total population of England and Wales is included in three categories: (*a*) London, (*b*) the County Boroughs, and (*c*) the Administrative Counties. London, which has been treated separately on account of its unique characteristics, here signifies the area under

---

[1] Kuczynski, *The Measurement of Population Growth.*   [2] Ibid.

TABLE I

GROSS REPRODUCTION RATES AND POPULATIONS

ADMINISTRATIVE COUNTIES, URBAN AND RURAL DISTRICTS

(In 1931 order of magnitude of Gross Reproduction Rates)

| | 1911 (Order) | Gross Reproduction Rates | | | | Populations | |
		1911	1921	1931	1911-31 (Decrease)	1911	1931
England and Wales (Whole) ..		*1·442*	*1·324*	*0·930*	*0·512*	*929,214*	*924,228*
Durham—							
Administrative County	(3)	2·153*	1·992	1·298	0·855		
Urban District		2·096*	1·968	1·314	0·782	528,095	520,033
Rural District		2·232	2·020	1·267	0·965	401,119	404,195
Lincolnshire (Holland)—							
Administrative County	(9)	*1·715*	*1·629*	*1·247*	*0·468*	*82,849*	*92,330*
Urban District		1·591	1·503	1·198	0·393	37,233	41,048
Rural District		1·831	1·741	1·305	0·526	45,616	51,282
Ely (Isle of)—							
Administrative County	(7)	*1·718*	*1·505*	*1·197*	*0·521*	*69,752*	*77,698*
Urban District		1·594	1·467	1·234	0·360	36,608	45,107
Rural District		1·886	1·547	1·141	0·745	33,144	32,591
Monmouthshire—							
Administrative County	(1)	*2·263*	*1·915*	*1·170*	*1·093*	*312,028*	*345,755*
Urban District		2·421	1·998	1·204	1·217	264,538	291,163
Rural District		1·560	1·362	0·999	0·561	47,490	54,592

	No.						
Lincolnshire (Kesteven)—							
Administrative County	(32)	1·420	1·380	1·157	0·263	111,324	110,060
Urban District		1·303	1·201	0·966	0·337	43,982	41,572
Rural District		1·509	1·507	1·296	0·213	67,342	68,488
Cumberland—							
Administrative County	(16)	1·554*	1·538	1·136	0·418	265,746	205,847
Urban District		1·596*	1·628	1·193	0·403	164,872	114,545
Rural District		1·480	1·425	1·063	0·417	100,934	91,302
Staffordshire—							
Administrative County	(5)	1·743	1·716	1·120	0·623	738,990	703,254
Urban District		1·775	1·775	1·140	0·635	529,948	490,632
Rural District		1·659	1·577	1·071	0·588	209,042	212,622
Huntingdonshire—							
Administrative County	(18)	1·552	1·428	1·108	0·444	55,577	56,206
Urban District		1·672	1·323	1·111	0·561	23,652	25,738
Rural District		1·455	1·516	1·106	0·349	31,925	30,468
Anglesey—							
Administrative County	(28)	1·448	1·246	1·098	0·350	50,928	49,029
Urban District		1·473	1·286	0·969	0·504	18,994	18,429
Rural District		1·432	1·220	1·181	0·251	31,934	30,600
Lincolnshire (Lindsey)—							
Administrative County	(12)	1·650	1·446	1·096	0·554	237,843	263,498
Urban District		1·574	1·383	1·005	0·569	96,120	128,636
Rural District		1·710	1·511	1·195	0·515	141,723	134,862
Norfolk—							
Administrative County	(17)	1·554	1·347	1·092	0·462	321,733	321,933
Urban District		1·332	1·073	0·923	0·409	60,885	61,143
Rural District		1·614	1·429	1·136	0·478	260,848	260,790
Radnorshire—							
Administrative County	(23)	1·493	1·166	1·089	0·404	22,590	21,323
Urban District		0·897	0·621	0·751	0·146	5,806	5,863
Rural District		1·757	1·489	1·251	0·506	16,784	15,460

TABLE I—continued

	1911 (Order)	Gross Reproduction Rates				Populations	
		1911	1921	1931	1911-31 (Decrease)	1911	1931
Glamorganshire—							
Administrative County	(2)	2·251	1·878	1·072	1·179	742,998	766,223
Urban District		2·342	1·957	1·098	1·244	537,096	585,508
Rural District		2·021	1·672	0·992	1·029	205,902	180,715
Brecknockshire—							
Administrative County	(6)	1·724	1·421	1·070	0·654	59,287	57,775
Urban District		1·626	1·238	1·057	0·569	17,556	16,493
Rural District		1·770	1·505	1·076	0·694	41,731	41,282
Southampton—							
Administrative County	(25)	1·475	1·312	1·057	0·418	433,566	472,229
Urban District		1·526	1·318	1·069	0·457	204,341	213,725
Rural District		1·428	1·307	1·047	0·381	229,225	258,504
Montgomeryshire—							
Administrative County	(34)	1·411	1·395	1·051	0·360	53,146	48,473
Urban District		1·341	1·198	0·909	0·432	19,140	17,408
Rural District		1·458	1·517	1·139	0·319	34,006	31,065
Suffolk East—							
Administrative County	(20)	1·526	1·419	1·046	0·480	203,223	207,475
Urban District		1·440	1·248	0·949	0·491	80,953	86,945·
Rural District		1·598	1·576	1·129	0·469	122,270	120,530
Shropshire—							
Administrative County	(21)	1·515	1·472	1·043	0·472	246,307	244,156
Urban District		1·404	1·383	0·954	0·450	109,673	115,091
Rural District		1·611	1·555	1·129	0·482	136,634	129,065

Northumberland—							
Administrative County	408,704	371,474	0·658	1·030	1·553	1·688	(10)
Urban District	305,117	246,181	0·749	1·087	1·707	1·836	
Rural District	103,587	125,293	0·547	0·860	1·143	1·407	
Merionethshire—							
Administrative County	43,201	45,565	0·292	1·018	1·139	1·310	(42)
Urban District	19,703	20,163	0·399	0·866	0·980	1·265	
Rural District	23,498	25,402	0·193	1·155	1·282	1·348	
Nottinghamshire—							
Administrative County	443,930	344,194	0·701	1·016	1·504	1·717	(8)
Urban District	270,495	214,878	0·809	0·977	1·560	1·786	
Rural District	173,435	129,316	0·513	1·079	1·396	1·592	
Yorkshire (North Riding)—							
Administrative County	331,101	314,779	0·555	1·016	1·322	1·571	(15)
Urban District	182,279	178,196	0·656	1·018	1·377	1·674	
Rural District	148,822	136,583	0·413	1·014	1·244	1·427	
Derbyshire—							
Administrative County	614,971	560,013	0·763	1·012	1·536	1·775	(4)
Urban District	316,476	287,689	0·701	0·948	1·488	1·649	
Rural District	298,495	272,324	0·807	1·086	1·592	1·893	
Rutland—							
Administrative County	17,401	20,346	0·410	1·008	1·396	1·418	(33)
Urban District	3,191	3,667	+0·054	0·929	1·107	0·875	
Rural District	14,210	16,679	0·516	1·026	1·467	1·542	
Yorkshire (East Riding)—							
Administrative County	169,392	154,768	0·476	0·992	1·214	1·468	(26)
Urban District	72,750	59,878	0·477	0·779	0·937	1·256	
Rural District	96,642	94,890	0·449	1·181	1·469	1·630	
Flintshire—							
Administrative County	112,889	92,705	0·625	0·990	1·280	1·615	(14)
Urban District	47,092	34,864	0·774	0·915	1·127	1·689	
Rural District	65,797	57,841	0·515	1·050	1·401	1·565	

TABLE I—continued

	1911 (Order)	Gross Reproduction Rates				Populations	
		1911	1921	1931	1911-31 (Decrease)	1911	1931
Pembrokeshire—							
Administrative County	(31)	1·433	1·415	0·989	0·444	89,960	87,206
Urban District		1·378	1·426	0·980	0·398	38,779	40,785
Rural District		1·478	1·406	0·998	0·480	51,181	46,421
Yorkshire (West Riding)—							
Administrative County	(19)	1·533*	1·406	0·986	0·547	1,398,888	1,530,405
Urban District		1·445*	1·316	0·902	0·543	1,016,236	1,090,432
Rural District		1·842	1·706	1·211	0·631	382,652	439,973
Oxfordshire—							
Administrative County	(27)	1·449	1·318	0·984	0·465	146,221	129,802
Urban District		1·324	1·272	0·905	0·419	46,175	36,356
Rural District		1·516	1·337	1·019	0·497	100,046	92,726
Herefordshire—							
Administrative County	(36)	1·385	1·430	0·977	0·408	114,269	111,767
Urban District		1·243	1·331	0·853	0·390	39,867	41,201
Rural District		1·476	1·493	1·061	0·415	74,402	70,566
Wiltshire—							
Administrative County	(29)	1·440	1·322	0·975	0·465	286,822	303,373
Urban District		1·282	1·204	0·870	0·412	125,100	144,743
Rural District		1·585	1·437	1·086	0·499	161,722	158,630
Denbighshire—							
Administrative County	(13)	1·622	1·366	0·973	0·649	144,783	157,648
Urban District		1·213	0·967	0·737	0·476	48,612	57,575
Rural District		1·893	1·642	1·131	0·762	96,171	100,073

Worcestershire—								
Administrative County	(38)	1·327	1·300	0·971	0·356	427,026	309,927	
Urban District		1·303	1·302	0·960	0·343	234,489	205,628	
Rural District		1·359	1·295	0·994	0·365	192,537	104,299	
Suffolk West—								
Administrative County	(22)	1·494	1·368	0·966	0·528	116,905	106,137	
Urban District		1·295	1·159	0·826	0·469	43,855	41,507	
Rural District		1·637	1·514	1·049	0·588	73,050	64,630	
Berkshire—								
Administrative County	(48)	1·251	1·146	0·956	0·291	195,811	214,304	
Urban District		1·218	1·185	0·928	0·290	57,512	71,943	
Rural District		1·266	1·125	0·971	0·295	138,299	142,361	
Warwickshire—								
Administrative County	(30)	1·438	1·353	0·943	0·495	408,227	365,321	
Urban District		1·348	1·229	0·835	0·513	241,038	177,172	
Rural District		1·592	1·459	1·053	0·539	167,189	188,149	
Leicestershire—								
Administrative County	(24)	1·476	1·323	0·939	0·537	249,331	302,692	
Urban District		1·440	1·282	0·903	0·537	98,519	121,244	
Rural District		1·502	1·354	0·964	0·538	150,812	181,448	
Essex—								
Administrative County	(35)	1·396*	1·196	0·937	0·459	865,651	1,198,672	
Urban District		1·370*	1·164	0·914	0·456	600,267	918,631	
Rural District		1·488	1·284	1·026	0·462	265,384	280,041	
Dorsetshire—								
Administrative County	(44)	1·295	1·173	0·931	0·364	223,266	239,352	
Urban District		1·215	1·068	0·876	0·339	118,458	134,491	
Rural District		1·398	1·315	1·011	0·387	104,808	104,861	
Carmarthenshire—								
Administrative County	(11)	1·670	1·562	0·924	0·746	160,406	179,100	
Urban District		1·481	1·551	0·832	0·649	60,844	74,650	
Rural District		1·791	1·571	0·994	0·797	99,562	104,450	

TABLE I—continued

	1911 (Order)	Gross Reproduction Rates				Populations	
		1911	1921	1931	1911–31 (Decrease)	1911	1931
Gloucestershire—							
Administrative County	(41)	1·310	1·286	0·923	0·387	329,014	336,051
Urban District		1·065	1·082	0·750	0·315	100,419	111,869
Rural District		1·440	1·385	1·019	0·421	228,595	224,182
Kent—							
Administrative County	(46)	1·284	1·163	0·917	0·367	1,020,965	1,194,827
Urban District		1·229	1·124	0·895	0·334	708,808	853,565
Rural District		1·432	1·270	0·974	0·458	312,157	341,262
Peterborough (Soke of)—							
Administrative County	(50)	1·247	1·299	0·917	0·330	44,718	51,839
Urban District		1·192	1·296	0·869	0·323	33,574	43,551
Rural District		1·450	1·310	1·212	0·238	11,144	8,288
Buckinghamshire—							
Administrative County	(43)	1·302	1·179	0·916	0·386	219,551	271,586
Urban District		1·318	1·125	0·927	0·391	79,955	124,169
Rural District		1·292	1·220	0·995	0·387	139,596	147,417
Sussex, West—							
Administrative County	(55)	1·174	0·980	0·899	0·275	176,308	222,995
Urban District		1·018	0·860	0·808	0·210	83,590	114,800
Rural District		1·341	1·119	1·002	0·339	92,718	108,195
Cornwall—							
Administrative County	(49)	1·248	1·172	0·884	0·364	328,098	317,968
Urban District		1·177	1·053	0·795	0·382	144,118	144,391
Rural District		1·310	1·274	0·963	0·347	183,980	173,577

Bedfordshire—							
Administrative County	(40)	1·311	1·147	0·866	0·445	194,588	220,525
Urban District		1·230	1·080	0·821	0·409	116,994	141,625
Rural District		1·465	1·276	0·959	0·506	77,594	78,900
Somersetshire—							
Administrative County	(51)	1·246	1·187	0·863	0·383	407,304	406,327
Urban District		1·170	1·027	0·757	0·413	157,356	174,788
Rural District		1·301	1·324	0·952	0·349	249,948	231,539
Westmorland—							
Administrative County	(56)	1·148	1·056	0·848	0·300	63,575	65,408
Urban District		0·971	0·883	0·713	0·258	26,875	28,828
Rural District		1·286	1·213	0·972	0·314	36,700	36,580
Caernarvonshire—							
Administrative County	(54)	1·196	0·946	0·840	0·356	125,043	120,829
Urban District		1·079	0·760	0·680	0·399	58,334	63,488
Rural District		1·322	1·212	1·035	0·287	66,709	57,341
Middlesex—							
Administrative County	(39)	1·313	1·105	0·826	0·487	1,126,465	1,638,728
Urban District		1·311	1·103	0·823	0·488	1,078,334	1,589,397
Rural District		1·366	1·146	0·908	0·458	48,131	49,331
Hertfordshire—							
Administrative County	(53)	1·217	1·114	0·825	0·392	311,284	401,206
Urban District		1·212	1·088	0·792	0·420	194,242	280,977
Rural District		1·226	1·174	0·906	0·320	117,042	120,229
Cheshire—							
Administrative County	(52)	1·232	1·158	0·816	0·416	597,771	675,296
Urban District		1·229*	1·176	0·814	0·415	414,523	469,184
Rural District		1·242*	1·117	0·821	0·421	183,248	206,112
Cambridgeshire—							
Administrative County	(45)	1·285	1·137	0·812	0·473	128,322	140,004
Urban District		1·053	1·034	0·616	0·413	51,561	66,789
Rural District		1·486	1·233	0·998	0·488	76,761	73,215

TABLE I—continued

	1911 (Order)	Gross Reproduction Rates				Populations	
		1911	1921	1931	1911–31 (Decrease)	1911	1931
Northamptonshire—							
Administrative County	(37)	1·360	1·221	0·807	0·553	213,733	217,133
Urban District		1·243	1·105	0·686	0·557	94,496	102,420
Rural District		1·470	1·333	0·925	0·545	118,237	114,713
Devonshire—							
Administrative County	(57)	1·131	1·026	0·805	0·326	457,331	458,757
Urban District		1·005	0·898	0·720	0·285	230,918	230,416
Rural District		1·285	1·174	0·899	0·386	226,413	228,341
Cardiganshire—							
Administrative County	(59)	1·073	1·084	0·803	0·270	59,879	55,184
Urban District		0·815	0·748	0·532	0·283	16,324	16,792
Rural District		1·179	1·275	0·943	0·236	43,555	38,392
Lancashire—							
Administrative County	(47)	1·269	1·196	0·797	0·472	1,739,320	1,795,073
Urban District		1·278	1·207	0·800	0·478	1,498,707	1,531,112
Rural District		1·212	1·124	0·781	0·431	240,613	263,961
Surrey—							
Administrative County	(58)	1·081	0·980	0·755	0·326	676,027	947,846
Urban District		1·049	0·971	0·750	0·299	452,788	765,000
Rural District		1·151	1·011	0·779	0·372	223,239	182,846
Sussex, East—							
Administrative County	(60)	1·010	0·952	0·749	0·261	242,146	276,795
Urban District		0·848	0·822	0·665	0·183	115,841	142,266
Rural District		1·168	1·099	0·841	0·327	126,305	134,529

	(61)					
Wight, Isle of—						
Administrative County	0·985	0·848	0·742	0·243	88,186	88,454
Urban District	0·905	0·816	0·725	0·180	57,127	58,472
Rural District	1·146	0·927	0·777	0·369	31,059	29,982
Aggregate Urban Districts	1·443	1·286	0·923	0·520	—	—
Aggregate Rural Districts	1·490	1·398	1·030	0·460	—	—

FOOTNOTE TO TABLES I AND II

* There has been a change of area in the following Districts since 1911. The Gross Reproduction Rates have been recalculated for 1911 on the basis of the area as constituted in 1931.

Plymouth County Borough (Devonport and Plymouth)	1·421	
Cheshire—		
Administrative County	1·249	
Urban District	1·254	
Cumberland—		
Administrative County	1·613	
Urban District	1·721	
Durham—		
Administrative County		2·200
Urban District		2·169
Essex—		
Administrative County		1·426
Urban District		1·375
Yorkshire, West Riding—		
Administrative County		1·542
Urban District		1·458

TABLE II

GROSS REPRODUCTION RATES AND POPULATIONS

COUNTY BOROUGHS

(In 1931 order of magnitude of Gross Reproduction Rate)

	1911 (Order)	Gross Reproduction Rates				Populations	
		1911	1921	1931	1911-31 (Decrease)	1911	1931
England and Wales		*1·442*	*1·324*	*0·930*	*0·512*	—	—
Aggregate of County Boroughs		*1·461*	*1·348*	*0·959*	*0·502*	—	—
Middlesbrough (Yorkshire, North Riding)	(6)	1·980	2·026	1·432	0·548	104,767	138,274
Sunderland (Durham)	(12)	1·800	1·801	1·365	0·435	151,159	185,824
Bootle (Lancashire)	(11)	1·846	1·662	1·324	0·522	69,876	76,770
South Shields (Durham)	(9)	1·890	1·876	1·316	0·574	108,647	113,455
Liverpool (Lancashire)	(20)	1·719	1·623	1·291	0·428	746,421	855,688
West Hartlepool (Durham) ..	(14)	1·791	1·826	1·275	0·516	63,923	68,135
St. Helens (Lancashire)	(1)	2·407	1·899	1·269	1·138	96,551	106,789
West Bromwich (Staffordshire) ..	(3)	2·025	1·890	1·250	0·775	68,332	81,303
Gateshead (Durham)	(8)	1·935	1·920	1·245	0·690	116,917	122,447
Dudley (Worcestershire)	(13)	1·794	1·781	1·171	0·623	51,079	59,583
Walsall (Staffordshire)	(16)	1·752	1·764	1·158	0·594	92,115	103,059
Tynemouth (Northumberland) ..	(24)	1·652	1·648	1·144	0·508	58,816	64,922
Rotherham (Yorkshire, West Riding)	(10)	1·865	1·931	1·128	0·737	62,483	69,691
Barnsley (Yorkshire, West Riding) ..	(5)	1·982	1·840	1·116	0·866	50,614	71,522
Kingston-on-Hull (Yorkshire, East Riding)	(19)	1·745	1·587	1·109	0·636	277,991	313,544

Birkenhead (Cheshire)	(26)	1·640	1·579	1·090	0·550	130,794	147,803
Stoke (Staffordshire)	(7)	1·979	1·773	1·084	0·895	234,534	276,639
Newcastle (Northumberland)	(33)	1·559	1·550	1·067	0·492	266,603	283,156
West Ham (Essex)	(4)	1·983	1·690	1·067	0·916	289,030	294,278
Wigan (Lancashire)	(28)	1·629	1·624	1·061	0·568	89,152	85,357
Grimsby (Lincolnshire, Lindsey)	(21)	1·703	1·593	1·056	0·647	74,659	92,458
Portsmouth (Southampton)	(40)	1·448	1·354	1·048	0·400	231,141	249,283
Warrington (Lancashire)	(15)	1·767	1·618	1·046	0·721	72,166	79,317
Southampton (Southampton)	(41)	1·443	1·389	1·043	0·400	119,012	176,007
Newport (Monmouthshire)	(22)	1·701	1·549	1·041	0·660	83,691	89,203
Barrow-in-Furness (Lancashire)	(25)	1·647	1·504	1·037	0·610	63,770	66,202
Merthyr (Glamorganshire)	(2)	2·197	1·819	1·034	1·163	80,990	71,108
Wolverhampton (Staffordshire)	(30)	1·598	1·496	1·030	0·568	95,328	133,212
Smethwick (Staffordshire)	(17)	1·751	1·513	1·015	0·736	70,694	84,406
Plymouth (Devonshire)	(53)	1·317*	1·313	1·003	0·314	193,708	208,182
Burton (Staffordshire)	(45)	1·387	1·464	0·993	0·394	48,266	49,486
Swansea (Glamorganshire)	(18)	1·750	1·450	0·991	0·759	114,663	164,797
Cardiff (Glamorganshire)	(34)	1·552	1·415	0·985	0·567	182,259	223,589
Nottingham (Nottinghamshire)	(52)	1·322	1·324	0·980	0·342	259,904	268,801
Gloucester (Gloucestershire)	(36)	1·536	1·504	0·977	0·559	50,035	52,937
Birmingham (Warwickshire)	(27)	1·635	1·355	0·972	0·663	840,202	1,002,603
Wakefield (Yorkshire, West Riding)	(46)	1·360	1·408	0·970	0·390	51,511	59,122
Derby (Derbyshire)	(39)	1·452	1·295	0·951	0·501	123,410	142,403
Ipswich (Suffolk, East)	(44)	1·411	1·385	0·938	0·473	73,932	87,502
York (Yorkshire)	(47)	1·354	1·195	0·927	0·427	82,282	84,813
Carlisle (Cumberland)	(49)	1·332	1·313	0·924	0·408	46,420	57,304
Doncaster (Yorkshire, West Riding)	(29)	1·620	1·438	0·924	0·696	30,516	63,316
Reading (Berkshire)	(50)	1·327	1·151	0·923	0·404	75,198	97,149

TABLE II—continued

	1911 (Order)	Gross Reproduction Rates				Populations	
		1911	1921	1931	1911–31 (Decrease)	1911	1931
Salford (Lancashire)	(31)	1·584	1·455	0·914	0·670	231,357	223,438
Norwich (Norfolk)	(58)	1·256	1·324	0·909	0·347	121,478	126,236
Worcester (Worcestershire)	(55)	1·298	1·121	0·906	0·392	47,982	50,546
Great Yarmouth (Norfolk)	(42)	1·433	1·197	0·901	0·532	55,905	56,771
Oxford (Oxfordshire)	(73)	1·057	0·915	0·899	0·158	53,048	80,539
Lincoln (Lincolnshire, Lindsey)	(38)	1·471	1·402	0·896	0·575	57,285	66,243
Sheffield (Yorkshire, West Riding)	(23)	1·682	1·466	0·891	0·791	454,632	511,757
Manchester (Lancashire)	(43)	1·423	1·345	0·886	0·537	714,333	766,378
Preston (Lancashire)	(51)	1·324	1·305	0·886	0·438	117,088	119,001
Darlington (Durham)	(32)	1·559	1·417	0·884	0·675	55,631	72,086
Chester (Cheshire)	(48)	1·343	1·193	0·873	0·470	39,028	41,440
Leicester (Leicestershire)	(59)	1·250	1·142	0·870	0·380	227,222	239,169
Coventry (Warwickshire)	(37)	1·527	1·258	0·861	0·666	106,349	167,083
Bristol (Gloucestershire)	(66)	1·185	1·228	0·860	0·325	357,048	397,012
Wallasey (Cheshire)	(70)	1·088	0·950	0·814	0·274	78,504	97,626
Leeds (Yorkshire, West Riding)	(54)	1·301	1·222	0·809	0·492	445,550	482,809
East Ham (Essex)	(35)	1·542	1·340	0·804	0·738	133,487	142,394
Dewsbury (Yorkshire, West Riding)	(65)	1·193	1·308	0·797	0·396	53,351	54,302
Bolton (Lancashire)	(60)	1·236	1·200	0·792	0·444	180,851	177,250
Brighton (Sussex, East)	(72)	1·074	1·024	0·792	0·282	131,237	147,427
Exeter (Devonshire)	(68)	1·158	1·064	0·786	0·372	48,664	66,029

Stockport (Cheshire)	(56)	1·291	1·128	0·786	0·505	108,682	125,490
Croydon (Surrey)	(61)	1·231	1·087	0·780	0·451	169,551	233,032
Bradford (Yorkshire, West Riding)	(76)	0·962	1·035	0·772	0·190	288,458	298,041
Northampton (Northamptonshire)	(63)	1·212	1·127	0·758	0·454	90,064	92,341
Oldham (Lancashire)	(57)	1·280	1·211	0·752	0·528	147,483	140,314
Canterbury (Kent)	(64)	1·198	1·324	0·746	0·452	24,626	24,446
Hastings (Sussex, East)	(80)	0·804	0·725	0·744	0·060	61,145	65,207
Burnley (Lancashire)	(62)	1·214	1·174	0·742	0·472	106,322	98,258
Bury (Lancashire)	(71)	1·079	1·117	0·712	0·367	58,648	56,182
Halifax (Yorkshire, West Riding)	(77)	0·930	0·927	0·698	0·232	101,553	98,115
Rochdale (Lancashire)	(67)	1·159	1·123	0·689	0·470	91,428	90,263
Huddersfield (Yorkshire, West Riding)	(74)	1·032	0·982	0·680	0·352	107,821	113,475
Blackburn (Lancashire)	(69)	1·131	1·051	0·670	0·461	133,052	122,697
Bath (Somersetshire)	(79)	0·842	0·888	0·668	0·174	50,721	68,815
Southend (Essex)	(75)	1·021	0·781	0·646	0·375	62,713	120,115
Eastbourne (Sussex, East)	(82)	0·757	0·605	0·629	0·128	52,542	57,435
Blackpool (Lancashire)	(78)	0·880	0·574	0·600	0·280	58,371	101,553
Southport (Lancashire)	(81)	0·767	0·763	0·594	0·173	51,643	78,925
Bournemouth (Southampton)	(83)	0·627	0·693	0·549	0·078	78,674	116,797

TABLE III

GROSS REPRODUCTION RATES AND POPULATIONS

LONDON BOROUGHS

(In 1931 order of magnitude of Gross Reproduction Rates)

	1911 (Order)	Gross Reproduction Rates				Populations	
		1911	1921	1931	1911–31 (Decrease)	1911	1931
London Administrative County ..		1·332	1·215	0·805	0·527	4,521,685	4,397,003
Poplar	(3)	2·031	1·779	1·101	0·930	162,442	155,089
Bermondsey	(2)	2·094	1·713	1·092	1·002	125,903	111,542
Shoreditch	(1)	2·190	1·942	1·037	1·153	111,390	97,042
Southwark	(7)	1·898	1·645	1·029	0·869	191,907	171,695
Finsbury	(6)	1·905	1·653	1·014	0·891	87,923	69,888
Stepney	(5)	2·002	1·528	0·999	1·003	279,804	225,238
Bethnal Green	(4)	2·008	1·578	0·970	1·038	128,183	108,194
Deptford	(8)	1·597	1·373	0·960	0·637	109,496	106,891
Battersea	(9)	1·576	1·297	0·916	0·660	167,743	159,552
Islington	(15)	1·377	1·309	0·915	0·462	327,403	321,795

Greenwich	(10)	1·567	1·396	0·898	0·669	95,968	100,924
Woolwich	(12)	1·444	1·372	0·872	0·572	121,376	146,881
Hammersmith	(17)	1·313	1·180	0·860	0·453	121,521	135,523
Lambeth	(16)	1·349	1·249	0·839	0·510	298,058	296,147
Fulham	(11)	1·494	1·207	0·833	0·661	153,284	150,928
Camberwell	(13)	1·430	1·365	0·829	0·601	261,328	251,294
St. Pancras	(14)	1·395	1·181	0·796	0·599	218,387	198,133
Hackney	(18)	1·237	1·198	0·794	0·443	222,533	215,333
Lewisham	(20)	1·091	1·091	0·785	0·306	160,834	219,953
Stoke Newington	(21)	1·013	1·101	0·753	0·260	50,659	51,208
Paddington	(23)	0·916	0·936	0·659	0·257	142,551	144,923
Wandsworth	(19)	1·123	1·020	0·629	0·494	311,360	353,110
Kensington	(26)	0·713	0·886	0·666	0·107	172,317	180,677
Chelsea	(24)	0·806	0·776	0·575	0·231	66,385	59,031
St. Marylebone	(25)	0·798	0·698	0·454	0·344	118,160	97,627
Hampstead	(28)	0·538	0·660	0·428	0·110	85,495	88,947
Westminster	(27)	0·575	0·570	0·425	0·150	160,261	129,579
Holborn	(22)	0·917	0·722	0·409	0·508	49,357	38,860

the administration of the London County Council and covers the more congested part of the city. Regarded as a residential unit, London spreads over a much larger area which now includes the whole of Middlesex, parts of Essex, Kent, Surrey, Herts, and Bucks. Even portions of Berkshire and Sussex are to some extent suburbs of London. The Administrative County of London is subdivided into separate boroughs. The County Boroughs include nearly all the large towns apart from London, though they vary greatly in size and importance from Birmingham, with a population of over a million, to Canterbury, with a population of 24,000. Liverpool and Birkenhead are contiguous and may be regarded as one city. Together they also have a population of over a million.

The Administrative Counties are subdivided into Urban and Rural Districts. The peculiar history of the growth of English local government excludes a rigid definition of the composition of these districts. Nevertheless certain differences are generally characteristic. The Urban Districts with few exceptions all have populations of less than 40,000. The exceptions all occur in the immediate vicinity of London, where large concentrations of populations have recently grown up but have not yet attained the status of a county borough. On the other hand, some urban districts in the more rural counties have populations of less than 20,000, though probably all could be described as small towns and would have a railway station and shopping centre. Generally speaking, the rural districts are characterized by a sparse and scattered population, though here again exceptions occur. Though rural districts taken together in all the counties except Middlesex, where the term rural has now become an anachronism, have a low density of population per acre, individual rural districts, especially in the mining areas, may have a population density greater than that of some urban districts. It may be useful to add as giving a general picture of the population distribution that at the present time about a quarter of the total population of the country is located in London and its environs and another quarter in the industrial belt of the North, including Yorkshire, Lancashire, and Cheshire. In some cases changes of area occurred between 1911 and 1931. These are referred to in a footnote to the tables. The occupational data used are all derived from the census returns.

III. REGIONAL DIFFERENCES IN FERTILITY

Gross reproduction rates for the Administrative Counties as a whole and for their Urban and Rural Districts, for the County Boroughs and for the London Boroughs are given in Tables I, II, and III respectively for 1911, 1921, and 1931. The same tables also give the total populations of the various districts in 1911 and 1931, the gross reproduction rates for England and Wales as a whole, and the aggregates of Urban Districts, Rural Districts, and County

TABLE IV

GROSS REPRODUCTION RATES FOR POPULATION AGGREGATES,
1911 AND 1931

			1911	1931	Percentage Drop
Aggregate of Rural Districts ..	..	..	1·490	1·030	30·9
Aggregate of County Boroughs	..	..	1·461	0·959	35·0
Aggregate of Urban Districts	..	.. ·	1·443	0·929	35·6
England and Wales (whole)	..	..	1·442	0·930	35·5
Administrative County of London ..		..	1·332	0·805	39·6

Boroughs. The rates are printed in their 1931 order, and the order in 1911 is shown in parenthesis. A large gain or loss in rank taken in conjunction with the amount of the change between the 1911 and 1931 rates indicates those districts where the change in fertility has been unusual.

In some countries a considerable difference in fertility between urban and rural populations has been found. Table IV summarizes the facts relating to large aggregates of population in England and Wales.

In 1911 no significant difference between urban and rural fertility is found, but that of London is markedly lower than the rest of the country. By 1931 rural fertility has fallen less than that of the country as a whole, while London fertility has fallen more. Only 20 per cent of the population is rural, and only 6·4 per cent is engaged in agriculture. The rural districts as a whole include large numbers of people living in either industrial or suburban conditions. Owing to the small area of England and Wales there are no districts very remote from large urban centres. What is perhaps significant is that fertility has been maintained somewhat better in the rural districts, the extent of the fall being less than in other aggregates.

The high fertility of the county boroughs is surprising. It is not obviously associated with size. Liverpool and Birmingham both have gross reproduction rates higher than England and Wales as a whole. If we consider the five cities, having a population of over half a million, namely London, Birmingham, Liverpool, Manchester, and

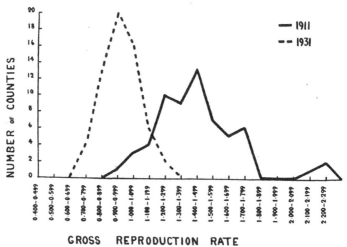

GROSS   REPRODUCTION   RATE

FIG. 1.—Distribution and range of gross reproduction rates, 1911 and 1931— Administrative Counties.

Sheffield—London has the lowest gross reproduction rate, and is also lower than any of the large aggregates of population. It may thus be considered to display a metropolitan as distinct from an urban pattern of fertility. The differences in fertility are, however, small, and since the gross reproduction rate of Liverpool is as high as that of any rural district, it is clear that no broad regional distinctions can be drawn. On the other hand, within each large aggregate very big differences in fertility existed in 1911. In that year among the County Boroughs we find St. Helens with a gross reproduction rate of 2·407 and Bournemouth with a gross reproduction rate of 0·627, though, as is pointed out later, the presence of large numbers of domestic servants in the latter district may tend to exaggerate the difference in fertility. In 1931 the range was from 1·432 to 0·549.

Population figures of local government areas do not indicate clearly the main centres of urban concentration. The larger cities outside London may include within the boundaries of a continuous urban area several County Boroughs, Municipal Boroughs, Urban and occasionally Rural Districts. The word "conurbation" has been applied by geographers to these areas. Professor Fawcett[1] has given

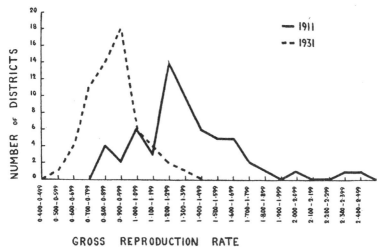

FIG. 2.—Distribution and range of gross reproduction rates, 1911 and 1931—
Urban Districts.

details of the composition of seventy-five such conurbations. Those in England and Wales with over a million inhabitants are London, Manchester, Birmingham, West Yorkshire, Merseyside, and Tyneside. While the gross reproduction rates for these conurbations cannot be given, their order of magnitude can be deduced approximately. The most fertile are clearly Tyneside and Liverpool. The five County Boroughs in Tyneside have gross reproduction rates ranging from 1·067 to 1·365, while the aggregate surrounding Urban Districts are 1·087 and 1·314. The gross reproduction rates of the two largest County Boroughs in Merseyside (Liverpool and Birkenhead) are 1·291 and 1·090. Bootle and Wallasey are smaller and are 1·324 and 0·814 respectively. The conurbation of Birmingham

[1] Fawcett, "Distribution of the Urban Population in Great Britain, 1931," *Geog. Journ.*, vol. lxxix, 1932.

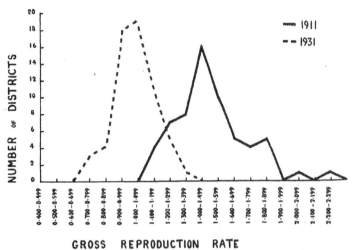

GROSS   REPRODUCTION   RATE

FIG. 3.—Distribution and range of gross reproduction rates, 1911 and 1931—
Rural Districts.

includes in addition to the principal city eight smaller County
Boroughs with gross reproduction rates ranging from 1·015 to 1·250.

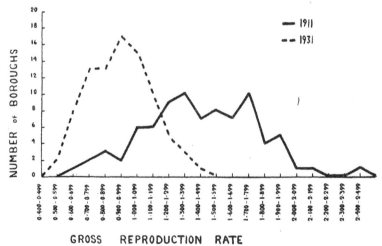

GROSS   REPRODUCTION   RATE

FIG. 4.—Distribution and range of gross reproduction rates, 1911 and 1931—
County Boroughs.

TABLE V

ADMINISTRATIVE COUNTIES, URBAN DISTRICTS, AND RURAL DISTRICTS

1911 AND 1931 DIFFERENCES IN FERTILITY EXPRESSED AS A PERCENTAGE OF 1911 RATE

England and Wales (Whole)   ..   ..   ..   *35·5*

	Percentage Drop		*Percentage Drop*
Glamorganshire—		Northumberland—	
Administrative County	.. *52·4*	*Administrative County*	.. *39·0*
Urban District ..	.. *53·1*	Urban District ..	.. *40·8*
Rural District ..	.. *50·9*	Rural District ..	.. *38·9*
Monmouthshire—		Flintshire—	
Administrative County	.. *48·3*	*Administrative County*	.. *38·7*
Urban District ..	.. *50·3*	Urban District ..	.. *45·8*
Rural District ..	.. *36·0*	Rural District ..	.. *32·9*
Carmarthenshire—		Brecknockshire—	
Administrative County	.. *44·7*	*Administrative County*	.. *37·9*
Urban District ..	.. *43·8*	Urban District ..	.. *35·0*
Rural District ..	.. *44·5*	Rural District ..	.. *39·2*
Derbyshire—		Lancashire—	
Administrative County	.. *43·0*	*Administrative County*	.. *37·2*
Urban District ..	.. *42·5*	Urban District ..	.. *37·4*
Rural District ..	.. *42·6*	Rural District ..	.. *35·6*
Nottinghamshire—		Middlesex—	
Administrative County	.. *40·8*	*Administrative County*	.. *37·1*
Urban District ..	.. *45·3*	Urban District ..	.. *37·2*
Rural District ..	.. *32·2*	Rural District ..	.. *33·5*
Northamptonshire—		Cambridgeshire—	
Administrative County	.. *40·7*	*Administrative County*	.. *36·8*
Urban District ..	.. *44·8*	Urban District ..	.. *39·2*
Rural District ..	.. *37·1*	Rural District ..	.. *32·8*
Denbighshire—		Leicestershire—	
Administrative County	.. *40·0*	*Administrative County*	.. *36·4*
Urban District ..	.. *39·2*	Urban District ..	.. *37·3*
Rural District ..	.. *40·3*	Rural District ..	.. *35·8*
Durham—		Staffordshire—	
Administrative County	.. *39·7*	*Administrative County*	.. *35·7*
Urban District ..	.. *37·3*	Urban District ..	.. *35·8*
Rural District ..	.. *43·2*	Rural District ..	.. *35·4*

E

TABLE V—*continued*

	Percentage Drop			Percentage Drop
Yorkshire, West Riding—		Hertfordshire—		
Administrative County	35·7	*Administrative County*		32·2
Urban District	37·6	Urban District		34·7
Rural District	34·3	Rural District		26·1
Suffolk, West—		Oxfordshire—		
Administrative County	35·3	*Administrative County*		32·1
Urban District	36·2	Urban District		31·6
Rural District	35·9	Rural District		32·8
Yorkshire, North Riding—		Suffolk, East—		
Administrative County	35·3	*Administrative County*		31·5
Urban District	39·2	Urban District		34·1
Rural District	28·9	Rural District		29·3
Warwickshire—		Shropshire—		
Administrative County	34·4	*Administrative County*		31·2
Urban District	38·1	Urban District		32·1
Rural District	33·9	Rural District		29·9
Bedfordshire—		Pembrokeshire—		
Administrative County	33·9	*Administrative County*		31·0
Urban District	33·3	Urban District		28·9
Rural District	34·5	Rural District		32·5
Cheshire—		Somersetshire—		
Administrative County	33·8	*Administrative County*		30·7
Urban District	33·8	Urban District		35·3
Rural District	33·9	Rural District		26·8
Lincolnshire, Lindsey—		Ely—		
Administrative County	33·6	*Administrative County*		30·3
Urban District	36·1	Urban District		22·6
Rural District	30·1	Rural District		39·5
Essex—		Surrey—		
Administrative County	32·9	*Administrative County*		30·2
Urban District	33·3	Urban District		28·5
Rural District	31·0	Rural District		32·3
Yorkshire, East Riding—		Caernarvonshire—		
Administrative County	32·4	*Administrative County*		29·8
Urban District	38·0	Urban District		37·0
Rural District	27·5	Rural District		21·7
Wiltshire—		Norfolk—		
Administrative County	32·3	*Administrative County*		29·7
Urban District	32·1	Urban District		30·7
Rural District	31·5	Rural District		29·6

TABLE V—*continued*

	Percentage Drop		Percentage Drop
Buckinghamshire—		**Lincolnshire, Holland—**	
Administrative County	29·6	*Administrative County*	27·3
Urban District	29·7	Urban District	24·7
Rural District	30·0	Rural District	28·7
Gloucestershire—		**Radnorshire—**	
Administrative County	29·5	*Administrative County*	27·1
Urban District	29·6	Urban District	16·3
Rural District	29·2	Rural District	28·8
Herefordshire—		**Cumberland—**	
Administrative County	29·5	*Administrative County*	26·9
Urban District	31·4	Urban District	25·3
Rural District	28·1	Rural District	28·2
Cornwall—		**Worcestershire—**	
Administrative County	29·2	*Administrative County*	26·8
Urban District	32·5	Urban District	26·3
Rural District	26·5	Rural District	26·9
Rutland—		**Peterborough (Soke of)—**	
Administrative County	28·9	*Administrative County*	26·5
Urban District	+6·2	Urban District	27·1
Rural District	33·5	Rural District	16·4
Devonshire—		**Westmorland—**	
Administrative County	28·8	*Administrative County*	26·1
Urban District	28·4	Urban District	26·6
Rural District	30·0	Rural District	24·4
Huntingdonshire—		**Sussex, East—**	
Administrative County	28·6	*Administrative County*	25·8
Urban District	33·6	Urban District	21·6
Rural District	24·0	Rural District	28·0
Kent—		**Montgomeryshire—**	
Administrative County	28·6	*Administrative County*	25·5
Urban District	27·2	Urban District	32·2
Rural District	32·0	Rural District	21·9
Southampton—		**Cardiganshire—**	
Administrative County	28·3	*Administrative County*	25·2
Urban District	29·9	Urban District	34·7
Rural District	26·7	Rural District	20·0
Dorsetshire—		**Wight (Isle of)—**	
Administrative County	28·1	*Administrative County*	24·7
Urban District	27·9	Urban District	19·9
Rural District	27·7	Rural District	32·2

TABLE V—*continued*

	Percentage Drop			Percentage Drop
Anglesey—		Sussex, West—		
Administrative County	24·2	Administrative County		23·4
Urban District	34·2	Urban District		20·6
Rural District	17·5	Rural District		25·3
Berkshire—		Merionethshire—		
Administrative County	23·6	Administrative County		22·3
Urban District	23·8	Urban District		31·5
Rural District	23·3	Rural District		14·3

Lincolnshire, Kesteven—
Administrative County .. 18·5
Urban District .. .. 25·9
Rural District .. .. 14·1

URBAN DISTRICTS

1911 AND 1931 DIFFERENCES IN FERTILITY EXPRESSED AS A PERCENTAGE
OF 1911 RATE

England and Wales (*Whole*) .. .. .. 35·5

	Percentage Drop		Percentage Drop
Glamorganshire	53·1	Hertfordshire	34·7
Monmouthshire	50·3	Anglesey	34·2
		Suffolk, East	34·1
Flintshire	45·8	Cheshire	33·8
Nottinghamshire	45·3	Huntingdonshire	33·6
Northamptonshire	44·8	Bedfordshire	33·3
Carmarthenshire	43·8	Essex	33·3
Derbyshire	42·5	Cornwall	32·5
Northumberland	40·8	Montgomeryshire	32·2
		Shropshire	32·1
Cambridgeshire	39·2	Wiltshire	32·1
Denbighshire	39·2	Oxfordshire	31·6
Yorkshire, North Riding	39·2	Merionethshire	31·5
Warwickshire	38·1	Herefordshire	31·4
Yorkshire, East Riding	38·0	Norfolk	30·7
Yorkshire, West Riding	37·6		
Lancashire	37·4	Southampton	29·9
Durham	37·3	Buckinghamshire	29·7
Leicestershire	37·3	Gloucestershire	29·6
Middlesex	37·2	Pembrokeshire	28·9
Caernarvonshire	37·0	Surrey	28·5
Suffolk, West	36·2	Devonshire	28·4
Lincolnshire, Lindsey	36·1	Dorsetshire	27·9
Staffordshire	35·8	Kent	27·2
Somersetshire	35·3	Peterborough (Soke of)	27·1
Brecknockshire	35·0	Westmorland	26·6
Cardiganshire	34·7	Worcestershire	26·3

TABLE V—*continued*

URBAN DISTRICTS

	Percentage Drop		Percentage Drop
Lincolnshire, Kesteven	.. 25·9	Sussex, West	20·6
Cumberland ..	.. 25·3		
Lincolnshire, Holland	.. 24·7	Wight, Isle of ..	.. 19·9
Berkshire	.. 23·8	Radnorshire	.. 16·3
Ely	.. 22·6		
Sussex, East	.. 21·6	Rutland	.. +6·2

RURAL DISTRICTS

1911 AND 1931 DIFFERENCES IN FERTILITY EXPRESSED AS A PERCENTAGE
OF 1911 RATE

England and Wales (*Whole*) .. .. .. 35·5

	Percentage Drop		Percentage Drop
Glamorganshire ..	.. 50·9	Buckinghamshire ..	.. 30·0
		Devonshire	.. 30·0
Carmarthenshire ..	.. 44·5		
Durham	.. 43·2	Shropshire	.. 29·9
Derbyshire	.. 42·6	Norfolk	.. 29·6
Denbighshire ..	.. 40·3	Suffolk, East ..	.. 29·3
		Gloucestershire ..	.. 29·2
Ely	.. 39·5	Yorkshire, North Riding ..	28·9
Brecknockshire ..	.. 39·2	Radnorshire	.. 28·8
Northumberland ..	.. 38·9	Lincolnshire, Holland ..	28·7
Northamptonshire ..	.. 37·1	Cumberland	.. 28·2
Monmouthshire ..	.. 36·0	Hereford	.. 28·1
Suffolk, West ..	.. 35·9	Sussex, East	.. 28·0
Leicestershire.. ..	.. 35·8	Dorsetshire	.. 27·7
Lancashire	.. 35·6	Yorkshire, East Riding ..	27·5
Staffordshire	.. 35·4	Worcestershire ..	.. 26·9
Bedfordshire	.. 34·5	Somersetshire ..	.. 26·8
Yorkshire, West Riding ..	34·3	Southampton . ..	.. 26·7
Cheshire	.. 33·9	Cornwall	.. 26·5
Warwickshire.. ..	.. 33·9	Hertfordshire ..	.. 26·1
Middlesex	.. 33·5	Sussex, West ..	.. 25·3
Rutland	.. 33·5	Westmorland ..	.. 24·4
Flintshire	.. 32·9	Huntingdonshire ..	.. 24·0
Cambridgeshire ..	.. 32·8	Berkshire	.. 23·3
Oxfordshire	.. 32·8	Montgomeryshire ..	.. 21·9
Pembrokeshire ..	.. 32·5	Caernarvonshire ..	.. 21·7
Surrey	.. 32·3	Cardiganshire ..	.. 20·0
Nottinghamshire ..	.. 32·2		
Wight, Isle of ..	.. 32·2	Anglesey	.. 17·5
Kent	.. 32·0	Peterborough (Soke of) ..	16·4
Wiltshire	.. 31·5	Merionethshire ..	.. 14·3
Essex	.. 31·0	Lincolnshire, Kesteven ..	14·1
Lincoln, Lindsey ..	.. 30·1		

TABLE VI

COUNTY BOROUGHS

1911 AND 1931 DIFFERENCES IN FERTILITY EXPRESSED AS A PERCENTAGE
OF 1911 RATE

	Percentage Drop
England and Wales	*35·5*
Merthyr (Glamorganshire) ..	52·9
East Ham (Essex)	47·9
St. Helens (Lancashire) ..	47·3
Sheffield (Yorkshire, West Riding) .. |.. ..	47·0
West Ham (Essex)	46·2
Stoke (Staffordshire) ..	45·2
Barnsley (Yorkshire, West Riding)	43:7
Coventry (Warwickshire) ..	43·6
Swansea (Glamorganshire) ..	43·4
Darlington (Durham) ..	43·3
Doncaster (Yorkshire, West Riding)	43·0
Salford (Lancashire) ..	42·3
Smethwick (Staffordshire) ..	42·0
Oldham (Lancashire) ..	41·3
Blackburn (Lancashire) ..	40·8
Warrington (Lancashire) ..	40·8
Birmingham (Warwickshire)	40·6
Rochdale (Lancashire) ..	40·6
Rotherham (Yorkshire, West Riding)	39·5
Lincoln (Lincolnshire, Lindsey)	39·1
Stockport (Cheshire) ..	39·1
Burnley (Lancashire) ..	38·9
Newport (Monmouthshire) ..	38·8
West Bromwich (Staffordshire)	38·3
Grimsby (Lincolnshire, Lindsey)	38·0
Leeds (Yorkshire, West Riding)	37·8
Canterbury (Kent)	37·7
Manchester (Lancashire) ..	37·7
Northampton (Northamptonshire)	37·5
Great Yarmouth (Norfolk) ..	37·1

	Percentage Drop
Barrow-in-Furness (Lancashire)	37·0
Southend (Essex)	36·7
Croydon (Surrey)	36·6
Cardiff (Glamorganshire) ..	36·5
Gloucester (Gloucestershire)	36·4
Kingston-on-Hull (Yorkshire, East Riding)	36·4
Bolton (Lancashire)	35·9
Gateshead (Durham) ..	35·7
Wolverhampton (Staffordshire)	35·5
Chester (Cheshire)	35·0
Wigan (Lancashire)	34·9
Dudley (Worcestershire) ..	34·7
Derbyshire (Derby)	34·5
Huddersfield (Yorkshire, West Riding)	34·1
Bury (Lancashire)	34·0
Walsall (Staffordshire) ..	33·9
Birkenhead (Cheshire) ..	33·5
Ipswich (Suffolk)	33·5
Dewsbury (Yorkshire, West Riding)	33·2
Preston (Lancashire) ..	33·1
Exeter (Devonshire)	32·1
Blackpool (Lancashire) ..	31·8
Newcastle (Northumberland)	31·6
York (Yorkshire, West Riding)	31·5
Tynemouth (Northumberland)	30·8
Carlisle (Cumberland) ..	30·6
Leicester (Leicestershire) ..	30·4
Reading (Berkshire) ..	30·4
South Shields (Durham) ..	30·4
Worcester (Worcestershire) ..	30·2
West Hartlepool (Durham) ..	28·8
Wakefield (Yorkshire, West Riding)	28·7

TABLE VI—*continued*

COUNTY BOROUGHS

	Percentage Drop		Percentage Drop
Burton (Staffordshire) ..	28·4	Liverpool (Lancashire) ..	24·9
Bootle (Lancashire)	28·3	Sunderland (Durham) ..	24·2
Middlesbrough (Yorkshire, North Riding)	27·7	Plymouth (Devonshire) ..	23·8
Southampton (Southampton)	27·7	Southport (Lancashire) ..	22·6
Norwich (Norfolk)	27·6	Bath (Somersetshire) ..	20·7
Portsmouth (Southampton)..	27·6		
Bristol (Gloucestershire) ..	27·4	Bradford (Yorkshire, West Riding)	19·8
Brighton (Sussex, East) ..	26·3	Eastbourne (Sussex, East) ..	16·9
Nottingham (Nottinghamshire)	25·9	Oxford (Oxfordshire) ..	14·9
Wallasey (Cheshire)	25·2	Bournemouth (Southampton)	12·4
Halifax (Yorkshire, West Riding)	24·9	Hastings (Sussex, East) ..	7·5

TABLE VII

LONDON BOROUGHS

1911 AND 1931 DIFFERENCES IN FERTILITY EXPRESSED AS A PERCENTAGE OF 1911 RATE

	Percentage Drop		Percentage Drop
London	*39·6*	Battersea	41·9
Holborn	55·4	Deptford	39·9
Shoreditch	52·6	Woolwich	39·6
Bethnal Green	51·7	Lambeth	37·8
Stepney	50·1	Hackney	35·8
		Hammersmith	34·5
Bermondsey	47·9	Islington	33·6
Finsbury	46·8		
Poplar	45·8	Chelsea	28·7
Southwark	45·8	Paddington	28·1
Fulham	44·2	Lewisham	28·0
Wandsworth	44·0	Westminster	26·1
St. Marylebone	43·1	Stoke Newington	25·7
St. Pancras	42·9	Hampstead	20.4
Greenwich	42·7		
Camberwell	42·0	Kensington	15·0

The total gross reproduction rate may thus be unity or a little more. The two remaining conurbations, Manchester and West Yorkshire, contain no County Boroughs with a gross reproduction rate higher than 0·9, and almost certainly show a total fertility less than that of England and Wales as a whole. Thus of the six "million" cities in England and Wales, three have a higher fertility than that of the country as a whole and three a lower fertility.

The range and distribution of gross reproduction rates in the various aggregates are shown in Figs. 1–4.

These charts bring out the fact that on the whole the higher fertility rates have fallen more than the lower, the result being a general levelling down. This is seen best in the Administrative Counties and County Boroughs, and less so in the Rural Districts. At both extremes the range of urban fertility rates is larger than that of fertility in the Rural Districts. The percentage drop of fertility in the different districts is given in Tables V, VI, and VII.

The general levelling illustrated in Figs. 1–4 may be visualized from another point of view, when the mean percentage drop over the period studied is plotted against the 1911 gross reproduction rate classified in groups of equivalent range. This has been done in Figs. 5–9. The correspondence, most striking in the London Boroughs and least so in the Rural Districts, indicates that on the whole the fall has been greatest where fertility was formerly highest. Since it can hardly be argued that this effect is mainly due to migration, we are driven to the conclusion which has already been put forward on the basis of several recent Continental studies. This is that the high differential fertility noted by Bertillon and others about the beginning of the present century in highly industrialized countries is not a permanent feature of their social organization and may indeed disappear in a few decades.

The nature of the local differences can be most easily appreciated by the aid of maps (Figs. 11–16). The maps for the Administrative Counties cover the whole population of the country outside the County Boroughs, but those for Urban and Rural Districts only refer to a part of the population, though the whole area is shaded. Fig. 10 gives a key to the shading used in the maps.

A preliminary scrutiny of these maps reveals certain outstanding features. In 1911 the highest fertility was mainly found in five districts, the coalfields of South Wales, Northumberland and

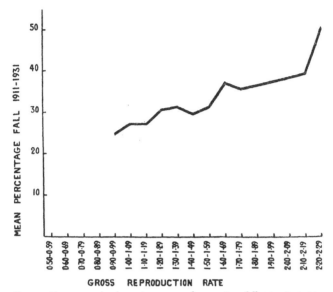

FIG. 5.— Gross reproduction rates, 1911 and percentage fall, 1911 to 1931—
Administrative Counties.

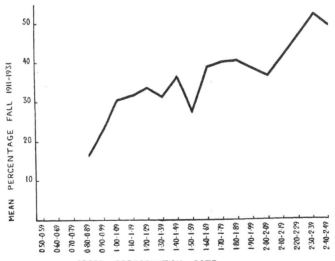

FIG. 6.—Gross reproduction rates, 1911 and percentage fall, 1911 to 1931—
Urban Districts.

E*

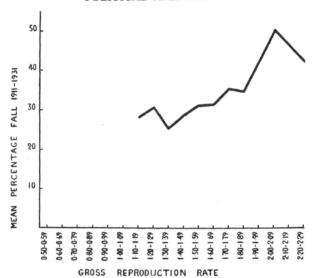

Fig. 7.—Gross reproduction rates, 1911 and percentage fall, 1911 to 1931—
Rural Districts.

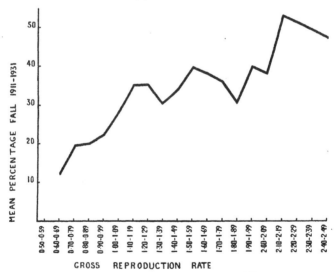

Fig. 8.—Gross reproduction rates, 1911 and percentage fall, 1911 to 1931—
County Boroughs.

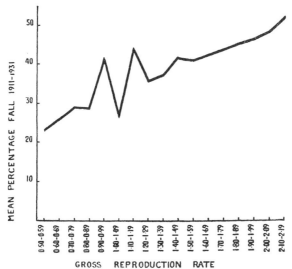

FIG. 9.—Gross reproduction rates, 1911 and percentage fall, 1911 to 1931—
London Boroughs.

Durham and Derbyshire, the industrial counties Stafford and Notts
(also a mining county), and the agricultural district of Lincolnshire.
Low fertility was mainly found in the textile district of Lancashire,
the London area, and the south and west of the country generally.

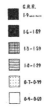

FIG. 10.—Key to shading used in maps.

In 1931, apart from the levelling-out tendency, a more conspicuous
decline in fertility is seen in the South Wales and Derbyshire coalfields and in Notts. Otherwise the relative fertility of different parts
of the country remains in broad outline unchanged.

In connection with these changes migratory movements in popula-

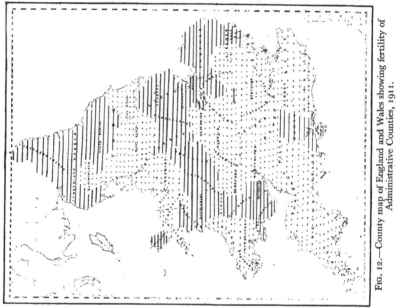

FIG. 12.—County map of England and Wales showing fertility of Administrative Counties, 1911.

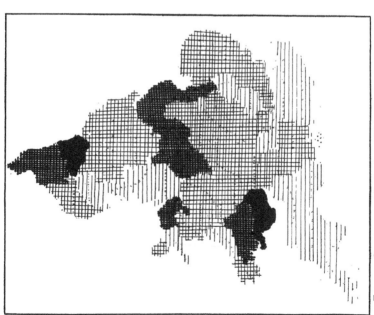

FIG. 11.—County map of England and Wales showing fertility of Administrative Counties, 1911.

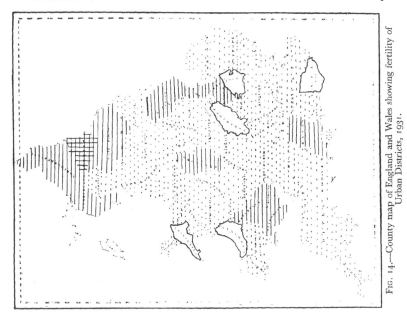

Fig. 14.—County map of England and Wales showing fertility of Urban Districts, 1931.

Fig. 13.—County map of England and Wales showing fertility of Urban Districts, 1911.

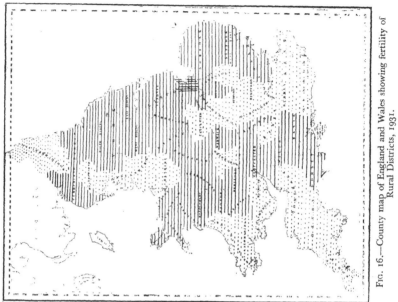

Fig. 16.—County map of England and Wales showing fertility of Rural Districts, 1931.

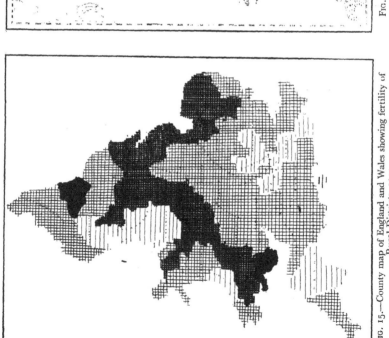

Fig. 15.—County map of England and Wales showing fertility of Rural Districts, 1911.

tion must be considered. The principal movements have been from the South Wales and Northern coalfields, the North Riding of Yorkshire, the textile towns, and the rural districts generally, particularly in the South and West. The chief accessions of population have been in the districts adjoining London, Notts, and in the County Boroughs of Doncaster, Oxford, and Coventry. Population has thus moved both from the fertile coalfields and rural districts and the infertile textile towns. It has, however, moved uniformly to regions of relatively low fertility. The two towns which have received large accessions of population, Doncaster and Coventry, have had drops in fertility of 43 and 44 per cent respectively. The only instance where a large increase of population has changed the character of the district in the direction of higher fertility is Oxford, which has changed from a residential and academic town to a partly industrialized one.

To sum up the general conclusions arrived at in this section, we see that the differences in fertility associated with mining and textile industry already demonstrated by census studies continue to show themselves. We have also seen a general tendency for the higher fertility rates to fall nearer to those of less fertile regions, coupled with a general movement of the population from regions of high fertility to those of lower fertility. The development of new industries in the London area has not been associated with any increase in the fertility of these districts. It follows from this scrutiny that the most propitious line of approach to an analysis of local difference is a more detailed study of the geographical distribution of the principal occupations. This will be done in the next section.

IV. THE OCCUPATIONAL ANALYSIS OF LOCAL DIFFERENCES IN FERTILITY

In this section a complete occupational analysis has not been attempted. Certain important occupations have been selected for analysis. The two occupations which have been referred to as having a clear relationship to fertility differences also carry with them well-marked conditions affecting the employment of women. In mining districts there are practically no avenues of employment open to women outside the home, whereas in textile districts the bulk of the work is carried on by women. This suggested the tabulation of districts according to the percentage of women employed, together with fertility. The figures obtained are shown in

Tables VIII and IX for the Administrative Counties and County Boroughs.

The tables show that on the whole there is a considerable degree of correlation between a high incidence of employment among women and relative infertility. The difference was more marked in 1911 than in 1931. The main avenues of employment for women are the textile industries and personal service. The counties constitute a somewhat heterogeneous assembly from this point of view. Among those with a high percentage of women employed in 1931, Lancashire, Cheshire, Leicester, and Worcester have textile industries, while Middlesex, Surrey, and Bedford are residential. The drop in the percentage of women employed in Cardigan was associated with a low fall but little change in rank.

The County Boroughs form more homogeneous occupational units. Of the twenty-one County Boroughs with 40 per cent or more women employed in 1931, only four had a gross reproduction rate higher than that of England and Wales as a whole. These were Stoke, Wigan, Nottingham, and Birmingham. Both Stoke and Birmingham showed an increase in the percentage of women employed since 1911, together with a large percentage drop in fertility. Wigan contains a large number of men engaged in mining. Of the twenty-one County Boroughs with less than 30 per cent of women employed in 1931, Doncaster, Lincoln, and Darlington had a gross reproduction rate below that of England and Wales as a whole. These three towns will be referred to again. There are, on the other hand, County Boroughs with a high fertility where the percentage of women employed is not particularly low—for example, Liverpool, Bootle, and West Bromwich. At the other end of the scale the towns with low fertility and apparently comparatively little employment of women are all seaside and holiday resorts.

It has already been said that personal service still constitutes one of the main categories of employment for women. This raises a difficulty in the interpretation of the fertility data in districts where there are large numbers of domestic servants. If the domestic service is of a permanent character, it is reasonable to conclude that the women concerned are less fertile than they might otherwise have been. Then the low fertility of residential districts would give a true picture of the effects of conditions in those districts, even though some of the women affected might have come from other districts. If, on the other hand, the domestic service is of a temporary nature,

TABLE VIII

PERCENTAGE OF WOMEN OCCUPIED* AND
GROSS REPRODUCTION RATE

ADMINISTRATIVE COUNTIES

Percentage of Women Occupied	1911		1931	
	Number of Administrative Counties	Mean Gross Reproduction Rates	Number of Administrative Counties	Mean Gross Reproduction Rates
35 and over	3	1·218	5	0·870
30–34·9	20	1·278	11	0·887
25–29·9	30	1·481	28	0·960
20–24·9	5	1·606	14	1·055
15–19·9	3	2·222	3	1·180
	61		61	

* Per 1,000 females aged 14 years and over.
The names of Administrative Counties in each category are as follows:
1911—35 and over : Lancashire, Bedfordshire, Cardiganshire. *30–34·9 :* Cheshire, Leicestershire, Westmorland, Radnorshire, Worcestershire, Somersetshire, Surrey, Montgomeryshire, Warwickshire, Devonshire, Sussex (East), Middlesex, Hertfordshire, Berkshire, Northamptonshire, Sussex (West), Isle of Wight, Yorkshire (West Riding), Gloucestershire, Pembrokeshire. *25–29·9 :* Carmarthenshire, Rutland, Herefordshire, Dorsetshire, Merionethshire, Kent, Cambridgeshire, Oxfordshire, Anglesey, Suffolk (West), Buckinghamshire, Cumberland, Brecknockshire, Shropshire, Staffordshire, Caernarvonshire, Yorkshire (East Riding), Essex, Southampton, Nottinghamshire, Suffolk (East), Peterborough, Yorkshire (North Riding), Wiltshire, Derbyshire, Cornwall, Denbighshire, Huntingdonshire, Lincolnshire (Holland), Flintshire. *20–24·9 :* Norfolk, Ely, Lincolnshire (Kesteven), Lincolnshire (Lindsey), Northumberland. *15–19·9 :* Glamorganshire, Monmouthshire, Durham.
1931—35 and over : Lancashire, Leicestershire, Middlesex, Worcestershire, Chester. *30–34·9 :* Surrey, Bedfordshire, Northamptonshire, Westmorland, Warwickshire, Staffordshire, Hertfordshire, Sussex (East), Yorkshire (West Riding), Berkshire, Sussex (West). *25–29·9 :* Somersetshire, Cambridgeshire, Buckinghamshire, Isle of Wight, Essex, Gloucestershire, Nottinghamshire, Kent, Herefordshire, Derbyshire, Devonshire, Dorsetshire, Oxfordshire, Rutland, Shropshire, Southampton, Peterborough, Yorkshire (East Riding), Suffolk West, Radnorshire, Cardiganshire, Flintshire, Yorkshire (North Riding), Wiltshire, Montgomeryshire, Suffolk East, Caernarvonshire, Lincolnshire (Holland). *20–24·9 :* Denbighshire, Merionethshire, Cumberland, Huntingdonshire, Pembrokeshire, Norfolk, Cornwall, Anglesey, Northumberland, Lincolnshire (Lindsey), Lincolshire (Kesteven), Ely, Brecknockshire, Carmarthenshire. *15–19·9 :* Durham, Glamorganshire, Monmouthshire.

TABLE IX

PERCENTAGE OF WOMEN OCCUPIED AND
GROSS REPRODUCTION RATES

COUNTY BOROUGHS

Percentage of Women Occupied	1911		1931	
	Number of County Boroughs	Mean Gross Reproduction Rates	Number of County Boroughs	Mean Gross Reproduction Rates
50 and over	4	1·187	8	0·801
40–49·9	14	1·133	13	0·829
35–39·9	16	1·225	21	0·915
30–34·9	15	1·444	20	0·919
25–29·9	19	1·633	16	1·108
Under 25	15	1·806	5	1·101
	83		83	

The names of County Boroughs in each category are as follows:
1911—50 and over : Blackburn, Burnley, Preston, Bury. *40–49·9 :* Rochdale,
Leicester, Oldham, Nottingham, Bradford, Stockport, Bolton, Halifax, East-
bourne, Huddersfield, Stoke, Bournemouth, Bath, Dewsbury. *35–39·9 :* Oxford,
Northampton, Manchester, Birmingham, Worcester, Hastings, Salford, Blackpool,
Southport, Leeds, Norwich, Bristol, Brighton, Wigan, Exeter, Carlisle. *30–34·9 :*
Great Yarmouth, Walsall, Chester, Canterbury, Smethwick, York, Coventry,
Liverpool, Ipswich, Reading, Southend, Gloucester, Croydon, Derby, Wolver-
hampton. *25–29·9 :* Warrington, Wallasey, Wakefield, West Ham, Birkenhead,
Portsmouth, Sheffield, Dudley, Newcastle, Cardiff, Barnsley, Plymouth, West
Bromwich, Bootle, Kingston-on-Hull, Southampton, East Ham, Newport, Darling-
ton. *Under 25 :* Grimsby, Doncaster, Lincoln, Swansea, Burton, Gateshead, Sunder-
land, Tynemouth, West Hartlepool, Barrow, St. Helens, Middlesbrough, South
Shields, Rotherham, Merthyr.
1931—50 and over : Blackburn, Burnley, Rochdale, Preston, Oldham, Bury,
Leicester, Stoke. *40–49·9 :* Salford, Bolton, Stockport, Manchester, Bradford,
Leeds, Halifax, Nottingham, Birmingham, Dewsbury, Huddersfield, Eastbourne,
Wigan. *35–39·9 :* Northampton, Worcester, Carlisle, Smethwick, Blackpool,
Walsall, Norwich, Bournemouth, West Ham, Bath, Oxford, Liverpool, Chester,
Warrington, Southport, Brighton, Bristol, Dudley, Wolverhampton, Coventry,
West Bromwich. *30–34·9 :* York, Bootle, Hastings, East Ham, Great Yarmouth,
Croydon, Reading, Derby, Newcastle, Exeter, Sheffield, Birkenhead, Gloucester,
Wallasey, Southend, Ipswich, Canterbury, Wakefield, Cardiff, Kingston-on-Hull.
25–29·9 : Gateshead, Sunderland, Burton, Tynemouth, Grimsby, Southampton,
Barnsley, Darlington, Lincoln, Doncaster, Portsmouth, St. Helens, Newport,
West Hartlepool, Plymouth, Middlesbrough. *Under 25 :* Barrow, Swansea,
South Shields, Rotherham, Merthyr.

so that the women concerned merely fill in the time thus when they would in any case have been infertile, then the populations of the districts in which they engage in domestic service are artificially swollen at the expense of those of the districts in which they marry and have children. It is quite possible that this may have some effect in exaggerating the difference in fertility between, for example, Hampstead and South Wales.

Turning to the occupations of males, attention has been focused in Tables X and XI on three occupations—agriculture, mining, and metal—which have fairly well-defined regional distributions. Other important occupations which are not considered, such as building, are more evenly distributed over the whole country. The districts which are included in the categories mining and metal had in 1911 over 30 per cent and over 20 per cent respectively of employed males in these categories. Owing to the great unemployment in these industries the figures for 1931 are more elastic, the limits being 26 and 13 per cent respectively.

The most striking feature of the table relating to the Administrative Counties is the very high fertility of the predominantly mining counties in 1911, together with the fact that fertility in these four counties taken together has been halved in twenty years. We may perhaps also infer from the difference between groups I (a) and I (b) that fertility tends to be higher in counties which have a high proportion of cultivated land and are at the same time remote from large urban centres. Examples are Anglesey, Lincoln, and the East Riding of Yorkshire. Intensity of cultivation, as measured by the number of labourers per acre, does not connote high fertility. This ratio is high in the infertile Home Counties where there is a considerable development of market gardening. From the rank of the counties given in Table I, the four which have gained most rank are Lincoln (Kesteven), Anglesey, Merioneth, and Montgomery. All these except Merioneth are included in group I (a) of Table X. In Merioneth agriculture is more important than mining.

In Table XI (County Boroughs) both the metal and mining industries are seen to be associated with relatively high fertility, and the fall in fertility has been greatest in the more exclusively mining centres. These two industries are dominant in all the County Boroughs with high fertility except Liverpool, Bootle, Stoke, Kingston, and West Ham. The high fertility of West Ham is surprising as it is practically part of London. However, fertility was nearly halved in

TABLE X

OCCUPATIONS AND MEAN GROSS REPRODUCTION RATES FOR
ADMINISTRATIVE COUNTIES

	Number	1911 Mean Gross Reproduction Rates	1931 Mean Gross Reproduction Rates
I. Agriculture—			
(a) Counties with more than 30 per cent of men employed in agriculture	18	1·456	1·032
(b) Counties with less than 30 per cent and more than 18 per cent of men employed in agriculture	13	1·286	0·905
(c) Mean of (a) and (b) ..	31	1·385	0·979
II. Mining (approximately 30 per cent or over employed in Mining)	4	1·994	1·071
III. Agriculture and Mining ..	8	1·481	0·985
IV. Agriculture and Metal	6	1·355	0·927
V. Mining and Metal	4	1·675	1·050
VI. Agriculture and Mining and Metal	3	1·574	0·952
VII. Miscellaneous	5	1·212	0·835

The Administrative Counties in each category are as follows:

I (a). Ely (Isle of), Lincolnshire (Holland), Radnorshire, Montgomeryshire, Norfolk, Huntingdonshire, Cardiganshire, Yorkshire (East Riding), Herefordshire, Suffolk (West), Anglesey, Lincolnshire (Kesteven), Lincolnshire (Lindsey), Suffolk (East), Rutland, Cambridgeshire, Oxfordshire, Westmorland. (N.B.—In 1931, Cambridgeshire and Westmorland are slightly under 30 per cent.)

I (b). Pembrokeshire, Devonshire, Shropshire, Sussex (West), Sussex (East), Somersetshire, Berkshire, Buckinghamshire, Dorsetshire, Gloucestershire, Northamptonshire, Hertfordshire, Southampton.

II. Glamorganshire, Monmouthshire, Northumberland, Derbyshire.

III. Merionethshire, Cornwall, Leicestershire, Cumberland, Brecknockshire, Denbighshire, Caernarvonshire, Nottinghamshire. (N.B.—In 1931 Cornwall was chiefly agricultural, and Nottinghamshire chiefly mining.)

IV. Yorkshire (North Riding), Bedfordshire, Cheshire, Peterborough, Worcestershire, Wiltshire.

V. Yorkshire (West Riding), Lancashire, Staffordshire, Durham.

VI. Carmarthenshire, Flintshire, Warwickshire.

VII. Middlesex, Essex, Kent, Surrey, Wight (Isle of).

TABLE XI

OCCUPATIONS AND MEAN GROSS REPRODUCTION RATES FOR
COUNTY BOROUGHS

	Number	Mean Gross Reproduction Rates	
		1911	1931
I. Metal	24	1·660	1·049
II. Mining	4	2·054	1·120
III. Metal and Mining	4	1·763	1·165
. Aggregate County Boroughs	*83*	*1·461*	*0·959*

The County Boroughs in each category are as follows:
I. Barrow, Coventry, Smethwick, West Bromwich, Sheffield, Middlesbrough, Wolverhampton, Lincoln, Warrington, Darlington, West Hartlepool, Sunderland, Dudley, Birmingham, Derby, Swansea, Newcastle, Doncaster, Oldham, Walsall, Birkenhead, Tynemouth, Ipswich, Newport.
II. Merthyr, Wigan, Barnsley, St. Helens.
III. Rotherham, South Shields, Gateshead, Wakefield.

the twenty years considered. In West Bromwich, Dudley, Walsall, and Wigan the predominance of metal and mining is associated with high fertility in spite of a moderately high percentage of employed women. The metal towns, with a gross reproduction rate below that of England and Wales as a whole, are interesting. They are Doncaster, Lincoln, Darlington, Sheffield, Coventry, and Oldham. Of these Oldham is also a textile town. Coventry and Lincoln are seats of comparatively new and developing industries, namely cycles and motor-cars and agricultural machinery respectively. Doncaster has increased its population and also its percentage of employed women, so is presumably prospering in some direction. Sheffield and Darlington remain obscure. Both have experienced a pronounced fall in fertility. In these cases it may be the effects of depression, for it appears that two entirely different complexes of social conditions may operate to reduce fertility, unemployment and poverty in a formerly fairly prosperous area as in South Wales, and recent prosperity as in parts of the London area. However, the depressed areas have not all shown the great loss of rank found in South Wales.

It is a possibility that districts with a high percentage of males engaged in commerce may possess an ideology unfavourable to reproduction. Districts are tabulated from this point of view in Tables XII and XIII. The very low fertility of the highly commercialized County Boroughs is suggestive.

TABLE XII

GROSS REPRODUCTION RATES IN COMMERCIAL COUNTIES

(COUNTIES WITH MORE THAN 10 PER CENT MALES ENGAGED IN COMMERCE)

Number of Counties	Mean G.R.R. for 1931
17	0·861

Owing to the difficulty of estimating similar figures from the 1911 census, *1931 rates only* have been calculated.

The Administrative Counties in this category are as follows: Middlesex, Surrey, Sussex (East), Sussex (West), Essex, Wight (Isle of), Hertfordshire, Kent, Cheshire Peterborough, Bedfordshire, Caernarvonshire, Berkshire, Cambridgeshire, Somersetshire, Yorkshire (East Riding), Dorsetshire.

TABLE XIII

COMMERCIAL OCCUPATIONS AND GROSS REPRODUCTION RATES, 1931

COUNTY BOROUGHS

Percentage of Males employed				Number	Mean G.R.R.
Above 18 per cent	..	..	..	9	0·683
13–18 per cent	..	..	..	19	0·865
All ..	..	..	..	28	0·806

The County Boroughs in each category are as follows:

Above 18 per cent: Southend, Southport, Bournemouth, Blackpool, Hastings, Wallasey, Eastbourne, Croydon, Brighton.

13–18 per cent: Great Yarmouth, Canterbury, Bath, Exeter, Reading, Stockport, Manchester, Cardiff, Leeds, Bristol, Ipswich, Norwich, Bradford, Nottingham, Worcester, Carlisle, East Ham, Gloucester, Leicester.

V. OTHER FACTORS ASSOCIATED WITH DIFFERENCES IN FERTILITY

The gross reproduction rates of districts having different densities of population per acre was tabulated, but no significant correlation was found except in the London boroughs. The persistently high fertility of the more densely populated boroughs as compared with the others suggests, though it does not prove, that a differential

fertility rate between more and less prosperous groups has not altogether disappeared in London. The figures are given in Table XIV.
The presence of immigrants from countries with a higher fertility
pattern suggests itself as being possibly associated with high gross
reproduction rates. Fertility in Ireland is higher than in England

TABLE XIV

MEAN DENSITY PER ACRE AND GROSS REPRODUCTION RATE

LONDON BOROUGHS

Density per Acre	1911		1931	
	Number	Mean Gross Reproduction Rates	Number	Mean Gross Reproduction Rates
100 and over	9	1·558	7	0·946
70–99	8	1·377	8	0·758
Under 70	11	1·215	13	0·753
	28		28	

The London Boroughs in each category are as follows:
1911—100 and over: Bethnal Green, Chelsea, Finsbury, Holborn, Islington,
Shoreditch, Southwark, Stepney, Paddington. *70–99 :* Battersea, Bermondsey,
Deptford, Fulham, Kensington, Lambeth, St. Marylebone, St. Pancras. *Under
70:* Camberwell, Greenwich, Hackney, Hammersmith, Hampstead, Lewisham,
Poplar, Stoke Newington, Wandsworth, Westminster, Woolwich.
1931—100 and over: Bethnal Green, Finsbury, Islington, Paddington, Shore-
ditch, Southwark, Stepney. *70–99:* Battersea, Bermondsey, Chelsea, Fulham,
Holborn, Kensington, Lambeth, St. Pancras. *Under 70:* Camberwell, Deptford,
Greenwich, Hackney, Hammersmith, Hampstead, Lewisham, Poplar, St.
Marylebone, Stoke Newington, Wandsworth, Westminster, Woolwich.

and Wales. A large percentage of Irish immigrants is generally
associated with high fertility, notably in Liverpool, Birkenhead,
Bootle, St. Helens, and Middlesbrough. On the other hand it is
associated with comparatively low fertility in Manchester and
Salford, and there are many towns similar to Middlesbrough which
have not a high percentage of Irish. Possibly only in Liverpool and
the adjoining towns could the presence of the Irish element be
regarded as having a marked influence on fertility.

The proportion of foreign immigrants is too small and scattered to be significant except in London, where possibly owing to the numbers of foreigners engaged in the hotel and restaurant trade there is some inverse correlation between the presence of immigrants and high fertility. The percentage of Catholics in the community is difficult to obtain directly, but the ratio of Catholic marriages to all marriages is recorded for counties. Judged by this criterion the counties with a markedly high proportion of Catholics are Lancashire, Cumberland, Durham, Yorkshire (North Riding), Northumberland, and Cheshire. These counties have very varying degrees of fertility. Possibly a more detailed analysis might reveal a closer connection between Catholicism and fertility, but it appears from the Catholic Register that many textile workers are Catholics, in which case no such connection could be established. The counties referred to here are the Registration Counties, but in the case of Lancashire the bulk of the Catholic marriages take place outside Liverpool.

VI. SEXUAL PATTERNS AFFECTING FERTILITY

Since the proportion of married persons in the community has not altered significantly during the period of declining fertility, it is clear that changes in the frequency of marriages are not important in relation to the general level of fertility. Nevertheless they may play a part in determining local differences. Hence fertility differences were compared with the percentage of married women in three age-groups: 20–24 years, 25–29 years, and 30–34 years. Attention will be confined to the 20–24 and 30–34 age-groups. The first of these gives a measure of the rate of early marriage, while the latter includes all marriages likely to affect fertility significantly. In England and Wales as a whole the marriage rates for these two age-groups were in 1911 24 and 73 per cent, and in 1931 26 and 75 per cent. The increase was greatest in the rural districts, where the proportion of married women between 20 and 25 was 24 per cent in 1911 and 28 per cent in 1931. Wide differences were found between different districts, the ranges over the whole set of data being from 9 to 44 per cent for the younger age-group and from 43 to 88 per cent for the older age-group. Table XV shows the correlations found between marriage percentages and gross reproduction rates.

A very high degree of correlation appears between local fertility differences and marriage rates. The amount of correlation is least in the Rural Districts, and in every case is less in 1931 than in 1911. These facts seem to indicate that where opportunities for marriage are adequate the connection is ceasing to be important, but that

TABLE XV

CORRELATION BETWEEN GROSS REPRODUCTION RATES AND PERCENTAGES OF MARRIED WOMEN

	Year 1911	
	Age-group	
	20–25	30–35
Urban Districts	+ 0·909 ± 0·024	+ 0·785 ± 0·053
Rural Districts	+ 0·741 ± 0·062	+ 0·695 ± 0·071
County Boroughs	+ 0·853 ± 0·030	+ 0·837 ± 0·033
London Boroughs	+ 0·934 ± 0·024	+ 0·917 ± 0·030

	Year 1931	
	Age-group	
	20–25	30–35
Urban Districts	+ 0·847 ± 0·039	+ 0·735 ± 0·063
Rural Districts	+ 0·551 ± 0·096	+ 0·373 ± 0·119
County Boroughs	+ 0·726 ± 0·053	+ 0·716 ± 0·054
London Boroughs	+ 0·842 ± 0·055	+ 0·882 ± 0·042

where restricted marriage is combined with a low fertility pattern the marriage rate is a decisive factor. The smaller correlations in 1931 are in part due to a similar tendency to uniformity as was seen in gross reproduction rates. Although the range of variation in marriage rates was not appreciably less in 1931, there were fewer examples at the extremes, since on the whole the higher marriage rates had fallen, while the lower had risen.

The changes in gross reproduction rates between 1911 and 1931 were compared with the changes in the marriage rates between these two years. Table XVI shows the correlations obtained. These results confirm the conclusions derived from the previous table.

The facts cited suggest the possibility that the connection previously demonstrated between the employment of women and fertility may operate through the mechanism of differences in marriage rates. In Table XVII the groups of County Boroughs with different percentages of employed women shown in Table IX have been regrouped. Those boroughs with a marriage rate above the average for England and Wales as a whole have been put in separate groups.

It will be seen that those County Boroughs with less than 30 per

TABLE XVI

CORRELATION BETWEEN FALL IN GROSS REPRODUCTION RATE
AND RISE IN PERCENTAGE OF MARRIED WOMEN

			Age-group 20–24	*Age-group 30–34*
Rural Districts	..	..	− 0·631 ± 0·083	− 0·323 ± 0·123
Urban Districts	..	..	− 0·753 ± 0·059	− 0·527 ± 0·099
County Boroughs	..	..	− 0·779 ± 0·044	− 0·664 ± 0·062
London Boroughs	..	..	− 0·764 ± 0·079	− 0·841 ± 0·055

cent occupied women form a distinct category with uniformly high marriage rates, while only a small proportion of these high rates occur in the other groups. When we consider the two separate categories we see that the series of mean gross reproduction rates are discontinuous. The correspondence between employment of women and fertility is mainly associated with differences in marriage rates. When this factor is kept constant there is still some rise in fertility as the employment of women declines. Table XVIII shows the same effects in the Administrative Counties and should be compared with Table VIII. The position is not so clearly marked since the counties are more complex units.

Differences in marriage rates are correlated to some extent with differences in the sex ratio. The ratio of females to males in the age-group 20–24 is 1·057 for England and Wales as a whole. It is lowest in the rural districts and highest in London. In the London Boroughs and County Boroughs a low sex ratio is usually associated with a high marriage rate, but not so much so in the Rural Districts. Everywhere a sex ratio of about 1·2 or more is associated with a

TABLE XVII.—PERCENTAGE OF WOMEN OCCUPIED, GROSS REPRODUCTION RATE, 1931, AND PERCENTAGE OF MARRIED WOMEN

COUNTY BOROUGHS

Percentage of Occupied Women	Number of County Boroughs	Percentage of County Boroughs with Normal or Sub-normal Number of Women Married aged 20–25	Mean Gross Reproduction Rates	Percentage of County Boroughs with Supra-normal Number of Women Married aged 20–25	Mean Gross Reproduction Rates	Percentage of County Boroughs with Normal or Sub-normal Number of Women Married aged 30–35	Mean Gross Reproduction Rates	Percentage of County Boroughs with Supra-normal Number of Women Married aged 30–35	Mean Gross Reproduction Rates
50 and over	8	75	0·742	25	0·977	87·5	0·760	12·5	1·084
40–49·9	13	92	0·816	8	0·980	100	0·829	0	—
35–39·9	21	76	0·860	24	1·091	62	0·817	38	1·075
30–34·9	20	80	0·917	20	0·924	65	0·903	35	0·949
25–29·9	16	6	0·884	94	1·123	0	—	100	1·108
Under 25	5	0	—	100	1·101	0	—	100	1·101
	83								

TABLE XVIII.—PERCENTAGE OF WOMEN OCCUPIED, GROSS REPRODUCTION RATE, 1931, AND PERCENTAGE OF MARRIED WOMEN

ADMINISTRATIVE COUNTIES

Percentage of Occupied Women	Number of Administrative Counties	Percentage of Administrative Counties with Normal or Sub-normal Number of Women Married aged 20–25	Mean Gross Reproduction Rates	Percentage of Administrative Counties with Supra-normal Number of Women Married aged 20–25	Mean Gross Reproduction Rates	Percentage of Administrative Counties with Normal or Sub-normal Number of Women Married aged 30–35	Mean Gross Reproduction Rates	Percentage of Administrative Counties with Supra-normal Number of Women Married aged 30–35	Mean Gross Reproduction Rates
35 and over	5	80	0·844	20	0·971	60	0·809	40	0·955
30–34·9	11	82	0·850	18	1·053	64	0·842	36	0·964
25–29·9	28	54	0·922	46	1·003	68	0·941	32	0·999
20–24·9	14	43	0·981	57	1·111	57	1·011	43	1·113
Under 20	3	0	—	100	1·180	0	—	100	1·180
	61								

low marriage rate. A high ratio of females to males is thus a very definite limiting factor to marriage and fertility. There are a considerable number of districts in this category. In 1931, 11 out of the 28 London Boroughs had sex ratios between 20 and 25 of 1·18 or over, all had low marriage rates and were the eleven lowest in fertility. There were 19 County Boroughs in a similar position. The highest sex ratios are associated with seaside resorts and residential districts and clearly imply large numbers of domestic servants. The combination of a high sex ratio and a low marriage rate is also usually associated with a high percentage of illegitimate births. These districts are not negligible in point of size, since several have populations of over 100,000.

In addition to the residential group two other groups can be distinguished as possessing features of special interest. The first is the Irish Catholic pattern seen in Liverpool, Birkenhead, Bootle, and Southampton. This consists of high fertility relatively well maintained combined with marriage rates markedly below that of other districts with similar fertility. There is nothing unusual about the sex ratio or amount of illegitimacy in these towns. The same pattern is also found in Newcastle and Wigan. The second pattern is found in some Welsh rural districts. We have seen that a low marriage rate and a high percentage of illegitimacy often occur together, but this combination is usually associated with very low fertility. In the rural districts of Anglesey, Merioneth, and Montgomery referred to it is associated with relatively high fertility. The relevant facts are set out in Table XIX, together with those for three other Welsh counties with quite different patterns.

Carmarthen and Glamorgan are mining counties, and their rural districts, particularly those of Glamorgan, are highly industrialized.

In conclusion, since a slight rise in marriage rates both at earlier and later ages during the last two decades has been associated with a 35 per cent drop in fertility, it is obvious that any rise in marriage rates would not avert further decline. It is, of course, impossible to say whether the decline would not have been steeper if marriage rates had fallen. Further, the high correlation found between local differences does not necessarily imply that an equalization of marriage rates would have any effect on the general level of fertility. This would occur only if the gains in those districts with low marriage rates were not counterbalanced by losses in those with high rates. A consideration of the sex ratios in infertile districts

TABLE XIX

SEXUAL PATTERNS IN WELSH RURAL DISTRICTS

	1931 Gross Reproduction Rates	Gain or Loss in Rank	1931 Marriage Rates, 20–24	1931 Marriage Rates, 30–34	1931 Sex Ratio, 20–24	Ratio Illegitimate to Legitimate Female Births
Anglesey	1·181	+30	23	66	0·95	0·171
Merionethshire	1·155	+36	20	65	0·85	0·084
Montgomeryshire	1·139	+22	22	68	0·81	0·106
Carmarthen	0·994	−22	25	73	0·92	0·046
Glamorganshire	0·992	−40	31	80	0·99	0·036
Cardiganshire	0·943	+ 8	18	59	1·04	0·099
Mean of Rural Districts, England and Wales	1·030	—	28	76	0·92	0·050

suggests that if the young female population were more evenly distributed some slight favourable effect might be produced.

VII. GENERAL CONCLUSIONS

In two previous memoirs by one of the writers the future populations of England and Wales and of Scotland were computed according to certain different estimates of further changes in fertility and mortality. The results were necessarily divergent, and a plausible objection to accepting these estimates as defining an upper and lower limit of population decline in the absence of further information can now be brought forward. This is that fertility might continue to fall for a long while by a unilateral process affecting some stocks only. With the elimination of these stocks the reverse process would set in. While the present study does not exclude the possibility that relatively fertile stocks which do not respond to prevailing fashions of family limitation are distributed in all sections of the community, whether classified from a regional or occupational standpoint, one conclusion about which we can now be definite is that all sections of society are participating in the present decline. In certain quarters it has been held that the well-known differential fertility rates of town and country, rich and poor, set a limit to the continued fall of fertility. The picture of differential fertility which emerges from this enquiry makes it difficult to believe that the fall in fertility will be arrested in the near future, and, while it is impossible to disprove the assertion that a reversal will eventually ensue when all except the most fertile stocks have been eliminated, we are at least entitled to urge that *such a contingency is too remote*

TABLE XX

DISTRICTS WHICH GAINED MOST IN FERTILITY RANK (I.E. WHERE THE FALL IN FERTILITY HAS BEEN RELATIVELY SMALL) BETWEEN 1911 AND 1931

ADMINISTRATIVE COUNTIES	RURAL DISTRICTS
Lincolnshire (Kesteven)	Merionethshire
Merionethshire	Peterborough
Anglesey	Anglesey
Montgomeryshire	Kesteven
URBAN DISTRICTS	Montgomeryshire
Berkshire	Southampton
COUNTY BOROUGHS	
Oxford	
Plymouth	
Portsmouth	
Nottingham	

to prevent a large-scale decline in the total population during the next half-century. We have seen that the largest fall has occurred in in congested areas where high fertility formerly prevailed. In spite of this the present level of fertility is still higher than that of areas where the growth of population has been associated with new industrial developments. On the whole the regions of high fertility are associated with declining industries and the shifting of their personnel to regions where there is no pre-existing tradition of high fertility must be expected to encourage further decline.

The main result of this enquiry, therefore, is to remove any justification for a complacent view of the possibilities examined elsewhere. We may anticipate that there will be a considerable fall in fertility during the next two decades. In these circumstances we may naturally ask whether our data admit of any conclusions which throw light on social agencies which are propitious to the maintenance of reproductive capacity. Table XX gives the districts which have gained most in fertility rank between 1911 and 1931. Fertility has been relatively well maintained in some rural areas, conspicuously so in those which are remote from urban centres and the holiday resorts of urban dwellers. On the other hand no rural areas are apparently immune to the urban fertility pattern. One is driven to ask whether it is possible to maintain a stationary population in a community where urban congestion is sufficiently prevalent to dictate the *mores* of family life.

Perhaps an even more striking conclusion which emerges from this study is the association of low fertility with female employment. The low fertility of the textile areas has long been the subject of comment; and its association with the employment of women has not escaped notice. American statistics show that female employment is generally associated with low fertility;[1] and the present survey shows that this is true of England and Wales as a whole. In the data of this enquiry the effect of employment on the fertility of women who do marry is relatively small. Its chief influence on net fertility appears to lie in reducing the proportion of women who get married.

VIII. SUMMARY

(i) Gross reproduction rates are given for the Administrative Counties of England and Wales, the Counties subdivided into Urban and Rural Districts, the County Boroughs and the London Boroughs for the years 1911 and 1931.

(ii) Comparing local differences in the two years in question shows a general tendency for the higher rates to fall more than the lower so that differences were less pronounced in 1931. At the same time it was noted that there had been a movement of population on the whole from regions of high fertility to those of low fertility.

(iii) The fall in fertility between 1911 and 1931 was greatest in the coalfields and least in certain rural districts.

(iv) There is a definite correlation between low fertility and a high percentage of employed women.

[1] Charles: "Differential Fertility," *Soc. Review,* July 1937.

(v) The mining and metal industries, and to a somewhat less degree agriculture, are associated with relatively high fertility.

(vi) There is a high correlation between differences in fertility and differences in the percentages of married women in various age-groups. Low marriage rates account for a large part of the infertility of districts with high percentages of employed women.

CHAPTER IV

CHANGES IN FERTILITY IN ENGLAND AND WALES
1851 TO 1931

by

D. V. GLASS[1]

I. METHOD AND SCOPE OF INQUIRY

PAST studies of changes in fertility in England and Wales have generally made use of one or more simple fertility rates—either the number of live births per thousand women aged 15 to 45 or the number of legitimate live births per thousand married women in the same thirty-year age-group. Apart from the distortion which may be introduced into these rates by changes in the age distribution of women within the thirty-year group, they suffer from a further inadequacy. Fertility rates lose most of their value unless they show, in addition to spatial, temporal, and social class differences, how these differences and changes are related to the measuring-rod of replacement. That is, we are interested not only in changes in fertility but also in the degree to which they affect a community's ability to reproduce itself. From this point of view simple fertility rates are unreal.

Realistic studies of fertility therefore demand the use of a reproduction rate, and the most straightforward rate of this variety is the one used extensively by Kuczynski. The precise form of the rate depends upon the aim of the particular study undertaken. The total specific fertility rate shows the number of children who will be born to a woman passing through the fertile period—here assumed to be 15 to 49 years—if the specific fertility of a given time were to remain constant. The gross reproduction rate shows the number of female children born to a woman in the same circumstances; and the net reproduction rate, by adding survival ratios to the terms of the equation, shows the number of potentially fertile women who, in the succeeding generation, will replace a woman now passing through the fertile period.

[1] The grant for this research was provided by the Population Investigation Committee of which the author is the Research Secretary.

F

If the study aims mainly at estimating the probability of a future increase or decrease in the population, the net reproduction rate is most suitable. If, on the other hand, changes or differentials in fertility are of primary concern, the gross reproduction rate is more appropriate. The significance of this rate in terms of actual replacement can be seen by computing from the Life Table for the period or the region the minimum number of children per woman passing through the ages 15 to 49 necessary for maintaining a net reproduction rate of unity. At the same time the reproductivity of married women can be gauged by slight variations in the basic rates—by allowing for illegitimacy (through illegitimate fertility rates) and marriage (through Nuptiality Tables).

For the construction of accurate reproduction rates we must know the ages of the mothers at the birth of their children, and this information has at no time been available for England and Wales. Even without this knowledge, however, it is possible to compute reproduction rates by making use of the specific fertility rates of other European countries for which full information is available. The method consists in applying these specific rates to the five-year age-groups of potentially fertile women in this country at the particular time chosen, calculating the expected births and adjusting the total specific fertility rate employed by the ratio between expected and actual births. The procedure is then completed in the same way as if the ages of the mothers had been given.[1] The accuracy of the method depends, of course, upon the degree to which the relative fertility of the seven quinquennial age-groups of potentially fertile women varies between countries and over periods of time. Theoretically the range of relative fertility is extremely wide; it might be equal for each five-year age-group or concentrated entirely upon one of them. If this theoretical range were actually found in practice, and if at the same time the relative proportions of women in the seven groups between 15 and 49 years varied very considerably, the substitute method would be far too inaccurate to be used. But in fact the actual range of relative fertility, so far as can be ascertained, is very much narrower than the theoretical.

For the purpose of checking the accuracy of the method, two of the most divergent series of specific fertility rates were applied to the females recorded by the 1861 census of England and Wales. This census was chosen because of the large differences shown in the

---

[1] The method was suggested by Dr. Kuczynski.

proportions of females in each of the five-year groups between the ages of 15 and 49, the differences being of such a magnitude that there were 2·04 times as many in the group 15 to 19 years as in that of 45 to 49 years. The fertility rates used were those for Sweden in 1891–95 and Bulgaria in 1921–26.[1] The relative fertilities of the quinquennial age-groups are shown in the following table.

TABLE I

RELATIVE FERTILITIES OF QUINQUENNIAL AGE-GROUPS OF WOMEN AGED 15–49

(BASE = FERTILITY OF AGE-GROUP 15–19 YEARS = 100)

Age-Group	SWEDEN 1891–95		BULGARIA 1921–26	
	Actual Fertility	Relative Fertility	Actual Fertility	Relative Fertility
15–19	11·6	100·0	35·1	100·0
20–24	107·9	930·2	246·4	702·0
25–29	193·4	1,667·2	272·7	776·9
30–34	208·8	1,800·0	208·7	594·6
35–39	180·1	1,552·6	155·4	442·7
40–44	102·7	885·3	78·9	224·8
45–49	14·4	124·1	35·8	102·0

The average annual number of live births in England and Wales for the period 1860–62 was 697,713, and the application of the Swedish rates gave a total of 609,744 births, or 12·6 per cent below the actual figure, while the application of the Bulgarian rates gave a total of 813,705 births, or 16·6 per cent above the actual number. Simple adjustment of the specific fertility rates used, in the ratio of actual to expected births, yielded gross reproduction rates of 2·291 and 2·166, the former being only 5·77 per cent higher than the latter. In view of the extreme divergencies both in the relative fertility rates used and in the expected births they yielded, this range of error may justifiably be regarded as a maximum. This is still more the case because in practice two factors tend to keep the actual error well below that figure. In the first place, proceeding from 1861 to the present day, the divergence between the proportions of potentially

[1] From R. R. Kuczynski, *The Measurement of Population Growth*, pp. 122–4.

fertile women in each of the seven quinquennial age-groups becomes decreasingly marked. In 1931 the number of women aged 20 to 24 years was only 1·31 times that in the group 45 to 49 years, and this age range showed the maximum divergence for the 1931 census. The closing-up of the age-group differences automatically increases the accuracy of the substitute method employed. By reference to the theoretical range of fertility mentioned earlier, it can be seen that even so great a range would make no difference in the final gross reproduction rates if the numbers of women in each five-year group were constant. Automatically, therefore, the computed gross reproduction rates would tend to become increasingly accurate as the present period was approached. Further, the gross reproduction rate tends to become more accurate as the margin of error between actual and computed births is reduced. In the example given above the error was very large and the difference in the final rates was 5·77 per cent. Applying for the same period two widely divergent series of fertility rates (Denmark 1878–84 and Germany 1891–1900) which, however, gave a difference between actual and computed births of only 4·4 and 6·8 per cent respectively, the gross reproduction rates arrived at were 2·255 and 2·185, the former being only 3·2 per cent higher than the latter. In view of this relation between the correspondence of computed with actual births and the accuracy of the final reproduction rate, the calculations made in the course of this study have followed the rule of using, for each particular case, only that set of specific fertility rates which yielded computed births differing by less than 10 per cent from actual births. In the circumstances, the range of error which may be taken as maximal is plus or minus 3 per cent. In many cases the error is considerably less, but it is extremely unlikely ever to be more than that amount.

So small a range of error means that gross reproduction rates constructed by the method described are sufficiently accurate for most of the requirements of fertility studies. They would not, of course, be accurate enough for studies of annual deviations of fertility from the secular trend. But since the births recorded in the Annual Reports of the Registrar-General are those registered in the year, not those which actually took place, such studies are in any case precluded in this country.

The present inquiry is concerned with changes in fertility over rather longer periods of time—namely, between successive census years—and its aim is to analyse movements in England and Wales as a whole, and in the constituent parts of the country. It is hoped that the elucidation of these movements will be interesting in itself and that, in addition, it may help to throw light on some of the general factors responsible for the marked fall in fertility in the last sixty years. For the country as a whole, the analysis begins with 1841,[1] but, since county analyses of age and sex distribution were not constructed at that census, the regional study only goes back to 1851. Some difficulty is caused by the change from registration to local government divisions in 1911, but in the main the shape and area of the counties have not been affected fundamentally. In those few cases where the change appeared considerable an attempt has been made to obtain consistency by corresponding corrections of the figures in the 1911 and 1931 censuses, and in the births for the same periods. An earlier investigation (Chapter III) by Dr. E. Charles and Dr. P. Moshinsky, included in this volume, gives a detailed survey of fertility changes in England and Wales between 1911 and 1931, and the present study therefore refers more especially to earlier periods. However, the 1911 and 1931 periods have also been included, both for the sake of historical perspective and because the paper mentioned deals with administrative units and not with registration counties.

II. THE COUNTRY AS A WHOLE

The course of fertility and replacement for the country as a whole is shown in four tables, numbers II–V, and illustrated in an accompanying graph. So far as the course of fertility is concerned—shown by the trend of gross reproduction rates—two facts are interesting. First, between 1841 and 1871 the rise in fertility was very small, amounting to only about 11 per cent. Remembering that there is a maximum error of ± 3 per cent, the total certain increase shown by the figures is not more than 5 per cent. At the same time a glance at the intercensal increases between 1841 and 1871 shows that the highest took place between 1841 and 1851, when the country was recovering from a severe depression. Bearing in mind the recent figures for Germany, showing the effect of economic depression on the postponement of marriage, and the consequent piling up of births towards the end of such a period, it is possible

---

[1] The births used for computing reproduction rates are averages for the three years centring on each census.

that the apparent increase between 1841 and 1851 is a real one. But it is unlikely that the same can be said of the increase between 1851 and 1871. When we also take into account the fact that the system of registration was in process of completion during the period, and was not really made compulsory until 1874, the most reasonable

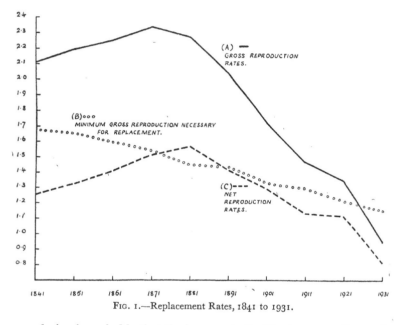

ENGLAND AND WALES.

REPLACEMENT RATES, 1841 TO 1931.

FIG. 1.—Replacement Rates, 1841 to 1931.

conclusion is probably that the increase in fertility between 1841 and 1871 was at most rather small, and more likely to have occurred between 1841 and 1851 than between 1851 and 1871.

The second fact is that in the comparable period after 1871—that is, up to 1901—the fall was really marked. Even assuming the error in the rates to be at its maximum, the fall was not less than 20 per cent. In the succeeding thirty years the fall was even greater, amounting to at least 40 per cent. It is also interesting to note the relatively small effect of the abnormally high post-war births. Assuming that a straight line drawn from 1881 through 1911 is a fairly accurate representation of the trend that would have been shown but for the interruption of the war, the positive deviation in 1921 was just over 10 per cent. Even with this deviation the 1921 gross reproduction rate was below that of 1911.

The course of the net reproduction rates shows a number of differences. In the first place, the peak appeared later. Secondly, the total fall between the peak and 1931 was smaller—allowing for a maximum error, it amounts to about 43 per cent, as compared with a fall of at least 54 per cent in the gross reproduction rates. Thirdly, with the exception of the period 1921 to 1931 the rate of decline was considerably less rapid than for the gross reproduction rates. Finally, the positive deviation in 1921 appears to have been about 17 per cent, and the 1921 net reproduction rate was only very slightly—less than 2 per cent—below that of 1911. All these differences are, of course, explained by the changes in mortality during the period under examination. In studying reproductive capacity we are only concerned with female mortality in the first fifty years of life, and the change in this from 1841 to the present day is most clearly shown in column 6 of Table II, or in column 1 of Table V, though in the latter there are slight differences introduced by fluctuations in the sex ratio at birth. Taking the former set of figures the decrease in female mortality in the first fifty years of life is seen to be about 30 per cent between 1841 and 1931. In view of the effect of reductions in mortality as a counterpoise for declining fertility, it is interesting to estimate the range within which mortality in the first fifty years of life may fall in the future. If there were no mortality in the first fifty years, the number of children per woman necessary to maintain adequate replacement would be 2·05 (assuming a sex ratio at birth equal to that in 1930–32). At present mortality rates about 2·36 children are necessary[1] to give a unity replacement rate. Assuming that mortality is reduced by 50 per cent in the future, so that only 2·21 children are necessary, fertility at its present level would still be inadequate for replacement. In fact, no amount of reduction in mortality would be enough, by itself, to raise the net reproduction rate to unity.[2]

---

[1] Calculated from Table II, column 1 multiplied by the reciprocal of column 5, or column 2 multiplied by the reciprocal of column 5 and divided by female/male sex ratio at birth.

[2] In constructing net reproduction rates the following Life Tables were used: for 1838–54, 1871–80, 1881–90, and 1891–1900 from the *Supplement to the 65th*

[*Continued at foot of p.* 169

TABLE II.—ENGLAND AND WALES: REPLACEMENT RATES I

Period	Total Fertility (1)	Gross Reproduction Rates			Net Reproduction Rate (5)	Minimum Gross Reproduction Rate necessary to maintain Net Reproduction Rates of Unity (6)
		Rates (2)	Indices Base 1841 (3)	Intercensal Change (per cent) (4)		
1840–42	4,322	2·107	100·0	—	1·259	1·673
1850–52	4,488	2·195	104·2	+ 4·2	1·325	1·657
1860–62	4,613	2·256	107·1	+ 2·8	1·411	1·599
1870–72	4,781	2·344	111·2	+ 3·9	1·519	1·543
1880–82	4,641	2·278	108·1	- 2·8	1·572	1·449
1890–92	4,158	2·043	97·0	- 10·3	1·419	1·439
1900–02	3,514	1·725	81·9	- 15·6	1·295	1·333
1910–12	2,997	1·469	69·7	- 14·8	1·132	1·297
1920–22	2,757	1·345	63·8	- 8·4	1·113	1·209
1930–32	1,904	0·929	44·1	- 30·9	0·807	1·152

TABLE III.—FEMALE NUPTIALITY TABLES (FIRST MARRIAGES ONLY), 1851–1931

NUMBER OF FEMALES REMAINING UNMARRIED AT SPECIFIC AGES

Ages	1851–52*	1860–62	1870–72	1880–82	1890–92	1900–1902	1910–12	1921†	1930–32
15	1,000	1,000	1,000	1,000	1,000	1,000	1,000	1,000	1,000
20	900	886	875	898	922	938	945	929	919
25	474	456	436	478	517	548	574	516	534
30	293	276	263	290‡	295‡	310‡	328	278	288
35	218	211	196	204	207	211	243	202	216
40	180	179	164	175‡	175‡	175‡	209	172	188
45	160	162	146	156	158	164	192	158	175
50	149	152	135	146‡	148‡	155‡	182	150	167

* No age-distribution data available for 1850.   † 1921 only—1920 and 1922 figures too divergent.
‡ Evaluated—10-year age-groupings given in census.

To estimate the effect which changes in marriage habits have had on reproductivity, it is necessary to compute the probability of marriage at the various census periods. This is shown by the nuptiality tables in Table III. A nuptiality table is based on the principle of a life table; but first marriages are substituted for deaths, and the single female for the total population. Thus the survivors recorded in the table are the unmarried left at particular ages. An examination of the tables[1] brings out two points—first, the decrease of early marriages in the pre-war period after 1870, and the slight increase after the war, and, secondly, the relatively small change in the number of survivors at age 50 over most of the nine census periods. 1871 was the peak year and 1911 the lowest, the survivors in the latter year being almost 35 per cent more than in the former. With these two exceptions, however, the range is small. It is also interesting to note that in spite of the abnormally high marriage frequency of 1921 and the abnormally low frequency of 1911, the survivors at age 50 in 1911 were only about 21 per cent higher than in 1921. Generally speaking, marriage in England and Wales strikes a midway point as compared with other countries in Europe. In Sweden marriage is at a lower level, because it has long been customary for unmarried couples to

Continued from p. 167]
Annual Report of the Registrar-General (an estimate for 1860 being made by simple interpolation between 1838–54 and 1871–80); for 1901–10 and 1910–12 from the *Supplement to the 75th Annual Report of the Registrar-General*, Part I; for 1920–22 from the Registrar-General's *Decennial Supplement* for 1921, Part I; and for 1930–32 from the Registrar-General's *Decennial Supplement* for 1931, Part I.

[1] The tables were constructed on the basis of the single female populations recorded at each census, and the marriages of spinsters in the three years centred on each census, the marriages at unstated ages being distributed in the same proportions as those for which ages were given. As 1921 was an abnormal year it was thought better to use the marriages of that year alone, rather than make a fictitious average of 1920–22. For the sake of comparability, the age of 15 years has been chosen as zero-point, and where marriages below that age were noticed, they were included in the age-group 15 to 19 years. The results throughout are given in quinquennial age-groups, and two points should be noted in this connection. First, at two censuses, 1921 and 1931, it was possible to construct tables for single years of age. Comparison of these results with the quinquennial computations of survivors at age 50 showed differences of less than 5 per cent. Secondly, at three censuses the marital condition of females was given, after the age of 25, in ten-year periods only. The computations were made on this basis, and the intermediate points evaluated by graphical interpolation. However, since the probability of marriage is higher in the first five years of each ten-year period than in the second, it is likely that the number of survivors at age 50 is higher than should be the case for the years 1880, 1890, and 1900.

live together and bring up families. In Ireland, on the other hand, it has been suggested that late marriage and celibacy have been used as a means of birth-control, thus providing quite different reasons for low marriage frequency. France is at the other extreme, showing a very high marriage frequency. In 1930–32, for example, there were only about 816 unmarried survivors left at age 20, as compared with 919 for this country, and only about 75 at age 50, as compared with 167 here.[1]

For constructing marital or nuptial reproduction rates we are concerned only with the chances of marriage in the potentially fertile age-group, and these chances are sufficiently well expressed by the number of women married by age 50 out of 1,000 single women at the zero-point of age 15. Were there no illegitimacy, a nuptial gross reproduction rate could be computed simply by dividing the ordinary gross reproduction rate by the reciprocal of the single survivors at age 50. Since, however, there is a certain amount of illegitimacy and since, also, this amount varies over time, the proportion of women married by age 50 must be divided into the legitimate gross reproduction rate. The simplest method of obtaining this last rate is by subtracting from the total gross reproduction rate an illegitimate gross reproduction rate computed on the basis of the total potentially fertile female population. The nuptial net reproduction rate is then computed by including Life Tables in the process described. It must be remembered that these rates are considerably less accurate than the ordinary gross and net reproduction rates. They contain not only the errors involved in computing nuptiality and illegitimacy, but also, in the case of the nuptial net reproduction rate, the additional error incurred by applying the same mortality to married and unmarried females, though it is doubtful if this last error is any longer very significant. But in any case the marital fertility rates are intended only as rough guides to trends, not as

---

[1] The French figures are, however, rather unsatisfactory, as marital condition figures after age 20 are only given by ten-year periods in the censuses. As a correcting factor it was decided to allocate the marriages between the first and second halves of each ten-year period in the proportions of relative marriage frequency given in the *Bulletin de la Statistique Generale de la France* of January–March 1933 ("Tables de Nuptialité et de Fécondité pour la France, 1925–27). The allocation of marriages was thus: 20–24/25–29, 1·612 to 1; 30–34/35–39, 1·594 to 1; 40–44/45–49, 1·569 to 1. But it should be remembered that the marriage frequencies given in the article are themselves based on interpolations for obtaining the basic unmarried population at each age at the 1926 census.

accurate interpretations of them, and the approximate computations will suffice as such. The illegitimate gross reproduction rates for the various periods are:

TABLE IV*a*

Period	Illegitimate Gross Reproduction Rates (on Total Potentially Fertile Female Population)
1850–52	0·126
1860–62	0·124
1870–72	0·113
1880–82	0·094
1890–92	0·073
1900–02	0·060
1910–12	0·057
1920–22	0·058
1930–32	0·040

and the nuptial gross and net reproduction rates derived from them are given in Table IV*b*. For gauging the influence of marriage upon changes in replacement rates, column 3 in Table V was standardized

TABLE IV*b*

ENGLAND AND WALES—REPLACEMENT RATES II

Period	Net Reproduction Rates (1)	Nuptial Gross Reproduction Rates (2)	Nuptial Net Reproduction Rates (3)	Minimum Nuptial Gross Reproduction Rate necessary for Adequate General Replacement (4)
1850–52	1·325	2·431	1·462	1·835
1860–62	1·411	2·514	1·567	1·782
1870–72	1·519	2·579	1·667	1·698
1880–82	1·572	2·557	1·761	1·627
1890–92	1·419	2·312	1·603	1·629
1900–02	1·295	1·970	1·478	1·521
1910–12	1·132	1·726	1·328	1·525
1920–22	1·113	1·514	1·252	1·360
1930–32	0·807	1·067	0·927	1·322

on the basis of 1930–32 nuptiality. Comparing this with column 2 in the same table, it is evident that at no time would the application of present nuptiality have made so much as a 4 per cent difference in the replacement. Column 2, of course, represents the combined influence of mortality, nuptiality, and illegitimacy, and the height of the figures for 1890–92 as compared with 1880–82, and for 1910–12 as compared with 1900–02 is due to the fall in illegitimacy and nuptiality being greater than that in mortality during these periods.

So far as the present day is concerned—as shown by the period 1930–32—column 3 of Table IV*b* shows that not even married women are reproducing themselves. Even if there were no illegi-

TABLE V

ENGLAND AND WALES—REPLACEMENT RATES III

Period	Number of Children per Woman necessary to maintain a Net Reproduction Rate of Unity (1)	Number of Children per Married Woman necessary to maintain a Net Reproduction Rate of Unity (2)	Number required to maintain Unity Rate if Nuptiality were constantly at 1930–32 level (3)
1850–52	3·39	3·75	3·83
1860–62	3·27	3·64	3·71
1870–72	3·15	3·47	3·60
1880–82	2·95	3·31	3·40
1890–92	2·93	3·32	3·40
1900–02	2·71	3·10	3·14
1910–12	2·65	3·11	3·06
1920–22	2·48	2·79	2·84
1930–32	2·36	2·72	2·72

timacy, the introduction of universal marriage would not raise the general reproduction rate to unity. But as in fact 40 out of the 929 girls born to a thousand women passing through the childbearing ages are illegitimate, the introduction of universal marriage would have still less effect. No doubt many of the married women are replacing themselves, but this could only be shown by a census analysis of families by the age of the mother, the duration of marriage, and the number of live births. An analysis on these lines would show us if there is a solid core of the population which would act as an eventual brake upon the decline of numbers in the future. It would not, however, alter the fact that the population as a whole is not being replenished by natural increase, and the approximate deficits are shown in the following summary table:

TABLE VI

MINIMUM NUMBERS OF CHILDREN PER WOMAN NECESSARY FOR
REPLACEMENT AND ACTUAL NUMBERS (ON THE BASIS OF
FERTILITY, MORTALITY, NUPTIALITY, AND THE SEX RATIO
AT BIRTH IN 1930–32)

	Number of Children Needed (1)	Actual Number of Children (2)	Approximate Deficit (Percentage) (3)
(a) Per Woman for adequate total replacement	2·36	1·90	19
(b) Per Married Woman for replacing Married Women	2·36	2·19	7
(c) Per Married Woman for replacing all Women (assuming 1930–32 illegitimacy) ..	2·72	2·19	19
(d) Per Married Woman for replacing all Women (assuming no illegitimacy)	2·84	2·19	23

III. THE REGISTRATION COUNTIES

The basic information about the fertility of the counties is given in eleven tables and five maps. Table VII gives the actual gross reproduction rates by counties for seven census periods from 1851 to 1931. Tables VIII to XI give comparable figures for five census periods from 1861 to 1931 for selected districts. These four tables constitute an attempt to link up the work in the present paper with the results in the previously mentioned paper by Charles and Moshinsky, which dealt with the years 1911 and 1931. Since for the analysis of these years administrative divisions were adopted, no direct comparison with registration counties is possible. But it seemed worth while to try to build up county boroughs and administrative counties from the registration districts in the earlier censuses. For this purpose the 1911[1] rank of administrative counties and county boroughs was analysed, and those with the highest and lowest gross reproduction rates were chosen. Comparable units were then constructed at three of the earlier censuses. In the present paper the computed gross reproduction rates for these districts are included only for the sake of completeness. It is intended, however, to include a detailed analysis

[1] The 1911 position was chosen, because the census of 1911 was the last "normal" census before replacement fell below unity for England and Wales.

of them in the final report. The remaining tables in this section express the changes in the fertility of each census as indices on the base of the 1871 census. The five maps show pictorially the fertility of each county at selected censuses and the falls in fertility by counties over the period 1871 to 1931.

Three questions which immediately come to one's mind when considering the fertility of the counties are: first, how high were their gross reproduction rates in the past; secondly, when did the rates begin to fall; and thirdly, how far have the rates fallen. These questions are answered by the tables and maps mentioned above. Taking the registration counties, the highest rate occurred in 1871, when Durham had a gross reproduction rate of 2·975. The county boroughs showed even higher figures—Dudley, for example, having a gross reproduction rate of 3·304 in 1871. In terms of net replacement these figures would be approximately 1·9 and 2·1, rates which imply an eventual doubling of the population about every generation. The highest rates in 1931 were 1·275 for Durham county and 1·432 for Middlesbrough county borough. The lowest rate for counties in 1871 was 1·762 for London, considerably above the rate for the highest county in 1931.

A glance at the maps shows the relative distribution of fertility at various periods. In particular it is evident that the highest fertility has not been associated with agricultural districts. Throughout the period Durham and Monmouth have shown the highest rates, and at different times Staffordshire, Glamorgan, Derby, and the West Riding of Yorkshire have been in the upper ranks. The persistence of high fertility in Durham and Monmouth would seem to suggest an important connection with heavy industry, and perhaps also with the rapidly growing demand for labour in the new industrial areas. It should be noticed, however, that Lancashire, which also experienced a similar growth in demand, has been an area of relatively low fertility for most of the time. Other areas of relatively low fertility throughout the period were the Home Counties and the counties of the South-West (with the exception of Cornwall in 1851). In the Home Counties this might well have been due to metropolitan influence (though London itself was not generally the area of lowest fertility), but the south-west counties have long been agricultural. Among the counties the lowest rate has generally been found in Cardigan, another almost entirely agricultural county.

The degree of regionalization in fertility varies considerably from

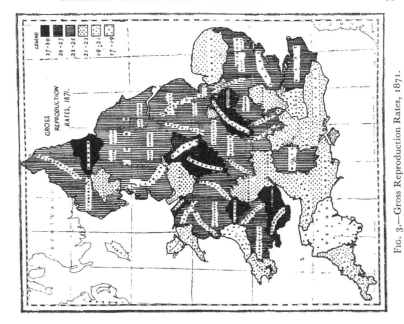

Fig. 3.—Gross Reproduction Rates, 1871.

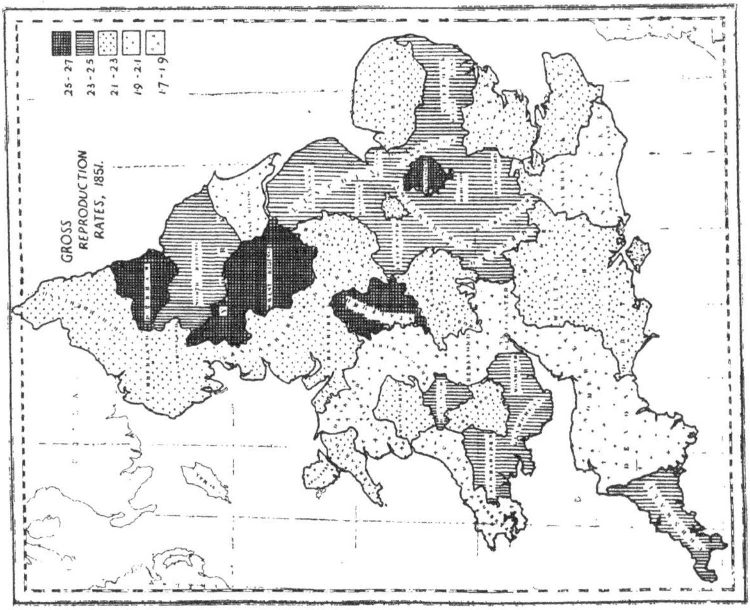

Fig. 2.—Gross Reproduction Rates, 1851.

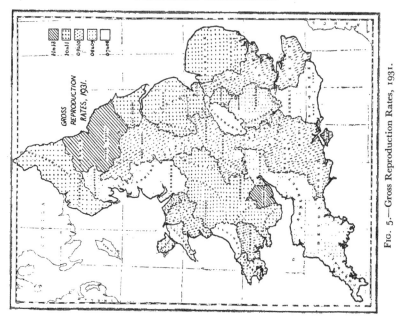

Fig. 5.—Gross Reproduction Rates, 1931.

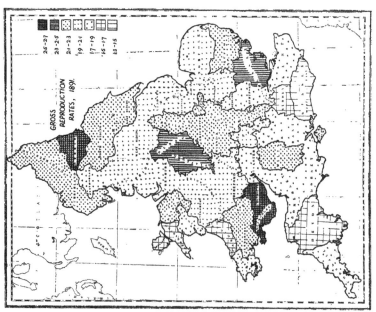

Fig. 4.—Gross Reproduction Rates, 1891.

census to census. So far as the maps are concerned the most clear-cut divisions are shown in 1871. At this period a line drawn north-west from the Kent–Sussex border to the Cardigan–Montgomery boundary would leave the bulk of the high fertility districts to the

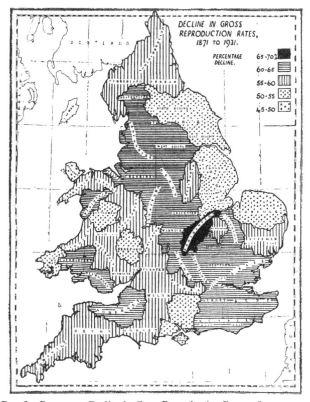

Fig. 6.—Percentage Decline in Gross Reproduction Rates, 1871 to 1931.

north, with the exception of the South Wales high-fertility zone. Differences, however, are more marked in 1891, though the regional divisions are less apparent. In 1891 the four highest regions—Durham, Glamorgan–Monmouth, Stafford–Derby, and Essex—have secondary high zones attached to them, while the rest of the country has gross reproduction rates mainly below 2·1. The 1851 map shows more dis-persion of the high-fertility areas. One stretches across Durham and

TABLE VII

ENGLAND AND WALES—REGISTRATION COUNTIES GROSS REPRODUCTION RATES, 1851–1931

Registration Counties	1851	1861	1871	1881	1891	1911	1931
1. Surrey	1·996	2·018	2·062	1·945	1·526	1·119	0·767
2. Kent	2·292	2·246	2·304	2·248	1·894	1·258	0·919
3. Sussex	2·096	2·016	2·142	1·991	1·493	1·006	0·772
4. Hampshire	2·139	2·166	2·157	2·158	1·742	1·300	0·976
5. Berkshire	2·260	2·240	2·268	2·307	1·866	1·332	0·916
6. Middlesex	1·910	1·915	2·103	2·171	1·796	1·286	0·806
7. Hertfordshire	2·323	2·214	2·223	2·304	1·893	1·143	0·829
8. Buckinghamshire	2·389	2·456	2·429	2·368	2·130	1·251	0·898
9. Oxfordshire	2·314	2·338	2·346	2·278	1·941	1·297	0·935
10. Northamptonshire	2·419	2·433	2·558	2·525	2·238	1·323	0·787
11. Huntingdonshire	2·517	2·422	2·588	2·191	2·023	1·456	1·089
12. Bedfordshire	2·410	2·193	2·326	2·184	1·774	1·174	0·863
13. Cambridge	2·364	2·338	2·447	2·296	2·020	1·487	0·931
14. Essex	2·262	2·379	2·450	2·537	2·306	1·471	0·917
15. Suffolk	2·308	2·348	2·408	2·397	2·136	1·447	1·030
16. Norfolk	2·169	2·178	2·283	2·324	2·056	1·458	1·005
17. Wiltshire	2·295	2·337	2·361	2·362	2·109	1·424	0·994
18. Dorsetshire	2·190	2·265	2·222	2·204	1·830	1·249	0·939
19. Devonshire	2·004	2·097	2·096	2·073	1·691	1·133	0·847
20. Cornwall	2·335	2·370	2·178	2·059	1·800	1·209	0·875
21. Somerset	2·046	2·166	2·188	2·189	1·893	1·186	0·837
22. Gloucestershire	1·985	2·048	2·172	2·136	1·857	1·183	0·898
23. Herefordshire	2·090	2·268	2·238	2·207	1·987	1·363	1·027
24. Shropshire	2·094	2·346	2·425	2·259	1·990	1·541	1·034
25. Staffordshire	2·661	2·663	2·853	2·672	2·480	1·807	1·074
26. Worcestershire	2·214	2·273	2·316	2·233	1·942	1·071	0·971
27. Warwickshire	2·293	2·325	2·386	2·370	2·153	1·593	0·924

28. Leicestershire	2·304	2·324	2·485	2·495	2·155	1·399	0·907
29. Rutland	2·175	2·318	2·247	2·187	1·857	1·433	1·040
30. Lincolnshire	2·359	2·349	2·399	2·437	2·086	1·567	1·096
31. Nottinghamshire	2·243	2·340	2·402	2·452	2·203	1·645	1·000
32. Derbyshire	2·283	2·327	2·540	2·532	2·330	1·553	0·995
33. Cheshire	2·163	2·244	2·299	2·218	1·987	1·236	0·836
34. Lancashire	2·281	2·202	2·369	2·286	1·996	1·363	0·898
35. Yorkshire, West Riding	2·530	2·356	2·469	2·245	2·003	1·450	0·903
36. Yorkshire, East Riding	2·067	2·290	2·371	2·358	2·181	1·523	1·083
37. Yorkshire, North Riding	2·315	2·373	2·497	2·514	2·212	1·644	1·137
38. Durham	2·580	2·731	2·975	2·754	2·566	2·080	1·275
39. Northumberland	2·268	2·359	2·473	2·393	2·285	1·652	1·031
40. Cumberland	2·263	2·312	2·383	2·438	2·141	1·513	1·073
41. Westmorland	2·121	2·328	2·255	2·317	1·896	1·113	0·847
42. Monmouthshire	2·316	2·501	2·702	2·552	2·533	2·066	1·140
43. Glamorganshire	2·352	2·564	2·689	2·614	2·565	2·078	1·029
44. Carmarthenshire	2·355	2·298	2·337	2·321	2·143	1·674	0·916
45. Pembrokeshire	2·070	2·336	2·262	2·276	1·980	1·513	1·021
46. Cardiganshire	1·908	1·976	1·862	1·825	1·569	1·211	0·759
47. Brecknockshire	2·228	2·349	2·387	2·364	2·272	1·699	1·029
48. Radnorshire	2·307	2·407	2·532	2·477	2·034	1·340	1·028
49. Montgomeryshire	2·153	2·371	2·392	2·367	1·976	1·486	1·086
50. Flintshire	2·285	2·279	2·542	2·389	2·248	1·552	1·002
51. Denbighshire	2·076	2·197	2·435	2·298	2·114	1·552	0·993
52. Merionethshire	2·029	2·146	2·457	2·285	1·861	1·416	0·964
53. Carnarvonshire	2·232	2·049	2·115	2·045	1·567	1·248	0·860
54. Anglesey	1·992	1·847	2·004	1·949	1·624	1·209	1·044
55. London	1·762	1·918	2·022	2·023	1·774	1·304	0·780

TABLE VIII

GROSS REPRODUCTION RATES, 1861–1931

A. HIGHEST ADMINISTRATIVE COUNTIES (1911 ORDER)

	1861	1871	1881	1911	1931
1. Monmouthshire	2·724	2·725	2·540	2·263	1·170
2. Glamorganshire	2·679	2·844	2·720	2·251	1·072
3. Durham	2·909	3·207	2·864	2·153	1·298
4. Derbyshire	2·374	2·581	2·539	1·775	1·012
5. Staffordshire	2·342	2·692	2·607	1·743	1·120
6. Brecknockshire	2·349	2·387	2·364	1·724	1·070
7. Isle of Ely	2·422	2·547	2·358	1·718	1·197
8. Nottinghamshire	2·508	2·666	2·775	1·717	1·016
9. Lincolnshire (Holland)	2·237	2·415	2·326	1·715	1·247
10. Northumberland	2·186	2·328	2·227	1·688	1·030
11. Carmarthenshire	2·298	2·337	2·321	1·670	0·924
12. Lincolnshire (Lindsey)	2·389	2·393	2·339	1·650	1·096
13. Denbighshire	2·197	2·435	2·298	1·622	0·973
14. Flintshire	2·279	2·542	2·389	1·615	0·990
15. Yorkshire (North Riding)	2·373	2·497	2·514	1·571	1·016

TABLE IX

GROSS REPRODUCTION RATES, 1861–1931

B. LOWEST ADMINISTRATIVE COUNTIES (1911 ORDER)

	1851	1871	1881	1911	1931
1. Merionethshire ..	2·146	2·457	2·285	1·310	1·018
2. Buckinghamshire	2·456	2·429	2·368	1·302	0·916
3. Dorsetshire	2·265	2·222	2·204	1·295	0·931
4. Cambridgeshire	2·324	2·432	2·255	1·285	0·812
5. Kent ..	2·256	2·296	2·295	1·284	0·917
6. Lancashire	2·102	2·301	1·986	1·269	0·797
7. Berkshire	2·240	2·268	2·307	1·251	0·956
8. Cornwall	2·370	2·178	2·059	1·248	0·884
9. Soke of Peterborough ..	2·477	2·604	2·480	1·247	0·917
10. Somerset	2·395	2·331	2·288	1·246	0·863
11. Cheshire	2·415	2·328	2·289	1·232	0·816
12. Hertfordshire	2·214	2·223	2·304	1·217	0·825
13. Carnarvonshire	2·049	2·115	2·045	1·196	0·840
14. West Sussex	2·217	2·303	2·198	1·174	0·899
15. Westmorland	2·328	2·255	2·317	1·148	0·848
16. Devonshire	2·100	2·171	2·099	1·131	0·805
17. Surrey ..	2·065	2·070	1·954	1·081	0·755
18. Cardiganshire	1·976	1·862	1·825	1·073	0·803
19. East Sussex	2·273	2·339	2·274	1·010	0·749

Table X

GROSS REPRODUCTION RATES, 1861–1931

C. Highest County Boroughs (1911 order)

	1861	1871	1881	1911	1931
1. St. Helens (Lancs.)	2·793	2·822	2·900	2·407	1·269
2. Merthyr Tydfil (Glamorganshire)	2·744	2·826	2·535	2·197	1·034
3. West Bromwich (Staffs.) ..	2·759	3·021	2·588	2·025	1·250
4. West Ham (Essex)	2·179	2·497	2·675	1·983	1·067
5. Barnsley (Yorks., West Riding) ..	2·860	3·234	3·035	1·982	1·116
6. Middlesbrough (Yorks., North Riding)	—*	—*	—*	1·980	1·432
7. Stoke (Staffs.)	2·552	2·873	2·828	1·979	1·084
8. Gateshead (Durham)	2·834	3·018	2·756	1·935	1·245
9. South Shields (Durham) ..	2·624	2·982	2·856	1·890	1·316
10. Rotherham (Yorks., West Riding) ..	2·729	3·064	2·973	1·865	1·128
11. Bootle (Lancs.)	2·093	2·250	2·992	1·846	1·324
12. Sunderland (Durham)	2·478	2·644	2·616	1·800	1·365
13. Dudley (Staffs.)	3·247	3·304	2·939	1·794	1·171
14. West Hartlepool (Durham) ..	2·726	3·063	2·823	1·791	1·275
15. Warrington (Lancs.)	2·667	2·779	2·814	1·767	1·046
16. Walsall (Staffs.)	2·915	3·024	2·726	1·752	1·158
17. Smethwick (Staffs.)	—†	—†	—†	1·751	1·015
18. Swansea (Glamorganshire)	2·455	2·570	2·589	1·750	0·991
19. Kingston-on-Hull (Yorks., East Riding)	1·992	2·274	2·327	1·745	1·109
20. Liverpool (Lancs.)	1·904	2·063	2·042	1·719	1·291

* Included with Stockton.   † Included in Birmingham area.

TABLE XI

GROSS REPRODUCTION RATES, 1861–1931

D. LOWEST COUNTY BOROUGHS (1911 ORDER)

	1861	1871	1881	1911	1931
1. Leeds (Yorks., West Riding)	2·247	2·456	2·220	1·301	0·809
2. Worcester (Worcs.)	1·988	2·155	2·217	1·298	0·906
3. Stockport (Cheshire)	2·073	2·117	1·972	1·291	0·786
4. Oldham (Lancs.)	2·380	2·376	2·203	1·280	0·752
5. Norwich (Norfolk)	1·988	2·176	2·310	1·256	0·909
6. Leicester (Leics.)	2·280	2·553	2·453	1·250	0·870
7. Bolton (Lancs.)	2·488	2·471	2·284	1·236	0·792
8. Croydon (Surrey)	1·822	1·878	1·811	1·231	0·780
9. Burnley (Lancs.)	2·375	2·452	2·396	1·214	0·742
10. Northampton (Northants.)	2·445	2·557	2·566	1·212	0·758
11. Canterbury (Kent)	2·015	2·155	2·059	1·198	0·746
12. Dewsbury (Yorks., West Riding)	2·721	2·561	2·187	1·193	0·797
13. Bristol (Glos.)	2·019	1·988	2·123	1·185	0·860
14. Rochdale (Lancs.)	2·357	2·137	1·788	1·159	0·689
15. Exeter (Devon)	1·789	1·918	1·776	1·158	0·786
16. Blackburn (Lancs.)	2·585	2·488	2·237	1·131	0·670
17. Wallasey (Cheshire)*	1·895	2·305	2·268	1·088	0·814
18. Bury (Lancs.)	2·190	2·247	2·169	1·079	0·712
19. Brighton (East Sussex)	1·566	1·715	1·647	1·074	0·792
20. Oxford (Oxon.)	1·971	2·061	1·953	1·057	0·899
21. Huddersfield (Yorks., West Riding)	2·350	2·234	1·963	1·032	0·680
22. Southend (Essex)	2·709	2·460	2·840	1·021	0·646
23. Bradford (Yorks.)	2·172	2·331	2·033	0·962	0·772
24. Halifax (Yorks., West Riding)	2·689	2·186	1·989	0·930	0·698
25. Blackpool (Lancs.)	2·195	2·107	2·023	0·880	0·600
26. Bath (Somerset)	1·328	1·483	1·496	0·842	0·668
27. Hastings (East Sussex)	1·422	1·524	1·437	0·804	0·744
28. Southport (Lancs.)	2·319	2·157	1·963	0·767	0·594
29. Eastbourne (East Sussex)	2·159	2·058	1·935	0·757	0·629
30. Bournemouth (Hants.)	1·576	1·488	1·450	0·627	0·549

* Wallasey and Birkenhead.

the West Riding of Yorkshire; a second centres on Huntingdonshire; Stafford constitutes a third; a fourth is found in South Wales, and Cornwall forms a fifth. By 1931 only two regions of high fertility remain—Monmouth and the Durham–North Riding region. Zones of secondary height stretch along the east coast and are also attached to the northern side of Monmouth. But the central and southern sections of the country show gross reproduction rates below 1·0.

TABLE VIIa

MINIMUM ADEQUACY GROSS REPRODUCTION RATES AND LOWEST ACTUAL RATES

Period	Minimum Adequacy Gross Reproduction Rates	Lowest Actual Rates*		
		Registration Counties	Selected Administrative Counties	Selected County Boroughs
1850–52	1·657	1·762	—	—
1860–62	1·599	1·847	1·976	1·328
1870–72	1·543	1·862	1·862	1·483
1880–82	1·449	1·825	1·825	1·437
1890–92	1·439	1·526	—	—
1910–12	1·297	1·006	1·010	0·627
1930–32	1·152	0·759	0·749	0·549

* Reading from top to bottom the locations of the actual rates are:—
(a) Registration Counties: London, Anglesey, Cardigan, Cardigan, Surrey, Sussex, Cardigan.
(b) Administrative Counties: Cardigan, Cardigan, Cardigan, East Sussex, East Sussex.
(c) County Boroughs: Bath, Bath, Hastings, Bournemouth, Bournemouth.

In Table II, column 6 gives a series of minimum gross reproduction rates necessary to produce a net reproduction rate of unity at various periods from 1841 onwards. Comparison of these minima with the actual gross reproduction rates in Tables VII to XI shows approximately the extent to which the different parts of the country were replacing themselves by natural increase at the successive census periods.[1] The results are summarized in Table VIIa. From

[1] This is only approximate because it assumes constant mortality throughout the country. But it is close enough to give a general idea of the position.

the summary table it appears that while the registration counties were all more than replacing themselves until 1911, and administrative counties up to the same time, fertility below the replacement level could be observed among county boroughs as early as 1861. The numbers of county boroughs—in the selected lists—below replacement level at various periods were: 4 in 1861; 3 in 1871; 1 in 1881; 29 in 1911; and 39 in 1931.[1] These boroughs, it will be remembered, have been selected from the 1911 order, so that the 1911 figure of 29 represents the total below replacement level. In 1931, however, there were considerably more than 39 mentioned above. By turning to the paper by Charles and Moshinsky and comparing the figures with the minimum adequacy rate for 1931, it will be seen that there were then 72 county boroughs actually below the replacement level. Of the administrative counties in the selected lists, 18 appeared to be below replacement level in 1911[2] and—by examination of the complete lists in the paper mentioned—56 in 1931.[3] Of the 55 registration counties 18 appeared not to be replacing themselves in 1911,[4] while only one—Durham—appeared to have a net reproduction rate above unity in 1931.

Such a change in the position implies a very considerable fall in fertility in all parts of the country, and this brings us to the second

[1] In 1861 these were: Brighton, Bath, Hastings, and Bournemouth; in 1871, Bath, Hastings, and Bournemouth; in 1881, Hastings; in 1911, Worcester, Stockport, Oldham, Norwich, Leicester, Bolton, Croydon, Burnley, Northampton, Canterbury, Dewsbury, Bristol, Rochdale, Exeter, Blackburn, Wallasey, Bury, Brighton, Oxford, Huddersfield, Southend, Bradford, Halifax, Blackpool, Bath, Hastings, Southport, Eastbourne, and Bournemouth. It will be noticed that seaside resorts and spas are notable in these lists. In 1931 the only county boroughs above replacement level were: Middlesbrough, Sunderland, Bootle, South Shields, Liverpool, West Hartlepool, St. Helens, West Bromwich, Gateshead, Dudley, and Walsall. Among these the centres of heavy industries form the majority.

[2] Including the Isle of Wight. The other 17 were: Dorset, Cambridge, Kent, Lancashire, Berkshire, Cornwall, Soke of Peterborough, Somerset, Cheshire, Hertford, Carnarvon, West and East Sussex, Westmorland, Devon, Surrey, and Cardigan.

[3] Of the total of 61 administrative counties, only 5 appeared to be above replacement level in 1931. They were: Durham, Holland and Kesteven (Lincs.), Isle of Ely, and Monmouth.

[4] These were: Surrey, Kent, Sussex, Middlesex, Herts, Bucks, Bedford, Dorset, Devon, Cornwall, Somerset, Gloucester, Worcester, Cheshire, Westmorland, Cardigan, Carnarvon, and Anglesey. It is interesting that London still appeared to be replacing itself, probably because of the large numbers of foreign immigrants.

TABLE XII

REGISTRATION COUNTIES IN ENGLAND AND WALES

GROSS REPRODUCTION RATES AS PERCENTAGES OF 1871 GROSS REPRODUCTION RATES

	1851	1861	1881	1891	1911	1931
Surrey	97	98	94	74	54	37
Kent	100	98	98	82	55	40
Sussex	98	94	93	70	47	36
Hampshire	99	100	100	81	60	45
Berkshire	100	99	102	82	59	40
Middlesex	91	91	103	85	61	38
Hertfordshire	105	100	104	85	51	37
Buckinghamshire	98	101	98	88	52	37
Oxfordshire	99	100	97	83	55	40
Northamptonshire	95	95	99	88	52	31
Huntingdonshire	97	94	85	78	56	42
Bedfordshire	104	94	94	76	51	37
Cambridgeshire	97	96	94	83	61	38
Essex	92	97	104	94	60	37
Suffolk	96	98	100	89	60	43
Norfolk	95	95	102	90	64	44
Wiltshire	97	99	100	89	60	42
Dorsetshire	99	102	99	82	56	42
Devonshire	96	100	99	81	54	40
Cornwall	107	109	95	83	56	40
Somerset	94	99	100	87	54	38
Gloucestershire	91	94	98	85	55	41
Herefordshire	93	101	99	89	61	46
Shropshire	86	97	93	82	64	43
Staffordshire	93	93	94	87	63	38
Worcestershire	96	98	96	84	46	42
Warwickshire	96	97	99	90	67	39
Leicestershire	93	94	100	87	56	37
Rutland	97	103	97	83	64	46
Lincolnshire	98	98	102	87	65	46
Nottinghamshire	93	97	102	92	69	42
Derbyshire	90	92	100	92	61	39
Cheshire	94	98	97	86	54	36
Lancashire	96	93	97	84	58	38
Yorkshire, West Riding	103	95	91	81	59	37
Yorkshire, East Riding	87	97	100	92	64	46
Yorkshire, North Riding	93	95	101	89	66	46
Durham	87	92	93	86	70	43
Northumberland	92	95	97	92	67	42
Cumberland	95	97	102	90	64	45
Westmorland	94	103	103	84	49	38
Monmouthshire	86	93	94	94	77	42
Glamorganshire	88	95	97	95	77	38
Carmarthenshire	101	98	99	92	72	39
Pembrokeshire	92	103	101	88	67	45
Cardiganshire	103	106	98	84	65	41
Brecknockshire	93	98	99	95	71	43
Radnorshire	91	95	98	80	53	41
Montgomery	90	99	99	83	62	45
Flintshire	90	90	94	88	61	39
Denbighshire	85	90	94	87	64	41
Merionethshire	83	87	93	76	58	39
Carnarvonshire	106	97	97	74	59	41
Anglesey	99	92	97	81	60	52
London	87	95	100	88	65	39

TABLE XIII
ENGLAND AND WALES
REGISTRATION COUNTIES IN 1871 AND 1931 ORDER OF GROSS REPRODUCTION RATES

Registration Counties	1871 order	1931 order	Registration Counties	1871 order	1931 order
Durham	1	1	Wiltshire	29	24
Staffordshire	2	8	Oxfordshire	30	30
Monmouthshire	3	2	Carmarthenshire	31	35
Glamorganshire	4	15	Bedfordshire	32	43
Huntingdonshire	5	5	Worcestershire	33	27
Northamptonshire	6	51	Kent	34	33
Flintshire	7	21	Cheshire	35	48
Derbyshire	8	23	Norfolk	36	20
Radnorshire	9	17	Berkshire	37	35
Yorkshire, North Riding	10	3	Pembrokeshire	38	19
Leicestershire	11	37	Westmorland	39	45
Northumberland	12	13	Rutland	40	11
Yorkshire, West Riding	13	38	Herefordshire	41	18
Merionethshire	14	28	Hertfordshire	42	49
Essex	15	34	Dorsetshire	43	29
Cambridgeshire	16	31	Somerset	44	47
Denbighshire	17	25	Cornwall	45	42
Buckinghamshire	18	39	Gloucestershire	46	39
Shropshire	19	12	Hampshire	47	26
Suffolk	20	14	Sussex	48	53
Nottinghamshire	21	22	Carnarvonshire	49	44
Lincolnshire	22	4	Middlesex	50	50
Montgomeryshire	23	6	Devon	51	46
Brecknockshire	24	15	Surrey	52	54
Warwickshire	25	32	London	53	52
Cumberland	26	9	Anglesey	54	10
Yorkshire, East Riding	27	7	Cardiganshire	55	55
Lancashire	28	39			

TABLE XIV

HIGHEST ADMINISTRATIVE COUNTIES

GROSS REPRODUCTION RATES AS PERCENTAGES OF 1871 GROSS REPRODUCTION RATES

	1861	1881	1911	1931
Monmouthshire	100	93	83	43
Glamorganshire	94	96	79	38
Durham	91	89	67	40
Derbyshire	92	98	69	39
Staffordshire	87	97	65	42
Brecknockshire	98	99	72	45
Isle of Ely	95	93	67	47
Nottinghamshire	96	106	66	39
Lincolnshire—Holland	93	96	71	52
Northumberland	94	96	73	44
Carmarthenshire	98	99	71	40
Lincolnshire—Lindsey	100	98	69	46
Denbighshire	90	94	67	40
Flintshire	90	94	64	39
Yorkshire, North Riding	95	101	63	41

TABLE XV

LOWEST ADMINISTRATIVE COUNTIES

GROSS REPRODUCTION RATES AS PERCENTAGES OF 1871 GROSS REPRODUCTION RATES

	1861	1881	1911	1931
Merionethshire	87	93	53	41
Buckinghamshire	101	97	54	38
Dorset	102	99	58	42
Cambridgeshire	96	93	53	33
Kent	98	100	56	40
Lancashire	91	94	55	35
Berkshire	99	103	55	42
Cornwall	109	95	57	41
Soke of Peterborough	95	95	48	35
Somerset	99	98	53	37
Cheshire	104	98	53	35
Hertfordshire	100	104	55	37
Carnarvonshire	97	97	57	40
West Sussex	96	95	53	41
Westmorland	103	103	51	38
Devonshire	97	97	52	37
Surrey	100	94	52	36
Cardiganshire	106	98	58	43
East Sussex	97	97	43	33

TABLE XVI

HIGHEST COUNTY BOROUGHS

GROSS REPRODUCTION RATES AS PERCENTAGES OF 1871 GROSS REPRODUCTION RATES

	1861	*1881*	*1911*	*1931*
St. Helens	99	103	85	45
Merthyr Tydfil	97	90	78	37
West Bromwich	91	86	67	41
West Ham	87	107	79	43
Barnsley	88	94	61	35
Stoke	89	98	69	38
Gateshead	94	91	64	41
South Shields	88	96	63	44
Rotherham	89	97	61	37
Bootle	93	133	82	59
Sunderland	94	99	68	52
Dudley	98	89	54	35
West Hartlepool	89	92	58	42
Warrington	96	101	64	38
Walsall	96	90	58	38
Swansea	96	101	68	39
Hull	88	102	77	49
Liverpool	92	99	83	63

TABLE XVII

LOWEST COUNTY BOROUGHS

GROSS REPRODUCTION RATES AS PERCENTAGES OF 1871 GROSS REPRODUCTION RATES

	1861	*1881*	*1911*	*1931*
Leeds	91	90	53	33
Worcester	92	103	60	42
Stockport	98	95	61	37
Oldham	100	93	54	32
Norwich	91	106	58	42
Leicester	89	96	49	34
Bolton	101	92	50	32
Croydon	97	96	66	42
Burnley	97	98	50	30
Northampton	96	100	47	30
Canterbury	94	96	56	35
Dewsbury	106	85	44	31
Bristol	102	107	60	43
Rochdale	110	84	54	32
Exeter	93	93	60	41
Blackburn	104	90	45	27
Wallasey	82	98	47	35
Bury	97	97	48	32
Brighton	91	96	63	46
Oxford	96	95	51	44
Huddersfield	105	88	46	30
Southend	110	115	42	26
Bradford	107	87	41	33
Halifax	123	91	43	32
Blackpool	104	96	42	28
Bath	90	101	57	45
Hastings	93	94	53	49
Southport	108	91	36	28
Eastbourne	105	94	37	31
Bournemouth	106	97	42	37

question—when did the fall begin? But before answering this question it is worth while reconsidering one of the points mentioned in an earlier section—the extent to which fertility actually rose between 1851 and 1871—in the light of the data for the registration counties. In Table XII the gross reproduction rates of the counties have been expressed as percentages of their 1871 levels, and a scrutiny of the column for 1851 will provide an indication of the extent of the rise in fertility in the succeeding twenty years. Assuming that the error in computation is at its maximum—and the part played by the divergencies in the numbers of women in each five-year age-group will tend to make the error larger here than for later periods—there remain only 24 registration counties showing more than 6 per cent increase in the period 1851 to 1871. For these counties the average percentage rise *above* 6 *per cent* is only 4·8 per cent, a rise which might, partly at any rate, be accounted for by the growing completeness of registration statistics. Further examination of the counties which make up this average shows that 13 out of the 24 indicate rises under 4 per cent. If any rise actually occurred it is likely that it applied only to the remaining eleven counties.[1] But so far as the fall in fertility in the period 1871 to 1891 is concerned, in only three was it at all doubtful. These counties were: Essex, Glamorgan, and Brecknock.

The fall in fertility did not, of course, begin at the same time in all counties, though for many it appears to have taken place after 1881. Among the registration counties there are only ten cases in which a fall between 1871 and 1881 seems definite, while for the rest the period 1861 to 1881 shows fertility at about the same level.[2] Of the ten cases mentioned, one—the West Riding of Yorkshire—appears rather as if it had been falling throughout the period 1851 to 1881. There are also three other cases in which the fall appears to have begun before 1881. In Cornwall, Cardigan, and Carnarvon it seems to have been noticeable during the period 1861 to 1871. In the selected lists, 9 of the 34 administrative counties indicate a fall in fertility between

[1] These were Shropshire, Derby, East Riding of Yorkshire, Durham, Monmouth, Montgomery, Flint, Denbigh, Merioneth, and London. Even here the amount of the rise is dubious. The Registrar-General's *Annual Reports* of the period stress the incomplete statistics of illegitimate births. In many of these counties illegitimacy was likely to be an important factor, and part of the apparent increase in births would be due merely to a more complete recording of this factor.

[2] The ten counties are: Sussex, Huntingdon, Bedford, Cambridge, Shropshire, Staffordshire, West Riding of Yorkshire, Durham, Flint, and Merioneth.

1871 and 1881,[1] and two others—Cornwall and Cardigan—appear to have shown a fall between 1861 and 1871. Of the 48 selected county boroughs 20 show a fall beginning between 1871 and 1881, while of these, 7 appear to have had declining fertility from 1861 onwards. These 7 were Dewsbury, Rochdale, Blackburn, Bradford, Halifax, Southport, and Eastbourne.[2] Bournemouth also shows a fall between 1861 and 1871, though its fertility does not appear to have dropped any further by the 1881 census. No general rule applies to the dates when the fall in fertility began, but there is some evidence that many of the areas of relatively low fertility in 1871 had already experienced a decline by that date, while the areas

TABLE XVIII

PERCENTAGE INTERCENSAL CHANGE IN FERTILITY IN THE REGISTRATION COUNTIES

Period	Average Percentage Change	Standard Deviation	Coefficient of Variation
1851–71	+ 5·5	5·95	108·2
1871–91	− 14·6	5·45	37·3
1891–1911	− 29·6	6·06	20·5
1911–31	− 31·6	7·34	23·2
1871–1931	− 59·3	3·56	6·0

of relatively high fertility showed indications of a rise in fertility between 1851 and 1871.

These notes on the dates at which fertility began to fall, and the extent to which there appeared to be a rise or fall in fertility up to 1881, make it clear that the trend in the early periods was not very consistent. In fact there was a good deal of variation in the movements between successive censuses. Perhaps the clearest method of showing this is to give the average intercensal changes in fertility as percentages together with the standard deviations and the coefficients of variation.[3] These facts are summarized, for the registration counties, in Table XVIII. The table brings out two facts. First,

---

[1] They were: Monmouth, Durham, Ely, Denbigh, Flint, Merioneth, Cambridge, Lancashire, and Surrey.

[2] The other thirteen were: Merthyr Tydfil, West Bromwich, Barnsley, Gateshead, Dudley, West Hartlepool, Walsall, Leeds, Oldham, Bolton, Huddersfield, and Hastings.

[3] The coefficient of variation—used as a measure of divergence of the individual data from the general trend—is a percentage, being $\dfrac{100 \times \text{Standard Deviation}}{\text{Arithmetic Mean}}$

that the rate of decline of fertility for the counties in general showed a regular increase over each twenty-year period from 1871. Secondly, that over each twenty-year period there was a high degree of variability in the percentage decline of individual counties. But it is also evident that there must, in one of the periods, have been a reversal of the trends of decline shown in the previous period, for over the whole sixty years from 1871 to 1931 the fall in fertility in the individual counties shows a remarkably high consistency, the coefficient of variation being only 6 per cent. Even if we take the decline in the selected administrative districts—where by reason of selection for highest and lowest rates a much higher variability would be expected —the average percentage decline from 1871 to 1931 for the 82 districts was 61, with a standard deviation of 6·5 and a coefficient of variation of only 10·7 per cent.

In the chapter by Charles and Moshinsky a number of graphs have been drawn to show, for the period 1911 to 1931, the relation between the size of the initial gross reproduction rates of the various administrative districts and the percentage decline in the following twenty years. These graphs showed a general tendency for the highest initial rates to have the largest percentage falls. It seemed worth while to test the application of this tendency to registration counties for the whole period, and for that purpose correlations were computed between the height of gross reproduction rates at the beginning of a period and percentage falls during that period. The coefficients[1] obtained were:

(1)	1871–1891	− 0·374 ± 0·116
(2)	1891–1911	− 0·154 ± 0·132
(3)	1911–1931	+ 0·703 ± 0·068
(4)	1871–1931	+ 0·122 ± 0·133

Of these coefficients only two are significant—for 1871–91 and for 1911–31—and these show the movement in opposed directions, which was suggested above. In the early period the lowest initial rates experienced the largest percentage falls, while in the later period the reverse took place. It seems likely that this movement should have an influence upon the fertility differentials of the counties. The trend of the fall in the early period ought to increase

---

[1] The measure of the standard deviation of the correlation coefficient adopted in this paper is $\pm \dfrac{1 - r^2}{\sqrt{n}}.$

the differential, while that of the later period ought to lower it again. To test this, an analysis of the gross reproduction rates of the registration counties was made for seven censuses, and the results are given in Table XIX. From this table the trend is evident—the differential increasing fairly consistently from 1851 till 1911 (it might, of course, have continued till 1921) and then falling sharply to below the 1891 level. The trend of the fall in fertility in the registration counties between 1911 and 1931, and the closing up of the county differentials in the same period are rather suggestive. It

TABLE XIX

DIFFERENTIALS IN THE FERTILITY OF REGISTRATION COUNTIES
AT SPECIFIC CENSUSES, 1851–1931

Period	Mean Gross Reproduction Rates of Registration Counties	Standard Deviation	Coefficient of Variation (Percentage)	Indices of Coefficient of Variation (Base = 1871 = 100)
1850–52	2·225	0·171	7·70	90
1860–62	2·275	0·169	7·42	87
1870–72	2·353	0·200	8·52	100
1880–82	2·298	0·184	8·02	94
1890–92	2·013	0·249	12·37	145
1910–12	1·420	0·237	16·65	195
1930–32	0·957	0·108	11·29	133

seems likely from these facts that regional differentials in fertility are only marked in a period when industrial expansion has still not proceeded far enough to urbanize the whole community. In 1911 not only was farming prosperous in England and Wales, but also large sections of the country still remained untouched by urban developments. The development of railways in the nineteenth century was on the lines of relatively long-distance traffic rather than the penetration of rural areas by branch lines. Not till the development of widespread road transport, the creation of national newspapers, and the introduction of the cinema and the radio as means of spreading ideas and information was the isolation of the rural from the urban areas really broken down. Since 1911 such changes have tended to produce a more universal pattern of life, a more generally accepted set of social *mores*. The attitude of married couples towards

G

the family would thus tend to be less divergent in different parts of the country and would result in a more marked similarity in the regional fertility rates. The closing up of the regional differential does not throw any light upon differentials between social classes, but it does indirectly suggest that the same process may be at work here. If the differences between the various parts of the country are breaking down, there is no reason to believe that the social classes are impervious to similar influences.

IV. THE FACTORS ASSOCIATED WITH THE DECLINE IN FERTILITY

This section of the present investigation does not attempt to break new ground. Its scope is limited from the beginning by the fact that the smallest areas with which it deals are registration counties. As each county is a complex of many patterns of social life, it is highly possible that factors which might be noticeable if small, homogeneous groups were analysed are merged and invisible in the large and heterogeneous areas. For the present, therefore, attention will be paid only to those factors which satisfy two requirements—first, that they would appear, *a priori*, to have a bearing upon fertility; and secondly, that they affect sufficiently large sections of the population for their influence, if it is real, to be clearly visible. The factors which come within this category are: the amount of marriage, the amount of female employment, the general occupational type of the area, and, finally, the degree of child labour. The last factor has been included because it clearly has an important influence upon the economic attraction of large families.

(a) Marriage

The analysis of marriage has been approached from its obverse side—the amount of celibacy—merely because it is simpler to extract information from the census in that form. Since we are concerned only with the fertility of the potentially fertile women, the basic data used are the percentages of unmarried women[1] out of all women between the ages of 20 and 45 years. This information is summarized in Table XX. Two kinds of analysis of the relationship between celibacy and fertility are possible—at a point of time or over

[1] That is, women who have not been married, thus excluding widows.

TABLE XX

REGISTRATION COUNTIES IN ENGLAND AND WALES

PERCENTAGES OF UNMARRIED FEMALES, AGED 20–45

	1851	1871	1891	1911	1931
Surrey	41	41	47	46	41
Kent	37	34	40	41	35
Sussex	39	41	47	46	43
Hampshire	37	34	40	40	35
Berkshire	38	37	40	43	39
Middlesex	42	40	40	40	38
Hertfordshire	35	38	41	44	40
Buckinghamshire	34	34	36	40	36
Oxfordshire	37	36	41	45	39
Northamptonshire	33	30	33	38	36
Huntingdonshire	30	32	37	36	33
Bedfordshire	35	38	42	41	36
Cambridgeshire	33	32	36	39	36
Essex	33	31	30	35	35
Suffolk	35	33	36	40	36
Norfolk	37	35	36	40	36
Wiltshire	37	35	37	38	34
Dorsetshire	39	38	41	43	37
Devonshire	41	39	43	43	37
Cornwall	39	39	43	43	38
Somerset	42	39	42	46	40
Gloucestershire	42	39	42	43	40
Herefordshire	41	37	43	45	40
Shropshire	40	37	42	42	38
Staffordshire	29	26	30	34	34
Worcestershire	37	36	41	40	36
Warwickshire	34	31	34	37	36
Leicestershire	36	33	35	39	36
Rutland	39	37	42	41	37
Lincolnshire	35	33	35	35	32
Nottinghamshire	36	32	33	36	34
Derbyshire	36	30	32	32	32
Cheshire	38	36	40	42	39
Lancashire	37	33	36	39	39
Yorkshire, West Riding	33	30	35	36	35
Yorkshire, East Riding	36	32	34	37	36
Yorkshire, North Riding	40	35	35	39	35
Durham	29	22	26	30	30
Northumberland	38	33	35	36	36
Cumberland	42	38	39	43	38
Westmorland	44	40	46	50	44
Monmouthshire	29	27	29	28	28
Glamorganshire	31	26	27	29	31
Carmarthenshire	42	42	43	41	38
Pembrokeshire	46	44	45	45	40
Cardiganshire	49	50	53	57	52
Brecknockshire	38	36	40	38	37
Radnorshire	44	39	46	48	43
Montgomeryshire	43	38	44	47	53
Flintshire	33	30	36	40	39
Denbighshire	39	35	39	40	39
Merionethshire	41	37	41	48	44
Caernarvonshire	40	40	45	46	45
Anglesey	40	42	43	45	43
London	40	37	40	43	43

a period—and correlation coefficients for both kinds of analysis were computed. For the former analysis they are given in Table XXI. The rise in the coefficients up to 1890–92 is associated with the fall in illegitimacy during the period (see Table IV*a*). At the same time the height of the coefficients in the first three periods and the fall after 1890–92 shows the change in the biological function of marriage. Although marital fertility was falling between 1871 and 1891, marriage almost inevitably involved the raising of children. But the fall in marital fertility between 1891 and 1931 has been accompanied by a loosening of the relationship between marriage and birth. Not only do marriages now produce fewer children, but also the likelihood of any children being produced in a marriage is

TABLE XXI

CORRELATION BETWEEN HEIGHT OF GROSS REPRODUCTION
RATES AND PERCENTAGE OF UNMARRIED WOMEN AMONG ALL
WOMEN AGED 20–45

(1)	1850–52	$-0\cdot740 \pm 0\cdot061$
(2)	1870–72	$-0\cdot841 \pm 0\cdot040$
(3)	1890–92	$-0\cdot849 \pm 0\cdot038$
(4)	1910–12	$-0\cdot724 \pm 0\cdot064$
(5)	1930–32	$-0\cdot433 \pm 0\cdot110$

considerably less than it was. This should be remembered when considering the coefficients in Table XXII. Only two of these are significant—those for 1871–91 and 1911–31—and their significance is not identical. In the period 1871–91 the percentage of celibacy rose, but in the period 1911–31 it fell.[1] So that whereas in the former case the coefficient means that the larger the fall in marriage the larger the fall in fertility, in the second it means the larger the rise in marriage the smaller the fall in fertility. But although these coefficients are significant the extent of the influence of mar-

[1] The extent of celibacy among women aged 20–45 is shown by the following average percentages for the registration counties:

	Percentage of Unmarried Women Aged 20–45	Standard Deviation
1850–52	38	$4\cdot25$
1870–72	35	$4\cdot84$
1890–92	39	$5\cdot32$
1910–12	41	$5\cdot20$
1930–32	38	$4\cdot53$

riage in the decline of fertility is, as was shown in the first section of this investigation, quite small. Even if all women had married in the period 1930–32 the average number of children per woman passing through the fertile period would only have been $2 \cdot 19$[1] instead of the $1 \cdot 9$ actually found, and still considerably below the $2 \cdot 36$ necessary for adequate maintenance of the population.

TABLE XXII

CORRELATION BETWEEN PERCENTAGE CHANGE IN GROSS REPRODUCTION RATES AND PERCENTAGE CHANGE IN PROPORTIONS OF UNMARRIED WOMEN AGED 20–45

(1)	1871–1891	$+0 \cdot 520 \pm 0 \cdot 098$
(2)	1891–1911	$+0 \cdot 165 \pm 0 \cdot 131$
(3)	1911–1931	$+0 \cdot 510 \pm 0 \cdot 100$
(4)	1871–1931	$+0 \cdot 185 \pm 0 \cdot 130$

(b)   *The Employment of Women*

The analysis of the influence of the employment of women upon fertility is made difficult by the changes in occupational classification and age-grouping from census to census. Strictly speaking, we should study the employment of women in specific age-groups, or, failing that, in the group of 20 to 45 years. But in some censuses no age divisions are given for the counties, while, taking the country as a whole, the 1931 census adopts a division at 21 instead of at the customary 20 years of age. The subsequent tables and analysis represent an attempt to make comparable groups which, if there is any significance in the relationship between female employment and fertility, should show that relationship.

The basic figures for the country as a whole are given in Table XXIII, which summarizes female employment in general, as well as in the major occupations, for five census periods. Strictly speaking, the 1931 figures, since they refer to women aged 21 and over, are not comparable with the earlier data for women aged 20 and over. But a figure for the total employment of women aged 20 and over has been included,[2] and it is unlikely that the distri-

---

[1] This may be an exaggeration, since it is possible that the incidence of sterility among women who have not married is greater than among those who have.

[2] The figures for calculating this figure were kindly provided by the Registrar-General.

TABLE XXIII

ENGLAND AND WALES, 1851–1931—EMPLOYMENT OF WOMEN

Occupied Women Aged 20 Years and over—Absolute Numbers and Percentages of all Occupied Women aged 20 years and over

	1851		1871		1891		1911		1931*	
	Number	Per cent	Number	Per cent	Number	Per cent	Number	Per cent	Number	Per cent
1. Teaching	59,271	3·3	80,934	3·5	120,985	4·4	179,039	4·8	191,127	4·7
2. Domestic Service	554,993	31·3	822,615	35·7	966,714	35·4	1,055,689	29·5	1,075,087	26·2
3. Nursing	25,775	1·5	28,205	1·2	53,198	1·9	85,666	2·4	131,744	3·2
4. Clothing Manufacture	464,774	26·2	594,671	25·8	636,172	23·3	649,269	18·2	441,893	10·8
5. Distribution	78,452	4·4	108,449	4·7	109,272	4·0	349,438	9·8	417,671	10·2
6. Catering	21,820	1·2	59,786	2·2	71,423	2·6	204,444	5·7	247,035	6·0
7. Agriculture	187,528	10·6	133,925	5·8	44,540	1·6	72,659	2·0	43,724	1·1
8. Textile Manufacture	273,497	15·4	334,453	14·5	370,100	13·5	390,362	10·9	440,309	10·7
9. Commerce	—†	—	4,667	0·2	13,965	0·5	82,861	2·3	381,448	9·3
10. Professions	1,924	0·1	8,531	0·4	14,687	0·5	25,578	0·7	35,222	0·9
11. Central and Local Government	2,169	0·1	5,552	0·2	13,146	0·5	44,794	1·3	—‡	—‡
Total of 1 to 11	1,670,203	94·1	2,172,788	94·3	2,414,202	88·3	3,130,209	87·7	3,405,260	83·1
Total Occupied Women aged 20 and over	1,775,699	100·0	2,305,198	100·0	2,733,061§	100·0	3,571,183§	100·0	4,097,409§	100·0
Total Women aged 20 and over	5,099,584	—	6,463,645	—	8,363,491	—	11,423,330	—	14,032,386	—
Percentage of Women aged 20 and over in employment	34·8		35·7		32·7		31·3		29·2 (21 and over)‖ 30·3 (20 and over)‖	

* The 1931 figures are for women aged 21 years and over.

† The Commerce figure for 1851 is not comparable with subsequent censuses.

‡ This figure is not comparable with preceding ones, since clerks and typists were excluded in 1931.

§ The totals include women who had retired from paid employment, since it was not possible to exclude the retired from the occupied at the 1851 and 1871 censuses.

‖ From unpublished figures kindly provided by the Registrar-General.

bution of women between the various occupations differs significantly for the group 21 and over as compared with 20 and over. Since the 1851 and 1871 censuses did not distinguish women who had retired from gainful employment, the retired category was added for 1891, 1911, and 1931. But this only swells the totals of the occupied by 2·6, 2·3, and 4·4 per cent respectively.

Leaving aside, for the moment, the changes in the type of female employment, the most striking feature of Table XXIII is that there is less female employment to-day than there was in any previous point in the period under examination. But since 1871—taking that date as marking the peak of fertility—the age composition of the population has changed considerably. The population is now much

TABLE XXIV

PERCENTAGES OF WOMEN OCCUPIED IN SPECIFIC AGE-GROUPS

			Age-Groups		
Period	20–25	25–35	35–45	20–45	45 and over
1851	57·4	36·1	27·2	38·8	27·2
1871	58·4	35·5	28·8	39·1	29·4
1891	58·2	33·2	25·4	37·2	24·5
1911	62·1	34·0	24·4	37·1	20·9
1931	67·5	36·6	24·9	39·2	15·6

older than it was, and percentages for the totals of employed women aged 20 and over may mask the real facts. The trends in specific age-groups are shown in Table XXIV. It is evident that throughout the period there has been a marked tendency for the older women to drop out of employment and a less marked tendency for the younger women to go into it. But it is no less evident that only in the age-group 20–25 has the increase in employment been significant. For the age-group 20–45 which concerns us most, there was a fall of 5 per cent between 1871 and 1891, no significant fall between 1891 and 1911, and a rise of 6 per cent between 1911 and 1931. Since the position now is almost what it was in 1871, it is impossible to explain the decline in fertility between 1871 and 1931 in terms of an increase in the general employment of women for the country as a whole. Of course it is possible that significant differences in the counties cancel each other when the country is taken as a whole, and to test this possibility it was decided to make a similar analysis for the individual counties. The problem of comparability was particularly difficult here and the analysis was limited to three censuses—1871, 1911, and 1931. To include the 1931 census meant analysing the employment of women aged 15 and over, and even then the Welsh counties, with the exception of Monmouth, had to be excluded as the necessary information for these counties was not given in the 1871 census. The study was thus restricted to 43 registration counties, and in order to allow for the influence of changes in the age composition of the females over the period, the employment percentages were standardized for the age-group 20–45 years.[1] The unstandardized percentages are given in Table XXV and the standardized in Table XXVI.[2] The coefficients for the correlation between changes in fertility and changes in the employment of women were[3]:

$$\begin{array}{ll} \text{(1) } 1871\text{--}1911 & -0\cdot010 \pm 0\cdot152 \\ \text{(2) } 1911\text{--}1931 & -0\cdot384 \pm 0\cdot130 \end{array}$$

Neither correlation is significant. For the censuses of 1871 and 1911 it was possible to obtain the actual percentages of employed women aged 20–45 years, and to allow for the change in employment in the younger section of this group, the percentages were standardized for the age-group 20–30 years. The resultant correlation was − 0·061 ± 0·152, which is also not significant.

Having seen that the time analysis of the registration counties yields the same impression regarding the relation between fertility and the general employment of women as that of the whole of England and Wales, it is now worth while to return to a closer analysis of the position in the country in general. For 1911 and 1931 the censuses give rather more details of employment, dividing the women into married and unmarried as well as into a number of age-groups. It has been shown that there was more marriage among women aged 20–45 years in 1931 than in 1911, so that the influence of women's employment upon fertility would appear only through

[1] On the basis of the percentage which women aged 20–45 years formed in the total female population aged 15 years and over in each county in 1871.

[2] These tables include percentages for 1851, not used in this particular correlation.

[3] The correlations were between the relative level of fertility at the end of the period and the relative level of female employment at the end of the period. In interpreting the signs it must be remembered that employment fell between 1871 and 1911 and rose between 1911 and 1931.

TABLE XXV

ENGLAND AND WALES: REGISTRATION COUNTIES, 1851–1931

PERCENTAGE OCCUPIED (INCLUDING RETIRED) OF ALL FEMALES 15 AND OVER

	1851	1871	1911	1931
Surrey	33·8	40·6	37·7	35·7
Kent	30·9	34·5	32·9	30·3
Sussex	35·0	40·8	38·5	35·2
Hampshire	32·5	35·1	32·4	29·5
Berkshire	37·2	39·3	35·1	32·9
Middlesex	36·9	39·9	35·9	36·7
Hertfordshire	41·2	45·7	35·7	33·3
Buckinghamshire	48·1	50·1	31·7	30·0
Oxfordshire	36·8	41·6	35·7	32·4
Northamptonshire	38·8	39·9	35·3	34·2
Huntingdonshire	29·9	36·4	27·9	24·5
Bedfordshire	57·3	66·3	40·3	34·6
Cambridgeshire	31·3	35·0	30·7	28·1
Essex	31·6	34·3	31·3	31·8
Suffolk	31·5	35·2	31·4	28·1
Norfolk	33·9	36·5	32·8	29·2
Wiltshire	39·4	39·0	29·6	26·6
Dorsetshire	38·6	41·0	33·0	28·9
Devonshire	40·9	42·0	35·1	28·9
Cornwall	33·1	37·7	28·6	24·0
Somerset	44·7	45·8	38·1	32·4
Gloucestershire	43·5	45·1	38·2	33·6
Herefordshire	36·1	38·3	33·6	29·3
Shropshire	32·8	36·0	31·2	27·7
Staffordshire	32·0	34·1	33·9	37·4
Worcestershire	43·0	44·6	37·5	36·5
Warwickshire	44·2	44·5	41·1	39·8
Leicestershire	47·3	46·8	44·7	44·3
Rutland	30·8	34·5	32·7	27·4
Lincolnshire	31·5	34·0	26·4	24·6
Nottinghamshire	46·3	46·1	38·7	35·4
Derbyshire	40·9	39·8	29·3	29·2
Cheshire	43·2	44·7	38·3	36·9

G*

TABLE XXV—*continued*

ENGLAND AND WALES: REGISTRATION COUNTIES, 1851–1931

PERCENTAGE OCCUPIED (INCLUDING RETIRED) OF ALL FEMALES, 15 AND OVER

	1851	*1871*	*1911*	*1931*
Lancashire	47·3	49·7	43·1	44·4
Yorkshire, West Riding ..	39·5	40·8	35·8	36·0
Yorkshire, East Riding* ..	33·9	35·1	30·9	30·2
Yorkshire, North Riding† ..	—	—	28·1	26·2
Durham‡	—	—	20·6	21·2
Northumberland	31·2	33·1	26·4	27·7
Cumberland	39·5	41·2	32·0	28·2
Westmorland	41·4	42·1	38·3	33·7
Monmouthshire	27·8	30·1	22·4	18·5
Glamorganshire	—	—	23·1	20·3
Carmarthenshire	—	—	34·3	21·7
Pembrokeshire	—	—	34·5	24·8
Cardiganshire	—	—	39·9	27·3
Brecknockshire	—	—	31·4	22·2
Radnorshire..	—	—	38·2	27·4
Montgomeryshire	—	—	37·3	26·7
Flintshire	—	—	28·4	26·8
Denbighshire	—	—	29·1	25·5
Merionethshire	—	—	33·1	25·2
Caernarvonshire	—	—	30·6	26·3
Anglesey	—	—	31·8	24·0
London	42·6	43·8	44·3	45·5
Aggregate North Wales ..	33·8	36·3	30·9	25·9
Aggregate South Wales ..	33·5	36·2	26·6	21·2
Yorkshire, North Riding‡ ..	34·9	36·3	29·6	26·4
Durham†	24·5	22·6	20·8	21·6
England and Wales ..	39·0	41·1	36·1	35·1

* Including York.   † Including Middlesbrough.

‡ Excluding Middlesbrough.

TABLE XXVI

ENGLAND AND WALES—REGISTRATION COUNTIES

PERCENTAGE OF WOMEN EMPLOYED

(Women employed aged 15 and over, as percentage of all women aged 15 and over, standardized for 20–45 age-group—base year 1871)

	1851	*1871*	*1911*	*1931*
Surrey	35·7	40·6	38·4	41·1
Kent	30·5	34·5	32·9	33·9
Sussex	34·3	40·8	39·4	43·0
Hampshire	31·9	35·1	31·9	33·5
Berkshire	36·9	39·3	35·5	36·7
Middlesex	37·4	39·9	34·5	38·8
Hertfordshire	39·6	45·7	34·4	34·8
Buckinghamshire	47·2	50·1	31·5	32·0
Oxfordshire	35·2	41·6	36·2	35·0
Northamptonshire	37·4	39·9	34·7	36·2
Huntingdonshire	27·6	36·4	28·5	26·1
Bedfordshire	55·7	66·3	41·6	38·1
Cambridgeshire	28·8	35·0	30·9	29·8
Essex	30·7	34·3	29·6	34·3
Suffolk	29·6	35·2	30·9	30·4
Norfolk	31·6	36·5	32·3	30·9
Wiltshire	38·0	39·0	28·6	27·7
Dorsetshire	37·6	41·0	32·6	31·6
Devonshire	38·8	42·0	33·9	31·3
Cornwall	31·8	37·7	28·9	26·4
Somerset	42·6	45·8	37·5	35·5
Gloucestershire	41·9	45·1	38·3	36·6
Herefordshire	35·8	38·3	34·4	32·6
Shropshire	31·9	36·0	31·0	29·5
Staffordshire	31.1	34·1	33·6	40·1
Worcestershire	42·3	44·6	36·9	39·8
Warwickshire	50·1	44·5	39·7	42·3
Leicestershire	46·3	46·8	42·4	45·5
Rutland	29·0	34·5	31·7	29·7
Lincolnshire	29·7	34·0	25·3	25·8
Nottinghamshire	45·4	46·1	36·8	36·5
Derbyshire	40·5	39·8	28·1	30·5
Cheshire	42·1	44·7	37·4	41·2
Lancashire	45·7	49·7	43·4	50·5
Yorkshire, West Riding	39·4	40·8	35·8	39·9
Yorkshire, East Riding*	32·6	35·1	29·6	31·9
Yorkshire, North Riding†	35·1	36·3	28·3	28·3
Durham‡	24·8	22·6	20·7	23·6
Northumberland	30·9	33·1	25·0	29·4
Cumberland	38·4	41·2	31·3	29·9
Westmorland	41·3	42·1	38·3	37·1
Monmouthshire	26·2	30·1	20·8	18·9
London	41·2	43·8	45·0	52·0
England and Wales	38·2	41·1	35·5	38·2

* Including York.   † Excluding Middlesbrough.   ‡ Including Middlesbrough.

the married women who were at work. The percentages of married women employed in 1911 and 1931, in the various age-groups, are given in Table XXVII.

Applying the 1911 percentages to the absolute figures of 1931 yields a total of 528,555 employed married women aged 20–45 years, instead of the actual number 626,608, giving an excess of actual over expected numbers of 98,053. This may be regarded as the increase due to changes in female employment between 1911 and 1931. To obtain an idea of the extent to which this increase might have affected fertility, let us assume that married women who are at work do not bear any children at all. This assumption would show the maximum possible effect of the increase in employment. In that case the 1930–32 annual average of 603,362 legitimate live

TABLE XXVII

PERCENTAGES OF MARRIED WOMEN EMPLOYED OUT OF ALL MARRIED WOMEN IN SPECIFIC AGE-GROUPS

Period	Age-Group Percentages		
	20–25	25–35	35–45
1911	12·9	10·6	10·6
1931	19·2	13·8	10·5

births would be attributed only to the 4,259,727 unoccupied married women aged 20–45 years, giving a legitimate fertility rate of 141·6 per 1,000 women. If the increase of employed married women had not taken place, there would, at this rate, have been an addition of 13,884 live births in 1931. But this addition to the total live births would only have raised the gross reproduction rate from 0·929 to 0·949. The fall in fertility between 1911 and 1931 would still have been about 35 per cent. The additional fertility attributed to the married women is, of course, very much exaggerated. And the effect of employment is still more exaggerated because the numbers of women returned in 1931 as employed were probably too high. The 1931 census made a special survey of female "operatives," normally in employment, who were actually unemployed at the time of the census. The unemployed amounted to 19·5 per cent of all the women who returned themselves as normally in employment. Since 1931 was the end point of a series of depressed years, it is probable that many of the "normally employed" women then returned as unemployed had long been out of work and were really out of the labour market.

The employment of married women shown by the 1931 census would therefore be inflated and effect of female employment upon the decline of fertility would be still smaller than has been estimated. It is important, then, to remember that such facts as are available show no relationship between changes in the extent of female employment and the decline of fertility over any part of the period 1871 to 1931. But if the position at any point of time is examined, the results are rather different. The correlations between female employment and fertility are shown in Table XXVIII.

TABLE XXVIII

CORRELATIONS BETWEEN GROSS REPRODUCTION RATES AND
EMPLOYMENT OF WOMEN AGED 15 AND OVER, BY
REGISTRATION COUNTIES

	Unstandardized	Standardized[1]
1850–52	$- 0 \cdot 167 \pm 0 \cdot 148$	$- 0 \cdot 156 \pm 0 \cdot 149$
1870–72	$- 0 \cdot 408 \pm 0 \cdot 127$	$- 0 \cdot 422 \pm 0 \cdot 125$
1910–12	$- 0 \cdot 611 \pm 0 \cdot 096$	$- 0 \cdot 708 \pm 0 \cdot 067$
1930–32	$- 0 \cdot 625 \pm 0 \cdot 093$	$- 0 \cdot 622 \pm 0 \cdot 083$

TABLE XXIX

CORRELATION BETWEEN PERCENTAGES OF WOMEN, AGED 15
AND OVER, WHO WERE EMPLOYED AT SPECIFIC DATES, AND
THE PERCENTAGES OF UNMARRIED WOMEN OUT OF
ALL WOMEN AGED 20–45 YEARS

(IN 43 REGISTRATION COUNTIES)

1851	$+ 0 \cdot 252 \pm 0 \cdot 143$
1871	$+ 0 \cdot 460 \pm 0 \cdot 120$
1911	$+ 0 \cdot 580 \pm 0 \cdot 101$
1931	$+ 0 \cdot 530 \pm 0 \cdot 110$

From 1871 onwards these coefficients show a significant relation between fertility and the employment of women, and this appears to contradict the conclusions of the historical survey. But the difference can be explained by a further correlation—between the percentages of women employed and the percentages of women aged 20–45 years who were unmarried, for the same points of time as in the previous correlation. The results are given in Table XXIX.

[1] Standardized to eliminate the variations between counties of the proportion which women aged 20–45 years formed of the total female population aged 15 and over. The correlations of the standardized series for 1910–12 and 1930–32 cover 55 items; in the other correlations 43 items were used.

The coefficients show a trend similar to those in Table XXVIII —a significant relationship from 1871 onwards, the correlation being more marked for 1911 and 1931 than for 1871. It is therefore evident that in so far as there is a relationship between fertility and the employment of women, it acts not through the fertility of married women who are employed, but largely by means of dissuading women from marriage. Interpreting the change between 1851 and 1931 in terms of these coefficients, it would appear that whereas marriage and employment were not competing fields in 1851, employment at the present time tends to cause women not to marry, or at least to postpone marriage.

(c) The Occupational Type of the District

In studying the relation between the occupational pattern of counties and their fertility, some index of occupational type must be chosen. The bulk of the working population consists of adult males, and the percentage of these engaged in each of a number of occupations was used as a guide to the character of districts. The two censuses which, in this preliminary investigation, seemed most worth analysis are for 1871 and 1931. For the 1871 census adult males were taken to be those aged 20 and over, but as the 1931 census did not make the division at this age, the index used in the latter case refers to males aged 21 and over. But it is highly unlikely that the difference would introduce significant errors in analysing the relationship between fertility and occupation at the two points of time. No survey of the relation over time has been included, because at this stage of the enquiry it did not seem profitable. It has already been shown that the average fall in fertility in the registration counties between 1871 and 1931 was about 59 per cent. The coefficient of variation between counties was only about 6 per cent, so that the fall has been too general to attribute it, in a county analysis, to changes in specific occupations. Fig. 6 makes clear that the areas of differential decline in fertility are linked to no broad or simple changes in employment. A study of the changes over time needs closer analysis of districts within the counties, and this has been postponed for presentation in the final report on the investigation. Further, as the present study deals with no units smaller than registration counties, only those occupations which employed a relatively large proportion of men could be used as indices, and it was decided to limit them to kinds

TABLE XXX

REGISTRATION COUNTIES IN ENGLAND AND WALES

PERCENTAGES OF MEN EMPLOYED IN AGRICULTURE AND FISHING

	1871 Percentage of Males 20 and over	1931 Percentage of Males 21 and over		1871 Percentage of Males 20 and over	1931 Percentage of Males 21 and over
Surrey	22·9	8·1	Rutland	52·4	35·8
Kent	28·7	12·8	Lincolnshire	49·7	29·0
Sussex	35·4	17·5	Nottinghamshire	21·0	6·4
Hampshire	24·7	10·5	Derbyshire	17·5	6·6
Berkshire	38·6	16·9	Cheshire	19·8	8·3
Middlesex	19·3	2·6	Lancashire	7·7	3·1
Hertfordshire	40·3	15·2	Yorkshire, West Riding	11·1	4·0
Buckinghamshire	43·7	17·2	Yorkshire, East Riding	27·0	13·1
Oxfordshire	43·5	20·3	Yorkshire, North Riding	37·9	15·6
Northamptonshire	35·1	13·0	Durham	6·9	2·6
Huntingdonshire	55·7	38·6	Northumberland	16·8	6·4
Bedfordshire	44·3	16·4	Cumberland	27·3	16·1
Cambridgeshire	49·2	35·1	Westmorland	36·8	27·6
Essex	39·6	7·2	Monmouthshire	15·2	5·1
Suffolk	47·1	29·6	Glamorganshire	9·1	2·5
Norfolk	42·8	30·8	Carmarthenshire	35·0	16·9
Wiltshire	41·9	21·9	Pembroke	34·7	33·9
Dorsetshire	37·9	22·3	Cardiganshire	46·4	40·9
Devonshire	29·9	18·6	Brecknockshire	38·9	23·1
Cornwall	31·4	27·3	Radnorshire	60·2	49·1
Somerset	32·0	21·7	Montgomeryshire	45·5	48·3
Gloucestershire	22·2	9·9	Flintshire	18·5	13·6
Herefordshire	46·6	41·2	Denbighshire	31·3	17·6
Shropshire	36·9	28·2	Merionethshire	37·4	29·4
Staffordshire	11·6	4·7	Carnarvonshire	27·8	17·7
Worcestershire	21·7	14·4	Anglesey	39·3	34·0
Warwickshire	14·8	3·9			
Leicestershire	25·5	8·2	England and Wales	20·4	8·6

which might *a priori* appear to have a relationship to fertility. They are: agriculture, because of the rural background; mining and quarrying, because they are generally associated with a low female employment; and commerce, because it is in part a reflection of a distinctive type of urbanism. But the last category was omitted from the 1871 analysis because of the small proportions of men engaged in it at the time. Finally, London was omitted because it is entirely urban. It is hoped to publish a detailed analysis of occupation and fertility relationships in its constituent parts at a later date.

The first stage in the analysis was to test the general relationship between agriculture and fertility. The percentages of agricultural employment are given in Table XXX, and when these were correlated with gross reproduction rates for 54 registration counties, the resultant coefficients were: $- 0\cdot287 \pm 0\cdot125$ for 1871, and $+ 0\cdot120 \pm 0\cdot134$ for 1931, neither being significant. But this is not conclusive evidence of the absence of a relationship between agriculture and fertility. Closer examination shows that it only means an absence of relationship between agriculture and the highest fertility rates. The highest rates are found in counties in which mining is important, and mining is generally associated with low agricultural employment. Omitting the counties in which mining employed 10 per cent or more of the males,[1] a further analysis was made, and is given in Table XXXI.

The difference between the groups is, of course, very small, never amounting to as much as 6 per cent. Yet the consistency of the gradation does suggest that within the non-mining group of counties agriculture is positively correlated with fertility, though apparently less so in 1871 than in 1931. Two further conclusions are possible. The average of the gross reproduction rates of the mining counties was $2\cdot507$ in 1871 and $1\cdot020$ in 1931. Thus in both years mining was associated with the highest fertility, though it was less above the fertility of the most highly agricultural counties in 1931 than it was in 1871. Finally, for 1931 the percentages of males engaged in commerce were computed for the non-mining counties in which less than 20 per cent of the employment was agricultural. The average

---

[1] Fifteen counties in 1871 and fourteen in 1931. In 1871 they were Cornwall, Stafford, Warwick, Derby, Yorkshire (North Riding), Durham, Northumberland, Cumberland, Monmouth, Glamorgan, Brecon, Flint, Denbigh, Merioneth, and Caernarvon. By 1931 Cornwall, Warwick, and Flint had dropped out and Nottingham and Carmarthen were added.

of the commerce percentages was computed and the counties divided into two groups—above and below this average.[1] The counties below had an average gross reproduction rate of 0·939, and those above an average of 0·843. The difference is large enough to be significant of a negative association between commerce and fertility.

TABLE XXXI

AGRICULTURE AND FERTILITY IN REGISTRATION COUNTIES

(EXCLUDING MINING COUNTIES)

1871			1931		
Percentage of Males engaged in Agriculture	Average Gross Reproduction Rate	Number of Counties	Percentage of Males engaged in Agriculture	Average Gross Reproduction Rate	Number of Counties
—	—	—	Under 20 per cent	0·903	21
Under 30 per cent	2·277	13	20–30 per cent	0·954	9
30–40 per cent ..	2·283	11	30 per cent and over	1·003	10
40 per cent and over	2·339	15	—	—	—

(d) The Employment of Children

When child labour is mentioned in relation to industrialism in the early nineteenth century, the term generally refers to the employment of children below ten years of age. But this meaning has no relevance to the study of changes in fertility in England and Wales, for child labour in that sense was largely abolished by 1851. But the employment of children aged 10 to 15 years persisted after 1851 and was still significant in 1911. The available figures for the registration counties are given in Table XXXII. Taking the country as a whole the percentages fell slightly between 1851 and 1871, unaccompanied by a fall in fertility. Between 1871 and 1911 they fell very considerably—the average of the percentages for the registration counties was 25·6 in 1871 and 13·5 in 1911. Since the fall in fertility was very

[1] The average was 17·3 per cent. Below the average were Warwick, Leicester, Lancashire, Hampshire, Berkshire, Buckingham, Northampton, Bedford, Devon, Worcester, Yorks (East Riding and North Riding), and Flint. Above were Surrey, Middlesex, Essex, Gloucester, Cheshire, Kent, Sussex, and Hertford.

Table XXXII
REGISTRATION COUNTIES IN ENGLAND AND WALES
PERCENTAGE OF CHILDREN OCCUPIED, AGED 10–15 YEARS

	1851	*1871*	*1911*
Surrey ..	18·5	15·2	8·3
Kent ..	17·6	16·1	7·9
Sussex ..	22·0	21·0	10·0
Hampshire	21·9	17·6	9·7
Berkshire	25·2	23·8	11·2
Middlesex	13·0	11·5	8·4
Hertfordshire ..	34·1	30·8	11·0
Buckinghamshire	39·1	33·6	14·7
Oxfordshire ..	25·9	26·8	14·5
Northamptonshire	39·9	36·4	23·9
Huntingdonshire	29·0	33·7	18·8
Bedfordshire ..	50·1	45·4	16·6
Cambridgeshire	22·2	29·2	15·2
Essex ..	24·8	22·4	9·8
Suffolk ..	22·4	25·5	15·3
Norfolk ..	23·0	25·2	12·3
Wiltshire	29·4	30·4	12·9
Dorsetshire	13·7	25·7	10·6
Devonshire	27·9	23·6	12·0
Cornwall	31·7	28·0	9·2
Somerset	28·5	27·6	15·8
Gloucestershire..	23·4	22·2	12·7
Herefordshire ..	22·5	19·7	11·8
Shropshire	25·4	23·2	11·2
Staffordshire ..	34·7	27·7	16·8
Worcestershire ..	31·6	25·9	14·3
Warwickshire ..	34·8	29·5	15·2
Leicestershire ..	38·3	33·2	20·1
Rutland ..	18·7	20·0	14·4
Lincolnshire	18·5	22·6	13·1
Nottinghamshire	38·6	32·5	19·2
Derbyshire	37·7	33·5	18·0
Cheshire	33·9	30·7	15·2
Lancashire	38·7	38·7	22·7
Yorkshire, West Riding	43·8	39·3	24·7
Yorkshire, East Riding*	22·2	19·9	11·4
Yorkshire, North Riding†	20·1	18·5	9·5
Durham‡	22·3	19·7	8·5
Northumberland	18·4	17·4	9·9
Cumberland ..	19·0	17·7	7·7
Westmorland ..	17·5	17·2	11·5
Monmouth	27·2	24·2	12·9
London..	17·4	16·5	9·6
England and Wales ..	28·3	26·3	14·4

* Including York.   † Excluding Middlesbrough.   ‡ Including Middlesbrough.

marked in the same period, a relation between changes in the two factors might be assumed. But even if the decrease in child labour is a broad factor influencing the fall in fertility, it does not account for the differential fall in the registration counties. A correlation between the decline of fertility and the decrease of child labour in the 43 counties between 1871 and 1911 yields a coefficient of only $+ 0 \cdot 145 \pm 0 \cdot 149$, which is insignificant. Nor does the distribution of child labour account for differences in the fertility of the counties at points of time. Correlations between fertility and child labour yielded coefficients of $+ 0 \cdot 489 \pm 0 \cdot 116$ for 1851, $+ 0 \cdot 291 \pm 0 \cdot 140$ for 1871, and $+ 0 \cdot 043 \pm 0 \cdot 152$ for 1911. Of these coefficients, only that for 1851 is significant. By 1871, after a very small decrease in child labour—the average of the percentages for the registration counties was $27 \cdot 1$ in 1851 and $25 \cdot 6$ in 1871—the relation between this factor and fertility had ceased to be important. This change may be suggestive. It may perhaps mean that the attitude towards children as an economic asset had changed completely by 1871, and thus prepared the ground for the pressure of less tangible influences upon fertility. But in that case we must reckon with a time lag of a generation before the influence upon fertility was felt, for the real decrease in child labour took place before 1851.

V. CONCLUSION

This chapter records an investigation which will be continued, if circumstances permit. So far the smallest regions which have been analysed are registration counties, and these are relatively large units containing wide ranges of occupational and social types. A more detailed analysis might alter the significance of many of the results obtained, and it would therefore be unwise to make definite assertions on the basis of present conclusions. But even from this broad study one conclusion seems inevitable. In any particular year for which statistics are available, we can trace a relationship between the fertility of the various parts of the country and a number of concomitant social factors such as marriage, the employment of women, and the occupational type of the district. But if we try to link up pro-gressive changes in the operation of these social factors with the decline of fertility from one period to another, the relationship breaks down. The data do not show that changes in the amount of marriage, in the extent of female employment, or in the occupational type of the district have been significantly responsible for the decline in the fertility of the various counties between 1871 and 1931. The small coefficient of variation between the falls in fertility experienced by the different counties would suggest that the factors at work must be common to all parts of the country and equally powerful on all types of occupational patterns. Whereas in 1871 practically every part of the country had a high fertility, in 1931 practically every part had a fertility inadequate for replacement. Perhaps a clue to the problem is given in the analysis of the relation between child labour and fertility. The correlations showed that in 1850–52 there was a definite association, and that it disappeared after this period. Social developments before 1851 began to decrease the economic incentive to the raising of large families and by the eighteen-seventies had turned what had probably been a net economic advantage before into what was certainly a net economic disadvantage subsequently. Of itself this change may not have affected fertility, but it is likely that it threw open the family to the increasing influence of less tangible factors which, so far, we have not been able to measure.

CHAPTER V

THE CHANGING STRUCTURE OF THE FAMILY IN AUSTRALIA

by

ENID CHARLES

I. INTRODUCTION

THE existence of declining fertility in all highly industrialized countries is now well known. Since fertility in Western and Northern Europe and the United States has now reached a level which, if maintained, must eventually lead to a declining population, it is now advisable to analyse in greater detail the changes which have taken place in the reproductive behaviour of people in these countries. Before an effective programme can be devised to arrest or reverse falling fertility we need to know how far the fall has been accompanied by a reduction in the number of large families and to what extent it entails an increase in the number of women having no children. The present chapter is mainly an attempt to throw some light on these two questions, and in so doing to ascertain the proportions of families of various sizes appropriate to different fertility levels. Such considerations are fundamental to a housing programme designed to arrest population decline.

Owing to the defective system of birth registration it is impossible to get direct information concerning Great Britain. The country selected for study is the Commonwealth of Australia over the period 1909 to 1933. For any study of size of family from year to year the essential data are records of births by age of mother and order of birth of child. For the Commonwealth of Australia the data are first given for 1909, so that a period of twenty-five years has been covered. Details of the data and methods employed will be found in later sections.

At the beginning of the twenty-five-year period fertility was rising, though doubtless it had already fallen below the level of an earlier period of Australian history. During the period studied the highest point was reached in 1912, with a gross reproduction rate of 1·781. From this year fertility fell steadily, except for the post-war recovery, till in 1933 the gross reproduction rate was 1·052, a drop of 41 per cent in twenty-one years, so that in the period covered fertility changed from a figure characteristic of a quite rapidly increasing population to one just too low to maintain a stationary population. In 1933 the net reproduction rate was 0·96. In 1931 it was 1·03, i.e. in that year fertility and mortality were in equilibrium.

During the twenty-five-year period the population of Australia increased from 4,300,000 to 6,600,000.[1] In the early years there was a large inward balance of migration reaching its maximum in 1912, when the rate of increase by migration is given as 2·04 per cent[2] of the total population as against a natural increase of 1·7 per cent. During the war there was outward migration, which ceased in 1919. Since then inward migration maintained a fairly steady level until 1929 of about 0·65 per cent of the total population. Since 1930 there has been a slight excess of departures over arrivals.

There are many aspects of Australian history which might throw light on the problem studied. Only two will be mentioned. There has been throughout a steady increase in the proportion of the population living in cities. The metropolitan population is given as 38·53 per cent[3] in 1909 and 46·87 per cent in 1933. Employment of women fluctuated considerably during the period. It was at a maximum in the year 1922–23, when 386 women per 10,000 were returned as employed in factories. The number was nearly as large in 1933, when it was 379. It was at a minimum in 1930, when it was 291.[4]

Needless to say, the greatest interruption to the normal course of events was provided by the World War. Among other effects, 329,883 men served overseas and the number of war deaths was 59,342.[5] The changes in fertility will be examined in detail later. Throughout this communication fertility and sterility are used in a purely statistical sense as referring to women who have or have not borne children.

II. THE CHANGE IN FERTILITY

The method of calculating the gross reproduction rate has been fully set out by Kuczynski.[6] For Australia the yearly births by age of mother in five-year age-periods were obtained from the Demographic

---

[1] *Australian Demography*, Bulletin No. 51 (1933).
[2] Ibid.   [3] Ibid.   [4] *Official Year Book.*
[5] Data obtained from Australia House.   [6] *Fertility and Reproduction.*

Bulletins. The age composition of the population was only obtainable for the census years 1911, 1921, and 1933. For the intervening years it was obtained by graphical interpolation, and is therefore subject to error. The maximum possible error due to this cause in the gross

TABLE I

GROSS REPRODUCTION RATE, AUSTRALIA, 1909–33

Year	Ex-nuptial	Nuptial	Total
1909	0·087	1·575	1·662
1910	0·085	1·569	1·654
1911	0·087	1·606	1·692
1912	0·087	1·694	1·781
1913	0·085	1·660	1·745
1914	0·081	1·651	1·732
1915	0·078	1·572	1·651
1916	0·069	1·512	1·580
1917	0·070	1·469	1·539
1918	0·074	1·401	1·475
1919	0·070	1·341	1·410
1920	0·069	1·466	1·535
1921	0·069	1·438	1·507
1922	0·065	1·430	1·495
1923	0·066	1·379	1·445
1924	0·064	1·363	1·427
1925	0·063	1·342	1·405
1926	0·062	1·287	1·349
1927	0·059	1·269	1·328
1928	0·059	1·250	1·310
1929	0·056	1·196	1·252
1930	0·054	1·180	1·235
1931	0·053	1·074	1·128
1932	0·047	1·007	1·054
1933	0·047	1·005	1·052

PERCENTAGE FALL

1912–33	46	41	41

reproduction rate for the intercensal years around 1916 and 1927 would be about 3 per cent. The occurrence of censal years at the beginning, middle, and end of the period makes this possible error of little significance in studying the trend of fertility. The ratio of women in the reproductive period to total population and also the ratio of younger to older women were highest at the beginning of the period. The proportion of women between 15 and 50 fell in

1921, but later recovered, so that in 1933 it was 53·6 per cent of the total female population, nearly as high as in 1911. The ratio of younger to older women, however, continued to diminish. In 1911 there were 2·1 times as many women 15–20 as women 45–50, but in 1933 only 1·5 times as many. The 1921 census showed the largest number of women in the age-group 25–30, whereas the other two censal years showed the largest number in the age-group 15–20.

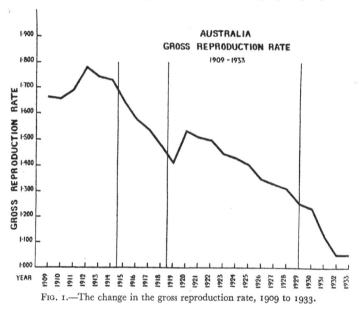

FIG. 1.—The change in the gross reproduction rate, 1909 to 1933.

Table I sets out the gross reproduction rate for each year from 1909 to 1933. The change in the total gross reproduction rate is shown graphically in Fig. 1.

The ex-nuptial rate is chiefly of interest as showing the proportionately greater falling off in illegitimate births. The illegitimate births in later years appear to have been replaced to some extent by births conceived before marriage. In Australian statistics the terms "ex-nuptial" and "nuptial" are used in place of "illegitimate" and "legitimate." The latter terms have been used in the text as being more familiar to readers in Great Britain.

From 1909 onwards the pre-war and wartime fall in fertility was associated with little change in the mean age of mothers at birth of all children. This was because, while fertility of the older age-groups fell rapidly, there was also a considerable fall in the 15–25 age-group together with a considerable reduction in the illegitimate birth-rate which mainly affects this age-group. Since 1921 the mean age of mothers has fallen from 29·3 years to 28·3 years. This is because fertility has not fallen greatly in the younger age-groups. In the 15–20 group fertility in 1933 was practically the same as in 1920, and during the intervening period had been much higher. Table II shows the percentage fall in specific fertility rates.

TABLE II

PERCENTAGE FALL IN SPECIFIC FERTILITY RATES, 1912–33

Age-group	Ex-nuptial	Nuptial	Total	Percentage Ex-nuptial Fertility of Total in 1933
15–19	40·3	2·6	16·2	20·9
20–24	50·6	30·8	32·6	6·4
25–29	55·7	38·8	39·3	2·5
30–34	42·0	45·2	45·1	2·2
35–39	34·6	52·9	52·7	2·5
40–44	35·9	57·7	57·3	3·0
45–49	43·0	62·4	61·9	4·4

It will be seen that the legitimate fertility of the 15–19 age-group has fallen very little. The fall in total fertility is almost wholly due to the fall in illegitimate fertility. Illegitimate births are most important in this age-group, since in 1933 30 per cent of all illegitimate births were due to mothers under twenty. The number of illegitimate births after thirty-five is so small that the differences in the percentage fall in illegitimate fertility in these age-groups are probably not significant.

III. CHANGES IN THE SIZE OF THE FAMILY

(a) Data and Methods

The data available consist in the main of an annual table of order of birth in the Demographic Bulletins entitled "Birth Total, Mothers' Ages, Duration of Marriages and Issue." A note states that "Ex-nuptial children, previous issue by the same father, are included, but children by former marriages are not, nor are still-born children."

As, however, the table includes married mothers only, it is clear that ex-nuptial children only affect the order of birth of later children and do not themselves appear in the table. The principal omission is therefore that of ex-nuptial ·children whose mothers afterwards marry and have legitimate children by the same father, and who may therefore be regarded for all practical purposes as part of the legitimate family. Further, it should be noted that the table records current marriages only and takes no account of former marriages. The method for dealing with these figures was suggested by Kuczynski. It involves first calculating gross reproduction rates in the usual way for first, second, third, etc., children respectively. For each thousand women between 15 and 50 we thus obtain the number who will have in the course of their lives a first child, a second child, etc., on the basis of the fertility of a given year. By subtraction the size of the families of a thousand women can be obtained. For example, if it is found that out of every thousand women 800 will have a first child, 700 a second, and 500 a third, it is clear that out of every thousand women there will be 200 with no children, 100 with a family consisting of one child only, and 200 with a family of two children only, while 500 will have families of three or more children. While the gross reproduction rates given in § II were calculated for female births only as is customary, the rates given in this and later sections are based on all births, since the main object is to ascertain family sizes.

Tables III and IV show the results thus obtained from the tables cited. They refer only to children legitimately born of a single marriage. They take no account of illegitimate children except in so far as they affect the order of later-born children. Modifications will be dealt with later, but as these involve estimates which can at best be only very rough approximations the data are presented first in their simplest form which directly depend on accredited data. Owing to great fluctuation in the rates for first and second children, as will be described later, the rates are presented as five-yearly averages round the most suitable years.

(b) *Illegitimacy and Remarriage*

The size of family so obtained does not represent any very clear-cut sociological entity. Some attempt must be made to estimate the number of illegitimate children whose parents later marry. The only data which bear directly on this point are the number of legitima-

TABLE III

REPRODUCTION RATES PER 1,000 WOMEN BY ORDER OF BIRTH

FIVE-YEARLY AVERAGES

(*Nuptial Children of Single Marriages only*)

Order of Birth of Child	1909–13	1911–15	1922–26	1925–29	1929–33
1	793	835	769	744	660
2	626	654	618	578	528
3	502	508	434	409	351
4	388	385	296	281	235
5	291	284	207	189	157
6	214	209	146	128	106
7	157	151	103	91	71
8	109	104	71 .	62	48
9	76	70	48	41	31
10	51	47	31	27	19
11	31	27	17	16	12
12	18	16	10	8	7
13	10	9	5	4	4
14	5	4	2	2	2
15 and over	4	3	2	2	1

TOTAL GROSS REPRODUCTION RATE

	1·707	1·720	1·424	1·329	1·144

TABLE IV

SIZE OF FAMILY PER 1,000 WOMEN

FIVE-YEARLY AVERAGES

(*Nuptial Children of Single Marriages only*)

Size of Family	1909–13	1911–15	1922–26	1925–29	1929–33
0	207	165	231	256	340
1	167	181	151	166	132
2	124	146	184	169	177
3	114	123	138	128	116
4	97	101	89	92	78
5	77	75	61	61	51
6	57	58	43	37	35
7	48	47	32	29	23
8	33	34	23	21	17
9	25	23	17	14	12
10	20	20	14	11	7
11	13	11	7	8	5
12	8	7	5	4	3
13	5	5	3	2	2
14	1	1	—	—	1
15 and over	4	3	2	2	1

tions under the Legitimation Acts of the various States. These were first recorded in the *Official Year Book* for 1929 for the year 1924 onwards. It is of course impossible to say in what years the births occurred which were legitimatized in any particular year. Relating the legitimations to births of the same or the previous year, they range from 15·6 to 14 per cent of all illegitimate births, but relating them to the births of two years earlier the range is lowered to 13·6 per cent. The best approximate figure for the number of illegitimate births afterwards legitimatized seems to be 14 per cent. This figure has been applied throughout the period, though possibly the proportion of children who later became members of a legitimate family may have been greater at the beginning of the period. The question of remarriage will be discussed later, and it will be shown

TABLE V

REPRODUCTION RATES PER 1,000 WOMEN AND SIZE OF FAMILY
CORRECTED FOR LEGITIMATIZED CHILDREN

Year ..			*1909–13*	*1911–15*	*1922–26*	*1925–29*	*1929–31*
First children	··	··	817	859	787	761	675
No legitimate children	··		183	141	213	239	325
One child	··	··	191	205	169	183	147

that it does not greatly affect the size of the family. For the present the addition of a percentage of illegitimate births gives a table of families which represent definite biological and sociological entities, i.e. the families produced by two parents who at some time or another marry. Apart from remarriage the families of women who do not marry are also omitted. The illegitimate birth-rate in Australia is not very large. In 1909 it was 6·01 per cent of all births, and fell fairly continuously to 4·71 per cent in 1933. The remaining 86 per cent of illegitimate births will be considered later, but for the present they are omitted from the discussion of size of family. Table V sets out the figures obtained by the addition of legitimatized children to the figures in Tables III and IV.

A possible source of error is that more than one illegitimate child of the same parents may later form part of a legitimate family. No account has been taken of this, but there is some reason to think that the error involved cannot be large. In Czechoslovakia in 1925 the proportion of children legitimatized who were firstborn appears to have been 89 per cent as compared with 67 per cent first births among all illegitimate births. We should therefore expect the percentage of first births among legitimatized children in Australia to be about 90 per cent at the beginning of the period and considerably higher at the end (vide § v(b)). Considering the number of mothers of illegitimate first births not later legitimatized as shown in § v(b), we can apply the current ex-nuptial infant mortality death-rate to these births. Assuming, then, that the mothers of illegitimate children who die under a year old are as likely as other women to marry and have legitimate children, it appears that this would reduce the number of legitimate first births at the beginning of the period by about 1 per cent and by less than 1 per cent at the end of the period. The maximum error due to this source thus appears to be 1 per cent in the pre-war period only. Against this could be set the fact that legitimations may have been more than 14 per cent in this period. In the pre-war period there was no legal legitimation; but it has been assumed that illegitimate children whose parents later married occupied a family status which was nearly equivalent to that enjoyed by those who at a later period were legally legitimatized.

The tables presented indicate a significant trend over the period with several features which are sufficiently clearly marked to be outside the limits of any statistical error. It will be seen that the proportion of families of only children has not increased, but on the other hand has become slightly less. Looking at this from another angle, the ratio of second to first births for the 1911 five-year period was 77 and for the 1931 five-year period was 78. Both these rates fluctuate considerably from year to year; but it seems safe to say that there appears no tendency for the proportion of women who, having had one child, follow it up with a second, to diminish. After the second child the rates rapidly diminish, giving an increase in families of two children only and a marked diminution in the numbers of large families. The difference between the proportions of families of various types in 1911 and 1931 is shown in the form of pyramids in Fig. 2. Perhaps the most significant feature of the change is the emergence of the fashionable family of two children.

The data can be presented in another form by considering only women who have at least one legitimate child. Table VI sets out the percentages of such women having families of different sizes in the two five-year periods 1909–13 and 1929–33.

Table VI illustrates the same points that were brought out in previous tables. There is no significant change in the proportion of one-child families, a great increase in the proportion of two-child, and to a lesser extent of three-child families, while the number of families of seven or more has been halved.

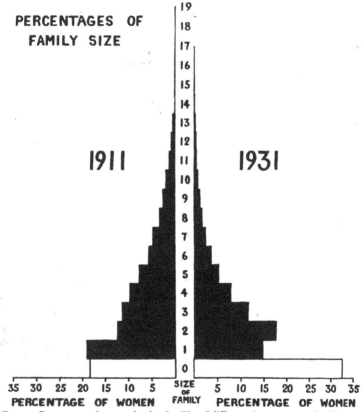

FIG. 2.—Percentages of women having families of different sizes at current fertility rates 1911 and 1931 (five-yearly averages).

(c) Completed Marriages

The most easily grasped way of thinking about fertility in relation to population growth is in connection with the size of completed families. If the gross reproduction rates were stable for sufficiently long, they would of course have a simple relation to the number of children in all completed families. The fact that they are based on figures which change from year to year gives them a somewhat artificial nature. It therefore seemed desirable to make some attempt to compare the trend of the gross reproduction rates calculated for the period with the results of completed marriages. Previous studies of completed marriages have been open to the objection that the survivors to an advanced age of a group of marriages may be a highly selected sample. The present study does not appear to be open to that objection though complicated by other factors, particularly those due to high migration. Nevertheless it is hoped that it may prove suggestive for purposes of comparison. The annual Demographic Bulletins give tables of the issue of deceased parents.

TABLE VI

PERCENTAGES OF DIFFERENT SIZES OF FAMILY AMONG 100 WOMEN HAVING AT LEAST ONE LEGITIMATE CHILD

Size of Family	1909–13	1929–33
1	23	22
2	15	26
3	14	17
4	12	12
5	9	8
6	7	5
7	6	3
8 or more	13	7

These cannot be used to give completed[1] families, since for any one year and for a given duration of marriage they represent a selected sample of the marriages contracted.

The annual births in Australia are recorded for duration of marriage as well as for order of birth and age of mother. It is therefore theoretically possible by working backwards to tabulate all the births, by order of birth, resulting from the marriages of any particular year. This can only be done for three years—1909, 1910, 1911—marriages in these years being at least 99 per cent complete by 1933. The ratio of second to first children can, however, be traced for some years later. During these years there was a considerable inward balance of migration of married women, some with

---

[1] As the word is used here the family is completed if further issue is stopped either by the natural cessation of fertility or by the termination of the marriage by divorce or death. The families obtained refer to current marriages only and no account is taken of remarriage.

children, so that some of the marriages and some of the first children corresponding to the births of second children will not have been recorded in Australia. Table VII sets out the results obtained by this method.

As the gross reproduction rates refer to all women whether married or unmarried, they can only be directly compared with completed marriages as regards the ratio of second to first children and so on. In Fig. 3 the families resulting from the marriages of

TABLE VII

PERCENTAGES OF DIFFERENT SIZES OF FAMILIES RESULTING
FROM MARRIAGES OF 1909, 1910, AND 1911

Size of Family	1909	1910	1911
0	12·9	12·4	10·5
1	10·7	11·4	15·5
2	16·2	17·1	17·6
3	17·2	17·7	17·7
4	13·4	13·7	13·3
5	10·1	9·6	8·9
6	6·7	6·4	6·0
7	4·5	4·3	4·1
8	3·1	3·0	2·6
9	2·2	1·9	1·7
10	1·2	1·2	1·1
11	0·8	0·6	0·5
12	0·5	0·4	0·2
13	0·2	0·2	0·2
14 and over	0·3	0·2	0·1

1911 are compared with those derived from the gross reproduction rates—(a) the five-yearly average for 1911, and (b) the 1933 rate. As all the women married do not live to the end of the reproductive period it would be more correct to make the comparison with the net reproduction rates. The figure therefore shows also the 1911 net reproduction rates. But while the substitution of net for gross reproduction rates materially affects the number of first children born, as will be seen, it does not greatly alter the ratios of second to first children, etc.

Comparing the completed families of marriages contracted in 1911 with gross reproduction rates according to order of birth in 1911 and 1933, we find that the ratio of second to first children was higher than that shown by the gross reproduction rates in either year. This may have been due to the high immigration at this period. The ratio of third to second children was very near to the 1911 rate. Later ratios diverged from the 1911 rates until sixth to

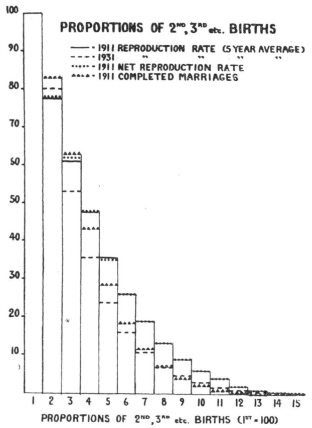

PROPORTIONS OF 2ND, 3RD etc. BIRTHS

——· 1911 REPRODUCTION RATE (5 YEAR AVERAGE)
– – –· 1931 " " " "
······· 1911 NET REPRODUCTION RATE
▲▲▲▲· 1911 COMPLETED MARRIAGES

PROPORTIONS OF 2ND, 3RD etc. BIRTHS (1ST = 100)

FIG. 3.—Proportions of second, third, etc., births to first in completed marriages of 1911 and according to 1911 and 1931 reproduction rates.

fifth and later ratios were very close to the 1933 rates. The fact that the later ratios are lower than would be expected may be accounted for in two ways: (a) The war may have prevented births which would have occurred among later children. Consideration of the widowhood data does not lead to the view that much weight

H

should be attached to this. (*b*) It can be shown algebraically[1] that when, for example, rates of births of third and fourth children are decreasing but the latter is decreasing faster, the current gross reproduction rates must overestimate the ratio of fourth to third children actually produced.

The relation between gross reproduction rates and completed fertility can be looked at in either of two ways. (*a*) It may be that the fertility pattern of a marriage is largely determined at the time when it is contracted. If so it is little affected by social changes occurring during the period of the marriage. The current gross reproduction rate in a period of declining fertility would then be made up of births at different fertility levels, the older women being more fertile and the younger women less so. The families which will be produced by the women commencing child-bearing would then be smaller than would be indicated by the current gross reproduction rate. (*b*) On the other hand, if social changes equally affect all stages in the history of a marriage, fertility of completed marriages simply represents a cross section of the gross reproduction rates over a period of time. The problem of stabilizing or raising the current gross reproduction rate would then be simpler.

The ratio between second and first children is 99 per cent complete for marriages of 1909 to 1919. This ratio is probably disturbed in

---

[1] Let a be the number of third births per thousand women in a given year A. Let the ratio of fourth to third births be l, so that the number of fourth births per thousand women can be written $l.a$, where l may be equal to or less than unity. Let us suppose that all the fourth births occurring to women who had their third births in year A occur in year B. If fertility is falling yearly the third births per thousand women in year B will be less than in year A and can be written $m.a$, where m is less than unity. If the fourth births were falling off at the same rate as the third births they could be written $m.l.a$. But if they are falling off faster, the number of fourth births per thousand women in year B can be written $n.m.l.a$, where n is again less than unity. The number of births per thousand women in the two years will thus be

		Third Births		Fourth Births
Year A ..	..	a	..	$l.a$
Year B ..	..	$m.a$	..	$n.m.l.a$

The ratio of fourth to third births given by reproduction rates would be l in year A and $n.l$ in year B. But the ratio of fourth to third births actually produced by women who had their third births in year A is $n.m.l$. Since both n and m are less than unity, $n.m.l$ is less than either l or $n.l$. Therefore under the conditions assumed the ratio of fourth to third births resulting from marriages in a given year will be less than the ratios given by the reproduction rates obtained at the time of birth of either the third or the fourth child.

the earlier years by migration and from 1915 onwards by war. Taking 1912 and 1919 as most representative of pre- and post-war marriages the ratios are 80·6 and 80·1. The uncompleted ratio for 1923 is 80·2. So that there is here no evidence of a reduction in the proportion of second children.

Another point emerges from the consideration of the ratio of

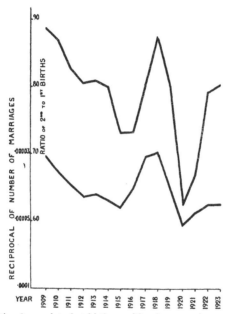

FIG. 4.—The ratio of second to first births resulting from marriages, 1909 to 1923, and the reciprocal of the absolute number of marriages in those years.

second to first children. Taking the period as a whole there is a high correlation between the ratio of second to first children and the reciprocal of the absolute number of marriages, i.e. when marriages were numerous, the ratio of second to first children resulting from them was low and vice versa. This is shown in Fig. 4. The figures are incomplete from 1920 onwards. The correlation in the early years may be solely due to migration, but from 1918 onwards migration maintained a fairly steady level. In the later years the figure suggests that in a period of few marriages those that are postponed to later years are those of older and more infertile women. The data are, of course, much too scanty to do more than suggest a possible field for investigation.

To sum up, a study of completed marriages confirms the conclusions derived from a study of gross reproduction rates in the two most significant conclusions, (1) that the proportion of second to first children has not decreased, and (2) that the births of all later children are becoming progressively fewer.

TABLE VIII

NUMBER OUT OF EVERY 1,000 CHILDREN BORN BELONGING TO FAMILIES OF DIFFERENT SIZES ACCORDING TO THE FERTILITY OF 1911 AND 1931

(FIVE-YEAR AVERAGES)

Size of Family	1909–13	1929–31
1	58	65
2	75	157
3	104	155
4	117	139
5	117	113
6	104	93
7	102	72
8	80	60
9	68	48
10	61	31
11	43	24
12	29	16
13	20	12
14 and over	24	13

(d) *The Position of Children in the Family*

An increasing amount of attention is being devoted to a study of the order of birth of a child and the size of its family as correlated with intelligence and psychological adjustment. The two most important points to note in this connection are the proportion of first-born to all children and of only children to all children. Including illegitimate children the proportion of first-born to all children appears to have increased from about 28 per cent in 1909 to about 34 per cent in 1933. In view of the evidence as to handicapping of the first-born any further rise in this percentage would point to the urgent need for research on such problems as uterine environment that might affect this factor.

The proportion of only children and of children from families of different sizes out of every 1,000 children born according to the 1911 and 1931 fertility rates is shown in Table VIII.

The table shows that considering all children born there has been a slight increase in the proportion of only children. The most striking feature, however, is that the proportion of children from two-child families has doubled and in 1931 was the most frequent family size, while in 1911 more children came from four-child families than from those of any other size. This is especially significant in view of the probably self-perpetuating nature of the family pattern. Taking one-, two-, and three-child families together, in 1911 they accounted for about 24 per cent of all children born, and in 1931 for about 38 per cent. In 1931 62 per cent of all children born still came from families of four or more, a fact which is of some importance in connection with housing, seeing that fertility in 1931 was only just about adequate to maintain a stationary population.

IV. FLUCTUATIONS IN BIRTH-RATES

The last twenty-five years have seen a very large fluctuation in the birth-rate due to the war, and in the last few years most countries have experienced a similar though much smaller fall and rise due to post-war depression and recovery. The most important factor in both cases was the fluctuation in the number of marriages. In Australia in 1918 the crude marriage rate was 6·65, and in 1920 9·62. In 1931 it was 5·96, and in 1933 7·03. With the increasing proportion of first births to which attention has already been drawn, such fluctuations have a more marked effect not only on the crude birth-rate but also on the gross reproduction rate. It is of interest, therefore, to see whether we can detect any general trend in fertility unaffected by changes in the number of marriages from year to year.

Table IX shows the yearly reproduction rates per 1,000 women for each order of birth separately from the first to the sixth. The rates for first to third children show clearly changes due to changes in the marriage rate. The rates for third to sixth children show slight rises in 1917. As these are all in the same year midway between two censal years, they suggest some error in the proportions of older to younger women. Apart from this the fall in the rates for fifth and sixth births is continuous from 1912 onwards.

Fig. 5 shows the yearly changes in the rates for first and fourth births, together with the changes in the crude marriage-rate. The graph for fourth births is drawn to a scale twice as large as that for

TABLE IX

YEARLY REPRODUCTION RATES ACCORDING TO ORDER OF
BIRTH PER 1,000 WOMEN

Year	Order of Birth					
	1st	2nd	3rd	4th	5th	6th
1909	753	593	484	374	285	213
1910	756	600	490	390	296	215
1911	809	617	497	385	287	215
1912	876	658	525	396	300	220
1913	891	661	515	394	288	208
1914	881	678	509	387	280	206
1915	839	657	495	363	266	196
1916	800	652	484	355	253	184
1917	713	629	495	357	262	184
1918	653	600	481	350	250	177
1919	661	547	457	334	241	170
1920	893	586	455	334	240	169
1921	911	583	423	321	225	165
1922	836	645	432	313	225	161
1923	798	643	428	292	217	148
1924	779	626	442	290	203	144
1925	769	600	442	295	202	143
1926	755	579	426	291	191	133
1927	767	577	406	285	188	128
1928	776	570	397	275	185	124
1929	741	565	376	261	175	114
1930	731	578	362	249	168	113
1931	659	512	350	232	155	108
1932	609	494	334	218	144	101
1933	633	492	334	217	140	94

first births. The figure brings out both the less fluctuating character of the rate for fourth births and also its much steeper fall.

In assessing the trend of fertility from year to year it is clearly important to be able to distinguish between first and second and later births. A very considerable rise in the crude birth-rate may have no permanent significance if the rate of production of fourth or more children continues to fall. On the other hand, if the numbers of these rise, as apparently occurred in Germany in 1935, it would appear that some change in reproductive habits has taken place, whether temporary or permanent.

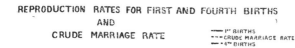

REPRODUCTION RATES FOR FIRST AND FOURTH BIRTHS AND CRUDE MARRIAGE RATE

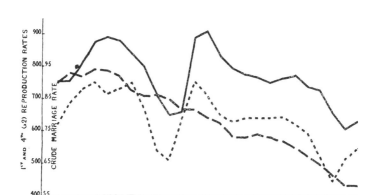

FIG. 5.—Reproduction rates for first and fourth births and the crude marriage rate, 1909 to 1933.

V. THE PERCENTAGE OF STERILE WOMEN

In section III an estimate was made of the sizes of single families without taking into account remarriages or the illegitimate children born to women who did not later marry. To obtain the percentage of childless women it is necessary to make some estimate of these two factors. Unfortunately the data do not exist for measuring these accurately for Australia. It is, however, so important to discover whether the percentage of childless women is increasing or decreasing, and to what extent, that it seems advisable to make some attempt to answer it even if largely based on guesswork, in the hope that in the future statistics may become available for dealing with it adequately. The only material which throws any light on the problem is that contained in the vital statistics of Czechoslovakia for 1925 to 1927.

(a) Remarriage

In the Czechoslovakian statistics the previous fertility of widows and divorcées remarrying is given. The average percentage for the three years 1925 to 1927 is given in Table X. The percentage of brides who were either widows or divorcées in Australia was between 5 and 6 per cent from 1909 to 1916, and then began to rise. The post-war peak was reached in 1922, when the percentage was 7·2. It then gradually fell, being below 6 per cent in 1932 and 1933.

TABLE X

PERCENTAGE OF WIDOWS AND DIVORCÉES REMARRYING WHO HAD PREVIOUSLV HAD A CHILD

CZECHOSLOVAKIA, 1925–27

Age-group	Widows	Divorcées
15–25	49·515	27·605
25–30	57·542	37·962
30–35	67·807	43·795
35–40	72·979	50·771
40–45	71·019	52·889
45–50	64·504	53·501

The Czechoslovakian fertility percentages were applied to the first births resulting from marriages in 1911, when the percentage of remarriage was 5·4, and those resulting from the marriages of 1924, when the percentage of remarriage was 6·8. The assumption was made that the fertility of remarriages was the same as that of first marriages. On this assumption it appeared that of the births to marriages of 1911 98·5 per cent were actual first births, and of the births to marriages of 1924 98 per cent were actual first births. It was therefore assumed as a rough approximation that when the percentage of remarriage was below 6·1, 98·5 per cent, and above 6·1, 98 per cent of first births were actually first births. In Table XI column (a) gives the legitimate first births per 1,000 women together with 14 per cent of all illegitimate births. In column (b) these figures have been corrected for remarriage by applying the percentages stated above. It should therefore give approximately the percentage of women having at least one legitimate child.

(b) *Illegitimate Births*

Account has already been taken of 14 per cent of all the illegitimate births which have been regarded as legitimatized after birth. To determine the total percentage of fertile women the remaining

TABLE XI

FIRST BIRTHS PER 1,000 WOMEN

Year	(a) First Births, + 14 per cent Illegitimate Births	(b) First Births as (a) corrected for Remarriage	(c) First Births as (b) +remaining Illegitimate First Births	(d) Five-yearly Averages of (c)
1909	753·470	742·168	833·104	—
1910	756·405	745·059	833·502	—
1911	809·354	797·214	894·238	*902*
1912	876·351	863·206	966·175	—
1913	890·805	877·443	982·800	*946*
1914	880·570	867·361	967·356	—
1915	838·944	826·360	919·048	—
1916	800·270	788·266	871·550	—
1917	712·744	702·053	774·646	—
1918	653·344	640·277	709·018	—
1919	661·046	647·825	734·806	—
1920	893·167	875·304	975·291	—
1921	911·266	897·597	999·317	—
1922	836·150	819·427	905·760	—
1923	797·906	781·948	866·116	—
1924	778·981	763·401	845·005	*854*
1925	768·509	753·139	833·714	—
1926	755·171	740·068	820·912	—
1927	766·551	751·220	833·668	*828*
1928	775·802	760·286	844·737	—
1929	741·163	726·340	806·335	—
1930	730·837	716·220	793·862	—
1931	658·936	645·757	719·242	*735*
1932	609·469	600·327	666·180	—
1933	632·758	623·267	691·576	—

illegitimate births must be considered. No data exist for Australia giving the percentage of illegitimate births which are first births. Australian statisticians treat all illegitimate births as first births, evidently considering the error involved in doing so to be negligible. Considering the Czechoslovakian statistics, the percentage of illegitimate births which were first births in 1925-27 was 67 per cent. On examining the figures for the four different provinces separately

H*

the percentage was found to range from 46 to 74 per cent. It appeared that the percentage of first births among illegitimate births was higher when the proportion of legitimate first births was higher, and also when the ratio of illegitimate to legitimate births was low. On these grounds, then, one would expect the proportion of illegitimate first births in Australia to be considerably above 67 per cent, both on the grounds of a lower illegitimate birth-rate throughout the period and a lower fertility at the end of the period.

In order to combine the Czechoslovakian experience with the generally held Australian opinion a formula was used to express the fact that the percentage of illegitimate first births varies in direct proportion to (a) the percentage of legitimate first births, and inversely as (b) the illegitimate birth-rate. If x is the percentage of first births to all legitimate births and y is the percentage of illegitimate births to all births, then $3x-2y$ is taken to be the percentage of first births among illegitimate births. This formula fitted the Czechoslovakian data fairly well, and applied to the Australian data gave percentages of illegitimate first births ranging from 61 to 86 per cent. Column (c) in Table XI shows the figures obtained by applying the formula, and is therefore a rough estimate of the number of women in every thousand having at least one child in the course of their lives on the basis of the fertility of the given year.

In column (d) five-yearly averages for the years centring on 1911, 1913, 1924, 1927, and 1931 are given. The figure for 1913 is probably greatly affected by migration. Taking the 1911 figure as more representative of the pre-war period, it appears that the proportion of fertile women has fallen in twenty years from about 90 per cent to about 74 per cent. It might be well to recapitulate the principal sources of error involved in this estimate. The first is in assuming that the fertility of remarriages and first marriages is the same. Although no data on the subject are known to the writer it seems likely that remarriages are probably less fertile. There is a further error in assuming that the previous fertility of the remarried is accurately represented by the Czechoslovakian fertility of 1926. It was probably greater than this at the beginning of the period and less at the end. This source of error would lead to an overestimate of fertility at the beginning and an underestimate at the end of the period, but the amount of this error cannot be very great. Finally, it might appear that fertility has been underestimated by taking too low a percentage of illegitimate births. Thus both the principal sources of error would lead to an underestimate of fertility. On the other hand there seems no reason to think that they would falsify the trend from 1909 to 1933. Moreover, any higher estimate of fertility would seem, even allowing for the effects of migration, to lead to improbably high figures in the earlier part of the period.

The error due to women whose illegitimate children die, and who later marry and have a legitimate child recorded as a first birth, has been dealt with in § III. It was there shown that this source of error would not be likely to reduce the percentage of fertile women by more than 1 per cent in the pre-war period and by considerably less in the post-war period. There still remain to be considered the women who have illegitimate children by other fathers than those they later marry. It is impossible to make any guess at the number of these women. On balance the errors enumerated in this paragraph appear to tend in the opposite direction to those enumerated in the last paragraph, so that there does not appear to be any reason to alter the figures given.

The figures given in column (c) for 1920 and 1921 call for some comment. It is obviously impossible that at any time or place 100 per cent of the women in a community should be fertile. There is no error in the numbers of women on whom the rate is based, since 1921 was a census year. Nor is any significantly different result obtained by computing the gross reproduction rate by single years instead of by five-yearly age-groups. The total number of first births per 1,000 women obtained for 1921, working with single years of age, was 998. Clearly the result is due to the accumulation of postponed births. Gross reproduction rates express current fertility in terms of the total fertility of women over the whole reproductive period. When fertility is such that it could not possibly continue as in 1921, gross reproduction rates, like all other indices of fertility, cease to have any significance as measures of total fertility.

If the figures given in Table XI are accepted as a rough estimate, it is possible to make some estimate of the relative weight to be attached respectively to increasing sterility and decreasing size of family. In 1911 the gross reproduction rate was 1·69, and in 1931 it was 1·13. If the family sizes of 1911 were associated with the 1931 percentage of sterility, a gross reproduction rate of 1·38 would ensue. The same gross reproduction rate would be obtained by associating the family sizes of 1931 with the sterility of 1911. It would therefore seem that increasing sterility and decrease in the number of large families were about equally important during these twenty years.

A further point merits consideration. In the light of what was said in § III about the relation between the gross reproduction rate and completed families, it seems probable that although the 1931 gross reproduction rate was sufficiently high to maintain a stationary population, the proportion of fertile women was already too low for this. In view of the attitude of present-day communities to large families it would appear likely that when the proportion of sterile women rises above 25 per cent fertility will fall below the level adequate to maintain a stationary population.

VI. FERTILITY OF MARRIAGE

In order to arrive at an estimate of the proportion of fertile marriages on the lines of the work hitherto recorded it would be necessary to determine the proportion of women who marry at least once before reaching the age of fifty. The numbers recorded at the census as never married in the age-group 50–54 have increased steadily from 6 per cent in 1891 to 16 per cent in 1921. These figures reflect the marriage rates over the period of thirty-five years previous to the census. The crude marriage rate has fluctuated widely since 1860 without displaying any very marked fall. It is possible that the consistent trend of the census figures above quoted may be illusory in that the high percentage of never-married in 1921 may reflect the low crude marriage rate in the period 1892 to 1898, when it was below 7 per 1,000. The rate did not fall below 7 again until the war years and again in 1930. It is possible to arrive at a percentage of never-married based on the rate at which women are marrying in a particular year by constructing a nuptiality table based on the same principles as a life table. The numbers of single and married women for each age-group must be known, and in Australia these are only available for the census years. Unfortunately the 1933 data are not yet available, and both 1911 and 1921 were years with an exceptionally high marriage rate. Nuptiality tables calculated for these years give a percentage of never-married at exactly fifty years of age of 12 and 10 per cent respectively. In the absence of more data it is only possible to make a guess at the true marriage rates corresponding to the gross reproduction rates of

1911 and 1931. It seems most likely that the nuptiality table giving 12 per cent of never-married women at fifty for 1911 may represent the true rate for that period, and that the 1921 census figure of 16 per cent may represent the rate for the 1931 period. Accepting these figures the conclusions arrived at are presented in Table XII.

From the figures in Table XII it appears that 91·5 per cent of all marriages in the 1911 period were fertile and 78·5 per cent of all marriages in the 1931 period. While these figures are largely guesswork they can to some extent be corroborated or otherwise by a study of the fertility of completed marriages on the lines referred to in § III. As far as could be ascertained the mean fertility of marriages contracted in the five years 1909 to 1913 was 88 per cent. For the three years 1924, 1925, and 1926 fertility during the first seven years after marriage could be studied. This period covers

TABLE XII

PERCENTAGES OF FERTILE AND STERILE MARRIED WOMEN
PER 1,000 WOMEN

Year	Married Women	Fertile	Sterile
1911	88	80·5	7·5
1931	84	66	18

98 per cent of all first births. Seventy-nine per cent of the marriages contracted in these three years were found to be fertile, probably corresponding to a total fertility of about 80 per cent. The study of the fertility of completed marriages therefore agrees fairly well with the figures arrived at from a study of current data. The final conclusion, then, is that in the 1911 period about 90 per cent of all marriages were fertile, and at the present time probably rather less than 80 per cent are fertile.

VII. AGE OF WOMEN AT MARRIAGE AND BIRTH OF CHILDREN

It is generally believed that declining fertility is associated with a postponement of marriage and child-bearing. In the Australian period studied this has not been so. Table XIII gives the mean age at marriage, at birth of the first child, and at the birth of all children. The figures are higher in 1921 for all three on account of the postponement of marriages and births during the war. There is a very slight rise in the age at marriage. This clearly affects chiefly

the more infertile marriages, since the mean age of the mother shows
a slight fall over the twenty-five-year period.

TABLE XIII

MEAN AGE OF WOMEN AT MARRIAGE AND BIRTH OF CHILDREN

Year	Mean Age at Marriage	Mean Age at Birth of First Child	Mean Age at Birth of all Children
1909	25·2	25·4	29·4
1912	25·2	25·4	29·2
1921	26·2	25·8	29·3
1931	25·3	25·1	28·8
1933	25·4	25·0	28·3

While there has been some tendency to the postponement of
marriages and births among older women, this has been more than
counterbalanced by the high marriage rate and high fertility of the

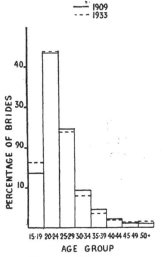

FIG. 6.—Percentages of brides in different age-groups, 1909 and 1933.

younger women. Fig. 6 shows the distribution of ages at marriage
in 1909 and 1933. It is seen that the 15–20 age-group constitutes a
larger proportion of all brides in 1933 than in 1909. The percentage
of marriages of minors is given in the official statistics as 20·5 in
1909 and 23·4 in 1933. There are also more marriages among the

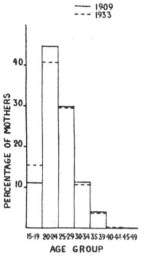

FIG. 7.—Percentages of mothers in different age-groups at birth of first child, 1909 and 1933.

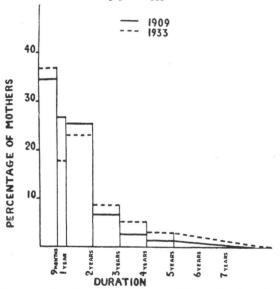

FIG. 8.—Percentage of mothers of first children at different durations of marriage, 1909 and 1933.

40–50 age-group, so that the average remains practically the same. Fig. 7, which gives the distribution of ages at birth of the first child, shows the same phenomena, greater frequency in the youngest age-group with some tendency to postponement of births to a later age. Since the fertility of the later age-groups is relatively insignificant the net effect is a reduction of the mean age.

The same tendency to a bimodal distribution is seen when the period elapsing between marriage and the birth of the first child is considered. The mean length of the period was 15·2 months in 1909 and 19·4 months in 1933. Fig. 8 gives the age distribution in these two years. The increase in the numbers born less than nine months after marriage has to some extent replaced a number of illegitimate births. The increase is so marked that in 1931–33 more first children were born in the sixth month after marriage than in any other single month. Considering the post-nuptial conception alone there has been a more considerable increase in the period elapsing between marriage and birth than is reflected in the mean duration.

VIII. THE SIZE OF THE FAMILY IN THE UNITED STATES

The data already presented refer to Australia alone. It does not necessarily follow that similar phenomena will be found in any other population group. Unfortunately the Australian data do not appear to be exactly paralleled elsewhere, though some material exists in several other countries. As a step towards a comparative study some estimates have been made of sizes of families in the United States, grouping the mothers by race and country of origin.

The data relate to a single year—1930—which was a census year. The populations used are the census populations for that year. Where the foreign-born mothers are subdivided by country of origin the precise age-groups required were not given in the census returns. So it was necessary to redistribute the figures given. This introduces an element of error into this part of the work. It is believed to be not more than 2 per cent for any single group.

A serious source of error arises at the outset in connection with the numbers of births. This is the admitted incompleteness of birth registration in the United States. According to Whelpton,[1] complete-

[1] Whelpton, "The Completeness of Birth Registration in the United States," *Journ. Am. Stat. Ass.*, 1934.

ness of birth registration for whites in the year April 1929 to April 1930 varied from 98 per cent in the original registration states to 85 per cent in those admitted in 1926–29. For negroes, completeness varied similarly from 98 to 77 per cent. American statisticians sometimes apply a correction factor to the recorded births, but as the amount of the correction cannot be precisely determined it seemed best to leave the figures as they stand with the warning that the number of births is certainly understated by an amount which is not known. It may well be greater for negro births than for white births.

The order of births is given in a table headed "Births (Exclusive of Stillbirths) with the Number of Child in order of Birth, by Colour, and for White by Nativity of Mother," in the annual volume of United States Vital Statistics. The total number of births given in the table corresponds to the total number of births, both legitimate and illegitimate, given elsewhere. The table should therefore correspond to the total number of children born to a woman during her lifetime. No official information ever appears to have been published which would throw light on the degree of accuracy obtained in this table, and in the absence of such information the table is taken at its face value. The entries under age not stated and order of birth not stated were redistributed proportionately so that no births were omitted. These entries were negligible in amount except for coloured mothers, where they amounted to nearly 3 per cent of the total births. The number of births used is the average for the three years 1929–31, except in the case of foreign-born women by country of origin when births for 1930 alone were used. The table excludes Colorado, Maine, Massachusetts, New Hampshire, and Rhode Island. In addition, South Dakota and Texas were not included in the registration area, so that all the data which follow refer to the United States exclusive of the seven states mentioned. The area covered includes 89 per cent of the total population of the United States. The states omitted are scattered over the country and have very varying degrees of fertility, so that their omission should not affect the results very greatly in any particular direction.

An attempt was made to study the families of foreign-born mothers by country of origin. It seemed only possible to do so for Great Britain, Germany, Ireland, Canada, and Italy. Some other countries were excluded on account of the small numbers involved. For mothers from Russia and Poland the total number of births seemed much too low when compared with the census population. It is, of course, possible that women born in Russia and Poland have a lower fertility than native-born white women in the United States. Since this is improbable it seemed better to assume some undiscoverable source of error and leave the data for further investigation. Austria-Hungary was omitted as being a probable location for the missing Russian and Polish births. If such an error exists, it may to some extent affect the whole subdivision of foreign-born women by country of origin. A further caution needs to be stated with reference to this group. Owing to the slowing down of immigration all the foreign-born groups have a quite abnormal age composition, heavily

TABLE XIII

GROSS REPRODUCTION RATES OF WOMEN IN THE
UNITED STATES, 1930*

Native-born white	1·086
Coloured	1·109
Foreign-born white	1·286

Born in Great Britain	0·938
Germany	1·003
Ireland	1·086
Canada	1·172
Italy	1·864

* Uncorrected for incomplete birth registration.

weighted in the older age-groups. The least abnormal are those from Canada and Ireland. Hence the data for foreign-born women are not directly comparable to those for the native-born.

Table XIII gives the gross reproduction rates of the different groups for 1930. The correction often made for incomplete birth registration would make the coloured[1] rate more nearly equal to that of the foreign-born white. Comparing these rates with the gross reproduction rates for Australia, we see that the rate given for U.S. native white women in 1930 lies between the Australian rates for 1931 and 1932. Taking the Australian average rate for the five-year period round 1931, all the rates in Table XIII are below it except those for foreign-born whites as a whole and for women

[1] The heading "coloured" includes negro, Indian, Chinese, Japanese, Mexican, and all other non-white races. At the 1930 census negroes constituted 85 per cent of this assemblage.

born in Canada and Italy. None of these rates, however, except the Italian, are as high as the Australian 1928 rate. The Italian rate corresponds roughly to the fertility found at the beginning of the Australian period.

Table XIV gives the percentages of families of different sizes found. The same data are represented in Figs. 9 and 10. These can be

TABLE XIV

SIZE OF FAMILY PER 1,000 WOMEN, UNITED STATES, 1930

Size of Family	Native-born White	Coloured	Foreign-born White	Born in				
				Great Britain	Germany	Ireland	Canada	Italy
0	330	419	165	244	0	186	41	114
1	175	212	243	241	499	258	385	141
2	167	90	223	231	286	220	257	170
3	105	52	124	132	98	137	119	127
4	67	40	79	66	50	81	80	117
5	43	32	46	36	24	39	36	94
6	32	33	32	19	12	32	34	72
7	22	23	20	13	9	19	12	35
8	18	25	17	7	6	8	11	29
9	13	16	14	4	6	13	9	26
10	11	19	14	4	3	1	6	26
11	7	10	9	—	5	5	2	18
12	5	11	6	1	1	2	5	16
13	3	6	4	1	1	—	1	8
14 and over	3	11	5	1	2	1	2	9

compared with the Australian data in Tables IV and V and Fig. 2. They do not represent precisely the same entities, since the Australian figures do not include all illegitimate children, nor do they take account of remarriage.

The data for United States native-born white women most closely resemble the latest Australian data. The percentage of childless found in this group was 67. This is practically the same as the Australian figure for 1932. The distribution of family sizes is somewhat similar to that in Australia, 1931. The principal differences are (a) the higher proportion of first children, and (b) the somewhat higher proportion of very large families. The numbers of one- and two-child families are nearly equal. This suggests that, while the increase in the percentage of childless women has proceeded at the same rate in the United States and Australia, there has been less concentration on the two-child family in the United States.

The data for the coloured group are difficult to interpret. The percentage of childless women is very high. It would seem probable

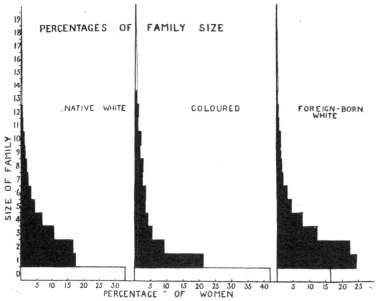

FIG. 9.—Distribution of family sizes among women in the United States, 1930.

that with more complete birth registration it might be reduced, particularly as the proportion of coloured women married at all ages is greater than in the other groups. The pattern of family sizes is not dissimilar to that for Australia for 1911. The high ratio of first to second children is consonant with a high general fertility. In fact, the family pattern suggests a higher gross reproduction rate for coloured women than can be obtained even after the usual allowance has been made for incomplete registration. Possibly the employment of a large number of coloured women in personal service may account for a number of childless women. An alternative view suggested to me by Dr. Kuczynski is that owing to the very

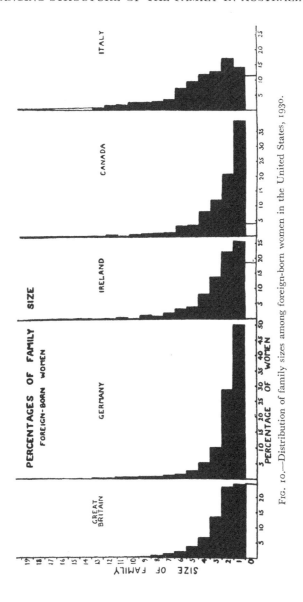

Fig. 10.—Distribution of family sizes among foreign-born women in the United States, 1930.

rapid and sudden fall in fertility among coloured women the effects of the spread of contraception appear in a more erratic manner. So we may now have childless women among urban workers together with large families among rural negroes. In this connection the high illegitimate rate among coloured women needs to be borne in mind.

With regard to the foreign-born women, the percentage of childless ones is largely determined by the conditions of immigration. Canada, Ireland, and Great Britain may possibly represent stages in the standardization of the two-child family. The picture for Germany is to be looked at remembering the very low fertility found. If it were associated with the same proportion of childless women as in native-born white women, it would represent a gross reproduction rate of about 0·7. It may therefore indicate a still later stage in the elimination of all except first and second children. The fact that the rate obtained for Germany shows no childless women at all is in large part a statistical accident due to the unavoidable necessity of using a single year's births. This occurred also for a single year in the Australian data for 1921, when the number of first births was fluctuating widely. The picture for Italy, although it shows an excess of two-child families as in Australia 1931, is clearly quite different owing to the very much greater proportion of larger families.

Table XV gives the percentages of different sizes of family among women having at least one child and is perhaps more easily comparable with the similar Australian table. This table shows the general similarity of the native-born white and British patterns to the Australian 1931 pattern, though the British mothers appear to have gone much further in the reduction of large families, as have some of the other groups. The coloured and Italian patterns are not dissimilar to the Australian 1911 pattern. The deficiency of first births among the Italian women may be due to the great preponderance of older women.

The position of children in the family is illustrated in Table XVI. Twenty-nine per cent first births among coloured women and 33 per cent among native white may be compared with 28 and 34 per cent at the beginning and end of the Australian period. The percentage of first births among foreign-born women increases in passing from the more fertile to the less fertile groups. The table also shows a high proportion of children from one- and two-child families, though nowhere is the two-child family the most frequent size as in Australia 1931. Only in the Italian group do we find the most popular size between four and five as in Australia 1911. The percentage of all children born coming from one-, two-, and three-child families was 38 per cent in Australia 1931. Among native-born white women in the United States it was 37 per cent, 40 per cent among British mothers, 50 per cent for Irish, 52 per cent for Canadian, and 67 per cent for German. The percentages were

TABLE XV

PERCENTAGES OF DIFFERENT SIZES OF FAMILIES AMONG
100 WOMEN HAVING AT LEAST ONE CHILD

Size of Family	Native-born White	Coloured	Foreign-born White	Born in				
				Great Britain	Germany	Ireland	Canada	Italy
1	26	36	29	32	50	32	40	16
2	25	16	27	30	29	27	27	19
3	16	9	15	17	10	17	12	14
4	10	7	9	9	5	10	8	13
5	6	6	6	5	2	5	4	11
6	5	6	4	3	1	4	4	8
7	3	4	2	2	1	2	1	4
8 or more	9	17	8	2	2	4	4	15

lower for coloured and Italian mothers—24 and 23 per cent respectively.

In conclusion, the United States data are too scanty to be more than suggestive, particularly in view of the abnormal age composition of the foreign-born. As far as they go they suggest the following conclusions. (a) The rapid increase in the percentage of childless women has proceeded in much the same way among native-born women in the United States as in Australia. (b) The same is true of the reduction in large families, but this process has gone even further in some of the foreign-born groups. (c) The concentration on the two-child family is not found to the same extent in any of the American groups studied. This suggests that the Australian phenomenon may be a temporary phase to be succeeded by a larger proportion of only-child families, or on the other hand it may be peculiar to Australia. It is hoped that further study of other family patterns may elucidate this. (*d*) Italian-born mothers show a pattern of family sizes characteristic of high fertility consistent with their high gross reproduction rate. (*e*) Coloured mothers show a similar pattern, which does not agree with their

TABLE XVI

NUMBER OUT OF EVERY 1,000 CHILDREN BORN BELONGING TO FAMILIES OF DIFFERENT SIZES AND PERCENTAGE OF FIRST BIRTHS TO ALL BIRTHS

Size of Family	Native-born White	Coloured	Foreign-born White	Born in				
				Great Britain	Germany	Ireland	Canada	Italy
1	78	94	92	125	244	116	160	37
2	150	80	170	240	279	197	214	89
3	141	69	141	205	143	184	149	100
4	119	72	121	138	98	145	134	122
5	97	71	88	95	57	87	75	122
6	87	88	72	59	34	86	86	113
7	68	72	54	49	29	59	34	64
8	65	88	52	28	22	29	36	60
9	53	63	47	19	28	51	34	62
10	48	86	53	23	16	3	25	68
11	32	51	36	1	24	23	9	51
12	26	56	29	9	6	11	26	49
13	17	37	21	4	8	2	4	27
14 and over	19	73	26	6	12	6	15	36
Percentage first births	33	29	24	34	43	32	37	15

recorded fertility. Possibly this is because the number of births is greatly understated. Alternatively, the unusual social pattern shown may be due to the exceptionally sudden fall in fertility.

IX. SUMMARY

(i) The particulars elucidated at birth registration in Australia since 1909 make it possible to estimate within certain limits the changing distribution of families of a given size. It is thus possible to infer the contribution of (a) an increasing proportion of marriages which have no issue, and (b) diminution of large families towards declining fertility.

(ii) The gross reproduction rate was calculated for the years 1909 to 1933 inclusive. It was 1·78 in 1912 and 1·05 in 1933. There was thus a 41 per cent fall in fertility in twenty-one years. The fall was more striking in illegitimate than in legitimate fertility and greater in the older age-groups than in the younger.

(iii) The foregoing tables show the distribution of sizes of families resulting from current marriages. They also show that over the period 1911 to 1931 (a) the proportion of sterile marriages had considerably increased, (b) there was little change in the proportion of one-child families, (c) there was a considerable increase in the proportion of two-child families, and (d) there was a reduction in the proportion of all families of four or more children. The result of these changes was to make two children the fashionable family size.

(iv) The data recorded may be compared with fertility of completed marriages from 1909 to 1911. This leads to the conclusion that the completed families resulting from marriages contracted at the present time are likely to be smaller than is indicated by the current gross reproduction rate even if no further social changes reducing fertility take place.

(v) The proportion of firstborn to all children has risen from 28 to 34 per cent. In 1909–13 more children came from four- and five-child families than from any other size, but in 1929–33 more children came from two-child families than from any other size. In 1929–33, when the gross reproduction rate was just sufficient to maintain a stationary population, 62 per cent of all children came from families of four or more.

(vi) The crude birth-rate and also the gross reproduction rate have fluctuated widely during the last twenty-five years. These fluctuations are accentuated by the increasing proportion of first births. The reproduction rates for fourth and later births have been much more steady. Hence they form a better index of the general trend of fertility.

(vii) The proportion of sterile women (using the term in a purely statistical sense) is estimated at 10 per cent in 1909–13 and 26·5 per cent in 1929–33. The latter percentage is probably incompatible with the maintenance of a stationary population so long as the present attitude to large families persists.

(viii) The fall in fertility between 1912 and 1933 appears to have been due in about equal measure to the increasing proportion of sterile women and the reduction in the numbers of large families.

(ix) The fall in fertility has not been accompanied by any increase in the mean age at marriage or at childbirth. The tendency to later marriages and postponement of birth among older women has been more than counterbalanced by the relatively better-maintained fertility of younger women.

CHAPTER VI

MARRIAGE FREQUENCY AND ECONOMIC FLUCTUATIONS IN ENGLAND AND WALES, 1851 TO 1934

by

D. V. GLASS[1]

INDICES now used for the analysis of marriage frequency range from the crude rate at one end of the scale to the nuptiality table at the other. The intervening "twilight continuum" is filled with refined rates which attempt to correct the inadequacies of the crude marriage rate and to approximate to the accuracy of the nuptiality table.

The crude marriage rate is obviously unsatisfactory. Relating marriages to the total population, it would only be accurate as an index of changes in marriage habits if the age composition of the population remained constant. Changes such as have been caused by movements in mortality and fertility in the last seventy years in England and Wales cause the rate to exaggerate the amount of marriage at one moment and underestimate it at another. Thus it may lead to incorrect conclusions concerning the trend in marriage and in deviations from that trend. Like the birth-rate, its use should be avoided if other methods of measurement are available.

At the other end, the nuptiality table summarizes, for any particular time, the frequency of marriage in successive years of individuals' lives. As is shown in the example given in an article by Dr. R. R. Kuczynski,[2] it is a life-table in which unmarried persons are substituted for all persons, and marriages for deaths. From it may be calculated the expectation of marriage at birth. However, the compilation of a nuptiality table requires accurate information concerning the marital status in each age-group, and at present this information can only be obtained for census periods. Until such time as the records of death and migration allow us to make accurate

---

[1] This research was undertaken on a grant provided by the Population Investigation Committee, of which Mr. D. V. Glass is the Research Secretary.

[2] "The Decrease of Fertility," *Economica*, May 1935.

mid-year estimates of the population by age, sex, and marital condition, the nuptiality table will remain a method of measuring intercensal changes and cannot be used for examining year-to-year

TABLE I

(A)

PROPORTIONS OF UNMARRIED MEN AT VARIOUS AGES

(*Percentages*)

	20–45	*25–45*	*20–25*	*25–35*	*35–45*
1851	40·56	27·18	79·68	35·55	16·22
1861	37·47	23·91	77·48	31·84	14·21
1871	37·14	23·78	76·71	31·59	13·70
1881	37·62	23·86	77·71	31·70	13·78
1891	39·55	25·72	80·56	34·26	14·66
1901	41·00	27·12	82·62	35·89	15·84
1911	41·58	28·75	85·72	38·55	16·87
1921	37·46	24·79	82·21	34·11	15·01
1931	39·28	25·00	86·12	35·23	12·54

(B)

PROPORTIONS OF UNMARRIED WOMEN AT VARIOUS AGES, 1851–1931

(*Percentages*)

	20–45	*25–45*	*20–25*	*25–35*	*35–45*
1851	37·00	25·86	68·73	32·90	16·28
1861	35·02	24·08	66·38	30·50	15·85
1871	34·18	23·63	65·16	29·80	15·56
1881	34·37	23·18	66·54	29·22	15·35
1891	37·17	25·67	70·11	32·60	16·44
1901	38·88	27·38	72·59	33·98	18·53
1911	39·27	28·45	75·70	35·53	19·63
1921	36·96	26·82	72·64	33·72	19·22
1931	37·17	26·62	74·19	33·00	19·40

fluctuations. Consequently it is in the same category, though the conclusions derived from it are more accurate, as the census analysis of the percentage of persons unmarried in successive age-groups. Table I summarizes the main features of an analysis of each census since 1851, and their graphical form is given in Figs. 1 and 2.

For examining year-by-year variations in marriage some modification of the crude marriage rate is required. One such example was used by Professor Udney Yule in a paper read at the Royal Statistical Society in 1906.[1] He constructed an adjustment factor for correcting the crude marriage rate, the factor being based on

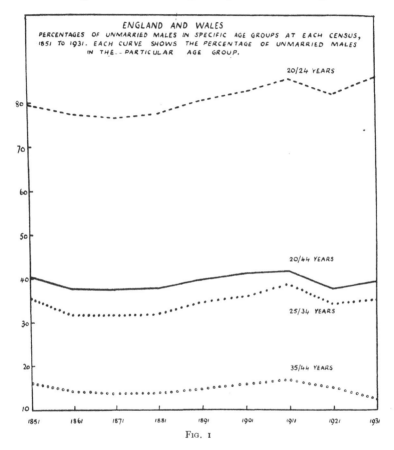

ENGLAND AND WALES

PERCENTAGES OF UNMARRIED MALES IN SPECIFIC AGE GROUPS AT EACH CENSUS, 1851 TO 1931. EACH CURVE SHOWS THE PERCENTAGE OF UNMARRIED MALES IN THE PARTICULAR AGE GROUP.

FIG. 1

the proportions of marriageable persons in the total population, compared with the position in 1901. My only criticisms are, first, that in correcting for the age-composition of marriageable persons Professor Yule assumed for his period a constant relative marriage-

[1] G. Udney Yule, "On Changes in the Marriage and Birth Rates in England and Wales in the Past Half Century," *J.R.S.S.*, 1906 (March).

ability of unmarried persons of different ages. He adopted the proportions found in 1901, when the ratios of new marriages to unmarried persons were 8 per 1,000 for the age-group 15 to 19

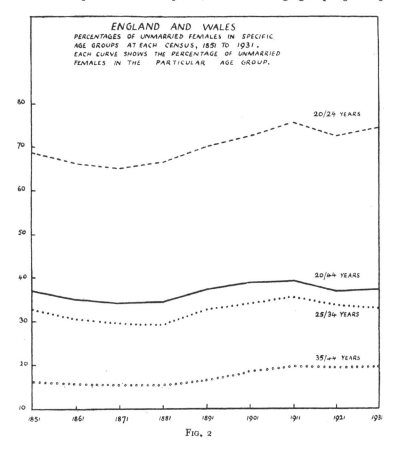

FIG. 2

years, 99 for the 20 to 34 years age-group, and 21 for the group aged 35 years and over. This is rather begging the question, for changes in the age at marriage will alter the relative marriageability of the different age-groups. Secondly, instead of using a correction factor, it would be more useful to compute the basic unmarried population by simple intercensal interpolation. Such a method would have no less a claim to accuracy than the one used by Professor Yule—its claim would really be higher, for no assumptions as to relative marriageability would be made—and at the same time it would greatly facilitate the construction of moving averages for smoothing out trends, as such averages should be calculated on the original data, and not on the annual rates derived from them. Finally, it might be slightly better to compute a marriage rate for males only, as this would obviate any need for discounting the fluctuating excess of females over males in the marriageable age-groups.

The marriage rates used in this paper attempt to meet the criticisms made above. They are computed on the basis of the unmarried (that is, single, widowed, and, when the figures became available, divorced) male population. On examination of the statistics of the ages at which men marry,[1] it was seen (shown in Table II) that from 1851 onwards never less than 90 per cent of males married between the ages of 20 and 44 years. On the basis of this information, two marriage rates were constructed: (1) the number of marriages per 1,000 unmarried males aged 15 years and over, the male population being standardized for the age-group 20 to 44 years on the base of 1900, and (2) the number of marriages of males aged 20 to 44 years per 1,000 unmarried males aged 20 to 44 years. The first rate was rather in the nature of a test for comparison with the crude rate. The second rate has been used for all the subsequent analysis of general marriage trends. Finally, it was decided to attempt some analysis of trends in specific age-groups. For this purpose the two extremes of the marriage range were chosen for comparison—the marriages of males aged 20 to 24 years per 1,000 unmarried males aged 20 to 24, and a similar rate for the marriages of males aged 45 to 54 years. In the absence of more accurate data the basic unmarried male populations were estimated by simple intercensal interpolation, which, as has been indicated, was really also the method used by Professor Yule in constructing a correction factor for the crude marriage rate. The age analysis of the marriages of males was taken from tables given in the Annual Reports and Reviews of the Registrar-General for each year from 1851 to 1934. These tables depend for their completeness upon the ability and willingness of people to give their ages when signing the marriage

[1] In the Annual Reports of the Registrar-General for each year from 1851 to 1934.

TABLE II

MARRIAGES OF MALES IN SPECIFIC AGE-GROUPS AS PERCENTAGES OF ALL MARRIAGES

	Age 20–24	Age 20–44		Age 20–24	Age 20–44
1851	46·58	92·42	1889	43·57	92·28
1852	46·47	92·33	1890	43·20	92·20
1853	46·74	92·39	1891	42·56	92·29
1854	46·71	92·28	1892	42·09	92·24
1855	45·80	91·91	1893	41·32	92·35
1856	46·11	91·94	1894	41·60	92·69
1857	46·77	91·97	1895	41·36	92·82
1858	46·80	91·69	1896	41·58	92·98
1859	46·91	91·62	1897	41·38	93·21
1860	47·15	91·44	1898	41·51	93·17
1861	46·77	91·33	1899	41·26	93·29
1862	47·42	91·41	1900	41·54	93·06
1863	48·00	91·53	1901	40·49	92·89
1864	48·49	91·63	1902	39·30	93·30
1865	48·15	91·28	1903	39·12	93·60
1866	48·24	91·12	1904	38·93	93·68
1867	47·34	90·98	1905	38·32	93·61
1868	47·59	90·95	1906	38·18	93·60
1869	47·34	90·80	1907	37·73	93·57
1870	47·51	91·00	1908	37·17	93·42
1871	47·38	90·65	1909	36·12	93·29
1872	48·06	90·73	1910	35·17	93·45
1873	48·85	90·56	1911*	34·79	93·24
1874	48·48	90·29			
1875	48·32	90·39	1921	35·17	91·64
1876	48·29	90·52	1922	34·90	91·73
1877	48·57	90·70	1923	35·72	91·90
1878	48·15	90·82	1924	35·93	91·84
1879	47·68	91·04	1925	35·88	91·69
1880	47·73	91·40	1926	35·65	91·46
1881	47·20	91·40	1927	35·29	91·51
1882	47·29	91·57	1928	34·90	91·36
1883	46·61	91·64	1929	34·52	91·57
1884	45·98	91·65	1930	34·29	91·53
1885	45·30	91·48	1931	34·16	91·61
1886	44·67	91·69	1932	33·41	92·34
1887	44·32	91·96	1933	32·35	92·41
1888	43·56	92·07	1394	31·88	92·78

* The marriage percentages for the period 1912–20 (not used in the computations for this paper) are:—

	Age 20–24	Age 20–44		Age 20–24	Age 20–44
1912	34·76	93·05	1917	32·09	89·76
1913	34·95	92·93	1918	31·79	89·31
1914	35·13	92·84	1919	31·57	90·92
1915	35·28	93·51	1920	34·70	91·79
1916	33·02	91·47			

register, instead of merely stating that they are of full legal age, and the proportion of marriages for which such information was given has varied considerably. To-day it is not far short of a 100 per cent completeness. But even in 1851 it amounted to almost 40 per cent

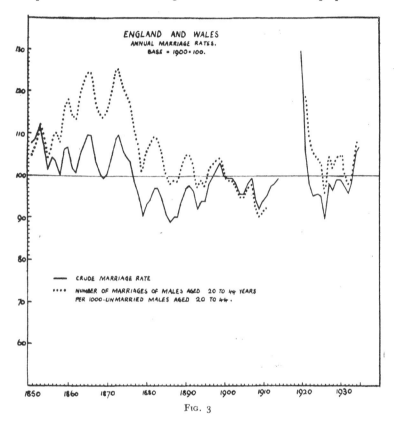

ENGLAND AND WALES
ANNUAL MARRIAGE RATES.
BASE = 1900 = 100.

—— CRUDE MARRIAGE RATE

•••• NUMBER OF MARRIAGES OF MALES AGED 20 TO 44 YEARS
PER 1000-UNMARRIED MALES AGED 20 TO 44.

FIG. 3

of all marriages. The marriages for which the age was given may have been specially selected, but the likelihood of this appears to be lessened by the consistency of the proportions of marriages in the age group 20 to 44 years during the whole period. In any case, lacking more accurate information, the annual totals of marriages have been distributed between the various age-groups in the same proportions as those for which ages were given.

I

Some interesting facts are shown by comparing the two general marriage rates—the crude rate and the rate for unmarried males

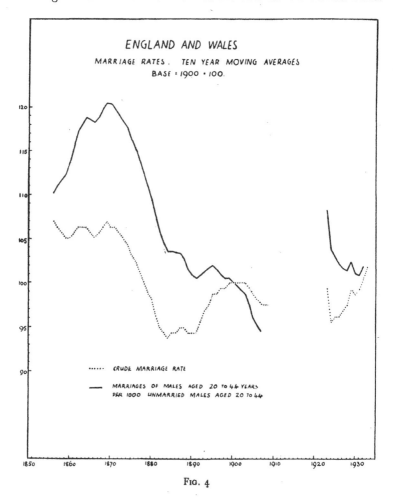

ENGLAND AND WALES

MARRIAGE RATES.   TEN YEAR MOVING AVERAGES
BASE = 1900 = 100.

········ CRUDE MARRIAGE RATE

——— MARRIAGES OF MALES AGED 20 TO 44 YEARS
PER 1000 UNMARRIED MALES AGED 20 TO 44

FIG. 4

aged 20 to 44 years. First, although the peaks and depressions in marriage frequency appear to occur at the same times in both rates, yet the refined rate shows a considerably greater range of oscillation. This is made evident in Fig. 3. Omitting the period 1912 to

1920 inclusive, for which there are no comparative figures for the refined rate, the crude rate shows a range from 17·9 to 14·2, the highest point being 26 per cent above the lowest. The refined rate

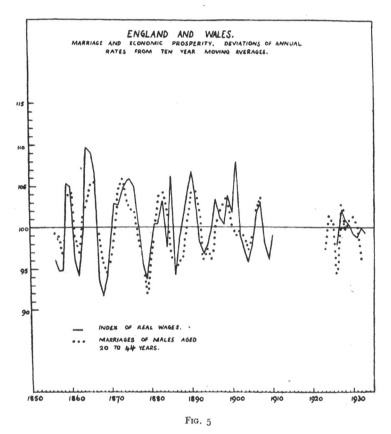

ENGLAND AND WALES.
MARRIAGE AND ECONOMIC PROSPERITY. DEVIATIONS OF ANNUAL RATES FROM TEN YEAR MOVING AVERAGES.

FIG. 5

shows a range from 122·1 to 87·1, the difference in this case being 40 per cent. A similar difference in range is also shown for the ten-year moving averages, the crude rate showing a range of 14 per cent, and the refined rate one of about 28 per cent. Secondly, whereas the crude rate shows a maximum marriage frequency in 1853, for the refined rate it does not appear until 1873. The earlier maximum for the crude rate was due partly to the high proportion of males of marriageable age in the total population. The existence of a similar situation in 1900 to 1911 was also partly responsible for keeping

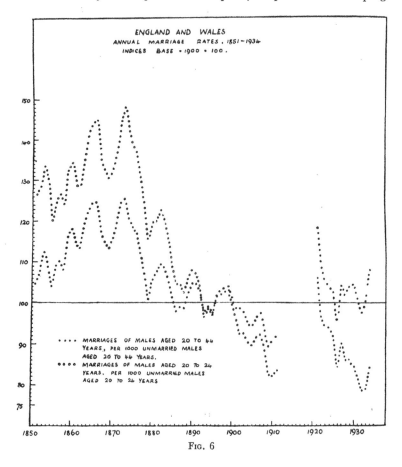

ENGLAND AND WALES
ANNUAL MARRIAGE RATES. 1851–1934
INDICES BASE · 1900 · 100.

•••• MARRIAGES OF MALES AGED 20 TO 44 YEARS, PER 1000 UNMARRIED MALES AGED 20 TO 44 YEARS.
•••• MARRIAGES OF MALES AGED 20 TO 24 YEARS, PER 1000 UNMARRIED MALES AGED 20 TO 24 YEARS

FIG. 6

up the crude marriage rate. Thirdly, the relative balance of marriage frequency as between the post-war and immediate pre-war periods appears differently in the two rates. The relative shortage of marriageable males kept down the crude marriage rate after 1921, so that up to 1934 it appeared to be below the 1900 level. But the refined rate shows that in ten of the twelve years marriage frequency was above the 1900 level. Also the rise in the crude rate from 1930 to 1935 is about 11 per cent, while the refined rate shows an increase of only about 7 per cent. The smaller increase shown by the refined

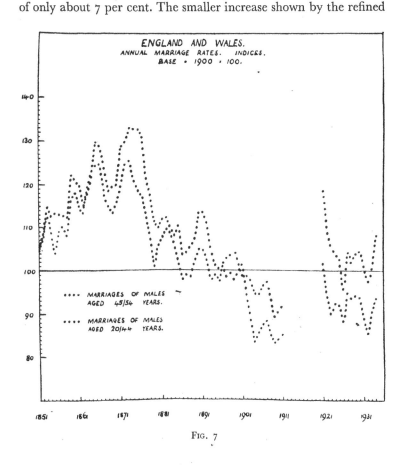

FIG. 7

rate is what might well be expected if the effect of depression is to postpone marriages and thus swell the numbers of marriageable persons. Professor Yule suggested that those who postpone marriage in one year tend to marry in the next. Judging from German experience, there is good reason to believe that marriages may be postponed for considerably more than one year. Finally, the trends shown by the two rates are sometimes dissimilar. For example, the crude rates appeared to be fluctuating about a point of stability

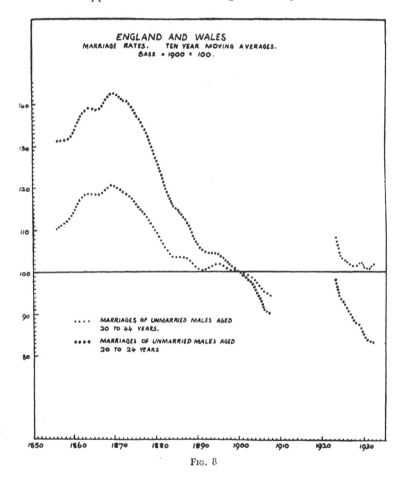

FIG. 8

in 1860 to 1870, whereas the refined rate moved steadily upwards. Also the upward trend of the crude rate from 1891 to 1900 is contradicted by the downward trend of the refined rate from 1895, and a similar situation is shown in the post-war period.

The main point of this paper is not, however, to analyse the general course of marriage frequency, but to relate its fluctuations to the economic changes which appear to influence it. The aim is

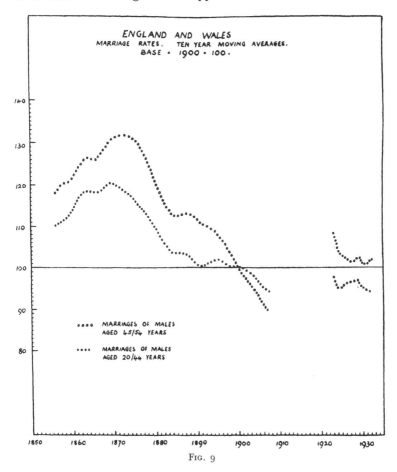

FIG. 9

by no means new. In her book, *Social Aspects of the Business Cycle*,[1] Dr. D. S. Thomas gives an excellent account of the numerous statistical investigations of this problem. The only new aspect brought into the present attempt is the use of a refined marriage rate, and its correlation with an economic index somewhat different

[1] Published 1925: See especially chapter 2.

from those used in previous researches. The index used here is that constructed by Dr. Jürgen Kuczynski,[1] and represents the changes in net real wages for unemployed and employed workers. This index is used because it seems *a priori*, that if there is any economic influence

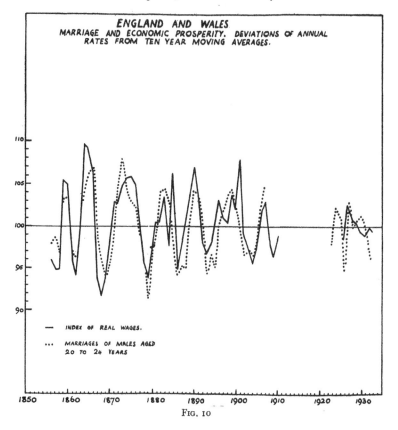

ENGLAND AND WALES
MARRIAGE AND ECONOMIC PROSPERITY. DEVIATIONS OF ANNUAL
RATES FROM TEN YEAR MOVING AVERAGES.

FIG. 10

upon marriage, it should make itself most strongly felt through real earnings discounted for unemployment. Moreover, real wages are more relevant to the actual economic situation than *per capita* real income. They relate to wage-earning workers, but even if they

[1] See *Labour Conditions in Western Europe* (1937), especially p. 71. The Wage Index refers to the United Kingdom and not just to England and Wales, but the difference can scarcely be great.

and their immediate dependents constituted only two-fifths of the total population, it is likely that the repercussions of their prosperity would in turn affect another two-fifths of the population. *Per capita* real income, on the other hand, does not relate to any class of people,

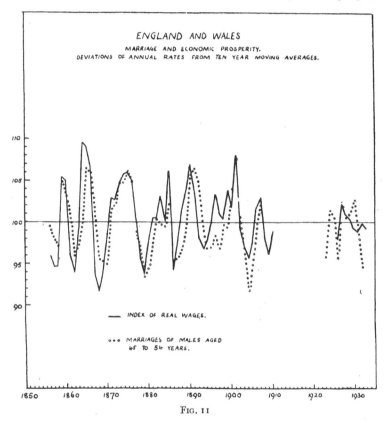

FIG. 11

but is simply a fictitious arithmetical expression of the national dividend discounted for the number of inhabitants in the country. Changes in the resultant figure may show only a rough relation to the prosperity of the bulk of the population.

In correlating real wages and marriage frequency, the simplest methods were used. This was partly to reduce the amount of calculation involved, but also because the basic figures being approximate,

I*

it would have been inappropriate to apply highly refined methods to their analysis. As Hooker pointed out in 1901,[1] any correspondence between the two time series must lie in the similarity of their oscillations about the trend. For the purpose of this paper the trend was estimated by computing ten-year moving averages. Such averages reduce considerably the work of calculation from the original data, and do not disagree with Dr. Thomas's own conclusions that "since the trend may be determined by several methods, and since it may take any one of many different forms, it is obvious that we cannot find the absolute trend of the data and must regard any trend as being empirical."[2] The period for which deviations from the moving averages were computed—that is, 1856 to 1932—was divided into four sections. One section consisted of the seven post-war years 1926 to 1932, and it is obvious that with so few items a correlation coefficient can have no real significance. But at the same time the seven years represented a period markedly different from the pre-war sections and could scarcely be included with them. The post-war items have therefore only been used in computing a coefficient for the whole fifty-two years. The pre-war forty-five years were divided into three equal periods, each of sixteen years, the equality being obtained by including the last year of the previous period as the first year of the next.

On such a basis the correlation coefficients yielded were:

REFINED MARRIAGE RATE AND INDEX OF REAL WAGES

(1)	1856–1932	+ 0·706 ± 0·065
(2)	1856–1873	+ 0·870 ± 0·057
(3)	1873–1890	+ 0·709 ± 0·117
(4)	1890–1907	+ 0·603 ± 0·150
(5)	1926–1932	+ 0·677 ± 0·206

Leaving aside for a moment the implications of these coefficients, it is interesting to compare them with the results obtained by correlating the index of real wages and the crude marriage rate. They are:

CRUDE MARRIAGE RATE AND INDEX OF REAL WAGES

(1)	1856–1932	+ 0·721 ± 0·062
(2)	1856–1873	+ 0·857 ± 0·063
(3)	1873–1890	+ 0·714 ± 0·115
(4)	1890–1907	+ 0·658 ± 0·134
(5)	1926–1932	+ 0·705 ± 0·190

[1] "Correlation of the Marriage Rate with Trade," *J.R.S.S.*
[2] *Social Aspects of the Business Cycle*, pp. 168–9.

The differences obtained by using the refined marriage rate for correlation are evidently small, and do not alter the major facts—that there is a high correlation for the whole period and that the correlation is highest for the section 1856 to 1873. Both sets of correlations show a steady decline in the value of the coefficients with the passage of the nineteenth century. The exception for the section 1926 to 1932 is not significant since there are only seven items in the series. The importance of the particular economic index used, and the relative unimportance of the particular marriage rate in this case, is brought out by four additional correlations in which, instead of the index of real wages, the Beveridge index of *per capita* real income is used. This index is not adjusted for unemployment.[1] All the coefficients are considerably lower for this series.

BEVERIDGE INDEX AND REFINED MARRIAGE RATE

(1)	1865–1907	+ 0·497 ± 0·115
(2)	1865–1873	+ 0·746 ± 0·148
(3)	1873–1890	+ 0·448 ± 0·188
(4)	1890–1907	+ 0·431 ± 0·192

In fact, bearing in mind both the numbers of items in the series and the relative magnitudes of the coefficients and their probable errors, it is doubtful if there is any significance in the correlations for the three sub-sections.

When Dr. Thomas made her analysis of the relation between marriage and the business cycle,[2] she found the following coefficients:

(1)	1854–1913	+ 0·67 ± 0·07
(2)	1854–1874	+ 0·64 ± 0·13
(3)	1875–1894	+ 0·84 ± 0·07
(4)	1895–1913	+ 0·57 ± 0·15

They show important differences from the results obtained by correlating the refined marriage rate and real wages. In the first

[1] From Sir William Beveridge's "The Fall of Fertility Among European Races," *Economica*, March 1925.

[2] *Social Aspects of the Business Cycle.* Her economic index was constructed from the following items: Value of total exports of British produce; Sauerbeck index numbers of all materials; percentage unemployed in "all trades"; production of pig-iron in the United Kingdom; production of coal in the United Kingdom; railway freight traffic receipts; and provincial bank clearings (Manchester and Birmingham).

TABLE III

UNITED KINGDOM, 1851–1935

INDEX OF REAL WAGES OF EMPLOYED AND UNEMPLOYED
POPULATION

	A	B	C		A	B	C
1851	60	—	—	1894	92	95·7	97·8
1852	59	—	—	1895	95	96·8	99·8
1853	63	—	—	1896	99	97·4	103·4
1854	57	—	—	1897	98	98·7	101·0
1855	55	—	—	1898	98	99·4	100·3
1856	56	59·3	96·1	1899	102	99·9	103·9
1857	55	59·1	94·7	1900	100	100·0	101·7
1858	55	59·0	94·8	1901	106	99·9	107·9
1859	61	58·9	105·4	1902	97	99·7	99·0
1860	62	60·1	104·9	1903	95	99·6	97·0
1861	58	61·5	95·9	1904	93	99·0	95·6
1862	58	62·8	94·0	1905	94	97·8	97·8
1863	62	63·4	99·5	1906	97	97·0	101·7
1864	69	64·0	109·7	1907	97	95·8	103·0
1865	69	64·3	109·2	1908	92	95·3	98·2
1866	68	64·9	106·6	1909	90	95·3	96·1
1867	61	66·3	93·6	1910	93	95·6	98·9
1868	61	67·9	91·5	1911	94	—	—
1869	64	69·3	94·0	1912	92	—	—
1870	68	70·2	98·6	1913	95	—	—
1871	72	71·2	102·9	1914	96	—	—
1872	73	72·3	102·7	1915	—	—	—
1873	76	73·9	104·7	1916	—	—	—
1874	78	75·1	105·7	1917	—	—	—
1875	79	75·9	105·9	1918	—	—	—
1876	79	76·6	104·9	1919	—	—	—
1877	76	77·2	100·1	1920	—	—	—
1878	73	77·7	95·5	1921	—	—	—
1879	72	78·2	93·6	1922	—	—	—
1880	75	78·2	97·5	1923	—	—	—
1881	78	79·0	100·4	1924	90	—	—
1882	78	79·0	100·4	1925	93	—	—
1883	81	79·9	103·2	1926	91	94·6	97·8
1884	78	81·4	97·5	1927	96	95·6	102·1
1885	87	83·3	106·2	1928	95	95·8	100·8
1886	79	85·4	94·2	1929	95	96·4	100·2
1887	84	86·9	98·4	1930	94	96·4	99·2
1888	88	88·1	101·6	1931	94	96·8	98·7
1889	91	89·0	104·0	1932	96	97·9	99·8
1890	95	90·4	106·9	1933	97	99·5	99·2
1891	93	91·3	103·7	1934	100	—	—
1892	90	93·3	98·1	1935	102	—	—
1893	90	94·7	96·7				

A = Annual Indices, 1900 = 100. B = Ten-Year Moving Averages, 1900 = 100.
C = Deviations from Moving Averages.
Five-Year Moving Averages used in Post-War Period.

TABLE IV

MARRIAGE RATES, ENGLAND AND WALES, 1851–1935

1. ANNUAL RATES

	A	B	C		A	B	C
1851	17·2	56·6	102·0	1894	15·0	53·3	96·4
1852	17·4	58·3	105·0	1895	15·0	52·7	95·3
1853	17·9	60·8	109·5	1896	15·7	54·8	99·2
1854	17·2	59·2	106·5	1897	16·0	55·2	100·3
1855	16·2	56·6	101·4	1898	16·2	55·5	100·7
1856	16·7	59·4	106·4	1899	16·5	55·8	101·5
1857	16·5	59·7	107·0	1900	16·0	53·7	97·4
1858	16·0	58·9	105·2	1901	15·9	53·1	96·1
1859	17·0	63·6	113·5	1902	15·9	52·9	96·1
1860	17·1	64·7	115·2	1903	15·7	52·0	94·9
1861	16·3	62·6	111·5	1904	15·3	50·5	92·3
1862	16·1	62·2	110·7	1905	15·3	50·6	92·3
1863	16·8	65·1	116·1	1906	15·7	51·7	94·3
1864	17·2	66·8	119·4	1907	15·9	52·3	95·2
1865	17·5	68·3	121·4	1908	15·1	49·3	89·7
1866	17·5	68·4	121·5	1909	14·7	47·9	87·1
1867	16·5	64·7	114·6	1910	15·0	48·5	88·5
1868	16·1	63·0	111·8	1911	15·2	49·4	89·8
1869	15·9	62·6	110·8	1912	15·6	—	—
1870	16·1	63·6	112·9	1913	15·7	—	—
1871	16·7	66·0	116·5	1914	15·9	—	—
1872	17·4	68·6	121·3	1915	19·4	—	—
1873	17·6	69·1	122·1	1916	14·9	—	—
1874	17·0	66·9	117·8	1917	13·8	—	—
1875	16·7	65·7	115·6	1918	15·3	—	—
1876	16·5	64·6	114·1	1919	19·8	—	—
1877	15·7	61·5	108·7	1920	20·2	—	—
1878	15·2	59·2	104·8	1921	16·9	64·8	115·6
1879	14·4	55·9	99·1	1922	15·7	59·6	106·5
1880	14·9	57·8	103·0	1923	15·2	57·3	102·6
1881	15·1	58·7	104·6	1924	15·3	57·3	102·5
1882	15·5	59·7	106·7	1925	15·2	56·3	100·6
1883	15·5	59·4	106·0	1926	14·3	52·5	93·6
1884	15·1	57·6	102·8	1927	15·7	57·1	101·8
1885	14·5	55·0	97·9	1928	15·4	55·3	98·5
1886	14·2	53·5	95·6	1929	15·8	56·3	100·6
1887	14·4	53·9	96·4	1930	15·8	55·9	99·7
1888	14·4	53·7	96·2	1931	15·6	54·5	98·0
1889	15·0	55·5	99·8	1932	15·3	52·9	95·2
1890	15·5	56·8	102·2	1933	15·8	53·6	97·9
1891	15·6	56·8	102·1	1934	16·9	58·1	105·1
1892	15·4	55·7	100·0	1935	17·1	58·9	—
1893	14·7	52·7	94·7				

A = Number of Marriages per 1,000 Total Population.

B = Number of Marriages per 1,000 Unmarried Males aged 15 years and over, standardized for the age-group 20–45 years.

C = Number of Marriages of Males aged 20 to 45 years per 1,000 Unmarried Males aged 20–45 years.

TABLE V

MARRIAGE RATES, ENGLAND AND WALES, 1851–1935

2. INDICES.—(a) ANNUAL RATES (1900 = 100)

	A	B	C		A	B	C
1851	107·5	105·4	104·7	1894	93·8	99·3	99·0
1852	108·8	108·6	107·8	1895	93·8	98·1	97·8
1853	111·9	113·2	112·4	1896	98·1	102·0	101·8
1854	107·5	110·2	109·3	1897	100·0	102·8	103·0
1855	101·3	105·4	104·1	1898	101·3	103·4	103·4
1856	104·4	110·6	109·2	1899	103·1	103·9	104·2
1857	103·1	111·2	110·3	1900	100·0	100·0	100·0
1858	100·0	109·7	108·0	1901	99·4	98·9	98·7
1859	106·3	118·4	116·5	1902	99·4	98·5	98·7
1860	106·9	120·5	118·3	1903	98·1	96·8	97·4
1861	101·9	116·6	114·5	1904	95·6	94·0	94·8
1862	100·6	115·8	113·7	1905	95·6	94·2	94·8
1863	105·0	121·2	119·2	1906	98·1	96·3	96·8
1864	107·5	124·4	122·6	1907	99·4	97·4	97·7
1865	109·4	127·2	124·6	1908	94·4	91·8	92·1
1866	109·4	127·4	124·7	1909	91·9	89·2	89·4
1867	103·1	120·5	117·7	1910	93·8	90·3	90·9
1868	100·6	117·3	114·8	1911	95·0	93·0	92·2
1869	99·4	116·6	113·8	1912	97·5	—	—
1870	100·6	118·4	115·9	1913	98·1	—	—
1871	104·4	122·9	119·6	1914	99·4	—	—
1872	108·8	127·7	124·5	1915	—	—	—
1873	110·0	128·7	125·4	1916	—	—	—
1874	106·3	124·6	120·9	1917	—	—	—
1875	104·4	122·3	118·7	1918	—	—	—
1876	103·1	120·3	117·1	1919	—	—	—
1877	98·1	114·5	111·6	1920	126·3	—	—
1878	95·0	110·2	107·4	1921	105·6	120·7	118·7
1879	90·0	104·1	101·1	1922	98·1	111·0	109·2
1880	93·1	107·6	105·8	1923	95·0	106·6	105·2
1881	94·4	109·3	107·4	1924	95·6	106·4	104·0
1882	96·9	111·2	109·5	1925	95·0	104·9	102·8
1883	96·9	110·6	108·8	1926	89·4	97·7	95·8
1884	94·4	107·3	105·5	1927	98·1	106·4	104·4
1885	90·6	102·4	100·5	1928	96·3	102·9	101·7
1886	88·8	99·6	98·2	1929	98·8	104·8	104·4
1887	90·0	100·4	99·0	1930	98·8	104·0	104·6
1888	90·0	100·0	98·8	1931	97·5	101·5	100·6
1889	93·8	103·4	102·5	1932	95·6	98·5	97·7
1890	96·9	105·8	104·9	1933	98·8	99·8	100·5
1891	97·5	105·8	104·8	1934	105·6	108·2	107·9
1892	96·3	103·7	102·7	1935	106·9	109·7	—
1893	91·9	98·1	97·2				

A = Crude Rates.
B = Rates for Unmarried Males 15 and over, standardized for age group 20–45 years.
C = Rates for Unmarried Males aged 20–45 years.

TABLE VI

MARRIAGE RATES, ENGLAND AND WALES, 1856–1933

3. TEN-YEAR MOVING AVERAGES

	A	B		A	B
1856	16·9	107·1	1895	15·6	99·2
1857	16·8	108·1	1896	15·6	98·8
1858	16·7	108·7	1897	15·7	98·2
1859	16·6	109·3	1898	15·7	97·8
1860	16·6	110·6	1899	15·8	97·8
1861	16·7	112·7	1900	15·8	97·3
1862	16·8	114·2	1901	15·8	97·0
1863	16·8	115·0	1902	15·8	96·5
1864	16·8	115·6	1903	15·8	96·0
1865	16·7	115·3	1904	15·7	94·9
1866	16·6	115·1	1905	15·6	93·4
1867	16·7	115·6	1906	15·5	92·5
1868	16·8	116·6	1907	15·4	91·9
1869	16·9	117·2	1908	15·4	—
1870	16·8	117·1	1909	15·4	—
1871	16·8	116·5	1910	—	—
1872	16·7	115·8	1911	—	—
1873	16·6	115·2	1912	—	—
1874	16·5	114·4	1913	—	—
1875	16·3	113·1	1914	—	—
1876	16·2	112·0	1915	—	—
1877	16·0	110·8	1916	—	—
1878	15·8	109·4	1917	—	—
1879	15·6	107·9	1918	—	—
1880	15·5	106·4	1919	—	—
1881	15·2	104·6	1920	—	—
1882	15·0	102·8	1921	—	—
1883	14·9	101·6	1922	—	—
1884	14·8	100·7	1923	15·7	105·5
1885	14·9	100·8	1924	15·1	101·1
1886	14·9	100·7	1925	15·2	100·2
1887	15·0	100·5	1926	15·2	99·4
1888	15·0	99·9	1927	15·3	99·0
1889	14·9	98·8	1928	15·4	98·8
1890	14·9	98·1	1929	15·7	99·7
1891	14·9	97·9	1930	15·6	98·4
1892	15·1	98·2	1931	15·7	98·2
1893	15·3	98·6	1932	15·9	99·2
1894	15·4	99·0	1933	16·1	—

A = Crude Marriage Rates.
B = Marriage Rates for Unmarried Males aged 20–45 years.
In the Post-War Period Five-Year Moving Averages are used.

TABLE VII

MARRIAGE RATES, ENGLAND AND WALES, 1856–1933

4. INDICES.—(b) TEN-YEAR MOVING AVERAGES (1900 = 100)

	A	B		A	B
1856	107·0	110·1	1895	98·7	102·0
1857	106·3	111·1	1896	98·7	101·5
1858	105·7	111·7	1897	99·4	100·9
1859	105·1	112·3	1898	99·4	100·5
1860	105·1	113·7	1899	100·0	100·5
1861	105·7	115·8	1900	100·0	100·0
1862	106·3	117·4	1901	100·0	99·7
1863	106·3	118·2	1902	100·0	99·2
1864	106·3	118·8	1903	100·0	98·7
1865	105·7	118·5	1904	99·4	97·5
1866	105·1	118·3	1905	98·7	96·0
1867	105·7	118·8	1906	98·1	95·1
1868	106·3	119·8	1907	97·5	94·5
1869	107·0	120·5	1908	97·5	—
1870	106·3	120·3	1909	97·5	—
1871	106·3	119·7	1910	—	—
1872	105·7	119·0	1911	—	—
1873	105·1	118·4	1912	—	—
1874	104·4	117·6	1913	—	—
1875	103·2	116·2	1914	—	—
1876	102·5	115·1	1915	—	—
1877	101·3	113·9	1916	—	—
1878	100·0	112·4	1917	—	—
1879	98·7	110·9	1918	—	—
1880	98·1	109·4	1919	—	—
1881	96·2	107·5	1920	—	—
1882	94·9	105·7	1921	—	—
1883	94·3	104·4	1922	—	—
1884	93·7	103·5	1923	99·4	108·4
1885	94·3	103·6	1924	95·6	103·9
1886	94·3	103·5	1925	96·2	103·0
1887	94·9	103·3	1926	96·2	102·2
1888	94·9	102·7	1927	96·8	101·7
1889	94·3	101·5	1928	97·5	101·5
1890	94·3	100·8	1929	99·4	102·5
1891	94·3	100·6	1930	98·7	101·1
1892	95·6	100·9	1931	99·4	100·9
1893	96·8	101·3	1932	100·6	102·0
1894	97·5	101·7	1933	101·9	—

A = Crude Marriage Rates.
B = Marriage Rates per 1,000 Unmarried Males aged 20–45 years.
In the Post-War Period Five-Year Moving Averages are used.

TABLE VIII

MARRIAGE RATES, ENGLAND AND WALES, 1856–1932

5. DEVIATIONS FROM TEN-YEAR MOVING AVERAGES

(*Moving Average is 100 in each year*)

	A	B		A	B
1856	98·8	99·3	1895	96·2	96·1
1857	98·2	99·0	1896	100·6	100·4
1858	95·8	96·8	1897	101·9	102·1
1859	102·4	103·8	1898	103·2	103·0
1860	103·0	104·2	1899	104·4	103·8
1861	97·6	98·9	1900	101·3	100·1
1862	95·8	96·9	1901	100·6	99·1
1863	100·0	101·0	1902	100·6	99·6
1864	102·4	103·3	1903	99·4	98·9
1865	104·8	105·3	1904	97·5	97·3
1866	105·4	105·6	1905	98·1	98·8
1867	98·8	99·1	1906	101·3	101·9
1868	95·8	95·9	1907	103·2	103·6
1869	94·1	94·5	1908	98·1	—
1870	95·8	96·4	1909	95·5	—
1871	99·4	100·0	1910	—	—
1872	104·2	104·7	1911	—	—
1873	106·0	106·0	1912	—	—
1874	103·0	103·0	1913	—	—
1875	102·5	102·2	1914	—	—
1876	101·9	101·9	1915	—	—
1877	98·1	98·1	1916	—	—
1878	96·2	95·8	1917	—	—
1879	92·3	91·8	1918	—	—
1880	96·1	96·8	1919	—	—
1881	99·3	100·0	1920	—	—
1882	103·3	103·8	1921	—	—
1883	104·0	104·3	1922	—	—
1884	102·0	102·1	1923	96·8	97·3
1885	97·3	97·1	1924	101·3	101·4
1886	95·3	94·9	1925	100·0	100·4
1887	96·0	95·9	1926	94·1	94·2
1888	96·0	96·3	1927	102·6	102·8
1889	100·7	101·0	1928	100·0	99·7
1890	104·0	104·2	1929	100·6	100·9
1891	104·7	104·3	1930	101·3	101·3
1892	102·0	101·8	1931	99·4	99·8
1893	96·1	96·0	1932	96·2	96·0
1894	97·4	97·4			

A = Crude Marriage Rates.

B = Marriage Rates per 1,000 Unmarried Males aged 20–45 years.

In the Post-War Period, Deviations from Five-Year Moving Averages are used.

TABLE IX

ENGLAND AND WALES, 1851–1934

MARRIAGES OF MALES AGED 20–24 YEARS

	A	A'	B	B'	C		A	A'	B	B'	C
1851	112·7	126·5	—	—	—	1889	95·0	106·6	94·2	108·0	100·8
1852	114·8	128·8	—	—	—	1890	96·8	108·6	92·8	106·4	104·3
1853	119·3	133·9	—	—	—	1891	95·4	107·1	91·7	105·2	104·0
1854	115·1	129·2	—	—	—	1892	92·5	103·8	91·4	104·8	101·2
1855	107·0	120·1	—	—	—	1893	86·0	96·5	91·2	104·6	94·3
1856	111·9	125·6	114·3	131·1	97·9	1894	88·0	98·8	91·2	104·6	96·5
1857	113·1	126·9	114·5	131·3	98·8	1895	86·5	97·1	91·0	104·4	95·1
1858	110·5	124·0	114·5	131·3	96·5	1896	90·5	101·6	90·2	103·4	100·3
1859	118·5	133·0	114·8	131·7	103·2	1897	90·9	102·0	89·3	102·4	101·8
1860	120·0	134·7	116·0	133·0	103·4	1898	91·7	102·9	88·4	101·4	103·7
1861	114·3	128·3	118·2	135·6	96·7	1899	91·9	103·1	88·0	100·9	104·4
1862	115·0	129·1	119·9	137·5	95·9	1900	89·1	100·0	87·2	100·0	102·2
1863	122·0	136·9	120·5	138·2	101·2	1901	86·0	96·0	86·5	99·4	99·4
1864	126·6	142·1	121·2	139·0	104·5	1902	82·6	92·7	85·7	98·3	96·4
1865	128·5	144·2	120·9	138·6	106·3	1903	82·6	92·7	84·9	97·4	97·3
1866	129·1	144·9	120·8	138·5	106·9	1904	80·5	90·3	83·5	95·8	96·4
1867	119·8	134·5	121·6	139·4	98·5	1905	79·9	89·7	81·6	93·6	97·9
1868	117·5	131·9	123·0	141·1	95·5	1906	82·0	92·0	80·1	91·9	102·4
1869	116·1	130·3	124·0	142·2	93·6	1907	82·5	92·6	78·9	90·5	104·6

Year	A	A'	B	B'	C
1870	118·5	133·0	124·0	142·2	95·6
1871	122·5	137·5	123·6	141·7	99·1
1872	129·0	144·8	122·8	140·8	105·0
1873	132·1	148·3	122·4	140·4	107·9
1874	126·6	142·1	121·6	139·4	104·1
1875	123·6	138·7	120·1	137·7	102·9
1876	121·5	136·4	118·8	136·2	102·3
1877	116·0	130·2	117·2	134·4	99·0
1878	110·6	124·1	115·3	132·2	95·9
1879	103·2	115·8	112·9	129·5	91·4
1880	106·8	119·9	110·5	126·7	96·7
1881	107·0	120·1	107·9	123·7	99·2
1882	109·4	122·8	105·1	120·5	104·1
1883	107·2	120·3	102·8	117·9	104·3
1884	102·9	115·5	100·9	115·7	102·0
1885	96·9	108·8	100·1	114·8	96·8
1886	93·4	104·8	99·1	113·6	94·2
1887	93·3	104·7	98·0	112·4	95·2
1888	91·6	102·8	96·4	110·6	95·0
1908	77·2	88·6			
1909	73·6	82·6			
1910	73·2	82·2			
1911	74·3	83·4			
1921	94·6	106·2			
1922	85·8	96·3			
1923	83·9	94·2	85·8	98·4	97·8
1924	83·8	94·1	82·0	94·0	102·2
1925	81·7	91·7	81·0	92·9	100·9
1926	75·3	84·5	79·5	91·2	94·7
1927	80·4	90·2	78·1	89·6	102·9
1928	76·6	86·0	76·8	88·1	99·7
1929	76·8	86·2	76·3	87·5	100·7
1930	75·2	84·4	74·2	85·1	101·3
1931	72·7	81·6	73·0	83·7	99·6
1932	69·9	78·5	72·7	83·4	96·1
1933	70·5	79·1			
1934	75·2	84·4			

A = Annual Rates.

A' = Annual Rates, Indices, Base = 1900 = 100.

B = Ten-Year Moving Averages (in the Post-War Period, Five-Year Moving Averages are used).

B' = Ten-Year Moving Averages, Indices, Base = 1900 = 100.

C = Deviations of Annual Rates from Moving Averages (Moving Average = 100 in each year).

TABLE X

ENGLAND AND WALES, 1851–1934

MARRIAGES OF MALES AGED 45–54 YEARS

	A	A'	B	B'	C
1851	36·0	105·3	—	—	—
1852	37·3	109·1	—	—	—
1853	39·3	114·9	—	—	—
1854	38·5	112·6	—	—	—
1855	38·8	113·5	—	—	—
1856	38·7	113·2	38·9	118·2	99·5
1857	38·6	112·9	39·4	119·8	89·0
1858	38·5	112·6	39·6	120·4	97·2
1859	41·8	122·2	39·7	120·7	105·3
1860	41·3	120·8	40·0	121·6	103·3
1861	41·0	119·9	40·6	123·4	101·0
1862	39·4	115·2	41·1	124·9	95·9
1863	40·4	118·1	41·5	126·1	97·3
1864	41·8	122·2	41·7	126·7	100·2
1865	44·3	129·5	41·6	126·4	106·5
1866	44·0	128·7	41·5	126·1	106·0
1867	42·3	123·7	41·9	127·4	101·0
1868	40·5	118·4	42·4	128·9	95·5
1869	40·9	119·6	42·9	130·4	95·3

	A	A'	B	B'	C
1889	36·8	107·6	37·0	112·5	99·5
1890	38·7	113·2	36·8	111·9	105·2
1891	38·8	113·5	36·4	110·6	106·6
1892	38·1	111·4	36·3	110·3	105·0
1893	35·9	105·0	36·1	109·7	99·4
1894	34·7	101·5	35·9	109·1	96·7
1895	34·4	100·6	35·5	107·9	96·9
1896	34·5	100·9	35·1	106·7	98·3
1897	33·6	98·2	34·7	105·5	96·8
1898	34·0	99·4	34·1	103·6	99·7
1899	33·4	97·7	33·6	102·1	99·4
1900	34·2	100·0	32·9	100·0	104·0
1901	34·7	101·5	32·4	98·5	107·1
1902	32·2	94·2	32·0	97·3	100·6
1903	30·6	89·5	31·6	96·0	96·8
1904	28·6	83·6	31·2	94·8	91·7
1905	29·3	85·7	30·7	93·3	95·4
1906	30·0	87·7	30·1	91·5	99·7
1907	30·3	88·6	29·6	90·0	102·4

Year	A	A'	B	B'	C	Year	A	A'	B	B'	C
1870	41·0	119·9	43·2	131·3	94·9	1908	29·3	85·7	—	—	—
1871	44·0	128·7	43·3	131·6	101·6	1909	28·5	83·3	—	—	—
1872	44·4	129·8	43·4	131·9	102·3	1910	28·8	84·2	—	—	—
1873	45·5	133·0	43·4	131·9	104·8	1911	29·1	85·1	—	—	—
1874	45·4	132·7	43·3	131·6	104·8						
1875	45·3	132·5	43·0	130·7	105·3	1921	34·8	101·8	—	—	—
1876	44·8	131·0	42·7	129·8	104·9	1922	32·3	94·4	—	—	—
1877	41·6	121·6	42·1	128·0	98·8	1923	30·8	90·1	32·2	97·9	95·7
1878	40·3	117·8	41·5	126·1	97·1	1924	31·7	92·7	31·3	95·1	101·3
1879	38·2	111·7	40·7	123·7	93·9	1925	31·5	92·1	31·3	95·1	100·6
1880	37·6	109·9	39·8	121·0	94·5	1926	30·2	88·3	31·6	96·0	95·6
1881	38·3	112·0	39·1	118·8	98·0	1927	32·5	95·0	31·7	96·4	102·5
1882	38·4	112·3	38·2	116·1	100·5	1928	32·0	93·6	31·8	96·7	100·6
1883	37·5	109·6	37·6	114·3	99·7	1929	32·2	94·2	31·9	97·0	100·9
1884	36·9	107·9	37·1	112·8	99·5	1930	32·1	93·9	31·3	95·1	102·6
1885	37·8	110·5	37·0	112·5	102·2	1931	30·7	89·8	31·1	94·5	98·7
1886	35·4	103·5	37·1	112·8	95·4	1932	29·3	85·7	31·0	94·2	94·5
1887	35·6	104·1	37·2	113·1	95·7	1933	31·0	90·6	—	—	—
1888	36·1	105·6	37·2	113·1	97·0	1934	32·0	93·6	—	—	—

A = Annual Rates.

A' = Annual Rates, Indices, Base = 1900 = 100.

B = Ten-Year Moving Averages (in the Post-War Period Five-Year Moving Averages are used).

B' = Ten-Year Moving Averages, Indices, Base = 1900 = 100.

C = Deviations of Annual Rates from Moving Averages (Moving Average = 100 in each year).

place, there is not much divergence between Dr. Thomas's coefficients for 1854 to 1874 and 1895 to 1913. Our own coefficients for analogous periods are, however, quite dissimilar: + 0·870 for 1856–1873, and + 0·603 for 1890–1907. Secondly, whereas the coefficients used by Dr. Thomas show the strongest relationship for the period 1875 to 1894, those computed on the basis of fluctuations in real wages show the peak in period 1856 to 1873, and decline consistently from then to 1907. In explaining the differences between Dr. Thomas's results and those obtained by using an index of real wages, it is important to consider the analysis which Dr. Thomas herself gave of the trend of her coefficients. She noticed two main factors. First, 50 per cent of the population of England and Wales lived in rural districts in 1851, while by 1891 this proportion had fallen to only 28 per cent. In the first period there was, therefore, a strongly agricultural population which, she believed, would be less affected by business cycles than the more industrialized population of the later period. Secondly, changes in the economic and social *milieu* towards the end of the century tended to lessen the burdens which marriage implied for the husband. Of these the most important, according to Dr. Thomas, was "the development of effective methods of birth-control and the gradual diffusion of the knowledge of these methods."

Reconsideration of the factors mentioned above tends to increase the probable validity of our own correlation coefficients. In the first place, although a strongly agricultural population might not be markedly influenced by business cycles,[1] it might be very responsive to changes in real wages. This would be even more likely when, as was the case in earlier sections of the period under analysis, it was the custom for marriages to yield a relatively large number of children. The growth of industry and commerce saw the passing of Acts prohibiting child labour, and the introduction of compulsory education. Both these changes reduced the economic value of children. At the same time the struggle of parents for higher standards of life for themselves and their children gave a considerable basis for any tendencies to reduce the size of families. If, when Dr.

---

[1] Though even here it depends upon the type of agricultural economy. An agricultural system based largely upon hired labour and catering mainly for export would be very strongly affected. And even an economy which produced only for the home market would be severely hurt by a depression which, like that of the 1870's, saw the home market flooded with foreign agricultural produce.

Thomas speaks of the development and diffusion of effective methods of birth-control, she is referring to contraception in its modern sense, it is doubtful if her argument is realistic. It is not very probable, even at the present time, that modern methods of contraception are used by the bulk of the population, and it is highly unlikely that the Bradlaugh–Besant trial was followed by any considerable increase in the use of contraceptives. What is far more likely is that the Bradlaugh–Besant trial acted as a crystallizer of public opinion, and made clear the personal disadvantages of large families. Such a change in *mores* would increase the use of the methods of birth-prevention which were already well known, that is, especially of abortion. The references given by Dr. Ethel Elderton in her monumental work[1] clearly point to a wide popular knowledge of many crude and harmful, but nevertheless effective, methods of abortion with which to supplement the practice of *coitus interruptus*. With this change in *mores* it is only to be expected that the marriage rate should become less strongly linked to fluctuations in real wages. The smaller the size of the family the less would children have to be taken into account in forecasting the possible expenses entailed by marriage.

At the beginning of this paper two further analyses of marriage frequency were mentioned—the marriages of males aged 20 to 24 years and of those aged 45 to 54 years. Relatively speaking, the marriage rates for both these age-groups were considerably higher than the general rate for males aged 20 to 44 years before the war, and considerably lower after it. For males aged 20 to 24 years this change is a function of the rise in the age at marriage. For males aged 45 to 54 years it is probably due to the decrease in the number of children born to a marriage. Since most of these males are widowers, the possibility of remarriage would be greatest if a number of young children had been left from the first marriage. Among the working class in particular, remarriage would be a method of obtaining an unpaid housekeeper to look after the children. With the fall in the size of the family this factor has lost much of its importance, and thus correspondingly reduced the relevant marriage rate.

The correlations between oscillations in these rates and changes in real wages are shown below.

[1] "Report on the English Birth Rate," Part 1, England North of the Humber (*Eugenics Laboratory Memoirs*, XIX and XX, 1914).

INDEX OF REAL WAGES AND

		(A) Marriages of Males aged 20–24 Years	(B) Marriages of Males aged 45–54 Years
(1)	1956–1932	+ 0·737 ± 0·059	+ 0·716 ± 0·064
(2)	1856–1873	+ 0·871 ± 0·057	+ 0·768 ± 0·097
(3)	1873–1890	+ 0·702 ± 0·120	+ 0·876 ± 0·055
(4)	1890–1907	+ 0·661 ± 0·133	+ 0·692 ± 0·123
(5)	1926–1932	+ 0·686 ± 0·200	+ 0·562 ± 0·259

For the marriages of males aged 20 to 24 years the coefficients show the same general decline between 1856 and 1907 as was noted in the earlier analysis. The coefficient for the whole period is slightly higher than in the case of the general marriage rate, this being due to the considerably stronger relationship shown for the section 1890 to 1907. If this difference has any real meaning, it is probably connected with class changes in the age at marriage. The rise in the average age at marriage towards the end of the nineteenth century probably affected the middle class most of all. In that case the males marrying between the ages of 20 and 24 years would consist more largely of members of the working class than in previous periods, and a stronger correlation between marriage and real wages would be expected.

The course of the correlation coefficients for the marriages of males aged 45 to 54 years has probably been influenced by three main factors. In the first period, 1856 to 1873, the results of the unhealthy conditions in factories and towns promoted by the Industrial Revolution were still being felt. They were probably most clearly apparent in the average length of life of men in different social classes. It is likely, therefore, that the large proportion of the males aged 45 to 54 years belonged to economic grades which were not closely affected by changes in real wages.[1] The increasing general expectation of life, the result no less of the extension of public health services than of the progress of curative medicine, would gradually raise the proportion of working-class males in the older age-groups as the end of the century was approached, and two other factors would tend to strengthen the correlation coefficients. First, the

---

[1] For information concerning the average age at death of the various social classes in the early nineteenth century, see the *First Report of the Commissioners for Inquiring into the State of Large Towns and Populous Districts*, 1844, p. 411, and Appendix, pp. 99 and 149–50. Also the Supplement to the *Report on the Sanitary Conditions of the Labouring Population of Great Britain*, Appendix 11.

bulk of the males who marry between the ages of 45 and 54 years are widowers, and their desire to remarry is influenced by motives rather different from those affecting younger and hitherto unmarried men. It is likely that they would be more strongly affected by changes in prosperity than the younger men. Secondly, men in these older age-groups are probably at the peak of their earnings. The onset of depression would therefore make them ripe for dismissal in an attempt on the part of employers to reduce costs, and their ability to undertake marriage would be more closely related to changes in prosperity.

CONCLUSION

Although the whole period, 1856 to 1932, showed a close connection between marriage and prosperity, it is evident that this connection was becoming more tenuous with the approach of the twentieth century. Although the figures for the present time are not adequate for accurate analysis, there is no reason to believe that this tendency has been reversed. On the contrary, the increase in employment of women, the extension of unemployment and health insurance, and the declining fertility of marriage should reinforce the tendency. So far as the future is concerned, two possible factors may work still more in the same direction. The invention of a really efficient contraceptive would do so. On the other hand, a similar effect would also be produced by the introduction of family allowances or other forms of subsidy for the same purpose.

SUMMARY

1. A refined general marriage rate—the number of marriages of males aged 20 to 44 years per 1,000 unmarried males in the same age-group—shows considerable differences from the marriage trends apparent in the crude marriage rate.
2. But the correlations of annual deviations of both these rates from their ten-year moving averages with comparable deviations from an index of real wages (discounted for unemployment) shows little difference.
3. The correlations were high for the whole period 1856 to 1932 and showed a consistent decrease of intensity in successive periods during the nineteenth century. This is probably explained by

the changes in social *mores*, and does not conflict with the somewhat different results obtained by Dr. Thomas.

4. Similar correlations for the marriages of males aged 20 to 24 years do not show much difference from coefficients obtained with the general marriage rate. But for the marriages of males aged 45 to 54 years, markedly higher coefficients were found for the periods 1873 to 1890 and 1890 to 1907.

5. There is reason to believe that the relation between real wages and marriage will continue to decrease in importance in the future.

CHAPTER VII

BRITISH DEMOGRAPHERS' OPINIONS ON FERTILITY,
1660 to 1760[1]

by

R. R. KUCZYNSKI

FECUNDITY AND FERTILITY

THERE was a consensus of opinion among British demographers in the century preceding the Industrial Revolution that fertility, i.e. the actual production of children, lagged considerably behind fecundity, i.e. the child-bearing capacity. Some writers of the period thought that this had always been so. Thus David Hume ([15], p. 159) states (1752) that "there is in all men, both male and female, a desire and power of generation more active than is ever universally exerted." Other writers rather emphasize the big gap between fecundity and fertility in the England of their time as compared with former periods or with the American colonies. Most demographers contented themselves with pointing to the fact, but some made attempts actually to measure fecundity.

Reproductive Age

The founder of vital statistics, John Graunt (1662), estimated ([10], pp. 49, 60) the child-bearing period at 25 years ("between 16 and 40, or between 20 and 44"), and the reproductive period of men at 40 years.

Sir William Petty (1671) in a fragment "Observations" ([23], **2**, 232-3) and at one place in *A Treatise of Ireland*, 1687 ([22], **2**, 603), likewise counts 25 years for females and 40 years for males, but at another place of the *Treatise* ([22], **2**, 604), and in a manuscript of the same year, "Magnalia Regni" ([23], **1**, 267), figures the child-bearing period at 27 years (between 18 and 44 years). In *Another Essay in Political Arithmetick*, 1682 ([19], p. 13), he assumes 30 years to be the reproductive period for women (15 to 44 years) and 42 years for men (18 to 59 years), and in "An Essay for the Emprovement of London, 1687" he speaks of the "teeming women of between 16 and 45 years old" ([23], **1**, 34).

---

[1] Reprinted by permission of Professor R. A. Fisher from the *Annals of Eugenics*, 1935.

Edmund Halley (1693) considers ([13], p. 656) 29 years as the child-bearing period ("above 16 and under 45").

Thomas Short (1750) states ([25], p. 71) that "Women are generally sooner marriagable than Men by four or five Years." On the other hand ([25], p. 72) men "are longer capable of Procreation; for if they have a good Constitution, and have lived temperately and chastly in their Youth, they are capable till 80 or 90; Women seldom beyond 45, but very rarely above 50." He reckons ([25], p. 247) the child-bearing period at 30 years ("between 15 Years of Age and 45").

Reproductive Capacity

Graunt (1662), having ascertained ([10], pp. 48–9) that in London the baptisms of boys exceeded those of girls "by about a thirteenth part," states that "a man be *Prolifique* fourty years, and a woman but five and twenty, which makes the Males to be as 560 to 325 Females." He adds, however, that the excess of males over females at the reproductive age is actually smaller because "more men die violent deaths then women, that is, more are slain in Wars, killed by mischance, drowned at Sea, and die by the Hand of Justice. More-over, more men go to Colonies, and travel into foreign parts, then women." As to the married women at child-bearing age, he estimated them at one-sixteenth of the total population.[1]

---

[1] The method ([10], p. 60) through which he obtained this result was as follows: "I considered, that the number of *Child-bearing women* might be about double to the *Births*: forasmuch as such women, one with another, have scarce more then one Childe in two years. The number of *Births* I found, by those years, wherein the *Registries* were well kept, to have been somewhat less then the *Burials*. The *Burials* in these late years at a *Medium* are about 13000, and consequently the *Christnings* not above 12000. I therefore esteemed the number of *Teeming women* to be 24000: then I imagined, that there might be twice as many Families, as of such women; for that there might be twice as many women *Aged* between 16 and 76, as between 16 and 40, or between 20 and 44; and that there were about eight Persons in a Family, one with another, *viz.* the Man, and his Wife, three Children, and three Servants, or Lodgers: now 8 times 48000 makes 384000."

This estimate probably includes "the 97 Parishes within the Walls"; "the 16 Parishes without the Walls, standing part within the Liberties, and part without: in Middlesex, and Surrey"; and ten "out Parishes, in Middlesex, and Surrey," situated without the liberties but adjacent to London. It does not include the city of Westminster and the six circumjacent parishes of Islington, Lambeth, Stepney, Newington, Hackney, and Redriff. Graunt estimated the population of all the 130 parishes "in and about London" at 460,000. ([10], pp. 6–7, 10, 42, 62–3; see also "An Appendix" to 3rd ed. (1665), p. 161.)

Graunt assumed for London proper 384,000 inhabitants, 24,000 married women of child-bearing age, and 12,000 yearly births. This implies a birth-rate of 31¼ per 1,000, and a fertility rate for married women at child-bearing age of 500 per 1,000. It is possible that he guessed the birth-rate right; but he doubtless underestimated the number of married women at child-bearing age, and he doubtless overestimated their fertility rate.[1]

[1] According to the census of 1851, the first at which the civil condition was ascertained, the married women between 15 and 40 years constituted two-nineteenths and those of between 20 and 45 years one-eighth of the total population of London (see *Census of Great Britain, 1851, Population Tables II, Ages, Civil Condition, Occupations, and Birth-Place of the People,* **1**, 1, 6).

It may be mentioned incidentally that Graunt very likely also underestimated the proportion of females among the total population and the number of men at reproductive age.

Having ascertained that "from the year 1628, to the year 1662, *exclusivè*, . . . there have been Christned . . . 139782 Males, and but 130866 Females" (p. 47), he says: "We have (though perhaps too much at Random) determined the number of the inhabitants of London to be about 384000: the which being granted, we assert, that 199112 are Males, and 184886 Females" (p. 61). Graunt apparêntly took it for granted that the ratio of males to females in the total population of London corresponded to the sex proportion at birth (14 : 13). Gregory King (1696) ([16], p. 39) perhaps came nearer to the truth when, 34 years later, he estimated the ratio of males to females at 10 to 13. According to the census of 1801, the ratio was 10 : 12 (see *Abstract of the Answers and Returns, Made persuant to . . . "An Act for taking an Account of the Population of Great Britain, and the Increase or Diminution thereof,"* p. 503, London, 1802).

As to the men at reproductive age, Graunt did not explicitly compute their numbers, but he apparently assumed that they comprised one-third only of the total male population. He had indeed, after a fashion, constructed a life table according to which 40 per cent of all newly born survived the age of 16 years and 6 per cent the age of 56 years: "there are therefore of Aged between 16, and 56, the number of 40, less by six, *viz.* 34 . . . Wherefore, supposing there be 199112 Males, and the number between 16, and 56, being 34; it follows, there are 34 per Cent. of all those Males fighting Men in London, that is 67694, *viz.* near 70000" (p. 62). Westergaard rightly objects: "He does not see that he has found the number of *deaths* between the two ages, instead of the number of *living*"; and shows that the proportion of living between 16 and 56 years, according to Graunt's life table, was 41 per cent (see Harald Westergaard, *Contributions to the History of Statistics,* p. 23, London, 1932). But quite apart from that, Graunt makes here the mistake of assuming an equal mortality for males and females. He does, moreover, not realize that, as a consequence of the large influx of country people to London (and for many other reasons), the actual age composition of the population of London differed very much from the age composition of the stationary population derived from a life table. It is safe to assume that the males between 16 and 56 years actually constituted the majority of the male population of London.

Petty ([(22)], **2**, 604), in one passage of *A Treatise of Ireland*, 1687, follows rather closely Graunt's argument. He first states: "That in Mankind at London, there are 14 Males for 13 Females, and because Males are prolific 40 Years, and Females but 25, there are in Effect 560 Males for 325 Females." He then assumes for London 684,000 inhabitants, "above" 114,000 women of child-bearing age, "above" 38,000 married women at child-bearing age, and "about" 19,000 births.[1]

This implies a birth-rate of 27·8, a general fertility rate of less than 167 for 1,000 women at child-bearing age, and a fertility rate of less than 500 for 1,000 married women at child-bearing age. This tendency to estimate fecundity lower than Graunt had done is more evident still in Petty's independent attempts to measure fecundity:

(1) *Another Essay in Political Arithmetick*, 1682. Assuming as a maximum that "in the Countrey" 25 are born per 600 people (see p. 314), he argues as follows ([(19)], pp. 13–14):

I might here Insert, That although the Births in this last Computation be 25 of 600, or a Twenty fourth part of the People; yet that in Natural possibility, they may be near thrice as many, and near 75. For that by some late *Observations*, the *Teeming* Females between 15 and 44, are about 180 of the said 600, and the *Males* of between 18 and 59, are about 180 also, and that every Teeming *Woman* can bear a *Child* once in two Years; from all which it is plain, that the *Births* may be 90 (and abating 15 for *Sickness*, Young *Abortions*, and *Natural Barrenness*) there may remain 75 Births, which is an Eighth of the People; which by some Observations we have found to be but a *two and thirtieth part*, or but a *quarter* of what is thus shewn to be Naturally possible.

Petty here assumes that the women at child-bearing age (15–44 years) and the males at reproductive age (18–59 years) constitute 30 per cent each of the total population and that there might be 5 yearly births for every 12 women at child-bearing age. He thus indicates that "in Natural possibility" the birth-rate may be 125—four times as much as in London, and three times as much as in the country—and the general fertility rate 417.[2]

---

[1] ". . . if there be about 19000 Births per Ann. at London, the Number of the marry'd teeming Women must be above 38000; and of the whole Stock of the Teeming Women must be above 114000, and of the whole People Six Times as many vizt 684000 . . ." ([(22)], **2**, 605). This estimate apparently comprises 134 parishes (see [(20)], p. 21).

[2] Petty did not then realize that if the general fertility rate were so much higher, the age constitution would differ very much from what it actually was, so that the birth-rate would by no means increase proportionally.

(2) In "An Essay for the Emprovement of London, 1687" Petty states that of the total population of 720,000 "180^m are males of between 16 and 60 yeares old," and "140 are teeming women of between 16 and 45 years old, who may beare 40^m children per annum, or above double the present number" ([23], **1**, 34).[1] Petty's judgment about the proportion of the males and females at reproductive age is here certainly sounder; he estimates the proportion of males between 16 and 60 years at 25 per cent (instead of 30 per cent for those between 18 and 59 years),[2] and the proportion of females between 16 and 45 years at 19 or 20 per cent (instead at 30 per cent for those between 15 and 44 years). His figures indicate that the birth-rate might be 56 per cent and the general fertility rate 286—2⅔ times of what, he here assumes, they were in London; but he probably did not intend to suggest that this was the maximum that might possibly be attained.

(3) In *A Treatise of Ireland*, 1687 [21] Petty contends:

1. The sixth Part of the People are teeming Women of between 18 and 44 Years old.

2. It is found by Observation That but ⅓ Part or between 30 and 40 of the teeming Women are Married.

3. That a Teeming Woman, at a Medium, bear a child every two Years and a half ([22], **2**, 604).

He thus reduces the proportion of women at child-bearing age to 16⅔ per cent of the total population.[3] If all these women were married, the birth-rate would be 66⅔, and the general fertility rate 400. But according to him, one-third only of the women at child-bearing age are married.[4] He assumes here that the married women

---

[1] He figures the "registered christenings" in the 137 parishes which this estimate covers at 15,000 only.

[2] In "Magnalia Regni" (1687) ([23], **1**, 268) he likewise assumes that in Great Britain and Ireland the males between 16 and 60 years constitute 25 per cent of the total population. This assumption agrees well with the estimate of Gregory King (1696) who figures that 1,310,000, or 24 per cent of the population of England (5,500,000), were males between 16 and 60 ([16], p. 40).

[3] In 1671 he even states that in England the "males aged between 16 and 60" constitute only one-sixth of the total population; see the fragment "Observations" ([23], **2**, 239).

[4] We also find in the draft of an essay "Concerning Marriages": "The way of marriage is now such, that of 100 capable women only 32 are maryed . . ." ([23], **2**, 49). See further "Magnalia Regni" (1687): "Now though there be in
[*Continued at foot of p.* 288.

at child-bearing age (18–44 years) constitute one-eighteenth only of the total population, which is still less than the one-sixteenth assumed by Graunt (16–40 or 20–44 years).[1]

Petty, then, seems inclined to estimate the maximum possible fertility rate at 400 or 417 per 1,000 women at child-bearing age. He is less consistent in his statements on the actual birth-rate and general fertility rate of London. His figures in *Another Essay in Political Arithmetick* indicate a birth-rate of 31¼ (agreeing with Graunt) and a general fertility rate of 104 (per 1,000 females of 15–44 years). In "An Essay for the Emprovement of London" he suggests a birth-rate of about 21 and a general fertility rate of about 107 (per 1,000 females of 16–45 years)[2]. In *A Treatise of Ireland* he indicates a birth-rate of about 22 and a general fertility rate of about 133 (per 1,000 females of 18–44 years). But at another place of the same *Treatise* he indicates a birth-rate of about 28 (and a general fertility rate of less than 167).

His statement in *Another Essay in Political Arithmetick* that the number of births in London is only one-quarter of what would be "Naturally possible" implies that the fertility rate even of married women lagged behind their fecundity rate. In his draft of an essay "Concerning Marriages" he explicitly says so by asserting that each 32 married women of child-bearing age "brought 11 children per annum, whereas 100 teeming women may well bring 40 children per annum" ([23], **2**, 49).

---

efect 112 males for 65 females, yett it is found by observation that but between 30 & 40 of the teeming women are att present married . . ." ([23], **1**, 267). It is hard to believe that the proportion of married women among the females at child-bearing age should actually have been so low. According to Gregory King ([16], p. 39), the married women of all ages constituted about 35 per cent of the total female population of London. According to the census of 1851 that proportion for London was 33 per cent, and about 52 per cent of the women between 18 and 44 years were married (*Census* 1851, *Population Tables II*, **1**, 1, 6).

[1] As to Ireland, however, he assumes that "about ¹⁄₁₂ are maryed teeming women" (see "Heads of Irish Revenue" ([23], **1**, 96). See further *A Treatise of Ireland*, 1687 ([22], **2**, 608): "For in England, the Proportion of Marry'd Teeming Women, is not so great as in Ireland; Where they marry upon the first Capacity, without staying for Portions, Jointures, Settlements, &c." See also William Brakenridge ([5], p. 878): "But in Scotland and Ireland this increase may be reasonably supposed to be more, in proportion as there are more marriages than in England" (see further ibid., p. 884).

[2] He similarly indicates a general fertility rate of 110 in the draft of an essay "Concerning Marriages" ([23], **2**, 49).

Halley (1693) concluded ([13], p. 656) from his figures for Breslau:

. . . it is plain, that there might well be four times as many Births as we now find. For . . . I find that there are nearly 15000 Persons above 16 and under 45, of which at least 7000 are Women capable to bear Children. Of these notwithstanding there are but 1238 born yearly, which is but little more than a sixth part: So that about one in six of these Women do breed yearly, whereas were they all married, it would not appear strange or unlikely, that four of six should bring a Child every year.

Halley assumed for Breslau 34,000 inhabitants ([12], p. 600), 7,000 women at child-bearing age, and 1,238 births. This implies a birth-rate of 36, and a general fertility rate of 177, while he thinks that if all women at child-bearing age were married a general fertility rate of 667 "would not appear strange or unlikely."

Short (1750) in one passage ([25], p. 247) refers to what fertility might be: "For were only 3 Women of 17, between 15 Years of Age and 45, married, and bear Children yearly, we might expect several more Children every Year (allowing for dry Pairs)."

CAUSES REDUCING FERTILITY

The demographers of the period give manifold reasons why fertility is lower than fecundity.

Diseases

In 1662 Graunt [10] found that the number of births decreased considerably in times of plagues. "The Question is, Whether Teeming-women died, or fled, or miscarried?" A study of the trend of baptisms and deaths in 1603 showed him that in the first months of the plague (March to July) weekly baptisms in London decreased from 110 or 130 to under 90, while "there died not above twenty per Week of the Plague,[1] which small number could neither cause the death, or flight of so many Women, as to alter the proportion ¼ part lower." He therefrom concluded that in the initial stage of the plague the reduction of births was mainly due to miscarriages.

From the 21 of *July* to the 21[2] of *October*, the *Plague* increasing, reduced the *Christnings* to 70 at a *Medium* . . . Now the cause of this must be

[1] This statement is evidently inaccurate. According to a table included from the third edition (1665) on, the weekly number of deaths from the plague exceeded 20 from May 19th on.

[2] From the second edition (1662) the date stated is October 12.

flying, and death, as well as miscarriages, and Abortions; for there died within that time about 25000, whereof many were certainly *Women with childe*, besides the fright of so many dying within so small a time might drive away so many others, as to cause this effect ([10], pp. 37–8).

He further states that "except in a very few Cases," quite apart from the plague, "the more sickly the years are, the less fecund, or fruitfull of Children also they be" (p. 40), and "that healthfull years are also the most fruitfull" (p. 65).[1] But his figures are by no means conclusive, and Short (1750), using in part the data of Graunt, in part more recent data, pointed ([25], pp. 191, 231) to the lack of a close relation between mortality and fecundity: "Sometimes we find the sickliest Years the fruitfullest . . . and the healthiest Years the barrenest . . ."

Both writers discussed also the trend of baptisms after "mortal" years, and in this matter Graunt ([10], p. 50) was more realistic than Short. His argument runs as follows:

That although in the very year of the *Plague* the *Christnings* decreased, by the dying and flying of *Teeming-women*, yet the very next year after, they increased somewhat, but the second after, to as full a number as in the second year before the said *Plague*: for I say again, if there be encouragement for an hundred in *London*, that is, a Way how an hundred may live better then in the Countrey, and if there be void housing there to receive them, the evacuating of a ¼th, or ⅓ part of that number, must soon be supplied out of the Countrey . . .

Short, on the other hand, says ([25], p. 191):

Sometimes a very fruitful Year is followed by a very mortal and sickly one . . . and mortal ones often succeeded by very fruitful . . . as though Nature sought either to prevent, or quickly repair the Loss by Death. In general, the next Year after sickly or mortal ones, is prolific in Proportion to the Breeders left; for many of the weak, sickly, declining Constitutions being cut off, Health returning gives Vigour and Vivacity to the Survivers.

The cases which he mentions in order to prove that sometimes a very fruitful year is followed by a very mortal and sickly one are few and not conclusive; but he affords ample proof for his contention that mortal years are often succeeded by years with a large number of baptisms. Corbyn Morris (1751) also discusses ([17], pp. 3–5) this fact rather fully. He does, however, attribute it neither

---

[1] We may compare the following reference by Petty ([18], p. 4): "It hath been formerly observ'd, That *in the years wherein most dye, fewest are born, & vice versâ*."

to an intention of Nature to repair quickly the loss by death nor to a greater vigour and vitality of the survivors, but rather to the influx of people from the country (like Graunt) and to the increase of marriages.

Robert Wallace (1753) called attention ([27], p. 82) to the effects of syphilis on fertility. He quotes an opinion given to him by "the learned Author of *An Essay on the vital and other involuntary Motions of Animals*," according to which "the *Lues Venerea*, or *Great Pox*, . . . frequently renders both sexes unfruitful, or at best debilitates them, so as to make their posterity sickly, infirm, and often barren."

Graunt (1662) had stated ([10], p. 46) that "there should be none extraordinary in the Native Air of the place" which could cause the greater "Barrenness in London," but King (1696) said ([16], p. 44) that one 'reason why each marriage in London produces fewer children than the country marriages, seems to be . . . the unhealthfulness of the coal smoke," and the editor of the *Collection of the Yearly Bills of Mortality* (1759)[1] mentioned ([8], pp. 14–15) among the

---

[1] It is still a controversial question who was the editor. Richard Price, in a letter to Benjamin Franklin, dated April 3, 1769, and published in the *Philosophical Transactions* for the year 1769, referred (p. 122) to "the preface to Dr. Birch's *collection of the bills of mortality*." But when he republished this letter in his *Observations on Reversionary Payments*, etc. (1771), he referred (p. 204) to "the preface to the *Collection of the London Bills of Mortality*" without giving credit to Dr. Birch.

William Godwin, in his book *Of Population* (p. 315, London, 1820), speaks of "Dr. Birch's Collection of the Yearly Bills of Mortality."

Joshua Milne, in an article "Bills of Mortality" in the *Supplement to the Fourth, Fifth, and Sixth Editions of the Encyclopædia Britannica* (2, 307, Edinburgh, 1824), states that the Collection "has been generally attributed to Dr. Birch, the Secretary and Historian of the Royal Society," but adds:

"For the following history of this publication, the author of the present article is indebted to the kindness of Dr Heberden:—'The bills were collected into a volume by his father, the late Dr Heberden. He procured likewise, observations from several of his friends, rectors of some large parishes, or others likely to give him information; particularly from Bishop Moss, Bishop Green, Bishop Squire, and Dr Birch. These, together with some of his own remarks, were thrown into the form of a preface; and the whole was committed to the care of Dr Birch. . . .' "

William Ogle ("An Inquiry into the Trustworthiness of the Old Bills of Mortality," *J. R. Statist. Soc.* 55 (1892), 442) says: "The writer is believed to have been Dr. Birch, as much of the preface exists in manuscript in the papers of that gentleman now in the British Museum. (The copy in the Museum was given by Dr. William Heberden, who received it from the editor.)"

Charles Henry Hull (1899; [22], 2, 641) believes in the editorship of Heberden.

The *Dictionary of National Biography* (2 (1908), 531) mentions the Collection among the principal books of Thomas Birch.

factors reducing fertility in London "the crowded manner of living in our cities," and "the unhealthfulness of many occupations."

Birth Control

Graunt (1662) points ([10], p. 51) to the "unlawfull Copulations," which "beget Conceptions but to frustrate them by procured Abortions." The Lord Chief Justice Hale (1667) speaks ([11], p. 230) of "Abortions voluntary or accidental." Short (1750) complains ([25], p. 74) of the "Destruction of real Beings in the Womb" and the "nefarious Practices used by wicked Wretches to prevent Conceptions from their carnal Gratification."[1] But it is doubtful whether he is really opposed to deliberate abortion in the case of illegitimate children, since, in discussing the number of births in "the Prussian Dominions," he speaks ([25], p. 243) of the "Bastards, which make one 30th of the whole, whose Procreation and Expences licensed public Stews might have prevented"; and, in explaining the existence of the "Foundling Hospital" in Paris, says (p. 244): "the most Christian King being both too Christian and too Politick, legally, for the Lucre of a small Tax, to allow Stews, to prevent Procreation by common Prostitutes there."

Abstention of Wives

Graunt ([10], p. 45) and Morris (1751) ([17], pp. 1–2) both point to the reduction of fertility caused by the temporary abstinence of country women whose husbands for one reason or another spend some time in London. Graunt mentions also the long periods of abstention on the part of the wives of seamen.

Short (1750) attributes ([25], p. 181) the increase of London baptisms from December to January in part to the abstention of married couples in Lent:

That *January*, the fruitfullest Month, is to *June* the barrennest, near as 21½ to 17; the Fertility of *January* being owing either to the ecclesiastic

---

[1] See also ibid., p. 162: "Many of the Army give themselves up to Whoredom and Adulteries, whereby Children are several wicked Ways . . . artfully prevented." Short discusses the prevention of conception and some other phases of fertility more fully in *A Comparative History of the Increase and Decrease of Mankind in England, and several Countries abroad* (London, 1767), to which volume readers interested in demographers' opinions during the period immediately following the one discussed here may be referred.

Interdict being taken off the Marriage Bed at *Easter*; or to the religious Abstinance and other *Lent* Severities, whereby the *City Ladies* have reduced their Bodies to a more impregnable State; or because in *Lent*, *Plays, Assemblies, Masquerades*, and other Occasions of Night *Revellings* and *Intrigues*, happen not to be quite so fashionable as in Winter.[1]

Suckling of Children

Petty, in *Of Lands and Hands*, suggests ([23], **1**, 194) that "long suckling of children" be a "hindrance to the speedier propagation of mankind."

Polygamy

Graunt, Arbuthnott, Short, and Wallace are of the opinion that polygamy reduces fertility.[2]

Graunt (1662) in the Dedicatory Epistle of his book to Lord Roberts states: "That the irreligious Proposals of some, to multiply People by Polygamy, is withall irrational, and fruitless." "From the difference between Males and Females [excess of Males], we see the reason of making Eunuchs in those places where Polygamy is allowed, the latter being useless as to multiplication, without the former . . ." ([10], pp. 50–1).

John Arbuthnott (1710), in "An Argument for Divine Providence, taken from the constant Regularity observ'd in the Births of both Sexes," reaches the conclusion ([1], p. 189):

that Polygamy is contrary to the Law of Nature and Justice, and to the Propagation of Human Race; for where Males and Females are in equal number, if one Man takes Twenty Wives, Nineteen Men must live in Celibacy, which is repugnant to the Design of Nature; nor is it probable that Twenty Women will be so well impregnated by one Man as by Twenty.

[1] But on p. 151 he has noted: ". . . married Men cannot be watched that they cohabit not with their Wives in *Lent*."

[2] Petty, however, in discussing "Californian Marriages" where "6 men were conjugated to 6 women in order to beget many and well conditioned children, and for the greatest venereall pleasure," asserts: "The encrease of children will be great and good" ([23], **2**, 52–3). In his "Advices about American plantations" (1685), he proposes "That the English may buy Indian girles of under 7 yeares old and use them as wives, even with polygamy regulated by authority" (**2**, 113).

It may be remembered that a few years before (1681), the Poet Laureate Dryden, in his poem *Absalom and Achitophel*, likewise advocated polygamy (and promiscuous sexual intercourse in general).

Short (1750), who discusses polygamy more fully ([25], pp. 151–8), gives the following reasons for its hampering fertility:

But allow of Polygamy for once, then some Men must necessarily be mutilated, or deprived of their Right, or prevented complying with their natural Inclinations, from want of Females; and the greater Part of the Women denied, or come short of the Duty due to them from their Husbands, one Woman being only caressed, and the rest made Slaves to the Pride and extravagant Humours of the Husband and favourite Bride, whose Height is but precarious, and liable to be kicked down by a new Successor. . . .

Policy forbids Polygamy on a double account, for the probable Safety of a Nation depends on the Number of its People and Riches; then the incapacitating a great Number of its Males from lawful Procreation, is inconsistent both with the Increase of People, and native couragious Soldiers. Hence Countries, where Polygamy is used, are the thinnest of Inhabitants, so many of their Males being castrated, and so many Women unmarried. . . .

Polygamy is inconsistent with the natural, as well as civil Strength of a People; for as it requires too frequent Gratifications of the amorous Passion, few of them will prove prolific, and still fewer productive of strong-bodied Men, from the Inelaboratedness of the too often drained genital Liquor. . . .[1]

As it is inconsistent with both civil and natural Strength, so with the necessary Means of Self-preservation which every Man owes himself, these frequent Dalliances enervating the Vigour both of Body and Mind, whilst each of his Wives may justly sollicite and expect their own due Gratifications.

It is inconsistent with the Love and Duty which every Man owes his Wife, whom he is obliged to love, cherish, and provide for suitable to his Station, and cohabit with: But in Polygamy all these Duties must dwindle away, and be divided among several, to the defrauding every one of their Right; for a number of Wives is only a Number of Slaves to the Ambition of the Husband.

[1] A different reason for the reduction of fertility through polygamy was given ([24], pp. 103–4) a few years later by James Porter, British Ambassador at Constantinople, who had been asked by his friend Dr. Maty: "Whether plurality of wives is in fact, as it was confidently affirmed to be, *in the order of nature*, favourable to the increase of mankind?" He replied on February 1, 1755: "I can affirm, with truth, what may seem a paradox, that in general, Mahometans, notwithstanding their law, procreate less than Christians. . . . I take this to arise from a cause different from that which is commonly assigned, not from their being enervated by variety, but rather from their law. The frequent ablutions, required by the doctrine of purity and impurity, perhaps may check the libidinous passion; or when it is at its height, they find themselves prohibited enjoyment."

Wallace (1753) likewise states ([27], pp. 84–5) that "polygamy is a hindrance to the propagation of mankind":

Whatever strange and wonderful accounts have been given of the disproportion between males and females, and the more numerous births of the latter in some Eastern nations; according to the best observations, which have been made in the Western parts, the proportion between the births of males and females appears to be nearly equal. To provide therefore most equally for the whole human race, and make all of them most useful in propagating, one man ought to be allowed to marry but one woman at once. Thus polygamy, by which many men are deprived of wives, and several women being married to one man, become less fruitful, must have a baneful influence. Hence Mahometanism is pernicious in this respect; and if, to the influence of polygamy, we add the institution of eunuchs for guarding the fair, and of female slaves who assist these eunuchs, and seldom marry; this must have no inconsiderable effect in all those countries, where the Mahometan religion is established at present, and where polygamy and eunuchs were not allowed in antient times. This is the case with the more Eastern places of *Europe*, and Western parts of *Asia*. But whatever changes have been wrought in those nations which are situated farther to the East, cannot be accounted for in this way, since polygamy prevailed, and eunuchs swarmed in those countries from very antient times.

Promiscuous Sexual Intercourse

Most demographers of the period are convinced that sexual intercourse with another man than the husband and promiscuous sexual intercourse in general seldom are followed by conception.

Graunt (1662) repeatedly expressed ([10], pp. 46, 51) this view:

. . . Adulteries and Fornications . . . do certainly hinder breeding. For a Woman, admitting 10 Men, is so far from having ten times as many Children, that she hath none at all.
. . . admitting Men as Whores (that is more then one) . . . commonly procreates no more then if none at all had been used . . .
From what hath been said, appears the reason why the Law is, and ought to be so strict against Fornications and Adulteries, for if there were universal liberty, the Increase of Man-kind would be but like that of *Foxes* at best.

King (1696) likewise states ([16], p. 44) that one "reason why each marriage in London produces fewer children than the country marriages, seems to be . . . the more frequent fornications and adulteries."

D'Avenant (1699) illustrates ([9], pp. 31–2) the barrenness of promiscuous sexual intercourse through the example of the unmarried soldiers:

Indeed, all Armies whatsoever, if they are over large, tend to the dispeopling of a Country, of which our Neighbour Nation [Spain] is a sufficient Proof; where, in one of the best Climates in *Europe*, Men are wanting to Till the Ground. For Children do not proceed from the intemperate Pleasures taken loosly and at random, but from a regular way of Living, where the Father of the Family desires to rear up and provide for the Off-spring he shall beget.

Morris (1751) states ([17], p. 2) that the people who temporarily come to London "can add nothing to the Amount of the Christnings, except by promiscuous Venery with other Mens Wives, or with common Women; which Practices are found rather to prevent than promote the Procreation of Children."

Wallace (1753) thinks ([27], p. 13) that "irregular amours" weaken "the generating faculties of men."

Intemperance

One of the reasons why Short thought that polygamy reduced fertility was that "it requires too frequent Gratifications of the amorous Passion." Intemperance in sexual intercourse also seemed to him to be the main cause for the low fertility of many marriages. Other writers attributed it rather to intemperance in feeding and drinking. But all agreed that steady physical labour and a simple uncomplicated manner of life promote reproduction.

Graunt (1662) states ([10], p. 46) that "intemperance in feeding" in London does "certainly hinder breeding." Moreover, "the minds of men in London are more thoughtfull and full of business then in the Country, where their work is corporal Labour, and Exercizes. All which promote Breedings, whereas Anxieties of the minde hinder it."

King (1696) also states ([16], p. 44) that two reasons "why each marriage in London produces fewer children than the country marriages" seem to be "a greater luxury and intemperance," and "a greater intenseness to business."

Short (1750) discusses ([25], pp. 143–9) this phase more fully than any other demographer of the period. His starting-point is a table showing 58,553 "Christenings of eight different Places" by months:

That *March* is the fruitfullest Month of the twelve by almost 1/11th; and that *July* is the barrenest, the former being to the latter near as 57 to 44. The Proportion of the first five Months is to the second five as 13 to 11. The Product of the last two Months of the Year is to the Product of the first two Months, near as 9 to 10. Thus we find that the most laborious and toilsome Months prove the best for Impregnation and Conception, viz. *April, May, June, July* and *August*; and the Months of the greatest Ease, Repletion, Indolence, and smallest Discharge, are most improper for Procreation, as *October, November, December,* and *January. Corrol.* Seeing that in the Months of hardest Labour, least Rest, longest Days, and Exercise, People beget 2/13ths more Children than in time of the longest Rest, least Labour, most liberal and invigorating Feeding, freest sensible, but least insensible Discharges; then the most laborious Part of Mankind are also most fruitful in proportion to their Numbers; and the most voluptuous, idle, effiminate and luxurious are the barrenest. . . .

As to the Effects of Labour and Exercise on Mens Bodies during the busy Season of the Year. 1. It causes plentiful Perspiration, and promotes other necessary Evacuations, whereby all the Animal Juices are attenuated and diminished, and the more serous, saline and excrementitious Parts are carried off. 2. As a daily continued Perspiration gives Vent to Abundance of superflous Humours, so it brings the viscous genital Liquor to its greatest Maturity, most perfect and elaborated State, much of its useless Serum is otherwise discharged; the seminal Vesicles are not so soon filled with poor spiritless Stuff, as its Bulk or Quantity must force an immature Expulsion; and the poor Country Labourer's Drink at his hard Work, being seldom strong, it carries no stock of Salts into the Blood, and such as were in it before, are so thinned and diluted, that much of the useless Part of them is carried off by Sweat and Urine; hence less seminal Stimulus, and seldomer Provocation to Venery. By the same Means the Blood is freed from so great a Quantity of Mucosity in the Uterus and its Appendages, which occasions a Slipperyness, that the best genital Liquor is lost, *re infecta*, or expelled or carried off the small tender Embryo; or that laid in the Way, so that the prolific Aura of the Semen reached not the *Fallopian Tubes* and *Ovaria* to impregnate them. Daily Labour not only wastes the superflous serous and saline Humours, but braces the Fibres, Membranes and Vessels, and proper Parts of both Sexes for the fuller Preparation and longer Retention of this prolific Humour in the Males, and Reception and due Residence in the Females. Hard Labour, and a promoted Perspiration, not only lessen the Quantity, and mend the Consistence, and takes off not only an

K*

useless, but injurious Stimulus at that Time, yet hinders not a prolific one, attended with all pleasurable Satisfaction. Hence it follows: 1st, That tho' Idleness may be a Friend to Venery, yet it is not to Prolificness. Nor, 2dly, does a constant thin watery Diet promise a numerous healthy Progeny, as that Diet is liable to fill the seminal Vescicles with insipid watery Sperm. Nor, 3dly, are high stimulant Food, Drinks or Sauces, Promoters of Fertility, especially before or at the Meridian of Life, seeing they both provoke to immature Acts, and, by the Irritation of the Semen on the Recipient, may procure its Expulsion. 4thly, As Idleness, so Night-revelling and unseasonable Hours, which as they load the Body with unperspired Humours, so they distend the seminal Repositories with inelaborated Matter, which hastens its Expulsion. 5thly, Hence it's plain that Procreation is often prevented by too frequently repeated Gratifications. This is still more evident from the Decrease of Births in *June*, *July*, and *August*, the Months answering the idlest and plentifullest Season; and from the young vertuous Breeders, seldom coming with their first Load within the Year,[1] till they have a little sated themselves; and the young Husbands put off their pale, lank, thin looks, and somewhat recovered their Batchelor-like Complexion. Would the just Odiousness and Nastyness of the Subject allow it, I could fully and clearly from hence prove, how injurious to Procreation all unnatural or illegal Gratifications are in either Sex, whether before or after Marriage. Thus it is plain, that all too frequent or promiscuous Emition, and all needless, frequent, or profuse Loss of the Semen; the Slipperyness, Laxness, or Insensibility, or too great Moisture of the Recipient Parts, prevent or protract Conception, and also Stimulants, which provoke an unnatural and unfruitful Desire, without due Repletion of proper Matter (except to dull flegmatic Bodies) and likewise too low and innutritive a Diet answer not the Design of Fertility, for they all taint the Semen, either in Quantity or Quality, make it too much, too little, too watery, acrid, insipid, saline, or stimulant.[2]

[1] See also [25], p. 150: "our new-married Women seldom come in the Year, (except their Husbands are very chaste)."

[2] While Short thus is convinced that intemperance and idleness reduce the fertility of married couples, he thinks that they increase the number of illegitimate births:

"The greater or less Number of Bastards in a Country or Place, I find depends much on the prevailing Vices or Virtues of the Age, or State of Religion, publick Plenty or Prosperity, or Calamities: For times of Poverty, Sickness, Famine, or Plague, are as great Enemies to Sensuality, as Trade, Plenty, Riches, Peace, general Health, Fulness, and Idleness, are to Piety and Virtue" (p. 74).

". . . there are more Bastards in Towns than in the Country, from the Peoples more plentiful Eating and Drinking, greater Idleness, Immodesty, Intemperance, and other Incitements and Opportunities to Wantonness" (p. 121).

Short also mentioned intemperate drinking quite casually as a factor reducing fertility. That he thought that it rather increased mortality is shown on [25], pp. 209–10. Having found that convulsions had become more numerous, he states:

Were the Cause of this prodigious Increase enquired into, perhaps the *Aera* would be found to commence from Parents too general and fatal Acquaintance with spirituous Liquors, for between 1670 to 88, this Article rose from 1600 to 4000. This is the more probable, if we look into Inland remote Country Places, which tho' fully exposed to the Inclemency of Weather, yet have in a great Measure the Happiness to be unacquainted with Spirits, and other strong Liquors, Ale excepted; there this Disease keeps to its old State.

The small importance for fertility which he attaches to spirits is rather surprising since the consumption of gin had reached its peak exactly at the time he wrote his *New Observations*.[1] Morris (1751), on the other hand, considered ([17], pp. 3, 23) intemperance in drinking as the main cause for the low fertility of so many married couples:

But above all, the present increasing Diminution of the Christnings in *London* beneath the Burials, with many other Evils, is particularly to be attributed to the enormous Use of *spirituous Liquors*. For it is beyond all Dispute, that such Liquors are become the common *Drink*, and even the *Food* too, if it may be so termed, of these People. The Effects of which therefore must necessarily appear.—And the certain notorious ones are, that it debilitates and enervates the Drinkers, drying up and burning

---

[1] See Richard Price, *An Essay on the Population of England, from the Revolution to the present Time*, 2nd ed., London, 1780, p. 20: "The use of spirituous liquors prevailed most in 1750 and 1751." "Since 1751 it has been so much checked by new regulations, additional duties, and other causes, that most probably it does not prevail much more now than it did at the Revolution." He gives as "the *annual* average of spirits drawn from malted corn, cyder, melasses, and brewers' wash":

1692–93:	2,329,487 gallons
1730–31:	6,658,788 ,,
1750–51:	11,326,976 ,,
1752–53:	7,500,000 ,,
1767–68:	3,663,568 ,,

It may be mentioned, however, that Short, in a book published in 1767 and therefore not analysed in this study, repeatedly points to the reduction of fertility through spirituous liquors. See *A Comparative History of the Increase and Decrease of Mankind*, pp. 21, 34.

their radical Strength and Moisture, so as to render them less capable of Labour, or the Procreation of Children.—With *adult* Persons, these fatal Draughts operate in enfeebling them, and carrying many to their Graves.—But they *trebly* operate in respect to *Infants*; 1st, In preventing many from being begotten, by the Debility of the Males. 2dly, Where the Weakness is not on the Male Side, by preventing many Conceptions, by the Sterility of the Females; which Sterility is known to be a certain Consequence of the drinking of these Potions. And, lastly, By rendering such as are born meagre and sickly, and unable to pass through the first Stages of Life.—This last Effect therefore contributes to *increase* the *Burials*, and the two former to *diminish* the *Christnings*.—No Wonder then, under the shocking Influence of this *single* Cause, that the *Christnings* in *London* should be inferrior to the *Burials*. And that they are not only so, but that the Christnings have proceeded, of late Years, since the Use of these Liquors, in a continually *decreasing* Proportion, in respect to the Burials, is a serious Truth, evident beyond all Contradiction, by the annexed annual Amounts of both, extracted from the Bills of Mortality. . . .

It appears by these Bills, that the Amount of the Births in *London* went on annually *increasing* to the Year 1724; in which Year they amounted to upwards of 19000: But since then, have continually sunk to the present Time; and now scarcely arise to 14,500 annually.—Nor have actually for ten Years past amounted to this last Sum, upon a Medium. Whereby it appears, that this *Diminution* of the *Births* set out from the *same* Time that the *Consumption* of these *Liquors* by the common People became enormous; and that as this *Consumption* hath been constantly *increasing* since that Time, the *Amount* of the *Births* hath likewise been continually *diminishing*. But let this *Diminution*, and the Number of *Infants* lost thereby within this City, be strictly computed.—Now the Amount of the *Christnings* in the Year 1724, was 19370; and had proceeded in a gradual Course of *Increase* up to that Number.—Admit then, that they would have *stood* only to this Amount from that Time to the present, without *advancing*, *beyond* this *Level*, though that was their evident *Tendency*. Then for the Twenty-six Years past, from 1725, to 1750, both Years inclusive, the Amount of the *Births* would have been 26 × 19370, that is, 503,620. But the *actual Amount* of the *Births* for these Years hath been no more than 419,635. The Difference between which Numbers is 83985, falling short, by only the small Number of *Fifteen*, of *Fourscore and Four Thousand Infants*;—which, at a very moderate Computation, have been lost, during this short Term, within this *Capital* only, by the Drinking of *spirituous Liquors*.—Besides what have been lost in all other Parts of the Kingdom, wherein this Consumption hath been prevalent.

Obstacles to Divorces

Robert Wallace thought ([27], pp. 85–6) that the difficulty of obtaining divorces slightly reduced fertility:

> Some reckon the difficulty of obtaining divorces, according to the Christian institution, another hinderance of the increase of mankind, as persons may be childless by being improperly matched, tho' either of them might have children in another marriage, if divorces could be easily obtained. But, as there are many dangers both to parents and children, from allowing divorces to be procured too easily; and as whatever loss is sustained by the difficulty of procuring them, is more than compensated by other advantages; allowing divorces, merely for want of children, must have but an inconsiderable effect, as few instances can be supposed, where a married couple, pleased in other respects, would separate on this account alone.

Josiah Tucker (1755) believed ([26], pp. 23, 29) that "the Difficulty of obtaining a Divorce in Cases of Adultery" was a discouragement "of the Married State" and therefore reduced fertility. If "the Remedy of a Divorce would be at hand . . . this itself might be a Means to engage many Persons to venture upon that State, which, at the worst, would not then be, as it is now, without a Remedy."[1]

Age at Marriage

King (1696) from his "Observations from a certain great town in the middle of the kingdom," concluded ([16], pp. 45–6) "that a just equality, or too great an inequality of age, in marriages, are prejudicial to the increase of mankind; and that the early or late marriages, in men and women, do tend little to the propagation of the human race." But the "great town" which he had studied was Lichfield, "consisting of near 3000 souls," and even there his figures are not conclusive.

Tucker (1755) emphasizes ([26], pp. 15–16) the infertility of late marriages:

> The Nobility and Gentry of *England* are deterred from entering into the married State during the *Prime* of Life, because they can have little or no

---

[1] Hume held a different view: "It may justly be thought, that the liberty of divorces in *Rome* was another discouragement to marriage" ([15], p. 182; see also [14], **2**, 192).

Command over their Children, when they advance towards Years of Maturity. And a Father is by no Means desirous of being treated disrespectfully by his Son, merely because he is not likely to make a Vacancy as soon as the young Heir could wish him. Yet this consequence, bad as it is, too frequently happens to a middle-aged Man, as his Son draws towards the Years of twenty one. For at that Period of Life (such is our wrong Polity) the Parental Authority is almost at an End, and the Son can shew an undutiful Behaviour with Impunity. . . .

But in general, as I said before, Men of Fashion do not marry in the Prime of Life. And it is observable, that they stay later in *England*, than in any other Country in *Europe*,—as if it were on purpose to be ready to move off the Stage, when their Successors come on. But alas! if they continue single during the Prime of their Years, in what manner do they spend their Time?—Generally in all the Excesses of Riot and Debauchery: so that those of higher Rank, who ought to set the Example, seldom think of raising a Family, till they are fitter for an Hospital than the Bridal Bed. What an Offspring! what Members of Society, or Defenders of their Country, are we to expect from such Parents!

The very Liberty which the *English* enjoy above other Nations, becomes in the Event, as Matters are *now* circumstanced, a means of dispeopling the Country. For it currupts their Morals, hurries them into Vice and evil Courses, shortens their Days, and destroys the natural Fertility of the Sexes.[1]

Celibacy

All demographers of the period agreed that the obstacles or the disinclination to marriage were a most important factor in reducing fertility. We must confine ourselves to summarizing briefly the main causes mentioned in the course of the discussion:

(1) *Monks and Nuns*

Graunt emphasizes ([10], p. 51) very strongly the influence of the Catholic celibacy upon fertility:

In *Popish* Countries, where *Polygamy* is forbidden, if a greater number of *Males* oblige themselves to *Cœlibate* then the natural overplus or difference between them and *Females* amounts unto; then multiplication is hindred; for if there be eight Men to ten Women, all of which eight men are married to eight of the ten Women, then the other two bear no Children, as

---

[1] Again ([26], p. 40) he says: "For good Morals . . . prevent the *barren* and *unfruitful* Vices of Lewdness and Debauchery . . ."

either admitting no Man at all, or else admitting Men as Whores (that is more then one) which commonly procreates no more then if none at all had been used: or else such unlawfull Copulations beget Conceptions but to frustrate them by procured Abortions or secret Murthers, all which returns to the same reckoning. Now, if the same proportion of women oblige themselves to a single life likewise, then such obligation makes no change in this matter of encrease.

Wallace (1753) holds ([27], pp. 86–7) the same view:

Undoubtedly the great number of unmarried priests in all the *Roman* catholick countries, which make so great a part of *Europe*, and the multitude of women who live unmarried in convents, and profess perpetual virginity, foolishly imagining, that celibacy is a more holy state than marriage, may justly be accounted one of the causes of the scarcity of people in all the countries under the Pope's dominion.[1]

[1] See also ibid., pp. 147, 165–6; [25], p. 161; [5], p. 885. Hume (1752), however, questioned ([15], p. 179) the strength of this argument: "Our modern convents are, no doubt very bad institutions . . . And tho' we have reason to detest all these popish institutions, as nurseries of the most abject superstition, burthensome to the public, and oppressive to the poor prisoners, male, as well as female; yet may it be question'd, whether they be so destructive to the populousness of a state as is commonly imagin'd. Were the land, which belongs to a convent, bestow'd on a nobleman, he wou'd spend its revenue on dogs, horses, grooms, footmen, cooks, and chamber-maids; and his family wou'd not furnish many more citizens than the convent."
He then compared the confinement of nuns with infanticide and came to the conclusion that infanticide was less unfavourable to the propagation of mankind (ibid., pp. 180–1):
"The common reason why parents thrust their daughters into nunneries, is, that they may not be overburthen'd with too numerous a family; but the antients had a method almost as innocent and more effectual to that purpose, *viz.* the exposing their children in the earliest infancy. . . .
"Shall we then allow these two circumstances to compensate each other, *viz.* monastic vows and the exposing of children, and to be unfavourable, in equal degrees, to the propagation of mankind? I doubt the advantage is here on the side of antiquity. Perhaps, by an odd connexion of causes, the barbarous practice of the antients might rather render those times more populous. By removing the terrors of too numerous a family, it wou'd engage many people in marriage; and such is the force of natural affection, that very few, in comparison, wou'd have resolution enough, when it came to the push, to carry into execution their former intentions.
"*China*, the only country, where this barbarous practice of exposing children prevails at present, is the most populous country we know; and every man is married before he is twenty. Such early marriages cou'd scarce be general, had not men the prospect of so easy a method of getting rid of their children."

(2) *Servants*

Mórris (1751) lays great stress ([17], p. 25; see also p. 2) upon the large number of unmarried servants:

> The *Luxury* of great Families, in their present general Use of *unmarried* Servants, considerably obstructs the *annual Produce* of *Children*;—Thus, suppose a fashionable Family in *London*, to consist of half a dozen Persons, and upwards;—and of these, perhaps at most, only the Master and the Mistress *married*; the rest, all Servants *marriageable*, and *unmarried*. . . .

Wallace (1753) states ([27], p. 87) that one "cause of the scarcity of people in modern times, is the difference of antient and modern customs, with respect to servants." He praises Greek and Roman masters who encouraged their slaves to marry (pp. 89–92, 168–206),[1] and regrets the celibacy of the servants of his time ([27], p. 91):

> *God* forbid! that I should ever be an advocate for slavery, ecclesiastic, civil, or domestic, on account of any accidental advantages which it may happen to produce; yet it must be confessed, that considering it only with respect to the phænomenon we are at present examining, it seems probable, that the antient condition of servants contributed something to the greater populousness of antiquity, and that the antient slaves were more serviceable in raising up people, than the inferior ranks of men in modern times.

(3) *Apprentices*

Graunt (1662) mentions ([10], p. 45) as one reason why "the Breeders in London are proportionally fewer then those in the Country . . . That many Apprentices of London, who are bound seven, or nine years from Marriage, do often stay longer voluntarily."

(4) *Soldiers*

D'Avenant and Short, as has been shown, point to the unmarried state of numerous soldiers as an impediment to reproduction. Wallace ([27], p. 95) takes the same view:

> Another cause of the want of people, is the great number of soldiers in modern armies, among whom there are few who marry, and by whose means so many women are debauched, and venereal distempers spread

---

[1] On this as on many other points he opposes the views of Hume ([15], pp. 165–79).

so wide and so fatally. This is an unhappy policy on many accounts, adapted in particular to increase idleness, and lessen the numbers of the people, and is entirely different from the policy of the most antient ages. (See also [15], pp. 188–9.)

(5) *The Poor*

Many factors prevent the poor from marrying:

(*a*) *Taxes*. D'Avenant (1699), after having described the encouragements to marriage given by the Jews, the Romans, and France, says ([9], pp. 32–3):

> But we in *England* have taken another Course, laying a Fine upon the Marriage-Bed, which seems small to those who only contemplate the Pomp and Wealth round about 'em, and in their View; but they who look into all the different Ranks of Men, are well satisfied that this Duty on Marriages and Births, is a very grevious Burthen upon the poorer Sort, whose Numbers compose the Strength and Wealth of any Nation. This Tax was introduc'd by the Necessity of Affairs. . . .[1]

Short (1750) mentions ([25], pp. 159–62; see also pp. xv–xvi, 144, 185) among the obstacles to marriages of the poor:

1. Laying on heavy Taxes on the common Necessaries of Life, whilst many Articles for meer Luxury escape quite free.
2. Laying Dues or Duties on the Marriage-Bed and its Product; thus a Burden is directly laid on the porer Sort, which make up the Strength and Wealth of a Country. Taxes contrary to true Policy and Reason, though they may appear small to the legislative Donors, who see nothing but Pomp and Wealth around them, yet they are found too hard on such as can hardly maintain themselves. Such Burdens, however trifling they may appear, may hinder the Poor from marrying, and so prevent Procreation. . . .

. It is evident that one of the remotest, but surest Steps of an imperious Prince to make himself absolute, is to deter the poorer sort from Marriage, and so lessen the Proportion of his own Subjects. And there is no greater moral, nor civil Indiscretion, in castrating a great Part of the Males, like the Orientals, or shutting up a Part of the Females in Religious Houses, like several *European* Countries, than in hindering the Marriage of the

---

[1] In 1694 an Act had been passed "for granting to His Majesty certain Rates and Duties upon Marriages, Births, and Burials, and upon Bachelors and Widowers, for the term of five years, for carrying on the War against France with vigour."

poor Sort, by Imposts laid heavy on the Necessaries of Life, and hindering the Marriage-Bed and its lawful Product . . .

3. Marriage of the Poor is hindered by maintaining numerous, useless, standing Armies in time of Peace. 1. Because a Fund to support such Armies, must necessarily arise either from continuing many old heavy Taxes necessary in time of War and Danger, or by laying on and levying new ones, both which must unavoidably fall heavy on the Poor, however easily they may seem taxed.

Tucker (1755) likewise points out ([26], pp. 13–14) that "the Marriage State is loaded with many Taxes and Expences, from which a Single Life is free":

For this Burden has the same Effect in its Operations, as if the Legislature had actually passed a Law to discourage Marriage, and incourage Celibacy. For the Father of a numerous Family, in paying the several Duties and Excises laid on those Commodities which his Family consumes, is *fined* as it were in those respective Sums, from which a Batchelor is exempt: And yet the Batchelor is not put under any Discouragements of another Nature, whereby the Scale might be brought even, or rather inclined to favour the Matrimonial Side.

(*b*) *Other discriminations against the poor.* Short further says ([25], p. 163): "Marriage is discouraged . . . By squeezing, oppressing, and defrauding the Poor, either because they are poor, and have none to redress their Wrongs, or they want Money to obtain Right and Justice."

Tucker complains ([26], p. 21) that "even as to Marriage, the Overseers and the Justices frequently exercise a Power, for as to Right, in reality they have none, of forbidding the Banns of poor Persons, lest they should bring a Charge upon the Parish."

(*c*) *High cost of living.* Halley (1693), having ascertained the ratio of births to the women of child-bearing age in Breslau, 1687–91, concludes ([13], pp. 655–6):

A second Observation I make upon the said Table, is that the Growth and Encrease of Mankind is not so much stinted by any thing in the Nature of the *Species*, as it is from the cautious difficulty most People make to adventure on the state of *Marriage*, from the prospect of the Trouble and Charge of providing for a Family. Nor are the poorer sort of People herein to be blamed, since their difficulty of subsisting is occasion'd by the unequal Distribution of Possessions, all being necessarily fed from the Earth, of which yet so few are Masters. So that besides themselves and Families, they are yet to work for those who own the Ground that feeds them : And of such does by very much the greater part of Mankind consist . . .[1]

Morris (1751) in discussing "the Discouragement to Matrimony in London" which "is a grand operating Cause of the Diminution of the Christnings" states ([17], p. 2) :

And as to the vast Body of common Manufacturers, Labourers, and Porters, the Expences in *London* of House-Rent, including Taxes, together with the high Rate of Milk, Roots, and other Provisions proper for Children, are such, that, undoubtedly, such Persons enter at the same time into Matrimony, and Poverty and Distress.

Wallace (1753) states ([27], pp. 13, 15, 23; see also pp. 26–7, 87–8, 116, 127, 151) that "great poverty . . . prevents marriage," and that "plenty will always encourage the generality of the people to marry." "Where-ever living is cheapest, and a family can be most easily supported, there will be more frequent marriages . . ."

William Bell (1756) held similar views ([2], pp. 10, 13; see also pp. 3–4, 21) :

And where the whole people, from the highest to the lowest orders, are able by their industry to procure themselves, and their dependants, a sufficient support; it cannot be doubted, but that marriage will prevail universally . . .

Very few of those, who find it a matter of the greatest difficulty to subsist themselves, will lay themselves under the additional obligation of providing for others.

(6) *The Wealthy*

Many factors prevent the well-to-do from marrying :

(*a*) *Taste of luxury.* Morris (1751) considers ([17], p. 2) the taste for luxury and pleasures a "Discouragement to Matrimony in London" :

The unmarried Ladies and Gentlemen in this City, of moderate Fortunes, which are the great Bulk, are unable to support the Expence of a Family with any Magnificence; and therefore cannot intermarry together, without retiring from high Life, and submitting to relinquish those

---

[1] Hume says ([15], p. 183): "For tho' a man of an overgrown fortune, not being able to consume more than another, must share it with those who serve and attend him: Yet their possession being precarious, they have not the same encouragement to marriage, as if each had a small fortune, secure and independent."

Pleasures of the Town, to which their Appetites have long been raised;
they therefore acquiesce in Celibacy; Each Sex compensating itself, as it
can, by other Diversions.—Persons also of inferior Situation in *London*,
have their Taste for Pleasures inflamed; and avoid, with Caution, the
Marriage State with their Equals.[1]

Wallace (1753) over and over again ([27], pp. 24, 96–8, 114–17,
146–7, 149–50, 200) emphasizes that "when simplicity of taste is
lost, . . . mankind be less able to support families, and less encouraged to marry." Bell very fully ([2], pp. 4–5, 14–17, 21–2)
expresses the same opinion.

(*b*) *Education of children*. Short (1750) thinks ([25], pp. 164–6) that
it is in particular the luxurious education of the children of the well-
to-do that reduces the number of marriages:

There are still other Retarders or Hinderances of Marriage arising too
often from Parents themselves, in Towns especially. As when Parents
breed up their Daughters, and give them an Education much superior
to their Circumstance, or Fortune they intend to give them, or a Match
suitable to their Patrimony; instead of instilling into them early, true,
and just Notions of Religion and Virtue, and in training them up in
Housewifery to assist their Mothers in doing, ordering, directing, managing
or overseeing their Family and domestic Affairs, or being instructed in
the necessary relative Duties of Life; how to be dutiful Children, loving,
faithful, frugal Wives, discreet, prudent Mistresses, faithful Friends and
good Christians; or taught how to live comfortably and happily. They
are (to the Shame of the Christian Name) too often brought up the very
reverse; being first taught to mind and affect Gaiety, Dress, and Modes,
hear and learn unedifying Conversation; and when they can read a little,
they have fabulous Histories, Romances, Plays, Novels, or Pagan Fictions
put into their Hands. As soon as they are grown up a little, Misses are
packed off to Boarding-Schools, to learn Dancing, Musick, *French*, Gaming,
and withal get well tinctured with Pride, &c. When she comes home she
pursues the same Sort of Reading; now she is fit for visiting, going abroad,
is Mistress of every necessary Qualification, only is a Stranger to two
insignificant, antique, obsolete Trifles called Religion (save that she can
read her Prayers) and Housewifery. When married the way is paved for
Dress, Idleness, Luxury, Voluptousness, and Pleasures; which are so far

---

[1] Tucker also ([26], p. 14) says: ". . . as Places of Diversion are continually
multiplying, a Single Person with 200*l.* a Year, can make a more *modish* Appearance, and partake of a greater Variety of Pleasures, and consequently appear
in a Condition *more desirable* to the Generality of Mankind, than a married Man
with twice that Sum."

from engaging and charming the other Sex, that they deter even Rakes and Debauchees, who determine rather to gratify themselves in their former Course of Pleasures; or to keep a Mistress, which they can discard, than venture on a State that very few can support the Extravagance of. Whilst the virtuous and sober Youth is often obliged to leave his Fellow-citizens or Towns-women, and seek out for a suitable country Girl, who has not been bred up in those guilty Follies, which may often occasion shocking living Agonies of Mind, matrimonial Broils and a thorny dying Pillow.

Not only do some Parents give their Daughters Education unsuitable to their Rank; but many that have acquired by their own Industry a handsome Fortune, make their eldest Son a Gentleman to the Ruin of the rest, as though they were not their lawful Children, but either Bastards or adopted; hence not a few old Maids, and several kept Mistresses, to which last Course many indiscreet Parents have no small Accession.

(c) *Rules of succession.* The preferential treatment of the oldest son is also considered ([27], pp. 92–3) by Wallace (1753) a hindrance to marriages:

> The rules of succession, and the right of primogeniture, by which the eldest son, not only of the most opulent, but even of the middling and inferior families, carries off the greatest part of the father's estate, that the family may be supported in grandeur and affluence, while the younger children get but a small patrimony, may justly be accounted another cause of the scarcity of people in modern times. . . . This custom no doubt may be accompanied with great advantages, if it be consigned to a few great families, who by their grandeur and riches may be greatly serviceable to their country. . . . But if it becomes so extensive, as to produce a general inclination to raise and support families by such an unequal division of the father's estate, it will prove a source of idleness to the eldest, and prevent the other sons from marrying, since being born of the same parents, and educated in the same manner, they will naturally incline to live somewhat on a level with their elder brother; which they will seldom find possible, unless they keep themselves free from the embarrassments of a family. At *Venice* the custom is said to go so far, that often only one of the sons marries. This must surely have a bad effect in modern times, and make a sensible difference between the modern and the antient world, in which the estate being more equally divided among the children, all of them had greater encouragement to marry, and were more able to maintain families.[1]

[1] See further ibid., pp. 94–5: ". . . it is only among the *Swiss Cantons*, and in *Holland*, where estates are so equally divided among the children, and these two countries are the best peopled in *Europe* (see also [26], p. 14; [2], pp. 27–9).

(d) *Promotion of bachelors*. Short (1750) states ([25], p. 163) that "Marriage is discouraged, by promoting Batchelors, chiefly, to Places and Offices, publick and œconomical." Wallace also complains ([27], p. 94): ". . . married persons have no privileges . . . I do not know if batchelors are incapable of offices at present any where but in Switzerland."

(7) *Political and Economic System*

(a) *Liberty*. D'Avenant (1699) considered ([9], p. 26) the lack of political liberties as an impediment to marriages: "For Liberty encourages Procreation."[1] Short ([25], p. 124); Hume ([15], pp. 185–6, 191–2, 254–6); Tucker ([26], p. 21); and Bell ([2], p. 29) took the same view.[2] Tucker, at the same time, points out ([26], p. 12) that with a small population there is a lack of liberty: "Where a Country is thinly peopled, the Property of Lands will be the more easily ingrossed, and intailed in a few Families; by which means the Landholders become more absolute and despotic over their Vassals." Short adds in particular ([25], pp. 163–4) that "Persecution, for differing in mere Forms and Modes of Worship, when both Parties agreed entirely in all the published and professed Principles of the same Religion, has . . . been another Hindrance of Marriage."

(b) *Agriculture* versus *manufactures and commerce*. Wallace (1753) is of the opinion ([27], pp. 17–18; see also [26], p. 14, and [2], 27–8) that "an equal division of the lands, and into such small shares, that they can yield little more than what is necessary to feed and clothe the labourers in a frugal and simple manner," tends to increase the population. But agriculture, even if lands are unequally divided, promotes population increase more than manufactures ([27], pp. 29–30). He is not opposed ([27], p. 153) to manufactures altogether— "some must always be allowed to be necessary"—but ([27], pp. 25, 96) "a variety of manufactures diverts the attention of mankind from more necessary labour, and prevents the increase of the people." Moreover ([27], pp. 26–7) diversified manufactures increase the wants:

[1] See also ibid., p. 32: "Securing the Liberties of a Nation, may be laid down as a Fundamental for increasing the Numbers of its People."

[2] Wallace, however, as has been shown, considered ([27], p. 92) the slave system in Greece and Rome as promoting fertility. "Almost every page of antient history demonstrates the great multitude of slaves; which gives occasion to a melancholy reflexion, that when the world was best peopled, it was not a world of free men, but of slaves." He also points to the successful breeding of slaves through the planters "in our American colonies" ([27], pp. 207–8).

"But if by means of operose manufactures, such a variety of things becomes necessary, as the bulk of the people cannot purchase without difficulty, . . . multitudes will be discouraged from marrying" (see also [2], pp. 9–26).

Wallace thinks ([27], pp. 22–3, 95–6) that for similar reasons "trade and commerce, instead of increasing, may often tend to diminish the number of mankind"; but he lays more stress on the effects of manufactures. John Brown (1757), on the other hand, discusses ([7], pp. 184–7) exclusively the influence of highly developed commerce, —"the third or highest Period of Trade, of which England is now possessed"—upon fertility: "For first, the Vanity and Effeminacy which this exorbitant Pitch of Wealth brings on, lessens the Desire of Marriage. Secondly, the Intemperance and Disease which this Period of Trade naturally produceth among the lower Ranks in great Cities, bring on in some Degree an Impotence of Propagation."[1]

(8) *Public Opinion*

D'Avenant (1699) thinks ([9], p. 34) that the well-to-do should give the good example as to marrying: where 'tis once made a Fashion among those of the better Sort, 'twill quickly obtain with the lower Degree." Wallace (1753) complains ([27], p. 94) "the laugh is often against matrimony." Brakenridge (1754) speaks ([3], p. 798) of "the fashionable humour of living single, that daily increases" (see also [5], pp. 886, 889). Bell (1756) speaks ([2], pp. 7–8, 24) of "the force of publick example," that makes "celibacy a fashionable state, and marriage the general object of ridicule and contempt." The editor of the *Collection of the Yearly Bills of Mortality* (1759) states ([8], p. 15) that "the false ridicule thrown upon marriage, particularly by those great patrons of debauchery, who wrote for the stage towards the end of the last century and in the beginning of the present," seems to be one "of the causes, which restrain the natural fertility of mankind in Great Britain."

(9) *Religious Prohibition of Marriages*

Petty, in a Memorandum on "Religion," mentions ([23], 1, 117) among the "Disadvantages to the world by the same": "The world hath not increased, by reason of the needlesse restraints put upon conjugations."

---

[1] See also [2], pp. 9, 19–26; [6], p. 477. Hume, on the other hand, is of the opinion that both manufactures and commerce promote population increase ([15], pp. 208–10).

Short (1750) does not think ([25], pp. 150–1) that "the Denial of Matrimony in Lent, is consistent with the Prudence and Interest of a trading, warlike, singular People, whose Religion, Trade, and Liberty, render them hated by several of their Neighbours; and whose Numbers, Riches, Trade, and Policy, can only secure these to them."

(10) *Care for Illegitimate Children*

D'Avenant (1699) is of the opinion ([9], p. 35) that "the securing the Parish for Bastard-Children, is become so small a Punishment and so easily Compounded, that it very much hinders Marriage." Short (1750) likewise believes ([25], pp. 163, 248) that "the too easily compounding with, and passing by the Parents of Bastards, whose Maintainance become another Expence to mean Housekeepers," discourages marriage.

DIFFERENTIAL FERTILITY

Unmarried and Married Women

Starting from the assumption that unmarried women, having sexual intercourse, promiscuously admit numerous men, the demographers of the period agree that the sexual intercourse of unmarried women is less apt to lead to conceptions than that of wives with their husbands (see pp. 295–6).

Urban and Rural Dwellers

Most demographers emphasize the smaller fertility of married couples in the cities as compared with the country.

Graunt (1662) states ([10], pp. 44–5):

that in *London* the proportion of those subject to die unto those capable of breeding is greater then in the Countrey; That is, let there be an hundred Persons in *London*, and as many in the Country; we say, that if there be 60 of them Breeders in *London*, there are more then 60 in the Country . . .

Now that the Breeders in *London* are proportionally fewer then those in the Country arises from these reasons, *viz*.

1. All that have business to the Court of the King, or to the Courts of Justice, and all Country-men coming up to bring Provisions to the City, or to buy Foreign Commodities, Manufactures, and Rarities, do for the most part leave their Wives in the Country.

2. Persons coming to live in *London* out of curiosity, and pleasure, as also such as would retire, and live privately, do the same, if they have any.

3. Such, as come up to be cured of Diseases, do scarce use their Wives *pro tempore*.

4. That many Apprentices of *London*, who are bound seven, or nine years from Marriage, do often stay longer voluntarily.

5. That many Sea-men of *London* leave their Wives behind them, who are more subject to die in the absence of their Husbands, then to breed either without men, or with the use of many promiscuously.

It should be noted that only the last-mentioned reason bears on the fertility of married women residing in London. But Graunt is of the opinion that, quite apart from the reduction of the London birth-rate through the temporary presence of country people, through the celibacy of apprentices, etc.,[1] and through the temporary absence of seamen, the birth and the fertility rates are reduced by the greater barrenness of marriages in London, the main causes being ([10], p. 46) (1) "the intemperance in feeding, and especially the Adulteries and Fornications, supposed more frequent in London then else-where"; (2) "that the minds of men in London are more thought-full and full of business then in the Country."

But do the figures given by Graunt actually indicate a lower birth-rate for London than for the country? He reckoned, as has been shown, with a birth-rate of $31\frac{1}{4}$ for London. In the country, which was represented to him by "a certain Parish in Hampshire," he found (p. 65) for a period of 90 years an average of 70 births and 58 deaths, or "five Christnings for four Burials." From the number of communicants he then "concluded, that there must be about 27, or 2800 Souls in that Parish: from whence it follows, that little more then one of 50 dies in the Country, whereas in London, it seems manifest, that about one in 32 dies. . . ."[2] This implies a birth-rate of little more than 25.

Petty (1693) ([19], pp. 11–13) submits "two fair computations." Referring to Graunt, he states:

. . . we have good Experience (in the said 94 *pag.* of the afore-mentioned Observations) That in the Countrey, but one of fifty dye *per Annum*; and by other late Accounts, that there have been sometimes but

---

[1] At another place (p. 49) he mentions also "Fellows of Colleges."

[2] P. 69. At another place (p. 60), Graunt counts with 13,000 deaths for a population of 384,000 which implies that about one in thirty died.

24 *Births* for 23 *Burials* . . . Suppose there be 600 people, of which let a fiftieth part dye *per Annum*, then there shall dye 12 *per Annum* . . .

There are also other good *Observations*, That even in the Countrey, one in about 30, or 32 *per Annum* hath dyed, and that there have been five *Births* for four *Burials*. Now, according to this Doctrine. 20 will dye *per Annum* out of the above 600, and 25 will be Born . . .

The first statement implies a rural birth-rate of about 21, the second a rural birth-rate of 41⅔. Since, at the same place, he reckons for London with a birth-rate of 31¼ (like Graunt) but at other places, as has been shown, suggests rates varying from 21 to 28, his opinion on the subject cannot carry much weight.

King (1696) studied ([16], p. 44) the differential fertility of urban and rural dwellers more thoroughly. From the "assessments on marriages, births, and burials, and the collector's returns thereupon, and [from] the parish registers" he derived a set of data, which in so far as they relate to fertility may be summarized as follows:

Territory	Population	Yearly Marriages	Ratio of Births to Marriages	Yearly Births	Marriage Rate	Birth- Rate
London and bills of mortality ··	530,000	5,000	4	20,000	9·4	37·6
The cities and market towns ··	870,000	6,800	4·5	30,600	7·8	35·2
The villages and hamlets ··	4,100,000	29,200	4·8	139,400	7·1	34·3
Kingdom ··	5,500,000	41,000	4·64	190,000	7·5	34·7

King himself draws the conclusions:

That though each marriage in London produceth fewer people than in the country, yet London, in general, having a greater proportion of breeders, is more prolific than the other great towns; and the great towns are more prolific than the country. . . .

That the reason why each marriage in London produces fewer children than the country marriages, seems to be,

1. From the more frequent fornications and adulteries;
2. From a greater luxury and intemperance;
3. From a greater intenseness to business;
4. From the unhealthfulness of the coal smoke;
5. From a greater inequality of age between the husbands and wives.

King did not realize that the ratio of births to marriages of the same years does not afford an adequate measure of fertility, and that, since the population of London increased more rapidly than the population of the rest of the country (p. 43), the ratio of births to contemporaneous marriages was likely to be lower in London even if the actual fertility of marriages was the same. His estimate (p. 39) that the "husbands and wives" constituted 37 per cent of the total population in London, 36 per cent in the other cities and towns, and 34 per cent in the villages and hamlets, would indicate that the ratio of births to married persons was identical in the three groups, but his estimate may be wrong and even this ratio, while being more illuminating than the ratio of births to marriages, is by no means conclusive.

D'Avenant (1699), who used the manuscript of King, literally gave ([9], p. 22) the same five reasons for the smaller fertility of the marriages in London, and added: (6) "the Husbands and Wives not living so long as in the Country."

Short (1750) states ([25], p. 121) that "in general Country Breeders are more fruitful in proportion to their Numbers, than in large Towns." But he does not notice any difference between the fertility in smaller cities and the country. From a table ([25], p. 133) showing that in seven market towns with 5,978 families there were 916½ baptisms per year, while in 54 rural parishes with 4,456 families there were 659 baptisms, he concludes ([25], p. 265):

> That in Towns each 13 Families, one with another, have two Children, or six Families and a half have one Child yearly. But in Country Villages 6¾ Families only bring a Child yearly, or 27 Families have yearly four Children. This 27th Part greater Fruitfulness of Towns-people, is very near compensated by the greater Numbers of Bastards produced in them.

He finds also practically the same marriage rate in the market towns and in the country, but states ([25], p. 77) "that People often marry earlier in Towns than in the Country."

Morris (1751) gives [17] as reasons for the smaller fertility in London as compared with the country: (1) "the enormous Use of spirituous Liquors"; (2) "the Discouragement to Matrimony in London." Having shown the causes for the restriction of marriages (see pp. 304, 307–8) in London, he says ([17], p. 2):

> Hence therefore a great Checque to the Births in *London*, and a vast Body of People furnishing to the Amount of the Burials, and not at all to the Christnings.
> Whereas the Christnings in the *Country* exceed the Burials; for the chief

Part of the adult Inhabitants there are little Shopkeepers, Farmers, and Labourers; The two first are generally married for the Convenience of their Business; To which they are also encouraged by the Cheapness of House-Rent and Provisions; and even the Labourers there also, finding the Rent of a Cottage, together with Milk, Roots, and other Food proper for Children, cheap, and within their Income, usually marry, especially if they bend their Minds to reside in the Country.—All these, which are the general Body of the *provincial* Housekeepers, having little Luxury, and who live temperately, in a pure Air, with few Anxieties, are liable to rear great Numbers of healthy Children . . .[1]

Wallace (1753) lays great stress upon the greater fertility of people engaged in agriculture (see p. 310):

The same principle will teach us, that huge and overgrown cities, which are nurseries of corruption and debauchery, and prejudicial in many other respects, are in a particular manner destructive to the populousness of the world, as they cherish luxury, entice great numbers of all ranks to resort to them, and drain the rest of a country of useful labouring hands, who otherwise would be employed in agriculture and the most necessary arts ([27], pp. 22–3).

But neither Morris nor Wallace corroborates his statements by figures.

Brakenridge (1754) attributes ([8], p. 791) the large and increasing excess of deaths over births in London to "the multitude of people that live unmarried":

For in London and Westminster the one-half of the people at least live single, that are above twenty-one years of age; which must prevent almost as many more births, that might be reasonably expected. And this is not mere conjecture; for I have had some proof from a particular detail given me of one parish within the city; where the greater part of those that are above that age are single. In the natural state of mankind it seems plain, that the number of births should be greater than the burials, and I believe that in many parishes in the country they are near double. I found it so in the Isle of Wight, where I lived some time, and had an opportunity to see their registers; for there the births were generally near double.

---

[1] He gives ([17], pp. 1–2) two more reasons for the comparatively low birth-rate of London:

(1) "Multitudes of adult Persons are continually called to *London* from various Parts, by occasional Business. . . . Many of these Persons are not married, and few of those who are, bring their Wives with them to *London* upon these Occasions."

(2) "the large Number of Servants, of both Sexes . . . these Servants being generally unmarried . . ."

While he thinks that in London one-half of the people above twenty-one years of age are single, he estimates ([5], p. 886) the proportion for England at "above one-third." But he apparently believes ([4], pp. 269–70) that the marriages themselves are equally fertile all over the country: "For if we consider, that for every marriage there are four births, at an average, as Dr. Derham, Major Graunt, and others have shewn, and which I have found to be true from the Registers both in the Town and Country . . ."

John Brown (1757) states ([7], pp. 186–7) that "the Intemperance and Disease . . . among the lower Ranks in great Cities bring on in some Degree an Impotence of Propagation"; but he refrains from proving his assertion by figures.

The Poor and the Wealthy

Short (1750) states ([25], pp. 143–4) that "the most laborius Part of Mankind are also the most fruitful in proportion to their Numbers; and the most voluptuous, idle, effeminate and luxurius are the barrenest." ". . . hard Labour makes the Poor more fruitful."[1]

. . . they are less Slaves to the sensual Passion, are more fruitful, their Progeny more vigorous and healthy, have fewer hereditary Diseases, and sooner and more easily overcome the common ones, have stronger Constitutions, and better Stamina, relish a more natural and true Pleasure in Wedlock; they want no Whetters, Pickles, Sauces and Stimulants, or Bracers to procure Appetite and Digestion; they have not their fine covered Table garnish'd with Variety of Dishes and Sauces, but they have a good Stomach, sharp Appetite, true Relish, just Digestion, Distribution and Nutrition . . . ([25], p. 145).

Wallace (1753), while emphasizing that a taste for simplicity and simple manners increases the number of marriages and thereby fertility, thinks ([27], pp. 87–8; see also pp. 13, 151–2) that poverty itself is detrimental to reproduction:

For many ages *Europe* has been over-run with vast multitudes of beggars, and has also abounded with such as having no substance of their own, can only support themselves by daily labour. As frequently neither the first of these can be comfortably supported by begging, nor the second by the profits of their labour; and few of either kind are able to provide

---

[1] See also ibid., p. 35: ". . . and this is often the Lot of the poorer sort to have the greatest Offspring."

for more than themselves, little can be expected from persons in this situation: for either they do not marry at all; or their marriages are not fruitful; or their children die, or become sickly and useless, through the poverty or negligence of their parents.

MEANS OF PROMOTING FERTILITY

Graunt (1662), in order to promote fertility, recommended ([10], p. 52) "encouraging Marriage, and hindering Licentiousness."

Petty also was in favour ([23], **2**, 49) of encouraging marriage: "The first command of God was to encrease and multiply. Wherefore the law for marriages is that which will cause the most encrease of people."

In his "Advices about American plantations" ([23], **2**, 113) he demanded: "That no youth of between 18 & 58 yeares old, nor woman of between 16 & 41 yeares old, bee unmaryed, without manifest impediment allowed by the magistrate."

But as for England, he evidently believed that for the near future the economic obstacles to marriage constituted an unsurmountable barrier ([23], **1**, 267):

Now though there be in efect 112 males for 65 females [at reproductive age], yett it is found by observation that but between 30 & 40 of the teeming women are att present married, by reason the prolifick people are afraid they shall not be able to maintaine the Children they shall begett. . . .

Wherefore—leaving itt to God to punish the sin of women who become with Child against his Comandments, and leaving it to the world to punish such women with Contempt & Dirision, & leaving it to the women themselves to suffer for their folly in not obligding the men they deale with to provide for their Children,—Lett the Government in humanity make provision for every woman with Child for 30 days, the woman leaving her Child to be a servant to the Government for 25 yeares, suppressing the names of their parents (see also [23], **2**, 54–5).

At another place ([23], **2**, 49–50; see also **2**, 114) he went much further:

The way of marriage is now such, that of 100 capable women only 32 are maryed, and these 32 brought 11 children per annum. Whereas 100 teeming women may well bring 40 children per annum.

Wherefore:

(1) Let it be no sin or shame for a woman to bring a child.

(2) Let there be places for women to lye down in.

(3) For keeping the child.

(4) Let there be a tax upon all men of between 18 and 60, and upon all women of between 15 and 45, to defray the said charges of lying in and nursing; and the tax on the women but half that of the men.

But apart from an increase of births through a better care for illegitimate children, he urged a complete reorganization of the institution of marriage in order to promote fertility. His demands may be illustrated by an extract from his Memorandum "Of Marriages &c." concerning Ireland:

1. That none copulate without a covenant.[1]

2. That no youth under 18, and girle under 16, meddle with each other.

3. That such [shall] produce a child once in 3 yeares whilst they are teeming, under a penalty[2]; except in case of sickness, loathsomness &c.

4. That a covenant may bee dissolved in 6 monthes, in case of no conception, to be provd by proper signes; otherwise to continue till the delivery of the woman.

9. That a woman is not bound to declare the father, but to the officer who was privy to the contract and *habet sub sigillo*.

10. That this liberty for short marriages do not take away the present way, nor other covenants of cohabitation, estate, rewards &c.[3]

11. That both parties shall sweare they [are] free from any fowle disease.

13. When Ireland hath above 5 millions of people, that this liberty may cease.[4]

14. Women of above 45 yeares old may not use men, unlesse all under 45 be provided with men.

16. None under covenant shall meddle with another.

18. Incest shall extend but to mother, daughter, and sister.

19. Women that can produce 3 children in 3 yeares shall have[5] —

---

[1] See also "Concerning Marriages," [(23)], **2**, 50: "Let no woman, upon payne of being counted an whore, admitt any man without an indenture of covenants concerning (1) the time of cohabitation, (2) the allowance to the woman, (3) the disposal of the children and the power of inheritance, portion, name &c."

[2] See also "About the Encrease of Mankind," [(23)], **2**, 54–5: "That a woman of 18 yeares old do pay 10 shillings if shee has had no child, and 10 sh. more every yeare, if she has had no child since her last payment. The same to continue till shee be 44 yeares old. . . . Women of high quality to pay more in proportion . . ."

[3] Ibid., 55: "That the marriages already made bee sacredly observd."

[4] Petty estimated the population of Ireland at 1,260,000. See "Heads of Irish Revenue," [(23)], **1**, 96.

[5] The rewards are left blank in the manuscript.

reward, for 10 children —, for 15 children —, and — for 20, out of the public stock.[1]

Halley (1693), having shown that fertility is reduced by the small proportion of married women, recommends ([13], p. 656) to discourage celibacy through special taxes and military service, and to encourage marriage through privileges for families with numerous children and through better care for the poor:

> The Political Consequences hereof I shall not insist on, only the Strength and Glory of a King being in the multitude of his Subjects, I shall only hint, that above all things, Celibacy ought to be discouraged, as, by extraordinary Taxing and Military Service: And those who have numerous Families of Children to be countenanced and encouraged by such Laws as the *Jus trium Liberorum* among the *Romans*. But especially, by an effectual Care to provide for the Subsistence of the Poor, by finding them Employments, whereby they may earn their Bread, without being chargeable to the Publick.

D'Avenant (1699) infers ([9], pp. 34–5) from the figures given by King that "our Polity is some way or other Defective, or the Marriages would bear a nearer proportion with the gross Number of our People." ". . . a large Proportion of the Females remain unmarried, tho' at an Adult Age, which is a dead Loss to the Nation, every Birth being as so much certain Treasure; upon which Accompt, such Laws must be for the Publick Good, as induce all Men to marry whose Circumstances permit it."

To promote marriages, he recommends ([9], pp. 32–5) (1) "securing the Liberties of a Nation"; (2) abolishing the taxes on marriages and births; (3) granting privileges and tax exemptions to families with numerous children, and excluding bachelors from certain

---

[1] [23], **2**, 50–1. See also "Cogitata de Connubiis," ibid., **2**, 57:

"Foeminae omnes a 16 ad 40 annos habeant viros.

"Cesset matrimonium anno aetatis 40mo uxoris . . .

"Habetur illa sterilis quae duobus maritis p . . . ve habentis non pariet, nec alios plures habeat.

"Foeminae steriles, et 40^m annum superantes, liberae sunt ad quamlibet venerem cum viris innuptis et absolutis.

"Viri (post nuptas omnes foeminas 40^m annum nondum agentes) liberi sunt ad quamlibet venerem cum sterilibus et super-annuatis.

"Viri et foeminae a matrimonio soluti possunt alios contractus de cohabitando restaurare, vel inter se vel cum aliis."

offices; (4) compelling the father of an illegitimate child to marry its mother.

If this Tax [on marriages and births] be such a Weight upon the Poor, as to discourage Marriage and hinder Propagation, which seems the Truth, no doubt it ought to be abolish'd; and at a convenient time we ought to change it for some other Duty, if there were only this single Reason, That 'tis so directly opposite to the Polity of all Ages and all Countries.

In order to have Hands to carry on Labour and Manufactures, which must make us Gainers in the Ballance of Trade, we ought not to deterr but rather invite Men to marry, which is to be done by Priviledges and Exemptions, for such a Number of Children, and by denying certain Offices of Trust and Dignities to all unmarried Persons . . .

The Dutch compel Men of all Ranks, to marry the Woman whom they have got with Child; and perhaps it would tend to the farther Peopling of *England*, if the Common People here, under such a certain Degree, were condemn'd by some new Law to suffer the same Penalty.

Short (1750) is of the opinion ([25], pp. 158–66) that since the poor constitute the bulk of "all that are either the Defence or Encreasers of the Riches of a Nation" and since they "are generally the most prolific," all efforts to promote fertility should focus on encouraging the poor to marry:

Since the Bulk of Armies, Navies, Colonies, Manufactories, Agricultures, Mechanics, and Servants; or in a word, all that are either the Defence or Encreasers of the Riches of a Nation, are made up chiefly of the meaner Sort and Poor; and since People of that Rank are generally the most prolific . . .; then People of this Class should be encouraged to marry for Procreation, and all Hinderances removed as much as possible by the Legislature. Now these Hinderances are,[1]

1. Laying on heavy Taxes on the common Necessaries of Life . . .
2. Laying Dues or Duties on the Marriage-Bed and its Product . . .
3. Maintaining numerous, useless, standing Armies in time of Peace.
4. Promoting Batchelors, chiefly, to Places and Offices, publick and œconomical.
5. Squeezing, oppressing, and defrauding the Poor . . .
6. Not executing the present, or not making, and rigorously executing better Laws against Whoredom, Adultery, Drunkenness and Idleness,

---

[1] We give here the full catalogue of "Hinderances" enumerated by Short, although obviously not all 13 hinder marriages of the poor, and although we have quoted some before.

these great Funds of national Expences; from which the Poor that have Families are often not exempted.

7. The Want of, or not executing such Laws as may duly punish the Promoters and Practisers of such impious Arts, as prevent Conception by Whoredom.

8. If all Gratifiers of unnatural Lust are not rigorously punished.

9. The too easily compounding with, and passing by the Parents of Bastards . . .

10. The Neglect of early instilling into the Minds of Youth, the Evil, Danger, and Consequences of Whoredom, Adultery, &c. and the Honourableness, Usefulness, and Convenience of Marriage.

11. Persecution, for differing in mere Forms and Modes of Worship . . .

12. . . . when Parents breed up their Daughters, and give them an Education much superior to their Circumstance, or Fortune they intend to give them . . .

13. . . . many that have acquired by their own Industry a handsome Fortune, make their eldest Son a Gentleman to the Ruin of the rest . . .

He concludes the main part of his book (pp. 247–8):

with the Observation of an eminent Judge of this Nation; that the Growth and Encrease of Mankind is more stinted, from the cautious Difficulty People make to enter on Marriage, from the Prospect of the Trouble and Expences in providing for a Family, than from any thing in the Nature of the Species . . .

Since the Strength and Glory of a King depends on the Multitudes of Subjects; and the Flourishing of Trade and Agriculture, on the Number and Diligence of People, then Cœlibacy, Whoredom, Adultery, and Gratification of unnatural Lust, ought by all means to be discouraged or suppressed, by making the last capital and unpardonable in all Ranks of Men, and laying the first under heavy Taxes (toward the Support of the married Poor,) and drawing out the second into Military Service, when wanted, or sending them into the Plantations, and making the Third severely punishable, which many Countries, both Pagan and Christian, have made Death. And to make Taxes, Fees and Cessments on married poor easy, only find them Employment for their own and Families Maintainance; punish Drunkenness, and Idleness; discard useless Pensioners, and Deputy Officers in the Government; suppress Luxury, Voluptousness, and Intemperance; let arable Grounds be improved, and other enclosed; oblige every Man at home to marry his Whore, or pay a smart Fine toward the Support of the fruitful married Poor, instead of paying Cessments toward the Maintainance of Bastards; but make the Parents keep them, or go into the Army or Colonies; or lay a special, distinct Tax on all Whore-masters, whether they have Children or not, to keep their Bastards.

Morris (1751) demands a tax on keeping numerous unmarried servants and further proposes ([17], p. 25) that only married people be permitted to start a retail business:

> It is further proposed . . . That all *unmarried* Persons be prohibited from setting up *anew*, in any *Retail* Business; such Persons not meriting the Indulgence of this Liberty from the Publick.—Under this Regulation many Persons who would otherwise continue single, would enter into *Matrimony*; whereby the *annual Produce* of *Children* would be promoted, and the rising National Strength and Wealth greatly increased.

He finally (p. 25) urges "the Clergy of the Realm" to "zealously unite in warning their respective Flocks of the fatal Mischiefs flowing upon the Nation, from the Use of . . . Spirituous Liquors by the common People," which he considers the main cause for the decrease of fertility.

According to Wallace ([27], pp. 147–8) it were "to be wished, that as the bountiful Author of nature formed this earth chiefly for an habitation to man, and as with right culture it might support a much greater number than actually live upon it, the present scarcity of people in so many countries was more attended to, and that proper schemes were proposed for putting things on a better footing."

He is rather shy in making concrete proposals, and we shall confine ourselves to quoting that paragraph (pp. 154–5) in which he first recommends one particular scheme for encouraging marriage and then summarizes his views:

> A scheme might also be devised, for supporting the families of such as can easily provide for themselves and their families while alive, but cannot so certainly provide for their widows and children, if they happen to die at an early time of life. This scheme might be somewhat after the model of that lately established by law, for a provision for the widows and children of the ministers of the church, and the masters in the universities of *Scotland, viz.* by erecting one large, or several small societies of married men, who should pay either all at once, or annually, during their lives, certain sums, greater or less, as they might judge convenient, on condition, that proportional sums be paid after their death to their widows or children, in such manner, and with such provisions, as might be thought most proper. Such societies might be a security for the support of widows and children, on the event of the husband's or parent's death, be as useful in policy as banks, cash accounts, and insurance offices in the mercantile

world, and be a great encouragement to marry. It is chiefly by encouraging marriage, by keeping our youth at home, and by taking a greater turn to agriculture and the most useful manufactures, that it seems possible, in the present circumstances of the world, to increase the number of the people in any one country, without draining other places of a proportional number of their inhabitants.

According to Tucker (1775) "the married State is the only efficacious Method of increasing the Numbers of Mankind, and rendering a Country truly populous" ([26], pp. 16, 40).

The methods he recommends for encouraging matrimony are (pp. 17–23):

Now the Way to render Marriage a Matter of universal Choice, and the Aim of both Sexes, is,

I. To cause a Law to be enacted, That no Persons shall either elect, or be elected to any Post of Honour or Profit throughout the Kingdom, but those who either are, or have been married: And with regard to conferring Titles of Honour, and to the Disposal of such Civil Imployments as are lucrative or honourable, but not elective, they may likewise be subject to the same Regulations. . . .

II. It is proposed, That all Persons shall be adjudged to be *Minors*, till they arrive at the Age of *Twenty Five* Years,—unless they *marry* before that time, *with* the *Consent* of their Parents or Guardians, and so be admitted to be of Age at the present Period of *Twenty One*. . . .

III. It is proposed, That the Statute made in the fifth Year of Queen *Elizabeth* against Persons exercising any Mystery, Craft, or *mechanic* Trade, who have not served an Apprenticeship for seven Years, be repealed as to *married* Men, but remain in force against *Batchelors*. . . .

IV. It is proposed, That *married* Men shall be *free*, not only to work as Journeymen, but also to set up all Sorts of *mechanic* Trades in every City and corporate Place whatever, without *Fee*, or Acknowledgment in any Shape or Form. . . .

V. It is proposed, That *married* Men shall be free to reside where-ever they please, with their Wives and Children, without regard to Parish Settlements or Certificates . . .

VI. It is proposed, That Men shall not be allowed to work at, to set up, or carry on certain Trades, which properly belong to Women,— unless they *marry*, and so may be considered as *Assistants* to their Wives. . . .

VII. It is proposed, That all Men for the first twelve Calendar Months after Marriage, shall be exempted from serving any Offices they shall please to decline; also be freed from paying all *personal* Duties and Taxes whatsoever. . . .

Bell (1756), in studying the factors which through an increase of marriages "principally contribute to render a Nation populous," came to the following conclusions ([2], pp. 4-8) :

1. Whatever employments, manners, or political constitutions, are calculated to make the necessary supports of life more easily, and more universally attainable, must essentially tend to promote the populousness of a nation.

2. Whatever is calculated to preserve a frugal simplicity of taste and manners, to regulate the luxurious fancies, and restrain the fruitless indulgencies of a people; is so far adapted to increase the populousness of a nation.

3. Whatever serves to create or improve a general spirit of industry in a nation, does in a very high degree promote the speedy and great increase of a people.

4. Whatever promotes a virtuous regularity of manners, and restrains growth of vice and debauchery, cannot but be greatly instrumental in increasing the populousness of a nation.

These therefore appear to be certain and effectual methods of rendering a nation populous:

The procuring a great plenty of every thing requisite to their support.

The diminishing the number of their imaginary wants.

The universal encouragement and increase of industry.

And the restraining debauchery, and preserving a due regard to the principles of modesty and virtue.

Since "those arts, by which we are supplied with food and all other necessaries, tend directly to promote the populousness of a nation" through each of those four methods, while "commerce and the arts of elegance and refinement . . . are far less adapted to promote the increase of a people," he recommends the utmost promotion of "agriculture and the more necessary employments," and with this object in view demands "an equal division of lands," supported by suitable laws of succession "in a well-constituted republick" ([2], pp. 19, 25, 27-30).

CONCLUSION

A perusal of the British demographic literature during the century preceding the Industrial Revolution affords very scanty testimony on the practice of birth-control. There were, to be sure, writers who, in discussing population growth, pointed to practices preventing conception and procuring abortion, and also to differential fertility between urban and rural dwellers, between the well-to-do and the poor. They referred, however, merely to birth control by unmarried women and they did not intimate that differential fertility of married women was due to any deliberate action but rather to physical disability. To encourage matrimony and to hinder intemperance and licentiousness seemed to them the best and practically the only means of promoting fertility.

REFERENCES

(1) JOHN ARBUTHNOTT. "An Argument for Divine Providence, taken from the constant Regularity observ'd in the Births of both Sexes," *Philosophical Transactions, Giving some Account of the Present Undertakings, Studies, and Labours of the Ingenious, in many Considerable Parts of the World*, **27**, No. 328, for the Months of October, November, and December, 1710, pp. 186–90.

(2) WILLIAM BELL. *A Dissertation on the following Subject: What Causes principally contribute to render a Nation populous? And what Effect has the Populousness of a Nation on its Trade?* Cambridge, 1756.

(3) WILLIAM BRAKENRIDGE. "A Letter to George Lewis Scot, concerning the Number of Inhabitants within the London Bills of Mortality," Nov. 20, 1754, *Philos. Trans.* **48**, part 2, for the year 1754, pp. 788–800.

(4) ——"A Letter to George Lewis Scot, concerning the Number of People in England," Nov. 19, 1755, *Philos. Trans.* **49**, part 1, for the year 1755, pp. 268–85.

(5) ——"A Letter to George Lewis Scot, concerning the present Increase of the People in Britain and Ireland," Nov. 25, 1756, *Philos. Trans.* **49**, part 2, for the year 1756, pp. 877–90.

(6) ——"A Letter to the Earl of Macclesfield, containing an Answer to the Account of the Numbers and Increase of the People of England, by the Rev. Mr. Forster," March 16, 1758, *Philos. Trans.* **50**, part 1, for the year 1757, pp. 465–79.

(7) JOHN BROWN. *An Estimate of the Manners and Principles of the Times*, 2nd. ed. London, 1757.

(8) *A Collection of the Yearly Bills of Mortality, from 1657 to 1758 inclusive.* London, 1759.

(9) CHARLES D'AVENANT. *An Essay upon the Probable Methods of making a People Gainers in the Ballance of Trade.* London, 1699.

(10) JOHN GRAUNT. *Natural and Political Observations Mentioned in a following Index, and made upon the Bills of Mortality.* London, 1662.

(11) MATTHEW HALE. *The Primitive Origination of Mankind.* London, 1677.

(12) EDMUND HALLEY. "An Estimate of the Degrees of the Mortality of Mankind, drawn from curious Tables of the Births and Funerals at the City of Breslaw; with an Attempt to ascertain the Price of Annuities upon Lives," *Philos. Trans.* **17**, No. 196, for the Month of January, 1693, pp. 596–610.

(13) ——"Some further Considerations on the Breslaw Bills of Mortality," *Philos. Trans.* **17**, No. 198, for the Month of March, 1693, pp. 654–6.

(14) DAVID HUME. *Essays, Moral and Political.* 2 vols. Edinburgh, 1742.

(15) ——*Political Discourses.* Edinburgh, 1752.

(16) GREGORY KING. *Natural and Political Observations and Conclusions upon the State and Condition of England,* 1696. London, 1810.

(17) CORBYN MORRIS. *Observations on the Past Growth and Present State of the City of London.* London, 1751.

(18) WILLIAM PETTY. *Observations upon the Dublin-Bills of Mortality MDCLXXXI and the State of that City.* London, 1683.

(19) ——*Another Essay in Political Arithmetick, concerning the Growth of the City of London: With the Measures, Periods, Causes, and Consequences thereof.* 1682. London, 1683.

(20) ——*Five Essays in Political Arithmetick.* London, 1687.

(21) ——*A Treatise of Ireland,* 1687; first printed in *The Economic Writings of Sir William Petty* (Ref. No. 22.), **2**, 545–621.

(22) ——*The Economic Writings of Sir William Petty.* Edited by Charles Henry Hull. 2 vols. Cambridge (U.S.A.), 1899.

(23) ——*The Petty Papers; Some Unpublished Writings of Sir William Petty.* Edited from the Bowood Papers by the Marquis of Lansdowne. 2 vols. London, 1927.

(24) JAMES PORTER. "Answer to Queries sent to a Friend in Constantinople by Dr. Maty, Feb. 1, 1755," *Philos. Trans.* **49**, part 1, for the year 1755, pp. 97–107.

(25) THOMAS SHORT. *New Observations, Natural, Moral, Civil, Political, and Medical, on City, Town, and Country Bills of Mortality.* London, 1750.

(26) JOSIAH TUCKER. *The Elements of Commerce and Theory of Taxes.* Privately printed, 1755.

(27) ROBERT WALLACE. *A Dissertation on the Numbers of Mankind in antient and modern Times: In which the superior Populousness of Antiquity is maintained.* Edinburgh, 1753.

PART II

THE RECRUITMENT OF SOCIAL PERSONNEL

INTRODUCTION TO PART II

by

LANCELOT HOGBEN

THE significance of differential fertility with respect to occupation, locality, and income has been dealt with in the introduction to the first part and in Chapters III and IV. It was there discussed with special reference to its bearing on the social agencies which favour or obstruct the maintenance of the survival minimum. Differential fertility, more particularly differential fertility with respect to occupation, raises issues of another kind. The personnel of different groups depends on a process of social selection involving many extraneous conditions. Thus choice of occupation is partly determined by the capability of the individual, and partly by social status, income, family tradition, and education. In so far as different individual capabilities depend upon genetic differences, differential fertility therefore involves a process of *genetic selection*.

Differencies of social behaviour are the end-products of a complex tradition, process of training, social environment, and material circumstances such as diet, sunlight, and sanitation. Individuals with similar endowments may acquire different levels of vocational proficiency according to the combination of circumstances incidental to their upbringing. Similarly, natural endowments of different individuals may be so different that identical upbringing would lead to noticeably different behaviour patterns. At present it is extremely difficult to decide whether an individual deviation from the norm of social behaviour is determined mainly by differences of genetic constitution or mainly by a specially propitious environment. This is just as true of vocational proficiency as of any other characteristic of social behaviour. The intensity of genetic selection which results from occupational fertility therefore depends on the extent to which differences of individual proficiency are due to one or the other. Among other things it also depends on the extent to which the recruitment of occupational personnel is based on individual proficiency or on extraneous circumstances.

The ensuing chapters are primarily concerned with one of two different issues involved in the qualitative aspect of differential fertility. We may take the fact that individuals are *different* as given. Without asking anything about the origins of these differences as influenced by nature or nurture, we may investigate how far the process of occupational recruitment is based on special aptitude for a particular occupation; and the problem of political arithmetic is then to estimate the remediable wastage due to defective social organization and the loss of social efficiency resulting therefrom.

If the use of the word *wastage* in this context is an offence against established conventions of academic discourse, it may be said that no objection is raised when a chemist seeks to assess the wastage of phosphates in sewage. The same word is equally appropriate to the class of social phenomena illustrated by the following from an article on Borstal in *The Times* (March 1, 1937). The official report cited in the article refers to:

a boy from a North Country industrial centre. His mother had died when he was four years old, and his father, who had been in trouble for cruelty to his children, had deserted him shortly afterwards. The lad had lived with relatives for several years. These people had not allowed him to avail himself of a scholarship which he had won while he was at his elementary school, and at the age of 14 he had found himself in a quite unsuitable warehouse job in a local mill. He had lost this, as he had later lost several others, through the trade depression, and for nearly two and a half years before the beginning of his Borstal training he had been unemployed. He was very unsociable, and most of his enforced leisure had been taken up with the working out of calculations and the writing of essays. He had an astonishing knowledge of Stock Exchange news and ran an imaginary exchange of his own. Some of his essays related to his ambition to become Prime Minister. He had prepared detailed schemes for dealing with the problems of agriculture, unemployment, India, and disarmament. In an attempt to run away to London to get office work he stole. He was caught and put on probation. Again he stole, and again he was caught. On this occasion his sentence was one of Borstal detention. His test results made it clear that he was a boy of outstanding intellectual ability. Although he was only $16\frac{1}{2}$ at the time he scored an intelligence test mark considerably above the average for university students. In a clerical test he did exceptionally well, and he had good practical abilities. He would probably have made an excellent rating surveyor.

This citation illustrates the social wastage of personnel. Another aspect of the problems which arise from the existence of differential fertility is the biological wastage of personnel. From the standpoint of genetic selection we may investigate the extent to which individual differences are determined by genetic constitution, and the deteriora-

tion of biological resources resulting from different rates of reproduction in different occupational or other social groups. Inquiry
into the social wastage of personnel can be undertaken from the
analysis of data already at hand, and the four ensuing chapters are
mainly concerned therewith. They open a field of inquiry which
has been conspicuously neglected and offers ample scope for further
investigations on class mobility and changing social structure.
Inquiry into the biological wastage of personnel cannot be undertaken until much more research into human heredity has been
prosecuted.

Meanwhile we should scrutinize dogmatic assertions about the
relation between genetic variability and social behaviour with due
regard to the difficulties of the problem and the paucity of relevant
information. Because differences in the intelligence quotient are
not much affected by school environment, many writers have given,
and still give, support to the view that differences of this kind
are a reliable index of inborn endowment. Such assertions are not
supported by the results of inquiries into twin resemblance.[1] They
overlook the significance of the uterine environment and the period
of social training before intelligence tests can be applied. Between
birth and the age at which formal education begins there is a
protracted and, it may be, highly significant period during which
differences of social behaviour may affect the behaviour of an
individual. Hence the comparative constancy of a psychological index
such as the intelligence quotient between four and fourteen years of
age offers no presupposition in favour of the view that it measures a
characteristic which is little affected by differences in the family
environment. In the light of new evidence derived from the study of
twins, conclusions about inborn differences based on intelligence
test score comparisons of different occupational and racial groups
have little scientific validity.

One aspect of genetic variability in human communities is the
subject of a final chapter. It is included in this volume because the
prevalence of racialist dogmas which have no scientific foundation is
profoundly affecting the qualitative distribution of population at the
present time.

[1] *Vide* Hogben, *Nature and Nurture*. (Allen & Unwin.)

CHAPTER VIII

ABILITY AND OPPORTUNITY IN ENGLISH EDUCATION

by

J. L. GRAY

and

PEARL MOSHINSKY

(*from the Department of Social Biology, University of London*)

I. INTRODUCTION

MODERN methods of psychological measurement, together with a growing interest in the qualitative aspects of the population problem both in England and in the U.S.A., have evoked numerous studies of the relative ability of different social groups within a community. The essential procedure adopted in these studies has been to compare average (mean) indices of ability, e.g. mean Intelligence Quotients. On this basis different social groups have been ranked in order of ability. Aside from the very dubious nature of the evidence adduced to support the general inference that any observed differences are exclusively or even predominantly genetic in origin, previous inquiries of this sort throw little light upon the fundamental problem to which this investigation is directed. However great may be the discrepancies recorded, the comparison of averages is of itself entirely inadequate to display the distribution of ability within a population of varied social composition.

The problem which we have set out to examine may be put thus: To what extent does the existing machinery of social selection adjust educational opportunity to individual ability? In comparing average figures for different social groups we are comparing in effect the net capability of groups of individuals which make very varied contributions to the net personnel of the society in which they live. Let us suppose that in a population one social group A is ten times more numerous than another social group B, and that the proportion of specially gifted individuals (e.g. those above a certain level of I.Q.) is three times as high in B as in A. This may result in a very considerable superiority of the mean ability of the smaller group. Now suppose further that all individuals in group B, but none in group A, have access to a type of education suitable to individuals of the selected level of ability. The result would be, in spite of the superficial correspondence between the class distribution of ability and the class distribution of opportunity, that only three-thirteenths of the available high ability of the community would be utilized by the educational facilities it provided.[1] Recognition of this issue might serve to exhibit the distribution of high ability in the population as a whole in a less alarming light. It would also make it less easy to conceal the extent to which individual ability is wasted by a defective mechanism of educational selection.

The facts are, of course, more complicated than those in the illustration, which is given simply to clarify the nature of the problem. It is no part of our intention to minimize differences between group averages nor to attempt to distinguish between such as are the result of environmental and such as are attributable to genetic differences. We may state in advance that this investigation is in no way contradictory to the observed findings of earlier studies. Indeed, in so far as our data differ from theirs, we have no hesitation in affirming that the mean differences which we disclose are actually greater than those previously recorded. We make the fullest allowance for the existence of genuine mean differences between the intelligence of different social groups within the population, and consequently accept for our present purpose a conservative or maximum estimate of the extent to which these differences are determined by genetic inequalities. This allowance is almost certainly too generous, but even when it is made a striking discrepancy still remains between the amount of good material in the community

---

[1] Let A consist of 10,000 individuals of whom a proportion x have an I.Q. over 130, B consist of 1,000 individuals of whom a proportion y have an I.Q. over 130 and $x = \dfrac{y}{3}$.

$$\text{In population A } \frac{10,000y}{3} \text{ have I.Q. } 130, \text{ and}$$

$$\text{In population B } 1,000y \text{ have I.Q. } 130.$$

Only $1,000y$ individuals are being used, when we have a total of $1,000y + \dfrac{10,000y}{3}$ superior individuals.

$$\frac{1,000y}{1,000y + \dfrac{10,000y}{3}} \text{ are being used } = \frac{1}{1 + \dfrac{10}{3}} = \frac{3}{13}.$$

and the extent to which the existing machinery of social selection utilizes it. The inequality of the distribution of educational facilities in relation to the distribution of educational ability within the several social classes in this country, as described in this investigation, affords no ground for complacency. On the contrary, it discloses a defect in our social organization more extensive than is commonly recognized.

Sections II–IV of this study are concerned with the principles on which we constructed our survey of the distribution of ability within the largest sample of the English school population yet examined, and contain the raw material of the investigation. The remaining sections consist of a more detailed institutional analysis of the data and present the main conclusions. In subsequent papers we hope to carry the argument still further by an analysis of the factors of parental occupation and fertility in the selective process.

No attempt has hitherto been made to compare adequate samples of children educated in schools of widely varied educational and social type. The recent nation-wide inquiry into *The Intelligence of Scottish Children* (1933) of a single age-group included private as well as elementary pupils, but the data are not separately distinguished. In countries like the U.S.A. or Scotland, where the vast majority of children of different social levels are educated in State schools of similar type, such an undertaking may well appear of little consequence. Two selective factors in English education demand careful control when the ability of the school population as a whole is the subject of investigation. The first is that a large number of children receive an education the cost of which is defrayed, either wholly or in part, by their parents. The second is that in the public elementary school population the agency responsible for the selection of pupils for free education of a higher type operates in the great majority of cases once and for all at the age of 11 plus. Below this age the school population is divided into two parts, free and fee-paying pupils. Above it, this division persists and classification is further complicated by the selection from pupils of elementary school origin of a certain number who proceed to other types of schools. This selection is based mainly on ability, although its effect is limited by the extent of state expenditure on higher education. The majority remain in the ordinary elementary school until they leave at the age of 14, some proceed with scholarships to secondary schools, others are drafted into elementary schools of a higher type, i.e. central schools. Valid norms for the performances of school children at different ages on standardized psychological tests cannot be obtained unless adequate samples of every type of pupil are tested and combined in their proper proportions. In addition, account must be taken of pupils in fee-paying schools.

In this study more than ten thousand children from five different types of schools were examined during the year 1933–4. Data are presented concerning the distribution of ability in the entire group, in each type of school, in the group which receives the opportunity to pursue a higher education, and in the two contrasting groups of free and fee-paying pupils, with the aid of a system of weighting designed to take account of the selective factors mentioned above and of inequalities in our sampling.

II. THE NATURE OF THE SAMPLE

The kind of social behaviour selected for investigation is that measured by standardized intelligence tests of the type devised by Binet and Spearman in the beginning of the present century and developed by Burt, Terman, and others. Such tests enable comparisons to be made between the performances of different individuals educated in the characteristic manner of the twentieth century and for the most part in schools maintained by the State, on problems which form an essential part of the curriculum of schools in most modern communities. By general consent these performances are described by the adjective "intelligent," and it is in this sense alone that we employ the word intelligence for the characteristic under review. The test selected was the Otis Group Advanced Test, Form A, which has been used by the Department of Social Biology in two earlier investigations into the intellectual resemblance of relatives. This test possesses a high reliability, is completely objective in scoring, is simple to administer and is extensively used both in the U.S.A. and in this country. The original norms for the calculation of Mental Ages were based on the scores of more than 25,000 American school children between the ages of 8 and 18 years. When comparing individuals of different ages, the chief criterion of any such test is its ability to yield an index of intelligence independent of age. Intelligence Quotients determined on the basis of American norms for Mental Age have been shown both by Herrman and Hogben (1933) and Gray and Moshinsky (1933) to correlate very insignificantly with age. The Otis Test has already been adapted by the publishers for use with English children, and further modifications, both in the printed test and in the *Manual of Instructions*, were suggested by the present writers and incorporated in the new edition of the *Manual* (1934). These modifications, which have been employed throughout this investigation, were designed to simplify and clarify the verbal and printed instructions for the administration of the test. We have naturally considered the use of various tests of English origin, but these were found to be defective under one or more of the criteria enumerated above.

The Otis Test includes ten categories of performance, namely: (1) Following Directions, (2) Word Opposites, (3) Disarranged Sentences, (4) Proverbs, (5) Numerical Problems, (6) Geometrical Figures, (7) Analogies, (8) Similarities, (9) Narrative Completion, (10) Verbal Memory.

The conditions under which the tests were administered were made subject to as rigid a degree of standardization as was possible in the circumstances. In addition to the two authors, four other full-time investigators were employed, and all attempted to maintain the same technique of administration. All the children of this study were tested by these six examiners and in no case were tests given by teachers or any other person. In certain matters, e.g. the number of children tested in a group, the spatial distribution of the children in a classroom, the absence of all adults other than the examiners, etc., we were able to secure a large measure of uniformity. It was not possible, of course, to control every environmental factor of conceivable relevance. Different groups of children were tested on different days of the week at different times of the day, and thus probably in different conditions of physiological and psychological efficiency; nor could we control the differences in the amenities of school construction which characterize schools of different social type. Thus in addition to differences between individuals and between groups which might exert their influence prior to the administration of the test, such as those commonly discussed under the general heading of differences due to nurture, there were other environmental inequalities sufficient in themselves, however slight, to make us alive to the possibility of a certain amount of error in the constants denoting Intelligence Quotients.

In each school examined all children who were within our age range and present on the day of our visit were tested simultaneously in one or more groups. Where the numbers on the school roll were too large for our staff to cope with, we adhered to a strictly random method of selecting the group that was actually tested. Thus there is no possibility that the samples from each school are imperfect by reason of selection for ability.

Since we could only test comparatively small samples of the total populations with which we were concerned, we tried to make them as representative as possible. The schools in the public elementary group (junior, senior, and central) were selected in such a way that practically every district in the L.C.C. area was included. Our sample also contains the material that was collected by the present authors for a recent investigation into the intellectual resemblance of first-cousins and sibs. This was necessarily drawn from a much larger number of schools, since only a limited number of related pairs could be found in any one school. Altogether nearly one hundred schools were sampled in this group. We would add that we were careful also to include a certain number of non-provided schools, i.e. schools whose fabric is maintained by various religious denominations and other educational foundations, whose tradition is reflected in the personnel both of teachers and pupils, as also to some extent in the curriculum.

In the case of secondary schools, we were fortunate in being able to test approximately one-third of the total in London. These were likewise drawn from various parts of the city and include schools wholly maintained by the L.C.C. and those on the Grant List, both old and new foundations. In venturing to survey children in private and preparatory schools we were entering unknown territory. We could visit only such schools whose Heads responded to the invitation sent out by various interested bodies on our behalf. A study of the prospectuses of the schools tested and of the range of their means affords evidence of very considerable variety in both educational and financial status.

Table I shows the intellectual range of the schools in our sample. Figures for the mean I.Q. and I.B.[1] of every school were separately calculated and arranged in order of value. From this data we obtained the mean of the median school and the range of the means of the middle 50 per cent of schools within each group. The table does not include the cousins and sibs data.

All the children tested in our samples of various populations were between the ages of 9.0 and 12.6 years inclusive. The decision to

---

[1] For I.B., see below, p. 343.

restrict the age-range to these limits was based on the experience of the two previous investigations already mentioned. In these it was found that a significant proportion of children aged 8–9 years had to be rejected because they scored less than the norm for the earliest age for which norms have been calculated, namely, 8.0 years, and consequently could not be given an Intelligence Quotient. In other words, data for this year of age would be selected for high intelligence. Similarly, in the case of children above 12.6 a substantial number achieve or exceed the score yielding the highest Mental Age on the American norms, namely, 18.0, and in these

TABLE I

DISTRIBUTION OF MEANS OF SCHOOLS IN EACH GROUP

Type of School.	No. of Schools	Mean of Median School.		Range of Means of Middle 50 per cent. of Schools.	
		I.Q.	I.B.	I.Q.	I.B.
1. Elementary:					
(a) 9.0–11.0 [1] . .	16	113·7	99·8	108·7–121·6	89·6–104·0
(b) 11.1–12.6 [1] . .	17	116·1	98·5	110·3–118·6	90·0–101·9
2. Central . . .	23	137·5	126·2	135·5–140·8	123·6–131·1
3. Secondary:	30				
(a) Free pupils . .		148·8	147·3	146·9–151·4	143·3–151·4
(b) Fee-paying pupils.		131·7	119·2	126·2–133·8	111·9–122·2
(c) All pupils . .		136·9	129·2	135·3–139·8	124·5–131·9
4. Private . . .	14	122·9	109·7	119·9–126·7	104·8–112·1
5. Preparatory . .	26	134·0	123·9	129·0–137·0	115·9–128·3

[1] Excluding cousins and sibs data.

cases I.Q. does not rise with increasing score for children of constant age; in fact, it decreases with increasing chronological age, regardless of differences in score. It is thus impossible to compare the performances of children scoring more than 130 points on the Otis scale. I.Q. ceases to be independent of age and becomes entirely unreliable as an index of intelligence.

Table II shows the age distribution of the entire data classified according to different types of schools, together with the total numbers tested.

III.· RELIABILITY

Assuming that an intelligence test correlates highly with independent estimates of intelligence and is internally homogeneous, it remains to be proved that it is *reliable* in the sense that, when administered to the same group on two successive occasions, the order of the indices within the group is not materially altered on the second occasion, i.e. that there is a high correlation between the I.Q.s awarded on both occasions. Kelley (*The Interpretation of Educational Measurements*, p. 299) gives a reliability coefficient for the Otis Test of $r = + 0 \cdot 967$. The present authors examined the reliability of the Otis Test in two experiments. In the first 277 children aged 9.0–12.6,

TABLE II

AGE DISTRIBUTION OF THE DATA IN THREE-MONTHLY INTERVALS

Age.	Element-ary, 9.0–11.0.	Element-ary, 11.1–12.6.	Central.	Second-ary Free Pupils.	Second-ary Fee-payers.	Private.	Prep-aratory.
9.0– 9.2	234	—	—	—	36	26	34
9.3– 9.5	245	—	—	—	36	39	46
9.6– 9.8	272	—	—	—	46	39	80
9.9– 9.11	279	—	—	—	63	46	51
10.0–10.2	276	—	—	1	82	41	52
10.3–10.5	263	—	—	5	98	53	66
10.6–10.8	299	—	—	3	121	58	71
10.9–10.11	294	—	—	5	100	65	78
11.0–11.2	100	188	—	69	149	46	62
11.3–11.5	—	259	105	168	177	49	77
11.6–11.8	—	244	319	203	174	76	81
11.9–11.11	—	253	423	187	155	48	96
12.0–12.2	—	249	532	197	168	54	77
12.3–12.5	—	221	570	155	209	67	90
12.6	—	39	82	44	47	22	26
Totals	2,262	1,453	2,031	1,037	1,661	729	987

taken from three elementary schools, were tested with Form A and ten days later with the alternative Form B. The value of the correlation between the I.Q.s was $r = + 0 \cdot 89 \pm 0 \cdot 0007$. The corresponding figure for the Index of Brightness (see below) was $r = + 0 \cdot 95 \pm 0 \cdot 0002$. In the second experiment 110 children from another elementary school were tested with Form A and retested with the same form after an interval of one year. The correlations were: I.Q., $r = + 0 \cdot 85 \pm 0 \cdot 027$; and I.B., $r = + 0 \cdot 92 \pm 0 \cdot 015$. These correlations are very high and demonstrate that the performance of an individual on the Otis Test bears a constant relation to the performance of other members of the group in which he is tested, when all are tested on two successive occasions. In other words, the test appears to measure the same thing when given on two different occasions.

The most essential requirement of a test of intelligence is that it should be capable of yielding an index independent of age, i.e. that it should enable us to compare on an absolute scale the intelligence of persons of different ages. Herrman and Hogben found correlations between age and I.Q. for twins and siblings between the ages of 8.0 and 14.0 of $r = -0\cdot16$ and $r = -0\cdot12$ in two groups of children arranged so as to eliminate the factor of genetic relationship. In the case of sibs only, the data were divided into two sections, composed respectively of the older and the younger members of each related pair. The correlations were $r = -0\cdot08$ for the younger and $r = -0\cdot35$ for the older group. Their sample was drawn from junior and senior elementary schools only. They drew attention to the selective factor introduced at the age of 11 plus by the Junior County Scholarship Examination. The children who did not proceed to central or secondary schools constituted a relatively backward group, which would partly account for the negative correlation between age and I.Q. in the older group. It should also be noted that the same thing will occur when a large proportion of the children in a group score above the maximum for which Mental Ages are assigned. Herrman and Hogben showed further that between the ages of 9.0 and 12.6 the mean I.Q. of different age-groups was subject to less variation than was the case below or above these limits. In consequence, Gray and Moshinsky in a later study of cousin and sib resemblance restricted their data to this age-range. They obtained for two samples of 610 and 611 respectively correlations between age and I.Q. of $r = +0\cdot005$ and $r = +0\cdot02$. Primarily because these correlations were so close to zero, we decided to adopt for the present investigation the same restriction of age.

Column I of Table III gives the values for the correlation between age and I.Q. for each separate type of school. It will be noticed at once that the figures for central and secondary scholarship children are in striking contrast with the rest. These two groups are selected for high intelligence, and thus by far the largest proportion of individuals have scores above the figure for the computation of maximum Mental Age. For the Otis Test the raw score corresponding to the maximum Mental Age is 130. So, if a sample of children be selected all of whom attain or exceed this score, and thus have the same maximum Mental Age of 18.0, the magnitude of their I.Q.s will vary inversely with their chronological age, and the correlation coefficient for age and I.Q. would be negative in sign and unity in value. Thus in the testing of school populations selected on the basis of ability the I.Q. technique is gravely defective. In such cases it is

TABLE III

I.Q.—AGE AND I.B.—AGE CORRELATIONS

Type of School.	Age and I.Q.		Age and I.B.	
	r	N	r	N
1. *Elementary*, 9.0–11.0:				
(*a*) Present investigation	+ ·0008± ·026	1,419	— ·01 ± ·026	1,496
(*b*) Cousins and sibs [1] (i)	+ ·03 ± ·052	371	+ ·03 ± ·049	370
(ii)	— ·01 ± ·053	360		
2. *Elementary*, 11.1–12.6:				
(*a*) Present investigation	— ·16 ± ·031	994	— ·18 ± ·030	1,011
(*b*) Cousins and sibs [1] (i)	+ ·02 ± ·066	231	— ·01 ± ·064	235
(ii)	— ·11 ± ·063	244		
3. *Central Schools*	— ·09 ± ·022	2,026	— ·04 ± ·022	2,026
4. *Secondary Free Pupils:*				
(*a*) Junior county scholars	— ·50 ± ·028	700	— ·05 ± ·038	700
(*b*) Other free pupils .	— ·30 ± ·050	337	— ·07 ± ·052	338
(*c*) All free pupils. .	— ·41 ± ·026	1,037	— ·04 ± ·031	1,038
5. *Secondary Fee-payers* .	+ ·02 ± ·025	1,652	+ ·02 ± ·025	1,661
6. *Private* . . .	+ ·04 ± ·038	706	+ ·05 ± ·037	728
7. *Preparatory* . .	— ·02 ± ·032	982	+ ·06 ± ·032	988
8. *Private and Preparatory combined* . . .	+ ·001 ± ·024	1,688	+ ·06 ± ·024	1,716

[1] In the cousins and sibs data two samples have been taken for the I.Q. to avoid having related pairs in the same table. Only one of the two samples has been worked out for the I.B.

impossible to make valid comparisons between the intellectual indices of different individuals.

These considerations made it necessary for us to seek for an alternative index by which individuals could be reliably assessed for performance on the Otis Scale. It was decided to adopt in this investigation, side by side with the more familiar I.Q., a device invented by Dr. Otis for use with his intelligence scale, namely, the Index of Brightness. I.B., as it will henceforth be described, is a measure of the increment or decrement of an individual's score from the normal score of persons of his exact chronological age, the norm being in all cases expressed as 100. For example, if an individual scores 10 points more than the norm for his age, his I.B. will be 110. Similarly, if he scores 10 points less, his I.B. will be 90. It follows that the I.B. of an individual of given chronological age rises with increasing score without limit. Thus the I.B. makes it possible to compare the intellectual rank of children, even in groups highly selected for ability. Moreover, where the variability of the distribution of the scores at each age is approximately identical, the I.B. provides a reliable absolute scale on which to assess the intelligence of children of different chronological age.

In the calculation of I.B.s it is not necessary to know the normal scores for any individuals outside the age-group actually assessed. We therefore took the opportunity of deriving new norms for the Otis Test administered to English school children. It has long been evident to us that the American norms, on which the I.Q.s in this investigation are based, are throughout of a much lower order than the scores actually made by children in the London area. It would be highly desirable to calculate English norms for the whole age-range comprehended by the Otis Test. If this were done and if it were found that they are throughout on a higher level than the American norms, then the point at which the I.Q. becomes unreliable by reason of the upper limit of Mental Age would be considerably postponed, and hence the I.Q. technique would become more useful than it is at present. But the construction of a complete set of norms based on samples of adequate size for each month of age would have been too formidable a task to be undertaken as part of the present investigation. We do not believe that it could be successfully accomplished with fewer than twenty to thirty thousand individuals. We had, therefore, to be content with deriving new norms applicable to English school children in the London area between the ages of 9.0 and 12.6 years. This restricted age-range, together with the largeness of our total sample, enabled us to base the norms for each unit of age on a much greater number of cases than has been used, to the best of our knowledge, in any previous attempt to derive norms for any group test.[1]

The second column of Table III shows the superiority of the I.B. over the I.Q. as an index of the intellectual rank of children in

[1] Comparative tables of the original American and the new English norms will be found in the *Manual of Directions for Administering the Otis Test* (Harrap, revised edition, 1934).

selected populations. It may be useful to add, since elsewhere in this investigation the data of I.Q. and I.B. are printed side by side, that in the case of secondary school scholarship children and central school children the I.B. figures are to be regarded as more reliable than those for I.Q. This conclusion also applies in a lesser degree to the cases where such data are combined with other data to produce weighted figures referring to the whole population of elementary-school origin. It should further be noted that the manner in which the I.B. is determined makes it a more sensitive index than I.Q. and that consequently the standard errors of the various mean figures herein presented are greater in the case of I.B. than of I.Q.

IV. THE STRUCTURE OF THE ENGLISH EDUCATIONAL SYSTEM

To obtain a representative sample of English school children within our age-range, no less than five different types of schools require to be included. These are Public Elementary (usually divided into Junior and Senior schools), Central (for administrative purposes, part of the Elementary school system), Secondary, Private, and Preparatory. In the case of the secondary schools, moreover, the pupils must be further divided into two groups, one consisting of children selected by scholarship examinations from the elementary schools, the cost of whose education is wholly or in great part defrayed by the State, and the other of fee-paying pupils amongst whom there exists little or no selection for intelligence.

The school population of England and Wales falls naturally into two great groups of strikingly unequal size: (1) free pupils, and (2) fee-paying pupils. Under (1) are grouped pupils in both types of elementary schools, in central schools and those in secondary schools who possess scholarships or free places. (2) includes secondary-school fee-payers and children attending private and preparatory schools. ·

(1) *Free Pupils*

The great majority of children in this country begin their education round about the age of 5 in schools provided by the State and are compelled to remain at school at least until the age of 14. But they do not all remain at the same type of school. The elementary school population is subdivided at the age of 11 plus as a result of a scholarship examination attempted by a large proportion of all children, with the exception of the few who have been drafted into special schools for the physically and mentally retarded. Only up to the age of 11, therefore, would a random sample of the population of elementary school origin be found in one type of school.

In order to obtain mean figures for the ability of children of elementary school origin over the age of 11.0, we have combined samples of elementary, secondary scholarship and central school children and weighted them according to the proportions in which they respectively occur. Our samples of these three types of schools are elementary 11.1 to 12.6 = 1,457, central = 2,026, and secondary scholarship pupils = 1,038. As will be seen, the last two samples are disproportionately large, but we were anxious to ascertain as reliably as possible the distribution of ability amongst free pupils in central and secondary schools, who, so far as we know, have not been included in any previous investigation of this kind.

The Education Officer of the L.C.C. kindly supplied figures referring to the numbers of junior county scholars, central school pupils, and residual elementary school pupils aged 11.0 to 12.0 for the year 1932–33. Our sample of the last group stood in the ratio of 1 : 53 of the total in London, and of the central school pupils in the ratio of 1 : 7·8. We estimated that the total number of free pupils in secondary schools in London other than junior county scholars bore the same relation to the figure for junior county scholars as in our sample, namely, five-twelfths. We are thus able to state that our sample of all free pupils in secondary schools stood in the ratio of 1 : 3·6 of the London total. We assumed, further, that the same proportions would hold in all three cases for children between 11.1 and 12.6 years as between 11.0 and 12.0. The weights finally employed were elementary 11.1 to 12.6 × 14, central × 2 and secondary school free pupils × 1.

In order to make statements concerning the mean of all free pupils over our entire age-range of 9.0–12.6, it was only necessary to assume that children aged 9.0–11.0, of whom we tested 2,261, were in the proportion 4 : 3 to children aged 11–12.6, since the age-range of the former is $\frac{4}{3}$ of the latter and our samples of both were in approximately the same proportion to the total number in London.

(2) Fee-paying Pupils

While no unanimity exists in the classification of schools outside the public elementary system, we believe that a clear line of demarcation may be found in the acceptance or otherwise of financial aid from the State. Accordingly, we have restricted the term Secondary to schools either wholly maintained by or in receipt of financial grants from the State. These grants are conditional not only on a certain standard of efficiency being maintained, but on the provision by the school authorities of a certain number of scholarship places to pupils from elementary schools. Other schools exist which provide an education of a post-primary type, some of whom apply to the Board of Education for recognition as "efficient." There is no exact information available about the number of schools which are not inspected by the Board, nor is it known precisely what educational standards prevail among them. It is possible, however, to distinguish within the group of schools not on the Grant List one fairly homogeneous type commonly known as Preparatory schools. We have defined a preparatory school as one which is primarily concerned with preparing children for entrance to the public schools, i.e. schools belonging to the Headmasters' Conference, and which impose an upper age limit of 13 years. We have further confined the term to schools whose Heads are members of the two Associations of Headmasters and Headmistresses respectively of Preparatory Schools. Children in public schools, being for the most part upwards of 13 years, fall outside the scope of this investigation, but it will be seen that we have tested a sample of the same population at an earlier age.

Schools which are neither on the Grant List nor Preparatory, in the sense in which we have used the term, we have classified as Private. Like most of the preparatory schools, they are conducted for profit, but they offer an education alternative to both the elementary plus secondary school on the one hand, and the preparatory cum public school system on the other. As a rule they impose no upper age limit. There are a few large public day-schools in London which are neither on the Grant List nor conducted for profit. Where the scale of fees charged was comparable with that of grant-aided secondary schools, they were classified with the latter, not with private schools. They are all, of course, recognized as "efficient" by the Board of Education.

We are conscious of the imperfections of our samples of preparatory and private schools. We suspect, in the first place, that the figures in our data for the intelligence of such children are inflated by the inclusion of too high a proportion of the better schools. Secondly, there is no reliable evidence available concerning the relative proportions of private and preparatory schools. Hence we have had to group them together. Since the mean for preparatory schools is considerably higher than that for private schools, it follows that, according as the proportion of preparatory to private schools is greater or less, our figure for the combined group is either too low or too high. It must also be taken into account that twenty-six preparatory schools are represented in our data, compared with only fourteen private schools. Reference to a publication entitled *Schools 1934* (Truman and Knightley) shows that in the London Postal Area there are three times as many private as preparatory schools. But we do not know if this work is complete, nor if the distribution of pupils corresponds with that of schools. It would also be rash to conclude that the same proportion exists for the country as a whole. While we lack an estimate accurate enough to form the basis of any argument in this investigation, it is sufficiently clear that the assumptions adopted here lead to a considerable exaggeration of the average ability of children in the combined private and preparatory school population.

The task of determining figures for the intelligence of the entire class of fee-paying pupils is one of considerable difficulty. We tested 1,661 fee-payers in thirty secondary schools in the London area, or a proportion of approximately 1 : 3·6 of all schools on the Grant List (and including several which we have specially defined as secondary schools). Official statistics do not reveal the total number of *pupils* within our age-group in London secondary schools, and we had to assume that it stood in the same relation to our sample as did the total number of schools to the schools in our sample. The Report of a Departmental Committee of the Board of Education on Private Schools (1932) estimates that there are 350,000 children between the ages of 5 and 14 years in private and preparatory schools together. To find the approximate number in London within our age-group 9.0–12.6 the following method was adopted. We estimated that there were 217,000 children in London public elementary schools within this age-range. Now, the proportion of preparatory and private school children to public elementary school children in the country as a whole is one-fifteenth. Assuming that the same proportion held good in London within our age-range, our sample of 1,716 stood in the ratio of 1 : 8·5 to this figure. For convenience in arithmetic we employed the equivalent whole numbers 3 and 7 as weights for the secondary school fee-payers and preparatory and private school children respectively instead of 3·6 and 8·5.

V. THE SIGNIFICANCE OF MEAN DIFFERENCES

Table IV shows the means for each type of school population separately, together with the number of individuals tested.

It will be seen that the mean I.Q. of every type of school is considerably in excess of 100. This makes it impossible to compare I.Q.s for English children taking the Otis Test with those derived from

TABLE IV
MEANS OF DIFFERENT SCHOOL POPULATIONS

Type of School.	I.B.	N	I.Q.	N
Elementary, 9.0–11.0 .	97·2 ± 0·58	2,261	113·8 ± 0·47	2,150
Elementary, 11.1–12.6	93·2 ± 0·78	1,457	110·8 ± 0·57	1,469
Central . . .	126·8 ± 0·40	2,026	137·3 ± 0·29	2,026
Secondary Free Pupils	147·3 ± 0·57	1,038	148·8 ± 0·30	1,037
All Free Pupils .	98·4 ± 0·43	6,782	115·9 ± 0·34	6,682
Private . . .	108·4 ± 1·11	728	122·9 ± 0·88	706
Preparatory . .	126·9 ± 0·96	988	136·2 ± 0·72	982
Private and Preparatory .	119·0 ± 0·76	1,717	130·6 ± 0·58	1,688
Secondary Fee-payers.	118·8 ± 0·66	1,661	130·4 ± 0·52	1,652
All Fee-paying Pupils .	118·9 ± 0·57	3,378	130·6 ± 0·43	3,340
Mean of All . . .	100·1 ± 0·40	10,160	117·1 ± 0·31	10,022

other tests. The comparison of groups within the present investigation is not of course affected, although for reasons already mentioned it is less valid than comparisons using I.B. The fact that the mean for the random group of elementary school children (9.0–11.0) is less than the mean for the whole population of free pupils may be attributed to a certain amount of selection that occurs even under the age of 11. The decline in the mean of the residual elementary group (11.1–12.6) is evidence of the selection of many of the abler children over 11 years of age to secondary and central schools. It is interesting to observe that the mean of the secondary scholarship pupils is greatly in excess of the figure for any other group, while the central school mean is the same as the preparatory. The figures for I.Q. disguise the extent of the superiority of the secondary scholarship and central school means, because, as already explained, the I.Q. technique with the Otis Test artificially depresses the indices for children of exceptional ability. Taking the I.B. figures, the excess of the secondary scholarship mean over the mean of all free pupils is 48·9 points and over the mean of the entire school population, 47·2 points, as compared with the corresponding figures for I.Q. of 32·9 and 31·7 respectively.

The means for the two contrasting groups of free and fee-paying pupils and for the entire school population within our age-range were calculated in the following way. On the basis of official statistics relating to the year 1931–32, we estimated that there were 2,305,000 children in public elementary (including central) schools in England and Wales between the ages of 9.0 and 12.6. In secondary schools there were 106,000, of whom 41,000 were free pupils. This makes a total of 2,346,000 children in receipt of free education. The number of fee-paying pupils is approximately 215,000, of whom 65,000 are in secondary schools and 150,000 in private and preparatory schools. This last figure was calculated on the assumption that the proportion of private and preparatory school pupils aged 9.0–12.6 to the total aged 5–14 was the same as in the case of the elementary school population. Thus we find that for every one pupil within our age-group in a fee-paying school there are eleven receiving free education.

The difference between the means for the two contrasting groups of free and fee-paying pupils is 14·7 points of I.Q. and 20·5 points of I.B. For the present purpose, however, it would be highly misleading to restrict the comparison of the intellectual composition of these two groups to a comparison of their means. Knowledge of the two means would be valuable if we wanted to decide whether any other two random samples of the school population were more likely to belong to one group than to the other. But it would be useless if we wanted to know the proportion of individuals of high or of low ability in the combined groups. The proper statistical index by which to describe the nature of a population can be decided only with reference to the specific purpose for which information is required. For example, it may be more important to know the range of values for any variable whose frequency corresponds with the majority of the individuals in the population. Let us suppose that there are two populations of five individuals each. In the first the incomes of the individuals are £800, £100, £50, £25, and £25. In the second they are all £200. The mean income of the two groups is identical, but in the former 80 per cent of the individuals have an income of half or less than half the average. Here the measure of majority tendency would be in striking conflict with the measure of central tendency. In other words, the "average" income would be very different from the income of the "average" man. The indiscriminate use of measures of central tendency in social statistics is greatly to be deplored. When it is stated that the income of the

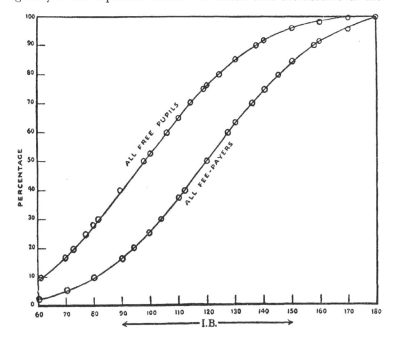

unemployed is, *on the average*, sufficient for the maintenance of a diet of given proportions, it is too readily assumed that no widespread under-nourishment exists. Many people make the utterly unwarranted inference that all or most of the unemployed do in fact possess this income. On the contrary, any number of income-values ranging up to just short of 100 per cent of all the values, may lie above or below the mean, according to the shape of the curve of the distribution of the values.

The prevailing conception of the superiority of the mean as a description of the essential nature of a group of values is bound up with its origin as the most probable estimate of the true value, when a series of measurements is made of the same variable in a single individual, and when the deviation of the measurements from the mean corresponds to what would be likely to happen if they had

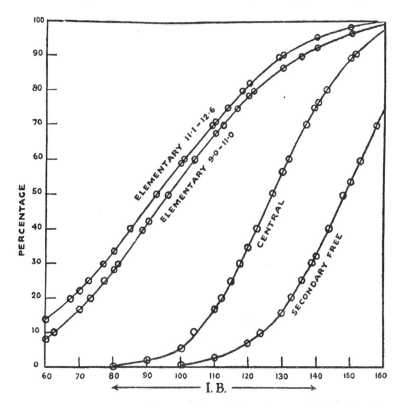

occurred by chance. It is no doubt sufficiently remarkable that the distribution of I.Q.s in a large sample of individuals should so often approximate to the curve of error, but this fact offords no ground for believing that there is a "true" value for the I.Q. of a group in the sense that there is a true value for the height of a mountain. Indeed, this would be a meaningless statement unless the group were completely homogeneous with respect to intelligence. Perhaps the temptation to believe that different racial or social groups are genetically homogeneous with respect to intelligence helped to encourage the habit of regarding mean differences with superstitious awe. In our case we are comparing the distribution of intelligence in two groups of contrasted social status, but not otherwise homogeneous with respect to intelligence. What we require is a picture of the total distribution of intelligence within each group, so that we can

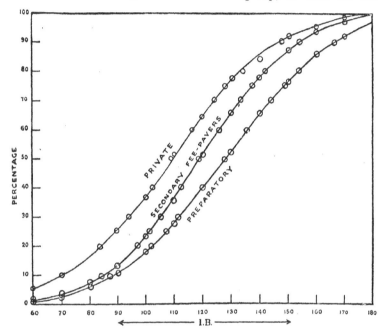

measure the extent of the resemblance and the difference between the two.

These considerations have led us to prefer to set out the differences between the intellectual composition of the two groups of free and fee-paying pupils in terms of their percentile distribution of I.Q. and I.B. and of the percentages in each group who attain a given level of intelligence.

Tables V–VIII give the percentile and percentage distribution both of I.Q and I.B. for pupils in the following four categories: all free, all fee-paying, all with opportunities of higher education and for the entire group. An explanation of the way in which the third

M

group was constituted will be found in Section VI. As shown in item 7 of Table X, it consists of all private and preparatory pupils plus actual and potential free and fee-paying secondary school pupils of

TABLE V

PERCENTILE DISTRIBUTION OF VARIOUS SCHOOL POPULATIONS—I.Q.

Percentile.	All Free Pupils.	All Fee-paying Pupils.	All Pupils with opportunities of higher education.	All Pupils.
10	86·5	100·0	105·8	87·0
20	93·6	110·2	118·8	94·3
25	96·6	114·1	123·4	97·3
30	99·5	118·1	127·8	100·5
40	105·7	124·7	136·6	106·8
50	111·9	131·2	142·8	113·3
60	118·4	139·0	147·3	119·8
70	126·1	145·4	151·6	127·8
75	130·3	148·5	153·6	132·3
80	135·6	152·0	155·6	·137·5
90	147·7	159·8	159·6	149·2

TABLE VI

PERCENTILE DISTRIBUTION OF VARIOUS SCHOOL POPULATIONS—I.B.

Percentile.	All Free Pupils.	All Fee-paying Pupils.	All Pupils with opportunities of higher education.	All Pupils.
10	61·2	80·3	89·1	61·9
20	72·8	94·3	104·6	73·7
25	77·3	100·0	110·5	78·4
30	81·6	104·1	115·4	82·7
40	89·3	112·2	124·7	90·8
50	97·7	119·7	133·0	99·4
60	105·9	127·4	140·6	107·5
70	114·3	135·9	147·6	116·1
75	118·8	140·5	151·4	120·6
80	124·1	145·5	155·5	126·0
90	137·4	158·2	165·9	139·4

elementary school origin. On the basis of the calculated total, the numbers corresponding to the percentage distribution of intelligence in the constituent populations were added together for each level of I.Q. and I.B. and a combined percentage and percentile distribution determined for the group as a whole.

TABLE VII

PERCENTAGE DISTRIBUTION OF VARIOUS SCHOOL POPULATIONS—I.Q.

I.Q.	All Free Pupils	All Fee-paying Pupils.	All Pupils with opportunities of higher education.	All Pupils.
190–9	—	0·2	0·1	—
180–9	0·4	0·9	0·6	0·4
170–9	0·7	2·7	1·8	0·8
160–9	2·2	5·9	6·5	2·5
150–9	5·0	12·8	25·0	5·6
140–9	7·6	16·1	22·1	8·3
130–9	9·4	12·9	11·3	9·6
120–9	12·2	16·1	11·6	12·5
110–19	15·5	12·7	8·4	15·3
100–9	16·2	9·8	6·3	15·7
90–9	16·9	6·6	4·2	16·2
80–9	11·1	2·8	1·8	10·5
70–9	2·6	0·5	0·3	2·5
60–9	0·1	0·1	0·1	0·1

TABLE VIII

PERCENTAGE DISTRIBUTION OF VARIOUS SCHOOL POPULATIONS—I.B.

I.B.	All Free Pupils.	All Fee-paying Pupils.	All Pupils with opportunities of higher education.	All Pupils.
200–9	—	0·1	—	—
190–9	0·1	0·4	0·6	0·1
180–9	0·2	1·5	1·9	0·3
170–9	0·3	2·5	4·2	0·5
160–9	1·2	4·2	7·8	1·4
150–9	2·4	6·8	12·1	2·7
140–9	4·2	9·9	14·2	4·6
130–9	6·4	11·1	13·0	6·7
120–9	8·9	13·0	11·6	9·2
110–19	11·2	13·3	10·0	11·4
100–9	12·4	12·1	8·4	12·4
90–9	11·8	8·9	5·8	11·6
80–9	13·0	6·4	4·1	12·5
70–9	11·0	4·5	2·9	10·5
60–9	7·9	2·7	1·7	7·5
50–9	5·6	1·4	0·9	5·3
40–9	2·1	0·9	0·6	2·0
30–9	0·9	0·3	0·2	0·9
20–9	0·3	0·1	—	0·3
10–19	0·1	—	—	0·1

Table IX shows the percentages in the various school populations who attain or exceed two levels of intelligence measured by I.Q. and I.B. respectively. The choice of I.Q. 130 and over as indicating

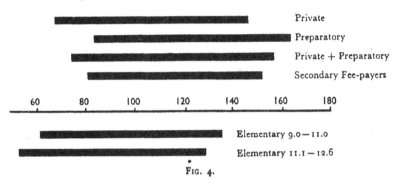

Fig. 4.

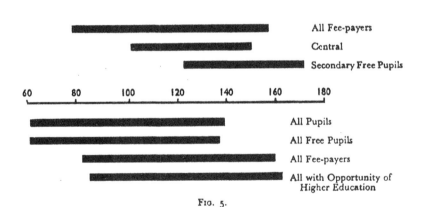

Fig. 5.

INDEX OF BRIGHTNESS

Range of Middle 80 per cent of various School Populations

the possession of high ability can be justified on two grounds. In the first place, it is the level attained by roughly 25 per cent of the entire school population and by more than 50 per cent of fee-paying children. Secondly, nearly all free pupils in secondary schools exceed it, and it may thus be taken as the minimum requirement imposed by the State in its rigorous selection of elementary school pupils for free education of a higher type. Analogous considerations apply to the choice of I.B. 120. We supply also data based on the figures of I.Q. 140 and I.B. 130, in order to provide an alternative criterion of exceptional ability.

VI. THE MEASUREMENT OF EDUCATIONAL OPPORTUNITY

We are now in a position to attempt an estimate of the total volume of high ability in the school population, of the character of its dis-

TABLE IX

PERCENTAGE OF PUPILS IN VARIOUS SCHOOL POPULATIONS AGED 9.0–12.6
WITH HIGH ABILITY

	I.Q.		I.B.	
	130 and over.	140 and over.	120 and over.	130 and over.
1. Elementary, 9.0–11.0 . .	21·4	13·3	21·2	13·1
2. Elementary, 11.1–12.6 . .	21·8	11·4	17·6	9·4
3. Central Schools . . .	71·7	51·6	65·5	43·5
4. Secondary Free Pupils . .	95·3	86·7	93·3	84·2
5. Secondary Fee-payers . .	51·7	37·1	48·7	34·3
6. Private Schools. . . .	37·0	25·0	35·5	22·7
7. Preparatory Schools . . .	61·8	49·6	60·1	47·7
8. Private and Preparatory Schools (combined)	51·2	39·1	49·5	37·0
9. All Free Pupils . . .	25·3	15·9	23·7	14·8
10. All Fee-paying Pupils . .	51·5	38·6	49·6	36·6
11. All with Opportunities of Higher Education	67·4	56·1	65·4	53·8
12. All	27·2	17·6	25·5	16·3

tribution amongst different social groups and of the extent to which the existing machinery of social selection adjusts educational opportunity to individual ability. We proceed further to offer some quantitative indices of the prevailing inequality in the assignment of educational opportunities.

Table IX gave the percentage of children in various school categories who attained or exceeded two high levels of ability. We have now to translate these percentages into actual numbers. In order to do this it is first necessary to determine the total size of these categories, which is done in Table X.

TABLE X

ESTIMATED SIZE OF SCHOOL POPULATIONS IN AGE-GROUP 9.0–12.6

1. *Free Pupils* (present constitution) :
    - (a) Elementary 2,305,000
    - (b) Secondary 41,000
      - ——————— 2,346,000
2. *Free Pupils* (constitution at leaving age) . . .   2,286,000
3. *Fee-paying Pupils* (present constitution) :
    - (a) Secondary 65,000
    - (b) Private and Preparatory 150,000
      - ——————— 215,000
4. *Fee-paying Pupils* (constitution at leaving age) . .   275,000
5. *Total School Population*   2,561,000
6. *Total Population of Elementary School Origin* . . .   2,377,000
7. *Pupils who have or will have Opportunities of Higher Education:*
    - (a) Secondary Free 158,000
    - (b) Secondary Fee-payers 125,000
    - (c) Private and Preparatory. 150,000
      - ——————— 433,000
8. *Pupils who go or will go to Central Schools* . . .   252,000

The figures in items 1, 3, and 5 are taken directly from official sources. Items 2 and 4 express the numbers who will be free and fee-paying pupils at the time of leaving school, i.e. after allowance has been made for those elementary school children who, at various ages, will become fee-payers at secondary schools. We estimate them to be 60,000 by an application of the argument described below (p. 361). Item 6 was obtained by adding to the existing elementary school population those secondary school children who have originated in elementary schools. We know the number of secondary free pupils of elementary school origin, and we make the assumption that 50 per cent of the fee-payers within our age-group also come from elementary schools, since this is approximately true for fee-payers of all ages. Item 8 presented greater difficulty. Central schools are not separately distinguished in official returns from other types of public elementary schools. We relied in the first place on figures specially furnished to us by the Education Officer of the L.C.C. These gave us the total central school population in London in the age-group 11–12 years. Reference to the total London population of elementary school origin at the same age enables us to estimate that approximately 12·3 per cent of all such children proceed to central schools at that age. It follows, in the absence of any change in the number of central school places, that a similar proportion of the age-group 9–11 would normally proceed to central schools on reaching the age of admission. Assuming that the same proportion exists for England and Wales, we arrive for children aged 9 and over at a figure of 252,000 with opportunities of a central school education. Since, in fact, we have no information concerning the comparative distribution of the elementary school population between central and other types of schools outside London, this estimate must be taken with considerable reserve.

Item 7 is of critical importance in the present discussion and requires very careful treatment. It will be noted that in Table IX the category entitled All with Opportunities of Higher Education has already appeared.

By higher education we mean education continuing beyond the primary or preparatory stage into the secondary or public school. What number of individuals enjoy a higher education in the sense defined, or may expect to do so when they reach the appropriate age? We assume that all children in private, preparatory, and secondary schools fall into this category. Not all necessarily remain at school or go on to the university, but the normal expectation is that such children enjoy at least some educational and social advantages not possessed by those who finish their education in the elementary school. There is no means of estimating the average length of the school life of private and preparatory school pupils, but we do know, in the case of secondary school pupils, that they spend on the average about five years in the secondary school and that the average age of leaving is just under 17 years. We also know that more than 50 per cent remain at school after the age of 16. It is common knowledge that attendance at schools of this type, even when incomplete, carries with it a considerable prestige value in the outside world.

The paucity of official information respecting children in private and preparatory schools makes it impossible to determine with any accuracy the total numbers within our age-range of 9.0–12.6. On the assumption that the proportion of such children in this age-group to the estimated total aged 5–14 is the same as in the case of elementary school children, where the total is known, we arrive at a figure of approximately 150,000.

The calculation of the number of children who will proceed to secondary schools, while resting on official returns, is nevertheless a task of considerable complexity. It is necessary for our purpose to calculate the total numbers who will have the *opportunity* of a higher education. We know the numbers of both free pupils and fee-payers aged 9.0–12.6 who are actually in attendance at secondary schools. We have also to estimate the number of individuals who are not yet at secondary schools, but may expect to proceed there at a later date. Since we do not propose to separate in the final result children receiving a higher education in different types of schools, we need only consider transferences from public elementary schools. Those entering secondary schools from elsewhere are necessarily included in our total of private and preparatory school children.

The obvious method of arriving at such a figure would seem to be to obtain the proportion of children leaving elementary schools for secondary schools at all ages to the total number of elementary school leavers, on the basis of figures for any given year or series of years, and thus the total number in any given age-group. This was in essence the method adopted by Carr-Saunders and Jones in 1927, using figures relating to the years 1922–25. Their procedure is satisfactory as long as there are no great fluctuations in the total number of leavers in successive years. Since 1927, however, the requisite constancy of the number of leavers per annum has not persisted. For example, in the year 1931–32, on which the estimates in this investigation are based, the population in the age-group 14–15, which contains the majority of leavers, is unusually small on account of the great decline in the birth-rate that occurred during the war. The figure is 539,000 as compared with 529,000 in the age-group 13–14, 741,000 in the age-group 12–13, and 768,000 in the age-group 11–12. Hence the total number of leavers in the two years subsequent to 1933 would be approximately two-fifths greater than for the year 1931–32. The proportion of leavers who went to secondary schools would be artificially inflated, if account were taken only of years in which the total school population over the age of 11 was unusually small. For these reasons we were compelled to seek an alternative method of obtaining the required information.

It is possible to calculate the *proportion* of all children in elementary schools over the age of 9 who will eventually go to secondary schools, on the assumption that the proportion of admissions to secondary schools at each year of age to the total elementary school population at the same age remains constant. With few exceptions, the minimum age of transference from elementary to secondary schools is 9 and the maximum 14. Hence this method only involves a summation of the proportions admitted at different years of age between 9 and 14. We have calculated free and fee-paying pupils separately.

(a) *Secondary Free Pupils.*—Let the 1931–32 age-group of children of elementary school origin aged 9–10 be N_{9-10}, the admissions to secondary schools of free pupils from elementary schools at the age of 9–10 be Y_1. Then $P_1 = \dfrac{Y_1}{N_{9-10}}$, where P_1 is the proportion of such admissions to the total age-group of elementary school origin (i.e. including children already gone to secondary schools as free pupils or fee-payers).[1] Similarly, if the admissions for the age-groups 10–11, 11–12, 12–13, and 13–14 be Y_2, Y_3, Y_4, and Y_5, then—

$$P_2 = \frac{Y_2}{N_{10-11}}$$

$$P_3 = \frac{Y_3}{N_{11-12}}$$

$$P_4 = \frac{Y_4}{N_{12-13}}$$

$$P_5 = \frac{Y_5}{N_{13-14}}$$

Let P be the proportion of all children aged 9 and over who will eventually go to secondary schools as free pupils, then—

$$
\begin{aligned}
P &= P_1 + P_2 + P_3 + P_4 + P_5 \\
&= \frac{102}{630,801} + \frac{5,582}{685,857} + \frac{31,532}{728,893} + \frac{7,342}{661,778} + \frac{1,342}{484,394} \\
&= 0 \cdot 02\% + 0 \cdot 81\% + 4 \cdot 33\% + 1 \cdot 11\% + 0 \cdot 28\% \\
&= 6 \cdot 6\%
\end{aligned}
$$

Since the total population of elementary school origin aged 9.0–12.6

[1] The more rigorous form of this method would be to take N_{10-11}, N_{11-12}, N_{12-13}, and N_{13-14} as the size of these age-groups when each of them was at the minimum age of 9–10, i.e. $_{9-10}N_{1930-31}$, $_{9-10}N_{1929-30}$, etc. This would lead to virtually the same result as that given above, since the depletion of the age-groups between 9 and 14 by mortality or emigration is insignificantly small.

is 2,377,000, the number who may hope to obtain free places in secondary schools is approximately 157,000. Since also the great majority of transferences from elementary to secondary schools of free pupils takes place within this age-range, we can provisionally estimate that between 6 and 7 per cent of children starting life in the public elementary school enjoy the opportunity of a higher education, the cost of which is defrayed either wholly or in part by the State or other public authority.

(b) *Secondary Fee-payers.*—Similarly, we have calculated the percentage of individuals of elementary school origin who will eventually proceed to secondary schools as fee-payers to be 3·9 per cent and the total number approximately 93,000. The combined percentage relating to free pupils and fee-payers is 10·5 and the total number within our age-group, 251,000.

By this means we obtained the figures for item 7 of Table X. It remained only to add to the totals of children proceeding to secondary from elementary schools as free or fee-paying pupils those originating in schools of other types. On March 31, 1932, there were about 3 per cent of all free pupils in secondary schools, or 1,230, who had come from private or preparatory schools and approximately 32,000 fee-payers. It was necessary only to take account of such individuals in actual attendance at secondary schools: those who will eventually proceed there are already included in the total of private and preparatory school children.

Table XI expresses in terms of percentages the relationship between some of the totals given in Table X.

VII. THE VOLUME AND DISTRIBUTION OF HIGH ABILITY

Table IX shows the proportion of pupils in various categories of the school population who attain or exceed four different levels of high ability, ranging between a lower limit of I.Q. 130 and an upper limit of I.B. 130. While a substantial percentage in both the free and fee-paying groups achieve the selected standards, it will nevertheless be observed that there is a striking discrepancy between the two figures, which confirms the disparity between the mean values already noted. We may repeat that it is not the purpose of this investigation to determine whether this superiority of the fee-paying group is due to nature or nurture. The assumptions we adopt are decidedly conservative in that we do not take into account any possible improvement in the intellectual performance of children of elementary school origin that might result from a diminution of existing economic and cultural inequalities.

Before proceeding to the discussion of the major issues, we venture to draw attention to several points of detail that arise from a study of this table. It will be noted that according to the criterion employed not less than 84 per cent nor more than 95 per cent of all free pupils

TABLE XI

COMPARISON OF VARIOUS SCHOOL POPULATIONS AGED 9.0–12.6 (IN PERCENTAGES)

1. *As Percentage of Total School Population:*
   (a) All Free Pupils:
       (i) Present constitution . . . . 91·6
       (ii) Constitution at leaving age . . . . . . 89·3
   (b) All Fee-paying Pupils:
       (i) Present constitution . . . . 8·4
       (ii) Constitution at leaving age . . . . . . 10·7
   (c) All Pupils with Opportunities of Higher Education . . . 16·9
2. *As Percentage of All Pupils of Elementary School Origin:*
   (a) Pupils of Elementary School Origin with Opportunities of obtaining Free Places in Secondary Schools . . . . . 6·6
   (b) Pupils of Elementary School Origin with Opportunities of proceeding to Secondary Schools as Fee-paying Pupils . . 3·9
   (c) (a) + (b) . . . . 10·5
   (d) Pupils who go or will go to Central Schools . . . . 12·3
3. *As Percentage of All Free Pupils:*
   (a) All Fee-paying Pupils:
       (i) Present constitution . . . . 9·2
       (ii) Constitution at leaving age . . . . . . 12·0

in secondary schools possess high ability. This may be held to illustrate the way in which existing scholarship examinations are successful in excluding children of comparatively low ability. As Table IX shows, it does not mean that they have as their object the selection of all gifted children of elementary school origin. For example, the significantly high proportion of between 43 and 72 per cent of all pupils in central schools possess superior ability. Nevertheless, very few of them may hope to proceed to secondary schools either as free pupils or as fee-payers. Again, of the residual population in the elementary schools, i.e. those who have failed to be selected either for central or secondary schools at the ages at which the overwhelming majority of transfers occur, between 9 and 22 per cent fall within our category of gifted children. In their case also, only an insignificant proportion have any subsequent opportunity of proceeding at a later age to any other kind of school.

Within the fee-paying group itself there are highly significant differences. The superiority of the preparatory school children is in bold contrast with the inferiority of children attending private schools. It will be recalled that in the absence of even approximate official estimates concerning the relative proportion of preparatory and private school children in the country as a whole, we were compelled, in calculating the intellectual indices of the combined group, to assume that the two populations were of equal size. It is obvious that the combined mean and the proportion of high ability for the fee-paying group as a whole would be significantly lower were there any great superiority in the relative size of the private school population. We have argued in a preceding section that this is almost certainly true. In that event the discrepancy between the ability of the two social groups distinguished in this investigation would be less and the inequality of their educational opportunities greater. Thus again our data incline to the side of conservatism.

Table XII presents the prime data of Table IX, the percentage figures having been converted into actual numbers on the basis of the data set out in Table X. Table XII also shows the percentage contribution of each group to the total school population of high ability. Table XIII continues the analysis of the data classified according to the further requirements of this investigation.

The most striking conclusion that emerges from a study of these tables is that there is no shortage of gifted children in the community. Our figures, we may recall, refer only to a restricted age-group. On the assumption that the percentile distribution of I.Q. and I.B. would be the same at all ages of school life, it would be possible to estimate the corresponding figures for the entire population of school age. The figures given here themselves suffice to show, when compared with those in Table X, a large reservoir of unutilized high ability. The argument from the discrepancy between the mean ability and between the relative proportions of gifted children in schools of different social type is seen to lose much of its practical significance. It is overwhelmed by the enormously greater actual numbers of superior children who originate in elementary schools. We are far from suggesting that the inferiority of the mean intelligence of the children of the relatively poor does not create a problem which calls for immediate investigation. For the present discussion the relevant fact is that on their observed performances alone the

TABLE XII

Estimated Totals with High Ability in Various School Categories, aged 9.0–12.6, with Percentages of each in Terms of Total School Population with High Ability

School	I.Q.			
	130 and over.		140 and over.	
	No.	Per cent.	No.	Per cent.
Elementary, 9.0–11.0 . .	279,000	39·2	174,000	37·9
Elementary, 11.1–12.6 . .	190,000	26·7	100,000	21·8
Central	92,000	12·9	66,000	14·4
Secondary Free Pupils . .	39,000	5·5	36,000	7·8
Secondary Fee-payers . .	34,000	4·8	24,000	5·2
Private and Preparatory .	77,000	10·8	59,000	12·9
Total with High Ability .	711,000	100·0	459,000	100·0

School	I.B.			
	120 and over.		130 and over.	
	No.	Per cent.	No.	Per cent.
Elementary, 9.0–11.0 . .	277,000	42·0	171,000	40·5
Elementary, 11.1–12.6 . .	154,000	23·4	82,000	19·4
Central	84,000	12·7	56,000	13·3
Secondary Free Pupils . .	38,000	5·8	35,000	8·3
Secondary Fee-payers . .	32,000	4·8	22,000	5·2
Private and Preparatory .	74,000	11·2	56,000	13·3
Total with High Ability .	659,000	100·0	422,000	100·0

comparatively poor very greatly preponderate in the production of individuals of high ability. That being so, it follows that an educational policy concerned with the training of a sufficient

TABLE XIII

ESTIMATED TOTALS WITH HIGH ABILITY IN VARIOUS CATEGORIES OF THE SCHOOL POPULATION, AGED 9.0–12.6, AND PERCENTAGES OF EACH IN TERMS OF TOTAL SCHOOL POPULATION WITH HIGH ABILITY

	I.Q.				I.B.			
	130 and over		140 and over		120 and over		130 and over	
	No.	Per cent.	No.	Per cent.	No.	Per cent.	No.	Per cent.
Total with High Ability	711,000	100·0	459,000	100·0	659,000	100·0	422,000	100·0
All Free Pupils	600,000	84·4	376,000	81·9	553,000	83·9	344,000	81·5
All Fee-paying Pupils	111,000	15·6	83,000	18·1	106,000	16·1	78,000	18·5
All who will leave as Free Pupils	569,000	80·0	353,000	76·9	523,000	79·4	323,000	76·5
All who will leave as Fee-payers	142,000	20·0	106,000	23·1	136,000	20·6	99,000	23·5
All in Elementary (including Central) Schools	561,000	78·9	340,000	74·1	515,000	78·1	309,000	73·2
All in Secondary, Private and Pre-paratory Schools	150,000	21·1	119,000	25·9	144,000	21·9	113,000	26·8
All Pupils with Opportunities of Higher Education	293,000	41·2	243,000	52·9	283,000	42·9	232,000	55·0
All Pupils without Opportunities of Higher Education	418,000	58·8	216,000	47·1	376,000	57·1	190,000	45·0
All Pupils who go or will go to Central Schools	181,000	25·5	130,000	28·3	165,000	25·0	110,000	26·1

number of children to supply the social demand for highly educated persons will be mainly directed to the provision of adequate facilities for the higher education of children of elementary school origin.

When we compare present free with present fee-paying pupils, we find that the former contain between four and five times as many gifted children as the latter. Similarly, when we consider the status of children at the time of leaving school, we note that there are three or four times as many gifted free pupils as gifted fee-paying pupils. It will not fail to be observed that in the single case of children whose educational future is limited to the central school there are many more superior individuals than in the entire group of fee-paying pupils. Yet practically none of these has the opportunity of entry into the professions and the higher ranks of the business world enjoyed by those who have attended fee-paying schools.

The most unexpected and disturbing result of the analysis in Table XIII is that on the highest criterion of ability 45 per cent and on the lowest 59 per cent of the total number of gifted children in the school population do not enjoy the opportunity of a higher education. None of these belong to the group whose parents are able and willing to pay fees for their children's education. The entire mass of unutilized talent consists of children for whose education the requisite financial provision from public funds is not available.

VIII. THE MALADJUSTMENT OF ABILITY AND OPPORTUNITY

In order to obtain a clear picture of the existing disparity with reference to differences of ability and of opportunity, it has been necessary to adopt certain arbitrary levels of ability as a basis for comparison. For example, we noted that an I.Q. of 130 is the figure reached by approximately 25 per cent of the total school population. If we have regard only to these arbitrary levels, then for the purpose of the present discussion we can speak of maladjustment as occurring (a) when individuals who attain or exceed them do not have the opportunity of higher education, and (b) when individuals who fail to attain them nevertheless receive a higher education. It must be clearly understood that there is no justification for the assertion that only children with intelligence above these levels can *benefit* from higher education. This investigation is in no way concerned with the problem of deciding in what different senses the term "benefit" may be legitimately employed in the discussion of educational policy. It aims only at bringing into relation objective criteria of educational performance and quantitative indices of educational opportunity.

Table XIV describes the way in which the existing facilities for higher education are distributed between the two social groups and between those individuals who possess high ability and those who do not.[1]

For example, 569,000, or 25 per cent, of all children who will leave as free pupils attain or exceed an I.Q. of 130. The number of such gifted children who actually enjoy the opportunities of a higher education is only 151,000 or 26·5 per cent,[2] while those who have the ability but are not afforded the opportunity number 418,000 or 73·5 per cent. Thus the wastage of talent from this source alone is nearly three times the total that is at present utilized, or 16·3 per cent of the total school population. In addition, a maladjustment of a different kind takes place when children who fail to attain the selected levels of high ability receive higher education. Seven thousand, or 0·3 per cent, of children of elementary school origin fall into this category. This percentage is not greater than would be expected when individuals are selected mainly as a result of a mass examination. The corresponding maladjustment in the case of fee-

---

[1] Slight discrepancies will be noted between comparable percentage figures in Tables IX and XIV. The data of Table IX were calculated directly from the distributions of I.Q. and I.B. in our samples of various populations, the weights employed being taken generally as whole numbers. When translated into actual numbers they are taken correct to the nearest thousand. The percentages in Table XIV express the relation of these round numbers to the *estimated* total size of various educational categories. The discrepancies are insignificant and do not affect the order of magnitude of the differences disclosed in the argument that follows.

[2] Dr. Robert R. Rusk, in an article on the recent "Mental Survey of Scottish Children" (*The Year Book of Education*, 1935), estimates that on certain assumptions 28 per cent of Scottish children aged 11 may be said to have I.Q.s of over 110. He goes on to say that "from the little data we have we can infer that they might proceed to secondary education in Scotland." While the actual value of the constants denoting I.Q. cannot usefully be compared, for reasons stated in Section III of this study, it is interesting to notice that Rusk's figure is in relatively close agreement with our figure of 27·2 per cent for the proportion of London children aged 9.0–12.6 who attain an I.Q. of 130 or more. We have remarked that this level may be regarded as the minimum qualification for free pupils in London Secondary Schools. We may express the hope that the Scottish Council for Research in Education will analyse the data at its disposal to show what proportion of this 28 per cent of superior individuals does in fact proceed to Secondary Schools in Scotland.

TABLE XIV

MALADJUSTMENT OF ABILITY AND OPPORTUNITY IN HIGHER EDUCATION

(Age Group 9.0–12.6)

| | I.Q. | | | | I.B. | | | |
| | 130 and over | | 140 and over | | 120 and over | | 130 and over | |
	No.	Per cent.[1]	No.	Per cent.[1]	No.	Per cent.[1]	No.	Per cent.[1]
1. Free Pupils [2,286,000]:								
(a) No. with high ability of	569,000	24·9	353,000	15·4	523,000	22·9	323,000	14·1
(b) No. of (a) *with* opportunity	151,000	6·6	137,000	6·0	147,000	6·4	133,000	5·8
(c) No. of (a) *without* opportunity	418,000	18·3	216,000	9·4	376,000	16·5	190,000	8·3
(d) No. with opportunity but without high ability	7,000	0·3	21,000	0·9	11,000	0·5	25,000	1·1
2. Fee-paying Pupils [275,000]:								
(a) No. with high ability of	142,000	51·5	106,000	38·5	136,000	49·5	99,000	36·0
(b) No. of (a) *with* opportunity	142,000	51·5	106,000	38·5	136,000	49·5	99,000	36·0
(c) No. of (a) *without* opportunity	—	—	—	—	—	—	—	—
(d) No. with opportunity but without high ability	133,000	48·5	169,000	61·5	139,000	50·5	176,000	64·0
3. All Pupils [2,561,000]:								
(a) No. with high ability of	711,000	27·8	459,000	17·9	659,000	25·7	422,000	16·5
(b) No. of (a) *with* opportunity	293,000	11·5	243,000	9·5	283,000	11·0	232,000	9·1
(c) No. of (a) *without* opportunity	418,000	16·3	216,000	8·4	376,000	14·7	190,000	7·4
(d) No. with opportunity but without high ability	149,000	5·5	190,000	7·4	150,000	5·9	201,000	7·8
4. Total Maladjustment (3c + 3d)	558,000	21·8	406,000	15·9	526,000	20·5	391,000	15·2

[1] The percentages refer to the relation between the figures in the rows and the figures in square brackets in column 1.

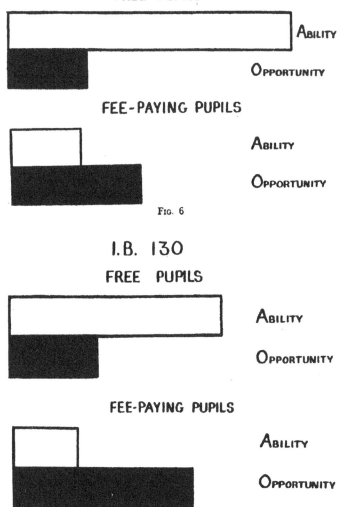

Fig. 6

Fig 7.

Comparison of total numbers with ability and numbers who have opportunity of higher education in the two groups of free and fee-paying pupils respectively (based on data of Table XIV). It should be noted that Figs. 6 and 7 are not drawn to the same scale.

paying pupils amounts to no less than 133,000, or 49 per cent, of the entire population of fee-paying pupils. Thus the overwhelming majority of sub-standard children who nevertheless obtain a higher education consists of fee-paying pupils. The final conclusion, taking I.Q. 130 as our criterion of ability, is that there are 558,000 individuals, or 22 per cent of the entire school population, aged 9.0–12.6, in whose case there is a maladjustment of ability and opportunity of one kind or the other. This total is considerably in excess of the total number who actually enjoy opportunities of higher education (irrespective of ability) and twice as great as the number of such children who also attain our selected levels of high ability.

There are other levels of ability which could be employed with equal justification. The figures given in the tables were obtained by calculation. It is also possible to use the method of graphical interpolation from the curves of the distribution of intelligence and so obtain rough estimates of the maladjustment that occurs when other levels are selected. Figures 1, 2, and 3 show the curves of the distribution of I.B. for various school populations. It will be seen that 25 per cent of fee-payers have an I.B. of less than 100. This level, however, is exceeded by 94 per cent of children in central schools. Hence, if we assume that 25 per cent of children who have access to a higher education by virtue of their parents' means are below the required level, then 95 per cent of children in central schools alone are above it, none of whom will receive a higher education. Likewise, if we assume that only 10 per cent of fee-payers are uneducable in this sense, which would mean that they failed to reach an I.B. of 80, it may be argued that the 72 per cent of free pupils who exceed this level ought to receive a higher education. In fact, only 10·5 per cent will receive it either as scholarship children or as fee-payers in secondary schools.

While the preponderance of State-assisted pupils among those of comparatively high ability is not surprising, it is less commonly recognized that they also provide the majority of individuals of exceptional intelligence. Dr. Cyril Burt, in a widely quoted estimate, defines the latter as the highest, 0·1 per cent of the population. It is not necessary to adopt the American ascription of "genius" to such individuals in order to believe that they are of unusual value to the community. According to Burt's view, not based, as far as we know, on a comparative study of children from different social strata, "these are rarely found in elementary schools; and are almost entirely confined to the families from the higher social and professional classes." Our data confirm neither of these statements. The present study shows that more than two-thirds of the number of individuals at this level of ability originate within the public elementary school. Of these no less than 70 per cent are of wage-earning parentage. Taking schools of every social type, we find that the "higher social and professional classes" contribute only 33 per cent of the total of exceptional children, while wage-earners are responsible for 50 per cent. The rest come from the shop-keeping and clerical and commercial classes.

Burt further states that the majority of those who constitute the top 1 or 2 per cent of the elementary school population win scholarships to secondary schools. In the present investigation the top 1·6 per cent of the elementary school population aged 9.0–11.0 attain an I.B. of 160 or over. Of these only 50 per cent become free pupils in secondary schools. He goes on to say that the next 10 per cent are in London usually drafted to central schools. According to our data the next 11·5 per cent have an I.B. between 130 and 160. In fact, more than 50 per cent of these do not proceed to central schools.

It can at once be remarked that a very considerable discrepancy appears between the two social groups when we consider individuals in whose case there exists a maladjustment between ability and opportunity. Table XV attempts to measure the amount of this disparity.

In the case both of free and fee-paying pupils the numbers with opportunities of further education irrespective of ability have been expressed as a percentage of the total number with high ability. The ratio of the two figures thus obtained affords an index of the inequality in the distribution of educational opportunities between the two social groups. Thus, according as we take the upper or the lower limit of high ability, an able fee-paying pupil has a chance of receiving a higher education either six or seven times greater than that of an equally able free pupil. We may recall that the evidence at our disposal makes it certain that this is a conservative estimate and that the extent of social inequality may well be greater than that here recorded.

Table XVI analyses inequality of the converse kind. It compares the percentages of sub-standard pupils of the two social groups who nevertheless enjoy educational privileges. Here the disparity is even more striking. A sub-standard child of the fee-paying group has an

TABLE XV

MEASURES OF SOCIAL INEQUALITY IN EDUCATIONAL OPPORTUNITY—I

(*The figures refer to pupils who will leave school as Free or Fee-paying Pupils*)

	I.Q.		I.B.	
	130 and over.	140 and over.	120 and over.	130 and over.
1. *Percentage of Pupils with Opportunities of Higher Education to Total Number with High Ability :*				
(*a*) Free Pupils	27·8	44·8	30·2	48·9
(*b*) Fee-paying Pupils	193·6	259·4	202·2	277·8
2. *Inequality of Opportunity:* [Proportion of (*a*) to (*b*)]	1 : 7·0	1 : 5·8	1 : 6·7	1 : 5·7

TABLE XVI

MEASURES OF SOCIAL INEQUALITY IN EDUCATIONAL OPPORTUNITY—II

(*The figures refer to pupils who will leave school as Free or Fee-paying Pupils*)

	I.Q.		I.B.	
	130 and over.	140 and over.	120 and over.	130 and over.
1. *Percentage of Pupils with Opportunities of Higher Education, but without High Ability, to Total Number in each category :*				
(*a*) Free Pupils	0·3	0·9	0·5	1·1
(*b*) Fee-paying Pupils	48·5	61·5	50·5	64·0
2. *Inequality of Opportunity:* [Proportion of (*a*) to (*b*)]	1 : 161·7	1 : 68·3	1 : 101·0	1 : 58·2

opportunity of receiving a higher education between 58 and 162 times greater than that of a similar child of the free group.

IX. SUMMARY

1. Over ten thousand individuals between the ages of 9 years and 12 years 6 months, drawn from public elementary (including central), secondary, private and preparatory schools in the London area, were tested with the Otis Advanced Group Intelligence Test (Form A) and assigned Intelligence Quotients on the basis of the existing American norms.

2. Norms based on the data of the present investigation were used to derive Indices of Brightness for all subjects examined.

3. Correlation coefficients which were obtained for Age and I.Q. and Age and I.B. demonstrated the superiority of the latter in the comparison of individuals in populations selected for intelligence.

4. The reliability coefficient for I.Q. was found to be $r = 0.85 \pm 0.027$ and for I.B. $r = 0.92 \pm 0.015$.

5. A system of weighting was designed to take account of the selective factors in English education and inequalities in sampling.

6. Mean figures and percentile distributions were calculated for the I.Q. and I.B. of various categories of the school population.

7. Estimates are given of the percentages and numbers of individuals of different social and educational status who attain various selected levels of high ability.

8. The proportion of individuals of elementary school origin who are afforded the opportunity of a secondary school education at the expense of the State was found, on the basis of official statistics for 1931–2, to be 6·6 per cent.

9. Similarly, the proportion of such individuals who normally proceed to secondary schools as fee-payers is 3·9 per cent.

10. If we take the level of ability attained by approximately 50 per cent of children who are educated at their parents' expense (I.Q. 130 or I.B. 120), then approximately 25 per cent of pupils educated at the expense of the State attain the same level. When account is taken of the unequal size of these two social groups, it is found that the numerical contribution at this level of ability of the last-named group amounts to 80 per cent of the total. Of these only a little more than a quarter have the opportunity of proceeding as free pupils to secondary schools. Individuals at this level of ability, whose education is limited to the central school, alone exceed the numbers of all fee-paying pupils of similar ability. In the whole school population more than 50 per cent of the able pupils are without the opportunity of

higher education. While only three per thousand of free pupils in secondary schools fall below the selected level of ability, the corresponding figure for the entire group of fee-paying pupils (all of whom nevertheless enjoy the opportunity of a higher education) is nearly 50 per cent. In other words, taking children of equally high ability, seven fee-paying pupils will receive a higher education for every one free pupil. Conversely, if we consider children who fall below the selected level of ability, for every one free pupil who is afforded the opportunity of a higher education, there are one hundred and sixty-two fee-paying pupils who enjoy the same advantages.

11. Similar calculations have been made, using higher criteria of ability.

12. If, instead of 50 per cent, we assume that only 10 per cent of children educated at their parents' expense are ineligible by virtue of inferior ability for receiving a higher education, then 72 per cent of free pupils are eligible.

13. At a very high level of ability, represented by the attainment of the uppermost one per thousand in the general school population, two-thirds of the total originate in elementary schools, of whom 70 per cent are of wage-earning parentage. Of the entire group of such exceptional individuals, 50 per cent are the children of wage-earners, and 33 per cent of members of the higher social and professional classes.

BIBLIOGRAPHY

1. Burt, C. (1924): "The Principles of Vocational Guidance, ii," *Brit. Jour. of Psych.*, Vol. XIV, Pt. 4.
2. Carr-Saunders, A. M., and Jones, D. Caradog (1927): *The Social Structure of England and Wales.*
3. Gray, J. L., and Moshinsky, Pearl (1933): "Studies in Genetic Psychology: The Intellectual Resemblance of Collateral Relatives," *Proc. Roy. Soc. Edin.*, Vol. LIII, Pt. 2, No. 14.
4. Herrman, L., and Hogben, L.(1933) : "The Intellectual Resemblance of Twins," *Proc. Roy. Soc. Edin.*, Vol. LIII, Pt. 2, No. 9.
5. Kelley, T. L. (1927): *The Interpretation of Educational Measurements.* New York.
6. *Manual of Directions for Otis Group Intelligence Scale.* Revised edition 1934. (George G. Harrap & Co., Ltd.)
7. Report of Departmental Committee of the Board of Education on Private Schools, 1932

8. *Education in 1932, being the Report of the Board of Education and the Statistics of Public Education for England and Wales.* Cmd. 4364. (1933.)

9. *Education in 1933, being the Report of the Board of Education and the Statistics of Public Education for England and Wales.* Cmd. 4631. (1934.)

10. *Schools 1934.* Truman and Knightley.

11. Scottish Council for Research in Education (1933): *The Intelligence of Scottish Children.*

12. Rusk, Robert R. (1935): "The Mental Survey of Scottish Children," *The Year Book of Education.*

CHAPTER IX

ABILITY AND EDUCATIONAL OPPORTUNITY IN RELATION TO PARENTAL OCCUPATION

by

J. L. GRAY

and

PEARL MOSHINSKY

(from the Department of Social Biology, University of London)

I. THE NATURE OF THE SAMPLE AND PROCEDURE

In the previous chapter we attempted to assess the intellectual differences between the two contrasted social groups in the English school population, constituted respectively by children educated at the expense of the State (Free pupils), and children educated at the expense of their parents (Fee-paying pupils). Our object was to discuss the way in which the existing facilities for higher education were related to the distribution of intelligence within each of these two social groups.

The present chapter analyses further the social composition of the same sample of the London school population.[1] It aims at the classification of the subjects according to parental occupation and socio-economic status, and compares the educational opportunities enjoyed by the filial generation of different socio-economic groups. This throws some light upon the extent of the educational and thus, in part, of the economic mobility characteristic of various occupational levels in the London population.

A full description of the nature of the sample, the reliability of the test employed, and the conditions of its administration, has been given previously. Nearly 9,000 individuals[2] between the ages of 9 years and 12 years 6 months, drawn from Public Elementary (in-

---

[1] Special Schools and Home Office Approved Schools are not included in the sample. It is thus likely that certain very depressed social strata are inadequately represented.

[2] I.e. all the data used in the previous chapter, with the exception of those brought forward from an earlier investigation into the intellectual resemblance of first cousins and sibs, for whom occupational information was not obtained.

cluding Central), Grant-aided Secondary, Private and Preparatory
schools in the London area were tested during the year 1933–34 with
the Otis Advanced Group Intelligence Test (Form A), assigned
Intelligence Quotients on the basis of the American norms and
Indices of Brightness (I.B.) calculated from norms derived from our
own data. Figures for I.Q. and I.B. are printed side by side.

Not every child assigned an I.Q. and an I.B. provided data for the
special purpose of the present inquiry. Approximately 9 per cent of
the children in the two school groups were unable to furnish
sufficiently exact information concerning parental occupation and
are included under the description "occupations unknown." Each
child was individuallly examined by one or more of our staff concerning the occupation of his father or other guardian. If the father
was dead or not supporting the family, the source of the family
income was ascertained. Preliminary tests, supplemented by con-
sultation with the principals of various schools, enabled us to frame a
series of questions designed to check the accuracy of the children's
replies. We believe that the information so obtained possesses a high
degree of trustworthiness.

There is a general tendency, illustrated in the Census of Population,
for individuals to exaggerate the status of their employment. Children
are not immune from this frailty, but their greater *naïveté* renders it
less difficult to detect. There is little evidence, when we compare
the distribution of occupational orders in our data with that of the
Census Occupational Tables, of any serious over-estimation of
employment status. The possibility of error, however, remains. It was
manifestly impossible for us to exercise compulsion on the children or
to check their statements except by other cautious questions and by
reference to the knowledge possessed by teachers. Everywhere we
respected the wish of school principals that no pressure should be
brought to bear upon the children to provide information which
they might have thought it unusual or improper to divulge.

Inability to furnish the desired information may be correlated with
inferior intelligence. If this were true, we should expect to find that
the average intelligence of the children in the group "occupations
unknown" would be lower than that of the entire population
examined. Moreover, if low average ability is characteristic of
children classified in certain occupational groups, such occupations
may supply the majority of individuals who display ignorance of
parental occupation. Consequently the mean intelligence of the

occupational orders lowest in intelligence would be somewhat higher in our data than it should be. In the free group the mean of those ignorant of their parents' occupations is lower than the mean of the entire group. In the fee-paying group this is also true, but the difference is not so marked. We venture to suggest that in the latter group other considerations, e.g. delicacy, partly account for failure to supply the required information, whereas in the free group it is mainly the result of inferior intelligence. In spite of the correlation between failure to state parental occupation and inferior intelligence, we do not believe that this introduces any significant amount of error into our data. The numbers affected are small and are no doubt spread over many of the occupations ranked lowest in intelligence.

To avoid complicating the work of subsequent classification and reclassification, the information concerning parental occupation was collected in as complete and detailed a manner as the circumstances allowed. The primary object was to obtain the *occupational* condition of individuals in the sense employed in the Census of Population. However, we also ascertained the nature of the industry or service in which an individual was employed, since very often this affects the definition of socio-economic status. For example, clerks employed by national or municipal authorities were distinguished from other clerks, and shop assistants in large stores from those employed in small retail shops. In the group of free pupils we graded shopkeepers and owners of small businesses according to the numbers of persons employed, although it did not prove possible to utilize this information in the subsequent assignment of social status. We even noted all cases where parents were unemployed and the length of the period of their unemployment.

II. PRINCIPLES OF CLASSIFICATION

With few exceptions the numbers of children in the crude occupational groups were insufficient to justify the presentation of separate figures for their intellectual standing. We have found it advisable to group together cognate occupations in more general classes which we have called "Occupational Orders."[1] These have been further

---

[1] No great significance can be attached to the specificity of the occupational orders in Category A (1). Under the heads "manufacturers," "merchants," etc., are no doubt included sole proprietors, partners, and company directors with or without a substantial share-holding. In Category E (1), two of the occupational

classified in a series of wider socio-economic groupings designated "Social Categories." Tables IV and V show both these forms of classification.

The assumption that underlies any attempt to construct a socio-economic classification of crude occupational groups is that significant resemblances and differences exist amongst them which justify for certain purposes a further degree of abstraction. The morphological systems of Linnæus, Cuvier, and their successors call attention to differences among animals and plants universally recognized as significant for the purpose of classification by botanists and zoologists. No such agreement is found amongst students of contemporary institutions concerning the principles of social differentiation. Consequently detailed discussion of the various possible bases of a social morphology cannot be undertaken here. Any classification adopted inevitably involves some presupposition, as yet unverified, of the nature and causes of differentiation in society.

Existing classifications belong to two main groups, namely, those that employ a single qualitative criterion, e.g. industrial or contractual status, and those which adopt a composite criterion combining a number of supposed differentiæ both qualitative and quantitative. Thus the Census of Population uses the test of industrial status, distinguishing between managerial occupations, operatives, workers on their own account and persons out of work. The Census of Production, followed by Bowley and Stamp, makes a distinction between the salaried, wage-earning, and other classes. Less objective are the classifications of Terman and Thurstone in the U.S.A. and of Burt in this country, based on the assumed level of intelligence required for the due performance of different kinds of work. The most critical of all such single criteria, that of money-income, has not been generally adopted, owing to the failure of modern Governments to publish statistics relating to the distribution of incomes.

Composite criteria are less susceptible of statistical verification.

orders demand special mention. "Miscellaneous craftsmen" consists mainly of skilled men "working on their own account," while under "factory workers" is grouped a large and varied assortment of industrial operatives, whom we describe as skilled on the basis of the Population Census of 1931, supplemented by the data regarding average earnings and susceptibility to unemployment contained in the occupational volumes of *The London Survey of Life and Labour*. Similarly, in Category E (2) we have grouped together a wide range of factory operatives whose work is generally regarded as requiring a lesser degree of skill.

Taussig distinguishes five "non-competing" groups differing in psychological and economic characteristics. The English Population Census employs a five-fold division based on the kind of people an individual associates with in his everyday life. But this tells us little about the specific characteristics of each class. Duff and Thomson made an attempt to divide occupations into those requiring principally brain work of different kinds and those mainly consisting of hand work. It may be doubted, however, whether we have sufficient psychological knowledge to justify such a procedure.

The system adopted in this investigation is admittedly a compromise. While a unitary criterion has an obvious advantage, it has the correspondingly serious limitations that attach to its very simplicity. We decided to make the basic ground of differentiation that of the nature of the work performed, but we have not hesitated where it seemed advisable to combine it with differences in average income and "social status." By social status we mean the amount of approbation conventionally accorded to various types of economic personnel at the present time by the majority of English citizens. Such a procedure is subjective only in the sense that it is not possible to produce quantitative data in support of every allocation. We do not, however, attach any great importance to the *order* in which our categories are arranged. We make no further claim than that each is relatively homogeneous with respect to social prestige.

Another possible criterion of social differences, namely, that of the educational opportunities afforded to the filial generation, we have set out to investigate for ourselves. The conclusions arrived at in the final section of this study confirm our impression that the social categories herein distinguished are not merely arbitrary.

Category A. Employing and Directive Classes.—Category A is intended to contain all those whose incomes are obtained primarily from the ownership of property, or from the kinds of work usually performed by persons administering their own property or some property in which they have a share, together with the high-salaried officials of business corporations. To describe these latter we have introduced the convenient American term "business executives." The scope of this category is somewhat narrower than that of the Census "managerial" group, since we exclude from it managers of inferior grades of responsibility and remuneration. The class of "employers," as the Census has recently recognized, is no longer a useful one. The complexity of modern joint-stock company enterprise and the enormous growth in the numbers and scale of *personae fictae* render it impossible to classify the employing function, in the contractual sense, according to personnel.

Not less remarkable, however, is the persistence of large numbers of small businesses and retail shops. While the owners of such concerns may be regarded as capitalists and employers on a small scale, it would be absurd to argue that there exists any significant degree of social resemblance between them and the individuals whom we have put into the first sub-division of Category A. No one can doubt that entrepreneur and executive functions in large-scale industry denote both a characteristic type of personal occupation and by comparison the highest known range of income levels. Sub-divisions A (2) and A (3), on the other hand, probably enjoy an average income approximating to those of Categories C and D, and perhaps an even lower social prestige. Indeed, they constitute together what is, in contrast with A (1), a wholly different social class. We have kept them separate only on account of the interest they possess for the economic statistician.

While we were able to find representatives of the class of shop-keepers both among free and fee-paying pupils, we had great difficulty in deciding in the case of the latter when an individual should be regarded as a larger-scale or smaller-scale business man, and thus go into A (1) or A (2). In the end we decided to describe all business men whose children are educated at the expense of the State as smaller-scale and all who paid fees for their children's education as larger-scale. We have no doubt that closer examination or personal knowledge of the parental circumstances would have enabled us to classify a small percentage in the fee-paying group as small-scale business men of the type found in the free group. Probably, therefore, we exaggerate the disparity between the average intelligence of the filial generation in Categories A (1) and A (2). Nevertheless, as subsequent tables will show, there are real differences of other kinds between them, e.g. in average family size, which appear to justify our procedure.

Category B. Professional Occupations.—We have followed the distinction made by Carr-Saunders and Jones (1927) between those professions demanding a higher and those demanding a lower level of skill and educational equipment. Category B contains only the former. We believe that such individuals constitute a comparatively homogeneous social group. The nature of their work is generally recognized to be different from that performed by persons in Category A, and professional workers enjoy a characteristic measure of social esteem. Moreover, in spite of some overlapping, the range of income amongst professional workers is smaller than amongst persons in Category A (1).

Category C. Minor Professional and Other Highly Skilled Occupations.— This group is intended to be intermediate between Categories B and D. It contains occupations often described as professional, but recognized to require a lower degree of attainment than the more traditional professions of Category B. We have added to this a miscellaneous group of supervisory, technical and administrative workers in business, inferior in responsibility and reward to those we have designated "higher business executives." It should be noted that in a few cases the sub-divisions overlap with those of Category D.

Category D. Clerical and Commercial Employees.—We decided to make the ground of distinction between the subordinate employees of industry and commerce one between "black-coated" and "manual" workers. This corresponds to a social distinction widely accepted in the general population and based upon the difference in the nature of the work performed. On the whole, Category D is composed of persons whose average income and security of employment are superior to those of the great majority of individuals in Category E, although this superiority may not be a marked one. It should be observed that we have not used a distinction between salaried and wage-earning employees, and that consequently Category D does not exclusively represent the salariat.

Category E. Manual Workers.—All individuals in this category are wage-earners participating directly in the manipulative, tool, or machine processes of industry or engaged in personal service. They are divided into skilled and unskilled mainly on the basis of the Census of Population Occupational Tables. Casual workers of every kind have been included in the unskilled group. The sub-division E (3) is mainly recruited from the free group and contains a majority of unskilled occupations.

Category F. Occupations Unknown and Miscellaneous.—It may be remarked that the majority of those referred to as "occupations unknown" are likely to belong to the category of manual workers. We have described as "miscellaneous" certain groups concerning which the information we obtained was inexact and others which did not readily fit in with the principles on which we constructed our socio-economic classification.

Table I gives the number and percentage distribution of children in the separate social categories in each type of school examined. Table II gives a similar distribution for the two groups of free and fee-paying pupils, and also for the entire school population, suitably weighted.

It will at once be observed that differences in the educational status of the filial generation correspond with very marked differences in parental occupation. Thus in the free group no less than 75·6 per cent of pupils whose parental occupation is known are the children of manual workers, a proportion which would almost certainly be increased if the occupational condition of those in Category F could be ascertained precisely. By contrast only one-half of one per cent are the offspring of professional workers. The position is strikingly reversed in the fee-paying group. Here only 6·5 per cent come from the families of manual workers, while 22·9 per cent belong to the professional classes and 34·8 per cent, contrasted with 14·7 per cent in the free group, come from other non-manual salaried or wage-earning occupations. Adding together all classes of capitalists, traders and other business men, we find that they constitute 9·2 per cent of the free group and 35·8 per cent of the fee-paying group.

If we exclude secondary schools, the contrast between the public elementary on the one hand and the private and preparatory schools on the other is even more remarkable. Only one child of unskilled manual workers was found in the 1,718 subjects examined in the private and preparatory schools, and he was being educated at the expense of his father's employer. In general the professions and the higher ranks of business preponderate in schools of superior financial status. It is worth while pointing out that professional parents seem to show a preference for preparatory as compared with private schools.

London secondary schools are more mixed in social composition than any other type of school. Even so they do not by any means reflect the proportionate frequency of the various social categories in the entire school population. They contain almost exactly as many children of clerical and commercial employees as of skilled wage-earners, whereas in the elementary 9.0–11.0 group the former are

TABLE I

SOCIO-ECONOMIC DISTRIBUTION OF THE DATA

	Elementary 9.0–11.0		Elementary 11.1–12.6		Central		Secondary Free		Secondary Fee-payers		All Secondary		Private		Preparatory	
	N.	Per cent.	N.	Per cent.	N.	Per cent.	N.	Per cent.	N.	Per cent.	N.	Per cent.	N.	Per cent.	N.	Per cent.
A. Employing and Directive Classes.																
1. Larger Business Owners and Higher Executives	—	—	—	—	—	—	—	—	229	13·8	229	8·5	217	29·8	276	27·9
2. Smaller Business Owners	21	1·5	26	2·6	64	3·2	24	2·3	183	11·0	24	0·9	—	—	—	—
3. Shopkeepers	92	6·2	73	7·2	85	4·2	46	4·4			229	8·5	65	8·9	38	3·8
B. Professional Occupations	7	0·5	1	0·1	11	0·5	25	2·4	238	14·3	263	9·7	101	13·9	291	29·4
C. Minor Professional and Other Highly Skilled Occupations	51	3·4	31	3·1	139	6·8	83	8·0	265	15·9	348	12·9	131	18·0	182	18·4
D. Clerical and Commercial Employees	145	9·8	63	6·2	259	12·8	204	19·7	366	22·0	570	21·1	94	12·9	75	7·6
E. Manual Workers.																
1. Skilled Wage-earners	527	35·5	354	35·0	874	43·1	396	38·2	173	10·4	569	21·1	39	5·3	4	0·4
2. Unskilled Wage-earners	395	26·6	303	30·0	375	18·5	152	14·7	33	2·0	185	6·8	—	—	1	0·1
3. Fatherless Wage-earning Families	50	3·4	55	5·4	105	5·2	38	3·7	15	0·9	53	2·0	3	0·4	—	—
4. Total Manual Workers	972	65·5	712	70·4	1,354	66·8	586	56·6	221	13·3	807	29·9	42	5·7	5	0·5
F. Occupations Unknown and Miscellaneous	198	13·3	105	10·4	118	5·8	69	6·7	163	9·8	232	8·6	79	10·8	122	11·7
Total	1,486		1,011		2,030		1,037		1,665		2,702		729		989	

N

TABLE II
Socio-Economic Distribution of the Data (continued)

	All Free Pupils		All Fee-paying Pupils		All Pupils			Census.
	N.	Percentage (weighted).	N.	Percentage (weighted).	N.	Percentage (weighted).	Percentage (omitting Category F).	Percentage.
A. *Employing and Directive Classes.*								
1. Larger Business Owners and Higher Executives	—	—	722	24·3	722	2·0	2·3	—
2. Smaller Business Owners	135	1·9	—	—	135	1·7	2·0	—
3. Shopkeepers	296	6·3	286	7·5	582	6·4	7·3	—
4. Total	431	8·2	1,008	31·8	1,439	10·1	11·6	11·7[1]
B. *Professional Occupations*	44	0·4	630	20·3	674	2·1	2·3	3·6
C. *Minor Professional and Other Highly Skilled Occupations*	304	3·7	578	17·5	882	4·9	5·5	3·3[2]
D. *Clerical and Commercial Employees*	671	9·2	535	13·4	1,206	9·6	10·8	18·0[2]
E. *Manual Workers.*								
1. Skilled Wage-earners	2,151	36·0	216	4·8	2,367	33·4	37·8	36·0
2. Unskilled Wage-earners	1,225	26·6	34	0·6	1,259	24·4	27·7	27·4
3. Fatherless Wage-earning Families	248	4·1	18	0·4	266	3·8	4·3	—
4. Total	3,624	66·7	268	5·8	3,892	61·6	69·8	63·4
F. *Occupations Unknown and Miscellaneous*	490	11·8	364	11·1	854	11·7	—	—
Grand Total	5,564		3,383		8,947			

[1] This figure was obtained by subtracting the sum of the rest from the total. The Census elsewhere gives 12·9 per cent. as the proportion of non-cooperatives in business to total of occupied persons. This includes employers, managers, and certain groups working on their own account.

[2] Including managerial occupations.

only a quarter of the latter, and in the private and preparatory group these proportions are reversed.

Agreement is not to be expected between the percentage occupational distribution of our data and the corresponding figures of the Census of Population. In view of possible misconceptions it may serve a useful purpose to draw attention to some of the ways in which sample investigations like the present differ from the Census. Table II contrasts the occupational distribution of all pupils who were the subjects of this inquiry, appropriately weighted, with the corresponding figures calculated on the same basis from the data of the Census of 1931. The Greater London Area, to which the Census data refer, may be taken to be roughly the same as the area covered by our data for elementary and secondary schools. The Census percentages relate to the proportion of all occupied males aged 14 years and over with the exception of those classified as "retired." In certain cases it proved impossible to make the Census classification match with ours. For example, individuals included in our Category A, amounting to 11·7 per cent of the total, are not identical with those designated in the Census as non-operatives, forming 12·9 per cent of the Census total. The Census classification includes employers, managers, and certain persons working on their own account.

The disparities between our figures and those of the Census do not necessarily point to lack of randomness or of amplitude in our sample. It is vital to remember that our classification is of children, not of occupied persons themselves. Unmarried adult males and married males without children in the age-group 9 years to 12 years 6 months cannot appear in our data. One reason why our figure for clerical and commercial employees is lower than that of the Census is that clerks and shop assistants have a younger age composition, compared with the average for all occupied males. For example, in England and Wales 252 per thousand of all occupied males were over 14 and under 25. The corresponding figure for clerks was 342 and for salesmen and shop assistants 594. Similarly the proportions of married males were 63 per cent for all, 48 per cent for clerks, and only 31 per cent for shop assistants. Thus in examining a random sample of children, one would expect to find a higher proportion than that shown in the Census for social groups where the age of marriage is lower than the average and the frequency of marriages greater, and a smaller proportion for groups with a later age of marriage and a comparatively small proportion of married males.

The relative fertility of the married at various social levels also affects the issue. If school children are selected for examination entirely at random, it is more probable that representatives of large families will be chosen than those of small families, because there will be relatively more children of large families between the ages of 9 and 12½ years and a greater chance of selecting siblings. Now, if we assume the existence of occupational differential fertility, in the restricted

TABLE III

MEAN FAMILY SIZE IN SOCIO-ECONOMIC CATEGORIES

	All Free Pupils (weighted).	All Fee-paying Pupils (weighted).	All Pupils (weighted).
A. *Employing and Directive Classes :*			
1. Larger Business Owners and Higher Executives . .	—	2·59	2·59
2. Smaller Business Owners .	3·75	—	3·75
3. Shopkeepers .	3·66	2·59	3·52
B. *Professional Occupations* . .	3·28	2·61	2·70
C. *Minor Professional and Other Highly Skilled Occupations* .	3·31	2·49	2·99
D. *Clerical and Commercial Employees*	3·52	2·19	3·31
E. *Manual Workers :*			
1. Skilled Wage-earners . .	4·02	2·30	3·99
2. Unskilled Wage-earners .	4·62	2·33	4·61
Mean of All (*weighted*) . .	4·09	2·49	3·96

sense of the different average size of the families of married pairs with at least one child, then a random type of selection of their children will tend to over-estimate the frequency of occupations with a relatively high fertility, and under-estimate the frequency of occupations where the average family is comparatively small.

An examination of our data shows beyond question the existence of a factor of this kind. Table III gives the mean size of the families in the several social categories for free pupils, fee-paying pupils, and for the whole sample.

The figures illustrate a notable social difference between certain of these categories and confirm the view that they are not mere arbitrary occupational groupings without any special significance in other realms of social behaviour. The difference between the mean family size (in our restricted sense of the term "family") of the two contrasted populations of free and fee-paying pupils is sufficiently remarkable. Equally significant are the differences in this respect between the various social categories. It is clear, for example, that the type of parent belonging to the minor professional, clerical, skilled, and unskilled classes, who sends his child to a fee-paying school, is very different from the average of his kind. He has fewer children. It appears also that we were justified in distinguishing smaller from larger business men. In respect of mean family size the former approximate to skilled wage-earners, and the latter have the smallest mean family size of all.

IV. INTELLIGENCE AND SOCIO-ECONOMIC STATUS

The existence in the general school population of a small but positive correlation between the intelligence of children and the socio-economic status of their parents is now a generally accepted fact. Duff and Thomson obtained a value of $r = 0.28$ for public elementary and secondary school children in the County of Northumberland. For our entire data the corresponding figure is 0.25 ± 0.008. If, however, the two groups of free and fee-paying pupils are taken separately, we obtain values of 0.19 ± 0.028 and 0.08 ± 0.026 respectively.[1] These lower values depend partly upon the narrower range of social differences that exist within a comparatively homogeneous population. But there is another possibility, to which reference will be made later.

The magnitude of this correlation is only one quarter of the maximum possible value which would denote that each individual occupied the same ordinal rank in both series, i.e. intelligence and socio-economic ratings. Its usefulness for diagnostic purposes is slight.

[1] I.B. was used as the index of intelligence, and for socio-economic ranking a rather coarse nine-point scale, namely Categories A (1), B, C, D, A (3), A (2), E (1), E (3) and E (2), in that order. When, instead of employing actual numbers (weighted), we assume each social category to be of equal size and use the percentage distribution of I.B., we obtain the following results: All Pupils, 0.28 ± 0.01, Free Pupils, 0.25 ± 0.033, Fee-paying Pupils, 0.15 ± 0.035. This may be regarded as a maximum estimate of the correlation between social and intellectual status.

Because a group of individuals has a high average I.Q. we are not entitled to assert with any great degree of confidence that it must therefore be largely composed of children of high socio-economic status. The significant discrepancies between the mean intelligence of different social groups are compatible with the existence of a considerable proportion of able children within groups with a low mean.

For these reasons it would be quite unwarranted to assert that intelligence is *determined* by socio-economic status, a view which is widely held by those unaccustomed to the proper interpretation of correlation technique. We are equally unjustified in making dogmatic statements about the nature of the agencies associated with differences in socio-economic status which assist in producing differences in performance on intelligence tests. These remarks apply equally whether we are disposed to ascribe intellectual differences mainly to environmental inequalities, or, as is more often asserted, to differences in the genetic composition of various social classes.

It may be argued, of course, that performances on intelligence tests are not sensitive to differences in the environmental condition of individuals, and that differences in test results correspond perfectly with differences in inherited capacity. If this were true, the intellectual standing of children would be a reliable index of the intellectual standing of their parents, since the genotypic correlation between the parental and filial generations, theoretically deduced on the assumption that what is being compared has an exclusively genetic basis, has a value of $+$ $0 \cdot 5$. We should then be in a position to say that there was a significant but slight tendency for adults of superior intelligence to possess superior socio-economic status, and *vice versa*. In the light of the previous discussion, however, it would also follow that at inferior social levels there are large numbers of adults with superior intelligence and large numbers of persons of inferior ability in the higher social classes.[1] In other words, if selection for intelligence exists in the sorting out of individuals into occupations of higher and lower social status, it does not operate perfectly. Agencies of a different kind must also exist to account for individuals of comparatively low intelligence occupying superior social positions, and

---

[1] If, to take the opposite view, it were held that differences in intelligence are entirely due to differences in environment, similar difficulties would arise. There would be many exceptions to the rule that superior intelligence was produced by a superior environment.

individuals of comparatively high intelligence remaining in inferior social positions.

These considerations, as we have seen, depend upon the view that environmental differences contribute nothing to observed differences in intellectual performance. The problem becomes much more complicated if we recognize the likelihood that test scores are not independent of environmental influences. In the first place we cannot be sure that such influences would be restricted to those associated with differences in socio-economic status. Secondly, it is probable that environmental agencies would operate more powerfully at an early age than in adult life. In so far as the parental generation, when young, may have been reared in a different socio-economic environment from that which they provide for their offspring, it would not be possible to infer that its intellectual level was influenced by the same forces that affect the filial generation. A certain proportion of individuals move up, a smaller proportion move down the social scale. Moreover, the standard of life of the whole population has progressively improved in recent times, although perhaps not equally for all sections of the community.[1] There would be an increased number of cases in which the intelligence of various groups of children would no longer give a sure indication of the intellectual level of the parental group.

Whatever view we take, it is probable that evidence of the segregation of ability at different social levels would remain. Although the issue has never been directly investigated, it is also possible that promotion in the social scale tends to a small extent to follow the possession of superior ability. We should not, however, be justified in arguing that this affords proof of the genetic character of selection, nor that social selection with regard to ability is exclusively based on hereditary differences. The only conclusion which we may safely draw is that neither an extreme autogenetic nor an extreme environmentalist hypothesis accords with the observed data in this and in similar studies. Nor, without further evidence concerning the re-

[1] If a better environment produces better performance on intelligence tests, it would follow that the whole level of intelligence in the population has risen in recent times. As in the parallel case of longevity, this would be difficult to explain in terms of some simple natural selection hypothesis. The difficulty would be all the greater to those who bewail the alleged rapid multiplication of unfit stocks as contrary to natural selection. The view that the general level of ability is declining ultimately depends upon the denial that environmental agencies can affect intelligent performances.

spective roles of differences due to nature and nurture in performance on intelligence tests, do they give the slightest indication that one hypothesis is less wide of the mark than the other. Finally, the very low value which we find for the correlation between intelligence and socio-economic status among fee-paying pupils as a group suggests the need for the further analysis of particular social groups within the community, in order that the limits of social segregation of ability should be more accurately determined. Provisionally we may advance the view that above (and perhaps below) a certain level in the social scale, differences both in income and in the nature of the work performed by parents do not correspond so significantly with differences in the intelligence of their children as in certain intermediate social groups where the selective process seems to operate most conspicuously.

With these considerations in mind we may examine the figures in Tables IV and V for cases of exceptional interest.

(a) It will be observed in Table V that the offspring of teachers of every kind exceed the mean of the social category highest in intelligence.[1] In view of the construction of intelligence tests this result is not surprising.[2]

(b) The high level of insurance agents, seamen (all of elementary school origin), engineering draughtsmen, customs and tax officers, and the clerical grades of the Civil Service is remarkable, inasmuch as they do not enjoy a socio-economic status comparable with that of the other occupational groups with a mean I.B. exceeding 124. In some of these occupations individuals are selected by competitive examinations. Together with the cases of teachers and other professions at this level of I.B., this consideration suggests that the widespread use of public examinations for certain occupations, not in themselves enjoying superlative social esteem, tends to lower the correlation between intelligence and socio-economic status and thus

---

[1] The single exception to this statement is the group described as "Teachers Unspecified." It may be that the parents in this group are teachers in small private schools, but it is more likely that the mean is depressed because children ignorant of the exact status of their parents' professions are a group selected for inferior intelligence.

[2] On the other hand, it is curious to observe that the offspring of ministers of religion, who are generally regarded as a literate group, have the poorest mean ability of any professional workers. It is in fact the same as the mean for the Clerical and Commercial Employees, police constables, and the rank and file of the armed forces.

render still more ambiguous certain of the arguments already criticized in the previous pages.

(c) Measured by a purely pecuniary canon, there is little doubt that the social category which we have described as Larger Business Owners and Higher Executives is the highest. Nevertheless, their offspring are significantly inferior in mean intelligence to those of the professional classes, an observation confirmed by nearly all similar studies.

(d) It is notable also that the mean of Category A (1) is exceeded by groups so diverse as tailors, clerks, and chauffeurs. It is possible that tailors form a racially selected group largely composed of Jews whose intelligence is probably above the average. The high level reached by the children of clerks may, perhaps, be explained partly in terms of selection within the industrial population, among whom black-coated workers enjoy considerable prestige, partly because clerical abilities may be highly correlated with whatever is measured by intelligence tests.

(e) The mean ability of the children of Civil Servants of the highest (administrative) grade closely resembles that for clerks both in the Civil Service and elsewhere. The figures for officers and for the rank and file of the armed forces are very similar. The means of shopkeepers, shop managers, and shop assistants are practically identical.

(f) An inspection of Table V indicates that from the point of view of intellectual level Category C is the least homogeneous. It may be that comparatively new social strata exhibit much greater differences than those of a more traditional kind. In other words, they may not constitute a homogeneous social class in the usual sense of the term, but may nevertheless require to be distinguished from other social categories.

(g) We may hazard the generalization that the children of manual workers occupied in mechanical road transport, the public services, the newer and more flourishing industries, and in crafts requiring apprenticeship or learnership are more intelligent than the average of all manual workers. The children of tailors, seamen, chauffeurs, wireless operators, and stage hands are exceptionally able. Interesting also is the relatively high position of metal trades workers, police constables, transport and postal workers, and electrical engineers.

(h) With the exception of workers in the hotel and catering trades, no unskilled workers exceed the mean for the group of skilled workers

N*

TABLE IV

Occupational Means of Free and Fee-paying Pupils

Occupation	I.B. Free Pupils	N.	I.B. Fee-paying Pupils	N.	I.Q. Free Pupils	I.Q. Fee-paying Pupils
A. Employing and Directive Classes						
1. Larger Business Owners and Higher Executives:						
Bank Managers and Bankers	—	—	119·2 ± 3·70	44	—	130·5 ± 3·09
Brokers, Jobbers, and Financiers	—	—	112·5 ± 4·63	45	—	127·8 ± 3·37
Building Contractors	—	—	112·4 ± 8·93	8	—	132·1 ± 6·41
Commercial Business Owners	—	—	119·4 ± 2·09	227	—	131·0 ± 1·64
Directors	—	—	123·6 ± 2·81	101	—	133·5 ± 2·15
Estate Agents, Surveyors, and Auctioneers	153·0	1	129·3 ± 5·67	28	145·0	137·4 ± 4·17
Farmers			98·1 ± 4·46	37		115·2 ± 3·71
Manufacturers	—	—	112·9 ± 3·14	89	—	126·3 ± 2·58
Merchants	—	—	125·0 ± 2·44	133	—	134·6 ± 1·95
Plantation Owners	—	—	118·4 ± 7·68	10	—	131·6 ± 6·61
2. Smaller Business Owners:						
Number of Employees, 1-10	113·2 ± 5·89	36	—	—	127·7 ± 5·30	
Number of Employees, over 10	79·3 ± 11·08	3	—	—	100·0 ± 8·06	
Number of Employees not stated	97·6 ± 4·58	93	—	—	114·4 ± 3·53	
Bookmakers	111·0 ± 14·14	2	—	—	124·0 ± 12·73	
3. Shopkeepers:						
Number of Assistants, none	112·9 ± 3·71	46	109·0 ± 9·43	9	125·7 ± 3·28	121·0 ± 7·42
Number of Assistants, 1-10	110·3 ± 5·23	63	119·3 ± 4·94	48	124·2 ± 5·00	130·3 ± 4·13
More than 1 Shop or 10 Assistants	100·5 ± 3·18	2	100·9 ± 5·15	30	111·5 ± 1·80	116·4 ± 4·00
Number of Assistants not stated[1]	106·3 ± 2·68	149	111·3 ± 2·67	164	122·4 ± 2·37	124·4 ± 1·88
Publicans	—	—	109·7 ± 7·77	35	—	124·2 ± 7·73
Stall-holders	96·6 ± 4·85	36	—	—	112·9 ± 3·99	

[1] Not separately distinguished for Free pupils.

B. Professional Occupations						
Architects	—	—	123·6 ± 4·75	41	—	133·3 ± 3·73
Army, Navy, and Air Force Officers	—	—	120·7 ± 3·31	66	—	132·2 ± 2·74
Authors, Artists, and Composers	130·0	1	119·1 ± 7·06	23	141·0	129·0 ± 5·31
Barristers, Judges, and Solicitors	—	—	126·4 ± 4·02	57	—	136·4 ± 3·10
Chartered Accountants	—	—	120·6 ± 5·05	36	—	130·7 ± 3·79
Civil Servants (Administrative Grade)	—	—	121·5 ± 4·58	40	—	133·3 ± 3·63
Colonial Administrators	—	—	138·7 ± 13·46	7	—	141·0 ± 8·16
Consultant Engineers	—	—	128·8 ± 10·97	3	—	135·9 ± 9·55
Dentists	—	—	122·6 ± 4·91	27	—	132·9 ± 3·54
Doctors	—	—	122·1 ± 2·61	113	—	132·9 ± 2·04
Diplomatic Service	156·0	1	145·0 ± 2·83	2	168·0	153·0 ± 1·41
Editors	—	—	127·8 ± 8·54	18	—	138·0 ± 5·67
Ministers of Religion	83·0	1	122·5 ± 5·56	42	99·0	136·4 ± 4·43
Professional (Miscellaneous)	133·1 ± 5·15	16	—	—	141·2 ± 3·40	—
Scientists	—	—	128·7 ± 6·40	21	—	136·6 ± 5·40
Teachers (Elementary)	121·2 ± 5·91	21	138·5 ± 6·59	35	131·5 ± 4·84	140·8 ± 2·22
Teachers (Non-elementary)	152·0 ± 10·20	4	134·9 ± 4·55	55	149·0 ± 5·71	138·6 ± 2·94
Teachers (Unclassified)	—	—	111·6 ± 6·19	29	—	124·9 ± 4·40
Teachers (University)	—	—	147·5 ± 6·14	15	—	150·2 ± 4·53
C. Minor Professional and Other Highly Skilled Occupations						
Civil Engineers	—	—	103·4 ± 6·75	23	—	128·1 ± 4·29
Civil Servants (Customs and Tax Officers, etc.)	142·4 ± 6·46	9	127·5 ± 4·10	66	144·4 ± 3·18	138·3 ± 3·37
Engineering Draughtsmen	—	—	133·3 ± 7·99	7	—	141·1 ± 5·27
Engineers (other higher grades)	—	—	122·0 ± 3·20	92	—	132·6 ± 2·48
Foremen	105·6 ± 4·65	176	112·2 ± 4·92	31	123·1 ± 3·15	125·4 ± 4·05
Journalists	132·5 ± 6·63	8	125·4 ± 7·35	11	139·5 ± 5·97	137·5 ± 6·36
Managers (Commercial)	106·8 ± 4·84	66	107·6 ± 3·37	69	122·4 ± 4·29	124·1 ± 2·65
Managers (Industrial)	130·4 ± 4·33	12	123·2 ± 2·37	162	139·3 ± 3·34	132·6 ± 1·76
Mercantile Marine (Officers)	—	—	110·6 ± 7·35	13	—	124·9 ± 5·99
Newspaper Employees (Editorial Staff)	—	—	100·8 ± 8·20	10	—	115·8 ± 6·68

TABLE IV—*continued*

OCCUPATIONAL MEANS OF FREE AND FEE-PAYING PUPILS

Occupation	I.B.			I.Q.		
	Free Pupils.	N.	Fee-paying Pupils.	N.	Free Pupils.	Fee-paying Pupils.
Officials (Industrial and Commercial)	—	—	125·3 ± 5·20	45	—	135·6 ± 5·28
Officials of Public Bodies	132·2 ± 5·62	12	113·7 ± 5·23	25	144·4 ± 4·52	128·0 ± 4·50
Police Officials (Inspectors, etc.)	—	—	100·3 ± 9·38	11	—	113·4 ± 5·85
Professional Entertainers	118·2 ± 6·54	21	125·8 ± 10·25	13	131·6 ± 6·48	137·6 ± 8·29
D. CLERICAL AND COMMERCIAL EMPLOYEES						
Accountants	—	—	113·5 ± 6·07	31	—	125·4 ± 4·47
Advertising Workers	137·4 ± 14·34	4	—	—	142·1 ± 10·39	—
Buyers and Head Salesmen	125·5 ± 3·16	11	120·1 ± 19·20	18	135·6 ± 3·36	130·2 ± 9·14
Clerical (Bank)	—	—	118·3 ± 3·73	79	—	129·4 ± 2·85
Clerical (Civil Service)	124·0 ± 3·70	78	129·9 ± 4·66	40	133·8 ± 3·20	138·4 ± 3·11
Clerical (Inferior)	122·3 ± 4·25	221	120·6 ± 2·98	143	135·1 ± 3·40	131·8 ± 2·42
Clerical (Railway)	98·7 ± 7·52	9	—	—	112·5 ± 5·39	—
Clerical (Superior)	114·5 ± 8·32	54	124·4 ± 3·81	97	126·4 ± 6·56	135·0 ± 3·03
Commercial Artists	—	—	120·5 ± 15·92	2	—	135·5 ± 15·92
Commercial Travellers	117·0 ± 7·19	81	113·8 ± 4·03	86	131·4 ± 5·24	129·1 ± 3·09
Insurance Agents	139·3 ± 8·47	21	125·3 ± 6·32	11	145·4 ± 5·37	134·8 ± 4·71
Shop Assistants	106·2 ± 2·94	192	115·9 ± 4·67	28	120·5 ± 2·29	129·8 ± 3·83
E. MANUAL WORKERS						
1. *Skilled Wage-earners :*						
Building Trades Craftsmen	95·5 ± 1·97	320	106·8 ± 10·25	6	112·7 ± 1·49	121·8 ± 8·32
Bus Conductors	108·7 ± 5·28	59	125·5 ± 15·21	2	121·6 ± 4·33	136·0 ± 12·73
Bus Drivers	104·7 ± 3·82	53	107·8 ± 12·67	5	117·2 ± 3·00	135·5 ± 7·82
Chauffeurs	121·0 ± 5·68	40	—	—	134·0 ± 5·24	—
Craftsmen (Miscellaneous)	101·3 ± 5·19	46	112·0 ± 9·63	7	115·9 ± 4·10	126·1 ± 7·62
Dock Labourers (Regular)	83·1 ± 8·97	8	—	—	104·1 ± 7·69	—

Occupation	Mean ± SE	N	Mean ± SE	N	Mean ± SE	Mean ± SE
Electrical Engineers	108·6 ± 9·27	14	—	—	123·8 ± 8·17	—
Electricians	99·8 ± 4·90	73	—	—	116·9 ± 3·35	—
Engineers and Mechanics	101·3 ± 3·12	207	112·6 ± 5·01	85	117·4 ± 2·53	126·7 ± 4·23
Factory Workers (Miscellaneous)	100·3 ± 2·34	342	104·7 ± 4·09	54	117·3 ± 1·78	120·7 ± 3·61
Firemen	105·2 ± 5·54	27	—	—	118·3 ± 4·58	—
Furniture Trades Workers	105·2 ± 3·72	66	—	—	120·2 ± 2·91	—
Metal Trades Workers	114·8 ± 7·94	64	133·2 ± 9·41	5	128·2 ± 7·47	135·4 ± 5·90
Motor and Taxi Drivers	99·6 ± 2·31	208	129·3 ± 3·19	4	114·3 ± 1·85	140·5 ± 4·35
Police Constables	114·5 ± 5·20	124	117·2 ± 6·32	14	127·4 ± 4·62	127·8 ± 4·87
Postal Workers	108·6 ± 4·54	108	125·5 ± 6·83	8	123·8 ± 3·03	136·6 ± 5·91
Printers (General)	85·8 ± 4·66	81	126·5 ± 9·07	8	108·8 ± 3·48	136·5 ± 7·59
Printers (Newspaper)	96·9 ± 4·40	24	96·7 ± 20·74	4	111·5 ± 3·43	118·5 ± 17·40
Railway Workers (Engine Drivers)	83·3 ± 5·69	18	—	—	101·0 ± 3·56	—
Railway Workers (Skilled)	100·5 ± 4·45	62	—	—	115·2 ± 3·69	—
Railway Workers (Unspecified)	99·7 ± 3·83	88	—	—	116·4 ± 3·10	—
Stage Hands	116·9 ± 3·09	4	—	—	130·4 ± 2·65	—
Tailors	122·4 ± 4·76	64	108·4 ± 5·64	7	131·9 ± 4·23	122·0 ± 5·33
Tram Drivers and Conductors	110·8 ± 5·66	51	113·0 ± 6·94	3	126·1 ± 4·45	127·3 ± 6·84
Wireless Operators	—	—	118·3 ± 20·15	4	—	148·3 ± 1·20
2. Unskilled Wage-earners:						
Bargees	78·2 ± 5·00	11	—	—	100·4 ± 4·02	—
Building Trades Labourers	89·9 ± 4·21	68	—	—	111·2 ± 3·20	—
Carmen	89·9 ± 4·34	57	—	—	107·4 ± 3·61	—
Dock Labourers (Casual)	95·6 ± 4·98	40	—	—	113·8 ± 3·28	—
Dustmen and Roadmen	94·2 ± 4·05	67	—	—	111·0 ± 3·01	—
Factory Workers (Miscellaneous)	93·9 ± 1·91	272	—	—	111·9 ± 1·50	—
Hotel and Catering Trades Workers	103·4 ± 3·75	93	—	—	117·9 ± 3·14	—
Labourers (General)	90·3 ± 4·33	101	—	—	113·1 ± 3·45	—
Market Porters	101·7 ± 6·29	28	—	—	118·3 ± 4·92	—
Milk and Bakers' Roundsmen	94·5 ± 4·42	43	—	—	110·4 ± 3·41	—
Miscellaneous	—	—	—	—	—	—
Navvies	89·4 ± 4·19	56	115·1 ± 7·60	15	108·5 ± 3·29	127·2 ± 6·17
Packers and Porters	96·1 ± 2·39	156	—	—	112·2 ± 1·86	—
Personal Service Workers	101·0 ± 2·86	192	105·0 ± 6·45	19	116·6 ± 2·50	123·7 ± 4·75
Street Traders	87·4 ± 3·81	41	—	—	104·5 ± 2·81	—

TABLE IV—*continued*

OCCUPATIONAL MEANS OF FREE AND FEE-PAYING PUPILS

Occupation.	I.B.			I.Q.		
	Free Pupils.	N.	Fee-paying Pupils.	N.	Free Pupils.	Fee-paying Pupils.
3. *Fatherless Wage-earning Families :*						
Mother Charwoman	97·1 ± 3·41	105	—	—	113·8 ± 2·70	—
Mother or other Wage-earner in Family	103·6 ± 4·16	143	116·4 ± 15·65	18	119·1 ± 3·34	124·0 ± 10·42
F. OCCUPATIONS UNKNOWN AND MISCELLANEOUS						
Army and Navy (Privates and Non-commissioned)	118·7 ± 4·79	36	—	—	130·7 ± 4·60	—
Building Trades Workers (Unspecified)	91·1 ± 8·25	12	—	—	109·7 ± 7·06	—
Civil Servants (Unspecified)	—	—	135·3 ± 4·57	75	—	141·7 ± 3·89
Dock Labourers (Unspecified)	96·2 ± 4·18	49	—	—	111·9 ± 2·60	—
Occupations Unknown	91·9 ± 1·77	270	114·6 ± 2·01	237	109·9 ± 1·36	128·8 ± 1·56
Office Workers (Unspecified)	—	—	106·5 ± 4·41	52	124·5 ± 18·75	119·8 ± 3·47
Orphanage Children	111·0 ± 21·22	2	—	—	128·7 ± 5·68	—
Pensioners	114·9 ± 6·25	38	—	—	142·3 ± 2·26	—
Seamen (Unspecified)	135·7 ± 3·58	22	—	—	104·1 ± 2·44	—
Unemployed (Occupation Unknown)	81·7 ± 3·42	61	—	—	—	—

TABLE V

Occupational Means of All Pupils

Occupation.	Category.	N.	I.B.	I.Q.
Teachers (University) . .	B	15	147·5 ± 6·14	150·2 ± 4·53
Diplomatic Service . .	B	2	145·0 ± 2·83	153·0 ± 1·41
Colonial Administrators. .	B	7	138·7 ± 13·46	141·0 ± 8·16
Advertising Workers . .	D	4	137·4 ± 14·34	142·1 ± 10·39
Insurance Agents . . .	D	32	137·2 ± 7·72	143·8 ± 4·90
Seamen (Unspecified) . .	F	22	135·7 ± 3·58	142·3 ± 2·26
Teachers (Non-elementary) .	B	59	135·5 ± 9·28	139·0 ± 5·20
Civil Servants (Unspecified) .	F	75	135·3 ± 4·57	141·7 ± 3·89
Engineering Draughtsmen .	C	7	133·3 ± 7·99	141·1 ± 5·27
Professional (Miscellaneous) .	B	16	133·1 ± 5·15	141·2 ± 3·40
Estate Agents, Surveyors, and Auctioneers . . .	A (1)	28	129·3 ± 5·67	137·4 ± 4·17
Officials of Public Bodies .	C	37	129·2 ± 5·13	141·8 ± 4·13
Consultant Engineers . .	B	3	128·8 ± 10·97	135·9 ± 9·55
Scientists	B	21	128·7 ± 6·40	136·6 ± 5·40
Civil Servants (Customs and Tax Officers, etc.) . .	C	75	128·4 ± 5·88	138·6 ± 2·91
Journalists	C	19	127·9 ± 6·06	138·1 ± 5·46
Editors	B	18	127·8 ± 8·54	138·0 ± 5·67
Barristers, Judges, and Solicitors	B	57	126·4 ± 4·02	136·4 ± 3·10
Teachers (Elementary) . .	B	56	126·2 ± 5·41	134·2 ± 4·40
Officials (Industrial and Commercial)	C	45	125·3 ± 5·20	135·6 ± 5·28
Merchants	A (1)	133	125·0 ± 2·44	134·6 ± 1·95
Clerical (Civil Service) . .	D	118	124·9 ± 3·39	134·4 ± 2·92
Doctors	B	114	124·8 ± 2·61	135·7 ± 2·04
Professional Occupations (Mean of All)	*B*	*674*	*124·7 ± 4·79*	*134·5 ± 4·42*
Buyers and Head Salesmen .	D	29	124·6 ± 3·36	134·7 ± 3·17
Directors	A (1)	101	123·6 ± 2·81	133·5 ± 2·15
Architects	B	41	123·6 ± 4·75	133·3 ± 3·73
Managers (Industrial) . .	C	174	123·5 ± 3·94	132·9 ± 3·04
Dentists	B	27	122·6 ± 4·91	132·9 ± 3·54
Tailors	E (1)	71	122·3 ± 4·36	131·8 ± 3·88
Authors, Artists, and Composers	B	24	122·0 ± 7·06	132·2 ± 5·31
Engineers (other higher grades)	C	92	122·0 ± 3·20	132·6 ± 2·48
Clerical (Inferior) . . .	D	364	122·0 ± 3·87	134·5 ± 3·10
Civil Servants (Administrative Grade)	B	40	121·5 ± 4·58	133·3 ± 3·63
Chauffeurs	E (1)	40	121·0 ± 5·68	134·0 ± 5·24
Army, Navy, and Air Force Officers	B	66	120·7 ± 3·31	132·2 ± 2·74
Chartered Accountants . .	B	36	120·6 ± 5·05	130·7 ± 3·79
Commercial Artists . .	D	2	120·5 ± 15·92	135·5 ± 15·92
Commercial Business Owners .	A (1)	227	119·4 ± 2·09	131·0 ± 1·64

POLITICAL ARITHMETIC

TABLE V—*continued*

OCCUPATIONAL MEANS OF ALL PUPILS

Occupation.	Category.	N.	I.B.	I.Q.
Bank Managers and Bankers .	A (1)	44	119·2 ± 3·70	130·5 ± 3·09
Professional Entertainers .	C	34	119·1 ± 6·02	132·2 ± 5·94
Larger Business Owners and Higher Executives (Mean of All) .	A (1)	722	118·8 ± 1·10	130·6 ± 0·86
Army and Navy (Privates and Non-commissioned) . .	F	36	118·7 ± 4·79	130·7 ± 4·60
Plantation Owners . .	A (1)	10	118·4 ± 7·68	131·6 ± 6·61
Clerical (Superior) . .	D	151	118·4 ± 7·57	129·8 ± 5·97
Clerical (Bank) . . .	D	79	118·3 ± 3·73	129·4 ± 2·85
Wireless Operators . ,	E (1)	4	118·3 ± 20·15	148·3 ± 1·20
Stage Hands . . .	E (1)	4	116·9 ± 3·09	130·4 ± 2·65
Commercial Travellers . .	D	167	116·2 ± 6·55	130·9 ± 4·77
Unskilled Wage-earners (Miscellaneous) . . .	E (2)	15	115·1 ± 7·60	127·2 ± 6·17
Metal Trades Workers .	E (1)	69	114·9 ± 7·27	128·3 ± 6·81
Pensioners . . .	F	38	114·9 ± 6·25	128·7 ± 5·68
Police Constables . . .	E (1)	138	114·6 ± 4·76	127·4 ± 4·22
Clerical and Commercial (Mean of All)	D	1,206	114·6 ± 1·85	127·3 ± 1·43
Ministers of Religion . .	B	43	113·5 ± 5·56	127·6 ± 4·43
Accountants . . .	D	31	113·5 ± 6·07	125·4 ± 4·47
Smaller Business Owners — Number of Employees, 1–10	A (2)	36	113·2 ± 5·89	127·7 ± 5·30
Manufacturers . . .	A (1)	89	112·9 ± 3·14	126·3 ± 2·58
Shopkeepers—Number of Assistants, none . . .	A (3)	55	112·9 ± 3·48	125·7 ± 3·06
Brokers, Jobbers, and Financiers	A (1)	45	112·5 ± 4·63	127·8 ± 3·37
Minor Professional and Other Highly Skilled Occupations (Mean of All)	C	882	112·5 ± 3·19	127·4 ± 2·39
Building Contractors . .	A (1)	8	112·4 ± 8·93	132·1 ± 6·41
Teachers (Unclassified) . .	B	29	111·6 ± 6·19	124·9 ± 4·40
Shopkeepers—Number of Assistants, 1–10 . . .	A (3)	111	111·4 ± 4·78	125·0 ± 4·56
Bookmakers	A (2)	2	111·0 ± 14·14	124·0 ± 12·73
Orphanage Children . .	F	2	111·0 ± 21·22	124·5 ± 18·75
Tram Drivers and Conductors	E (1)	54	110·8 ± 5·18	126·1 ± 4·09
Mercantile Marine (Officers) .	C	13	110·6 ± 7·35	124·9 ± 5·99
Publicans	A (3)	35	109·7 ± 7·77	124·2 ± 7·73
Bus Conductors . . .	E (1)	61	108·8 ± 4·99	121·6 ± 4·10
Postal Workers . . .	E (1)	116	108·7 ± 4·17	123·9 ± 2·81
Electrical Engineers . .	E (1)	14	108·6 ± 9·27	123·8 ± 8·17
Shopkeepers—Number of Assistants not stated . .	A (3)	313	107·1 ± 2·45	122·7 ± 2·16

TABLE V—*continued*

OCCUPATIONAL MEANS OF ALL PUPILS

Occupation.	Category.	N.	I.B.	I.Q.
Shopkeepers (Mean of All) . .	*A (3)*	*582*	*107·1 ± 1·86*	*122·1 ± 1·55*
Managers (Commercial) .	C	135	107·0 ± 4·41	122·8 ± 3·91
Office Workers (Unspecified) .	F	52	106·5 ± 4·41	119·8 ± 3·47
Shop Assistants . . .	D	220	106·3 ± 2·71	120·5 ± 2·11
Foremen	C	207	105·7 ± 4·25	123·2 ± 2·89
Firemen	E (1)	27	105·2 ± 5·54	118·3 ± 4·58
Furniture Trades Workers .	E (1)	66	105·2 ± 3·72	120·2 ± 2·91
Bus Drivers	E (1)	58	104·7 ± 3·66	117·2 ± 2·82
Father Dead, Mother or Other Wage-earner in Family .	E (3)	161	103·9 ± 4·04	119·2 ± 3·18
Civil Engineers . . .	C	23	103·4 ± 6·75	128·1 ± 4·29
Hotel and Catering Trades Workers	E (2)	93	103·4 ± 3·75	117·9 ± 3·14
Engineers and Mechanics .	E (1)	292	102·2 ± 2·87	118·2 ± 2·33
Skilled Wage-earners (Mean of All)	*E (1)*	*2,367*	*101·8 ± 0·86*	*117·6 ± 0·68*
Market Porters . . .	E (2)	28	101·7 ± 6·29	118·3 ± 4·92
Skilled Craftsmen (Miscellaneous)	E (1)	53	101·4 ± 4·80	116·1 ± 3·79
Personal Service Workers .	E (2)	211	101·0 ± 2·67	116·7 ± 2·31
Smaller Business Owners (Mean of All)	*A (2)*	*135*	*100·9 ± 4·08*	*117·2 ± 3·19*
Newspaper Employees (Editorial Staff) . .	C	10	100·8 ± 8·20	115·8 ± 6·68
Shopkeepers—More than 1 Shop or 10 Assistants .	A (3)	32	100·7 ± 2·93	114·3 ± 1·68
Railway Workers (Skilled) .	E (1)	62	100·5 ± 4·45	115·2 ± 3·69
Skilled Factory Workers (Miscellaneous	E (1)	396	100·4 ± 2·16	117·4 ± 1·65
Fatherless Wage-earning Families (Mean of All) . . .	*E (3)*	*266*	*100·4 ± 2·81*	*116·4 ± 2·16*
Police Officials (Inspectors, etc.)	C	11	100·3 ± 9·38	113·4 ± 5·85
Electricians	E (1)	73	99·8 ± 4·90	116·9 ± 3·35
Railway Workers (Unspecified)	E (1)	88	99·7 ± 3·83	116·4 ± 3·10
Motor and Taxi Drivers .	E (1)	212	99·6 ± 2·12	114·3 ± 1·73
Clerical (Railway) . .	D	9	98·7 ± 6·34	112·5 ± 4·50
Farmers	A (1)	38	98·6 ± 4·46	115·5 ± 3·71
Smaller Business Owners—Number of Employees not stated	A (2)	93	97·6 ± 4·58	114·4 ± 3·53
Father Dead—Mother Charwoman . . .	E (3)	105	97·1 ± 3·41	113·8 ± 2·70
Printers (Newspaper) . .	E (1)	28	96·9 ± 4·42	111·6 ± 3·50
Stall-holders . . .	A (3)	36	96·6 ± 4·85	112·9 ± 3·99

TABLE V—*continued*

OCCUPATIONAL MEANS OF ALL PUPILS

Occupation.	Category.	N.	I.B.	I.Q.
Occupations Unknown and Miscellaneous (Mean of All) . .	F	*854*	*96·3* ± *1·32*	*114·0* ± *1·04*
Dock Labourers (Unspecified)	F	49	96·2 ± 4·18	111·9 ± 2·60
Packers and Porters . .	E (2)	156	96·1 ± 2·39	112·2 ± 1·86
Dock Labourers (Casual) .	E (2)	40	95·6 ± 4·98	113·8 ± 3·28
Building Trades Craftsmen .	E (1)	326	95·5 ± 2·02	112·7 ± 1·55
Unskilled Wage-earners (Mean of All)	E (2)	*1,259*	*95·0* ± *0·90*	*112·3* ± *0·71*
Milk and Bakers' Roundsmen	E (2)	43	94·5 ± 4·42	110·4 ± 3·41
Occupations Unknown . .	F	507	94·5 ± 1·62	112·1 ± 1·24
Dustmen and Roadmen .	E (2)	67	94·2 ± 4·05	111·0 ∓ 3·01
Unskilled Factory Workers (Miscellaneous) . .	E (2)	272	93·9 ± 1·91	111·9 ± 1·50
Building Trades Workers (Unspecified)	F	12	91·1 ± 8·25	109·7 ± 7·06
Labourers (General) . .	E (2)	101	90·3 ± 4·33	113·1 ± 3·45
Building Trades Labourers .	E (2)	68	89·9 ± 4·21	111·2 ± 3·20
Carmen	E (2)	57	89·9 ± 4·34	107·4 ± 3·61
Navvies	E (2)	56	89·4 ± 4·19	108·5 ± 3·29
Street Traders . . .	E (2)	41	87·4 ± 3·81	104·5 ± 2·81
Printers (General) . .	E (1)	89	86·0 ± 4·32	109·0 ± 3·24
Railway Workers (Engine Drivers)	E (1)	18	83·3 ± 5·69	101·0 ± 3·56
Dock Labourers (Regular) .	E (1)	8	83·1 ± 8·97	104·1 ± 7·69
Unemployed (Occupations Unknown)	F	61	81·7 ± 3·42	104·1 ± 2·44
Owners of Small Businesses— Number of Employees, over 10	A (2)	3	79·3 ± 11·08	100·0 ± 8·06
Bargees	E (2)	11	78·2 ± 4·97	100·4 ± 4·01

as a whole. Indeed, what emerges most remarkably from this and similar studies is the fact that unskilled workers are an exceptionally homogeneous group.

(*i*) The relatively low position of the children of railway employees of all kinds, building trades craftsmen and printers excites some surprise. We may suggest that possible causes may be found in the irregular and frequently depressed condition of employment in the building trades and in the fact that both in building and on the railways employment is non-progressive. None of the three trades can be regarded as expanding, their technique is inclined to be traditional, and it is likely that they do not attract adventurous or ambitious young men.

One possibility remains that has not hitherto been discussed. It may be that intelligent behaviour is stimulated to a high pitch of performance in occupational groups composed of individuals and families engaged in the rapid ascent of the social ladder. In other words, where the conditions of mobility are present, individuals already selected for other qualities as well as for intelligence will be making exceptional efforts both for themselves and for their children. On the other hand, when persons have achieved a comparatively high economic status which is no longer precarious, these efforts may slacken. Similarly in the case of unskilled manual workers, whose mobility is still probably small, lack of opportunity to rise in the social scale may deaden the response to intellectual stimuli.

We cannot conclude this section without reiterating our view that it is dubious in the extreme to argue from the achievement of children on intelligence tests, designed to test aptitude in the performance of school tasks, to the mental standing of their parents. If we could examine in the case of the parental generation the correlation between intelligence as measured by tests designed for school children and socio-economic status, we might discover that while positive it was insignificantly small. It remains to be proved that there is any necessary connection between such performances on the part of the filial generation and the agencies that have led their parents to practise certain occupations.

V. THE RELATION BETWEEN ABILITY AND OPPORTUNITY

In the previous chapter we described how a quantitative estimate could be made of the inequality in the distribution of opportunities of a higher education that exists between children educated at the expense of the State (free pupils) and those educated at the expense of their parents (fee-paying pupils). In this section we employ the same methods to determine the relation of educational opportunity to socio-economic status.

It is possible in the first instance to compute the distribution of the various social categories among children who enjoy opportunities of a higher education and compare it with that of the general population, without having regard to comparative ability. We can go on to measure the extent of the disparity that persists when ability is related to opportunity. For this purpose we have used the same arbitrary criteria of high ability that were described in Chapter VIII. These criteria do not attempt to measure educability on an absolute psychological scale. They are employed in a sociological context only. For example, we discovered that roughly 50 per cent of fee-

TABLE VI

SOCIO-ECONOMIC DISTRIBUTION OF ALL PUPILS AND OF ALL WITH
OPPORTUNITIES OF HIGHER EDUCATION (PERCENTAGES)

	1 All Pupils.	2 All with Opportunities.	3 Ratio of 1 to 2.
A. *Employing and Directive Classes* :			
1. Larger Business Owners	2·4	14·0	1 : 5·8
2. Smaller Business Owners	1·7	0·8	1 : 0·5
3. Shopkeepers	6·5	6·9	1 : 1·1
B. *Professional Occupations*	2·4	12·9	1 : 5·4
C. *Minor Professional and Other Highly Skilled Occupations*	5·1	13·8	1 : 2·7
D. *Clerical and Commercial Employees*	9·9	16·9	1 : 1·7
E. *Manual Workers :*			
1. Skilled Wage-earners	32·8	17·7	1 : 0·5
2. Unskilled Wage-earners	23·8	5·9	1 : 0·2
3. Fatherless Wage-earning Families	3·7	1·7	1 : 0·5
4. Total Manual Workers	60·3	25·3	1 : 0·4
F. *Occupation Unknown and Miscellaneous*	11·7	9·3	1 : 0·8

paying pupils attain or exceed an I.Q. of 130 and an I.B. of 120 on the Otis scale. We then enquired what proportion of free pupils attain the same level. The term "high ability" is used only on the assumption that we may say for the sake of argument that at least 50 per cent of pupils in fee-paying schools are held worthy of receiving a higher education.

The first column of Table VI gives the (weighted) percentage distribution of the social categories for the entire school population of London as it appears in our data. The second column shows the social composition of those pupils, both free and fee-paying, who are already pursuing a higher education or who will have the opportunity to proceed to secondary schools. By higher education we mean that kind of post-primary education which the majority of fee-paying parents would regard as necessary when considering the future their own children. This definition excludes central and senior of elementary schools, and technical schools maintained by the local education authority. The methods used in the computation of this group were similar to those described in detail in the previous chapter. To the account given there it is only necessary to add that we assume the social composition of potential secondary school pupils aged 9.0–12.6 to be the same as that of existing pupils.[1]

The last column in the table indicates to what extent the social composition of pupils with opportunities of higher education corresponds with that of the school population as a whole. It will be observed that the children of larger business owners and higher executives and of the professional classes are considerably over-represented, and those of manual workers greatly under-represented. The former groups are proportionately five times more numerous in schools providing a higher education than they are in the general school population, while unskilled workers are proportionately only one-fifth as numerous.

This table presents the facts without regard to the relative ability of the various social categories. It may be argued that opportunities for higher education should stand in some relation to the ability of individuals. In the case of free pupils the State already imposes a rigorous test of educational fitness on those selected for free places in secondary schools. Without necessarily committing ourselves to the implied view that only those above a certain level of intelligence, as measured by intelligence tests, can *benefit* from higher education, we may proceed to discuss the result of applying the criteria of high ability already described. As previously, we have taken I.B. 120 and 130 and I.Q. 130 and 140. First we calculated the percentile distribution of intelligence in the various social categories for the group of All Pupils, and from these data obtained the percentage that attain or exceed the four selected levels of ability. These figures form the first part of Table VII.

---

[1] A fuller treatment of some of the methods used in the estimation of the size of this group appeared in a paper entitled "The Measurement of Educational Opportunity," in *The Journal of Adult Education* for September 1935.

TABLE VII

Socio-economic Distribution of All Pupils with Ability

	Percentage of Able Individuals in Each Social Category.				Percentage Contribution of Each Social Category to Total Number with Ability.			
	I.B.		I.Q.		I.B.		I.Q.	
	120 and over.	130 and over.	130 and over.	140 and over.	120 and over.	130 and over.	130 and over.	140 and over.
A. Employing and Directive Classes:								
1. Larger Business Owners and Higher Executives	48·8	36·7	51·2	39·7	4·5	5·3	4·4	5·2
2. Smaller Business Owners	25·0	17·8	28·4	17·5	1·7	1·8	1·7	1·7
3. Shopkeepers	28·1	17·6	31·5	19·2	7·1	6·9	7·4	7·0
B. Professional Occupations	57·4	42·6	59·3	44·5	5·4	6·2	5·1	6·0
C. Minor Professional and Other Highly Skilled Occupations	40·6	28·5	43·7	32·0	8·1	8·9	8·1	9·2
D. Clerical and Commercial Employees	41·4	29·7	42·6	30·7	15·9	17·7	15·2	16·9
E. Manual Workers:								
1. Skilled Wage-earners	23·7	14·3	26·0	15·7	30·2	28·4	30·8	28·7
2. Unskilled Wage-earners	16·4	9·7	18·3	10·9	15·2	14·0	15·7	14·5
3. Fatherless Wage-earning Families	26·1	13·4	28·3	14·3	3·8	3·0	3·8	3·0
4. Total Manual Workers	—	—	—	—	49·2	45·4	50·3	46·2
F. Occupations Unknown and Miscellaneous	17·9	10·8	18·5	12·1	8·2	7·6	7·8	7·9

As we have shown in the previous chapter, the great disparity in the relative size of various social groups in the population renders the use of such percentage figures misleading when we are considering the relative *numerical* contribution of the various groups to the total numbers with high ability. For example, 10 per cent of a population of 1,000,000 is a larger absolute number than 30 per cent of 100,000. For this reason we transformed the percentage distribution of the social categories in our data into absolute numbers, taking as our base the total estimated school population of London aged 9.0–12.6. It then became possible to calculate, for example, what percentage of the total school population with an I.B. of 120 and over was represented by the 23·7 per cent of skilled manual workers who attain this level. These data constitute the second part of Table VII. A comparison of the two parts of the table illustrates the importance of this factor of relative numerical magnitude. As a source of individuals of high ability, the manual workers category is by far the largest, although it contains a smaller *percentage* of such individuals than others enjoying a superior socio-economic status. In spite of the higher average ability of children of the professional classes, their numerical contribution to the total of able children is relatively small. It may be that environmental as well as genetic agencies affect performance on intelligence tests. If we wish to increase the proportion of individuals of high ability, it would seem to follow that there would be a greater return to our efforts from measures taken to improve the environment of manual workers than from attempts to increase the birth-rate among the professional classes.

The table on page 408 gives the numbers at the various social levels possessing educational opportunities as a percentage of the total numbers in each category with high ability.

For example, the figures show that when we use an I.B. of 120 as our criterion of high ability the children of larger business owners who enjoy the opportunity of a higher education are twice as numerous as those who have high ability, while in the case of the offspring of unskilled workers, the number with such opportunities is only a quarter of the total with high ability.

On the basis of the figures in Table VIII, relating to I.Q. 130, Fig. 1 illustrates the amount of ability represented by each social category, compared with the numbers who receive opportunities of a higher education irrespective of their ability. (Category F has not been included in the figure.)[1] In Fig. 2 the manual workers are compared with all the rest put together. It will be observed that the three social groups in which the distribution of opportunities of higher education is in excess of the distribution of ability are larger business owners and higher executives, professional occupations, and, to a lesser extent, minor professional and other highly skilled

TABLE VIII

PERCENTAGE OF PUPILS WITH OPPORTUNITIES OF HIGHER EDUCATION TO TOTAL NUMBER WITH HIGH ABILITY IN EACH SOCIAL CATEGORY.

		I.B.		I.Q.	
		120 and over.	130 and over.	130 and over.	140 and over.
A.	*Employing and Directive Classes :*				
	1. Larger Business Owners .	204·9	272·5	195·3	251·9
	2. Smaller Business Owners .	33·2	46·8	29·2	47·6
	3. Shopkeepers . . .	63·4	101·5	56·5	92·7
B.	*Professional Occupations* . .	159·1	214·0	153·9	204·9
C.	*Minor Professional and Other Highly Skilled Occupations* . .	111·8	159·1	103·8	142·1
D.	*Clerical and Commercial Employees* .	70·1	97·7	68·0	94·3
E.	*Manual Workers :*				
	1. Skilled Wage-earners . .	38·5	63·9	35·1	58·3
	2. Unskilled Wage-earners . .	25·6	43·4	23·1	38·8
	3. Fatherless Wage-earning Families	29·1	56·8	26·9	53·0
	4. Total Manual Workers . .	33·8	57·1	30·7	51·8

occupations. Conversely, when account is taken of their ability, manual workers are considerably under-represented in schools providing a higher education.

We may next consider the result of ranking in ability those in receipt of higher educational opportunities. In order to measure the extent to which children in receipt of such opportunities also possess high ability in the sense already explained, we have calculated the percentile distribution of I.B. and I.Q. in the group entitled All With

[1] Table VIII and Fig. 1 correspond with Table XIV and Figs. 6 and 7 in the previous chapter.

Opportunities of Higher Education. From these data we have obtained the figures comprising the first part of Table IX.

It may be remarked that the very high percentage of able children

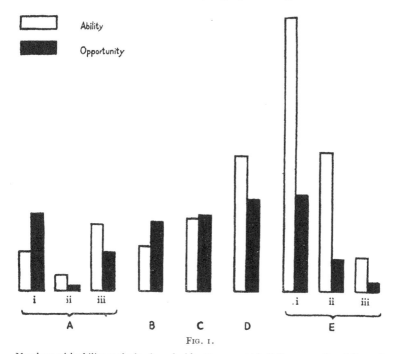

Fig. 1.

Numbers with ability at the level reached by 50 per cent of all Fee-payers (i.e. I.Q. 130) compared with the numbers who receive opportunities of a higher education in each social category.

A. Employing and Directive Classes: (i) Larger business owners and higher executives. (ii) Smaller business owners. (iii) Shopkeepers. B. Professional occupations. C. Minor professional and other highly skilled occupations. D. Clerical and commercial employees. E. Manual workers: (i) Skilled wage-earners. (ii) Unskilled wage-earners. (iii) Fatherless wage-earning families.

in Categories A (2), D, and E, results from the fact that children at these social levels enter secondary schools mainly through a competitive scholarship examination. On the other hand, in those cases where selection by examination plays little or no part, for example, Categories A (1) and B, between 40 and 50 per cent fail to reach the standard of I.Q. 130. The second section of the table takes into account the varying sizes of the several social categories and gives the percentage contribution of each to the total number of individuals with high ability.

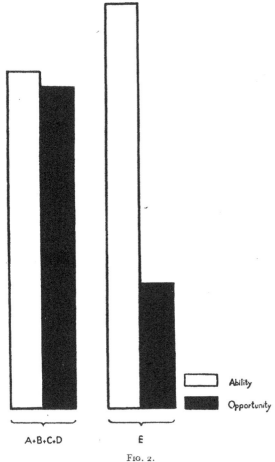

Fig. 2.

Amount of ability (at I.Q. 130) and of opportunities for higher education in the category of Manual Workers, compared with all the other categories added together (excluding F). A. Employing and Directive Classes.   B. Professional occupations.   C. Minor professional and other highly skilled occupations.   D. Clerical and commercial employees. E. Manual workers.

TABLE IX

Pupils with Opportunity Plus Ability

| | Percentage of Such Individuals to Total with Opportunity in Each Social Category. | | | | Percentage Contribution of Such Individuals in Each Social Category to Total Number with Ability. | | | |
| | I.B. | | I.Q. | | I.B. | | I.Q. | |
	120 and over.	130 and over.	130 and over.	140 and over.	120 and over.	130 and over.	130 and over.	140 and over.
A. *Employing and Directive Classes:*								
1. Larger Business Owners and Higher Executives	48·8	36·7	51·2	39·7	10·5	9·6	10·7	9·9
2. Smaller Business Owners	87·5	83·3	91·6	83·3	1·1	1·3	1·1	1·2
3. Shopkeepers	47·3	38·6	48·8	39·7	5·0	5·0	5·0	4·9
B. *Professional Occupations*	59·4	44·5	61·7	46·9	11·8	10·8	11·9	10·9
C. *Minor Professional and Other Highly Skilled Occupations*	59·4	47·4	62·3	49·3	12·6	12·3	12·8	12·2
D. *Clerical and Commercial Employees*	68·9	57·7	70·6	60·2	17·9	18·2	17·8	18·2
E. *Manual Workers:*								
1. Skilled Wage-earners	82·5	71·5	84·9	73·5	22·4	23·7	22·4	23·3
2. Unskilled Wage-earners	89·5	77·3	90·5	81·6	8·2	8·6	8·0	8·7
3. Fatherless Wage-earning Families	86·5	81·7	86·5	82·6	2·2	2·5	2·2	2·5
F. *Occupations Unknown and Miscellaneous*	57·7	46·3	58·8	48·8	32·8	34·8	32·6	34·5
					8·3	8·1	8·2	8·2

The data in the two previous tables enable us to make the calculations set out in Table X.

This gives the number of individuals possessing *both* ability and opportunity as a percentage of the entire number of individuals in each social category. The data in this table were in turn compared

TABLE X

NUMBERS WITH ABILITY AND OPPORTUNITY AS PERCENTAGES OF TOTAL NUMBERS IN EACH SOCIAL CATEGORY

	I.B.		I.Q.	
	120 and over.	13⁰ and over.	130 and over.	140 and over.
A. *Employing and Directive Classes :*				
1. Larger Business Owners and Higher Executives . .	48·8	36·7	51·2	39·7
2. Smaller Business Owners .	7·3	6·9	7·6	6·9
3. Shopkeepers . . .	8·4	6·9	8·7	7·1
B. *Professional Occupations* . .	54·2	40·6	56·3	42·8
C. *Minor Professional and Other Highly Skilled Occupations* . . .	27·0	21·5	28·3	22·4
D. *Clerical and Commercial Employees* .	20·0	16·7	20·5	17·5
E. *Manual Workers :*				
1. Skilled Wage-earners . .	7·5	6·5	7·8	6·7
2. Unskilled Wage-earners . .	3·8	3·3	3·8	3·4
3. Fatherless Wage-earning Families	6·6	6·2	6·6	6·3
F. *Occupations Unknown and Miscellaneous*	7·8	6·2	7·9	6·6

with the data in the first section of Table VII to produce the final figures in Table XI.

These ratios indicate the extent to which the distribution of able individuals at various social levels corresponds with the distribution of individuals who are both able and in receipt of opportunities for a higher education. For example, 26 per cent of all skilled wage-earners attain an I.Q. of 130 (see Table VII). 7·8 per cent have both this ability and the opportunity of a higher education. Thus 30 per cent of skilled wage-earners who possess this ability proceed to schools of a higher type. These indices reveal striking discrepancies in the educational opportunities enjoyed by individuals of equal ability, but of different socio-economic status.[1]

Table XII analyses inequalities of the converse kind.

It shows the proportion of children of different social origin who fail to attain the selected levels of ability, but who nevertheless enjoy

TABLE XI

NUMBERS WITH ABILITY AND OPPORTUNITY AS PERCENTAGES OF ALL WITH ABILITY IN EACH SOCIAL CATEGORY

	I.B.		I.Q.	
	120 and over.	130 and over.	130 and over.	140 and over.
A. *Employing and Directive Classes :*				
1. Larger Business Owners and Higher Executives	100·0	100·0	100·0	100·0
2. Smaller Business Owners	29·2	38·8	26·8	39·4
3. Shopkeepers	29·9	39·2	27·6	37·0
B. *Professional Occupations*	94·4	95·3	94·9	96·2
C. *Minor Professional and Other Highly Skilled Occupations*	66·5	75·4	64·8	70·0
D. *Clerical and Commercial Employees*	48·3	56·2	48·1	57·0
E. *Manual Workers :*				
1. Skilled Wage-earners	31·6	45·5	30·0	42·7
2. Unskilled Wage-earners	23·2	34·0	20·8	31·2
3. Fatherless Wage-earning Families	25·3	46·3	23·3	44·1
F. *Occupations Unknown and Miscellaneous*	43·6	57·4	42·7	54·5

the opportunity of higher education. It will be seen that this maladjustment is least in the groups of manual workers and smaller business owners, who are rigidly selected. On the other hand, 35 per cent of the offspring of professional workers, while receiving educational privileges, fail to attain the standard reached by the top 50 per cent of fee-paying and by the top 25 per cent of free pupils.

[1] The figure of 100 per cent for those in Category A (1) may be slightly misleading. It follows from the attribution to this category of all children in Fee-paying schools whose parents belong to the business classes.

Three general conclusions emerge from this study.

(a) We know that a minimum standard of educational equipment is an indispensable condition of entry into a large number of occupations. Lack of opportunities for higher education, imposed by the inadequacy of existing educational facilities upon the majority of

TABLE XII

NUMBERS WITH OPPORTUNITY BUT WITHOUT ABILITY AS PERCENTAGES OF TOTAL
NUMBERS IN EACH SOCIAL CATEGORY

	I.B.		I.Q.	
	Under 120.	Under 130.	Under 130.	Under 140.
A. *Employing and Directive Classes :*				
1. Larger Business Owners and Higher Executives . .	51·2	63·3	48·8	60·3
2. Smaller Business Owners .	1·0	1·4	0·7	1·4
3. Shopkeepers . . .	9·4	10·9	9·1	10·7
B. *Professional Occupations* . .	37·1	50·7	35·0	48·5
C. *Minor Professional and Other Highly Skilled Occupations* . . .	18·4	23·9	17·1	23·0
D. *Clerical and Commercial Employees* .	9·0	12·3	8·5	11·5
E. *Manual Workers :*				
1. Skilled Wage-earners . .	1·6	2·6	1·4	2·4
2. Unskilled Wage-earners . .	0·4	1·0	0·4	0·8
3. Fatherless Wage-earning Families	1·0	1·4	1·0	1·3
F. *Occupations Unknown and Miscellaneous*	5·7	7·2	5·6	6·9

children whose parents are manual workers, therefore constitutes a serious impediment to free movement in the labour market, and thus an important source of class stratification.

(b) The extent of educational opportunity afforded to the filial generation provides an objective criterion of social inequalities. In this study we have attempted to calculate quantitative indices of the extent of maladjustment of educational opportunity and educational ability at various social levels. It is much to be desired that some future investigation will accumulate data on a scale large enough to make possible the combination of occupations into wider social categories entirely on the basis of differences in amount of educational opportunity.

(c) The major part of these inequalities in educational opportunity remains after account has been taken of the relative ability of each social class. We are therefore dealing with disparities due to differences in social institutions, rather than to genetic inequalities. In other words, the ratios set forth in Table XI are a measure of nurtural as contrasted with natural differences in an important domain of social organization. Even so, they probably minimize the contribution of institutional agencies to differences in opportunity, since the inferior mean ability of the less prosperous social classes may itself arise partly from their environmental disadvantages.

VI. SUMMARY

1. The present study contains data based on nearly 9,000 individuals between the ages of 9 years and 12 years 6 months, drawn from public elementary (including central), secondary, private, and preparatory schools in the London area, tested with the Otis Advanced Group Intelligence Test (Form A), and assigned Intelligence Quotients on the basis of existing American norms and Indices of Brightness on the basis of new English norms. A full description of the general procedure, the nature and reliability of the test employed, and the system of weighting designed to take account of the selective factors in English education and of inequalities in sampling will be found in the previous chapter.

2. Information concerning parental occupation was obtained from more than 90 per cent of the children examined. The data were first classified into "occupational orders" and secondly into "social categories," on the basis of a socio-economic criterion depending mainly on the nature of the work performed by the parents.

3. The occupational distribution of our sample is compared with that of the Census of Population.

4. Differences in the educational status of the filial generation correspond with striking differences in parental occupation. In the group of children educated at the expense of the State (free pupils) 75·6 per cent are the offspring of manual workers, compared with 6·5 per cent in the group educated at the expense of their parents (fee-paying pupils). Professional workers contribute 0.5 per cent of

the children in the former and 22·9 per cent of children in the latter group.

5. The correlation between intelligence and socio-economic status is 0·25 ± 0·008 for the entire group of children examined, 0·19 ± 0·028 for free pupils alone and 0·08 ± 0·026 for fee-paying pupils alone.

6. Tables IV and V give the mean I.B. and I.Q. of the children in the various occupational orders and social categories.

7. The socio-economic composition of the entire school population is compared with that of the group with opportunities of a higher education (irrespective of ability). The offspring of larger business owners and higher executives and of the professional classes are proportionately five times more numerous in schools providing a higher education than they are in the general school population. Those of unskilled wage-earners are proportionately only one-fifth as numerous.

8. The data provide estimates of the percentage of individuals of different socio-economic status who attain various selected levels of ability and of the socio-economic composition of the total school population at these levels of ability. In spite of the higher average ability of the children of larger business owners and professional workers, their numerical contribution to the total of able children is relatively small. For example, manual workers contribute one-half of all children attaining the level of ability represented by the achievement of the top 50 per cent of fee-paying pupils, while children of larger business owners and professional workers together contribute less than 10 per cent.

9. In the case of larger business owners, the number of children with opportunities of a higher education is twice as great as the number achieving the level of ability stated in the preceding paragraph; in the case of professional workers one and a half times as great, and in the case of unskilled wage-earners less than a quarter as great.

10. Similarly, while nearly all the children of the larger business and the professional classes who possess ability have the opportunity of higher education, the corresponding figure for clerical and commercial employees is approximately 50 per cent, for skilled wage-earners 30 per cent, and for unskilled wage-earners 20 per cent.

11. Conversely, nearly one-half of all the children of larger business owners and 35 per cent of those of professional workers fall

below the level of achievement already stated. Nevertheless they receive the opportunity of higher education. Only 1 per cent of the children of skilled wage-earners and of smaller business owners and 0·4 per cent of the children of unskilled wage-earners with opportunities for higher education fall below the same level of achievement.

BIBLIOGRAPHY

1. Carr-Saunders, A. M., and Jones, D. Caradog (1927): *The Social Structure of England and Wales.*
2. *Census of England and Wales* 1911 (1917). General Report and Appendices.
3. *Census of England and Wales,* 1931 (1934). Occupational Tables.
4. Duff, James F., and Thomson, Godfrey H. (1924): "The Social and Geographical Distribution of Intelligence in Northumberland": *British Journal of Psychology,* Vol. XIV, Pt. 2.
5. Gray, J. L., and Moshinsky, Pearl (1935): "Ability and Opportunity in English Education." *Sociological Review,* Vol. XXVII, No. 2.
6. *London Survey of Life and Labour,* Vol. II (1931), Vol. V (1933), and Vol. VIII (1934).

CHAPTER X

OPPORTUNITY AND THE OLDER UNIVERSITIES

A STUDY OF THE OXFORD AND CAMBRIDGE SCHOLARSHIP SYSTEM

by

DAVID V. GLASS

and

J. L. GRAY

(from the Department of Social Biology, University of London)

I. INTRODUCTION

ORIGINALLY, the aims of the present study were three:

(*a*) To make a comprehensive survey of every class of financial assistance, other than family income, available in England and Wales to young men entering the Colleges of Oxford and Cambridge for the first time;

(*b*) To ascertain the distribution of such assistance among boys of widely different educational and social origins;

(*c*) To investigate significant social circumstances associated with disparity in the allocation of scholarship awards among schools of different types.

In examining the recruitment of social personnel, these issues are of great importance and there is a growing body of literature concerning them. With the aid of a grant from the Rockefeller Foundation, this inquiry has been conducted on a larger scale than has hitherto been possible. Circumstances compelled the authors to curtail the original scope of it. So it falls short of the completeness that they originally projected.

A previous research into the relation of educational ability and opportunity was restricted to the secondary school stage for which official statistics were to a large extent available. In discussing educational opportunity at later stages the investigator has no such help, owing to the substantial independence of the Universities from State control and the consequent lack of completeness and uniformity in the information they publish about themselves. For this reason our statistical conclusions are not so definitive as we had hoped, although in certain cases they are as complete as it is necessary for them to be. With the resources we had, some interesting problems could not be investigated at all. For other important topics, where comprehensiveness was very desirable, we have had to be content with samples.

From our knowledge both of the social urgency of the issues and the obstacles to unofficial research, we would suggest that nothing short of a Government inquiry, with full powers to examine witnesses and compel the production of documents, is likely to satisfy the public interest. Previous authors have shown how little justified is an attitude of complacency towards the rate at which the older Universities are opening their doors to students of the poorer classes. These views are abundantly confirmed by the data collected in the course of this study. If reform is wanted, it must be preceded by complete ascertainment of the facts, itself likely to be a lengthy task. Ignorance of these facts will help vested interests and flabby idealism to obstruct improvement if and when the legislature decides to act. Despite its imperfections, the present study clearly indicates the nature of the problem. To that extent it provides a recipe for action.

II. THE UNDER-REPRESENTATION OF THE ELEMENTARY SCHOOLS

In the academic year 1933–34 there were 21,727 full-time male undergraduates attending the Universities (excluding University Colleges) of England and Wales. Of this number, 8,381 were students of Oxford and Cambridge. When we consider how greatly they preponderate in the population of school age, the number of ex-Public Elementary schoolboys at the Universities is still very small. Table I shows that in 1933–34 they constituted 27 per cent of the total, while the corresponding figures for Oxford and Cambridge were respectively 12 and 13 per cent.

The remainder, with a few exceptions in the case of students from the Dominions, belonged to the class whose parents are able and willing to pay fees for their children's school education, and to send them to Preparatory and Public Schools not controlled by the State. Moreover, some undergraduates coming from Public Elementary Schools were fee-paying pupils at Secondary Schools. Taking only boys who receive free places at Secondary Schools, the figures in 1933–34 become 22 per cent for all University students, 10 per cent for Oxford, and 11 per cent for Cambridge.

TABLE I

EX-PUBLIC ELEMENTARY SCHOOLBOYS AT ALL UNIVERSITIES
IN ENGLAND AND WALES [1]

Year	Full-time Male Undergraduate Population	Number of ex-Public Elementary Schoolboys who paid no fees at Secondary School	Percentage of Male Undergraduate Population	Total number of ex-Public Elementary Schoolboys	Percentage of Male Undergraduate Population
(a) ALL UNIVERSITIES					
1934–35	22,069	4,796	21·73	6,109	27·68
1933–34	21,727	4,681	21·54	5,949	27·38
1932–33	21,006	4,311	20·52	5,537	26·36
1931–32	19,972	3,894	19·50	5,026	25·17
1930–31	19,326	3,664	18·96	4,674	24·19
1929–30	18,409	3,495	18·99	4,327	23·50
1928–29	17,722	3,371	19·02	4,108	23·18
1927–28	17,131	3,172	18·52	3,866	22·57
(b) OXFORD					
1934–35	3,509	361	10·29	434	12·37
1933–34	3,560	350	9·83	419	11·77
1932–33	3,605	344	9·54	415	11·51
1931–32	3,583	350	9·77	412	11·50
1930–31	3,515	351	9·99	407	11·58
1929–30	3,470	345	9·94	389	11·21
1828–29	3,421	313	9·15	356	10·41
1927–28	3,379	280	8·29	337	9·97
(c) CAMBRIDGE					
1934–35	4,816	536	11·13	647	13·43
1933–34	4,821	506	10·50	606	12·57
1932–33	4,775	455	9·53	561	11·75
1931–32	4,648	423	9·10	521	11·21
1930–31	4,649	423	9·10	506	10·88
1929–30	4,713	431	9·14	498	10·57
1928–29	4,703	457	9·72	528	11·23
1927–28	4,577	433	9·46	514	11·23

[1] Based on the Annual Reports of the Board of Education (Annual Output of Boys from Secondary Schools to the Universities), on the assumption that the average Undergraduate life is three years. (Excluding University Colleges of Nottingham, Exeter, and Southampton.)

The figures show that University students who did not originate in Elementary Schools outnumber those who did by nearly three (2·65) to one for all Universities, 7·5 to one at Oxford, and nearly seven (6·96) to one at Cambridge. However, this calculation under-

TABLE II

THE RELATIVE OPPORTUNITIES OF ELEMENTARY AND
NON-ELEMENTARY SCHOOLBOYS OF GOING TO OXFORD
AND CAMBRIDGE UNIVERSITIES

Estimates	Number of ex-Elementary School-boys in Male Under-graduate Population of Oxford and Cam-bridge in 1933–34	Number of non-ex-Elementary School-boys in Same Popu-lation	Population from which ex-Elementary School-boys Derived	Population from which non-ex-Elementary Schoolboys Derived	Non-ex-Elementary Schoolboy's Oppor-tunities compared with those of ex-Elemen-tary Schoolboy
A. Comparing all ex-Elementary Schoolboys with non-ex-Elementary Schoolboys ..	1,025	7,356	997,605	77,677	92·2 : 1
B. As in A, but including among ex-Elementary Schoolboys only those who paid no fees at Secondary Schools ..	856	7,356	997,605	77,677	110·37 : 1
C. As in B, but excluding pupils of Certified Special Schools from non-ex-Elementary School population ..	856	7,356	997,605	73,091	116·80 : 1

estimates the real discrepancy in the opportunities of the two classes of boys. The population of Public Elementary School origin is vastly greater than that of fee-paying schools. Assuming that the male undergraduates of 1933–34 were between 18 and 21 years old, they belonged to the age group which was not less than seven but not as much as ten years of age in the year 1922, which totalled 1,075,282. Of this number, 997,605 were in attendance at Public Elementary Schools (including a few at Non-Local and Certified Efficient Schools). Consequently the 5,949 ex-Elementary schoolboys who were undergraduates at all Universities in England and Wales in 1933–34 derived from a population of 997,605, i.e. they represent 0·596 per cent of this population. On the other hand, the 15,778 non-Elementary schoolboys at the Universities derived from a very diverse population. Those who were of English or Welsh birth or early education came from a population of, at the most, 77,677. We cannot estimate with any precision how many were of foreign or Empire origin. Moreover, the figure of 77,677 includes many native children who were not attending any school at all. It is perhaps safe to say that the non-Elementary schoolboys at the Universities and of native origin amounted to about 20 per cent of their appropriate age group. Their chances of proceeding to any University were thus about thirty times greater than those of ex-Elementary schoolboys, and in the case of Oxford and Cambridge perhaps ninety times as great.

If we compare non-Elementary schoolboys only with those Elementary schoolboys who paid no fees at their Secondary Schools, the disparities are naturally still greater, the opportunities of the former being about 40 times greater for all Universities in England and Wales and about 110 times greater for Oxford and Cambridge.

III. THE ENGLISH SECONDARY SCHOOL SYSTEM

AT present the only way in which an ex-Elementary schoolboy can proceed to the University is by the award of a scholarship or by obtaining some similar form of financial aid from some outside source. The chief object of this paper is to ascertain the facts concerning these awards and to analyse their allocation among boys of different social and educational origin. On account of the unique prestige they enjoy and the part they play in recruiting the personnel for many important and remunerative employments in the community, we decided to confine ourselves in the present instance to the Universities of Oxford and Cambridge.

Before proceeding to an account of the scholarships themselves, it is necessary to say something about the organization of Secondary School education in this country and to explain the classification which we have found useful to adopt. Secondary Schools may be divided into four main categories, viz.:

    I. *Public Schools.*—These are defined as those schools included in the *Public Schools' Yearbook* for 1934, all of which are eligible for representation on the Headmasters' Conference. According to the rules of this body, such schools (*a*) must not be run for private profit, and (*b*) they must send fair numbers of boys to the Universities, particularly to Oxford and Cambridge.

Public Schools, with a few exceptions, include all the most expensive boarding schools offering a secondary education and form an easily identifiable group. In England and Wales (excluding the Channel Islands) they numbered 160 in the year 1934.

For the purposes of this investigation, they have been further classified as "P" and "PD" Schools.

(*a*) "*P*" *Schools*, in which over 50 per cent of the pupils are boarders, or, where this is not the case, in which the tuition fees are over £31 10s. per annum. The great majority of schools in this class have more than 90 per cent boarders.

(*b*) "*PD*" *Schools*, having under 50 per cent of their pupils as boarders and with tuition fees of less than £31 10s. per annum. This class comprises all the Public Day Schools, except the most expensive, which are in subdivision (*a*).

The distinction drawn above is, of course, arbitrary, but it does make a fairly appropriate distinction between boarding and day school. The £31 10s. limit was adopted to separate such a school as the City of London from one like Westminster, the fees at the latter being so high as to place the school well above the ordinary Public Day School level. In England and Wales there were, in 1934–35, 96 "P" Schools and 64 "PD" Schools.

The term *Public Schools* is used throughout to refer to the group composed of both "P" and "PD" Schools.

II. "*SS*" *Schools* are those formerly known as Grammar Schools. They are largely self-governing, but receive grants-in-aid either direct from the Board of Education or from the Local Education Authority.

III. "*CS*" *Schools* are maintained wholly or largely by the Local Education Authority.

IV. "*SN*" *Schools* are private schools, whether boarding or day, not included in the *Public Schools' Yearbook*, nor in receipt of

Government grants, but recognized as "efficient" by the Board of Education.

Practically all the schools in these categories are termed "Secondary" schools by the Board, and information concerning fees, grants, free places, and numbers of pupils is contained in the Board of Education *List 60* for England and Wales.[1] The exceptions are those Public Schools which have not yet applied for recognition as "efficient" schools. Information concerning these was obtained from successive annual issues of the *Public Schools' Yearbook* and by direct questionnaire. There are, of course, a large number of non-recognized Private Schools. These we have been compelled to exclude from our study. There are no means of ascertaining how many there are, nor how many pupils attend them. It is unlikely that they send many pupils to Oxford and Cambridge with scholarships of the kind described hereafter.

The populations of the various types of school from 1913 to 1934 are given in Tables III and IV.

From the standpoint of socio-economic status our classification of schools is not entirely arbitrary. Analysis of the fees charged and the proportion of free places offered in schools of different type confirms the general view that English Secondary Schools are arranged in hierarchical order.

The weighted averages of fees charged by different types of schools in England and Wales are as follows:[2]

"P" Schools	..	£147·87 per annum (board and tuition)
"PD" Schools	..	£21·70 per annum (tuition only)
"SN" Schools	..	£27·25 per annum (tuition only)
"SS" Schools	..	£13·42 per annum (tuition only)
"CS" Schools	..	£11·40 per annum (tuition only)

[1] *List 60* was first issued for England in 1907–08 and for Wales in 1908–09. The English List for 1913–14 did not in all cases distinguish between boys and girls in the number of pupils stated. Where this occurred we have attempted to estimate the sex-distribution on the assumption that it was the same as in the previous year. Recently *List 60* has been issued biennially and interpolations have therefore been made to obtain estimates of the year-by-year populations.

[2] Information obtained from the *Public Schools' Yearbook*, *List 60* of the Board of Education, and by direct questionnaire. The figures include entrance fees and other obligatory expenses, but are perhaps slightly too low for "P" Schools as none of the heavy optional expenses have been included. The figures for other types of schools were calculated from official sources (*List 60*) and are thoroughly comprehensive.

Table III

SCHOOL POPULATIONS FOR ENGLAND AND WALES

Year	"P"	"D"	All Public	"SS"	"CS"	"SN"	Total
				Type of School			
1913–14	24,654	18,863	43,517	34,919	46,937	2,245	127,618
1919–20	30,282	28,107	58,389	54,008	72,796	1,636	186,829
1920–21	31,513	29,401	60,914	59,396	79,811	3,001	203,122
1921–22	32,445	30,486	62,931	61,203	86,697	3,286	214,117
1922–23	33,206	30,388	63,594	58,934	91,732	4,735	218,995
1923–24	33,983	30,290	64,273	56,666	96,766	6,183	223,888
1924–25	34,521	30,042	64,563	57,958	99,665	6,259	228,445
1925–26	34,751	29,801	64,552	59,378	103,469	6,337	233,736
1926–27	34,674	29,847	64,521	59,381	107,280	6,669	237,851
1927–28	34,802	29,892	64,694	59,384	111,091	7,001	242,170
1928–29	34,921	29,937	64,858	59,388	114,902	7,334	246,482
1929–30	35,042	29,949	64,991	59,699	120,356	7,590	252,636
1930–31	35,150	29,960	65,110	60,009	125,810	7,845	258,774
1931–32	34,066	31,121	65,187	61,162	132,672	7,773	266,794
1932–33	32,993	32,282	65,275	62,313	139,534	7,699	274,821
1933–34	30,216	32,178	62,394	63,643	142,897	7,978	276,912

In respect of the distribution of free places the hierarchy is no less evident. Public Schools in receipt of Government grants are generally required as a *quid pro quo* to provide a minimum proportion of free places to pupils of Elementary School origin. Public Schools financed independently of the Board or of Local Education Authorities make no provision for admitting boys from Elementary

TABLE IV

GRANT-AIDED SECONDARY SCHOOLS IN ENGLAND AND WALES

SCHOOL POPULATIONS, 1913–34

Year	"P"	"PD"	Total Grant-Aided "P" and "PD"	Total Grant-Aided Secondary Schools ("P" "PD" "CS" and "SS")
1913–14	1,456	18,100	19,556	101,412
1919–20	3,482	27,265	30,747	157,551
1920–21	3,795	28,554	32,349	171,556
1921–22	3,885	29,599	33,484	181,384
1922–23	3,909	29,500	33,409	184,075
1923–24	3,932	29,402	33,334	186,766
1924–25	3,964	29,152	33,116	190,739
1925–26	3,996	28,910	32,906	195,753
1926–27	4,025	28,959	32,984	199,645
1927–28	4,054	29,007	33,061	203,536
1928–29	4,083	29,054	33,137	207,427
1929–30	4,136	29,045	33,181	213,236
1930–31	4,189	29,036	33,225	219,044
1931–32	4,129	30,185	34,314	228,148
1932–33	4,068	31,334	35,402	237,249
1933–34	4,086	31,228	35,314	241,854

Schools.[1] We may safely conclude that such schools contain no boys from Elementary Schools and none whose parents cannot find the larger part of the money required for school fees.

Of the 154 Public Schools in England in 1933–34 74 were grant-aided (including twelve "P" Schools), while in Wales and the Isle of Man the corresponding number was two out of the total of six. According to the Education Act of 1902, which initiated a great extension of the free-place system, Secondary Schools, as a condition of receiving the full Government grant, were compelled to admit

[1] There are one or two exceptions to this statement, e.g. Harrow, but they are numerically insignificant.

25 per cent of "free placers."[1] But of the 74 grant-aided Public Schools in 1933–34 only 31 gave as many as 25 per cent of free places, although in all schools except one the grant was at the full rate. The exception was Blundell's School, where the grant was on a lower scale, but this school offered no free places at all to boys of Elementary School origin. Looking at the 74 English grant-aided schools, we find that:

31 gave 25 per cent of free places
6 ,, 20   ,,   ,,   ,,
3 ,, 15   ,,   ,,   ,,
5 ,, 12½   ,,   ,,   ,,
28 ,, 10   ,,   ,,   ,,
1 ,,   0   ,,   ,,

Public Schools appear to enjoy privileges with respect to free places not possessed by other classes of Secondary School. The Board of Education explains the matter as follows:

"Taking the country as a whole, children from Public Elementary Schools constituted, even in 1907, rather more than half the pupils in the [Secondary] Schools . . . but whilst some schools consisted almost entirely of such children, others had few or none of them and their incursion on a large scale was dreaded. Even where the social objection was not felt, the financial obligation remained, for the Regulations placed the responsibility directly on the school without regard to the school's ability to meet the cost. . . . The Board did something to alleviate these difficulties by adjusting the percentage of free places required to rates varying from the normal 25 per cent down to 10 per cent."[2]

The urbanity of the Board's reference to the financial difficulties of Public Schools does not disguise the truth that social objections were paramount in producing this anomalous situation.

The position in Wales is different. In that country the two "PD" Schools on the grant list offer well over 25 per cent of free places. The Welsh Grammar Schools, in contrast with those in England, had suffered a marked decay in the seventeenth century. Thus when

[1] See R. L. Archer, *Secondary Education in the Nineteenth Century*, chapter on "The Modern State System."

[2] Board of Education, Educational Pamphlets, No. 50, 1927.

educational progress began again in the 'forties of the nineteenth century, as a consequence of the religious revival, the Secondary-School system was founded on an entirely new model, being immediately dependent on the State. Even the older schools suffered from lack of adequate endowments and voluntarily converted themselves into County Council-managed schools under the Welsh Intermediate Education Act of 1889.

Considering England and Wales as a whole, the position with regard to free places may be summarized as follows: Public Schools not in receipt of grants give no free places to boys of Elementary School origin. In the case of grant-aided Public Schools having in 1933–34 a total population of 35,314 (see Table IV), 19,180 or 54·3 per cent of the boys were in schools offering less than 25 per cent free places. It will be recalled that only eight of these 74 grant-aided schools were boarding schools.

The "SS" and "CS" schools present, of course, a very different picture. Of "SS" Schools only 5,968 boys out of the total of 63,643 (9·38 per cent) were in schools giving under 25 per cent of free places, while the corresponding figures for "CS" Schools were 1,364 boys out of the total of 142,897 (0·955 per cent).

The "SN" Schools may be grouped for this purpose with the non-aided Public Schools—they were neither required to give, nor did they in fact give any significant proportion of free places.

The foregoing analysis makes it clear that only in the "SS" and "CS" Schools is there any considerable number of boys of Elementary School origin. The record of their successes in obtaining scholarships to Oxford and Cambridge will therefore be a reliable indication of the amount of upward educational movement that takes place in contemporary society, as measured by this criterion.

IV. THE UNIVERSITY SCHOLARSHIP SYSTEM

In this section we shall consider five main types of scholarships, viz.:

(1) *Scholarships and Exhibitions* awarded by the Colleges of Oxford and Cambridge:

(*a*) Open.
(*b*) "Closed."

(2) *County Major Scholarships.*
(3) *State Scholarships.*

(4) *Scholarships given by Institutions* independent of the University or the State, although their allocation may be influenced by State or University representatives.

(5) *Leaving Scholarships*, awarded by various schools to their own pupils.

(1) *College Scholarships and Exhibitions*

These constitute the most important, both numerically and in total value, of the forms of financial assistance available to intending students at the older Universities. At the same time they are not easy to analyse, since no single source gives a complete record of them, except for the year 1933–34, when a special inquiry was made by the Board of Education.[1] The data published in the official University periodicals, *The Oxford Gazette* and *The Cambridge Reporter*, are both ambiguous, in that open and "closed" scholarships are not clearly distinguished, and incomplete, since more open scholarships are awarded than they record.[2] Moreover, preliminary inquiries made it evident that the College officials of Oxford and Cambridge would not all be able, nor in some cases willing, to co-operate with us in making our investigation fully comprehensive.

The method actually followed was to use the data contained in *The Oxford Gazette* and *The Cambridge Reporter* as a basis, supplementing it by direct inquiry from the schools attended by scholarship-winners. No distinction is made in the earlier tables between open and "closed," which are grouped together. The position is shown in Tables V–VII. In Table V, the absolute and percentage distribution is given by different types of schools for the period 1913–34.

It is immediately obvious that at no time during this period have "P" Schools obtained less than 43 per cent of College scholarships. Indeed, in the case of Oxford Colleges they have never won less than 52 per cent. The minimum figures for "PD" Schools are 19·92 per cent for Oxford and 18·72 per cent for Cambridge. Taking

[1] *Education in 1934*, Board of Education, 1935, Table 48, p. 160.

[2] The discrepancy is shown by comparing the Board of Education Analysis for 1933–34 with the information printed in the University publications for the same year. The Board's figures give a total of 545 open scholarships to Oxford and Cambridge obtained by boys in all Secondary Schools, aided and non-aided. The Universities' figures give 558 as the total, but include "closed" scholarships, which form a relatively numerous class.

TABLE V

TOTAL COLLEGE SCHOLARSHIPS WON—BY TYPE OF SCHOOL

Year	Total Scholarships	"P"		"PD"		"CS"		"SS"		"SN"	
		Number	Percentage	Number	Percentage	Number	Percentage	Number	Percentage	Number	Percentage
To Cambridge											
1913–14	219	137	62·57	48	21·92	16	7·31	17	7·78	1	0·42
1919–20	187	113	60·45	35	18·72	11	5·89	25	13·37	3	1·57
1920–21	213	115	54·00	56	26·30	14	6·57	27	12·68	1	0·45
1921–22	195	102	52·33	47	24·11	14	7·18	30	15·39	2	0·99
1922–23	235	116	49·38	65	27·67	24	10·21	26	11·06	4	1·68
1923–24	256	133	51·97	72	29·13	24	9·38	23	8·99	4	0·53
1924–25	248	120	48·40	75	30·25	32	12·90	19	7·67	2	0·78
1925–26	247	116	46·97	61	24·70	31	12·55	35	14·17	4	1·61
1926–27	252	117	46·45	74	29·37	30	11·90	25	9·93	6	2·35
1927–28	232	106	45·70	62	26·73	31	13·36	31	13·36	2	0·85
1928–29	239	119	49·80	60	25·10	32	13·39	26	10·88	2	0·83
1929–30	236	110	46·62	75	31·78	20	8·48	27	11·42	4	1·70
1930–31	222	108	48·67	66	29·74	26	11·71	16	7·21	6	2·67
1931–32	274	121	44·17	91	33·22	31	11·31	27	9·86	4	1·44
1932–33	268	116	43·30	83	30·97	38	14·18	30	11·20	1	0·35
1933–34	308	142	46·10	84	27·28	41	13·31	38	12·34	3	0·97
To Oxford											
1913–14	213	135	63·40	54	25·35	13	6·10	10	4·70	1	0·45
1919–20	218	127	58·27	55	25·24	19	8·72	15	6·88	2	0·89
1920–21	213	128	60·10	56	26·30	15	7·04	13	6·15	1	0·41
1921–22	229	137	59·84	53	23·15	24	10·48	14	6·11	1	0·42

Year											
1922–23	0·43	1	5·36	12	6·70	15	24·11	54	63·40	142	224
1923–24	0·00	0	8·30	20	6·22	15	19·92	48	65·56	158	241
1924–25	0·41	1	6·90	16	9·92	23	25·87	60	56·90	132	232
1925–26	1·60	4	7·35	18	11·43	28	24·50	60	55·12	135	245
1926–27	0·00	0	6·28	15	10·46	25	26·36	63	56·90	136	239
1927–28	0·84	2	4·80	11	12·25	28	25·77	59	56·34	129	229
1928–29	0·76	2	6·38	16	11·96	30	25·90	65	55·00	138	251
1929–30	1·71	4	5·93	14	11·86	28	25·00	59	55·50	131	236
1930–31	1·20	3	6·80	17	16·00	40	23·20	58	52·80	132	250
1931–32	1·21	3	7·26	19	13·36	35	25·96	68	52·30	137	262
1932–33	0·80	2	8·68	21	11·57	28	26·45	64	52·50	127	242
1933–34	0·40	1	8·00	20	14·00	35	24·80	62	52·80	132	250

To OXFORD AND CAMBRIDGE (COMBINED)

Year											
1913–14	0·46	2	6·25	27	6·71	29	23·61	102	62·96	272	432
1919–20	1·23	5	9·88	40	7·41	30	22·22	90	59·26	240	405
1920–21	0·47	2	9·39	40	4·46	29	26·29	112	57·04	243	426
1921–22	0·71	3	10·38	44	8·96	38	23·58	100	56·37	239	424
1922–23	1·09	5	8·28	38	8·50	39	25·93	119	56·21	258	459
1923–24	0·80	4	8·65	43	7·85	39	24·14	120	58·55	291	497
1924–25	0·63	3	7·29	35	11·46	55	28·13	135	52·50	252	480
1925–26	1·63	8	10·77	53	11·99	59	24·59	121	51·02	251	492
1926–27	1·22	6	8·15	40	11·20	55	27·90	137	51·53	253	491
1927–28	0·87	4	9·11	42	12·80	59	26·25	121	50·98	235	461
1928–29	0·82	4	8·57	42	12·65	62	25·51	125	52·45	257	490
1929–30	1·69	8	8·69	41	10·17	48	28·39	134	51·06	241	472
1930–31	1·91	9	6·99	33	13·98	66	26·27	124	50·85	240	472
1931–32	1·31	7	8·58	46	12·31	66	29·66	159	48·13	258	536
1932–33	0·59	3	10·00	51	12·94	66	28·82	147	47·65	243	510
1933–34	0·72	4	10·39	58	13·62	76	26·16	146	49·10	274	558

"P", "PD", and "SN" Schools together,[1] as forming a fairly distinct socio-economic category measured by the cost of education, and comparing them with the "CS" and "SS" Schools, we obtain the following table:

TABLE VI

TOTAL COLLEGE SCHOLARSHIPS—BY TYPE OF SCHOOL
(PERCENTAGE DISTRIBUTION)

Year	To Cambridge		To Oxford	
	"P", "PD", "SN"	"CS", "SS"	"P", "PD", "SN"	"CS", "SS"
1913–14	84·91	15·09	89·20	10·80
1919–20	80·74	19·26	84·40	15·60
1920–21	80·75	19·25	86·81	13·19
1921–22	77·43	22·57	83·41	16·59
1922–23	78·73	21·27	87·94	12·06
1923–24	81·63	18·37	85·48	14·52
1924–25	79·43	20·57	83·18	16·82
1925–26	73·28	26·72	81·22	18·78
1926–27	78·17	21·83	83·26	16·74
1927–28	73·28	26·72	82·95	17·05
1928–29	75·73	24·27	81·66	18·34
1929–30	80·10	19·90	82·21	17·79
1930–31	81·08	18·92	77·20	22·80
1931–32	78·83	21·17	79·38	20·62
1932–33	74·62	25·38	79·75	20·25
1933–34	74·35	25·65	78·00	22·00

The belief that Cambridge is more favourably disposed to welcome the best men irrespective of social origin is borne out to some slight extent by the figures for "SS" and "CS" Schools. However, in neither University has the percentage of scholarships obtained by such schools risen much above 25, and although there has been a fairly steady increase in the last twenty years the relative proportions of Public and other Secondary Schools have not been radically changed. Starting with a very small percentage, "CS" and "SS"

[1] "SN" Schools are relatively unimportant in this connection since they have never obtained as much as 3 per cent of scholarships at either University during our period.

Schools have nearly doubled their 1913–14 figure. The proportion going to Public and Private Schools, which was very high to begin with, has only fallen by under 13 per cent. In 1913–14 these schools were receiving nearly seven times as many scholarships as "CS" and "SS." Schools, and in 1933–34 they still had more than three times as many.

The disparity is shown even more clearly if the number of scholarships is compared with the populations of the various types of schools.[1] The basic figures and rates are given in Tables VII and VIII and summarized in Table IX.

The figures set out in Table IX are very striking. First, it will be observed that the total number of scholarships available has not increased *pari passu* with the growth of the Secondary School population since 1913–14. In 1913–14 there were 430 scholarships awarded, or 3·43 per thousand of the entire Secondary School population. Twenty years later the number of scholarships had increased to 554, but this was only 2·06 per 1,000 of a much larger school population. In other words, while many more boys are eligible to proceed to Universities than in previous years, a smaller proportion of them may hope to obtain College scholarships to assist them. Second, there has been no significant change in the relative proportions of Public and other Secondary schoolboys awarded scholarships. Since the end of the war, the position has remained nearly stationary. In 1913–14 Public Schools obtained nearly thirteen times as many scholarships per thousand boys as "CS" and "SS" Schools. In 1919–20 this figure had fallen to ten, where it has remained with minor fluctuations ever since.[2]

Open Scholarships only.—So far the discussion relates to open and "closed" scholarships treated as one group. However, it is vital to attempt some means of distinguishing between them. When we speak of educational opportunity at the older Universities, we are accustomed to think mainly in terms of open scholarships. By definition, "closed" scholarships are restricted in various ways, to be described later on. Open scholarships, however, can be competed for by any intending student showing the necessary proficiency and able to pay

[1] No figure is given for the "SN" Schools in this section, since the "recognized" Private Schools, i.e., those of *List 60*, form only a very small proportion of all Private Schools.

[2] The calculations assume that the discrepancy between scholarships obtained and scholarships recorded remained constant over the period.

TABLE VII

TOTAL COLLEGE SCHOLARSHIPS—BY TYPE OF SCHOOL—
PER 1,000 OF SCHOOL POPULATION

Year	"P"			"PD"		
	School Population	Scholarships	Number of Scholarships per 1,000	School Population	Scholarships	Number of Scholarships per 1,000
To CAMBRIDGE						
1913–14	24,654	137	5·557	18,863	48	2·545
1919–20	30,282	113	3·732	28,107	35	1·245
1920–21	31,513	115	3·649	29,401	56	1·905
1921–22	32,445	102	3·144	30,486	47	1·542
1922–23	33,206	116	3·493	30,388	65	2·139
1923–24	33,983	133	3·914	30,290	72	2·377
1924–25	34,521	120	3·476	30,042	75	2·497
1925–26	34,751	116	3·338	29,801	61	2·047
1926–27	34,674	117	3·374	29,847	74	2·479
1927–28	34,802	106	3·046	29,892	62	2·074
1928–29	34,921	119	3·408	29,937	60	2·004
1929–30	35,042	110	3·139	29,949	75	2·504
1930–31	35,150	108	3·073	29,960	66	2·203
1931–32	34,066	121	3·552	31,121	91	2·924
1932–33	32,993	116	3·516	32,282	83	2·571
1933–34	30,216	142	4·699	32,178	84	2·610
To OXFORD						
1913–14	24,654	135	5·476	18,863	54	2·863
1919–20	30,282	127	4·194	28,107	55	1·957
1920–21	31,513	128	4·062	29,401	56	1·905
1921–22	32,445	137	4·223	30,486	53	1·739
1922–23	33,206	142	4·276	30,388	54	1·777
1923–24	33,983	158	4·649	30,290	48	1·585
1924–25	34,521	132	3·824	30,042	60	1·997
1925–26	34,751	135	3·885	29,801	60	2·013
1926–27	34,674	136	3·922	29,847	63	2·111
1927–28	34,802	129	3·707	29,892	59	1·974
1928–29	34,921	138	3·952	29,937	65	2·171
1929–30	35,042	131	3·738	29,949	59	1·970
1930–31	35,150	132	3·755	29,960	58	1·936
1931–32	34,066	137	4·022	31,121	68	2·185
1932–33	32,993	127	3·849	32,282	64	1·983
1933–34	30,216	132	4·369	32,178	62	1·927

TABLE VII—*continued*

TOTAL COLLEGE SCHOLARSHIPS—BY TYPE OF SCHOOL— PER 1,000 OF SCHOOL POPULATION

Year	"CS"			"SS"		
	School Population	Scholarships	Number of Scholarships per 1,000	School Population	Scholarships	Number of Scholarships per 1,000
			To CAMBRIDGE			
1913–14	46,937	16	0·341	34,919	17	0·487
1919–20	72,796	11	0·151	54,008	25	0·463
1920–21	79,811	14	0·175	59,396	27	0·454
1921–22	86,697	14	0·161	61,203	30	0·490
1922–23	91,732	24	0·262	58,934	26	0·441
1923–24	96,766	24	0·248	56,666	23	0·406
1924–25	99,665	32	0·321	57,958	19	0·328
1925–26	103,469	31	0·300	59,378	35	0·589
1926–27	107,280	30	0·280	59,381	25	0·421
1927–28	111,091	31	0·279	59,384	31	0·522
1928–29	114,902	32	0·278	59,388	26	0·438
1929–30	120,356	20	0·166	59,699	27	0·452
1930–31	125,810	26	0·207	60,009	16	0·267
1931–32	132,672	31	0·234	61,162	27	0·441
1932–33	139,534	38	0·272	62,313	30	0·481
1933–34	142,897	41	0·287	63,643	38	0·597
			To OXFORD			
1913–14	46,937	13	0·277	34,919	10	0·286
1919–20	72,796	19	0·261	54,008	15	0·278
1920–21	79,811	15	0·188	59,396	13	0·219
1921–22	86,697	24	0·277	61,203	14	0·229
1922–23	91,732	15	0·164	58,934	12	0·204
1923–24	96,766	15	0·155	56,666	20	0·353
1924–25	99,665	23	0·231	57,958	16	0·276
1925–26	103,469	28	0·271	59,378	18	0·303
1926–27	107,280	25	0·233	59,381	15	0·253
1927–28	111,091	28	0·252	59,384	11	0·185
1928–29	114,902	30	0·261	59,388	16	0·269
1929–30	120,356	28	0·233	59,699	14	0·235
1930–31	125,810	40	0·318	60,009	17	0·283
1931–32	132,672	35	0·264	61,162	19	0·311
1932–33	139,534	28	0·201	62,313	21	0·337
1933–34	142,897	35	0·245	63,643	20	0·314

TABLE VIII

TOTAL COLLEGE SCHOLARSHIPS—BY TYPE OF SCHOOL— PER 1,000 OF SCHOOL POPULATION

Year	Scholarships			School Population	Number of Scholarships per 1,000
	Cambridge	Oxford	Total		
To Oxford and Cambridge "P"					
1913–14	137	135	272	24,654	11·033
1919–20	113	127	240	30,282	7·926
1920–21	115	128	243	31,513	7·711
1921–22	102	137	239	32,445	7·366
1922–23	116	142	258	33,206	7·770
1923–24	133	158	291	33,983	8·563
1924–25	120	132	252	34,521	7·300
1925–26	116	135	251	34,751	7·223
1926–27	117	136	253	34,674	7·300
1927–28	106	129	235	34,802	6·752
1928–29	119	138	257	34,921	7·359
1929–30	110	131	241	35,042	6·877
1930–31	108	132	240	35,150	6·828
1931–32	121	137	258	34,066	7·574
1932–33	116	127	243	32,993	7·365
1933–34	142	132	274	30,216	9·068
"CS"					
1913–14	16	13	29	46,937	0·618
1919–20	11	19	30	72,796	0·412
1920–21	14	15	29	79,811	0·363
1921–22	14	24	38	86,697	0·438
1922–23	24	15	39	91,732	0·425
1923–24	24	15	39	96,766	0·403
1924–25	32	23	55	99,665	0·552
1925–26	31	28	59	103,469	0·570
1926–27	30	25	55	107,280	0·513
1927–28	31	28	59	111,091	0·531
1928–29	32	30	62	114,902	0·544
1929–30	20	28	48	120,356	0·399
1930–31	26	40	66	125,810	0·525
1931–32	31	35	66	132,672	0·497
1932–33	38	28	66	139,534	0·473
1933–34	41	35	76	142,897	0·532

TABLE VIII—*continued*

TOTAL COLLEGE SCHOLARSHIPS—BY TYPE OF SCHOOL—PER 1,000 OF SCHOOL POPULATION

| Year | Scholarships | | | School Population | Number of Scholarships per 1,000 |
	Cambridge	Oxford	Total		
		To Oxford and Cambridge "PD"			
1913–14	48	54	102	18,863	5·407
1919–20	35	55	90	28,107	3·202
1920–21	56	56	112	29,401	3·809
1921–22	47	53	100	30,486	3·280
1922–23	65	54	119	30,388	3·916
1923–24	72	48	120	30,290	3·962
1924–25	75	60	135	30,042	4·494
1925–26	61	60	121	29,801	4·060
1926–27	74	63	137	29,847	4·590
1927–28	62	59	121	29,892	4·048
1928–29	60	65	125	29,937	4·175
1929–30	75	59	134	29,949	4·474
1930–31	66	58	124	29,960	4·139
1931–32	91	68	159	31,121	5·109
1932–33	83	64	147	32,282	4·554
1933–34	84	62	146	32,178	4·537
		"SS"			
1913–14	17	10	27	34,919	0·773
1919–20	25	15	40	54,008	0·741
1920–21	27	13	40	59,396	0·673
1921–22	30	14	44	61,203	0·719
1922–23	26	12	38	58,934	0·645
1923–24	23	20	43	56,666	0·759
1924–25	19	16	35	57,958	0·604
1925–26	35	18	53	59,378	0·893
1926–27	25	15	40	59,381	0·674
1927–28	31	11	42	59,384	0·707
1928–29	26	16	42	59,388	0·707
1929–30	27	14	41	59,699	0·687
1930–31	16	17	33	60,009	0·550
1931–32	27	19	46	61,162	0·752
1932–33	30	21	51	62,313	0·818
1933–34	38	20	58	63,643	0·911

TABLE IX

SCHOLARSHIPS PER 1,000 SCHOOL POPULATION, 1913–34

(OXFORD AND CAMBRIDGE COMBINED)

Year	Scholarships "P" + "PD"	School Population "P" + "PD"	(a) Number of Scholarships per 1,000 Boys	Scholarships "SS" + "CS"	School Population "SS" + "CS"	(b) Number of Scholarships per 1,000 Boys	Ratio of (a) to (b)
1913–14	374	43,517	8·59	56	81,856	0·68	12·63
1919–20	330	58,389	5·65	70	126,804	0·55	10·27
1920–21	355	60,914	5·83	69	139,207	0·50	11·66
1921–22	339	62,931	5·39	82	147,900	0·55	9·80
1922–23	377	63,594	5·93	77	150,666	0·51	11·63
1923–24	411	64,273	6·39	82	153,432	0·53	12·06
1924–25	387	64,563	5·99	90	157,623	0·57	10·51
1925–26	372	64,552	5·76	112	162,847	0·69	8·35
1926–27	390	64,521	6·04	95	166,661	0·57	10·60
1927–28	356	64,694	5·50	101	170,475	0·59	9·32
1928–29	382	64,858	5·89	104	174,290	0·60	9·82
1929–30	375	64,991	5·77	89	178,055	0·50	11·54
1930–31	364	65,110	5·59	99	185,819	0·53	10·55
1931–32	417	65,187	6·40	112	193,834	0·58	11·03
1932–33	390	65,275	5·97	117	201,847	0·58	10·29
1933–34	420	62,394	6·73	134	206,540	0·65	10·35

the necessary dues. The Board of Education inquiry enables us to distinguish between open and "closed" scholarships for the year 1933–34. The figures show that in that year, 545 open scholarships and exhibitions were won by boys from all types of Secondary Schools in England and Wales, of which 302 went to pupils in grant-earning Secondary Schools. But we know that 74 of these schools, containing 35,314 boys, really belonged to the Public and Private School category. If we redistribute the scholarships on this basis, assuming that the 74 grant-earning Public Schools obtained scholarships only in direct proportion to their numbers, as compared with the total numbers in grant-earning Secondary Schools—which is almost certainly an under-estimate—we obtain the following results:

Scholarships obtained by "P", "PD", and "SN" Schools . 287
Scholarships obtained by "CS" and "SS" Schools . . 258

In other words, the Public and Private Schools obtained at least 52·7 per cent of the open scholarships and exhibitions to Oxford and Cambridge. Relating this to the school populations, we find that this former group won 4·08, while "CS" and "SS" schools won 1·25 scholarships per thousand boys.

"Closed" Scholarships only.—Concerning "closed" scholarships offered by various Colleges, a good deal of information is given in the Calendars of the two Universities and also in the *Students' Handbooks.* In the analysis that follows every attempt has been made to include only *entrance* scholarships and exhibitions available to students not already in residence at a College. But we cannot be certain that some of the exhibitions are not open to resident students as well. The awards are generally in the hands of the Colleges, being made out of College funds or Trust funds under College control, although in some cases the awards are in the gift of schools themselves. Our data are almost certainly incomplete, since there is no reason to suppose a higher degree of accuracy for "closed" scholarships than exists in the case of open scholarships recorded in official University publications. On the other hand, there is no reason to suspect bias in the distribution of the error.

The available information has been summarized in Tables X and XI.

Taking Oxford and Cambridge together, and treating scholarships and exhibitions as one group, we find from Table X that 241 are available to boys in Public Schools and only 50 to boys in "SS"

TABLE X

ENTRANCE SCHOLARSHIPS AND EXHIBITIONS CLOSED TO PARTICULAR SCHOOLS

(NUMBER OF SCHOOLS GIVEN IN BRACKETS)

	"P"	"PD"	All Public	"SS"	"CS"	"SS" + "CS"	Total
(A) OXFORD							
(i) Scholarships	83 (20)	31 (18)	114 (38)	15 (13)	2 (2)	17 (15)	131 (53)
(ii) Exhibitions	13 (7)	4 (2)	17 (9)	6 (6)	—	6 (6)	23 (15)
(B) CAMBRIDGE							
(i) Scholarships	37 (6)	4 (3)	41 (9)	3 (3)	—	3 (3)	44 (12)
(ii) Exhibitions	55 (17)	14 (8)	69 (25)	23 (14)	1 (1)	24 (15)	94 (41)[1]

[1] Including one to a Private School.

TABLE XI

ENTRANCE SCHOLARSHIPS AND EXHIBITIONS CLOSED IN OTHER WAYS

	Sons of Clergy	Members of Church of England	For Holy Orders or Divinity	Total Religious	Organ or Choral	Sons or Kin of Founders or other Persons	Locality	Miscellaneous	Total
(A) OXFORD									
(i) Scholarships	7	36	2	45	2	12	45	13	117
(ii) Exhibitions	9	—	2	11	1	—	11	2	25
(B) CAMBRIDGE									
(i) Scholarships	13	6	5	24	7	—	3	1	35
(ii) Exhibitions	9	1	6	16	1	1	1	5	24

and "CS" schools, a ratio of almost five to one. In terms of the respective school populations, the numbers available per thousand boys are 3·86 and 0·24 respectively, giving a ratio of sixteen to one in favour of boys from Public Schools. It is not possible to estimate how awards in Table XI are distributed between different types of school.

(2) *County Major Scholarships*

These are generally awarded, in the case of the older Universities at least, to boys who have already won an open College scholarship. As a rule, therefore, they duplicate the awards shown in the analysis of open scholarships. They assist poorer boys educated in "SS" or "CS" Schools to proceed to the Universities by supplementing the amount of the open scholarship won by a sum sufficient to pay the bulk of the necessary expenses of residence in College. They do not increase the total number of such boys proceeding thereto.

(3) *State Scholarships*

The State scholarship system was introduced as a result of a report of the Consultative Committee on Higher Education made in 1918. Originally the scheme provided for an annual number of two hundred scholarships tenable at any English or Welsh University, twenty-two being reserved for Wales (including Monmouth). Candidates were to be pupils in grant-aided Secondary Schools under 18 years of age on the July 31st preceding the examination. In England the candidates were required to pass one of the seven approved second examinations, and to be nominated for a scholarship by the Examining Body. In Wales, the scholarships were awarded on the results of a special examination conducted by the University of Wales. The awards consisted of a grant for approved tuition fees plus a maintenance grant not exceeding £80 per annum. Until 1930 they were distributed between the eight Examining Bodies in proportion to the total number of entrants, irrespective of sex. They were then divided equally between boys and girls, provided that sufficient numbers reached the qualifying standard. However, the number of male candidates greatly exceeded the females, and after 1930 the allocations were made in proportion to the number of candidates of each sex entering for the Higher School Certificate in one or more previous years. At the same time the annual number of scholarships was increased from two to three hundred. (It had remained at two hundred from the beginning except in 1922 and 1923 when, on the plea of economy, the scheme was entirely suspended.) Admittedly, the primary intention of the State Scholarship Scheme was to provide assistance for children who otherwise could not afford to go to University. It was provided that candidates must be pupils of grant-aided Secondary Schools only. However, many Public Schools are now in receipt of grants-in-aid. To discover how far the original object of increasing educational opportunities among the relatively poor has been achieved, it is necessary to examine the way in which State scholarships have been allocated between various types of grant-aided school. Our analysis refers only to male candidates proceeding to Oxford and Cambridge.

Table XII shows that, since the initiation of the programme, the grant-aided Public Schools have received the majority of the scholarships in relation to their populations.

This is even more clearly evident from Table XIII, where "P" and "PD" Schools have been grouped together and compared with the group formed by "SS" and "CS" Schools.

The conclusion to be drawn from this last table is that the bulk of State scholarships, in relation to school populations, is going to boys from wealthier families or from families of higher social status than was intended by the authors of the scheme.

During the last three years the discrepancy has been slightly decreasing. But the new Regulations of 1936 have once more raised the possibility that State funds will be used to assist children educated in expensive schools. Under these new rules, according to the statement published by the Board of Education,[1] State scholarships, instead of being closed to the pupils of grant-aided Secondary Schools, "are open to candidates who, at the date of the examination, had been pupils in full-time attendance for at least two years at Secondary Schools in England and Wales." At the same time the State Scholarship Regulations for 1936[2] defined the Secondary School as "a school for pupils who intend to remain for at least four years, and up to at least the age of sixteen, which provides a progressive course of general education of a kind and amount suited to an age-range at least from 12 to 17." In practice this means that any Secondary School recognized as "efficient" and included in *List 60*, may send in candidates for the examination. Among these are most of the big Public Schools. Since these new regulations

---

[1] Form I. U., 1936.   *Statutory Rules and Orders*, 1936, No. 391.

TABLE XII

STATE SCHOLARSHIPS TO OXFORD AND CAMBRIDGE

(GRANT-AIDED SCHOOLS ONLY)

Year	Total	Type of School									Total to all Universities
		"P"		"PD"		"SS"		"CS"			
		(a)	(b)	(a)	(b)	(a)	(b)	(a)	(b)		
1920–21	54	1	0·26	24	0·84	12	0·20	17	0·21		104
1921–22	62	4	1·03	27	0·91	16	0·26	15	0·17		100
1924–25	116	2	0·50	59	2·02	26	0·45	29	0·29		149
1925–26	79	3	0·75	31	1·07	15	0·25	30	0·29		100
1926–27	75	1	0·25	26	0·90	19	0·32	29	0·27		112
1927–28	81	1	0·24	31	1·07	19	0·25	30	0·27		106
1928–29	86	2	0·48	37	1·27	15	0·27	33	0·29		111
1929–30	80	2	0·48	37	1·27	16		25	0·21		108
1930–31	142	8	1·94	45	1·55	32	0·53	63	0·50		190
1931–32	161	5	1·23	70	2·32	40	0·65	43	0·32		188
1932–33	144	3	0·73	52	1·66	24	0·39	63	0·45		190
1933–34	148	2	0·49	55	1·76	36	0·57	54	0·38		196
1934–35	147			45	1·45	33	0·51	67	0·46		194

(a) Actual number of scholarships.
(b) Number per 1,000 boys.

were promulgated many Public Schools which had not formerly
sought Government inspection have now applied for recognition as
"efficient" schools. The inference is inescapable.

In defence it may be urged that even in the big Public Schools
there are many poor boys who require to be helped by scholarships.
It is not intended to reduce the number of scholarships going to boys
in "SS" and "CS" Schools. On the contrary, the total scholarships

TABLE XIII

DISTRIBUTION OF STATE SCHOLARSHIPS TAKEN TO OXFORD
AND CAMBRIDGE

NUMBER OF SCHOLARSHIPS PER 1,000 BOYS WON BY SCHOOLS
OF DIFFERENT TYPES (GRANT-AIDED SCHOOLS ONLY)

	"P" + "PD" (a)	"SS" + "CS" (b)	Ratio of (a) to (b)
1920–21	0·773	0·208	3·72
1921–22	0·926	0·210	4·41
1922–23	—	—	—
1923–24	—	—	—
1924–25	1·842	0·349	5·28
1925–26	1·033	0·276	3·74
1926–27	0·819	0·288	2·84
1927–28	0·968	0·287	3·37
1928–29	1·147	0·275	4·17
1929–30	1·175	0·230	5·11
1930–31	1·415	0·511	2·77
1931–32	2·273	0·428	5·31
1932–33	1·610	0·431	3·74
1933–34	1·642	0·436	3·77
1934–35	1·334	0·473	2·82

available each year have been increased to 360. To this it may be
answered that it is a notorious observation of social psychology that
there are few families rich enough to refuse financial aid for their
children's education. It is not improbable that two considerations
will be found to increase the proportion of Public School applications
for State scholarships. The number of scholarships is a fixed quantity,
but there is no minimum cost which the system must incur each
year to fulfil its obligations. Thus there might be a temptation to
save money by increasing the proportion of awards to boys from
relatively prosperous families, thus involving smaller grants per
head. Second, under the new regulations grants in aid of fees or

maintenance may be made to boys whose parents have incomes up to £1,000 per annum. The parental income of State secondary schoolboys seldom reaches this figure. When we consider their superior average examination performance, it becomes more than likely that a higher proportion of awards will be made to public school candidates with a parental income just below the maximum.

(4) Kitchener Scholarships

The fourth category of scholarships, those given by institutions independent of the Universities or the State, includes a substantial

TABLE XIV

KITCHENER SCHOLARSHIPS

Year	Total number of Scholarships given to boys from Schools in England and Wales	Total number of Scholarships taken up in Oxford or Cambridge	Scholarships taken up in Oxford or Cambridge as percentage of total
1925	65	35	53·8
1926	71	54	76·1
1927	82	56	68·3
1928	93	66	71·0
1929	95	72	75·8
1930	126	84	66·7
1931	116	73	62·9
1932	109	72	66·1
1933	97	54	55·7
1934	98	64	65·3

number in the gift of various City Corporations and special trusts. For example, the Grocers' and Drapers' Companies, the Mansbridge National Trust Fund, the Stapley Trust, the Vestey Memorial Fund, and the Wall Fund, to name but a few of the most important, give assistance to boys who intend to proceed to the University. But most of them only give supplementary assistance to boys who have already won scholarships, and thus merely duplicate the results we have already shown, without really extending facilities. In the discussion of entrance scholarship facilities the Kitchener scholarships are the most important. They were founded after the war in memory of Lord Kitchener, varying in number during the

TABLE XV

DISTRIBUTION OF KITCHENER SCHOLARSHIPS WON BY TYPE OF SCHOOL

(To OXFORD AND CAMBRIDGE ONLY)

Year	Total Oxford and Cambridge	Type of School from which Boys came											
		"P"		"PD"		"SS"		"CS"		"SN"		Others	
		Number	Percentage	Number	Percentage	Number	Percentage	Number	Percentage	Number	Percentage	Number	Percentage
1925	35	20	57·1	8	22·9	5	14·3	2	5·7	0	—	0	—
1926	54	19	35·2	15	27·8	9	16·7	11	20·3	0	—	0	—
1927	56	20	35·7	15	26·8	7	12·5	13	23·2	0	—	1	1·8
1928	66	27	40·9	15	22·7	7	10·6	17	25·8	0	—	0	—
1929	72	28	38·9	22	30·6	8	11·1	12	16·6	1	1·4	1	1·4
1930	84	40	47·6	17	20·2	11	13·1	15	17·9	1	1·2	0	—
1931	73	36	49·3	17	23·3	9	12·3	10	13·7	1	1·4	0	—
1932	72	34	47·2	15	20·8	10	13·9	11	15·3	0	—	2	2·8
1933	54	32	59·25	11	20·35	7	13·0	3	5·55	1	1·85	0	—
1934	64	39	60·9	8	12·5	6	9·4	9	14·1	2	3·1	0	—

period for which we have relevant statistics from 65 to 126 per annum. Kitchener scholarships are available only to the sons of officers and men or ex-officers and men of His Majesty's forces. Candidates must be between the ages of 17 and 20 on the January 1st preceding their application. The award, for which no examination is necessary, depends on the candidate's individual needs, with an upper limit of £250 per annum.

Tables XIV and XV give the position concerning the allocation of Kitchener scholarships between different Universities and different types of schools.

Summarizing the information contained in Table XV, we find that the percentage of Oxford and Cambridge scholarships awarded to public schoolboys was as follows:

TABLE XVI

KITCHENER SCHOLARSHIPS TO OXFORD AND CAMBRIDGE

PERCENTAGE AWARDED TO BOYS IN "P" AND "PD." SCHOOLS

1924–25	80·0
1925–26	63·0
1926–27	62·5
1927–28	63·6
1928–29	69·5
1929–30	67·8
1930–31	72·6
1931–32	68·0
1932–33	79·6
1933–34	73·4

An average of 70 per cent is very considerable. It is improbable that the children of privates and non-commissioned officers attend such schools. Since there were in 1935 fourteen times as many other ranks as officers in the armed forces, it is clear that a disproportionately large number of Kitchener scholarships go to children of comparatively high socio-economic status.

Table XVII summarizes the statistical conclusions reached so far.

(5) *School-Leaving Scholarships*

Finally, we have to consider the leaving scholarships given by schools themselves. These may be used either to give supplementary grants to boys who have already won other scholarships or may constitute

TABLE XVII

DISTRIBUTION OF SCHOLARSHIPS—BY TYPE OF SCHOOL—OXFORD AND CAMBRIDGE TOGETHER

Year	Open and Closed	State	Kitchener	Total Scholarships	School Population	Number of Scholarships per 1,000
			"P"			
1913–14	272	—	—	272	24,654	11·033
1924–25	252	2	20	274	34,521	7·937
1925–26	251	3	19	273	34,751	7·856
1926–27	253	1	20	274	34,674	7·902
1927–28	235	1	27	263	34,802	7·557
1928–29	257	1	28	286	34,921	8·190
1929–30	241	2	40	283	35,042	8·076
1930–31	240	2	36	278	35,150	7·909
1931–32	258	8	34	300	34,066	8·806
1932–33	243	5	32	280	32,993	8·487
1933–34	274	3	39	316	30,216	10·458
			"PD"			
1913–14	102	—	—	102	18,863	5·407
1924–25	135	59	8	202	30,042	6·724
1925–26	121	31	15	167	29,801	5·604
1926–27	137	26	15	178	29,847	5·964
1927–28	121	31	15	167	29,892	5·587
1928–29	125	37	22	184	29,937	6·146
1929–30	134	37	17	188	29,949	6·277
1930–31	124	45	17	186	29,960	6·208
1931–32	159	70	15	244	31,121	7·840
1932–33	147	52	11	210	32,282	6·505
1933–34	146	55	8	209	32,178	6·495
			"CS"			
1913–14	29	—	—	29	46,937	0·618
1924–25	55	29	2	86	99,665	0·863
1925–26	59	30	11	100	103,469	0·966
1926–27	55	29	13	97	107,280	0·904
1927–28	59	30	17	106	111,091	0·954
1928–29	62	33	12	107	114,902	0·931
1929–30	48	25	15	88	120,356	0·731
1930–31	66	63	10	139	125,810	1·105
1931–32	66	43	11	120	132,672	0·904
1932–33	66	63	3	132	139,534	0·946
1933–34	76	54	9	139	142,897	0·973
			"SS"			
1913–14	27	—	—	27	34,919	0·773
1924–25	35	26	5	66	57,958	1·139
1925–26	53	15	9	77	59,378	1·297
1926–27	40	19	7	66	59,381	1·111
1927–28	42	19	7	68	59,384	1·145
1928–29	42	15	8	65	59,388	1·094
1929–30	41	16	11	68	59,699	1·139
1930–31	33	32	9	74	60,009	1·233
1931–32	46	40	10	96	61,162	1·570
1932–33	51	24	7	82	62,313	1·316
1933–34	58	36	6	100	63,643	1·571

the whole of the financial assistance with which the recipients proceed to the Universities. No published sources furnish the necessary information for an analysis of these awards. Our data are derived solely from replies to a questionnaire sent to all the Secondary Schools in England and Wales. Some 25 per cent returned replies. The sample is small, but there is no particular reason to suspect bias. Moreover, the weighted averages of the fees charged by the schools in the sample correspond very closely to the figures for all

TABLE XVIII

COMPARISON OF AVERAGE SCHOOL FEES AND AVERAGE ANNUAL VALUE OF LEAVING SCHOLARSHIPS IN DIFFERENT TYPES OF SCHOOLS

Type of School	Number of Boys in Sample, 1934–35	Average Fee per Boy, 1934–35	Average Annual Value of Leaving Scholarships per 100 Boys, 1934–35
		£	£
"P"	9,471	149·46	216·79
"PD"	7,678	20·00	134·59
"SS"	16,348	14·88	38·03
"CS"	41,403	12·56	21·47

schools. It is not improbable, therefore, that our data approximately represent the actual situation.

Based on these data, Table XVIII compares the average fee in different types of schools with the average annual value of leaving scholarships. It shows that as the size of the average school fee increases, so also does the financial assistance provided for a university education.

In the "SS" and "CS" Schools, where monetary assistance for boys qualified to proceed to the University is most needed, it is least available. These results confirm the data of the previous sections relating to the distribution of open and closed scholarships and Kitchener scholarships. Schools charging the highest fees and offering the smallest proportion of free places to boys of Elementary School origin gain the majority of college and other public awards and give the greatest financial assistance to their pupils.

P

The Great Public Schools

Since Public Schools vary widely in the magnitude of the fees charged and in the public estimation of their social and educational advantages, it is interesting to compare the fifteen most expensive "P" schools with the rest in this class, numbering eighty-one. Moreover, since three schools, namely Eton, Harrow, and Winchester, enjoy a special reputation, these have been separated from the rest for comparison. The results are tabulated in Table XIX.

Thus the group of most expensive schools, constituting little more than 15 per cent of the total, obtained on the average just under 50 per cent of all college scholarships awarded to "P" Schools. Parents discussing the choice of a school will observe that boys in this group had twice and sometimes three times the chance of winning a college scholarship that boys in less expensive schools had. Eton, Harrow, and Winchester were even more fortunate. Constituting 3 per cent of all "P" Schools, they won about 14 per cent of the total scholarships. Seldom has a pupil of these schools an opportunity of winning a college scholarship less than three times greater than that of a boy in one of the "lesser" Public Schools.

Once more we would state that we are not concerned here with the relative ability of pupils in Secondary Schools of different type. If the distribution of ability, measured by some objective test, were such that in Eton, Harrow, and Winchester there were three times as many boys per hundred of scholarship standard as in the other Public Schools and sixteen times as many per hundred as in County Secondary Schools, the issue would be substantially different. We are not disposed to deny the possibility that certain able families select certain schools with a high scholastic reputation and that such schools do not base their entrance qualifications exclusively on the criterion of parental wealth. Even if we grant this, it does not mean that the existing situation is incapable of improvement. The higher scholarship ability observed in certain schools might not be due entirely to the genetic superiority of parents in the higher social classes over those who can only afford to begin their children's education in the Elementary School. It might be due partly to the special advantages afforded by expensive Public Schools in preparing their pupils for scholarship examinations. Some such advantages are clearly enjoyed by the group of most expensive schools. In order to test this possibility, when schools of different type are contrasted,

TABLE XIX

DISTRIBUTION OF TOTAL ENTRANCE SCHOLARSHIPS TO OXFORD AND CAMBRIDGE BETWEEN DIFFERENT TYPES OF PUBLIC SCHOOLS

Year	All "P" Schools		The 15 most expensive "P" Schools		The 81 less expensive "P" Schools		Eton, Harrow, and Winchester	
	(a)	(b)	(a)	(b)	(a)	(b)	(a)	(b)
1913–14	272	11·03	130	18·39	142	8·07	34	17·14
1919–20	240	7·93	94	11·97	146	6·51	25	11·57
1920–21	243	7·71	120	15·06	123	5·22	39	18·01
1921–22	239	7·37	124	15·03	115	4·75	39	17·84
1922–23	258	7·77	123	14·57	135	5·45	37	16·70
1923–24	291	8·56	144	16·55	147	5·81	44	19·72
1924–25	252	7·30	143	16·19	109	4·24	32	14·27
1925–26	251	7·22	133	14·83	118	4·58	39	17·24
1926–27	253	7·30	124	13·79	129	5·02	34	15·10
1927–28	235	6·75	114	12·62	121	4·70	34	15·07
1928–29	257	7·36	122	13·50	135	5·22	31	13·72
1929–30	241	6·88	127	14·06	114	4·38	30	13·35
1930–31	240	6·83	124	13·72	116	4·44	34	15·94
1931–32	258	7·57	125	13·82	133	5·32	35	15·69
1932–33	243	7·37	119	13·25	124	4·96	29	13·11
1933–34	274	9·07	132	14·75	142	6·68	35	15·80

(a) Number of scholarships.
(b) Number per thousand boys.

TABLE XXa

COLLEGE ENTRANCE SCHOLARSHIPS—BY TYPE OF SUBJECT

Year	Total Scholarships	Classics		Mathematics		Science		Modern Subjects		Miscellaneous		Unknown	
		Number	Percentage	Number	Percentage	Number	Percentage	Number	Percentage	Number	Percentage	Number	Percentage
CAMBRIDGE													
1913–14	219	81	36·99	51	23·29	50	22·83	28	12·79	2	0·91	7	3·19
1919–20	187	51	27·27	40	21·39	56	29·95	34	18·18	0	0·00	6	3·21
1920–21	213	58	27·23	50	23·47	52	24·41	44	20·66	0	0·00	9	4·23
1921–22	195	53	27·18	43	22·05	41	21·03	50	25·64	2	1·03	6	3·07
1922–23	235	68	28·94	44	18·72	56	23·83	65	27·66	0	0·00	2	0·85
1923–24	256	67	26·17	60	23·44	58	22·66	51	19·92	6	2·34	14	5·47
1924–25	248	69	27·82	52	20·97	56	22·58	58	23·39	1	0·40	12	4·84
1925–26	247	68	27·54	49	19·84	46	18·63	69	27·94	5	2·02	10	4·03
1926–27	252	72	28·57	46	18·26	49	19·45	62	24·60	5	1·98	18	7·14
1927–28	232	64	27·59	47	20·26	40	17·24	61	26·30	5	2·16	15	6·45
1928–29	239	75	31·38	40	16·74	47	19·67	61	25·52	6	2·51	10	4·18
1929–30	236	67	28·40	41	17·37	49	20·77	63	26·70	9	3·81	7	2·95
1930–31	222	50	22·52	45	20·28	46	20·72	64	28·83	10	4·50	7	3·15
1931–32	274	71	25·91	43	15·70	55	20·08	82	29·93	12	4·38	11	4·00
1932–33	268	68	25·38	44	16·42	52	19·41	84	31·34	10	3·73	10	3·72
1933–34	308	85	27·60	47	15·26	57	18·51	89	28·90	17	5·52	13	4·21
OXFORD													
1913–14	213	106	49·78	25	11·74	24	11·27	37	17·37	1	0·45	20	9·39
1919–20	218	92	42·20	26	11·93	33	15·14	41	18·81	5	2·29	21	9·63
1920–21	213	78	36·63	24	11·27	40	18·78	51	23·95	1	0·45	19	8·92
1921–22	229	91	39·74	20	8·73	36	15·72	52	22·71	2	0·87	28	12·23

Year													
1922–23	224	81	36·16	22	9·82	44	19·65	56	25·00	3	1·34	18	8·03
1923–24	241	101	41·92	21	8·72	47	19·51	60	24·90	7	2·91	5	2·04
1924–25	232	94	40·53	24	10·35	44	18·97	59	25·44	1	0·43	10	4·28
1925–26	245	96	39·20	21	8·58	43	17·56	69	28·17	3	1·22	13	5·27
1926–27	239	87	36·40	18	7·53	46	19·25	67	28·04	4	1·67	17	7·11
1927–28	229	95	41·50	18	7·65	41	17·91	64	27·95	2	0·87	9	4·12
1928–29	251	95	37·87	16	6·38	51	20·33	71	28·30	2	0·80	16	6·32
1929–30	236	89	37·73	24	10·17	39	16·53	70	29·67	2	0·85	12	5·05
1930–31	250	90	36·00	20	8·00	43	17·20	82	32·80	4	1·60	11	4·40
1931–32	262	100	38·19	23	8·78	50	19·09	78	29·78	4	1·53	7	2·63
1932–33	242	92	38·02	17	7·03	43	17·77	77	31·82	5	2·07	8	3·29
1933–34	250	93	37·20	25	10·00	51	20·40	71	28·40	5	2·00	5	2·00

OXFORD AND CAMBRIDGE

Year													
1913–14	432	187	43·29	76	17·59	74	17·13	65	15·05	3	0·46	27	6·25
1919–20	405	143	35·31	66	16·30	89	21·98	75	18·52	5	1·23	27	6·67
1920–21	426	136	31·92	74	17·37	92	21·60	95	22·30	1	0·23	28	6·57
1921–22	424	144	33·96	63	14·86	77	18·16	102	24·06	4	0·94	34	8·02
1922–23	459	149	32·46	66	14·38	100	21·79	121	26·36	3	0·65	20	4·36
1923–24	497	168	33·80	81	16·30	105	21·13	111	22·33	13	2·62	19	3·82
1924–25	480	163	33·96	76	15·83	100	20·83	117	24·38	2	0·42	22	4·58
1925–26	492	164	33·33	70	14·23	89	18·09	138	28·05	8	1·63	23	4·67
1926–27	491	159	32·38	64	13·03	95	19·35	129	26·27	9	1·83	35	7·13
1927–28	461	159	34·49	65	14·10	81	17·57	125	27·11	7	1·52	24	5·21
1928–29	490	170	34·69	56	11·43	98	20·00	132	26·94	8	1·63	26	5·31
1929–30	472	156	33·05	65	13·77	88	18·64	133	28·18	11	2·33	19	4·03
1930–31	472	140	29·66	65	13·77	89	18·86	146	30·93	14	2·97	18	3·81
1931–32	436	171	31·90	66	12·31	105	19·59	160	29·85	16	2·99	18	3·36
1932–33	510	160	31·37	61	11·96	95	18·63	161	31·57	15	2·94	18	3·53
1933–34	558	178	31·90	72	12·90	108	19·35	160	28·67	22	3·94	18	3·23

we now proceed to examine some aspects of the quality of the teaching available in its relation to college entrance examination requirements.

V. EDUCATIONAL ADVANTAGES OF CERTAIN SCHOOLS

Certain types of schools specialize in teaching certain subjects or enjoy a special reputation in connection with them. Table XX provides an analysis of the distribution of open and closed scholarships and exhibitions by the type of subject in which they were awarded. In order to obtain a small and manageable number of categories, the subjects of study were grouped into five main classes, viz.:

1. Classics, including Divinity and Moral Philosophy;
2. Mathematics;
3. The Natural Sciences;
4. Modern Subjects, including modern languages, literature, history and the social sciences;
5. Miscellaneous.

The most striking feature of this table is the high percentage of scholarships going to Classics, ranging from 43·29 per cent in 1913–14 to 31·90 per cent in 1933–34. Although it has suffered a significant reduction in the last twenty years, this group still remains pre-eminent in Oxford and has only been recently surpassed in Cambridge by Modern subjects. It is also notable that Mathematics should have undergone a decline in the same period from 17·59 to 12·90 per cent.

Tables XXI*a*, *b*, *c*, and *d* shed some additional light on the significance of these figures.

Table XXI*a*, giving the percentage of Classics scholarships won by different types of schools, shows that most of these are awarded to Public (including "SN") Schools. In 1913–14 the percentage was 96·79, and by 1933–34 it had only fallen to 92·13. In other faculties the original percentage of scholarships going to Public Schools was smaller and the fall during the last twenty years greater—in Mathematics from 81·58 to 66·67 per cent, in Natural Science from 71·62 to 60·19 per cent and in Modern Subjects from 80·00 to 70·63 per cent. Now it is certain that in England and Wales the Public Schools specialize in Classics to a greater extent than other

TABLE XXI*a*

PERCENTAGES OF CLASSICS SCHOLARSHIPS BY TYPES OF SCHOOLS

TO OXFORD

Year	"P"	"PD"	"P"+"PD"+"SN"	"CS"	"SS"	"CS"+"SS"
1913–14	73·58	22·64	96·23	2·83	0·94	3·77
1919–20	69·57	22·83	92·39	5·43	2·17	7·61
1920–21	67·95	24·36	92·31	5·13	2·56	7·69
1921–22	64·84	27·47	92·31	7·69	0·00	7·69
1922–23	75·32	18·52	93·83	4·94	1·23	6·17
1923–24	78·22	15·84	94·06	4·95	0·99	5·94
1924–25	68·09	24·47	92·55	6·38	1·06	7·45
1925–26	66·67	21·88	89·58	7·29	3·13	10·42
1926–27	66·67	25·29	91·95	4·60	3·45	8·05
1927–28	68·42	26·32	94·74	5·26	0·00	5·26
1928–29	77·89	16·84	94·74	3·16	2·11	5·26
1929–30	70·79	20·22	92·13	6·74	1·12	7·87
1930–31	65·56	22·22	87·78	10·00	2·22	12·22
1931–32	58·00	24·00	82·00	11·00	7·00	18·00
1932–33	65·22	26·09	91·30	7·61	1·09	8·70
1933–34	73·12	17·20	90·32	7·53	2·15	9·68

TO CAMBRIDGE

Year	"P"	"PD"	"P"+"PD"+"SN"	"CS"	"SS"	"CS"+"SS"
1913–14	87·65	9·88	97·53	1·23	1·23	2·47
1919–20	80·39	13·73	94·12	1·96	3·92	5·88
1920–21	81·03	15·52	96·55	0·00	3·45	3·45
1921–22	81·13	16·98	98·11	0·00	1·89	1·89
1922–23	60·29	35·29	95·59	2·94	1·47	4·41
1923–24	71·64	25·37	98·51	1·49	0·00	1·49
1924–25	62·32	34·78	97·10	2·90	0·00	2·90
1925–26	69·12	27·94	97·06	1·47	1·47	2·94
1926–27	72·22	20·83	94·44	2·78	2·78	5·56
1927–28	67·19	26·56	93·75	3·13	3·13	6·25
1928–29	66·67	28·00	94·67	1·33	4·00	5·33
1929–30	67·16	29·85	97·01	0·00	2·99	2·99
1930–31	62·00	34·00	96·00	4·00	0·00	4·00
1931–32	56·34	38·04	94·37	4·23	1·41	5·63
1932–33	66·18	26·47	92·65	2·94	4·41	7·35
1933–34	68·24	25·88	94·12	2·35	3·53	5·88

TO OXFORD AND CAMBRIDGE

Year	"P"	"PD"	"P"+"PD"+"SN"	"CS"	"SS"	"CS"+"SS"
1913–14	79·68	17·11	96·79	2·14	1·07	3·21
1919–20	73·43	19·58	93·01	4·20	2·80	6·99
1920–21	73·53	20·59	94·12	2·94	2·94	5·88
1921–22	70·83	23·61	94·44	4·86	0·69	5·56
1922–23	68·46	26·17	94·63	4·03	1·34	5·37
1923–24	75·60	19·64	95·83	3·57	0·60	4·17
1924–25	65·64	28·83	94·48	4·91	0·61	5·52
1925–26	67·68	24·39	92·68	4·88	2·44	7·32
1926–27	69·18	23·27	93·08	3·77	3·14	6·92
1927–28	67·92	26·42	94·34	4·40	1·26	5·66
1928–29	72·94	21·76	94·71	2·35	2·94	5·29
1929–30	69·23	24·36	94·23	3·85	1·92	5·77
1930–31	64·29	26·43	90·71	7·86	1·43	9·29
1931–32	57·31	29·82	87·13	8·19	4·68	12·87
1932–33	65·63	26·25	91·88	5·63	2·50	8·12
1933–34	70·79	21·35	92·13	5·06	2·81	7·87

Table XXI*b*

PERCENTAGES OF MATHEMATICS SCHOLARSHIPS BY TYPES OF SCHOOLS

TO OXFORD

Year	"P"	"PD"	"P"+"PD"+"SN"	"CS"	"SS"	"CS"+"SS"
1913–14	36·00	40·00	80·00	12·00	8·00	20·00
1919–20	30·77	34·62	65·38	11·54	23·08	34·62
1920–21	37·50	37·50	75·00	8·33	16·67	25·00
1921–22	50·00	20·00	70·00	20·00	10·00	30·00
1922–23	50·00	31·82	81·82	9·09	9·09	18·18
1923–24	38·10	28·57	66·67	14·29	19·05	33·33
1924–25	54·17	20·83	75·00	16·67	8·33	25·00
1925–26	47·62	9·52	66·67	23·81	9·52	33·33
1926–27	27·78	50·00	77·78	16·67	5·56	22·22
1927–28	50·00	22·22	72·22	11·11	16·67	27·78
1928–29	18·75	43·75	62·50	25·00	12·50	37·50
1929–30	29·17	33·33	66·66	12·50	20·83	33·33
1930–31	40·00	20·00	65·00	25·00	10·00	35·00
1931–32	34·78	30·43	69·57	21·74	8·70	30·43
1932–33	17·65	35·29	52·94	41·18	5·88	47·06
1933–34	40·00	28·00	72·00	20·00	8·00	28·00

TO CAMBRIDGE

Year	"P"	"PD"	"P"+"PD"+"SN"	"CS"	"SS"	"CS"+"SS"
1913–14	58·82	21·57	82·35	11·76	5·88	17·65
1919–20	57·50	17·50	75·00	5·00	20·00	25·00
1920–21	42·00	34·00	76·00	6·00	18·00	24·00
1921–22	41·86	34·88	76·74	11·63	11·63	23·26
1922–23	45·45	27·28	75·00	9·09	15·91	25·00
1923–24	58·33	16·67	75·00	11·67	13·33	25·00
1924–25	40·38	28·85	69·23	17·31	13·46	30·77
1925–26	40·82	26·53	67·35	18·37	14·29	32·65
1926–27	45·65	28·26	76·09	6·52	17·39	23·91
1927–28	46·81	25·53	72·34	10·64	17·02	27·66
1928–29	40·00	27·50	67·50	15·00	17·50	32·50
1929–30	41·46	34·15	75·61	12·20	12·20	24·39
1930–31	60·00	20·00	84·44	8·89	6·67	15·56
1931–32	51·16	30·23	81·40	11·63	6·98	18·60
1932–33	22·73	38·64	61·36	20·45	18·18	38·64
1933–34	38·30	25·53	63·83	21·28	14·89	36·17

TO OXFORD AND CAMBRIDGE

Year	"P"	"PD"	"P"+"PD"+"SN"	"CS"	"SS"	"CS"+"SS"
1913–14	51·32	27·63	81·58	11·84	6·58	18·42
1919–20	46·97	24·24	71·21	7·58	21·21	28·79
1920–21	40·54	35·14	75·68	6·76	17·57	24·32
1921–22	44·44	30·16	74·60	14·29	11·11	25·40
1922–23	46·97	28·79	77·27	9·09	13·64	22·73
1923–24	53·09	19·75	72·84	12·35	14·81	27·16
1924–25	44·74	26·32	71·05	17·11	11·84	28·95
1925–26	42·86	21·43	67·14	20·00	12·86	32·86
1926–27	40·63	34·38	76·56	9·38	14·06	23·44
1927–28	47·69	24·62	72·31	10·77	16·92	27·69
1928–29	33·93	32·14	66·07	17·86	16·07	33·93
1929–30	36·92	33·85	72·31	12·31	15·38	27·69
1930–31	59·85	20·00	78·46	13·85	7·69	21·54
1031–32	45·45	30·30	77·27	15·15	7·58	22·73
1932–33	21·31	37·70	59·02	26·23	14·75	40·98
1933–34	38·89	26·39	66·67	20·83	12·50	33·33

Table XXI*c*

PERCENTAGES OF SCIENCE SCHOLARSHIPS BY TYPES OF SCHOOLS

TO OXFORD

Year	"P"	"PD"	"P"+"PD"+"SN"	"CS"	"SS"	"CS"+"SS"
1913–14	37·50	29·17	66·67	12·50	20·83	33·33
1919–20	36·36	39·39	75·76	18·18	6·06	24·24
1920–21	37·50	45·00	82·50	7·50	10·00	17·50
1921–22	38·89	22·22	61·11	22·22	16·67	38·89
1922–23	52·27	31·82	84·09	9·09	6·82	15·91
1923–24	46·81	29·79	76·60	6·38	17·02	23·40
1924–25	40·91	27·27	68·18	18·18	13·64	31·82
1925–26	39·53	30·23	69·77	13·95	16·28	30·23
1926–27	36·96	34·78	71·74	10·87	17·39	28·26
1927–28	29·27	31·71	60·98	29·27	9·76	39·02
1928–29	27·45	45·10	72·55	15·69	11·76	27·45
1929–30	28·21	41·03	71·79	17·95	10·26	28·21
1930–31	41·86	27·91	72·09	20·93	6·98	27·91
1931–32	40·00	32·00	72·00	20·00	8·00	28·00
1932–33	39·53	25·58	69·77	13·95	16·28	30·23
1933–34	27·45	33·33	60·78	29·41	9·80	39·22

TO CAMBRIDGE

Year	"P"	"PD"	"P"+"PD"+"SN"	"CS"	"SS"	"CS"+"SS"
1913–14	36·00	38·00	74·00	6·00	20·00	26·00
1919–20	51·79	23·21	76·79	7·14	16·07	23·21
1920–21	42·31	32·69	76·92	11·54	11·54	23·08
1921–22	36·59	29·27	68·29	14·63	17·07	31·71
1922–23	44·64	26·79	73·21	16·07	10·71	26·79
1923–24	32·76	37·93	70·69	15·52	13·79	29·31
1924–25	37·50	33·93	71·43	19·64	8·93	28·57
1925–26	23·91	30·43	54·35	23·91	21·74	45·65
1926–27	32·65	30·61	63·27	20·41	16·33	36·73
1927–28	37·50	22·50	62·50	22·50	15·00	37·50
1928–29	38·30	23·40	61·70	25·53	12·77	38·30
1929–30	30·61	38·78	71·43	6·12	22·45	28·57
1930–31	30·43	36·96	69·57	19·57	10·87	30·43
1931–32	30·91	32·73	65·45	16·36	18·18	34·55
1932–33	34·62	36·54	73·08	13·46	13·46	26·92
1933–34	35·09	24·56	59·65	24·56	15·79	40·35

TO OXFORD AND CAMBRIDGE

Year	"P"	"PD"	"P"+"PD"+"SN"	"CS"	"SS"	"CS"+"SS"
1913–14	36·49	35·14	71·62	8·11	20·27	28·38
1919–20	46·07	29·21	76·40	11·24	12·36	23·60
1920–21	40·22	38·04	79·35	9·78	10·87	20·65
1921–22	37·66	25·97	64·94	18·18	16·88	35·06
1922–23	48·00	29·00	78·00	13·00	9·00	22·00
1923–24	39·05	34·29	73·33	11·43	15·24	26·67
1924–25	39·00	31·00	70·00	19·00	11·00	30·00
1925–26	31·46	30·34	61·80	19·10	19·10	38·20
1926–27	34·74	32·63	67·37	15·79	16·84	32·63
1927–28	33·33	27·16	61·73	25·93	12·35	38·27
1928–29	32·65	34·69	67·35	20·41	12·24	32·65
1929–30	29·55	39·77	71·59	11·36	17·05	28·41
1930–31	35·96	32·58	70·79	20·22	8·99	29·21
1931–32	35·24	32·38	68·57	18·10	13·33	31·43
1932–33	36·84	31·58	71·58	13·68	14·74	28·42
1933–34	31·48	28·70	60·19	26·85	12·96	39·81

TABLE XXI*d*

PERCENTAGES OF SCHOLARSHIPS FOR MODERN SUBJECTS BY TYPES OF SCHOOLS

TO OXFORD

Year	"P"	"PD"	"P"+"PD"+"SN"	"CS"	"SS"	"CS"+"SS"
1913–14	64·86	21·62	86·49	10·81	2·70	13·51
1919–20	63·41	21·95	87·80	4·88	7·32	12·20
1920–21	76·47	7·84	86·27	7·84	5·88	13·73
1921–22	76·92	17·31	84·62	7·69	7·69	15·38
1922–23	57·14	26·79	85·71	7·14	7·14	14·29
1923–24	68·33	18·33	86·67	5·00	8·33	13·33
1924–25	52·54	28·81	83·05	8·47	8·47	16·95
1925–26	46·38	31·88	79·71	11·59	8·70	20·29
1926–27	58·21	20·90	79·10	17·91	2·99	20·90
1927–28	56·25	21·88	81·25	14·06	4·69	18·75
1928–29	52·11	22·54	77·46	16·90	5·63	22·54
1929–30	55·71	22·86	80·00	15·71	4·29	20·00
1930–31	41·46	25·61	68·29	20·73	10·98	31·71
1931–32	55·13	23·08	80·77	11·54	7·69	19·23
1932–33	53·25	27·27	80·52	9·09	10·39	19·48
1933–34	47·89	28·17	76·06	11·27	12·68	23·94

TO CAMBRIDGE

Year	"P"	"PD"	"P"+"PD"+"SN"	"CS"	"SS"	"CS"+"SS"
1913–14	46·43	25·00	71·43	21·43	7·14	28·57
1919–20	50·00	17·65	73·53	11·76	14·71	26·47
1920–21	43·18	27·27	70·45	11·36	18·18	29·55
1921–22	46·00	18·00	66·00	6·00	28·00	34·00
1922–23	46·15	21·54	70·77	12·31	16·92	29·23
1923–24	33·33	35·29	74·51	13·73	11·76	25·49
1924–25	44·83	25·86	74·14	17·24	8·62	25·86
1925–26	42·03	17·39	65·22	14·49	20·29	34·78
1926–27	27·42	38·71	72·58	17·74	9·68	27·42
1927–28	26·23	31·15	59·02	22·95	18·03	40·98
1928–29	42·62	22·95	68·85	19·67	11·48	31·15
1929–30	36·51	25·40	66·67	19·05	14·29	33·33
1930–31	37·50	31·25	71·88	17·19	10·94	28·13
1931–32	32·93	35·37	71·95	14·63	13·41	28·05
1932–33	36·90	28·57	65·48	21·43	13·10	34·52
1933–34	31·46	32·58	66·29	15·73	17·98	33·71

TO OXFORD AND CAMBRIDGE

Year	"P"	"PD"	"P"+"PD"+"SN"	"CS"	"SS"	"CS"+"SS"
1913–14	56·92	23·08	80·00	15·38	4·62	20·00
1919–20	57·33	20·00	81·33	8·00	10·67	18·67
1920–21	61·05	16·84	78·95	9·47	11·58	21·05
1921–22	55·88	17·65	75·49	6·86	17·65	24·51
1922–23	51·24	23·97	77·69	9·92	12·40	22·31
1923–24	52·25	26·13	81·08	9·01	9·91	18·92
1924–25	48·72	27·35	78·63	12·82	8·55	21·37
1925–26	44·20	24·64	72·46	13·04	14·49	27·54
1926–27	43·41	29·46	75·97	17·83	6·20	24·03
1927–28	41·60	26·40	70·40	18·40	11·20	29·60
1928–29	47·73	22·73	73·48	18·18	8·33	26·52
1929–30	46·62	24·06	73·68	17·29	9·02	26·32
1930–31	39·73	28·08	69·86	19·18	10·96	30·14
1931–32	43·75	29·38	76·25	13·13	10·63	23·75
1932–33	44·72	27·95	72·67	15·53	11·80	27·33
1933–34	38·75	30·63	70·63	13·75	15·63	29·38

types of schools. It is in this subject that their pupils win most of their scholarships. It is highly probable that the preponderating share of college scholarships restricted to classical subjects is at least partly responsible for the large number of successful candidates from Public Schools. In other faculties the "CS" and "SS" Schools have been able to make headway, their percentages in the period 1913–34 having risen from 18·42 to 33·33 per cent in Mathematics, from 28·38 to 39·81 per cent in Science and from 20·00 to 29·38 in Modern Subjects.

In the discussion of educational advantages, of the kind that

TABLE XXII

NUMBER OF PUPILS PER MEMBER OF STAFF

Type of School	Number of Schools in Sample	Total number of Pupils	Total number of Staff	Pupils per one Member of Staff
"P"	74	25,459	1,812	14
"PD"	54	25,416	1,226	21
"SN"	21	2,827	201	14
"SS"	99	27,240	1,299	21
"CS"	243	87,692	3,889	23
"P" + "PD"	128	50,875	3,038	17
"P" + "PD" + "SN"	149	53,702	3,239	17
"SS" + "CS"	342	114,932	5,188	22

assist pupils to win college entrance scholarships, two further issues are important, namely, the number of pupils per member of regular full-time teaching staff and the proportion of graduate to non-graduate members thereof. Table XXII gives the data concerning the relation between the size of the teaching staff and the number of pupils in schools of different type.

Between the "P" Schools with 14 boys and the "CS." Schools with 23 boys per staff member there is a difference in educational practice which may contribute powerfully to the differential ability of boys to win scholarships to Oxford and Cambridge.

Table XXIII shows the graduate qualifications of the teaching staff in different types of schools.

While there is no significant difference with respect to the percentage of non-graduates, striking discrepancies are observed in the propor-

TABLE XXIII

GRADUATE QUALIFICATIONS OF STAFFS

Type of School	Oxford Graduates	Percentage	Cambridge Graduates	Percentage	Oxford and Cambridge Graduates combined	Percentage	Other University Graduates	Percentage	Non-Graduates	Percentage
"P"	713	39·3	806	44·5	1,519	83·8	198	10·9	95	5·2
"PD"	338	27·6	440	35·9	778	63·5	388	31·6	60	4·9
"SN"	31	15·4	49	24·4	80	39·8	96	47·8	25	12·4
"SS"	207	15·9	225	17·3	432	33·2	752	57·9	115	8·9
"CS"	300	7·7	340	8·7	640	16·4	2,896	74·5	353	9·1
"P" + "PD"	1,051	34·6	1,246	41·0	2,297	75·6	586	19·3	155	5·1
"P" + "PD" + "SN"	1,082	33·4	1,295	40·0	2,377	73·4	682	21·1	180	5·6
"SS" + "CS"	507	9·8	565	10·9	1,072	20·7	3,648	70·3	468	9·0

TABLE XXIVa

AVERAGE AGE AT AWARD OF ENTRANCE SCHOLARSHIP

To OXFORD

Type of School		1913–14	1919–20	1920–21	1921–22	1922–23	1923–24	1924–25	1925–26
"P"	Number in Sample	40	33	33	36	47	37	29	30
	Average Age	18·29	17·94	17·79	18·40	18·27	18·35	18·23	18·33
"PD"	Number in Sample	13	18	5	16	22	13	23	14
	Average Age	18·21	18·54	18·32	18·07	18·30	18·21	18·20	18·35
	Difference from "P"	−0·08	+0·60	+0·53	−0·33	+0·03	−0·14	−0·03	+0·02
"CS"	Number in Sample	3	2	8	13	13	9	17	15
	Average Age	18·19	18·21	17·22	18·10	17·74	17·99	17·58	17·96
	Difference from "P"	−0·10	+0·27	−0·57	−0·30	−0·53	−0·36	−0·65	−0·37
	Difference from "PD"	−0·02	−0·33	−1·10	+0·03	−0·56	−0·22	−0·62	−0·39
"SS"	Number in Sample	1	4	7	2	3	2	4	5
	Average Age	17·33	18·11	18·68	18·34	17·53	18·46	17·83	18·32
	Difference from "P"	−0·96	+0·17	+0·89	−0·06	−0·74	+0·11	−0·40	−0·01
"SN"	Number in Sample	0	1	1	1	0	0	1	3
	Average Age	0	18·33	17·84	17·84	0	0	17·50	18·19

Table XXIV*a*—*continued*

AVERAGE AGE AT AWARD OF ENTRANCE SCHOLARSHIP

To Oxford

Type of School		1926-27	1927-28	1928-29	1929-30	1930-31	1931-32	1932-33	1933-34
"P"	Number in Sample	37	36	32	31	29	36	43	35
	Average Age	18·27	18·31	18·43	18·34	18·18	18·43	18·44	18·21
"PD"	Number in Sample	25	22	30	19	18	29	18	20
	Average Age	18·47	18·26	18·35	18·38	18·43	18·35	18·26	18·22
	Difference from "P"	+0·20	−0·05	−0·08	+0·04	+0·25	−0·08	−0·18	+0·01
"CS"	Number in Sample	13	10	22	16	23	25	17	20
	Average Age	17·80	18·24	18·06	17·90	18·28	18·13	18·18	18·13
	Difference from "P"	−0·47	−0·07	−0·37	−0·44	+0·10	−0·30	−0·26	−0·08
	Difference from "PD"	−0·67	−0·02	−0·29	−0·48	−0·15	−0·22	−0·08	−0·09
"SS"	Number in Sample	4	8	7	10	6	10	6	12
	Average Age	17·50	18·09	18·35	18·38	18·06	18·23	18·14	18·23
	Difference from "P"	−0·77	−0·22	−0·08	+0·04	−0·12	−0·20	−0·30	+0·02
"SN"	Number in Sample	0	0	0	4	0	1	3	0
	Average Age	0	0	0	18·00	0	18·17	18·11	0

TABLE XXIV*b*

AVERAGE AGE AT AWARD OF ENTRANCE SCHOLARSHIP

To CAMBRIDGE

Type of School		1913–14	1919–20	1920–21	1921–22	1922–23	1923–24	1924–25	1925–26
"P"	Number in Sample	30	20	25	17	21	32	18	17
	Average Age	18·53	18·03	18·28	18·15	18·10	18·38	18·28	18·18
"PD"	Number in Sample	18	15	21	16	19	24	36	28
	Average Age	18·34	18·37	18·37	18·26	18·37	18·53	18·30	18·31
	Difference from "P"	−0·19	+0·34	+0·09	+0·11	+0·27	+0·15	+0·02	+0·13
"CS"	Number in Sample	4	3	3	7	10	10	15	14
	Average Age	18·19	18·14	18·39	17·70	18·08	18·28	18·02	18·18
	Difference from "P"	−0·34	+0·11	+0·11	−0·45	−0·02	−0·10	−0·26	0
	Difference from "PD"	−0·15	−0·23	+0·02	−0·56	−0·29	−0·25	−0·28	−0·13
"SS"	Number in Sample	11	2	9	25	10	11	10	14
	Average Age	18·39	18·21	18·42	18·09	18·37	18·06	18·53	17·92
	Difference from "P"	−0·14	+0·18	+0·14	−0·06	+0·27	−0·32	+0·25	−0·26
"SS"	Number in Sample	0	1	1	1	2	1	1	2
	Average Age	0	18·33	18·33	18·50	18·00	17·75	18·17	18·42

Table XXIV*b*—continued

AVERAGE AGE AT AWARD OF ENTRANCE SCHOLARSHIP

To Cambridge

Type of School		1926–27	1927–28	1928–29	1929–30	19_0–31	1931–32	1932–33	1933–34
"P"	Number in Sample	21	26	25	24	24	30	24	42
	Average Age	18·10	18·23	18·12	18·14	18·17	18·51	18·09	18·11
"PD"	Number in Sample	27	26	16	21	28	20	33	20
	Average Age	18·14	18·37	18·59	18·21	18·18	18·15	18·32	18·37
	Difference from "P"	+0·04	+0·14	+0·47	+0·07	+0·01	−0·36	+0·23	+0·26
"CS"	Number in Sample	16	16	5	11	12	23	23	26
	Average Age	17·98	18·48	18·19	17·94	18·08	18·01	18·05	18·24
	Difference from "P"	−0·12	+0·25	+0·07	−0·20	−0·09	−0·50	−0·04	+0·13
	Difference from "PD"	−0·16	+0·11	−0·40	−0·27	−0·10	−0·14	−0·27	−0·13
"SS"	Number in Sample	14	17	17	13	12	15	19	17
	Average Age	18·07	18·11	18·13	18·10	17·89	18·14	17·99	18·06
	Difference from "P"	−0·03	−0·12	+0·01	−0·04	−0·28	−0·37	−0·10	−0·05
"SN"	Number in Sample	2	0	2	0	2	2	0	2
	Average Age	17·96	0	18·58	0	18·34	18·63	0	17·63

TABLE XXIVc

AVERAGE AGE AT AWARD OF ENTRANCE SCHOLARSHIP

To Oxford and Cambridge

Type of School			1913-14	1919-20	1920-21	1921-22	1922-23	1923-24	1924-25	1925-26
"P"	Number in Sample	.. ..	70	53	58	53	68	69	47	47
	Average Age ..	.. ..	18·39	17·97	18·00	18·32	18·22	18·36	18·25	18·24
"PD"	Number in Sample	.. ..	31	33	26	32	41	37	59	42
	Average Age ..	.. ..	18·29	18·47	18·36	18·16	18·33	18·41	18·26	18·32
	Difference from "P"	.. ..	-0·10	+0·50	+0·36	-0·16	+0·11	+0·05	+0·01	+0·08
"P" & "PD"	Number in Sample	.. ..	101	86	84	85	109	106	106	89
	Average Age ..	.. ..	18·36	18·16	18·11	18·26	18·26	18·38	18·26	18·30
"CS"	Number in Sample	.. ..	7	5	11	20	23	19	32	29
	Average Age ..	.. ..	18·19	18·17	17·53	17·86	17·89	18·14	17·79	18·07
	Difference from "P"	.. ..	-0·20	+0·20	-0·47	-0·46	-0·33	-0·22	-0·46	-0·17
	Difference from "PD"	.. ..	-0·10	-0·30	-0·83	-0·30	-0·44	-0·27	-0·47	-0·25
	Difference from "P" + "PD"	.. ..	-0·17	-0·01	-0·58	-0·40	-0·37	-0·24	-0·47	-0·23
"SS"	Number in Sample	.. ..	12	6	16	27	13	13	14	19
	Average Age ..	.. ..	18·30	18·14	18·10	18·05	18·18	18·12	18·33	18·03
	Difference from "P"	.. ..	-0·09	+0·17	+0·10	-0·27	-0·04	-0·24	+0·08	-0·21
	Difference from "P" + "PD"	.. ..	-0·06	-0·02	-0·01	-0·21	-0·08	-0·26	+0·07	-0·27
"SN"	Number in Sample	.. ..	0	2	2	2	2	1	2	5
	Average Age ..	.. ..	0	18·33	18·09	18·18	18·00	17·75	17·84	18·28

TABLE XXIVc—*continued*

AVERAGE AGE AT AWARD OF ENTRANCE SCHOLARSHIP

To Oxford and Cambridge

Type of School			1926–27	1927–28	1928–29	1929–30	1930–31	1931–32	1932–33	1933–34	Averages
"P"	Number in Sample	.. ..	58	62	57	55	53	66	67	77	960
	Average Age	.. ..	18·21	18·28	18·29	18·25	18·18	18·47	18·31	18·16	18·25
"PD"	Number in Sample	..	52	48	46	40	46	49	51	40	673
	Average Age	..	18·30	18·32	18·43	18·29	18·28	18·27	18·30	18·29	18·32
	Difference from "P"	..	+0·09	+0·04	+0·14	+0·04	+0·10	−0·20	−0·01	+0·13	+0·07
"P" & "PD"	Number in Sample	.. ..	110	110	103	95	99	115	118	117	1,633
	Average Age	.. ..	18·25	18·29	18·36	18·27	18·22	18·38	18·31	18·20	18·28
"CS"	Number in Sample	.. ..	29	26	37	27	35	48	40	46	434
	Average Age	.. ..	17·90	18·39	18·11	17·92	18·21	18·07	18·11	18·19	18·06
	Difference from "P"	..	−0·31	+0·11	+0·18	−0·33	+0·03	−0·40	−0·20	+0·03	−0·19
	Difference from "PD" ..		−0·40	+0·07	−0·32	−0·37	−0·07	−0·20	−0·19	−0·10	−20·6
	Difference from "P" + "PD"		−0·35	+0·10	−0·25	−0·35	−0·01	−0·31	−0·20	−0·01	−0·22
"SS"	Number in Sample	.. ..	18	25	24	23	18	25	25	29	307
	Average Age	.. ..	17·94	18·10	18·19	18·22	17·95	18·18	18·03	18·13	18·14
	Difference from "P" ..		−0·27	−0·18	−0·10	−0·03	−0·23	−0·29	−0·28	−0·03	−0·11
	Difference from "P" + "PD"		−0·31	−0·19	−0·17	−0·05	−0·27	−0·20	−0·28	−0·07	−0·14
"SN"	Number in Sample	.. ..	2	0	2	4	2	3	3	2	—
	Average Age	..	17·98	0	18·58	18·00	18·34	18·65	18·11	17·67	—

tions of teachers educated at the older Universities. With their greater pre-knowledge of the requirements of college examinations teachers who are graduates of Oxford or Cambridge are obviously more useful to their pupils than those who come from other Universities. The extent of the discrepancy is remarkable. Whereas in "P" and "PD" Schools 75·6 per cent of the regular staff were graduates of Oxford or Cambridge, in "SS" and "CS" Schools the corresponding figure was only 20·7 per cent.

A final issue deserves attention. In "CS" and "SS" Schools the

TABLE XXV

MEAN AGES OF BOYS AT DATE OF SCHOLARSHIP AWARD

AVERAGE FOR PERIOD 1913-34

Type of School	Average Age in Years	Difference from "P" (+ or −)	Difference from "PD" (+ or −)	Difference from "P" and "PD" (+ or −)
"P"	18·25	—	—	—
"PD"	18·32	—	—	—
"P" + "PD"	18·28	—	—	—
"SS"	18·14	−0·11	−0·18	−0·14
"CS"	18·06	−0·19	−0·26	−0·22

fact that their parents are relatively poor means a continual time-pressure upon the boys. It must be their object, if destined for the University, to proceed thereto as quickly as possible in order to reduce the financial sacrifices of their parents. Thus the period of study between matriculation and the second approved examination or between it and entrance to the University is likely to be as short as custom will permit. In the Public Schools, however, such considerations do not weigh so heavily and it is highly probable that pupils spend a longer period in preparing themselves for scholarship examinations. Clearly, this would enhance their prospects of success. To test this possibility the sample of questionnaires returned to us was analysed and the results are tabulated in Tables XXIV*a*, *b*, and *c*.

Unfortunately the number of scholars for whom we have complete information is rather small, namely, 2,374 for the period 1913 to 1934, or some 30 per cent of the total. Nevertheless the figures are fairly consistent throughout. The tables show the difference in the mean ages of boys from different types of schools at the dates when scholarship results were announced. Taking "CS" Schools, the mean ages show a negative difference as compared with "P" Schools in twelve years out of sixteen and compared with "PD" Schools in fifteen years out of sixteen. The "SS" Schools show similar differences in thirteen years compared with "P" and in fifteen years compared with "PD" Schools. Table XXV averages the figures for the entire period.

It is not easy to assess the significance of these differences. In absolute terms they are small, but a difference of two or three months in preparation for a competitive scholarship examination may possibly be of critical importance in some cases.

VI. SUMMARY

1. In the academic year 1933–34 ex-Elementary School pupils constituted 27 per cent of the male undergraduate population of the Universities (excluding University colleges) of England and Wales. They amounted to just over one-half per cent of the appropriate age-group of Elementary School origin. The remainder probably represented about 20 per cent of the appropriate age-group of fee-paying school origin. Thus the opportunities enjoyed by the latter class of proceeding to a University were about thirty times greater than those of ex-Elementary School pupils.

2. If we consider only ex-Elementary School pupils whose Secondary School education was also free, they amounted to 22 per cent of the University population, and the disparity in University opportunities was over forty to one in favour of boys educated in fee-paying schools.

3. At Oxford University ex-Elementary schoolboys constituted 12 per cent, and at Cambridge University 13 per cent of the total male undergraduate population (Secondary School free-placers only —10 and 11 per cent respectively). Students beginning their education in fee-paying schools enjoyed opportunities of proceeding to these Universities ninety times greater than ex-Elementary schoolboys (one hundred and ten times, if we compare them only with Secondary School free-placers).

4. In general the higher the average fees paid in different types of grant-aided schools the lower was the proportion of free places

available to ex-Elementary schoolboys. Fifty-eight per cent of Public Schools in receipt of grants-in-aid offer less than the usual minimum of 25 per cent of free places.

5. In 1913–14 Public and Private Schools obtained 89 per cent of all college entrance scholarships (open and closed) at Oxford and 85 per cent at Cambridge. In 1933–34 the corresponding figures were 78 and 74 per cent.

6. When we consider their respective populations, Public Schools obtain about six such scholarships per thousand boys and other Secondary Schools about 0·6 per thousand, giving a ratio of about ten to one in favour of the former.

7. Taking open scholarships alone, 53 per cent are awarded to pupils of Public and Private Schools, whose chances of winning them are between three and four times greater than those of other Secondary schoolboys.

8. Of closed scholarships restricted to certain schools, 241 are available to Public Schools and 50 to other Secondary Schools, a ratio of sixteen to one in favour of the former when the figures are related to the respective school populations.

9. In the case of State scholarships tenable at Oxford and Cambridge at least three times as many per thousand boys are awarded to grant-aided Public Schools as are given to other Secondary Schools.

10. Of Kitchener scholars proceeding to the older Universities 70 per cent are boys from Public Schools. The children of the officer class probably receive ten times as many as they would on a purely population basis and the children of other ranks one-third, making a total disparity ratio in educational advantages of about thirty to one in favour of the former.

11. The average annual value per hundred boys of leaving scholarships awarded by schools themselves increases as the size of the average fee increases, as ascertained by a sample investigation.

12. The fifteen most expensive Public Schools obtained an average of 50 per cent of college scholarships awarded to all Public Schools. Eton, Harrow, and Winchester accounted for an average of 14 per cent of the total. Pupils attending these schools have a chance at least three times greater than other public schoolboys of obtaining a college scholarship at Oxford or Cambridge.

13. About 32 per cent of entrance scholarships at the older Universities are awarded in the subject of Classics. Of these 92 per

cent go to pupils of Public Schools. Under 30 per cent of scholarships are awarded in Modern Subjects and under 20 per cent in Natural Science. Public Schools obtained 70 per cent of the former and 60 per cent of the latter.

14. Public (boarding) Schools have one full-time teacher to every fourteen boys, and County Secondary Schools one to every twenty-three, as ascertained by a sample investigation.

15. Seventy-five per cent of the full-time teaching staff of Public Schools are graduates of Oxford and Cambridge, contrasted with 21 per cent in the case of other Secondary Schools, as ascertained by a sample investigation.

16. The average age of scholarship-winning boys at the date of the scholarship award was 18·28 years in the case of Public Schools and 18·06 in the case of County Secondary Schools, as ascertained by a sample investigation. This makes a difference of 2·6 months.

CHAPTER XI

THE RELATION BETWEEN INITIAL AND MAXIMUM EARNINGS AND DIFFERENTIAL FERTILITY OF SKILLED AND UNSKILLED WAGE-EARNERS

by

ENID CHARLES

and

DAVID MORGAN

I. INTRODUCTION

SINCE the existence of differential fertility with respect to occupational and social status was first emphasized by Bertillon at the beginning of this century, its significance from the standpoint of genetic selection has prompted vigorous discussion. A widespread view is summed up in the following assertions: (i) that existing inequalities of remuneration encourage the selection of individuals with special capabilities for social advancement, (ii) that individual differences with respect to vocational aptitude are largely due to differences in genetic constitution, and (iii) that since fertility is lowest at social levels to which individuals with specialized capability are promoted, social selection favours the survival of the less gifted section of the population. Hence it is argued that the biological resources of social efficiency are being squandered and that further improvement in the social machinery for the recruitment of gifted personnel will accentuate the disastrous consequences of existing class differences with respect to fertility.

How far this is true, and how far, therefore, it is a valid justification for failure to remove impediments to the wastage of human ability depends on several considerations which are commonly overlooked. One is, how far differential fertility is a relatively permanent or ephemeral feature of our civilization. Relevant information bearing on this question has been discussed in Chapters III and IV. A second is, how far the characteristics of different social groups are determined by social tradition and physical circumstances. At present there is little exact information which bears on this. A third is, the extent of mobility and the agencies which affect it. One aspect of this problem is the subject of this study.

Prevailing views about social selection may be compared with some of the speculations concerning natural selection current among biologists of an earlier generation. For instance, it is an attractive hypothesis to assume that such phenomena as mimicry or protective coloration are due to the selective advantages gained by a species in avoiding its enemies or remaining concealed from prey, and it was at one time customary for naturalists to indulge freely in speculations of this sort. From the standpoint of modern biology, such speculations may introduce a number of gratuitous assumptions which can only be justified by direct experiment. For instance, the fact that an animal which possesses the power of colour response is on that account difficult for a human being to recognize in certain situations does not necessarily signify that the chromatic function helps to conceal it from other animals which would devour it, or from other animals on which it feeds. It may be that its prey or natural enemies are chiefly guided by the sense of smell. It may be that its prey or natural enemies have a range of visual discrimination different from human beings. If so, the apparent similarity between the animal and its surroundings may be, as far as its chances of survival are concerned, negligible. In studying social selection we must be on our guard against the same teleological attitude. For instance, the fact that remuneration in occupations which call for special aptitude is often greater than for occupations which do not, does not necessarily imply that inequalities of remuneration provide an incentive to induce individuals with special aptitudes to take up vocations which make the fullest use of them.

That this is so is easily seen with the help of an example. Few will dispute that the calling of a surgeon demands more specialized capability than that of a country practitioner or that the rewards of the former may be far greater than those of the latter. On the other hand it would be foolish to argue that surgeons are recruited from a wider range of social personnel than country practitioners. While it is true that a surgeon's emoluments, taken over the whole period of his professional life, may be much greater than that of a medical man in country practice, it is equally true that the latter gains a modest competence soon after he qualifies, while the surgeon must work for many years, during which period he scarcely covers his living expenses. Clearly the so-called law of supply and demand has little relevance to the nature of social selection in this case.

If the parental income of two individuals of equal surgical

capability is the same, parental fertility will be a decisive feature of the selective process. A qualified man whose parents have other children to educate will have more inducement to choose a course which makes him self-supporting as early as possible. Similarly, if two individuals, both, let us say, only children, have parents whose incomes differ appreciably, parental income may be the decisive feature of the selective process. The individual whose parent has the larger income will be free to pursue the course which offers the possibility of a larger reward in the long run. Either way, the individual who chooses the latter course will generally delay marriage, and hence will be more likely to have a smaller family. Thus the inequality of reward diminishes the intensity of selection with respect to ability instead of reinforcing it, and the same agencies which operate to limit the efficiency of social selection also operate to favour differential fertility, instead of acting, as is commonly argued, in the opposite sense.

This example is chosen for illustrative reasons, and the fact that initial assumptions about scarcity of capability for surgical or general practice is an admittedly debatable issue, does not invalidate its usefulness in drawing attention to an aspect of social selection which is commonly overlooked. In general terms it is as follows. Whether inequality of remuneration restricts or enlarges the available fund of capability from which the personnel of a particular vocation is drawn depends on the inequality which exists *at the time when the decisive choice is made.* If high maximal earnings are associated with low initial earnings, or a prolonged and expensive course of training, they may operate to select such qualities as financial shrewdness, self-advancement, thrift, or infertility. Since there is no reason to suppose that any of these qualities are associated with special aptitudes for craftsmanship, technical performance, or creative intellectual work, the general effect of a high correlation between low initial and high maximal earnings will be to reduce the efficiency of social selection in so far as earning power affects the choice of a vocation.

Few people would assert that the machinery of social selection is such that the demand for specialized ability is perfectly adjusted to the supplies available, or that the so-called law of supply and demand operates smoothly over the whole range of vocational choice. Difference of opinion only arises concerning how far an example such as that given is representative or exceptional. For the large section of the population generally classified as wage-earners, there is ample material for reaching a decision.

The wage-earning classes are customarily divided into skilled, semi-skilled, and unskilled categories, according to the special capability required for the work performed. Broadly speaking, the maximal earnings of skilled wage-earners are greater than those of unskilled. The object of this study is to examine the effective financial inducement at the time when the dichotomy takes place, that is to say, at the age of leaving the elementary school and in the years which immediately follow it.

II. GENERAL SURVEY

The field of employment open to individual boys and girls is greatly circumscribed by the locality in which they live. As a general rule few seek employment far afield except through the medium of relatives or friends living at a distance. At one extreme this may limit a child's choice almost exclusively to one occupation, as in some coal-mining areas. At the other, most parts of London offer a wide choice of occupation. Further temporary fluctuations in unemployment may determine what vacancies are available at any given moment. Both these factors operate on single year age-groups in a small geographical area. In addition, factors determining the choice of employment are peculiar to the individual, such as the parents' knowledge and industrial experience, family circumstances, and the child's ability and initiative. A complete investigation of the problem would involve, therefore, following a group of children leaving almost every school up to the period of maximum earnings—a task of impracticable magnitude.

All that has been attempted in the present survey is a preliminary study of wage-rates applicable to different types of juvenile labour. Generally speaking, for any one industry juveniles engaged on different types of work may all be found in a single locality. For the large numbers of juveniles employed in London and in other big cities a comparison between rates of wages collected from several different industries is relevant. The rates of wages obtained cannot include every employee in any industry. Where they are the subject of national agreements or trade board regulations, there should be no employees getting less than the minimum stated. There may be some getting unascertained higher rates. Over the greater part of the field, however, there are no general agreements, and juvenile workers do not come within the scope of trade union organization. Thus little published material exists on juvenile wage-rates, and the lack of organization makes it very difficult to ascertain the general level of wages. An effort has been made to obtain fairly representative samples of wage-rates for juveniles in various industries, but it would seem likely that the sample rates obtained represent generally the better sections of the industry under investigation. Where the letter *c* occurs before a rate in the tables it indicates that the rate given is either the *median* or the *mode* (i.e. most frequent rate in a wide range). Where the range of wages only is known, the median is given, but where one rate was found to occur most frequently in a sample, this is given. Some of the corresponding ranges are shown in the figures.

Data have been obtained from four principal sources. (*a*) Ministry of Labour reports, in particular the Apprenticeship Report of 1928 and reports on standard Time-Rates. (*b*) Trade Board Regulations. (*c*) Lists of wage-rates furnished by various employers. (*d*) Agreements and sample wage-rates obtained from Trade Unions. In addition, the Clearing House Lists of the London Juvenile Employment Exchanges were analysed over a period of several weeks. It has not always been possible to obtain current rates of wages, but where the rates given relate to some years back, an endeavour has been made to ascertain whether there have been any significant changes in the ensuing period.

Types of juvenile labour fall into three main categories. (*a*) Apprentices. According to the Apprenticeship Report (vide supra), apprenticeship had decreased in amount between 1909 and 1928. We must distinguish here the main types of apprenticeship: ordinary apprenticeship, informal and involving no written agreement; indentured apprenticeship, involving a formally binding agreement, and premium apprenticeship, involving the payment of a premium as well as the signing of an agreement. While apprenticeship itself declined, informal apprenticeship increased relatively to the more rigid types of apprenticeship, the premium system especially declining rapidly. The importance of apprenticeship varies greatly from industry to industry. It is still the recognized mode of entry to certain skilled occupations, but in many large industries it is not found at all. No exact information exists as to the changes since 1928, but the general belief is that the proportion of apprentices has fallen still further. On the other hand, what appears to be a new type of apprenticeship has emerged. This will be referred to in the next section.

(*b*) Semi-skilled or learners. This is a very ill-defined category. In some of the newer and rapidly developing industries, a juvenile in this category may have the opportunity of acquiring a high degree of skill which may eventually place him or her almost if not quite on a level with the highly trained craftsmen in the older industries. At the other extreme, some branches of retail tailoring can be taken as an example. Here a skilled process has been highly subdivided, and although juveniles are taken on as learners, they do not acquire any skill beyond the aptitude for one very simple operation. In such industries a nominal system of learnership enables unskilled labour to be used for repetitive work at a low rate for this type of work.

(*c*) Unskilled. This category again covers a variety of types, including some in which increasing physical strength or length of experience may be an important factor.

Although this investigation is not specifically concerned with the question of blind-alley occupations, no discussion of rates of wages is possible without some consideration of the relation between juvenile and adult employment. In the 1931 census the ratio of juveniles to adults is given for each industry. Taken by themselves, however, these figures are not very informative. Those industries in which there was a high proportion of juvenile labour in 1931 were industries which had been rapidly expanding since 1921. Theoretically, the expansion which had occurred was sufficient in most cases to account for the excess of juveniles. Actually it is a matter of common knowledge that many trades and businesses are organized to run on a supply of juvenile labour or on juvenile and female labour. In some cases the wages are too low to attract adult males. Also the work may be so highly repetitive that a changing labour supply is almost inevitable, as in tailoring under the conveyor-belt system. In addition, there are the more specifically blind-alley jobs, such as van boys, errand boys and girls, and so on. Again theoretically, these juveniles might be absorbed into the industry as adults, but studies on this type of labour have shown that there is a great deal of drifting usually ending in the ranks of adult unskilled labour. The dislocation involved is reflected in the unemployment figures for juveniles, which show a big jump at the age of 18, and again at 21, when there is a tendency on the part of the juvenile worker to expect an adult wage, and a disinclination on the part of the employer to pay it. This point will be further discussed in connection with the separate industries.

In this connection, the fluctuations in the numbers of juveniles are not unimportant. In recent years the numbers of school-leavers have been small until 1935, which was a record 14–15 age-group, due to the post-war rise in births. From now onwards the numbers will decline, and the reduction in the supply of juvenile labour may have interesting repercussions in industry.

In most cases a very wide range of wages is found for any given type of labour, so that it is seldom easy to determine the typical or average wage. The same difficulty arises with adult rates of wages, though the gap between minimum rates for skilled and unskilled work is generally fairly clear. The material advantages of the skilled category have changed somewhat since the war. Before the war the skilled craftsman was in a privileged position. The pressure of armament manufacture during the war changed the position considerably, especially in engineering. It speeded up the subdivision and mechanization of processes, and broke down craft barriers, so that the less difficult work could be done by people who had had no regular apprenticeship. Changes of the same sort have gone on ever since, and have affected most branches of industry to some extent. This is reflected in the change in the relative wages of skilled and unskilled.

Before the war the skilled man who had served his apprenticeship was in a very favourable position both as regards higher wages and greater security of employment. Since the war employment has become less secure, and the wage difference in favour of the skilled adult worker has been reduced. The position varies from industry to industry; the levelling has been greatest in building, where in 1926 the rates of the semi-skilled were equal to those of the skilled, while those of the unskilled were 77 per cent of the skilled rate, as compared with 66 per cent in 1913 and 62 per cent in 1886. In most other industries the same process has gone on, though to a less marked extent.[1] The recent increase in armament production has, however, led to a shortage of highly skilled labour, and the position may be changing in the reverse direction.

A further factor which has to be considered is the rate of progress towards the maximum adult wage. The tendency for unskilled rates to rise somewhat suddenly at 18 and again at 21 (especially for

[1] Rowe, *Wages in Theory and Practice.*

males) has already been referred to. The full adult wage is usually reached at 21. Apprenticeship usually ends at 21 also, but there is often a period of two or three years at improver's rates before the craftsman's rate is reached. This difference is not shown in the tables.

Table I shows the principal industries investigated, together with the numbers of juveniles employed at the 1931 census. These figures are given in order to indicate the relative importance of the industry in the field of juvenile employment.

TABLE I

INDUSTRIES COVERED

NUMBER OF JUVENILES OCCUPIED (1931 CENSUS) (IN THOUSANDS)
In brackets Juveniles as Percentage of all Employees

Industry				Males		Females	
Engineering	..	..	..	223	(16·6 %)	41	(42·3 %)
Distribution:							
Shop Assistants	..	..	..	172	(40·4 %)	176	(43·2 %)
Warehousemen, etc.	..	..	..	45		78	
Messengers	..	..	..	160	(89·8 %)	15	(93·6 %)
Shop Roundsmen, etc.	..	..	..	34		—	
Personal Service	..	..	..	58	(12·4 %)	523	(27·2 %)
Building	..	..	..	49	(7·1 %)	—	
Railways	..	..	..	12	(4·2 %)	—	
Wood and Furniture	..	..	..	92	(18·4 %)	8	(38·9 %)
Tailoring	..	..	..	10	(16·2 %)	83	(35·2 %)
Printing	..	..	..	29	(19·3 %)	17	(45·4 %)
Woollen Manufacture	..	..	..	—		—	
All Textiles	..	..	..	40	(13·1 %)	134	(23·2 %)
Bricks, Pottery, Glass	..	..	..	13	(16·7 %)	*7	(27·4 %)
Chemicals	..	..	..	2	(5·0 %)	—	
Foods, Drinks, Tobacco	..	..	..	24	(15·6 %)	28	(36·9 %)
Mining	..	..	..	146	(15·6 %)	—	

*Pottery.

III. ENGINEERING

The time-rates obtained in the engineering industry are shown in Table II. The rates are not entirely comparable, since they refer to several distinct branches of the industry. The London time-rates for apprentices and unskilled are comparable, as are the Tyne fitters and turners' apprentice rates and the unskilled Tyne time-rates. Also rates are given for both groups by a Sheffield and a Middlesex firm. In London the apprentice rates are about 2s. a week lower right through as compared with an adult minimum rate 10s. per week higher. In the case of the two firms given, the difference is greater, being as much as 5s. or 6s. a week at some ages. Both show a larger increase at 18 characteristic of many unskilled rates, so that the unskilled rate at 18 in Sheffield is not reached by the apprentices until 20. It will be seen that the wage-rates paid in the recently established motor industry in Oxford lie quite outside the range of wages shown in the rest of the table.

The table gives time-rates only, but piece-work is very common in this industry. Where practised, it accentuates the wage difference between apprentices and others, as apprentices are not normally put on piece-work. Boys on piece-work usually earn about 25 per cent more than the standard time-rates. According to the Employers' Association, in Birmingham, Derby, Doncaster, Tyne, and Sheffield, the same time-rates generally apply to boys and apprentices, the only difference being that boys very often are on piece-work, while apprentices get the time-rates only. The time-rates referred to are shown in the table except those for Derby, which are almost the same as the Sheffield rates. Piece-work sometimes militates against the acquisition of skill, since a boy who has become adept on one machine at piece-rates is unwilling to go on to a different machine, where his earnings would be lower during the period of learning.

According to the Apprenticeship Report, 32 per cent of all juveniles in engineering were apprentices, and 11 per cent learners. Although no figures are available, it is generally believed that the proportion of apprentices has been falling since that date. The number of female metal workers is given in the 1931 census as 32·8 per cent of the whole, and no female apprentices were recorded. Their numbers had increased considerably, while those of male workers had diminished; 423 out of every 1,000 women were under 21, as compared with 166 out of every 1,000 men. The only specifically female rates ascertained were employers' agreed rates for London unskilled labour. These are similar to those for males. At the earlier ages they are very slightly higher, but lower from 18 onwards, the rate at 20 being 26s. 8d. compared with 32s. 3¾d. for males. Some of the more typical wage-rates given in Table II are shown graphically in Fig. 1 for Great Britain, and in Fig. 2 for London.

A modern development in engineering, associated with the general decline in apprenticeship and the need to retain a small

TABLE II

ENGINEERING WAGE-RATES: MALES

APPRENTICES / LEARNERS

Age	London Time-rates*	Middlesex Firm†	Sheffield Firm (Steel)†	Tyne Fitters and Turners‡	Ministry of Labour Apprentices Report	Clearing-house Lists, London	Ministry of Labour Apprentices Report
14	10/ 2·4	11/9	10/—	—	—	c. 12/—	—
15	12/ 0·3	15/8	12/6	—	c. 10/7	c. 12/9	c. 11/1
16	14/ 4·2	19/7	15/—	c. 10/—	—	c. 18/—	—
17	17/11·4	25/5	17/6	c. 12/3	—	c. 28/—	—
18	22/ 6·6	31/4	22/6	c. 15/—	—	—	—
19	27/ 1·8	37/2	30/—	c. 17/6	c. 25/8	—	c. 30/9
20	34/ 0·3	43/1	—	c. 21/3	—	—	—
21	—	58/9	—	—	—	—	—
22	—	—	—	—	—	—	—
Adult	—	—	—	—	54/— to 69/6	Usually piece-rates	

UNSKILLED

Age	London Time-rates*	Clearing-house Lists, London	Oxford Motors†	Birmingham Firm†	Doncaster‡ and Sheffield†	Birmingham Time-rates‡	Tyne Time-rates‡	Sheffield Time-rates
14	11/9	c. 12/—	18/4	16/4	13/—	10/—	c. 8/3	10/—
15	14/2¼	c. 15/—	27/6	18/8	15/—	12/—	c. 9/0½	12/6
16	16/7¼	c. 20/—	36/8	24/—	17/—	15/—	c. 14/—	15/—
17	20/6¾	c. 20/—	45/10	29/5	19/—	19/—	c. 16/3	17/6
18	24/5¾	—	55/—	35/1	28/—	23/—	c. 19/—	20/—
19	28/4¾	—	64/2	39/1	30/—	27/—	c. 23/—	25/—
20	32/3¾	—	73/4	47/5	32/—	31/—	c. 28/3	30/—
21	—	—	82/6	—	—	—	—	—
22	—	—	91/8	—	—	—	—	—
Adult	45/3½	—	—	—	—	45/6 to 49/—	—	—

* Agreed time-rates quoted in *Guide to Employment for Boys and Girls in London*, 1928.   † Rates given by individual firms.
‡ Rates of Employers' Associations.

corps of highly skilled technicians for tool-making and other vital processes, has been the emergence of a new type of apprentice, commonly called the "gentleman apprentice." A large motor works

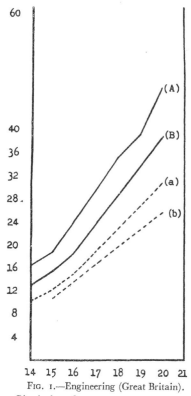

FIG. 1.—Engineering (Great Britain).

A. Rate given by a Birmingham firm.
B. Piece-work basis rate in Birmingham. For many juveniles, but not apprentices.
a. Time-rate in Birmingham for all juveniles.
b. Average apprentices' wages (1928 Report).

with 20,000 employees, for example, takes boys at 16 or 17 years for apprenticeship until the age of 21. The conditions for these apprentices give some indication of the social nature of this new class; they must have had a "public school or high-grade secondary school education, and have at least passed the School Certificate Examination. . . ." They start at 10s. a week, and they pay a compulsory subscription of £10 10s. to the Sports Fund, on entering the works. An additional allowance of 5s. per week is made to junior prefects, and 7s. 6d. a week to senior prefects. We have been informed

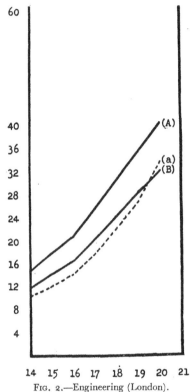

FIG. 2.—Engineering (London).

A. Recognized piece-work minimum rate.
B. Recognized time-rate minimum.
a. Recognized rate for apprentices.

that this practice in another large industrial undertaking has encouraged periodic contests between the gentlemen apprentices and authentic workmen as a leisure-time pursuit. Since we have not been able to obtain statistics of the frequency of such contests, the number of persons involved, or the injuries sustained, we cannot bring these within the scope of Sir William Petty's design for a Politicall Arithmitick.

Here we encounter a new type of social selection, which reserves a sphere of highly skilled industrial activity for a privileged class.

IV. DISTRIBUTION

The distributive industry is a large one, employing about nine hundred thousand people, males and females in about equal numbers. The proportion of juveniles is high, 404 per thousand for males, and 432 per thousand for females. The industry is badly organized, except in the Co-operative Wholesale and Retail Societies, and outside these societies a very wide range of wages and conditions of unemployment is found. Table III shows the rates of wages found in the distributive industry. Apprenticeship is unimportant. Where it exists the rates are given from Ministry of Labour reports, and appear to be somewhat lower than those paid to unskilled assistants.

The most significant difference is found in the prospects of future employment. Many co-operative societies have trade union agreements which limit the number of juveniles to one in four of all employees. This is not much more than half the ratio for the industry as a whole. Even where no definite agreement exists, the tradition in the co-operative societies is one of continuous employment. Their rates of wages can be best compared with those of other shops by taking the London area alone. The rates are shown graphically in Fig. 3. It is important to note that the co-operative rates are standardized, while rates elsewhere vary considerably. Generally the co-operative rates are somewhat lower than others at the ages 14 to 16, though later they are higher. Trade union opinion holds that the possibility of higher initial wages elsewhere is sufficient to deter many juveniles from co-operative employment, in spite of the better prospects in later life. The table given does not include any rates from individual firms of high repute as employers.

The relation between rates for apprentices and unskilled in grocery is shown in Fig. 4.

Further samples of juvenile wage-rates obtained from the Middlesex County Council Education Committee showed that the London Clearing-house samples were not typical even of the "prosperous South." In the newer industrial districts around London wages seem to be rather lower, although the samples obtained were not wide enough for a detailed comparison to be made. In Middlesex, too, examples were found of surprisingly low

TABLE III
DISTRIBUTION
A.—MALES

ENGLAND AND WALES

Age	Co-operative Wholesale Society			Drapery*		Grocery†		Meat‡
	Clerks and Salesmen	Warehouse Workers	Porters, etc.	Apprentices	Unskilled	Apprentices	Unskilled	
14	12/-	11/-	10/-	c. 10/-	c. 13/-	10/- to 12/6	c. 12/6	c. 14/6
15	15/-	14/-	13/-				c. 12/6	
16	19/-	18/-	17/-				c. 17/6	
17	24/-	23/-	21/-				c. 20/-	
18	30/-	29/-	26/-	15/- to 20/-	c. 27/-	20/-	c. 25/-	c. 25/-
19	38/-	35/-	32/-				c. 32/6	
20	46/-	42/-	39/-				c. 32/6	
21	56/-	52/-	48/-				c. 42/6	
22	60/-	56/-	52/-					
Adult	64/-	60/-	56/-		51/- to 86/-		55/- to 80/-	c. 55/- to 80/-

LONDON

PROVINCIAL

Age	Co-operative Wholesale Society			Drapery§			Miscellaneous‖	Grocery¶	Tailoring¶
	Clerks	Assistants	Warehouse Workers	Clerks and Assistants	Packers	Porters			
14	—	13/-	13/-	—	—	—	c. 15/-	c. 10/-	c. 10/-
15	16/6	15/-	15/-	—	—	—	c. 15/-	c. 11/6	c. 13/6
16	19/6	18/6	18/6	20/-	20/-	20/-	c. 20/-	c. 15/-	c. 15/-
17	27/6	22/6	22/6	25/-	25/-	25/-	c. 25/-	c. 15/-	c. 15/-
18	31/6	30/-	28/6	30/-	30/-	30/-	c. 30/-	c. 20/-	c. 18/9
19	39/6	36/-	34/6	35/-	35/-	35/-			
20	47/6	45/-	44/-	40/-	40/-	40/-			
21	56/-	55/-	53/-	48/-	48/-	46/-			
22	58/-	58/-	55/-	53/-	52/-	48/-			
Adult	65/- to 71/-	60/- to 63/-	57/-	59/- to 63/-	57/-	52/-		55/- to 80/-	

B.—FEMALES

ENGLAND AND WALES

Age	Co-operative Wholesale Society			Drapery*		Grocery†		Meat‡
	Clerks and Salesmen	Warehouse Workers	Porters, etc.	Apprentices	Unskilled	Apprentices	Unskilled	
14	11/-	10/-	10/-	—		⎫ 10/- to 12/6	c. 12/6	⎫
15	13/-	12/-	11/-	—	⎱ 13/-	⎬	c. 15/-	⎬ c. 14/-
16	16/-	15/-	14/-	—	⎰	⎭	c. 15/-	⎭
17	20/-	19/-	18/-	—			c. 20/-	
18	24/-	23/-	22/-	—	⎱ 23/-	20/-	c. 20/-	⎱ c. 24/-
19	29/-	27/-	25/-	—	⎰	—	c. 25/-	⎰
20	33/-	30/-	28/-	—		—	c. 25/-	
21	36/-	33/-	31/-	—		—	c. 30/-	
22	39/-	36/-	33/-	—	35/-	—	—	33/-
Adult	42/-	39/-	36/-	—	30/- to 45/-	—	30/- to 45/-	29/6 to 40/-

LONDON / PROVINCIAL

Age	Co-operative Wholesale Society			Drapery§			Miscellaneous‖	Grocery¶	Tailoring¶
	Clerks	Assistants	Warehouse Workers	Clerks and Assistants	Packers	Porters			
14	—	13/-	—	—	—	—	c. 12/-	c. 7/9	—
15	—	15/-	—	—	16/-	16/-	c. 15/-	c. 12/-	—
16	17/-	17/-	—	17/-	20/-	20/-	c. 20/-	c. 12/-	c. 10/6
17	21/-	18/-	—	20/-	24/-	24/-	c. 23/-	c. 12/-	c. 12/6
18	24/-	24/-	—	24/-	27/-	26/-	—	c. 13/-	c. 17/6
19	30/-	28/-	—	27/-	30/-	28/-	—	—	—
20	37/-	32/-	—	30/-	33/-	30/-	—	—	—
21	41/-	33/-	—	33/-	36/-	32/-	—	—	—
22	44/-	35/-	—	36/-	—	—	—	—	—
Adult	48/- to 52/-	40/-	—	39/-	—	—	—	—	—

* *Apprenticeship Report and Ministry of Labour Report on Drapery Trade, 1924.*
† *Apprenticeship Report and Ministry of Labour Report on Grocery Trade, 1925.*
‡ *Ministry of Labour Report on Meat Trade, 1924.*　　§ Standard Time-rates.
‖ London Clearing-house Lists, includes shop assistants, cycle boys, warehousemen, page-boys, messengers.
¶ Sample rates from Trade Unions.

rates for hairdressers' apprentices. Boys and girls in this trade were offered either no remuneration at all for the first two years, or, if a premium was paid, a scale of wages as follows:

Boys, at 14, 2s. 6d. a week; at 15, 5s.; at 16, 7s. 6d.; at 17, 10s. Girls, at 14, 2s. a week; thereafter as for boys.

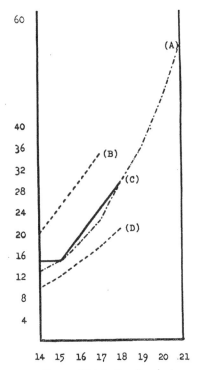

FIG. 3.—Distribution (London).

A. Rates for Co-operative assistants.
B–D. Range of Distributive wages (Clearing-house).
C. Median rates for Distributive wages (Clearing-house).

These striking figures do not seem explicable on the basis of an expectation of a high adult wage. Sample rates obtained by the Shop Assistants' Union indicated that, even in London, a typical rate was about 50s. a week. This anomaly seems rather to be connected with the extreme lack of integration in this trade, and the prospect each assistant has in mind of becoming one day the owner of his own small establishment. Such a prospect of independence

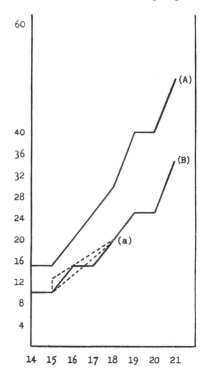

Fig. 4.—Distribution: Grocery (Great Britain).
A–B. Range of wages of grocers' assistants, from Ministry of Labour Report on Grocery Trade, 1925.
a. Typical range of apprentices' wages, from 1928 Report.

would provide an explanation for the exceptional conditions quoted for these apprentices.

V. BUILDING

The building industry is practically all male: 171 per thousand of the employees are juveniles. Of these, 61 per cent are apprentices, 21 per cent being indentured apprentices usually for five years from

TABLE IV

BUILDING

Age	APPRENTICES					LEARNERS				UNSKILLED				
							Kent and Sussex‖			Navvies				
	Apprenticeship Report	London*	Liverpool†	Scotland‡	Asphalt Workers§	London*	Bricklayers	Carpenters	Painters	Great Britain¶	London*	Kent and Sussex‖	Builders' Labourers, Kent and Sussex‖	Builders' Labourers, Middlesex**
14	—	—	9/6	—	10/-	—	—	—	—	c. 17/-	20/-	—	—	—
15	c. 13/-	—	11/6	—	12/6	—	25/8	c. 24/-	22/-	c. 17/-	20/-	—	—	—
16	c. 13/-	14/-	13/6	10/-	22/-	14/-	c. 33/-	c. 38/6	c. 31/-	c. 25/6	30/-	c. 36/8	36/8	—
17	—	17/6	16/-	13/-	25/8	17/6	c. 33/-	c. 38/6	c. 31/-	c. 25/6	30/-	c. 36/8	36/8	c. 35/-
18	—	26/8	20/-	17/-	33/-	26/8	c. 60/6	c. 59/7	c. 47/8	c. 34/-	40/-	c. 53/7½	57/9	—
19	—	35/-	25/6	24/-	40/4	35/-	c. 60/6	c. 59/7	c. 47/8	c. 34/-	—	c. 54/-	57/9	—
20	—	52/6	34/-	33/-	55/-	50/6	c. 60/6	c. 59/7	c. 47/8	—	—	c. 54/-	57/9	—
Adult	55/- to 78/10	62/4 to 69/8	—	—	73/4	—	—	—	—	42/- to 60/-	60/-	60/-	60/4	—

* Agreement of London Regional Joint Committee of the Building Industry, 1935.
† National Federation of Building Trades Employers.
‡ Scheme of the Scottish Regional Joint Council of the Building Industry.
§ Agreement for the Mastic Asphalt Industry, 1930.
‖ Supplied by Kent and Sussex builders.
¶ Standard Time-Rates.
** Middlesex Employment Bureaus.

the age of 15. The rest of the juveniles are mainly builders' labourers and navvies. The apprentices' rates are determined by agreements, but unskilled juveniles are usually outside the scope of trade union

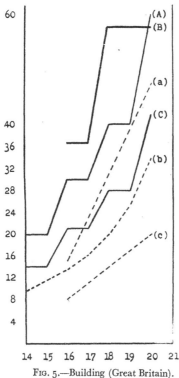

FIG. 5.—Building (Great Britain).

A–C. Range of wages for unskilled juveniles: 1928 Report.
B. Rates for brick labourers in a Kent and Sussex firm.
a–c. Range of apprentices' wages, 1928 Report.
b. Rate for apprentices in Liverpool.

action. They are supposed to get the full rate for adult unskilled labour as soon as they are able to do the work.

Table IV shows the rates obtained from several sources. In London, learners are paid the same as apprentices. No apprentice rates were obtained from Kent and Sussex, but the learners' rates given there are considerably higher than the agreed London rates

Q*

for this group. In London a navvy gets 16s. a week more than an apprentice at the age of 16, while the difference in adult wage in favour of the latter is not more than 10s. a week. The range of wages for the three different categories of juveniles is shown in Fig. 5.

VI. RAILWAYS

The conditions of labour in the railway service are somewhat different from those in any other large industry. According to

TABLE V

RAILWAYS

	I Locomotive Department				II Traffic Department (Conciliation Grades)	III Engineering Department		IV Clerical
15		16/-			16/-		12/-	13·2/-
16	Juveniles	20/-		24/-	20/-	Appren-	14/-	17·3/-
17	not yet	25/-		30/-	25/-	tices	16/-	21·15/-
18	cleaners	30/-	Cleaners →	36/-	Juveniles 30/-		22/-	30·8/-
19		35/-			35/-		24/-	
20					40/-		28/-	
21				42/-				
				↓	↓ Guards &	↓		↓
Adult		Firemen→Driver			Porters→Signalmen	Tradesmen		
Minimum ..	..	57/-	72/-		40/- 48/-	66/-		30·8/-
Maximum ..	..	72/-	90/-		56/- 75/-	—		76·9/-

Rowe,[1] experience in the railway service, rather than any particular kind of skill, is valuable. Hence we find numerous grades of workers, and a well-defined ladder of promotion from one grade to another. The numbers in the higher grades are roughly equal to those in the lower, and the percentage of juveniles employed is one in four, so that promotion is, or has been, until reductions in staff have tended to block avenues of promotion, reasonably certain though slow. The rates of pay for different grades are shown in Table V. The path of

[1] Rowe: *Wages in Practice and Theory.*

promotion is indicated by arrows. As regards the two large categories of workers in the locomotive and traffic departments, the wages paid to juveniles at starting are all the same. The most highly paid grade, and one requiring considerable specialized skill, starts from the same initial wage as the lower paid signalmen. The initial wage is higher than the usual apprentice wage, as can be seen by comparing it with the apprentice rates paid in the Engineering Department.

VII. FURNITURE

In the furnishing trades, 22 per cent of male workers and 38 per cent of female workers are juveniles. Apprenticeship is usually for five years from the age of 15. The wages of unskilled juvenile labour are not known. The Apprenticeship Report gives rates of wages for males at 16 as 6s. to 12s. 3d. for apprentices, and 10s. to 16s. for learners. At the age of 20 the rates are 22s. to 41s. 6d. for apprentices, 25s. to 59s. 6d. for learners. The rates for females are somewhat lower, and the difference between apprentices' and learners' rates is of the same order.

VIII. TAILORING

This forms about half of the garment trade, which employs a total of 160,000 workers, 75 per cent of whom are women and girls. The men consist firstly of the important skilled section, the cutters, and secondly of about an equal number of unskilled workers. In most parts of the trade, women are semi-skilled or unskilled. This is a development conditioned by the mechanization of the trade, a development typical of conditions in the trade to-day. The skilled sections of the trade still get comparatively good conditions, and they are generally well organized. In the retail bespoke section there is a separate scale for apprentices, learners, and other juveniles, showing very big differences in initial rates of remuneration. Cutters in the ready-made and wholesale bespoke section also have a special juvenile rate.

In the greater part of the trade, however, very different conditions prevail. The growing elimination of skill has meant the reduction of earnings and the possibility of running factories on cheap, unskilled youth labour. But in spite of the diminished prospects offered, the juvenile rates are still the learners' rates fixed when the trade was skilled to a much larger extent. These rates were more or less equivalent to apprentices' rates in other industries. Now juveniles are offered these wages for jobs which are largely unskilled

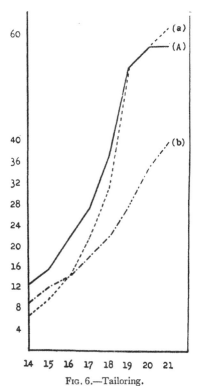

Fig. 6.—Tailoring.

A. Unskilled rate in Retail Bespoke Trade, London: Area B.
a. Apprentices' rate in Retail Bespoke Trade, London: Area B.
b. Learners' time-rate, in Ready Made and Wholesale Bespoke Tailoring, Great Britain.

and often blind-alley jobs. A result of this has been, at least in London, a shortage of juvenile labour in the tailoring trade.

IX. PRINTING

The position of juvenile labour in the printing industry differs from that found in the industries already discussed. It is a highly skilled trade for which apprenticeship is still common. The trade union organization is very strong, and has concerned itself with limiting the number of apprentices and regulating their rates of pay. As a result the rates paid are considerably higher than those found for any other group of apprentices. In the provinces they appear to be higher than those paid to unskilled juvenile labour in the same

TABLE VI

PRINTING

Age	Apprentices*		Unskilled†	
	London	Provinces	London	Provinces
14	16/–	c. 13/6	—	—
15	20/–	c. 17/–	—	—
16	24/–	c. 20/–	27/–	c. 13/–
17	32/–	c. 27/–	35/–	c. 19/–
18	40/–	c. 34/–	43/–	c. 25/–
19	48/–	c. 40/6	51/6	c. 30/6
20	56/–	c. 47/–	60/–	c. 39/6
21	—	—	—	c. 52/6
Adult	80/– to 160/–	62/6 to 103/–	60/– to 107/–	59/6 to 74/6

* Rates of Federation of Master Printers.
† Standard Time-Rates.

industry, though this is not the case in London. The rates obtained are shown in Table VI.

X. WOOLLEN INDUSTRY

In the woollen industry apprentices are very few and are almost exclusively maintenance workers. Fig. 7 shows the relation between the two grades of pay. The apprentices' rates are taken from the Apprenticeship Report. The rates for unskilled workers are standard time for Yorkshire. Apprentices reach adult wages of 61s. to 83s. 6d., while the adult rates for other grades are 23s. 8½d. to 72s. 4d. These rates apply to males only.

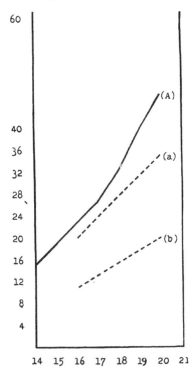

FIG. 7.—Woollen Manufacture.

A. Unskilled workers: Yorkshire.
a–b. Range of wages for apprenticed maintenance workers,
          Great Britain: 1928 Report.

XI. POTTERY AND GLASS

In the china section of the pottery industry, apprenticeship is
practically confined to males. The rates paid to males are shown in
Fig. 8. They are given by the Ministry of Labour. Adult rates
corresponding to the two grades are 70s. 6d. for engravers and
51s. 3d. for warehouse workers.

Females are chiefly on unskilled work. In glass manufacture,
apprentice rates only are available from the Apprenticeship Report.
They range from 11s. 6d. to 21s. at 15, and from 31s. to 41s. 3d.
at 20. The adult rate is 70s. 6d. to 86s. 2d. According to the report,

23 per cent of juveniles are apprentices, but half the boys entering before 16 leave before 21 owing to the arduous conditions of work.

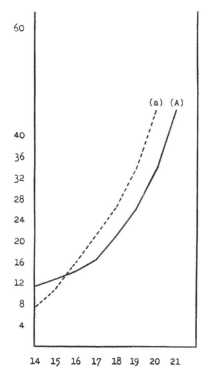

Fig. 8.—Pottery: China Section (Great Britain).
A. Warehouse workers' rates.
a. Apprentices' rates.

XII. CHEMICALS

The percentage of juveniles in the chemical industry is small, 20 per thousand. Apprenticeship has only been for chemists and maintenance workers, who constitute respectively 5 per cent and 10 per cent of all employees. The rates paid to different grades of workers are shown in Fig. 9. The chief point of interest is the very much lower initial rate paid to those entering upon the type of work generally supposed to demand exceptional intelligence. At the

present time, however, apprenticeship for chemists does not seem
to exist, and the tendency seems to be to raise the standard of

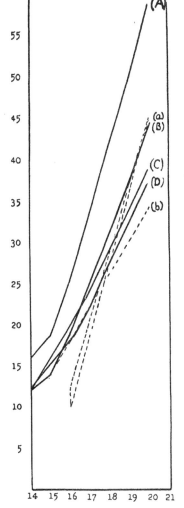

FIG. 9.—Chemical Industry
(Great Britain).

A. Piece-work basis rate in a
   big firm.

B. Time-rate in a big firm.

C. Agreed rate in the Drugs
   and Fine Chemical Trades.

D. Agreed rate in the Heavy
   Chemical Industry.

a. Range of wages for Chemists'
   apprentices.

b. Average wage of Maintenance Workers' apprentices.

qualifications demanded of skilled workers in the industry. Unskilled
adult rates range from 49s. 6d. to 65s. 11d. (piece-rates 25 per cent

more). Adult rates for skilled workers are unobtainable, and estimates of these vary widely. Juvenile wage-rates were obtained from the firms concerned.

The proportion of females employed is very small, with a high ratio of juveniles. Their rates of pay are slightly lower at the start; the difference increases as the age rises, until at the age of 20 they are 10s. to 20s. lower.

XIII. VARIOUS TYPES OF UNSKILLED AND SEMI-SKILLED LABOUR

A large group of industries, of which tobacco and chocolate manufacture are perhaps the most important examples, employs almost entirely unskilled and semi-skilled labour, mostly juvenile and female. These two industries, together with several others less important, come under the scope of Trade Board regulations. Some of the rates paid in these industries are shown in Fig. 10. In the following seven industries, laundries, aerated waters, sugar confection, boot and floor polish, button manufacture, cutlery, fur, the Trade Board rates do not diverge very greatly. The range, together with a typical rate, is shown as three heavy lines in the figure. The Trade Board rate for tobacco is shown separately. Individual firms frequently pay more than the Trade Board rates. Two of these scales are shown in the figure. Many of the workers in these industries are on piece-work, and when this is so the earnings would be higher than those shown, which are all time-rates or piece-work basis rates. In all cases the rate for 21 years appears to be the normal adult rate. Although no direct comparison is possible here with rates for more highly skilled labour in the same industries, these data affect such a large number of juveniles that it is instructive to compare them with the rates in more highly skilled and more lucrative occupations. For example, the upper limit of the Trade Board rates, exclusive of tobacco, corresponds fairly closely with the provincial rates for printing apprentices, which were found to be about the highest apprentices' rates.

XIV. SUMMARY

Previous sections have dealt with rates of wages within particular industries. Frequently the wage-rates of one such industry may dominate the situation in so far as the actions of any individual boy

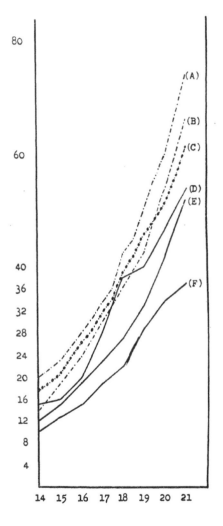

Fig. 10.—Trade Board Rates, and others.

A. Rate given by a large tobacco firm.

B. Rate agreed by several large chocolate firms.

C. Tobacco Trade Board Rate.

D–F. Range of seven Trade Board Rates.

E. Typical rate: Aerated Waters Trade.

or girl be concerned. Only rarely, if ever, can the general rate of wages for different types of work be relevant to individual choice.

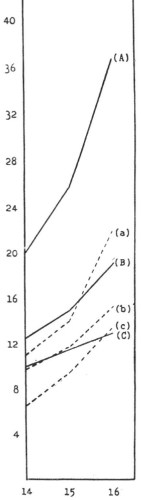

FIG. 11.—Summary for most industries (Great Britain).

A–C. Range of unskilled wages, 14–16 years.

B. Median of unskilled wages, 14–16 years.

a–c. Range of apprentices' wages, 14–16 years.

b. Median of apprentices' wages, 14–16 years.

Nevertheless, the general level of wage-rates sums up what is happening in particular cases, and so does, to some extent, give a picture of what is happening in the country as a whole. Fig. 11 gives a comprehensive picture of the wage-rates studied in this investigation for the age-groups 14 to 16 inclusive. The medians given are only suggestive, since any particular juvenile is not necessarily in the position of being able to earn one or other of the median rates. The difference between them may, however, be regarded as typical of the order of magnitude found between apprentices and unskilled rates at the school-leaving age. A difference of about 3s. a week at this age is not by any means a negligible factor in influencing decisions in families whose incomes are at or below subsistence level. At the age of 16 the difference of about 7s. 6d. is obviously a very serious deterrent to any juvenile starting on a skilled career at that age.

The range of unskilled wages is seen to be very large. The higher rates shown operate only in a few districts, but the number of juveniles affected is not inconsiderable, as these are invariably districts of expanding industry. Where these conditions are found, the financial inducements to enter into unskilled or semi-skilled occupations are obviously very much stronger.

It should perhaps be emphasized that the choice of occupation open to a child or its parents acting for it is not necessarily confined to the choice between apprenticeship and unskilled labour in a single industry. When the possibility of apprenticeship exists, the choice lies between such an apprenticeship and a variety of less skilled types of labour in the same district. For the purposes of this investigation any comparison between skilled and unskilled rates is valid provided both operate within the range of geographical mobility of the child.

The figure given may be compared with the rates given in the Apprenticeship Report for apprentices and other juveniles where similar results were obtained. The report also emphasized the greater disparity at the age of 16.

XV. CONCLUSIONS

The main results of this investigation may be summarized as follows:

1. A comparison between rates of remuneration for various types of juvenile work in several large industries shows that in general the remuneration of apprentices is less than that of learners or semi-skilled workers, and that these in turn receive less than unskilled juvenile workers.

This relationship was most striking for rates paid to juveniles in the two or three years following school-leaving age, and tended to grow less clear as adult status was approached.

2. Where apprenticeship begins at a higher age than 14 years, the difference between the rate paid to apprentices and the rate paid to unskilled juveniles is considerably greater.

3. The conclusions stated do not apply to the Printing Industry and the Railway Service. In the former the number of apprentices is limited, and this privileged position enables them to get as much as unskilled juveniles. In the latter all juveniles enter on the same conditions and have opportunities of promotion through various grades.

4. The range of wages for unskilled or semi-skilled work is greater than the range of apprentices' wages. The higher unskilled rates are confined to a few rising industries and localities, but where they exist they do add to the financial inducement, which tends to deter youth from entering skilled occupations.

The relationship which exists between initial earnings in skilled and unskilled occupations, as shown by the facts given above, is the inverse of the relationship between the adult, or maximum, earnings in skilled and unskilled occupations. At the time when the young worker actually makes the choice between entering a skilled or unskilled occupation, the differential payments are biassed in the opposite direction, and offer a financial inducement to the boy or girl taking up unskilled work. In so far as remuneration affects the choice of vocations, it is therefore clear that the existing inequalities restrict the fund of social personnel from which specialized ability is recruited.

Other things being equal, it seems likely that the boy or girl who is a member of the family with the highest margin above subsistence level will be best able to enter a skilled trade. Hence we are not surprised to learn that an investigation in 1923 showed that: "The economic position of the unskilled families is related to the prospects the children have of becoming skilled."[1]

The system of recruitment to skilled occupations by apprenticeship, as it has existed in this country, seems to involve two results. First, it restricts the vertical mobility of labour by making craftsmanship dependent upon a period of training begun within a year or two of leaving school. Secondly, it makes this training dependent upon

[1] E. L. Lewis, *The Children of the Unskilled.*

the sacrifice of opportunities of a higher immediate remuneration. The system emerges from this picture as one heavily weighted in favour of the recruitment to skilled occupations of those children who come from families with a superior economic position in virtue of high wages or low fertility, or the combination of both. Clearly the result is not the recruitment of the most naturally gifted or capable workers for the skilled occupations. If it encourages foresight, it chiefly ensures the recruitment of workers who have been the most far-sighted in the choice of their parents.

One reflection which is inescapable when we examine this relationship is the utter irrelevance of the economists' wage theory to the biological realities of human nature. Environment and heredity to a varying extent equip different individuals with different capabilities for the exercise of different social functions. The fundamental problem which the wage system raises is the relation between natural inequality and inequalities of remuneration. In a society whose social policy was enlightened by biological knowledge, social selection would be directed to explore the widest range of available personnel from which to secure candidates for necessary activities demanding the most specialized capabilities. It is arguable, though not by any means certain, that this might make it necessary to offer special rewards to widen the scope of recruitment for special occupations. Whether it would be necessary to do so, or whether it would not be, is irrelevant in this context. What is certain is that considerations of this kind have little relevance, if any at all, to the industrial policy of private enterprise. In so far as remunerative inequalities affect the choice of a vocation, they are at present weighted to secure a large fund of labour in grades which offer little scope for special skill. In a strictly behaviourist sense it is, therefore, the *policy* of employment to restrict the available fund of personnel from which native or acquired skill is recruited.

CHAPTER XII

THE DISTRIBUTION OF THE BLOOD-GROUPS AND ITS BEARING ON THE CONCEPT OF RACE

by

ALLISON DAVIS

A LARGE body of data concerning the geographical distribution of the iso-agglutination blood-groups, accumulated during the last fifteen years, is of special theoretical importance in connection with an analysis of the genetical significance of anthropological classifications. They involve the only type of ethnic differences concerning the genetic mechanism of which we possess definite information, based upon the application of rigorous quantitative treatment. So it is of the utmost significance to ask how far it is possible to establish any parallelism between the distribution of the iso-agglutination[1] reactions and single or grouped measurements of osteometric or other somatic characters which have been used by physical anthropologists as a basis for racial classification. The object of this survey is to set forth relevant information bearing upon the issue, and to discuss some theoretical implications emerging from its treatment.

The fact that our knowledge of the genetics of the blood-groups is of so definite a character makes it possible to ask what light their distribution may throw upon the migrations of peoples without raising controversial issues which arise in connection with the definition of a race as used by the geneticist on the one hand, and by different schools of anthropologists on the other. For any community living within a restricted geographical area we can determine the proportions of the several blood-groups. From these, with remarkable fidelity, as Bernstein has shown by a simple application of the

---

[1] Agglutination of blood by the clumping of the red blood corpuscles when brought into contact with the serum of another individual. Human beings fall into four main groups according to the presence in their red cells of one (A or B), both (A B), or neither (O) of two substances called agglutinogens. Blood transfusion between persons belonging to the same blood-group can always be successfully carried out. The free mixture of blood from persons of two different blood-groups results in agglutination.

principle of random mating,[1] we can derive the gene frequencies of the allelomorph system[2] involved. There is thus no temptation to confuse a statistical characteristic of the population so described with what may be a quite fictitious conception of the homogeneity of the individuals of which it is composed. Nor need we fall into the error of distinguishing between two groups on the basis of a mean difference, when the inter-group variance is not appreciably greater than the sum of the intra-group variances. In relation to a genetic analysis of the race concept, the study of blood-group distributions has a special merit because the phenotype classes are individually recognizable throughout the whole range of environment to which human populations are normally exposed. The iso-agglutinin reaction is not known to be affected by age, general health, climate, or by any common disease.

Before discussing how the distribution of the blood-groups compares with that of other somatic differences, some reference must be made to: (1) the most convenient form in which to represent the data statistically, and (2) the consistency of the available data. Various indices have been proposed for the description of blood-group distributions. The attempt to combine three variables in a single index only confuses the issue. The most satisfactory way to exhibit population statistics is either to give the total proportions of individuals with the B agglutinogen (genotypes bb, br, and ab), the total proportions of individuals with the A agglutinogen (aa, ar, and ab), and the total proportion of individuals who lack both (rr); or what is statistically equivalent, to give separately the gene frequencies[3] a, b, r.

---

[1] Since human beings cannot be brought under laboratory conditions, it is not possible to test a genetic hypothesis by crossing individuals from pure stock as Mendel did. A genetic hypothesis can only be tested experimentally by deducing the consequences of different systems of mating. When the genetic difference can only be identified by scientific tests, individual preference does not affect the choice of a mate, and we may treat the problem mathematically on the assumption that marriage is a lottery. This means that the relative proportions of matings between different genetic types only depends upon the proportions of the genetic types concerned (vide Hogben, *Nature and Nurture*, Chapter 2).

[2] Gene is the modern term for Mendel's unit factors. An allelomorph represents the alternative factor derived from the other parent, when an individual is genetically impure.

[3] Mendel's factors are now known to be located in the microscopic cell-organs called chromosomes. Any one gene may be present on one or both members of a particular pair of chromosomes. The probability that it will be present on a particular chromosome of the appropriate pair is called its gene frequency. If we

A population is then distinguished by relatively high or low gene frequency for one of the triple allelomorph series. In this way the relevant information is not confused.

As regards the consistency of different samples, three points are of foremost importance. (1) The first is errors arising from faulty administration of the tests. This point has been discussed by Bernstein (1930) and Lattes (1932), and is closely connected with a second to be mentioned later. In view of the fidelity with which mass data, as shown by Bernstein, conform to the principle of random mating, any sample may be rejected if the sum of the gene frequencies, a, b, r, departs significantly from unity. (2) Even if this test is satisfied, we cannot speak with confidence of the significance of a, when dealing with earlier samples, owing to the subsequent discovery of a second A group by Landsteiner. (3) A third point of importance is, of course, the size of the sample. The application of the goodness of fit criterion to blood-group data necessitates recourse to samples of at least 500 individuals to insure a probable error of no more than 2 per cent.

GENERAL DISTRIBUTION OF THE BLOOD-GROUPS

For the reason already stated, greatest importance is to be attached to the distribution of Group B. The first map[1] brings into prominence the following general conclusions. An exceptionally low gene frequency for B is highly characteristic of the bulk of western Europe (including Scandinavia, Britain, Spain, and France), the aboriginal population of Australia, and the entire aboriginal population of the American continent, Greenland, and Hawaii. In all of these the concentration of Group B is less than 10 per cent of the population, except in a few isolated samples, where it is never as high as 20 per cent. The southern Italians, with a very high B percentage ($27 \cdot 1$ per cent), constitute a class by themselves, whereas the Spanish and Portuguese, classified with the southern Italians by anthropologists as the purest "Mediterraneans," have a very low B ($6 \cdot 1$ and $3 \cdot 9$ per cent respectively).

An exceptionally high concentration of Group B, equivalent

consider a particular pair of Mendelian factors in a population containing a proportion N of recessive individuals, the gene frequency of the recessive gene is $\sqrt{N}$ and that of the dominant gene $1 - \sqrt{N}$. In a system of random mating the gene frequencies can be deduced directly from the proportions of the several genetic types.   [1] Maps on pp. 511–515.

to more than 30 per cent of the population, is characteristic of India, the Philippines, Turkestan, Mongolia, and northern Japan. In the remainder of Asia, and the Malay Archipelago, the concentration of Group B lies between 20 and 30 per cent of the population. The same applies to a considerable section of the aboriginal population of Africa; the Mediterranean regions, however, show in general a rather lower concentration of Group B. As regards Group O, the most noticeable fact is that the concentration is exceptionally high among the aborigines of America and exceptionally low over the entire continent of Asia.

If we wish to make a rough classification of the distribution of the blood-groups, we may distinguish between two main geographical regions: (1) one composed of Africa, the extreme east of Europe, and the whole Asiatic continent, including the islands west of Wallace's Line; (2) the other including the extreme west of Europe, Iceland, Greenland, and the aboriginal populations of America, Hawaii, and Australia. This orientation is notably determined by ocean barriers rather than by mountain ranges. Thus, there is no indication of any abrupt change in the blood-group distribution on either side of the Himalayas, Urals, or Andes. As far as they go, the data suggest the ebb and flow of populations from Africa and Asia across Mesopotamia. On the other hand, they throw absolutely no light on the settlement of the American continent or of the Australasian region. As regards the latter, it is noteworthy that New Guinea occupies a position midway between Australia and the Malay Archipelago with respect to the concentration of B. The most striking anomaly is the discontinuity between north-east Asia and north-west America. The only indication of any drift of population between the American and Asiatic mainlands appears to be found in the islands of the Tropic of Cancer, which seem to be a most unlikely route of migration.

Although it may harmonize with convincing conclusions, independently based upon historical data, to interpret the high concentration of B both in Africa and Asia in terms of migrations, it would be equally plausible, on the facts as they stand, to deduce the settlement of aboriginal America from western Europe or vice versa. If other evidence leads to the conclusion that these continents were peopled by Asiatic migrations, all that we are entitled to surmise from the blood-group distribution is that the settlement of Australia and America must have taken place at an exceedingly early date, when the composition of the Asiatic population was entirely different from what it is to-day. Such a conclusion is consistent with the usual ethnological view that America was peopled by Asiatic populations driven out of the latter continent by the present occupants. In the absence of any evidence from other sources, the distribution of the blood-groups would militate against the belief that America and Australia were settled by migration from the Asiatic mainland.

COMPARISON OF THE BLOOD-GROUP DISTRIBUTION WITH THAT OF OTHER ANTHROPOLOGICAL CRITERIA

In the preceding section, the issue dealt with might be expressed in the following form: To what extent does the geographical distribution of the blood-groups provide evidence that geographical isolation has segregated human populations which differ statistically in their genetical composition? This leads to a second question: How far are any conclusions drawn from blood-group data alone consistent with what may be inferred from the distribution of other single or grouped anthropological criteria?

It is unfortunate for this purpose that the statistical criteria employed are not strictly comparable. Thus, if such data were available, it would be better to compare the blood-group composition of different populations, as measured either by the percentage of Group B or by the gene frequency of b, with the percentage of persons in the same populations with a cephalic index higher or lower than a certain limit, instead of using an average measurement. The latter, taken by itself, may throw very little light upon the genetical structure of a population. Professor E. A. Hooton, of Harvard University, has clearly demonstrated the misleading nature of such anthropometric averages in his study of the ancient Teneriffe crania. Using twenty-two morphological features, each having five gradations, he found that, of 247 male crania, no two individual skull curves were alike. Furthermore, it is true that when any living European sample is analysed for its component groups, it is found to contain several distinct phenotypes; any group of statistical means, therefore, is liable to suggest an entirely unwarranted homogeneity.

In Maps 1 and 2 which illustrate the text, the percentage distribution of Group O and of Group B (Jansky I and III) is first represented. These are based upon adequate samples given by Lattes (1932). The world distribution of cephalic index, stature, and of nasal index on the skull is represented in figures which follow.

All of the anthropometric data are subject to the usual criticisms arising from the diversity of the techniques employed; the data for the nasal index are the most unreliable. The data constitute, nevertheless, the best available criteria at present used for the definition of human races. The traits chosen are those considered by all anthropologists to be the most significant for racial differentiation.

Cephalic Index and the Blood-groups.—The concentration of Group O (Jansky I) is highest both among the brachycephals, as in North and South American Indians (Peru and the Araucanos), North Italians, Dalmatians, and the Dutch, and among dolichocephals, as in Australia, New Guinea, and among Eskimos. The concentration of Group B (Jansky III) is likewise highest both among dolichocephals, such as the Basuto, Senegalese, Yoruba, Abyssinians, Hindus, and Buriats, and among brachycephals, as in Manchuria, Mongolia, Russia, Poland, and Java. Similarly, the concentration of each group can be found at its lowest among both dolichocephalic and brachycephalic peoples.

Blood-groups and Stature.—It will be seen, furthermore, that Group O may attain its highest concentration both among short peoples, as in Sumatra, the Malay Archipelago, the Philippine Islands, and Sardinia, and also among tall peoples, as in Senegal, England, Australia, and among North American Indians. In the same fashion, its lowest concentration can be found among both short and tall peoples. Group B, likewise, may reach its highest concentration among short peoples, as in Russia, the Philippines, Manchuria, Japan, and southern Italy, or among tall peoples, as in northern India, Senegal, and Madagascar. Similarly, its lowest concentration may be found among both short and tall peoples.

Blood-groups with Nasal Index, Skin-colour, and Hair-form taken together.—The highest concentration of Group O is attained either among (1) straight-haired, leptorrhine, yellow or white-skinned people, as among Eskimos and European Icelanders; or among (2) straight-haired, mesorrhine, or platyrrhine peoples, of reddish or brown skin-colour, as among North American Indians; or (3) among platyrrhine, wavy-haired people, of brown or yellowish skin-colour, as in Australia and parts of the Philippines and the Malay Archipelago. The lowest concentration of Group O may be found among peoples with equally divergent nasal index, skin-colour, and hair-form.

Similarly, *the highest concentration of Group B* may be found—and this fact has been overlooked by some who seek to relate existing classifications with blood-group distribution—either (1) among leptorrhine or mesorrhine, "white"-skinned, straight-haired peoples, as in southern Italy, Sicily, among the Buriats and Kirghiz Uzkegs, and the Russians of Krimtschack and Kasak (B over 30 per cent in samples of more than 1,000); or (2) among yellow peoples with leptorrhine noses (northern Chinese and Eskimos), or yellow peoples with mesorrhine noses (Japanese and southern Chinese), or yellow, brown, or black peoples with platyrrhine noses (Siamese, Sea-Dyaks, and in the Philippines, New Guinea, and parts of India). Hair among these highest B groups may be straight, wavy, frizzly or woolly (New Guinea). The very highest concentration of Group B is found in northern India, Samal, and Manchuria; in these three localities it cuts across hair-form, skin-colour, nasal index, stature, and cephalic index. Similar contrasts may be shown for the lowest concentration of Group B in relation to skin-colour, hair-form, and nasal index classifications (Sweden, Australia, Hawaii, Germany, Spain, North America, and among Lapps and Eskimos).

CORRESPONDENCE BETWEEN THE DISTRIBUTION OF ANTHROPOMETRIC DATA IN GENERAL

It has been emphasized already that the precise genetical knowledge which we now possess concerning the blood-groups makes the discussion of their geographical distribution an issue of pivotal importance in connection with any concept of race which can be interpreted in terms consonant with modern genetic theory. The inconsistencies which have appeared in the foregoing comparison between the geographical distribution of the blood-groups and that of other anthropological characteristics justify a brief survey of the correspondence between other types of anthropological data, before discussing whether it is impossible to harmonize the concept of race, as it is employed by physical anthropologists, with such a system of classification as would be based upon genetical analysis if adequate data were available.

It will not be necessary to deal with this issue in great detail, since the facts are familiar to every trained anthropologist. Ignoring, then, the well-known variation of certain characteristics among peoples who are usually grouped together (in Negro Africa, for example, Montandon (1928) and Struck (1922) find the mean cephalic index ranging from below 70 to above 87, and there would undoubtedly be a tremendous range, even if all the samples were statistically adequate), let us turn our attention to the distribution of the various measurements and observations with regard to each other.

Cephalic Index and Stature.—It is obvious that very dolichocephalic peoples may be short, as in Sardinia, Portugal, New Britain, Nigeria, and Ceylon; or very tall, as in East Africa (Nilotes), Scandinavia, Abyssinia, Australia, and northern India. Similarly, brachycephalic peoples may be short, as in Bavaria, Poland, Siberia, and the Caucasus, or tall, as in Dalmatia, Albania, Hawaii, and southern California.

Cephalic Index and Nasal Index.—Dolichocephalic peoples may be platyrrhine, as among the Basuto, Australians, and many tribes in China and India; or leptorrhine, as in England, southern Spain, Schleswig-Holstein, and among Eskimos. Similarly, brachycephalic peoples may be platyrrhine, as in the French and Belgian Congo, North America (west coast), and Mongolia; or leptorrhine, as in northern Germany, Poland, and parts of Russia and China.

Every gradation of *colour* can be found among both dolichocephals and brachycephals. I shall not point out, in detail, how both stature and nasal index also cut across all the other categories. It is important to notice, however, that platyrrhiny, regarded usually, along with woolly or frizzly hair and black or brown skin, as a distinguishing characteristic of negroes, can also be found among Hindus, American Indians, Chinese, North Caucasians, Sea-Dyaks, Japanese, Malays, and Polynesians, whose skin-colour and hair-form are quite different from negroes. Furthermore, mesorrhiny and leptorrhiny are found among Abyssinian tribes who have frizzly or woolly hair (Sergi (9) found the modal nasal index of 105 Tigre crania to be $47 \cdot 0$), as well as among the wavy-haired, almost black Somali and Danakil.

Even using the far too broad gradations of skin-colours and hair-form distinguished by anthropologists, it is obvious that both these categories also cut across each of the other traits dealt with in this communication—an observation fatal to the view that the "darker" and "lighter" races constitute monophyletic stocks. Dark-brown skinned people, with curly hair, for example, can be found with every gradation of cephalic index, nasal index, and blood-group proportions, as can also white-skinned peoples with straight hair. In the present state of knowledge, the following conclusions seem to be justified: (1) It is not difficult to devise for mankind, as a whole,

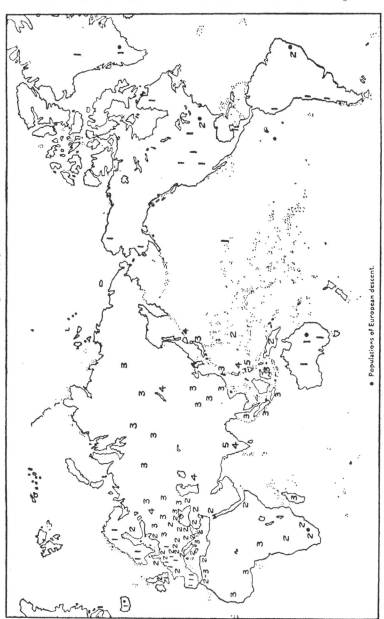

MAP I.—Blood-Groups.—"B" (Jansky III).   1 = less than 10%   4 = 30%–40%
2 = 10%–20%   5 = over 40%
3 = 20%–30%

• Populations of European descent.

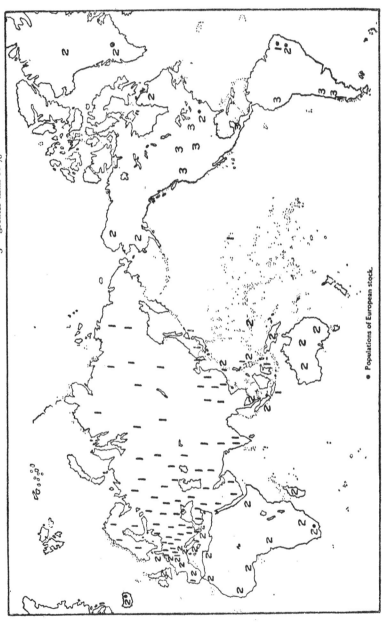

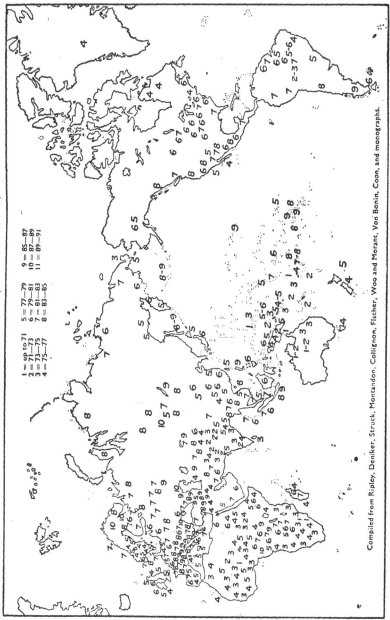

MAP III.—CEPHALIC INDEX (LIVING MEASUREMENT)

1 = up to 71   5 = 77—79   9 = 85—87
2 = 71—73   6 = 79—81   10 = 87—89
3 = 73—75   7 = 81—83   11 = 89—91
4 = 75—77   8 = 83—85

Compiled from Ripley, Deniker, Struck, Montandon, Collignon, Fischer, Woo and Morant, Von Bonin, Coon, and monographs.

R

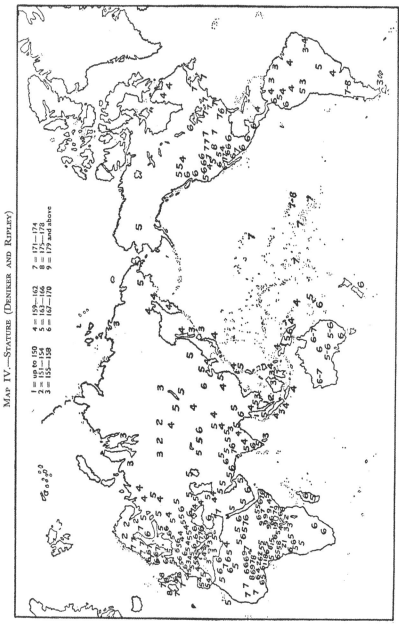

MAP IV.—STATURE (DENIKER AND RIPLEY)

1 = up to 150
2 = 151—154
3 = 155—158
4 = 159—162
5 = 163—166
6 = 167—170
7 = 171—174
8 = 175—178
9 = 179 and above

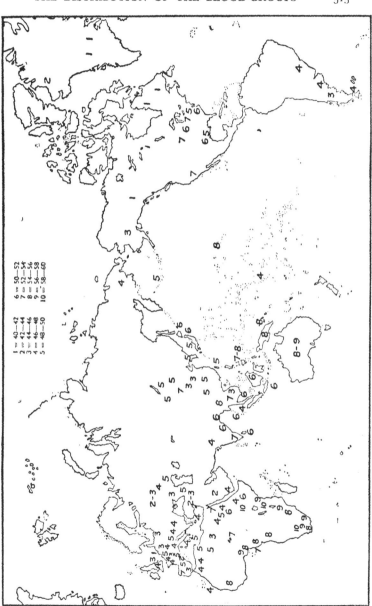

MAP V.—NASAL INDEX.—CRANIA   1. Thomson, Arthur and Buxton, L. H. Rudley—"Man's Nasal Index in Relation to Certain Climatic Conditions," *J. Roy. Anthro. Inst.*, Vol. LIII, 1923, pp. 92–122
2. Dixon, R. B.—*The Racial History of Man*, 1923
3. Deniker, J.—*Les Races*, 1924, and various monographs.

1 = 40–42   6 = 50–52
2 = 42–44   7 = 52–54
3 = 44–46   8 = 54–56
4 = 46–48   9 = 56–58
5 = 48–50   10 = 58–60

artificial systems of classification based upon the study of single attributes, which have very definite regional foci. (2) Nor can it be denied that we can readily recognize some groups of attributes with respect to which regional foci with comparative homogeneity can be isolated, as for example those African forest communities in which dark skin, platyrrhine nose, woolly hair, and alveolar prognathism may be practically universal. (3) Such foci which might be used to define a natural grouping based on unity of type or selective agencies are very much more *restricted* than the areas mapped out in early and, as is now recognized, essentially artificial systems of race classification. In the intervening regions we discern every sort of gradation. This might be put in simple terms by saying that while we can recognize certain restricted communities as natural races with well-defined limits, the bulk of mankind is not so classifiable. (4) In the light of recent experimental work on interspecific evolution, it is extremely doubtful whether the existence of natural races, defined in this sense, provides a sufficient basis for phylogenetic speculation. (5) This is true *a fortiori* when the concept of race is extended to the classification into distinct physical types of a community of individuals interbreeding with one another. The mechanism of segregation will ensure the reappearance of combinations with common features which they do *not* owe to common ancestors with the same group of characteristics. The existence of such physical types, characterized by an aggregate of physical peculiarities in excess of a purely random association, may arise from a variety of causes, which cannot be deduced from morphological study, and must be referred to the geneticist to unravel.

THE CONCEPT OF RACE PURITY

The practical utility of any classificatory system resides in its value as a device for identifying the objects of scientific study. While this defines in a general way what all naturalists are agreed upon, when they undertake the construction of a classificatory system, a precise interpretation of what is involved in the concept of identification is a matter of some difficulty. Two organisms are rarely, if ever, identical in the genetic sense, except where polyembryony, or spore formation without nuclear segregation, occurs. Even with this minor qualification, absolute identity is never realized by a perfectly symmetrical distribution of environmental variables. Consequently a unit of classification, be it variety, species, genus, or phylum, is an attempt to state, in as economical a way as possible, certain limits of variation which circumscribe the attributes of the individuals which are labelled as members of a group. The basic difficulty of classification, so conceived, arises from the immense variety of characteristics which may distinguish one organism from another. Classification is, in part, a statement of the limits of individual variability of single attributes, as when we distinguish Manx cats from all other cats by the absence of tails, or cordates from other phyla by the presence of pharyngeal clefts. It is also, and more especially, an attempt to indicate, with or without any explicit metric, the concurrent variability of a large group of attributes.

The criteria used in the definition of the attributes of organisms may depend either upon *discontinuous* variation, when the criterion for any given distinction is all or none, or upon *continuous* variation, in which case all the earlier classificatory work on organisms was quite content to use words like "large" and "small" as orders of magnitude to be interpreted as best they could by the context in which they occurred. All scientific inquiry starts from the common experience of mankind. It is an indisputable fruit of our common experience of plants and animals that there are concomitant limits of variability for large groups of attributes. For instance, few people with ordinary powers of observation would disagree in describing a particular bird as a "sparrow." In so far as this is so, the word "sparrow," or its Latin equivalent, is an instrument for the description of a well-defined group of animals. The real business of classification begins when we attempt to explain what we mean by a "sparrow" to someone who has never seen one.

Taxonomy has its historical roots closely intertwined with the practical task of providing guidance in distinguishing herbs with supposedly medicinal properties. The simplest conceivable unit of classification is the genetically pure line distinguished from parental or collateral stocks by virtue of some discrete all-or-none characteristics, or some single average measurement with its appropriate dispersion. Such a group rests upon a purely experimental basis. There is no obvious connection between the way in which it is defined and the definition of larger units of classification employed in describing the diversity of organisms as they occur in nature. Here the first task of the scientific investigator is to find a precise and economical way of expressing the association of a vast assemblage of

R*

characteristics which may be easily recognized as such by common observation and sustained experience in the field or museum, but are not easily communicated to the world of scientific discourse.

The issues raised by a radical examination of the scope and nature of classification are among the most recondite and fundamental, and at the same time, in the present context, among the most neglected, in the field of scientific methodology. Historically, they take us back to the medieval controversies of the realists and nominalists, if we are to see all that is involved. The problem of defining the concept of race, species, or phylum cannot be rightly undertaken apart from a consideration of the function of language in the communication of scientific truths.

Two of the words which are used as labels for classificatory units fell into the hands of biologists after they had served a long apprenticeship in philosophical controversies with a predominantly theological rather than scientific orientation. "Genus" and "species" seem to have passed from the Peripatetics and the Schoolmen, through the hands of the medieval herbalists, before they were brought into systematic use by Linnaeus. Around their meaning, and no less that of the race concept, still clings the aroma of the Aristotelian metaphysic. For the modern scientist, a "class" implies nothing more than a label for the common properties of a group of objects. In the disputations of the realists concerning *differentiæ* and *accidens*, the species was endowed with an existence independent of the objects classified as of the same species. In other words, the object retained its specific *substance*, when all its attributes had been stripped away. Something of this naïve realism persists in the peculiar indifference which taxonomists in general have shown to a critical analysis of the meaning of the terms they use.

At the opposite extreme, a clear statement of the scope and nature of classification in biology is not promoted by the naïve nominalism which is inclined to dismiss the existence of a phenomenon because the language in which it is described is not sufficiently definite. That we find it difficult to define a satisfactory criterion for a classificatory group does not dismiss the fact that we also encounter associated limits of variability for large assemblages of characters, and that we recognize with little difficulty hierarchies of such associations. Thus, although the distinction between an artificial and natural system of classification appears, at first sight, to savour of the old realist doctrine, it does embody a genuine recognition of the way in which the manifoldness of nature presents itself to human observation. The historical roots of the issue are clearly stated by John Stuart Mill [6] in the following passage:

> The Aristotelian logicians . . . did not admit every class which could be divided into other classes to be a genus, or every class which could be included in a larger class to be a species. . . . It was requisite, according to their theory, that genus and species should be of the *essence* of the subject . . . and in every classification they considered some one class as the lowest or *infima species*. . . . As applied to individuals, the word essence has no meaning except in connection with the exploded tenets of the realists. . . . Is there no difference, then, save this merely verbal one, between the classes which the Schoolmen admitted to be genera or species, and those to which they refused the title? Is it an error to regard some of the differences which exist among objects as differences in *kind* (genere or specie), and others only as differences in the *accidents*? Were the Schoolmen right or wrong in giving to some of the classes into which things may be divided the name of kinds, and considering others as secondary divisions grounded on differences of a comparatively superficial nature? Examination will show that the Aristotelians did mean something by this distinction, and something important; but which, being but indistinctly conceived, was inadequately expressed by the phraseology of essences and the various other modes of speech to which they had recourse. . . . There are as many actual classes as there are general names positive and negative together. But if we contemplate any one of the classes so formed such as the class animal or plant, or the class sulphur or phosphorus, or the class white or red, and consider in what particulars individuals included in the class differ from those which do not come within it, we find a very remarkable diversity in this respect between some classes and others. There are some classes the things contained in which differ from other things only in certain particulars which may be numbered, while others differ in more than can be numbered, more even than we need ever expect to know. . . .

What we have now to ask is why naturalists have found it difficult to give a precise formal definition of the groupings they recognize. Before attempting to answer this question, it will clarify further discussion if we examine the impact of the evolutionary doctrine on the growth of taxonomy.

Linnaeus may be described as the last of the herbalists for whom convenient identification with no ulterior pretensions was the main objective. The only respect in which the work of Linnaeus marks a philosophical advance upon that of his predecessors is that it created the problem of the origin of species by accepting the principle of biogenesis as a universal or wellnigh universal principle of nature. At the base of his classificatory system, Linnaeus implied that a species is a breeding unit. This limitation adopted as a formal definition by Illiger, if rigorously adopted, would relegate the finer ramifications of classification to experimental analysis. In fact, this practice has never been followed. Botanical taxonomists have endeavoured to extricate themselves from the dilemma by distinguishing between "Linnaeons" and "Jordanons," using these terms in a manner which corresponds, in a rough and ready way, with what zoologists respectively refer to as "species" and "local races." Zoologists in the broadest sense of the term, including anthropologists, have never reached any general agreement concerning the distinction so drawn. For instance, it is obviously unworkable as applied to fossil forms in general, and to man in particular. In practice, there is no universal consent concerning a criterion for different hierarchies of resemblance. If for practical reasons or from anthropomorphic bias a species has the good fortune to be the subject of very close study, gaps which would not be sufficient to separate species in a nearly related form are recognized as the basis for erecting new genera.

The Linnaean species was an experimentally valid concept, though the criterion it embodied could not commend itself to taxonomical routine. In his larger units of classification, Linnaeus, like the herbalists, was certainly concerned, in the main, with constructing a convenient key for the identification of species. For this purpose, a comparatively few clear-cut differentiæ were the prime desideratum. Cuvier's doctrine of the unity of type as a basis for natural classification drew attention to the facts that organisms fall into relatively discontinuous groups on the basis of complex assemblages of attributes, and that classificatory groups based upon such assemblages may be very difficult to differentiate in terms of a single or a small number of diagnostic peculiarities. In this way the distinction between a natural and an artificial system took shape. The evolutionary doctrine developed the distinction in a form which contained no explicit metaphysical implications such as those of Cuvier himself, who seems to have regarded the various manifestations of unity of type as different moods of a cosmic artificer. The destruction of types unable to compete with their contemporaries, extending over a long historic process, became at the same time an explanation of those discontinuities which make it possible to recognize organisms as members of discrete groups, and also of those inconsistencies which make a system of classification too severely dominated by economy of description an unsatisfactory way of representing different levels of resemblance for a wide range of attributes.

A natural classification thus acquired a new philosophic significance. Different levels in the hierarchy of classificatory units represent different levels in a genealogical tree. This is at least an intelligible objective for classification. Up to a point, it is accepted as a practicable one by all biologists. No one doubts, for example, that it can be successfully applied at the grosser levels of classification. All biologists will admit that reptiles, birds, and mammals constitute a natural triad in the sense that if we follow back the pedigrees of birds and mammals, respectively, to their common ancestry, the ancestral group would have characteristics which would lead us to describe it as a reptile if it were living to-day. In contradistinction to this broad basis of agreement, two noteworthy features of the influence of the evolutionary doctrine leave room for considerable controversy. (1) One is how far it is possible to carry the process of classification as an adequate representation of phyletic relationships. (2) The other is that by emphasizing the historical instability of any unit of classification, the evolutionary taxonomists shirked the responsibility of clarifying the meaning which they attached to the various units of classification which they adopted.

The first issue is of fundamental importance to anthropology in two ways. The confidence with which the early evolutionists undertook to express the phylogenetic relations of organisms knew no bounds except those prescribed by human fatigue. In pushing phyletic speculation into the finest ramifications of an ethnic system, it endowed a study of the geographical distribution of physical idiosyncrasies among mankind with the theoretical objective of arranging the peoples of the world in groups distinguished by a greater or less predominance of primitive, i.e. simian, characteristics. Behind this there was undoubtedly the disposition to hope that such a task, once accomplished, would throw light upon the cultural history of mankind.

This confidence has been shaken by the further progress of research along two divergent lines. Palaeontology has emphasized the existence of convergent and parallel evolution on a much larger scale than the early evolutionists would have been disposed to admit. For the assurance with which Darwinian naturalists were prepared to reconstruct pedigrees from the morphology of contemporary forms has given place to the belief that phylogenetic speculation is barren unless it is fortified by abundant fossil remains, a thesis amply sustained in the writings of Wood Jones and Le Gros Clark.

In another quarter, criticism of the optimism of an earlier generation has emerged from the studies which geneticists have lately undertaken in the fields of *interspecific evolution*. Such studies have now been carried out on animals and plants of widely separated groups. Hence the conclusions drawn from them have the most general validity. As it affects the practice of taxonomy the issue has been recently stated by Hogben [2] in the following passage:

> The ubiquitous occurrence of parallel evolution in the record of the rocks is fully consonant with the findings of experimental genetics, though systematic biology in general and physical anthropology in particular have pursued their course with a serenity unimpaired by the results of experimental investigation. This is perhaps because geneticists have refrained from commenting on the devasting consequences of their discoveries. It has long been known that similar varieties have emerged in closely allied species, but bodily similarities may result from entirely different changes in hereditary materials. Recent work on the fruit-fly Drosophila has shown that the germinal material of allied species is constantly changing in precisely the same way. In several species of the fruit-fly similar varieties have arisen as sports under experimental conditions. Modern genetical analysis makes it possible to allocate the genes responsible for the production of new varieties or mutants to the chromosomes on which they reside, and to indicate the actual position which they occupy along the length of the chromosomes. Metz and Sturtevant, who have constructed chromosome maps of several different species of the fruit-fly Drosophila, find that a large number of similar varieties have arisen through changes which have occurred at corresponding situations on corresponding chromosomes. They are therefore equivalent in a genetical as well as an anatomical sense. The consequences of this new body of information are immense, and few biologists have as yet realized how far-reaching is its significance. In *Drosophila simulans* Sturtevant has identified some twenty-five mutants, similar bodily to a series of mutants in *D. melanogaster*, with similar serial order on corresponding chromosomes. Thus yellow body, white eye, and rudimentary wing genes occur in the same order in both species on the X chromosome. A black-bodied, vestigial-winged, and a truncated-winged mutant have been found in *Drosophila simulans*. Their genes occur as in *D. melanogaster* on the second chromosome in the same serial relation. There is a sepia-eyed mutant

whose gene resides on the third chromosome as in *D. melanogaster*. There is a mutant "minute" with small fine bristles in both species, with its gene located on the fourth chromosome.

To appreciate the importance of Sturtevant's work it will suffice to consider two species, *A* and *B*, in each of which has appeared a series of recessive sports, *a*, *b*, *c*, *d*, *e*, *f*, and *g*. Their occurrence in nature will be occasional, and may well escape the observation of the field naturalist. The geneticist, who is on the look-out for them, at once isolates each. By simple and direct means he can then build up a stock of *A* and another stock of *B*, each characterized by the mutant characters *a*, *b*, *c*, *d*, *e*, *f*, and *g*. Unless previously initiated into the extent of variation exemplified by the parent stock under laboratory conditions, a taxonomist who visited his laboratory and examined these cultures would find himself confronted by two species resembling one another in a series of characteristics and differing from all other species of Drosophila with respect to the same characteristics. . . . Reassured by the convention that these characteristics are not 'adaptive,' he would infer a common ancestor characterized by the possession of a new constellation of mutant characters. On current assumption he would be justified in erecting a new sub-genus to represent the separation of this common ancestor from the ancestral stock of other species of Drosophila. Metaphorically speaking, it is possible that Nature is continually playing practical jokes of this sort.

It may be confidently predicted that experimental investigations upon interspecific evolution such as the researches of Metz and Sturtevant upon the fruit-fly will continue to progress and provide a basis for a less ambitious attitude to zoological classification. Eventually the principles of genetics will diffuse from the laboratories to the museums, and taxonomists will ask whether it is possible to draw legitimate inferences concerning family relationships without recourse to abundant fossil remains. We shall be compelled to abandon the hope of embodying the pedigrees of species in the terminal twigs of a classificatory system. *A fortiori* we can entertain no hope of reconstructing racial pedigrees within the limits of a single Linnaean species.

Without committing ourselves to so radical a standpoint as that which is expressed in the concluding sentence of this passage, it must be admitted that evolutionary speculation provides a very slender basis for clarifying the *infima species* which it is the aim of anthropologists to recognize. Consequently, we are thrown back upon direct observation in redefining our concepts. This task would not be as difficult as it is, if the issue were as simple as is implied in the passage quoted earlier from Mill's *Logic*. The concepts of taxonomy originated in a period when biological science was content with purely qualitative categories. If unity of type depended upon the existence of "multitudes of properties" all of which can be recognized in all members of a class, and none of which is encountered in members of other units, it would be easy to select a suitable number of readily detectable differentiæ on the basis of mere convenience. Sometimes this method of specification is possible, as when we define a group like the Mammalia, the birds, and the *Nematoda* or thread worms. Sometimes it is easy to give an approximate statement of the differentiæ of a group. Thus no animals except arthropods have an ostiate heart, and all arthropods, except the few which have lost the heart altogether, do possess an ostiate heart. In these few instances, the unity of type of the group is recognized by many other peculiarities none of which is absolutely universal for the group as a whole, though absent in all other groups. Even for the larger units of classification, the difficulties of a purely qualitative conception of the task of classification are great. Thus there is little that can be said concerning the existence of features common to all molluscs, and absent in all other phyla. The whole assemblage owes its unity to the interlocking of the several groups in the extent to which they share different properties.

From the evolutionary standpoint we should expect that the difficulties of defining the differentiæ of a unit in purely qualitative terms, i.e. all-or-none criteria, become greater as the size of the unit is reduced. Hence it is not surprising that anthropologists, alone among taxonomists, have applied statistical methods to the recognition of classificatory units. The value of this procedure lies in the fact that it directs attention to a conclusion which has emerged from the foregoing discussion. Although the earlier taxonomists were content with purely qualitative categories, unity of type is implicitly a statistical concept, and the meaning of a taxonomical unit can be clarified only when the statistical character of the concept is explicitly recognized. That the full implication of such a re-definition has not been recognized hitherto results from the fact that statistical methods were first introduced to deal with attributes which vary continuously within a group, and have been subsequently employed in the search for statistical averages, characteristic of the group. Exclusive preoccupation with statistical methods, having this end in view, deflects attention from the real business of the taxonomist. This is to recognize the characteristics which *individuals* have in common.

This task can be illustrated by the controversy concerning the existence of the "mongolian" idiot as a clinical category. Few students of mental defects fail to agree in classifying an institutional case as a "mongol." At the same time it may safely be said that while most writers agree about the characteristics commonly encountered among "mongols," no two authorities make the same statements concerning which, if any, of these characteristics are common to all "mongols." In a recent study, Penrose [8] compared a group of institutional cases (I.Q. of 15 to 30), designated "mongols" on grounds of superficial resemblance, with a group of unselected cases, for six stigmata: cephalic index < 82, epicanthic fold, fissured tongue, conjunctivitis, simian line, and presence of only one crease on the minimal digit of either hand. To the nearest integer, the percentage incidence of seven characters (including I.Q.) in the two groups of defectives was as follows:

	A	B	C	D	E	F	G
Mongols (50) . . .	70	44	52	74	30	44	18
Unselected (350) . .	26	17	3	7	1	4	0

It is clear that each of these characters, present in a large percentage of individuals who would be classified as "mongols" by superficial examination, is very much more common among "mongols" as a whole than in the general population, or even among a population of defectives. It is also seen that none of them is universal. "If," says Penrose, "we now note the number of these features present in any given patient, we find that two quite distinct frequency distributions are attained for the two groups of cases, thus:

Number of characters present	0	1	2	3	4	5	6	7
Number of "mongols" with a given number of characters	1	2	10	15	14	4	4	0
Number of unselected patients with a given number of characters	188	124	32	5	1	0	0	0

"almost three-quarters of the 'mongols' have three or more of these characters, but only six of 350 unselected patients have three or more."

These figures leave little doubt that if we had a census of the entire population, we should find that the number of associations of these relatively rare characters in groups of two or more is greatly in excess of the concurrent probability of two or more independent events. Their presence together in one and the same individual is more than a random circumstance. It betokens the existence of a *diathesis* of which, in response to different conditions of development, the various features, each characteristic of, but none common to, all "mongols" are the appropriate manifestation. This diathesis is the only thing common to all "mongols." If we like to give a modern scientific connotation to the terminology of the Schoolmen, it is the *essence* of "mongolism."

All practical taxonomists are agreed that the attempt to classify organisms in groups defined by characteristics which are common to all members of a group, and exhibited by no individuals belonging to other groups, only leads, when adopted as a general practice, to systems which are artificial; both in the theoretical sense that they fail to direct attention to evolutionary relationships, and in the practical sense that they fail to direct attention to large assemblages of attributes which are, metaphorically speaking, held together loosely. *A statistical concept of classification has its objective basis in the fact that certain associations of attributes occur much more often than their random combination inferred from their separate frequencies would lead us to predict, and the practical significance of an ascending hierarchy of classificatory units resides in the fact that what is true of a comparatively small number of individual attributes is also true of larger groups of attributes.*

Such associations as form the basis of biological classification may have their basis in: (1) a common diathesis or genetic constitution, of which the several manifestations are reactions to different conditions of development, as with clinical classifications; (2) geographical isolation, which may result in differential selection of genes; (3) the different conditions of environment which exist in different habitats, and which may possibly favour certain types; (4) different systems of mating adopted in different communities, affecting the frequency with which different gene combinations will occur; (5) differential exposure to pathogenic conditions, differences of fauna and mineral resources, different social tradition, or differential access to social intercourse with neighbours, all of which will affect the manifestations of such gene differences as may influence the social behaviour of individuals living in different localities. Of these, the second, third, and fourth provide the basis for any natural grouping which physical anthropology might be concerned to recognize. The last properly belongs to the domain of social anthropology. To what extent there exist groupings of the former kind is an empirical question.

That mankind can be classified with respect to a few single attributes, each of which shows a very striking concentration in different geographical areas, is beyond dispute. For instance, woolly or frizzly hair is almost universal among the indigenous populations domiciled in the part of Africa south of the Sahara, and practically unknown among the populations domiciled in Eurasia, north of the Mediterranean. It is this circumstance which first prompted the construction of classificatory schemes, and gave rise to the concept of race. Again, no one doubts the fact that there is a rough association between locality and certain simple groups of characters. For instance, it is possible to circumscribe localities where a particular type of pigmentation, hair-form, and nasal dimensions is practically universal, and other localities in which the same type of pigmentation, hair-form, and nasal dimensions is not found at all.

While these facts are universally admitted, they do not constitute in themselves any justification for the hope of dividing mankind as a whole into natural races. Among mankind we find a few communities living in restricted areas and displaying considerable homogeneity with respect to groups of characters, which are absent, or do not show the same amount of association, in other regions. To that extent such communities can be distinguished as natural races. *It will be noted that such a conception of race is consistent with the view that the vast majority of mankind is not divisible into races at all.* The only justification for using the term "race" for types based upon aggregates of physical characteristics, when such types inhabit the same locality and interbreed, lies in one of four assumptions, of which the first is difficult if not impossible to prove, the second is incapable of proof, the third has no foundation in genetical theory, and the fourth is not yet established. This may be illustrated by distinguishing between two types in the Scandinavian population, e.g. the Nordic and the Alpine. The substratum of fact for such racial categories is that people with blue eyes and fair hair are relatively more common in the north of Europe, and that if we take a more restricted geographical area we encounter a higher proportion of people in which these characteristics are combined with certain osteometrical features, such as dolichocephaly, depressed malars, long faces, and tall stature. That relative geographical isolation, inbreeding, or localized mutation have played a part in concentrating such a grouping is highly probable. Clearly we are at liberty to take one of four views.

(1) One is that the present population of northern Europe was formed by the mixing of what were at one time two or more fairly homogeneous groups, of which one was characterized by a comparatively homogeneous association of those characteristics used to define the Nordic type. If it were possible to prove this view, the term "Nordic race" would have a definite historical status. Clearly such a view could be established only if race-classification were based upon purely osteometric characteristics. There is, in fact, very little reason for believing that the aggregate of characters which define the Nordic type, taken as a whole, was ever concentrated in any particular region with a closer approximation than exists to-day.

(2) Alternatively, instead of regarding the concentration of this type in certain parts of northern Europe as evidence of the past existence of a population possessing greater homogeneity than any large population which exists to-day, we might regard the concentration of the same aggregate of physical characteristics in northern Europe as a stage in the formation of a homogeneous population. The plausibility of such a view must rest solely upon what opinion we hold about the future of international communications and public sentiment, tending to encourage assortative mating. While we might foreshadow a speculative significance for a distinction between Nordic and Alpine races when we direct attention to the concentration of certain aggregates of physical attributes studied over a large geographical area, such speculations do not confer any definite meaning on the term "race," when we speak of some Scandinavians belonging to the Nordic and some to the Alpine race. The mechanism of genetical segregation will ensure that in any freely interbreeding community all possible combinations of genes will make their appearance in the long run. Our examination of the statistical implications of any biological classification shows how important it is to establish the degree to which the existence of physical aggregates is or is not a random occurrence. The use of the term "race" implies that the frequency with which such aggregates occur takes place with something more than random assortment. From a genetical point of view, this seems to imply one of two things.

(3) The first is that the attributes of a given aggregate represent

different developmental aspects of a simple diathesis, depending upon a comparatively simple genetical mechanism, as is the case with a clinical classification like "mongolian" idiocy. No geneticist would admit such an interpretation to have any applicability to the problem under consideration.

(4) From the modern genetical standpoint, this leaves only one alternative, namely, that there is correlative assortative mating for the various attributes by which a racial type is defined. Such assortative mating might have its basis in social behaviour or in lack of homogeneity of local distribution.

As a concrete example of the extent to which association of the attributes used to define the Nordic type occurs in practice, the memoir of Lundborg and Linders on *The Racial Characters of the Swedish Nation* [5] may be cited. From a sample of 47,000 individuals, 87 per cent were classified as "light-eyed," 8 per cent "medium-eyed," and 5 per cent "dark-eyed." The percentage of light eyes among individuals with flaxen hair was 97, among persons with red hair 89, among persons with dark-brown hair 58, among persons with black hair 48. The figures may be contrasted alternatively in the following way. In the population as a whole, 7 per cent have flaxen hair. Among individuals with light eyes, 8 per cent have flaxen hair; among individuals with medium eyes, 2 per cent have flaxen hair; and among individuals with dark eyes less than 1 per cent have flaxen hair. In contrast with this association between eye and hair colour, a negligible correlation between hair and eye colour and either stature or cephalic index is seen in the same population. It is clear, therefore, that the aggregate of attributes which are commonly used to define the Nordic type do not all show a very high measure of correlation, *inter se*, when we examine a comparatively restricted locality of the order defined by national boundaries.

According to a literal interpretation of what is meant by the term "Linnaean species," the peoples of mankind indisputably constitute a single Linnaean species. The attempt, which anthropologists have undertaken, to extend the concept of a natural classification beyond the limits of a Linnaean species, *sensu stricto*, has received encouragement from two considerations. (1) The first is that quite distinct geographical varieties can sometimes be recognized within the limits of a single species of animals or plants. (2) The second is that artificial selection has succeeded in building up very complex and well-defined aggregates of physical attributes into distinct breeds or strains of domesticated species. With regard to the first, it is to be pointed out that *homo sapiens* is the most widely distributed species on this planet. Being so mobile, human beings are less subject to the selective effect of prolonged isolation than are less mobile species, especially when we take into account the fact that the human species is a comparatively recent one in units of geological time, and still more so in genetic time-units, i.e. generations. Another point is of importance in this connection. Because the tool-bearing habit of the human species has enabled it to transcend its physical environment, the distribution of the human species is peculiar not only in its range but in its spatial continuity. The analogy with domesticated races naturally prompts us to ask how far natural barriers such as oceans or mountain ranges, on the one hand, and social prohibitions, on the other, have achieved what the fancier or stock-breeder can encompass by the use of cages, wire-netting, or barbed-wire fences. The anthropologist is not entitled to assume that the answer is in the affirmative. He should approach the problem as one which awaits solution with the cooperation of the experimental geneticist.

WORKS CITED

1. BERNSTEIN, F. (1930) "Ueber die Erblichkeit der Blutgruppen." *Zeit f. Indukt. Abstamm. 4. Vererbungslehre*, Bd. LIV.
   (1931) "Zur Grundlegung der Chromosomentheorie der Vererbung beim Menschen mit besonderer Berucksichtingun der Blutgruppen." *Zeit. f. Indukt. Abstamm. 5. Vererbungslehre*, Bd. LVII, 2–3.
   (1931) "Die geographische Verteilung der Blutgruppen und ihre anthropologische Bedeutung." *Internat. Congr. for Studies regarding Population Problems*, Rome, 1931.
2. HOGBEN, LANCELOT, *Genetic Principles in Medicine and Social Science*, London, 1931, pp. 131–133.
3. HOOTON, E. A., *Methods of Racial Analysis, Science*, Vol. 63, January 22, 1926.
4. LATTES, L., *Individuality of the Blood*, tr. by. L. W. H. Bertie, Oxford University Press, 1932.
5. LUNDBORG, H., and LINDERS, F. J., *The Racial Characters of the Swedish Nation*, The Swedish State Institute for Race Biology, 1926.
6. MILL, JOHN STUART, *System of Logic*, Bk. I, Chap. 7.
7. MONTANDON, G., *L'Ologenèse Humaine*, Paris, 1928, p. 336.
8. PENROSE, L. S., *The Mental Defective*, 1932, Chap. 10, p. 101.

9. SERGI, S., *Crania habessinica*, 1912.

10. STRUCK, B., "Versuch einer Karte der Kopfindex in mittleren Afrika." *Zeit. f. Ethnologie*, Bd. LIV, 1922.

The distributions represented on the maps are based upon data given in the general works of DENIKER, MONTANDON, WOO and MORANT, VON BONIN, STRUCK, RIPLEY, COLLIGNON, DIXON, THOMSON and BUXTON, LATTES, and in numerous monographs.

Printed and bound by CPI Group (UK) Ltd, Croydon, CR0 4YY

08/05/2025

01864421-0001